ACCA

PAPER P4

ADVANCED FINANCIAL MANAGEMENT

S T U D Y   T E X T

BPP Learning Media is the **sole ACCA Platinum Approved Learning Partner – content** for the ACCA qualification. In this, **the only Paper P4 study text to be reviewed by the examiner**:

- We **discuss** the **best strategies** for studying for ACCA exams
- We **highlight** the **most important elements** in the syllabus and the **key skills** you will need
- We **signpost** how each chapter links to the syllabus and the study guide
- We **provide** lots of **exam focus points** demonstrating what the examiner will want you to do
- We **emphasise key points** in regular **fast forward summaries**
- We **test your knowledge** of what you've studied in **quick quizzes**
- We **examine** your understanding in our **exam question bank**
- We **reference** all the important topics in our **full index**

BPP's **Practice & Revision Kit, i-Pass and Interactive Passcard** products also support this paper.

FOR EXAMS UP TO JUNE 2014

First edition 2007
Sixth edition September 2012

ISBN 9781 4453 9656 9
(Previous ISBN 9781 4453 7770 4)

e-ISBN 9781 4453 9216 5

British Library Cataloguing-in-Publication Data

A catalogue record for this book
is available from the British Library

Published by

BPP Learning Media Ltd
BPP House, Aldine Place
London W12 8AA

www.bpp.com/learningmedia

Printed in the United Kingdom by

Polestar Wheatons
Hennock Road
Marsh Barton
Exeter
EX2 8RP

Your learning materials, published by BPP Learning
Media Ltd, are printed on paper obtained from
traceable sustainable sources.

We are grateful to the Association of Chartered Certified
Accountants for permission to reproduce past
examination questions. The suggested solutions in the
exam answer bank have been prepared by BPP Learning
Media Ltd, unless otherwise stated.

BPP
LEARNING MEDIA

Contents

A note about copyright

Dear Customer

What does the little © mean and why does it matter?

Your market-leading BPP books, course materials and elearning materials do not write and update themselves. People write them: on their own behalf or as employees of an organisation that invests in this activity. Copyright law protects their livelihoods. It does so by creating rights over the use of the content.

Breach of copyright is a form of theft – as well being a criminal offence in some jurisdictions, it is potentially a serious breach of professional ethics.

With current technology, things might seem a bit hazy but, basically, without the express permission of BPP Learning Media:
- Photocopying our materials is a breach of copyright
- Scanning, ripcasting or conversion of our digital materials into different file formats, uploading them to facebook or emailing them to your friends is a breach of copyright

You can, of course, sell your books, in the form in which you have bought them – once you have finished with them. (Is this fair to your fellow students? We update for a reason.) Please note the e-products are sold on a single user licence basis: we do not supply 'unlock' codes to people who have bought them second hand.

And what about outside the UK? BPP Learning Media strives to make our materials available at prices students can afford by local printing arrangements, pricing policies and partnerships which are clearly listed on our website. A tiny minority ignore this and indulge in criminal activity by illegally photocopying our material or supporting organisations that do. If they act illegally and unethically in one area, can you really trust them?

BPP
LEARNING MEDIA

Helping you to pass – the ONLY P4 Study Text reviewed by the examiner!

BPP Learning Media – the sole Platinum Approved Learning Partner – content

As ACCA's **sole Platinum Approved Learning Partner – content**, BPP Learning Media gives you the **unique opportunity** to use **examiner-reviewed** study materials for the 2013 exams. By incorporating the examiner's comments and suggestions regarding the depth and breadth of syllabus coverage, the BPP Learning Media Study Text provides excellent, **ACCA-approved** support for your studies.

The PER alert

Before you can qualify as an ACCA member, you do not only have to pass all your exams but also fulfil a three year **practical experience requirement** (PER). To help you to recognise areas of the syllabus that you might be able to apply in the workplace to achieve different performance objectives, we have introduced the '**PER alert**' feature. You will find this feature throughout the Study Text to remind you that what you are **learning to pass** your ACCA exams is **equally useful to the fulfilment of the PER requirement**.

Your achievement of the PER should now be recorded in your on-line *My Experience* record.

Tackling studying

Studying can be a daunting prospect, particularly when you have lots of other commitments. The **different features** of the text, the **purposes** of which are explained fully on the **Chapter features** page, will help you whilst studying and improve your chances of **exam success**.

Developing exam awareness

Our Texts are completely **focused** on helping you pass your exam.

Our advice on **Studying P4** outlines the **content** of the paper, the **necessary skills** the examiner expects you to demonstrate and any **brought forward knowledge** you are expected to have.

Exam focus points are included within the chapters to highlight when and how specific topics were examined, or how they might be examined in the future.

Using the Syllabus and Study Guide

You can find the syllabus and Study Guide on pages xii – xx of this Study Text

Testing what you can do

Testing yourself helps you develop the skills you need to pass the exam and also confirms that you can recall what you have learnt.

We include **Questions** – lots of them - both within chapters and in the **Exam Question Bank**, as well as **Quick Quizzes** at the end of each chapter to test your knowledge of the chapter content.

Chapter features

Each chapter contains a number of helpful features to guide you through each topic.

Topic list

Topic list	Syllabus reference

What you will be studying in this chapter and the relevant section numbers, together the ACCA syllabus references.

Introduction

Puts the chapter content in the context of the syllabus as a whole.

Study Guide

Links the chapter content with ACCA guidance.

Exam Guide

Highlights how examinable the chapter content is likely to be and the ways in which it could be examined.

> Knowledge brought forward from earlier studies

What you are assumed to know from previous studies/exams.

> FAST FORWARD

Summarises the content of main chapter headings, allowing you to preview and review each section easily.

Examples

Demonstrate how to apply key knowledge and techniques.

Key terms

Definitions of important concepts that can often earn you easy marks in exams.

Exam focus points

When and how specific topics were examined, or how they may be examined in the future.

Formula to learn

Formulae that are not given in the exam but which have to be learnt.

⚠ PER alert

Gives you a useful indication of syllabus areas that closely relate to performance objectives in your Practical Experience Requirement (PER).

Question

Gives you essential practice of techniques covered in the chapter.

Case Study

Real world examples of theories and techniques.

Chapter Roundup

A full list of the Fast Forwards included in the chapter, providing an easy source of review.

Quick Quiz

A quick test of your knowledge of the main topics in the chapter.

Exam Question Bank

Found at the back of the Study Text with more comprehensive chapter questions. Cross referenced for easy navigation.

Studying P4

As the name suggests, this paper examines advanced financial management topics and is particularly suited to those who are thinking about a career in treasury or are likely to be involved in strategic financial management decisions.

The P4 examiner

The examiner for this paper is **Shishir Malde**. He expects you to demonstrate a highly **professional approach** to all questions – not just presenting information in a professional manner, but also **integrating knowledge and understanding** of topics from across the syllabus. The examiner is also very keen for students to demonstrate evidence of **wider reading** and the ability to incorporate **real life examples** into their answers where relevant and appropriate. Professor Malde has written several articles in *Student Accountant*, which you should read.

1 What P4 is about

The aim of the syllabus is to develop students' ability to **apply relevant knowledge and skills**, and exercise the **professional judgement** expected of a senior financial advisor, in taking or recommending financial management decisions that are likely to have an impact on the entire organisation.

This is an **advanced level** optional paper which builds on the topics covered in Paper F9 *Financial Management*. As an advanced paper it tests much more than just your ability to perform calculations. You must be able to **evaluate** data, **assess** the potential financial and strategic consequences of taking investment decisions and **advise** on alternative courses of action, amongst other things, in both a **domestic** and **international** context.

The syllabus is divided into **seven** main sections:

(a) **The role and responsibility towards stakeholders**

More than ever, company management's responsibility towards all stakeholders is under scrutiny. They must be aware of different stakeholder groups' **conflicting needs** and be able to develop suitable financial strategies that fulfil each group's interests as much as possible. The impact of **environmental factors** should also be uppermost in their minds given the increasing importance placed on such factors in the modern business world.

Ethical issues cannot be ignored – ethics are expected to be a consistent theme in the examination, with the examiner expecting students to be able to take a **practical approach** to identifying such issues in given scenarios.

(b) **Economic environment for multinationals**

Multinational companies have their own unique set of challenges, including having operations in international locations. You will be expected to have detailed knowledge and understanding of how to manage international finances and strategic business and financial planning for companies with international operations.

(c) **Advanced investment appraisal**

This section revisits **investment** and **financing** decisions with the emphasis moving from straightforward technical knowledge towards the **strategic issues** associated with making investment decisions, both **domestic** and **international**.

(d) **Acquisitions and mergers**

You will be expected to distinguish between **different types** of acquisitions, **choose** and **apply** the most appropriate method of **valuation** and make **strategic decisions** regarding how the merger or acquisition should be **financed**. You will be required to act in an **advisory** as well as technical capacity.

(e) **Corporate reconstruction and re-organisation**

This section looks at how to put together a **restructuring package** and ways in which an organisation might be re-organised (for example, management buyouts and sell-offs). As above, you will be expected to act in both a **technical** and **advisory** capacity in questions on this section.

(f) **Treasury and advanced risk management techniques**

This section covers distinct areas of risk and how to measure and manage them. **Interest rate** and **currency risks** and the derivatives used to hedge against them are considered in detail. You will not only be required to know how the derivatives work but also to **advise** on the best methods of hedging in particular scenarios. This section also covers other risks such as **credit risk** and additional treasury functions such as **dividend policy**.

(g)   **Emerging issues in finance and financial management**

Financial management is a continually developing area and finance executives have to keep **up to date** with the new **tools** and **techniques** that are emerging, as well as **developments** in the **international financial markets**.

2 What skills are required?

- Be able to **integrate** knowledge and understanding from across the syllabus

- Think in a **strategic** way – you are assumed to be a senior financial adviser for the purposes of this paper

- Be able to **criticise** financial techniques as well as apply them, and be able to make **reasoned judgements** and give **objective advice** based on calculated results

- Be able to **think internationally** as well as from the viewpoint of the domestic market

- If you read the main capabilities listed by ACCA that students are expected to have on completion of P4, you will find continued reference to the verbs '**evaluate**', '**assess**', '**advise**' and '**explain**' – make sure you can do **all of these** in relation to the different aspects of the syllabus

3 How to improve your chances of passing

- Study the **entire** syllabus – questions may span a number of syllabus areas and you must be prepared for anything!

- **Practise** as many questions as you can under **timed conditions** – this is the best way of developing good exam technique. Make use of the **Question Bank** at the back of this text. **BPP's Practice and Revision Kit** contains numerous exam standard questions (many of them taken from past exam papers) as well as three mock exams for you to try.

- **Section A** questions in particular will be based on scenarios – make sure you relate your answers to the scenario rather than being generic. Answers that are simply regurgitated from texts are unlikely to score highly.

- Present your answers in a **professional** manner – there are **professional marks** available for setting answers out properly and for coherent, well structured arguments and recommendations. You should be aiming to achieve all of these marks.

- **Answer plans** will help you to focus on the requirements of the question and enable you to manage your time effectively.

- Answer the question that you are **most comfortable with** first – it will help to settle you down if you feel you have answered the first question well.

- **Answer all parts** of the question – leaving out a five mark discursive element for example may mean the difference between a pass and a fail.

- Read the financial press and relevant web sites for real life examples – the examiner is specifically looking for evidence of **wider reading**.

- Read **Student Accountant** (the ACCA's student magazine) regularly – it often contains technical articles written either by or on the recommendation of the examiner which can be invaluable for future exams.

4 Brought forward knowledge

As mentioned previously, this paper builds on knowledge brought forward from Paper F9 *Financial Management*. If you have not studied F9, you should be aware that the following topics are assumed knowledge and should be considered examinable.

- Management of working capital
- Business finance (including sources of finance and dividend policy)
- The capital structure decision
- Investment decisions
- Interest and discounting
- Investment appraisal
- Capital rationing
- Cost of capital (including CAPM and WACC)
- Business valuations
- Market efficiency
- Foreign currency and interest rate risk management

BPP
LEARNING MEDIA

The exam paper and exam formulae

Format of the paper

The format of the exam will change for exams from June 2013.

Section A contains one compulsory question worth 50 marks.

This question will cover topics from across the syllabus but will tend to be based on one major area – for example a cross-border merger question (major topic) might bring in ethical issues (smaller topic).

Section B contains a choice of two from three questions worth 25 marks each.

Professional marks are available. The examiner has emphasised that in order to gain all the marks available, students must write in the specified format (such as a report or memo). Reports must have terms of reference, conclusion, appendices and appropriate headings. Make sure you are familiar with how different types of documents are constructed to improve your chances of gaining maximum professional marks.

Time allowed - 3 hours with 15 minutes' reading time.

Syllabus and Study Guide

The P4 syllabus and study guide can be found below.

Syllabus

AIM

To apply relevant knowledge, skills and exercise professional judgement as expected of a senior financial executive or advisor, in taking or recommending decisions relating to the financial management of an organisation.

MAIN CAPABILITIES

On successful completion of this paper, candidates should be able to:

A Explain and evaluate the role and responsibility of the senior financial executive or advisor in meeting conflicting needs of stakeholders

B Evaluate the impact of macro economics and recognise the role of international financial institutions in the financial management of multinationals

C Evaluate potential investment decisions and assessing their financial and strategic consequences, both domestically and internationally

D Assess and plan acquisitions and mergers as an alternative growth strategy

E Evaluate and advise on alternative corporate re-organisation strategies

F Apply and evaluate alternative advanced treasury and risk management techniques

G Identify and assess the potential impact of emerging issues in finance and financial management.

RELATIONAL DIAGRAM OF MAIN CAPABILITIES

This syllabus develops upon the core financial management knowledge and skills covered in the F9, *Financial Management,* syllabus at the Fundamentals level and prepares candidates to advise management and/or clients on complex strategic financial management issues facing an organisation.

The syllabus starts by exploring the role and responsibility of a senior executive or advisor in meeting competing needs of stakeholders within the business environment of multinationals. The syllabus then re-examines investment and financing decisions, with the emphasis moving towards the strategic consequences of making such decisions in a domestic, as well as international, context. Candidates are then expected to develop further advisory skills in planning strategic acquisitions and mergers and corporate re-organisations.

The next part of the syllabus re-examines, in the broadest sense, the existence of risks in business and the sophisticated strategies which are employed in order to manage such risks. It builds on what candidates would have covered in the F9, *Financial Management,* syllabus and the P1,*Governance, Risk and Ethics,* syllabus. The syllabus finishes by examining the impact of emerging issues in finance.

DETAILED SYLLABUS

A   Role and responsibility towards stakeholders

1. The role and responsibility of senior financial executive/advisor

2. Financial strategy formulation

3. Conflicting stakeholder interests

4. Ethical issues in financial management

5. Impact of environmental issues on organisational objectives and on governance

B   Economic environment for multinational organisations

1. Management of international trade and finance

2. Strategic business and financial planning for multinational organisations

C   Advanced investment appraisal

1. Discounted cash flow techniques

2. Application of option pricing theory in investment decisions

3. Impact of financing on investment decisions and adjusted present values

4. Valuation and the use of free cash flows

5. International investment and financing decisions

D   Acquisitions and mergers

1. Acquisitions and mergers versus other growth strategies

2. Valuation for acquisitions and mergers

3. Regulatory framework and processes

4. Financing acquisitions and mergers

E   Corporate reconstruction and re-organisation

1. Financial reconstruction

2. Business re-organisation

F   Treasury and advanced risk management techniques

1. The role of the treasury function in multinationals

2. The use of financial derivatives to hedge against forex risk

3. The use of financial derivatives to hedge against interest rate risk

4. Dividend policy in multinationals and transfer pricing

G   Emerging issues in finance and financial management

1. Developments in world financial markets

2. Developments in international trade and finance

3. Developments in Islamic financing

APPROACH TO EXAMINING THE SYLLABUS

The P4, *Advanced Financial Management*, paper builds upon the skills and knowledge examined in the F9, *Financial Management*, paper. At this stage candidates will be expected to demonstrate an integrated knowledge of the subject and an ability to relate their technical understanding of the subject to issues of strategic importance to the organisation. The study guide specifies the wide range of contextual understanding that is required to achieve a satisfactory standard at this level.

Examination Structure

The examination will be a three-hour paper in two sections:

Section A:

Section A will contain a compulsory question, comprising of 50 marks.

Section A will normally cover significant issues relevant to the senior financial manager or advisor and will be set in the form of a case study or scenario. The requirements of the section A question are such that candidates will be expected to show a comprehensive understanding of issues from across the syllabus. The question will contain a mix of computational and discursive elements. Within this question candidates will be expected to provide answers in a specified form such as a short report or board memorandum commensurate with the professional level of the paper in part or whole of the question.

Section B:

In section B candidates will be asked to answer two from three questions, comprising of 25 marks each.

Section B questions are designed to provide a more focused test of the syllabus. Questions will normally contain a mix of computational and discursive elements, but may also be wholly discursive or evaluative where computations are already provided.

Total 100 marks

Study Guide

A ROLE AND RESPONSIBILITY TOWARDS STAKEHOLDERS

1. The role and responsibility of senior financial executive/advisor

a) Develop strategies for the achievement of the organisational goals in line with its agreed policy framework. [3]

b) Recommend strategies for the management of the financial resources of the organisation such that they are utilised in an efficient, effective and transparent way. [3]

c) Advise the board of directors or management of the organisation in setting the financial goals of the business and in its financial policy development [2] with particular reference to:
   i) Investment selection and capital resource allocation
   ii) Minimising the cost of capital
   iii) Distribution and retention policy
   iv) Communicating financial policy and corporate goals to internal and external stakeholders
   v) Financial planning and control
   vi) The management of risk.

2. Financial strategy formulation

a) Assess organisational performance using methods such as ratios, trends, EVA™ and MVA.[3]

b) Recommend the optimum capital mix and structure within a specified business context and capital asset structure.[3]

c) Recommend appropriate distribution and retention policy.[3]

d) Explain the theoretical and practical rationale for the management of risk. [3]

e) Assess the organisation's exposure to business and financial risk including operational, reputational, political, economic, regulatory and fiscal risk.[3]

f) Develop a framework for risk management, comparing and contrasting risk mitigation, hedging and diversification strategies.[3]

g) Establish capital investment monitoring and risk management systems.[3]

3. Conflicting stakeholder interests

a) Assess the potential sources of the conflict within a given corporate governance/ stakeholder framework informed by an understanding of the alternative theories of managerial behaviour. [3]
   Relevant underpinning theory for this assessment would be:
   i) The separation of ownership and control
   ii) Transaction cost economics and comparative governance structures
   iii) Agency Theory.

b) Recommend, within specified problem domains, appropriate strategies for the resolution of stakeholder conflict and advise on alternative approaches that may be adopted. [3]

c) Compare the different governance structures and policies (with particular emphasis upon the European stakeholder and the US/UK shareholder model) and with respect to the role of the financial manager. [3]

4. Ethical issues in financial management

a) Assess the ethical dimension within business issues and decisions and advise on best practice in the financial management of the organisation.[3]

b) Demonstrate an understanding of the interconnectedness of the ethics of good business practice between all of the functional areas of the organisation.[2]

c) Establish an ethical financial policy for the financial management of the organisation which is grounded in good governance, the highest standards of probity and is fully aligned with the ethical principles of the Association. [3]

d) Recommend an ethical framework for the development of an organisation's financial policies and a system for the assessment of its ethical impact upon the financial management of the organisation.[3]

e) Explore the areas within the ethical framework of the organisation which may be undermined by agency effects and/or stakeholder conflicts and establish strategies for dealing with them.[3]

5. Impact of environmental issues on organisational objectives and on governance

a) Assess the issues which may impact upon organisational objectives and governance from:[3]
   i) Sustainability and environmental risk
   ii) The carbon-trading economy and emissions
   iii) The role of the environment agency
   iv) Environmental audits and the triple bottom line approach.

B ECONOMIC ENVIRONMENT FOR MULTINATIONALS

1. Management of international trade and finance

a) Advise on the theory and practice of free trade and the management of barriers to trade.[3]

b) Demonstrate an up to date understanding of the major trade agreements and common markets and, on the basis of contemporary circumstances, advise on their policies and strategic implications for a given business.[3]

c) Discuss the objectives of the World Trade Organisation.[2]

d) Discuss the role of international financial institutions within the context of a globalised economy, with particular attention to the International Monetary Fund, the Bank of International Settlements, The World Bank and the principal Central Banks (the Fed, Bank of England, European Central Bank and the Bank of Japan).[2]

e) Assess the role of the international financial markets with respect to the management of global debt, the financial development of the emerging economies and the maintenance of global financial stability.[2]

2. Strategic business and financial planning for multinationals

a) Advise on the development of a financial planning framework for a multinational organisation taking into account:[3]
   i) Compliance with national regulatory requirements (for example the London Stock Exchange admission requirements)
   ii) The mobility of capital across borders and national limitations on remittances and transfer pricing
   iii) The pattern of economic and other risk exposures in the different national markets
   iv) Agency issues in the central coordination of overseas operations and the balancing of local financial autonomy with effective central control.

C ADVANCED INVESTMENT APPRAISAL

1. Discounted cash flow techniques

a) Evaluate the potential value added to an organisation arising from a specified capital investment project or portfolio using the net present value (NPV) model.[3]
   Project modelling should include explicit treatment and discussion of:
   i) Inflation and specific price variation
   ii) Taxation including capital allowances and tax exhaustion
   iii) Single period and multi-period capital rationing. Multi-period capital rationing to include the formulation of programming methods and the interpretation of their output
   iv) Probability analysis and sensitivity analysis when adjusting for risk and uncertainty in investment appraisal
   v) Risk adjusted discount rates.

b) Outline the application of Monte Carlo simulation to investment appraisal.[2]
   Candidates will not be expected to undertake simulations in an examination context but will be expected to demonstrate an understanding of:
   i) Simple model design
   ii) The different types of distribution controlling the key variables within the simulation

iii) The significance of the simulation output and the assessment of the likelihood of project success

iv) The measurement and interpretation of project value at risk.

c) Establish the potential economic return (using internal rate of return (IRR) and modified internal rate of return) and advise on a project's return margin. Discuss the relative merits of NPV and IRR.[3]

2. **Application of option pricing theory in investment decisions**

a) Apply the Black-Scholes Option Pricing (BSOP) model to financial product valuation and to asset valuation:[3]
   i) Determine and discuss, using published data, the five principal drivers of option value (value of the underlying, exercise price, time to expiry, volatility and the risk-free rate)
   ii) Discuss the underlying assumptions, structure, application and limitations of the BSOP model.

b) Evaluate embedded real options within a project, classifying them into one of the real option archetypes.[3]

c) Assess, calculate and advise on the value of options to delay, expand, redeploy and withdraw using the BSOP model.[3]

3. **Impact of financing on investment decisions and adjusted present values**

a) Identify and assess the appropriateness of the range of sources of finance available to an organisation including equity, debt, hybrids, lease finance, venture capital, business angel finance, private equity, asset securitisation and sale and Islamic finance. Including assessment on the financial position, financial risk and the value of an organisation.[3]

b) Calculate the cost of capital of an organisation, including the cost of equity and cost of debt, based on the range of equity and debt sources of finance. Discuss the appropriateness of using the cost of capital to establish project

and organisational value, and discuss its relationship to such value.[3]

c) Calculate and evaluate project specific cost of equity and cost of capital, including their impact on the overall cost of capital of an organisation. Demonstrate detailed knowledge of business and financial risk, the capital asset pricing model and the relationship between equity and asset betas.[3]

d) Assess an organisation's debt exposure to interest rate changes using the simple Macaulay duration method. [3]

e) Discuss the benefits and limitations of duration including the impact of convexity. [3]

f) Assess the organisation's exposure to credit risk, including: [3]
   i) Explain the role of, and the risk assessment models used by the principal rating agencies
   ii) Estimate the likely credit spread over risk free
   iii) Estimate the organisation's current cost of debt capital using the appropriate term structure of interest rates and the credit spread.

g) Assess the impact of financing and capital structure upon the organisation with respect to:[3]
   i) Modigliani and Miller propositions, before and after tax
   ii) Static trade-off theory
   iii) Pecking order propositions
   iv) Agency effects.

h) Apply the adjusted present value technique to the appraisal of investment decisions that entail significant alterations in the financial structure of the organisation, including their fiscal and transactions cost implications.[3]

i) Assess the impact of a significant capital investment project upon the reported financial position and performance of the organisation taking into account alternative financing strategies.[3]

4. Valuation and the use of free cash flows

a) Apply asset based, income based and cash flow based models to value equity. Apply appropriate models, including term structure of interest rates, the yield curve and credit spreads, to value corporate debt.[3]

b) Forecast an organisation's free cash flow and its free cash flow to equity (pre and post capital reinvestment).[3]

c) Advise on the value of an organisation using its free cash flow and free cash flow to equity under alternative horizon and growth assumptions.[3]

d) Explain the use of the BSOP model to estimate the value of equity of an organisation and discuss the implications of the model for a change in the value of equity.[2]

e) Explain the role of BSOP model in the assessment of default risk, the value of debt and its potential recoverability. [2]

5. International investment and financing decisions

a) Assess the impact upon the value of a project of alternative exchange rate assumptions.[3]

b) Forecast project or organisation free cash flows in any specified currency and determine the project's net present value or organisation value under differing exchange rate, fiscal and transaction cost assumptions.[2]

c) Evaluate the significance of exchange controls for a given investment decision and strategies for dealing with restricted remittance.[3]

d) Assess the impact of a project upon an organisation's exposure to translation, transaction and economic risk.[3]

e) Assess and advise on the costs and benefits of alternative sources of finance available within the international equity and bond markets.[3]

D ACQUISITIONS AND MERGERS

1. Acquisitions and mergers versus other growth strategies

a) Discuss the arguments for and against the use of acquisitions and mergers as a method of corporate expansion.[2]

b) Evaluate the corporate and competitive nature of a given acquisition proposal.[3]

c) Advise upon the criteria for choosing an appropriate target for acquisition.[3]

d) Compare the various explanations for the high failure rate of acquisitions in enhancing shareholder value.[3]

e) Evaluate, from a given context, the potential for synergy separately classified as:[3]
   i) Revenue synergy
   ii) Cost synergy
   iii) Financial synergy.

2. Valuation for acquisitions and mergers

a) Discuss the problem of overvaluation.[2]

b) Estimate the potential near-term and continuing growth levels of a corporation's earnings using both internal and external measures.[3]

c) Assess the impact of an acquisition or merger upon the risk profile of the acquirer distinguishing:[3]
   i) Type 1 acquisitions that do not alter the acquirer's exposure to financial or business risk
   ii) Type 2 acquisitions that impact upon the acquirer's exposure to financial risk
   iii) Type 3 acquisitions that impact upon the acquirer's exposure to both financial and business risk.

d) Advise on the valuation of a type 1 acquisition of both quoted and unquoted entities using:[3]
   i) 'Book value-plus' models
   ii) Market based models
   iii) Cash flow models, including EVA™, MVA.

e) Advise on the valuation of type 2 acquisitions using the adjusted net present value model.[3]

f) Advise on the valuation of type 3 acquisitions using iterative revaluation procedures.[3]

g) Demonstrate an understanding of the procedure for valuing high growth start-ups.[2]

3. **Regulatory framework and processes**

a) Demonstrate an understanding of the principal factors influencing the development of the regulatory framework for mergers and acquisitions globally and, in particular, be able to compare and contrast the shareholder versus the stakeholder models of regulation.[2]

b) Identify the main regulatory issues which are likely to arise in the context of a given offer and
   i) assess whether the offer is likely to be in the shareholders' best interests
   ii) advise the directors of a target entity on the most appropriate defence if a specific offer is to be treated as hostile.[3]

4. **Financing acquisitions and mergers**

a) Compare the various sources of financing available for a proposed cash-based acquisition. [3]

b) Evaluate the advantages and disadvantages of a financial offer for a given acquisition proposal using pure or mixed mode financing and recommend the most appropriate offer to be made.[3]

c) Assess the impact of a given financial offer on the reported financial position and performance of the acquirer.[3]

E **CORPORATE RECONSTRUCTION AND RE-ORGANISATION**

1. **Financial reconstruction**

a) Assess an organisational situation and determine whether a financial reconstruction is the most appropriate strategy for dealing with the problem as presented.[3]

b) Assess the likely response of the capital market and/or individual suppliers of capital to any reconstruction scheme and the impact their response is likely to have upon the value of the organisation.[3]

c) Recommend a reconstruction scheme from a given business situation, justifying the proposal in terms of its impact upon the reported performance and financial position of the organisation.[3]

2. **Business re-organisation**

a) Recommend, with reasons, strategies for unbundling parts of a quoted company.[3]

b) Evaluate the likely financial and other benefits of unbundling.[3]

c) Advise on the financial issues relating to a management buy-out and buy-in.[3]

F **TREASURY AND ADVANCED RISK MANAGEMENT TECHNIQUES**

1. **The role of the treasury function in multinationals**

a) Discuss the role of the treasury management function within:[3]
   i) The short term management of the organisation's financial resources
   ii) The longer term maximisation of corporate value
   iii) The management of risk exposure.

b) Discuss the operations of the derivatives market, including:[3]
   i) The relative advantages and disadvantages of exchange traded versus OTC agreements
   ii) Key features, such as standard contracts, tick sizes, margin requirements and margin trading
   iii) The source of basis risk and how it can be minimised.
   iv) Risks such as delta, gamma, vega, rho and theta, and how these can be managed.

2. **The use of financial derivatives to hedge against forex risk**

a) Assess the impact on an organisation to exposure in translation, transaction and economic risks and how these can be managed. [3]

b) Evaluate, for a given hedging requirement, which of the following is the most appropriate strategy, given the nature of the underlying position and the risk exposure:[3]
   i) The use of the forward exchange market and the creation of a money market hedge
   ii) Synthetic foreign exchange agreements (SAFEs)
   iii) Exchange-traded currency futures contracts
   iv) Currency swaps
   v) FOREX swaps
   vi) Currency options.

c) Advise on the use of bilateral and multilateral netting and matching as tools for minimising FOREX transactions costs and the management of market barriers to the free movement of capital and other remittances.[3]

3. **The use of financial derivatives to hedge against interest rate risk**

a) Evaluate, for a given hedging requirement, which of the following is the most appropriate given the nature of the underlying position and the risk exposure:[3]
   i) Forward Rate Agreements (FRAs)
   ii) Interest Rate Futures
   iii) Interest rate swaps
   iv) Options on FRAs (caps and collars), Interest rate futures and interest rate swaps.

4. **Dividend policy in multinationals and transfer pricing**

a) Determine a corporation's dividend capacity and its policy given:[3]
   i) The corporation's short- and long-term reinvestment strategy
   ii) The impact of capital reconstruction programmes such as share repurchase agreements and new capital issues on free cash flow to equity.
   iii) The availability and timing of central remittances

iv) The corporate tax regime within the host jurisdiction.

b) Advise, in the context of a specified capital investment programme, on an organisation's current and projected dividend capacity.[3]

c) Develop organisational policy on the transfer pricing of goods and services across international borders and be able to determine the most appropriate transfer pricing strategy in a given situation reflecting local regulations and tax regimes.[3]

G   EMERGING ISSUES IN FINANCE AND FINANCIAL MANAGEMENT

1. **Developments in world financial markets**

   Discuss the significance to the organisation, of latest developments in the world financial markets such as the causes and impact of the recent financial crisis; growth and impact of dark pool trading systems; the removal of barriers to the free movement of capital; and the international regulations on money laundering. [2]

2. **Developments in international trade and finance**

   Demonstrate an awareness of new developments in the macroeconomic environment, assessing their impact upon the organisation, and advising on the appropriate response to those developments both internally and externally. [2]

3. **Developments in Islamic financing**

   Demonstrate an understanding of the role of, and developments in, Islamic financing as a growing source of finance for organisations; explaining the rationale for its use, and identifying its benefits and deficiencies.[2]

Analysis of past papers

The table below provides details of when each element of the syllabus has been examined and the question number and section in which each element appeared. Further details can be found in the Exam Focus Points in the relevant chapters.

Covered in Text chapter		June 2012	Dec 2011	June 2011	Dec 2010	June 2010	Dec 2009	June 2009	Dec 2008	June 2008	Dec 2007	Pilot Paper
	ROLE AND RESPONSIBILITY TOWARDS STAKEHOLDERS											
1, 2	Role of senior financial executive/financial strategy formulation	2		5			2, 3		2a,b, c, 4	1a,c, 2c	4a, 5a	
3a	Conflicting stakeholder interests											
3b, 3c	Ethical/environmental issues		5	5				4	4	4	4b	5c
	ECONOMIC ENVIRONMENT FOR MULTINATIONALS											
4	Trading and planning in a multinational environment				5			4				5a,b
	ADVANCED INVESTMENT APPRAISAL											
5	Discounted cash flow techniques	4	1		2	1	1, 5	1, 5	1a,b, c. 2c	5b	1, 5b	3a
6	Application of option pricing theory to investment decisions	1		4	3	2	1d, 3	5			3	
7a, 7b	Impact of financing and adjusted present values / Valuation and use of free cash flows	1, 2, 3	1, 3	3	2			1b	3	5a	5	4a,b
8	International investment and financing decisions	5	1									
	ACQUISITIONS AND MERGERS											
9, 11, 12	Strategic/financial/regulatory issues			1			2			4	2b	1d
10	Valuation techniques	1		1		2			1b	2a,b		1a,b,c
	CORPORATE RECONSTRUCTION & REORGANISATION											
13	Financial reconstruction				1							
14	Business reorganisation		4		1	4		2				
	TREASURY & ADVANCED RISK MANAGEMENT TECHNIQUES											
15	Role of the treasury function							3				
16	Hedging foreign currency risk			2		5		3, 4		3		2
17	Hedging interest rate risk	3	2				5		5			
18	Dividend policy & transfer pricing in multinationals				4							
	EMERGING ISSUES											
19	Recent developments and trends in world financial markets and international trade	5			3	3	4					

Exam formulae

Set out below are the **formulae you will be given in the exam**. If you are not sure what the symbols mean, or how the formulae are used, you should refer to the appropriate chapter in this Study Text.

Chapter in Study Text

Modigliani and Miller Proposition 2 (with tax)

$$k_e = k_e^i + (1-T)(k_e^i - k_d)\frac{V_d}{V_e}$$

7a

The capital asset pricing model

$$E(r_i) = R_f + \beta_i(E(r_m) - R_f)$$

Assumed knowledge

The asset beta formula

$$\beta_a = \left[\frac{V_e}{(V_e + V_d(1-T))}\beta_e\right] + \left[\frac{V_d(1-T)}{(V_e + V_d(1-T))}\beta_d\right]$$

Assumed knowledge

The growth model

$$P_0 = \frac{D_0(1+g)}{(r_e - g)}$$

12

Gordon's growth approximation

$$g = br_e$$

5

The weighted average cost of capital

$$WACC = \left[\frac{V_e}{V_e + V_d}\right]k_e + \left[\frac{V_d}{V_e + V_d}\right]k_d(1-T)$$

7a

The Fisher formula

$$(1 + i) = (1 + r)(1 + h)$$

5

Purchasing power parity and interest rate parity

$$S_1 = S_0 \times \frac{(1+h_c)}{(1+h_b)}$$

8

$$F_0 = S_0 \times \frac{(1+i_c)}{(1+i_b)}$$

8

Modified internal rate of return

$$MIRR = \left[\frac{PV_R}{PV_I}\right]^{\frac{1}{n}}(1+r_e) - 1$$

5

The Black-Scholes option pricing model

$$c = P_a N(d_1) - P_e N(d_2)e^{-rt}$$ 6

Where $$d_1 = \frac{\ln(P_a/P_e) + (r + 0.5s^2)t}{s\sqrt{t}}$$ 6

$$d_2 = d_1 - s\sqrt{t}$$ 6

The put call parity relationship

$$p = c - P_a + P_e e^{-rt}$$ 16

Role and responsibility towards stakeholders

The role and responsibility of senior financial executive/advisor

Topic list	Syllabus reference
1 Financial goals and objectives	A (1) (c)
2 Non-financial objectives	A (1) (c)
3 Investment decision	A (1) (c)
4 Financing decision	A (1) (c)
5 Dividend decision	A (1) (c)
6 Financial planning and control	A (1) (c)
7 Risk management	A (1) (c)
8 Communicating policy to stakeholders	A (1) (c)
9 Strategies for achieving financial goals	A (1) (a) (b)

Introduction

In this chapter we discuss **the role and responsibility of the senior financial executive** in the context of setting strategic objectives, financial goals and financial policy development.

This chapter and the next four chapters underpin the rest of the syllabus therefore it is important to read them carefully. You have to understand the role and responsibility of senior financial executive in order to anticipate the types of decisions that might be made in particular circumstances.

Remember that non-financial objectives are at least as important as financial objectives and will have a significant impact on the three main financial management decisions – investment, financing and dividend.

Bear in mind at all times throughout the syllabus that the company is being run for the benefit of the **shareholders** therefore decisions should reflect their preferences as much as possible.

Study guide

		Intellectual level
A1	**The role and responsibility of senior financial executive/advisor**	
(a)	Develop strategies for the achievement of the organisational goals in line with its agreed policy framework.	3
(b)	Recommend strategies for the management of the financial resources of the organisation such that they are utilised in an efficient, effective and transparent way.	3
(c)	Advise the board of directors of the organisation in setting the financial goals of the business and in its financial policy development with particular reference to: (i) Investment selection and capital resource allocation (ii) Minimising the cost of capital (iii) Distribution and retention policy (iv) Communicating financial policy and corporate goals to internal and external stakeholders (v) Financial planning and control (vi) The management of risk	2

1 Financial goals and objectives   6/11

FAST FORWARD

In financial management of businesses, the key objective is the **maximisation of shareholders' wealth**.

1.1 The principal financial objective of a company

The principal role of the senior financial executive when setting financial goals is the **maximisation of shareholders' wealth** (which is equivalent to the maximisation of the market value of the company's ordinary shares).

A company is financed by ordinary shareholders, preference shareholders, loan stock holders and other long-term and short-term payables. All surplus funds, however, belong to the legal owners of the company, its ordinary (equity) shareholders. Any retained profits are undistributed wealth of these equity shareholders.

Question   Financial objectives

It is a common misconception that profit maximisation is the key objective of most publicly owned companies. Give reasons why this objective would be insufficient for investors.

Answer

There are several reasons why profit maximisation is not a sufficient objective for investors.

(a) **Risk and uncertainty**. This objective fails to recognise the risk and uncertainty associated with certain projects. Shareholders tend to be very interested in the level of risk and maximising profits may be achieved by raising risk to unacceptable levels.

(b) **Dividend policy**. Shareholders are interested in how much they will receive as dividends. Retained profits can be increased by reducing the dividend payout ratio or by not paying a dividend at all. This is not necessarily in the best interests of the shareholders who might prefer a certain monetary return on their investment.

(c) **Future profits**. Which profits should management be maximising? Shareholders may not want current profits to be maximised at the expense of future profits.

(d) **Manipulation of profits**. Unlike cash, profits can be easily manipulated – for example, by changing depreciation policy or provision for doubtful debts percentage. It is therefore not difficult to appear to be maximising profits when in reality the company is no better off.

You should remember however that, whilst the principal objective is the maximisation of shareholders' wealth, managers should not be pursuing this at any cost. They should not be taking **unacceptable business and financial risks** with shareholders' funds and must act within the law. Managers are aware that any actions that undermine their company's reputation are likely to be **very expensive** in terms of adverse effects on share price and public trust.

1.1.1 How do we measure shareholders' wealth?

Key term

> **Shareholders' wealth** comes from two sources – dividends received and market value of shares
> Shareholders' return on investment = dividend yield + capital gain on shares

In order to measure shareholders' wealth, we must be able to measure the value of the company and its shares. How do we do this?

(a) **Statement of financial position valuation**

Assets will be valued on a going concern basis. If retained profits increase year on year then the company is a profitable one. Statement of financial position values are not a measure of market value, although retained profits may give some indication of the level of dividends that could be paid to shareholders.

(b) **Break-up basis**

This basis will only be used when the business is being wound up, there is a threat of liquidation or management has decided to sell off individual assets to raise cash.

(c) **Market value**

Market value is the price at which buyers and sellers will trade shares in a company. Look at your local financial press (for example, Financial Times or Wall Street Journal) for a daily summary of market values of individual listed companies' shares. This value is the one that is most relevant to a company's financial objectives.

When shares are in a private company, and are not traded on any stock exchange, there is no easy way to measure their market value. However the principal objective of such companies should still be the maximisation of ordinary shareholders' wealth.

Shareholders' wealth comes from **two sources – dividends received** and the **market value** of the shares held.

Shareholders' **return on investment** is obtained from **dividends received** and **capital gains** resulting from increases in the market value of the shares.

1.1.2 How is the value of a business increased?

If a company's shares are traded on a stock market, the wealth of shareholders is increased when the share price goes up. The price of a company's shares may increase for a number of reasons, including the following.

- Potential takeover bid
- News of winning a major contract
- Better than expected profit forecasts and published results
- Change in senior staff, such as a new CEO
- Share buyback by the company (reduces supply of shares which should increase the price)

Case Study

In February 2012 a struggling US-based IT services company, Computer Sciences Corporation (CSC), announced that Mike Lawrie was to take over as chief executive and president. Following the announcement CSC's share price rose by 18.5% in one day.

Management should set targets for factors that they can influence directly, such as profits and dividend growth.

1.2 Earnings per share (EPS) growth

Formula to learn

$$\text{Earnings per share} = \frac{\text{Net profit (loss) attributable to ordinary shareholders}}{\text{Weighted average number of ordinary shares}}$$

EPS is particularly useful for comparing results over a number of years. Investors will be looking for grown in EPS year on year. In addition companies must demonstrate that they can sustain earnings for dividend payouts and reinvestment in the business for future growth.

 Question
Earnings per share

As an investor, why might you be wary of using EPS to assess the performance of a company?

Answer

EPS is based on past data whereas investors should be more concerned with future earnings. In addition, the measure is very easy to manipulate by changes in accounting policies and by mergers and acquisitions. In reality, the attention given to EPS as a performance measure is probably disproportionate to its true worth.

1.3 Other financial targets

In addition to targets for earnings, EPS, and dividend per share, a company might set other financial targets.

Examples of other financial targets	
Restriction on gearing	Ratio of debt: equity shouldn't exceed 1:1 or finance costs shouldn't be higher than 25% of profit from operations for instance
Profit retentions	Dividend cover (Profit for the year/Dividends) should exceed 2.5 for instance
Profit from operations	Target profit from operations: revenue ratio or minimum return on capital employed
Cash generation	As well as generating profits, businesses need to generate enough cash to ensure they remain liquid
Value added	Creation of economic value for shareholders, to be discussed later in this text

These targets are not primary objectives but can help a company to achieve its principal objective without incurring excessive risks. Such targets tend to be measured in the short-term (one year) rather than the long-term.

One problem with having several secondary financial targets is that they may conflict with one another. In this event, compromises may have to be made to ensure the overall principal objective is achieved.

 BPP LEARNING MEDIA

Singapore Airlines, in the 2010/11 Annual Report, states that the company was 'committed to continually enhancing shareholder value by maintaining high standards of corporate governance, professionalism, integrity and commitment at all levels, underpinned by strong internal controls and risk management systems'.

2 Non-financial objectives   6/11

FAST FORWARD Non-financial objectives may limit the achievement of financial objectives. Their existence suggests the assumption that the main purpose of a company is to maximise shareholders' wealth is too simplistic.

Many companies have non-financial objectives that may limit their ability to achieve their financial objectives. They do not negate the financial objectives but emphasise the need for companies to have other targets than the maximisation of shareholders' wealth.

 Question   **Non-financial objectives**

Suggest a non-financial objective for each of the following companies.

(a)   A major international airline
(b)   A provider of professional education courses
(c)   A large high-street supermarket
(d)   A major pharmaceutical company
(e)   A publicly-funded health service

Answer

Examples include

(a)   Development of enhanced on-board products (such as extra legroom, more spacious business class seating); improve the customer experience by for example enabling customers to choose their own seats in advance

(b)   Maximise pass rates; provide up-to-date technology in the classroom; continuous improvement of teaching materials

(c)   Provide services to the communities in which branches operate (for example, Coles supermarket chain in Australia has joined forces with a local council to create a community centre that will provide such support services as child day care and a health centre to support parents of children under the age of five); provide excellent staff facilities

(d)   Work with governments to tackle health issues on a global scale; develop new drugs to fight diseases

(e)   Eradicate any hospital-based bugs such as MRSA; reduce waiting times for treatment; improvement in doctor/patient ratio

3 Investment decision

FAST FORWARD

> In seeking to attain the financial objectives of the organisation or enterprise, a financial manager has to make three fundamental decisions – investment, financing and dividend. The investment decision involves selecting appropriate investment opportunities that will help to fulfil the company's primary objectives.

The three fundamental decisions that support the objective of maximising shareholders' wealth are

- Investment decision
- Financing decision
- Dividend decision

Underpinning these decisions is the **management of risk**, including the management of exchange rates and interest rates. At the same time, financial managers must monitor the company's **financial position** and plan for situations where cash injections may be needed. Control of how the money is used is also important, as the funds are being used on behalf of the shareholders.

At all times the financial managers should remember that they are making decisions with a view to **increasing shareholders' wealth**. It follows that all stakeholders (internal and external) should be kept informed of financial policy and corporate goals through effective communication channels.

As a financial manager you should always bear in mind that these decisions are not made in isolation but are **interconnected**.

This section deals with the first decision identified above – the **investment decision**.

The financial manager will need to **identify** investment opportunities, **evaluate** them and decide on the **optimum allocation of scarce funds** available between investments.

Investment decisions may be on the undertaking of new **projects** within the existing business, the **takeover** of, or the **merger** with, another company or the **selling off** of a part of the business. Managers have to take decisions in the light of strategic considerations such as whether the business wants to **grow internally** (through investment in existing operations) or **externally** (through expansion).

Investment decisions are considered more fully in Chapters 5 – 10 but some of the key issues are discussed below.

3.1 Organic growth

A company which is planning to grow must decide on whether to pursue a policy of 'organic' internal growth or a policy of taking over other established businesses, or a mix of the two.

Organic growth requires funding in cash, whereas acquisitions can be made by means of share exchange transactions. A company pursuing a policy of organic growth would need to take account of the following.

(a) The company must make the **finance available**, possibly out of retained profits. However, the company should then know how much it can afford, and with careful management, should not over-extend itself by trying to achieve too much growth too quickly.

(b) The company can **use its existing staff and systems** to create the growth projects, and this will open up career opportunities for the staff.

(c) **Overall expansion** can be **planned more efficiently**. For example, if a company wishes to open a new factory or depot, it can site the new development in a place that helps operational efficiency (eg close to other factories, to reduce transport costs).

(d) **Economies of scale** can be achieved from **more efficient use** of central head office functions such as finance, purchasing, personnel and management services.

3.2 Growth by acquisition

Companies may expand or diversify by developing their own internal resources, but they are also likely to consider growth through acquisitions or mergers. In both situations the result is a sudden spurt in company growth, which can clearly cause 'corporate indigestion' typified by problems of communication, blurring of policy decisions and decline in the staff's identity with company and products.

The aim of a merger or acquisition, however, should be to make **profits** in the long term as well as the short term. Acquisitions provide a **means of entering** a market, or building up a market share, more quickly and/or at a lower cost than would be incurred if the company tries to develop its own resources.

It will also be necessary to attempt an evaluation of the following.

- The **prospects** of **technological change** in the industry
- The size **and strength of competitors**
- The **reaction of competitors** to an acquisition
- The **likelihood of government intervention** and legislation
- The **state of the industry** and its long-term prospects
- The amount of **synergy** obtainable from the merger or acquisition

Whatever the reason for the merger or acquisition, it is unlikely to be successful unless it offers the **company opportunities** that cannot be found within the company itself and unless the new subsidiary fits closely into the strategic plan outlined for future growth.

3.3 Organic growth versus acquisition

Acquisitions are probably only desirable if **organic growth alone cannot achieve the targets** for growth that a company has set for itself.

Organic growth takes time. With acquisitions, entire existing operations are assimilated into the company at one fell swoop. Acquisitions can be made without cash, if share exchange transactions are acceptable to both the buyers and sellers of any company which is to be taken over.

However, acquisitions do have their **strategic problems**.

(a) They might be **too expensive**. Some might be resisted by the directors of the target company. Others might be referred to the government under the terms of anti-monopoly legislation.

(b) **Customers** of the target company might **resent** a sudden takeover and consider going to other suppliers for their goods.

(c) In general, the problems of assimilating new products, customers, suppliers, markets, employees and different systems of operating might create **'indigestion'** and management overload in the acquiring company.

 Case Study

During the global recession, organic growth has considerably slowed as companies struggle to find profitable investment opportunities. This has resulted in many companies having large stockpiles of cash for which they are looking for a suitable use.

In an article in the Financial Times (28 March 2012), the investment bank Citigroup said that large companies have an estimated $4.2 trillion of cash on their balance sheets. One option for these companies is to use this cash to expand through mergers and acquisitions, but this remains a risky option given the economic conditions.

This has led to an increase in foreign acquisitions in emerging economies such as China, India and Brazil.

Source: 'Emerging prospects', *Financial Times*, 28 March 2012

Acquisitions are dealt with in detail in Section D of the Study Text.

3.4 Capital resource allocation - capital rationing

> **Capital rationing** is a restriction on an organisation's ability to invest capital funds, caused by an internal budget ceiling being imposed on such expenditure by management (**soft capital rationing**), or by external limitations being applied to the company, as when additional borrowed funds cannot be obtained (**hard capital rationing**).
>
> *(CIMA Official Terminology)*

If an organisation is in a capital rationing situation it will not be able to invest in all available projects which have positive NPVs because there is not enough capital for all of the investments. Capital is **a limiting factor**.

3.4.1 Soft and hard capital rationing

Capital rationing may be necessary in a business due to **internal factors** (soft capital rationing) or **external factors** (hard capital rationing).

Soft capital rationing may arise for one of the following reasons.

(a) Management may be **reluctant to issue additional share capital** because of concern that this may lead to outsiders gaining control of the business.

(b) Management may be **unwilling to issue additional share capital** if it will lead to a dilution of earnings per share.

(c) Management may **not want to raise additional debt capital** because they do not wish to be committed to large fixed interest payments.

(d) There may be a desire within the organisation to **limit investment** to a level that can be financed solely from retained earnings.

(e) **Capital expenditure budgets** may restrict spending.

Note that whenever an organisation adopts a policy that restricts funds available for investment, such a policy may be less than optimal as the organisation may reject projects with a positive net present value and forgo opportunities that would have enhanced the market value of the organisation.

Hard capital rationing may arise for one of the following reasons.

(a) Raising money through the stock market may not be possible if **share prices are depressed**.

(b) There may be **restrictions on bank lending** due to government control.

(c) Lending institutions may consider an organisation to be too **risky** to be granted further loan facilities.

(d) The **costs** associated with making small issues of capital may be too great.

3.4.2 Divisible and non-divisible projects

(a) **Divisible projects** are those which can be undertaken completely or in fractions. Suppose that project A is divisible and requires the investment of $15,000 to achieve an NPV of $4,000. $7,500 invested in project A will earn an NPV of ½ × $4,000 = $2,000.

(b) **Indivisible projects** are those which must be undertaken completely or not at all. It is not possible to invest in a fraction of the project.

You may also encounter **mutually exclusive** projects when one, and only one, of two or more choices of project can be undertaken.

3.4.3 Single period rationing with divisible projects

With **single period capital rationing**, investment funds are a limiting factor in the current period. The total return will be maximised if management follows the decision rule of maximising the return per unit of the limiting factor. They should therefore **select those projects whose cash inflows have the highest present value per $1 of capital invested.** In other words, rank the projects according to their **profitability index**.

Formula to learn

$$\text{Profitability index} = \frac{\text{NPV of project}}{\text{Initial cash outflow}}$$

3.4.4 Single period rationing with non-divisible projects

The main problem if projects are non-divisible is that there is likely to be small amounts of unused capital with each combination of projects. The best way to deal with this situation is to use trial and error and test the NPV available for different combinations of projects. This can be a laborious process if there is a large number of projects available.

3.4.5 Practical methods of dealing with capital rationing

A company may be able to limit the effects of capital rationing and exploit new opportunities.

(a)   It might **seek joint venture partners** with which to share projects.

(b)   As an alternative to direct investment in a project, the company may be able to consider a **licensing** or **franchising agreement** with another enterprise, under which the licensor/franchisor company would receive royalties.

(c)   It may be possible to **contract** out parts of a project to reduce the initial capital outlay required.

(d)   The company may seek **new** alternative **sources of capital** (subject to any restrictions which apply to it) for example:

(i) Venture capital	(iv)	Grant aid
(ii) Debt finance secured on projects assets	(v)	More effective capital management
(iii) Sale and leaseback of property or equipment	(vi)	Delay a project to a later period

4 Financing decision

FAST FORWARD

Financing decisions included both long-term decisions (capital structure) and short-term decisions (working capital management).

The financial manager will need to determine the **source, cost** and effect on **risk** of the possible sources of long-term finance. A balance between **profitability** and **liquidity** (ready availability of funds if required) must be taken into account when deciding on the optimal level of short-term finance. A further issue with financing is that the financial manager will be wanting to **minimise the cost of capital** for an organisation as this means a lower return is required by the providers of capital.

4.1 Sources of funds

The various sources of funds for investment purposes was covered in Paper F9 – *Financial Management*. This section is a brief reminder of the sources of funds available. You should consult your previous study notes for details.

4.1.1 Short-term sources

(a) **Overdrafts**

Overdrafts arise when payments from a current account exceed income to the current account – the deficit is financed by an overdraft. Overdrafts are the most important source of short-term finance available to businesses (and individuals!) They can be arranged relatively quickly and offer a degree of flexibility. Interest is only charged when the current account is overdrawn.

(b) **Short-term loans**

This is a loan of a fixed amount for a specified period of time. The capital is received immediately and is repaid either at a specified time or in instalments. Interest rates and capital repayment structure are often predetermined.

(c) **Trade credit**

This is one of the main sources of short-term finance for businesses, as they can take advantage of credit periods granted by suppliers. It is particularly useful during periods of high inflation. However companies must consider the loss of discounts that suppliers may offer for early payment. Any unacceptable delays in payment will have an adverse effect on credit ratings.

(d) **Leasing**

Leasing is a popular source of finance and is a useful alternative to purchasing an asset. The two main types of lease are operational lease and finance lease. The difference between the two types of leases lies with the extent of responsibility the lessee has for the leased asset (maintenance etc).

4.1.2 Long-term sources

Debt

The choice of debt finance depends on

- The size of the business (a public issue of bonds is only available to large companies)
- The duration of the loan
- Whether a fixed or floating interest rate is preferred
- The security that can be offered

Bonds

Bonds are long-term debt capital raised by a company for which interest is paid, usually half-yearly and at a fixed rate. Bonds can be redeemable or irredeemable and come in various forms, including floating rate, zero coupon and convertible.

Bonds have a nominal value (the debt owed by the company) and interest is paid at a stated 'coupon' on this amount. The coupon rate is quoted before tax (ie gross).

One of the issues to be aware of with long-term debt is the ability to pay off debt when the redemption date arrives. The redemption date of current loans is an important piece of information in the statement of financial position as you can establish how much new finance is likely to be needed by the company and when.

Equity

Equity finance is raised through the sale of ordinary shares to investors via a new issue or a rights issue. Holders of equity shares bear the ultimate risk as they are at the bottom of the creditor hierarchy in the event of liquidation. As a result of this high risk, equity shareholders expect the highest return of long-term finance providers. The cost of equity is always higher than the cost of debt.

4.2 Pecking order

'Pecking order' refers to the preferred order in which some companies may use different sources of finance and is as follows.

(a) Retained earnings.
(b) Debt
(c) Equity

Pecking order will be discussed in more detail in Chapter 7a.

4.3 Level of gearing

The main focus of financing decisions is how much debt a company should use, which will obviously affect the company's gearing. The appropriate level of gearing depends on a number of practical issues.

(a) *Stage in the company's life cycle*

If a company is just starting up, or is in its early growth phase, a high level of gearing is discouraged. The company will find it difficult to forecast future cash flows with any degree of certainty and any debt that is obtained is likely to have high interest rates attached.

(b) *Stability of earnings*

This can be linked to the company's life cycle above. New companies tend to have fluctuating earnings, as do companies in volatile businesses. As interest still has to be paid regardless of earnings levels, unstable earnings are not conducive to high gearing ratios.

(c) *Operational gearing (contribution/PBIT)*

High levels of fixed costs mean that contribution (sales revenue – variable costs) will be high relative to profits after fixed costs – that is, operational gearing will be high. This cost structure means volatile cash flows, therefore high levels of gearing are not recommended.

(d) *Security/collateral for the debt*

If a company is unable to offer sufficient levels of security or collateral then debt will be difficult to obtain. Any debt that is granted will reflect the risk of insufficient collateral in high interest rates.

4.4 Optimal financing mix

Key term

> **Capital structure** refers to the way in which an organisation is financed, by a combination of long-term capital (ordinary shares and reserves, preference shares, loan notes, bank loans, convertible loan stock and so on) and short-term liabilities, such as a bank overdraft and trade creditors. The mix of finance can be measured by **gearing** ratios.

The assets of a business must be financed somehow. When a business is growing, the additional assets must be financed by additional capital.

However, using debt to finance the business creates financial risk. **Financial risk** can be seen from different points of view.

(a) **The company as a whole**

If a company builds up debts that it cannot pay when they fall due, it will be forced into liquidation.

(b) **Lenders**

If a company cannot pay its debts, the company will go into liquidation owing lenders money that they are unlikely to recover in full. Lenders will probably want a **higher interest yield** to compensate them for higher financial risk and gearing.

(c) **Ordinary shareholders**

A company will not make any distributable profits unless it is able to earn enough profit from operations to pay all its interest charges, and then tax. The lower the profits or the higher the interest-bearing debts, the less there will be, if there is anything at all, for shareholders.

Ordinary shareholders will probably want a **bigger expected return** from their shares to compensate them for a **higher financial risk**. The market value of shares will therefore depend on gearing, because of this premium for financial risk that shareholders will want to earn.

4.4.1 What determines the optimal financing mix?

When we consider the capital structure decision, the question arises of whether there is an **optimal mix** of **capital and debt** that a company should try to achieve. Under one view (the traditional view) there is an optimal capital mix at which the **average cost of capital**, weighted according to the different forms of capital employed, is **minimised**.

However, the alternative view of **Modigliani and Miller** is that the firm's overall **weighted average cost of capital** is **not influenced** by changes in its **capital structure**. Their argument is that the issue of debt causes the cost of equity to rise in such a way that the benefits of debt on returns are exactly offset. Investors themselves adjust their level of personal gearing and thus the level of corporate gearing becomes irrelevant. We shall discuss this debate further in Chapter 7a.

Taxes

The impact on the company's tax **overall tax position** will need to be considered, also how **tax efficient** the alternative sources of finance are.

Clientele effect

When considering whether to change gearing significantly, directors may take into account changes in the profile of shareholders. If gearing does change significantly, the company may adjust to a **new risk-return trade-off** that is unsuitable for many shareholders. These shareholders will look to sell their shares, whilst other investors, who are now attracted by the new gearing levels, will look to buy shares.

Bankruptcy risk

Increasing the level of debt may increase the probability of default as the company is much more exposed volatility in earnings. Higher levels of debt may also increase the cost of borrowing, making repayment of debt more difficult and triggering financial distress. The company may therefore choose a level of debt that balances the benefits of debt with the costs of bankruptcy.

Signalling

Some investors may see the issue of debt capital as a sign that the directors are confident enough of the future cash flows of the business to be prepared to commit the company to making **regular interest payments** to **lenders**.

4.5 Domestic and international borrowing

If the company is receiving income in a foreign currency or has a long-term investment overseas, it can try to limit the **risk of adverse exchange rate movements** by matching. It can take out a long-term loan and use the foreign currency receipts to repay the loan. Similarly it can try to **match its foreign assets** (property, plant etc) by a **long-term loan** in the foreign currency. However, if the asset ultimately generates home currency receipts, there will be a long-term currency risk.

In addition foreign loans may carry a lower **interest rate**, but the principle of **interest rate parity** (covered in Chapter 8) suggests that the **foreign currency** will ultimately strengthen, and hence loan repayments will become more expensive.

4.6 Risk attitudes

The choice of capital structure will not only depend on company circumstances, but also on the **attitudes** that directors and owners have towards the **principal risks**. This will include the risks that are specific to the business, more general economic risks, and also the risks of raising finance. It could for example adversely affect the company's reputation if it made a rights issue that was not fully subscribed. **Foreign exchange risk** will need to be considered if the company is considering using international sources of finance.

4.6.1 Loss of control

The directors and shareholders may be unwilling to accept the **conditions** and the **loss of control** that obtaining extra finance will mean. Control may be diminished whether equity or loan funding is sought:

(a)   **Issuing shares** to outsiders may **dilute** the **control** of the existing shareholders and directors, and the company will be subject to greater regulatory control if it obtains a stock market listing.

(b)   The price of additional debt finance may be **security** restricting disposal of the assets secured and **covenants** that limit the company's rights to **dispose of assets** in general or to pay dividends.

4.6.2 Costs

The directors may consider that the **extra interest costs** the company is committed to are too high; remember that companies are not legally obliged to pay dividends, although obviously if they don't do so, there may be an impact on the share price. On the other hand the effective **cost of debt** might be cheaper than the **cost of equity**, particularly if tax relief can be obtained.

The costs of **arranging new finance sources** may also be significant, particularly if the business is contemplating using a number of different sources over time.

4.6.3 Commitments

The interest and repayment schedules that the company is required to meet may be considered **too tight.** The collateral that loan providers require may also be too much, particularly if the directors are themselves required to provide **personal guarantees.**

4.6.4 Present sources of finance

Perhaps it's easy to find reasons why new sources of finance may not be desirable, but equally they may be considered more acceptable than drawing on current sources. For example shareholders may be **unwilling to contribute further funds** in a rights issue; the business may wish to improve its relations with its suppliers, and one condition may be lessening its reliance on trade credit.

4.7 Feasibility of capital structure

FAST FORWARD

The mix of finance chosen must be **feasible;** companies may face **restrictions** in the finance available, and may not be able to commit to repaying too much at any one time.

Even if directors and shareholders are happy with the implications of obtaining significant extra finance, the company may not be able to obtain that finance.

4.7.1 Lenders' attitudes

Whether lenders are prepared to lend the company any money will depend on the company's circumstances, particularly as they affect the company's ability to generate **cash** and **security** for the loan.

4.7.2 Availability and popularity of finance

If the **stock market** is **depressed**, it may be difficult to raise cash through share issues, so major amounts will have to be borrowed. On the other hand specific sources of finance may be particularly appealing to investors.

How quickly amounts are available may also be an issue.

4.7.3 Future trends

Likely **future trends** of **fund availability** will be significant if a business is likely to require a number of injections of funds over the next few years. The business needs to consider how much current decisions may affect its ability to raise funds in the future.

4.7.4 Restrictions in loan agreements

Restrictions written into agreements on current loans may prohibit a business from taking out **further loans**, or may require that its gearing does **not exceed specified limits**.

4.7.5 Maturity dates

If a business already has significant debt repayable in a few years' time, because of **cash flow restrictions** it may not be able to take out further debt repayable around the same time.

5 Dividend decision

FAST FORWARD The dividend decision is mainly a reflection of the investment decision and the financing decision.

The dividend decision is really an interaction between the investment decision and the financing decision, as the amount of money paid out as dividends will affect the level of retained earnings available for investment. Most companies follow a target dividend payout policy where a constant proportion of earnings is distributed as dividends each year.

Given the pecking order theory mentioned above, whereby companies generally prefer to use retained earnings first to finance investments, how do some companies manage to pay dividends at all? If companies have access to debt finance, they can borrow money to finance investments. This releases a proportion of retained earnings to be paid as dividends. Known as 'borrowing to pay a dividend', this practice is only legal if the company in question has accumulated realised profits.

5.1 Dividends and the company's life cycle

A company's dividend policy will vary depending on the stage of the company's life cycle.

A young, growing company with numerous profitable investment opportunities is unlikely to pay dividends as its earnings will be used for investment purposes. Shareholders should therefore have low or no expectations of receiving a dividend.

<--->

Young company

Zero / Low dividend

High growth / investment needs
Wants to minimise debt

Mature company

High stable dividend

Lower growth
Able & willing to take on debt
Possibly share buybacks too

More mature companies may have built up a sufficient surplus of cash to allow them to pay dividends whilst still being able to fund dividend payments. Shareholders in such companies may also benefit from share buybacks whereby their shares are re-purchased by the company – an alternative way of returning surplus cash to shareholders.

5.2 Interaction of investment with financing and dividend decisions

Managers will need to consider whether **extra finance** will be required, and if it will be, what will be the consequences of obtaining it. They will have to consider the demands of **providers of finance**, particularly of equity shareholders who require **dividends**. Will equity shareholders be content with projects that maximise their long-term returns, or will they require a minimum return or dividend each year?

When taking financial decisions, managers will have to fulfil the **requirements of the providers of finance**, otherwise finance may not be made available. This may be particularly difficult in the case of equity shareholders, since dividends are paid at the company's discretion; however if equity shareholders do not receive the dividends they want, they will look to sell their shares, the share price will fall and the company will have more difficulty raising funds from share issues in future.

Although there may be risks in obtaining extra finance, the long-term risks to the business of **failing to invest** may be even greater and managers will have to balance these up. Investment may have direct consequences for decisions involving the **management of finance**; extra working capital may be required if investments are made and sales expand as a consequence. Managers must be sensitive to this and ensure that a balance is maintained between receivables and inventory, and cash.

A further issue managers will need to consider is the **matching** of the **characteristics** of investment and finance. **Time** is a critical aspect; an investment which earns returns in the long-term should be matched with finance which requires repayment in the long-term.

The amount of surplus cash paid out as **dividends** will have a direct impact on **finance** available for **investment**. Managers have a difficult decision here; how much do they pay out to shareholders each year to keep them happy, and what level of funds do they retain in the business to invest in projects that will yield long-term income? In addition funds available from retained profits may be needed if debt finance is likely to be unavailable, or if taking on more debt would expose the company to undesirable risks.

5.3 Dividend payout policy

Senior management have to decide on a suitable payout policy that reflects the **expectations** and **preferences** of investors. As mentioned above, dividend payout is linked closely with the lifecycle of the company therefore it is unlikely that investors in a growing company will expect dividends in the near future.

The focus of all financial management decisions should be on the **primary objectives** of the company. If shareholders expect dividends to be paid senior management must balance the dividend payment and retention policies to meet these expectations whilst ensuring sufficient funds are available to finance profitable investment opportunities and fulfil the objective of maximising shareholder value.

You will often find that shareholders in a particular company have **similar** expectations and preferences regarding dividends. Those investing in a company that is not paying dividends will not be expecting dividends (or actually want them) whereas other investors expect dividends and newer shareholders may have purchased shares with this expectation in mind.

Dividend capacity (free cash flow to equity) is covered in Chapter 18 in a more detailed discussion of dividend policy. It is also covered in Chapter 10 in the context of company valuation and dividend policy is also covered in Chapter 2.

5.4 Share repurchase schemes

Dividends are not the only method of distributing retained earnings to shareholders. In many countries companies have the right to **buy back shares from shareholders** who are willing to sell them, subject to certain conditions. This is known as a share repurchase or a buy-back.

For a **smaller company** with few shareholders, the reason for buying back the company's own shares may be that there is no immediate willing purchaser at a time when a shareholder wishes to sell shares. For a public company, share repurchase could provide a way of withdrawing from the share market and 'going private'.

5.4.1 Benefits of a share repurchase scheme

(a) Finding a **use for surplus cash**, which may be a 'dead asset'.

(b) **Increase in earnings per share** through a reduction in the number of shares in issue. This should lead to a higher share price than would otherwise be the case, and the company should be able to increase dividend payments on the remaining shares in issue.

(c) **Increase in gearing**. Repurchase of a company's own shares allows debt to be substituted for equity, so raising gearing. This will be of interest to a company wanting to increase its gearing without increasing its total long-term funding.

(d) **Readjustment of the company's equity base** to more appropriate levels, for a company whose business is in decline.

(e) Possibly **preventing a takeover** or enabling a quoted company to withdraw from the stock market.

5.4.2 Drawbacks of a share repurchase scheme

(a) It can be **hard to arrive at a price** that will be fair both to the vendors and to any shareholders who are not selling shares to the company.

(b) A repurchase of shares could be seen as an **admission** that the company **cannot make better use of the funds** than the shareholders.

(c) Some shareholders may suffer from being **taxed on a capital gain** following the purchase of their shares rather than receiving dividend income.

Case Study

American technology giant Apple outlined plans in March 2012 to return $45 million to shareholders over a three year period, including a $10 billion buy back of shares, It was able to do this as it has generated large volumes of cash in recent years and was estimated to have a cash pile of more than $100 billion. Apple had not paid dividends in the previous 17 years as it previously felt that the cash reserves represented a security blanket for the company – when acquisition or R&D opportunities presented themselves there was no need to borrow a lot of money and put the company at risk, as the cash was already there. However, given Apple's cash reserves are growing rapidly (they increased by $38 billion in 2011) Apple decided to start making returns to shareholders.

6 Financial planning and control

FAST FORWARD

Financial planning covers the monitoring of the company's financial position, the evaluation of its productive capacity needs and the financing requirements of the company.

6.1 Strategic cash flow planning

In order to survive, any business must have an adequate net inflow of cash. Businesses should try to plan for positive net cash flows but at the same time it is unwise to hold too much cash.

When a company is cash-rich it may choose to do one (or more) of the following.

(a) **Plan to use the cash**, for example for a project investment or a takeover bid for another company

(b) **Pay out the cash** to shareholders as **dividends**, and let the shareholders decide how best to use the cash for themselves

(c) **Re-purchase its own shares** (share buyback)

Strategic fund management is an extension of cash flow planning, which takes into consideration the ability of a business to overcome unforeseen problems with cash flows. Where cash flow has become a problem, a company may choose to sell off some of its assets. However it is important to recognise the difference between assets that a company can survive without and those that are essential for the company's continued operation.

Assets can be divided into three categories.

(a)   Those that are needed to carry out the core activities of the business (eg plant and machinery)

(b)   Those that are not essential for carrying out the main activities of the business and can be sold off at fairly short notice (eg short-term marketable investments)

(c)   Those that are not essential for carrying out the main activities of the business and can be sold off to raise cash, but may take some time to sell (eg long-term investments, subsidiary companies)

Case Study

It was announced in July 2010 that BP was to sell off oil fields and production facilities to raise cash to pay for the Deepwater Horizon oil spill. The company reached a deal with American oil production company Apache Corp to sell a portfolio of oil assets in the US, Canada and Egypt. The sales are expected to raise $7 billion.

If a company is looking for cash quickly, it could perhaps arrange a higher overdraft facility, reduce inventory or ask customers to pay their outstanding balances immediately.

6.2 Financial controls

FAST FORWARD

Strategic planning and control is 'the process of deciding on objectives of the organisation, on changes in these objectives, on the resources used to attain these objectives, and on the policies that are to govern the acquisition, use and disposition of these resources'.

Tactical or management control is 'the process by which managers assure that resources are obtained and used effectively and efficiently in the accomplishment of the organisation's objectives'.

Operational control is 'the process of assuring that specific tasks are carried out effectively and efficiently'.

Management control is sometimes called **tactics** or **tactical planning**. Operational control is sometimes called **operational planning**.

	Investment	Financing	Dividend
Strategic	Selection of products and markets Required levels of profitability Purchase of fixed assets fundamental to the business	Target debt/equity mix	Capital growth or high dividend payout
Tactical	Other fixed asset purchases Efficient use of resources Effective use of resources Pricing	Lease versus buy	Scrip or cash dividends
Operational	Working capital management	Working capital management	N/A

It is quite common for strategic plans to be in conflict with the shorter term objectives of management control. Examples are as follows.

(a) It might be in the long-term interests of a company to buy more expensive or technologically advanced machinery to make a product, in the expectation that when market demand for the product eventually declines, customers will buy from producers whose output is of a slightly better quality – ie made on better machinery. In the short run, however, new and expensive machinery will incur higher depreciation charges and therefore **higher unit costs** for the same volume of production.

(b) Similarly, it may be in the long-term interests of a company to invest in research and development, in spite of the costs and loss of profits in the short term.

7 Risk management

FAST FORWARD

For investors to be persuaded to take on extra risk, they must be compensated in the form of higher returns.

7.1 The risk/return relationship

All businesses face some sort of risk, although the extent of the risk will vary. The risk/return relationship was covered in detail in Paper F9 – *Financial Management* therefore you should be familiar with the concept of investors requiring higher returns for taking on more risk.

In a risk-free investment (eg Treasury Bills, Gilts) investors will only be compensated for the fact that they are postponing consumption in favour of investment. As investors take on extra risk, the return they require will not only compensate them for delayed consumption but also include a premium for the additional risk.

The level of risk that a company is willing to expose itself to will depend on the risk appetite of its shareholders. Conservative shareholders are likely to be risk-averse, preferring less risk with lower returns, whereas risk-takers are prepared to take on more risk in exchange for the chance of higher returns.

The relationship between risk and return is demonstrated in the diagram below.

7.2 Risk preferences

Shareholders tend to invest in those companies that have a risk profile similar to their own portfolio. Therefore it would be extremely unlikely for a risk-averse investor to buy shares in a company that is perceived to be risky (for example, those involved in research and development or new technology companies).

Financial managers must be aware of the **risk preferences** of their company's shareholders and invest funds accordingly. They should avoid trying to change the risk profile of the company without the approval of the shareholders. This could lead to existing shareholders selling their shares, resulting in a **reduction** in the share price.

Managers should also avoid imposing their own risk preferences on their business decisions. Managers may be risk-averse (perhaps worried about their jobs) but if the shareholders are risk takers they will expect business decisions to reflect this. If shareholders are not satisfied they may again sell their shares, with a resultant fall in share price.

7.3 Managing risk

Risk can be managed in several different ways.

(a) **Hedging** – for example currency risk and interest rate risk (see Section F covered in Chapters 16 and 17). Hedging involves taking actions to make an outcome more certain.

(b) **Diversifying**. This was mentioned earlier in this chapter and is effectively the prevention of 'putting all your eggs in one basket'. (See systematic / unsystematic risk in Chapter 2 Section 6.2). A portfolio of different investments, with varying degrees of risk, should help to reduce the overall risk of the business. One way of achieving diversification is via acquisition or merger (see Section D of this Study Text).

(c) **Risk mitigation**. This involves putting control procedures in place to avoid investments in projects whose risk is above the shareholders' required level.

8 Communicating policy to stakeholders

FAST FORWARD

For financial strategy to be successful it needs to be communicated and supported by the **stakeholder groups**.

- **Internal** – managers, employees
- **Connected** – shareholders, banks, customers, suppliers
- **External** – government, pressure groups, local communities

Key term

Stakeholders are groups or individuals having a legitimate interest in the activities of an organisation, generally comprising customers, employees, the community, shareholders, suppliers and lenders.

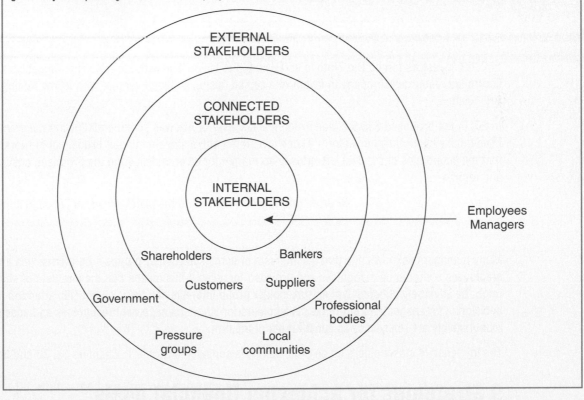

Exam focus point

You may be told in a question that a company aims to respect the interests of stakeholders, and determines its policies in the light of that aim. Even if you aren't, you will see at various times in this text circumstances when stakeholder interests become particularly important, for example in a merger and acquisition situation.

8.1 Objectives of stakeholder groups

The various groups of stakeholders in a firm will have different goals which will depend in part on the situation of the organisation.

STAKEHOLDER GOALS	
Shareholders	Providers of risk capital, aim to maximise wealth
Suppliers	Often other businesses, aim to be paid full amount by date agreed, but want to continue long-term trading relationship, and so may accept later payment
Long-term lenders	Wish to receive payments of interest and capital on loan by due date for repayment
Employees	Maximise rewards paid to them in salaries and benefits, also prefer continuity in employment
Government	Political objectives such as sustained economic growth and high employment.
Management	Maximising their own rewards

Exam focus point

You might be asked to comment on a situation where the interests of different stakeholders diverge.

8.2 Influence of stakeholders

The actions of stakeholder groups in pursuit of their various goals can exert influence on strategy. The **greater** the **power** of the **stakeholder**, the greater his influence will be.

 Case Study

There are numerous examples of the influence that stakeholders can have on business strategy.

In 2009, investors forced Rio Tinto to scrap its $28.1 billion deal with Chinalco (the Chinese state-controlled resources company in favour of a capital raising and joint venture with fellow mining group BHP Billiton.

In 2010, the proposed $35.5 billion Prudential takeover of AIA was scrapped following the stand taken by Prudential's institutional investors. Those investors (with a shareholding in Prudential of more than 20%) that the economics of the deal left virtually no margin for error in delivering the promised cost synergies and returns.

Source: 'Shareholders step up to the plate', *Financial Times*, 8 June 2010

Many managers acknowledge that the interests of some stakeholder groups – eg themselves and employees – should be recognised and provided for, even if this means that the interests of shareholders might be adversely affected. Not all stakeholder group interests can be given specific attention in the decisions of management, but those stakeholders for whom management recognises and accepts a responsibility are referred to as **constituents** of the firm.

The influence of stakeholders on an organisation is considered further in Chapters 3a, 3b and 3c.

9 Strategies for achieving financial goals   6/11

FAST FORWARD

Strategy is a course of action to achieve an objective. Strategies to accomplish the objective of maximising shareholder value are set at the corporate, business and operational levels.

9.1 Strategy

Key term

> **Strategy** may be defined as a course of action, including the specification of resources required, to achieve a specific objective.

Strategy can be **short-term** or **long-term**, depending on the time horizon of the objective to be achieved.

This definition also indicates that since strategy depends on objectives or targets, the obvious starting point for a study of corporate strategy and financial strategy is the **identification and formulation of objectives**.

9.2 Characteristics of strategic decisions

Johnson, Scholes and Whittington (2008) have summarised the characteristics of strategic decisions for an organisation as follows.

(a) Strategic decisions will be concerned with the **scope** of the organisation's activities.

(b) Strategy involves the matching of an organisation's activities to the **environment** in which it operates.

(c) Strategy also involves the matching of an organisation's activities to its **resource capability**.

(d) Strategic decisions therefore involve major decisions about the **allocation** or **re-allocation of resources.**

(e) Strategic decisions will **affect operational decisions**, because they will set off a chain of 'lesser' decisions and operational activities, involving the use of resources.

(f) Strategic decisions will be affected by:
   (i) Environmental considerations
   (ii) Resources availability
   (iii) The **values and expectations of the people in power** within the organisation

(g) Strategic decisions are likely to affect the **long-term direction** that the organisation takes.

(h) Strategic decisions have implications for change throughout the organisation, and so are likely to be **complex in nature**.

9.3 Levels of strategy

There are three main levels of strategy.

9.3.1 Corporate strategy

This is concerned with broader issues, such as 'what business are we in?' **Financial aspects** of this level of strategic decision-making include the choice of method in entering a market or business. Whether entry should be accomplished through an acquisition or through organic growth is a question with financial implications.   It is important to be clear about corporate strategy as this forms the basis of other strategic decisions.

9.3.2 Business strategy or competitive strategy

This covers the question of how strategic business units compete in **individual markets**, and therefore of the resources which should be allocated to them.   Business strategy relates to individual strategic business units (SBUs) – that is, parts of the organisation where there are distinct external markets for goods or services.

Competitive strategy examines the threat on the performance of the company of factors such as

(a) The potential changes in the industry in which the firm operates, through entry of new competitors

(b) The competition between existing firms in terms of costs, pricing and product quality

(c) The development of substitute products that may affect the industry as a whole

(d) The monopolistic power of individual companies in the input markets

(e) The monopolistic power of companies in the various product markets.

Competitive strategy allows a company to forecast revenue and costs much more accurately. Operating profits together with financing and distribution decisions determine ultimately the value of a company.

9.3.3 Operational strategy

This is to do with how different functions within the business – including the finance function – contribute to corporate and business strategies. In most businesses, the successful implementation of business strategies rely to a great extent on decisions that are taken at the operational level. For example, at BPP there are operational strategies in place in terms of updating study materials and the design and presentation of courses.

9.4 The management of financial resources

Key term

> The **management of financial resources** is part of the overall financial strategy and consists of the management of the balance sheet items to achieve the desired balance between risk and return.

Financial strategy determines the means for the attainment of stated **objectives** or **targets** An integral part of financial strategy is the **management of financial resources**.
The financial management process provides the framework for coordinating and controlling the firm's actions to achieve its financial objectives. It includes strategic financial plans which determines a company's actions and the resulting impact on shareholder value over a period of time, and which, in turn determine the short-term operating plans of the firm.

Long-term financial strategy is part of firm's overall strategy together with a company's marketing strategy, investment strategy and product development strategy. Financial strategy is expressed through a series of annual budget and profit plans.

The long-term financial strategy is supplemented by a **short-term financial strategy** which deals with the management of the financial resources of the company.

The goal of short-term financial management is to manage each of the firm's current assets and liabilities in order to achieve a balance between profitability and risk, which enhances shareholder value. Too much investment in current assets reduces profitability, whereas too little investment in current assets may impair the ability of a company to meet debt payments. Either way, the effect on the value on the firm may be negative.

The efficient management of financial resources of a company is achieved through the construction of annual cash budgets which reflect the firm's planned inflows and outflows of cash. The cash budget presents a useful tool for the estimation of the short-term cash requirements or surpluses of a company. If a company is predicted to face a deficit, the most efficient method of financing should be considered. This will normally involve the issue of short-term money market instruments.

If a company is predicted to have a surplus, then an appropriate investment in short-term money market instruments should be considered.

Case Study

The success of Four Seasons, one of the most luxurious hotel brands in the world, is based on four key strategic decisions that were made in the formative years of the business.

The 'Golden Rule' of the Four Seasons is based on service. However, whilst service is the backbone of any hotel chain, it is how service is delivered that sets Four Seasons apart. The founder and Chairman of the business Isadore Sharp has said that the 'Golden Rule' of the Four Seasons is 'to treat others as you would like to be treated yourself'.

The other key strategic decisions are

(a)   a focus on managing only medium-sized hotels of exceptional quality (thus ensuring that the values of the business are not blurred)

(b)   to manage, rather than own, the hotels

(c)   to make service the brand's distinguishing edge

Note that all the key strategic decisions compliment each other, thus ensuring that the business has clear direction and a sharp focus on what it is trying to deliver to its customers.

Chapter Roundup

- In financial management of businesses, the key objective is the **maximisation of shareholders' wealth**.

- Non-financial objectives may limit the achievement of financial objectives. Their existence suggests the assumption that the main purpose of a company is to maximise shareholders' wealth is too simplistic.

- In seeking to attain the financial objectives of the organisation or enterprise, a financial manager has to make three fundamental decisions – investment, financing and dividend. The investment decision involves selecting appropriate investment opportunities that will help to fulfil the company's primary objectives.

- **Financing decisions** include both long-term decisions (capital structure) and short-term decisions (working capital management).

- The mix of finance chosen must be **feasible**; companies may face **restrictions** in the finance available, and may not be able to commit to repaying too much at any one time.

- The dividend decision is mainly a reflection of the investment decision and the financing decision.

- Financial planning covers the monitoring of the company's financial position, the evaluation of its productive capacity needs and the financing requirements of the company.

- **Strategic planning and control** is 'the process of deciding on objectives of the organisation, on changes in these objectives, on the resources used to attain these objectives, and on the policies that are to govern the acquisition, use and disposition of these resources'.

- **Tactical or management control** is 'the process by which managers assure that resources are obtained and used effectively and efficiently in the accomplishment of the organisation's objectives'.

- **Operational control** is 'the process of assuring that specific tasks are carried out effectively and efficiently'.

- **Management control** is sometimes called **tactics** or **tactical planning**. **Operational control** is sometimes called **operational planning**.

- For investors to be persuaded to take on extra risk, they must be compensated in the form of higher returns.

- For financial strategy to be successful it needs to be communicated and supported by the **stakeholder groups**.

    - **Internal** – managers, employees
    - **Connected** – shareholders, banks, customers, suppliers
    - **External** – government, pressure groups, local communities

- **Strategy** is a course of action to achieve an objective. Strategies to accomplish the objective of maximising shareholder value are set at the corporate, business and operational levels.

Quick Quiz

1   Why is maximisation of the market value of shares the key objective in the theory of company finance?

2   State three ways of measuring the value of a company

3   What are the three main financial management decisions?

4   What are the main ways of growth for a company?

5   What are the three groups of stakeholders?

6   What is the objective of risk management policy?

Answers to Quick Quiz

1   Because it implies maximisation of the market value of shareholder wealth.

2   (1) Going concern basis
    (2) Break-up basis
    (3) Market values

3   (1) Investment decisions
    (2) Financing decisions
    (3) Dividend decisions

4   Organic growth or through acquisitions

5   Internal, Connected and External.

6   To choose the combination of risk and return which is consistent with the risk attitude of the company.

References

Johnson, G., Scholes, K. and Whittington, R. (2008). *Exploring Corporate Strategy: Test and cases*, 8th edition, Pearson, Harlow

Now try the question below from the Exam Question Bank

Number	Level	Marks	Time
1	Examination	20	36 mins

Financial strategy formulation

Topic list	Syllabus reference
1 Financial and non-financial characteristics of companies	A (2) (a)
2 Assessing corporate performance	A (2) (a)
3 Other information from companies' accounts	A (2) (a)
4 Optimal capital structure	A (2) (b)
5 Dividend policy	A (2) (c)
6 Risk management	A (2) (d), (f)
7 Different types of risk	A (2) (e)
8 Capital investment monitoring	A (2) (g)

Introduction

This chapter looks in greater detail into four areas of financial strategy, namely the capital structure policy, the dividend distribution policy, the capital investment monitoring process and the risk management process. The Capital Asset Pricing Model underpins a lot of what is covered in the following chapters.

Study guide

		Intellectual level
A2	**Financial strategy formulation**	
(a)	Assess organisational performance using methods such as ratios, trends, EVA™ and MVA	3
(b)	Recommend the optimum capital mix and structure within a specified business context and capital asset structure	3
(c)	Recommend appropriate distribution and retention policy	3
(d)	Explain the theoretical and practical rationale for the management of risk	3
(e)	Assess the organisation's exposure to business and financial risk including operational, reputational, political, economic, regulatory and fiscal risk	3
(f)	Develop a framework for risk management comparing and contrasting risk mitigation, hedging and diversification strategies	3
(g)	Establish capital investment monitoring and risk management systems.	3

Exam guide

You may be asked about the contents of a strategic financial plan. Alternatively, as part of a longer question assessing a specific proposal, you may need to draw on your knowledge of the reasons for mergers and acquisitions, or the differences between vertical integration and diversification.

1 Financial and non-financial characteristics of companies   6/08

In describing the state of a company, analysts normally rely on **financial characteristics**, as well as on characteristics such as **size**, **quality of management** and **industry structure**. It is possible of course that good management and monopolistic power in an industry would ultimately be reflected in financial performance. However, timing issues may also be important and therefore the effect of management change which is measured today may not be fully reflected within the time frame of our analysis. Thus one may want to investigate differences in companies in terms of **non-financial characteristics**.

So in addition to the analysis of the information contained in the financial statements, **non-financial factors** exist that may modify the evaluation of the company. Some of these **non-financial** factors are discussed below:

- Foreign exposure
- Quality of management
- Ownership structure

Foreign exposure is important for exporting or importing companies, as part of the revenue or expenses may be influenced by events outside the country of operation. Foreign currency exposure is an important possible source of risk, especially if the publication of information on hedging currency risk is not obligatory.

The **quality of management** and the depth of administrative structure in a company are more difficult to evaluate. **Positive aspects** of management will be reflected in a **steady growth pattern**. **Negative aspects** would include a firm founded and headed by one person who is approaching retirement and has made **no plan for succession**. Equally **negative** is the firm that has had **numerous changes of management** and philosophy. On the other hand excessive stability is not always desirable. Characteristics of a good management team include **depth**, a clear line of **succession** if the chief officers are nearing retirement, and a **diversity of age** within the management team.

Ownership of the firm should also be considered as a factor. If one family or group of investors owns a controlling interest in a firm, they may be too conservative in reacting to changes in the market. Owners should also be judged in terms of whether they are strategic or financial. Often financial buyers invest for the short to intermediate term, hoping to sell their positions (or the entire company) at a profit. In such a case a company may not plan for **longer-term growth** and it may be in its interest to boost **short-term growth** at the expense of **long term prospects**.

A second issue that faces the investigator is to determine when a financial characteristic of a company deviates from the norm. In other words we need a norm in order to compare these characteristics to other companies or to the industry. For example, a financial characteristic of a company such as sales growth may appear attractive on its own for a company, but for an industry it may not be. There are many industry considerations that should be taken account of such as:

- Economic cyclicality
- Growth prospects
- Research and development expenses
- Competitors
- Sources of supply
- Degree of regulation
- Labour relationships
- Accounting policies

An additional degree of complexity is added because these factors should be considered in a global context since the elimination of trade barriers seems to have increased the competitive pressures on all sectors of an economy. The economic crisis in the Far East, the Russian bond crisis, oil price volatility, all constitute factors that make the economic analysis of a company from the view point of domestic market seriously deficient.

2 Assessing corporate performance

FAST FORWARD

> Corporate performance can be measured using such means as ratios, trends and specialised techniques including Economic Value Added (EVA™) and Market Value Added (MVA).

The assessment of your own company's, or someone else's, corporate performance is an important foundation for the formulation of financial strategy. Knowledge of company performance will help management to determine new strategies or amend existing strategies to take account of changing circumstances.

2.1 Ratios

You should already be familiar with ratio analysis from Paper F9 – *Financial Management*. However as a reminder the main ratios are listed below. **Note that none of these ratios are given in the exam so you will have to learn them**.

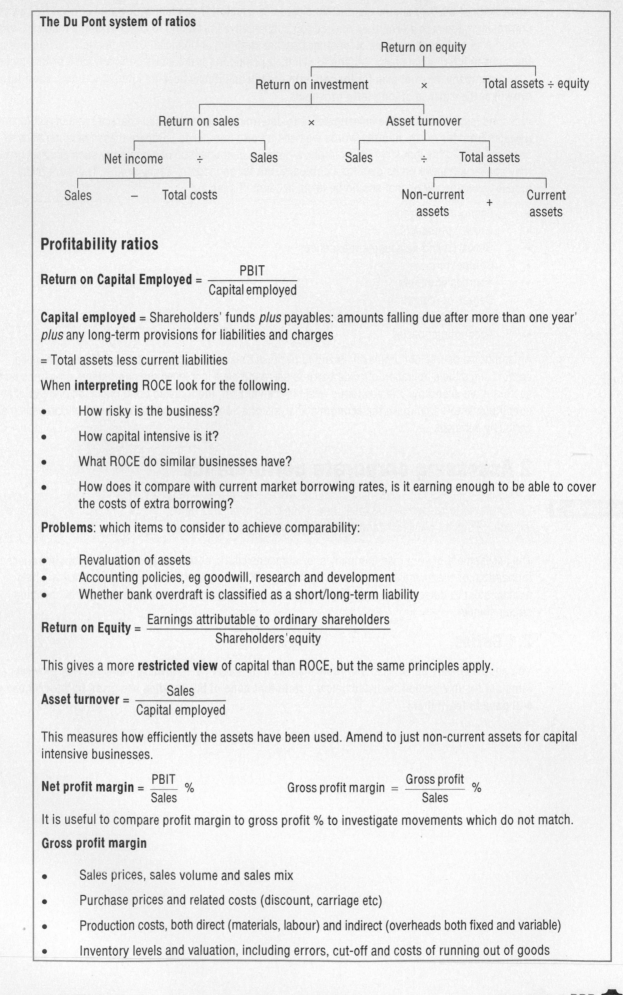

The Du Pont system of ratios

Return on equity

Return on investment × Total assets ÷ equity

Return on sales × Asset turnover

Net income ÷ Sales | Sales ÷ Total assets

Sales − Total costs | Non-current assets + Current assets

Profitability ratios

Return on Capital Employed $= \dfrac{\text{PBIT}}{\text{Capital employed}}$

Capital employed = Shareholders' funds *plus* payables: amounts falling due after more than one year' *plus* any long-term provisions for liabilities and charges

= Total assets less current liabilities

When **interpreting** ROCE look for the following.

- How risky is the business?

- How capital intensive is it?

- What ROCE do similar businesses have?

- How does it compare with current market borrowing rates, is it earning enough to be able to cover the costs of extra borrowing?

Problems: which items to consider to achieve comparability:

- Revaluation of assets
- Accounting policies, eg goodwill, research and development
- Whether bank overdraft is classified as a short/long-term liability

Return on Equity $= \dfrac{\text{Earnings attributable to ordinary shareholders}}{\text{Shareholders' equity}}$

This gives a more **restricted view** of capital than ROCE, but the same principles apply.

Asset turnover $= \dfrac{\text{Sales}}{\text{Capital employed}}$

This measures how efficiently the assets have been used. Amend to just non-current assets for capital intensive businesses.

Net profit margin $= \dfrac{\text{PBIT}}{\text{Sales}}$ %   Gross profit margin $= \dfrac{\text{Gross profit}}{\text{Sales}}$ %

It is useful to compare profit margin to gross profit % to investigate movements which do not match.

Gross profit margin

- Sales prices, sales volume and sales mix

- Purchase prices and related costs (discount, carriage etc)

- Production costs, both direct (materials, labour) and indirect (overheads both fixed and variable)

- Inventory levels and valuation, including errors, cut-off and costs of running out of goods

Net profit margin

- Sales expenses in relation to sales levels

- Administrative expenses, including salary levels

- Distribution expenses in relation to sales levels

Liquidity ratios

Current ratio = $\dfrac{\text{Current assets}}{\text{Current liabilities}}$

Assume assets realised at book level ∴ theoretical. 2:1 acceptable? 1.5:1? It depends on the industry. Remember that excessively large levels can indicate excessive receivables and inventories, and poor control of working capital.

Quick ratio (acid test) = $\dfrac{\text{Current assets - inventory}}{\text{Current liabilities}}$

Eliminates illiquid and subjectively valued inventory. Care is needed: it could be high if **overtrading** with receivables, but no cash. Is 1:1 OK? Many supermarkets operate on 0.3, as inventories of goods are very liquid and inventory turnover is very fast.

Receivables collection period (receivables days) = $\dfrac{\text{Trade receivables}}{\text{Credit sales}} \times 365$

Is it **consistent** with quick/current ratio? If not, Investigate.

Inventory days = $\dfrac{\text{Inventory}}{\text{Cost of sales}} \times 365$

Note that cost of sales excludes depreciation of any production equipment

The quicker the turnover the better? But remember:

- Lead times

- Seasonal fluctuations in orders

- Alternative uses of warehouse space

- Bulk buying discounts

- Likelihood of inventory perishing or becoming obsolete

Payables payment period = $\dfrac{\text{Trade payables}}{\text{Purchases}} \times 365$

Use **cost of sales (excluding depreciation)** if purchases are not disclosed.

Cash operating cycle

= Average time raw materials are in inventory

− Period of credit taken from suppliers

+ Time taken to produce goods

+ Time taken by customers to pay for goods

Reasons for changes in liquidity

- Credit control efficiency altered

- Altering payment period of suppliers as a source of funding

- Reducing inventory holdings to maintain liquidity

Shareholders' investment ratios (stock market ratios)

$$\text{Dividend yield} = \frac{\text{Dividend per share}}{\text{Market price per share}} \%$$

- **Low yield**: the company retains a large proportion of profits to reinvest

- **High yield**: this is a risky company or slow-growing

Dividend yield is generally less than interest yield. Shareholders will expect price rises, and wish for return (dividends + capital gains) to exceed return investors get from fixed interest securities.

$$\text{Earnings per share (EPS)} = \frac{\text{Profits distributable to ordinary shareholders}}{\text{Number of ordinary shares issued}}$$

Investors look for growth; earnings levels need to be sustained to pay dividends and invest in the business. In order for comparisons over time to be valid, must be consistent basis of calculation. EPS can be manipulated.

Need to consider possibility of dilution through exercise of warrants or options, or conversion of bonds.

$$\text{Dividend cover} = \frac{\text{EPS}}{\text{Dividend per share}}$$

This shows **how safe the dividend is**, or the extent of profit retention. Variations are due to maintaining dividend when profits are declining.

The converse of dividend cover is the **dividend payout ratio**.

$$\text{Dividend payout ratio} = \frac{\text{Dividend per share}}{\text{EPS}}$$

$$\text{P/E ratio} = \frac{\text{Market price per share}}{\text{EPS}}$$

The **higher the better** here: it reflects the confidence of the market in high earnings growth and/or low risk. A rise in EPS will cause an increase in P/E ratio, but maybe not to same extent.

P/E ratio will be affected by interest rate changes; a rise in rates will mean a fall in the P/E ratio as shares become less attractive. P/E ratio also depends on market expectations and confidence.

Debt and gearing ratios

$$\text{Financial gearing} = \frac{\text{Prior charge capital}}{\text{Equity capital (including reserves)}} \quad \text{(based on statement of financial position values)}$$

Financial gearing measures the relationship between shareholders' capital plus reserves, and either prior charge capital or borrowings or both.

Prior charge capital is capital which has a right to the receipt of interest or of preferred dividends in precedence to any claim on distributable earnings on the part of the ordinary shareholders.

OR

$$\text{Financial gearing} = \frac{\text{Market value of prior charge capital}}{\text{Market value of equity} + \text{Market value of debt}} \quad \text{(based on market values)}$$

$$\text{Operational gearing} = \frac{\text{Contribution}}{\text{Profit before interest and tax (PBIT)}}$$

Contribution is sales minus variable cost of sales.

$$\text{Interest coverage ratio} = \frac{\text{Profit before interest and tax}}{\text{Interest}}$$

Debt ratio = Total debts : Total assets

2.1.1 Uses of ratio analysis

The key to obtaining meaningful information from ratio analysis is **comparison**: comparing ratios over time within the same business to establish whether the business is **improving** or **declining**, and comparing ratios between similar businesses to see whether the company you are analysing is better or worse than average within its own business sector.

A vital element in effective ratio analysis is understanding the needs of the person for whom the ratio analysis is being undertaken.

(a)   **Investors** will be interested in the **risk and return** relating to their investment, so will be concerned with dividends, market prices, level of debt vs equity etc.

(b)   **Suppliers** and **lenders** are interested in receiving the payments due to them, so will want to know how liquid the business is.

(c)   **Managers** are interested in ratios that indicate how well the business is being run, and also how the business is doing in relation to its **competitors**.

2.1.2 Limitations of ratio analysis

Although ratio analysis can be a very useful technique, it is important to realise its limitations.

(a)   **Availability of comparable information**

When making comparisons with other companies in the industry, industry averages may hide **wide variations** in figures. Figures for 'similar' companies may provide a better guide, but then there are problems identifying which companies are similar, and obtaining enough detailed information about them.

(b)   **Use of historical/out-of-date information**

Comparisons with the previous history of a business may be of limited use, if the business has recently undergone, or is about to undergo, **substantial changes**.

(c)   **Ratios are not definitive**

'Ideal levels' vary industry by industry, and even they are not definitive. Companies may be able to exist without any difficulty with ratios that are rather worse than the industry average.

(d)   **Need for careful interpretation**

For example, if comparing two businesses' liquidity ratios, one business may have higher levels. This might appear to be 'good', but further investigation might reveal that the higher ratios are a result of higher inventory and receivable levels which are a result of poor working capital management by the business with the 'better' ratios.

(e)   **Manipulation**

Any ratio including profit may be distorted by **choice of accounting policies**. For smaller companies, working capital ratios may be distorted depending on whether a big customer pays, or a large supplier is paid, before or after the year-end.

(f)   **Other information**

Ratio analysis on its own is not sufficient for interpreting company accounts, and there are other items of information that should be looked at. These are considered below.

2.1.3 Other information

As well as ratios, other **financial** and **non-financial information** can give valuable indicators of a company's performance and position.

(a) **The revaluation of non-current assets**

Non-current assets may be stated in the statement of financial position at cost less accumulated depreciation. They may also be revalued from time to time to a current market value, which will lead to an increased depreciation charge.

(b) **Share capital and reserves**

The nature of any increase in share capital and accumulated profits will be of interest including **share issues** and **substantial profit retentions**. If a company has **issued shares in the form of a dividend**, are there obvious reasons why this should be so? For example, does the company need to retain capital within the business because of poor trading in the previous year, making the directors reluctant to pay out more cash dividend than necessary?

(c) **Loans and other liabilities**

Two aspects to look out for are whether or not loans are **secured** and the **redemption dates** of loans.

(d) **Contingencies**

Contingencies are conditions which exist at the balance sheet date where the outcome will be confirmed only on the occurrence or non-occurrence of one or more uncertain future events. For example, a pending lawsuit.

(e) **Events after the statement of financial position date**

Significant events occurring after statement of financial position date include mergers and acquisitions or the purchase and sales of major non-current assets and investments. Knowledge of such events allows the analyst to 'update' the latest published figures by taking account of their potential impact.

2.2 Trends

The use of trends is a popular method of assessing corporate performance. You will notice in most published financial statements that the previous year's figures, as well as those for the current year, are included. This allows users to quickly spot significant changes in such major financial categories as non-current assets and revenue. In addition five-year financial summaries are often provided towards the end of annual reports which means that trends can be identified easily.

Below is an extract of the five-year financial summary published in the Singapore Airlines Annual Report 2009/10.

	2009-10	2008-09	2007-08	2006-07	2005-06
CASH FLOW ($ million)					
Cash flow from operations	2,091.2	1,967.0	4,401.8	3,175.8	2,380.3
Internally generated cash flow [R1]	2,423.3	2,994.6	5,028.3	4,823.0	3,101.2
Capital expenditure	1,560.3	2,031.1	2,088.6	3,026.7	2,058.8
PER SHARE DATA					
Earnings before tax (cents)	24.1	101.2	209.5	185.2	136.3
Earnings after tax (cents) - basic	18.2	89.6	168.5	172.6	101.7
- diluted	18.0	89.1	166.1	170.8	101.3
Cash earnings ($) [R2]	1.67	2.36	2.94	2.84	2.08
Net asset value ($)	11.30	11.78	12.77	12.11	11.00
SHARE PRICE ($)					
High	15.94	16.34	20.20	18.00	14.90
Low	10.12	9.39	14.12	12.00	11.10
Closing	15.20	10.00	15.60	16.60	14.00
DIVIDENDS					
Gross dividends (cents per share)	12.0	40.0	100.0	100.0 [R3]	45.0
Dividend cover (times)	1.5	2.2	1.7	1.7	2.3
PROFITABILITY RATIOS (%)					
Return on equity holders' funds [R4]	1.6	7.3	13.6	14.9	9.6
Return on total assets [R5]	1.2	4.5	8.1	8.9	5.8
Return on turnover [R6]	2.2	7.2	13.4	15.2	9.8
PRODUCTIVITY AND EMPLOYEE DATA					
Value added ($ million)	4,276.4	5,570.8	7,082.1	6,510.1	5,534.0
Value added per employee ($) [R7]	159,151	174,995	235,380	223,523	193,781
Revenue per employee ($) [R7]	472,918	502,491	530,859	497,662	467,158
Average employee strength	33,222	31,834	30,088	29,125	28,558
S$ per US$ exchange rate as at 31 March	1.4005	1.5203	1.3807	1.5171	1.6181

Note the inclusion of key ratios which allows users of the reports to quickly spot trends or significant changes in results. Just by quickly scanning the figures, you can see that 2009/10 was a particularly challenging year for Singapore Airlines. Look for example at the dip in Earnings per Share between 2008/09 and 2009/10 – such a significant change in trend warrants further investigation.

2.3 Economic Value Added (EVA™)

We will discuss EVA™ as a means of valuing a company in Chapter 10. However this technique can also be used to measure company performance.

EVA™ was developed by, and is a trademark of, consulting firm Stern Stewart. The firm claims that this measure comes closest to capturing the true **economic profit** of an organisation and is most closely linked to **shareholder value** over time.

2.3.1 Calculating EVA™

EVA™ is an estimate of the amount by which earnings exceed or fall short of the required rate of return that investors could achieve from alternative investments of similar risk.

Formula to Learn

> EVA =NOPAT – (cost of capital x capital employed)
> Where NOPAT is net operating profit after tax adjusted for non-cash expenses

Adjustments to profit figures in the financial statements may include the following.

Adjustment to net (operating) profit	*Adjustment to capital employed*
Add the following	**Add the following**
Interest on debt	Cumulative goodwill and cumulative depreciation previously written off
Goodwill written off	Net book value of intangibles
Accounting depreciation (deduct economic depreciation)	Provisions (eg for bad debts)
Increases in provisions (eg for bad debts)	Debt to net assets
Net capitalised intangibles	

EVA™ is an annual measure of performance based on historical figures. It measures the extent to which funds have been used to either increase or diminish shareholder value.

The reasoning behind adding back the items listed in the table above is therefore simple. Depreciation, for example, is added as EVA™ sees this as funds that had been spent by management on non-current assets that could otherwise have been returned to the shareholders. Similarly, investment in intangibles is money that could also have been returned to shareholders or used to pay off debt obligations.

2.3.2 Advantages of EVA™ for assessing performance

As mentioned above EVA™ appears to come closer than any other performance measure to capturing the true economic profit of an organisation and is most directly linked to the creation of shareholder value over time. As the primary objective of any organisation is the maximisation of shareholder value, EVA™ should be the most relevant assessment of performance. The main advantages of this performance measure are given below.

(a)   **Keeps the focus on shareholder value**

Using EVA to monitor performance helps focus management's attention on shareholder value when making decisions. A company's value depends on the extent to which the actual return to the shareholders exceeds their minimum required rate of return (cost of capital). An increase in EVA™ should lead to an increase in company value. However remember it is the **increase** in EVA™ that will bring improvements in shareholder value.

(b)   **The most meaningful measure of profit for shareholders**

Shareholders will only improve their wealth if the return they receive from their investment exceeds their minimum required rate of return. EVA™ recognises this fact by including all capital costs in its calculation and forces management to appreciate that when they use capital they must be expected to pay for it.

(c)   **A single goal**

As we have seen above, there are numerous ratios that can be calculated to assess performance, each of which may have a target level. EVA™ links all these measures with a common focus – how do we improve EVA™ and thus shareholder value?

(d)   **Easy to understand**

The calculation of EVA™ starts with the familiar operating profit and deducts a capital charge. It is similar to residual income which is a widely used and understood concept. EVA™ is also calculated periodically, unlike NPV, and its results show the extent of change in shareholder value.

2.3.3 Disadvantages of EVA™

The main disadvantages of using EVA™ are summarised below.

(a)   **Easy to manipulate**

The results could be manipulated by choosing short-term projects with early (but low) yields over long-term projects whose cash flows do not yield benefits for several years. This type of decision-making may not be in the best interests of the company and its shareholders.

(b)   **Short-term focus**

EVA™ focuses only on the current accounting period, whilst ideally performance measures should have a longer-term focus.

(c)   **Makes comparisons difficult**

EVA™ is an absolute measure rather than a relative measure, which makes comparisons between firms difficult. Size adjustments would have to be made to make comparisons meaningful.

2.4 Market value added (MVA)

Market value added (MVA) is the difference between current total market value of the firm and the capital contributed by investors (debt and equity).

MVA is the difference between the market value and the book value of a company's invested equity and debt capital. It is not a performance measure but a wealth measure – it measures the level of value that a company has accumulated over time.

The higher the MVA, the more wealth the company has generated for its shareholders. A negative MVA means that the shareholders' wealth has been eroded.

When a company performs well, its accumulated retained earnings are likely to increase, which will improve the book value of the shares. Market expectations of future earnings are likely to bid up the market price of the shares. The MVA represents the excess price tag assigned to the company by the market for past successes and the expectation of future successes.

The main problem with MVA is that it does not take opportunity cost of capital into account as EVA™ does.

We will look at MVA in Chapter 10 in relation to business valuations.

3 Other information from companies' accounts

As well as ratios, **other information** can be used to analyse a company's performance and identify possible problem areas. This will include information relating to **non-current assets** and **financial obligations, contingencies** and **post balance sheet events.**

3.1 The revaluation of fixed assets

Fixed assets may be stated in the statement of financial position at cost less accumulated depreciation. They may also be revalued from time to time to a current market value to avoid understatement of current value. When this happens:

(a)   The increase in the statement of financial position value of the fixed asset is matched by an increase in the **revaluation reserve**

(b)   **Depreciation** in subsequent years is based on the revalued amount of the asset, its estimated residual value and its estimated remaining useful life

3.2 Share capital and share issues

The **capital and reserves** section of a company's accounts contains information which appears to be mainly the concern of the various classes of shareholder. However, because the shareholders' interest in the business acts as a **buffer for the creditors** in the event of any financial problems, this section is also of some importance to creditors.

For example, if a company has increased its total share capital and reserves in the year:

(a)   Did it do so by **issuing new shares** resulting in a higher allotted share capital and share premium account?

(b)   Did it do so by **revaluing some fixed assets**, resulting in a higher revaluation reserve?

(c)   Did it make a substantial profit and **retain a good proportion of this profit** in the business resulting in a higher income statement balance?

A **scrip issue** might also be of some interest. It will result in a **fall** in the **market price** per share. If it has been funded from a company's profit and loss account reserves, a scrip issue would indicate that the company recognised and formalised its long-term capital needs by now making some previously distributable reserves non-distributable.

If a company has **issued shares in the form of a dividend**, are there obvious reasons why this should be so? For example, does the company need to retain capital within the business because of poor trading in the previous year, making the directors reluctant to pay out more cash dividend than necessary?

3.3 Financial obligations

Financial obligations of a company may also be significant, and the timescale over which these become or could become repayable should be considered.

Examples are:

(a)   Levels of **redeemable debt**

(b)   **Earn out arrangements**

(c)   **Potential or contingent liabilities,** such as liabilities under unresolved legal cases or insurance claims

(d)   **Long-term commitments** (eg the Private Finance Initiative in the UK)

3.4 Debentures, loans and other liabilities

Two points of interest about debentures, loans and other liabilities are:

- Whether or not loans are **secured**
- The **redemption dates** of loans

For debentures and loan stock which are **secured**, the details of the security are usually included in the terms of a trust deed. Details of any **fixed or floating charges against assets** must be disclosed in a note to the accounts.

In analysing a set of accounts, particular attention should be paid to some significant features concerning **debenture or loan stock redemption**. These are:

(a)   The **closeness of the redemption date**, which would indicate how much finance the company has to find in the immediate future to repay its loans. It is not unusual, however, to repay one loan by taking out another, and so a company does not necessarily have to find the money to repay a loan from its own resources.

(b)   The **percentage interest rate** on the loans being redeemed, compared with the **current market rate of interest**. This would give some idea, if a company decides to replace loans by taking out new loans, of the likely increase (or reduction) in interest costs that it might face, and how easily it might accommodate any interest cost increase.

3.5 Contingencies

Contingencies are conditions which exist at the balance sheet date where the outcome will be confirmed only on the occurrence or non-occurrence of one or more uncertain future events.

Contingencies can result in contingent gains or contingent losses. The fact that the condition **exists at the statement of financial position date** distinguishes a contingency from a post balance sheet event.

Some of the **typical types of contingencies** disclosed by companies are as follows.

- Guarantees given by the company
- Discounted bills of exchange
- Uncalled liabilities on shares or loan stock
- Lawsuits or claims pending
- Tax on profits where the basis on which the tax should be computed is unclear

Again, knowledge of such contingencies will enhance the quality of the information used in analysis.

3.6 Events after the reporting period

Events after the reporting period are those events both favourable and unfavourable which occur between the statement of financial position date and the date on which the financial statements are approved by the board of directors.

The following are examples of events after the reporting period which should normally be disclosed.

- Mergers and acquisitions
- The issue of new shares and debentures
- The purchase and sale of major fixed assets and investments
- Losses of fixed assets or stocks as a result of a catastrophe such as fire or flood
- The opening of new trading activities
- The closure of a significant part of the trading activities
- A decline in the value of property and investments held as fixed assets
- Changes in exchange rates (if there are significant overseas interests)
- Government action, such as nationalisation
- Strikes and other labour disputes
- The augmentation of pension benefits to employees

Knowledge of such events allows the analyst to 'update' the latest published figures by taking account of their potential impact.

Exam focus point

You should try to develop a mental checklist of areas where accounts can be distorted, whether intentionally or unintentionally. These may include:
- Asset values
- Off balance sheet items
- Events after the reporting period
- Equity restructuring
- Loan terms

4 Optimal capital structure 12/08, 6/12

FAST FORWARD

Decisions on how to finance the acquisition of assets are based on the cost of the various sources of finance.

Exam focus point

Part of a 20 mark optional question in December 2007 asked for a discussion of the advantages and disadvantages of debt as a mode of financing. Part of a compulsory question in June 2012 asked for a assessment of different proposals for funding a company.

4.1 The capital structure decision

Suppose that a company has decided to expand its operations and has decided that the expansion will take place through organic growth rather than by acquiring another company. The company has therefore decided to expand its operation by increasing its productive capacity. This entails investment in plant and machinery. The increase in productive capacity need to generate cash flows that will increase the value of the firm. The question that the financial manger needs to address is how to finance the new investment.

4.2 Sources of finance

The main sources of finance for corporations are:

(a) Retained earnings
(b) Proceeds from the issue of new ordinary shares to existing or new shareholders
(c) Proceeds from a flotation of a company
(d) Preference shares
(e) Debt

4.3 The choice between debt and equity

4.3.1 Advantages of debt

(a) Debt is a **cheaper form of finance** than shares because, as debt interest is tax-deductible in most tax regimes.

(b) Debt should be **more attractive** to investors because it will be **secured** against the assets of the company.

(c) **Debt holders** rank above **shareholders** in the event of a liquidation.

(d) **Issue costs** are normally **lower** for debt than for shares.

(e) There is **no immediate change** in the existing structure of control, although this may change over time if the bonds are convertible to shares.

(f) There is **no immediate dilution** in earnings and dividends per share.

(g) Lenders do not participate in high profits compared with shares.

4.3.2 Disadvantages of debt

(a) **Interest** has to be paid on debt no matter what the company's profits in a year are. In particular the company may find itself locked into long-term debt at unfavourable rates of interest. The company is not legally obliged to pay dividends.

(b) Money has to be made available for **redemption** or **repayment** of debt. However, redemption values will fall in real terms during a time of inflation.

(c) Heavy borrowing **increases the financial risks** for ordinary shareholders. A company must be able to pay the interest charges and eventually repay the debt from its cash resources, and at the same time maintain a healthy balance sheet which does not deter would-be lenders. There might be insufficient security for a new loan.

(d) Shareholders may demand a **higher rate of return** because an increased interest burden increases the risks that dividends will not be paid.

(e) There might be restrictions on a company's power to borrow. The **company's constitution** may limit borrowing. These borrowing limits cannot be altered except with the approval of the shareholders at a general meeting of the company. **Trust deeds of existing loan stock** may **limit borrowing**. These limits can only be overcome by redeeming the loan stock.

4.4 Debt instruments

FAST FORWARD

> Debt capital takes various forms such as **loan capital**, **debentures**, **zero coupon bonds** and the interest on debt is tax-deductible

4.4.1 Types of corporate debt

Corporate debt takes many forms which are differentiated in terms of maturity as **redeemable** or **irredeemable**, in terms of the coupon as fixed rate loan notes, **floating rate loan notes**, or **zero coupon bonds**. Finally there are callable bonds which can be redeemed before maturity and **convertible loan stock** which can be converted into equity.

(a) **Debentures** are **secure loan capital** secured either by a floating charge on all assets of the company, or by a fixed charge on specific assets of the company.

(b) **Unsecured loan stock** is debt which is not secured on any of the assets of the company and it carries a higher interest.

(c) **Deep Discount bonds** are bonds offered at a large discount on the face value of the debt so that a significant proportion of the return to the investor comes by way of a capital gain on redemption, rather than through interest payment. Deep discount bonds pay a low coupon and have **low servicing costs** but a high cost of redemption at maturity. The only tax advantage is that the gain gets taxed (as **income**) in one lump on maturity or sale, not as amounts of interest each year.

BPP
LEARNING MEDIA

(d) **Zero coupon bonds** are bonds offering no interest payments, all investor return being gained through capital appreciation. They are issued at a discount to their redemption value, and the investor gains from the difference between the issue price and the redemption value. The advantage for borrowers is that zero coupon bonds can be used to raise cash immediately, and there is no cash repayment until redemption date. The cost of redemption is known at the time of issue, and so the borrower can plan to have funds available to redeem the bonds at maturity. The advantage for lenders is that that there is no exposure to interest rate risk and if held to maturity are free of market risk. The investor is of course exposed to credit risk.

(e) **Convertible unsecured debt** are debt instruments that give the option to the holder to convert them into equity at some time in the future at a predetermined price.

(f) **Mezzanine debt** is debt with conversion options. It is a subordinated debt because it ranks in terms of seniority of claims below straight debt like debentures and it requires a higher rate of return. Mezzanine debt is the preferred way of financing leveraged buyouts.

(g) **Leasing** is used for the financing of certain assets such as buildings, ship or aircraft.

(h) **Eurobonds** are bonds denominated in currency other than that of the issuer, usually dollar, yen or Euro, and trade in the international financial markets.

4.4.2 Trust deed

A **loan note (or debenture)** is a written acknowledgement of a debt by a company, usually given under its seal and normally containing provisions as to payment of interest and the terms of repayment of principal. A loan note may be secured on some or all of the assets of the company or its subsidiaries.

A **trust deed** would empower a trustee (such as an insurance company or a bank) to **intervene** on behalf of loan note holders if the conditions of borrowing under which the debentures were issued are not being fulfilled. This might involve:

- **Failure** to **pay interest** on the due dates
- An **attempt** by the company to **sell off important assets** contrary to the terms of the loan
- A company taking out **additional loans** and thereby exceeding previously agreed borrowing limits established either by its constitution or by the terms of the loan note trust deed. (A trust deed might place restrictions on the company's ability to borrow more from elsewhere until the loan notes have been redeemed.)

4.4.3 Issuing corporate bonds

A company that wants to issue corporate bonds will need to appoint an investment bank as the lead manager. The lead manager in turn sets up an underwriting syndicate which purchases the entire issue at an agreed price. The price reflects the coupon of the bond and the credit rating of the bond. The syndicate will then sell the issue to final buyers who are normally clients of the investment banks involved or other investment banks.

4.4.4 Cost of debt

The cost of debt capital is the after-tax cost of raising debt in the capital markets. It is the rate of return that investors require for investments with that specific risk. Other factors that influence the cost of debt capital include:

(a) The general level of interest rate

(b) The credit rating of the bond which is reflected in the spread over the risk-free rate .

(c) The maturity of the bond.

(d) The type of debt issue. For example callable bonds will be more expensive than non callable bonds.

(e) The cost of issuing a bond.

4.5 Preference shares

Preference shares have priority over ordinary shares in divided payments and capital repayment.

4.5.1 Characteristics of preference shares

Preference shares carry priority over ordinary shareholders with regard to dividend payments. They do not carry voting rights. They may be attractive to corporate investors, as (unlike interest receipts) dividends received are generally not subject to tax. However, for the issuing company, dividend payments (unlike interest payments) are generally not tax-deductible.

Preference shares are shares carrying a fixed rate of dividends, the holders of which, subject to the conditions of issue, have a prior claim to any company profits available for distribution. They are an example of prior charge capital.

Preferred shareholders may also have a prior claim to the repayment of capital in the event of winding up.

4.5.2 Types of preference shares

Cumulative preference shares are preference shares where any arrears of dividend are carried forward. When eventually the company decides to pay a dividend, the cumulative preference shareholders are entitled to all their arrears before ordinary shareholders are paid a dividend.

Participating preference shares are shares that have an additional entitlement to dividend over and above their specified rate. Participating preferred shareholders are entitled to participate along with ordinary shareholders in available profits, normally once the ordinary shareholders have themselves received a specified level of dividend.

Convertible preference shares are shares that can be converted into ordinary shares.

4.5.3 Advantages and disadvantages of preference shares

From the company's point of view, preference shares have some positive features.

- Dividends do **not have** to be **paid** in a year in which **profits are poor**, whilst this is not the case with interest payments on long-term debt.
- Since they do not normally carry voting rights, preferred shares **avoid diluting** the **control** of existing shareholders whilst an issue of equity shares would not.
- Unless they are redeemable, issuing preference shares will **lower** the company's **gearing**. Redeemable preference shares are normally treated as debt when gearing is calculated.
- The issue of preference shares does **not restrict** the company's **borrowing power**, at least in the sense that preferred share capital is not secured against assets of the business.
- The non-payment of dividend does **not give** the preferred shareholders the **right** to **appoint a receiver**, a right which is normally given to debenture holders.

From the point of view of the investor, preference shares are less attractive than loan stock because:

- They **cannot be secured** on the company's assets.
- The **dividend yield** traditionally offered on preferred dividends has been much **too low** to provide an attractive investment compared with the interest yields on loan stock in view of the additional risk involved.
- **Dividend payments on preference shares may not be tax deductible** in the way that interest payments on debt are. Furthermore, for preferred shares to be attractive to investors, the level of payment needs to be **higher than** for **interest on debt** to compensate for the additional risks.

4.5.4 Cost of preferred stock

The key feature of preferred stock is the **constant interest** that it pays to investors. The cost of preference shares should therefore be calculated in the same way as the cost of corporate bonds.

4.6 Retained earnings

Retained earnings are the **cumulative undistributed earnings** of the company and can be used to finance the **capital expenditure** programme of the company.

For many businesses, the cash needed to finance investments will be available because the earnings the business has made have been retained within the business rather than paid out as dividends. This interaction of investment, financing and dividend policy is the most important issue facing many businesses.

Advantages of using retentions

Retentions are a **flexible source** of finance; companies are not tied to specific amounts or specific repayment patterns. Using retentions does **not involve** a **change in the pattern** of **shareholdings**.

Disadvantages of using retentions

Shareholders may be **sensitive** to the **loss of dividends** that will result from retention for re-investment, rather than paying dividends.

4.6.1 Cost of retained earnings

Retained profits is not a cost-free method of obtaining funds. There is an **opportunity cost** in that if dividends were paid, the cash received could be invested by shareholders to earn a return. The cost of retained earnings is the rate of return that stockholders require on equity capital that the company has obtained by retaining profits.

The shareholders could have received these earnings as dividends and invested them elsewhere, therefore, the company needs to earn at least as good a return as the investors could have got elsewhere for comparable risk. If the company cannot achieve this return they should return the funds to the shareholders and let them invest them elsewhere.

4.7 Cost of equity

There are three alternatives for calculating the cost of retained earnings.

- Theoretical models such as the **Capital Asset Pricing Model (CAPM)** or the **Arbitrage Pricing Theory (APT)**.
- The **bond yield-plus-premium approach**. This is a model used where analysts do not have confidence in the CAPM or the APT approach, they instead simply add a judgmental risk premium to the interest rate on the firm's own long-term debt.
- **Market implied estimates** using variants of the discounted cash flow (DCF) approach. This model is however, based on particular assumption on the growth rate of earning of the company.

4.7.1 CAPM

We have already discussed in Chapter 1 that companies and investors in general will earn a return above the yield of a risk-free asset only if they are prepared to undertake extra risk. The difference between the expected return from a risky investment and the risk-free return is called the **risk premium**. The capital asset pricing model (CAPM) and the other valuation models make the assumption that the risk premium is proportional to the risk premium of the market as a whole.

Risk premium on a portfolio = beta of portfolio x risk premium on the market

The formula for the CAPM is given below

Exam Formula

$$E(r_i) = r_f + \beta_i(E(r_m) - r_f)$$

CAPM is assumed knowledge from Paper F9 – *Financial Management* .

4.7.2 Valuation models – beyond the CAPM

The CAPM specifies that the only risk factor that should be taken into account is the market risk premium. Subsequent empirical research has shown that there may be other factors in addition to market risk premium that explain differences in asset returns, such as **interest rates** and **industrial production**.

Unlike the CAPM, which analyses the returns on a share as a function of a single factor – the return on the market portfolio, the APM assumes that the return on each security is based on a number of **independent factors**. The actual return r on any security is shown as:

$$r = E(r_j) + \beta_1 F_1 + \beta_2 F_2 \ldots + e$$

where $E(r_i)$ is the expected return on the security

β_1 is the sensitivity to changes in factor 1

F_1 is the difference between actual and expected values of factor 1

β_2 is the sensitivity to changes in factor 2

F_2 is the difference between actual and expected values of factor 2

e   is a random term

Factor analysis is used to ascertain the factors to which security returns are sensitive. Four key factors identified by researchers have been:

- Unanticipated inflation
- Changes in the expected level of industrial production
- Changes in the risk premium on bonds (debentures)
- Unanticipated changes in the term structure of interest rates

It has been demonstrated that when no further arbitrage opportunities exist, the expected return $E(r_j)$ can be shown as:

$$E(r_j) = r_f + \beta_1(r_1 - r_f) + \beta_2(r_2 - r_f) \ldots$$

where r_f is the risk-free rate of return

r_1 is the expected return on a portfolio with unit sensitivity to factor 1 and no sensitivity to any other factor

r_2 is the expected return on a portfolio with unit sensitivity to factor 2 and no sensitivity to any other factor

The **Arbitrage Pricing Theory** (APT) generalises the CAPM and postulates the following model for the risk premium of a portfolio

$$E(r_i) = r_f + (E(r_A) - r_f)\beta_A + (E(r_B) - r_f)\beta_B + \ldots\ldots + (E(r_m) - r_f)\beta_m + \ldots\ldots$$

Where $(E(r_A) - r_f)\beta_A$ is the risk premium on factor A.

$E(r_B) - r_f)\beta_B$ is the risk premium on factor B and so on

The APT model calculates the risk premium by constructing a portfolio with a **beta of** 1 in relation to the factor under consideration (such as the interest rate) and a **beta of zero** in relation to all the other factors. The risk premium of that specific portfolio is then used as a proxy for the risk premium for the factor under consideration.

Fama and French identified **two factors** in addition to the **market portfolio** that explain company returns namely **size** and **distress.**

The **size factor** is measured as the difference in return between a portfolio of the smallest stocks and a portfolio of the largest stocks, whereas the **distress factor** is proxied by the difference in return between a portfolio of the highest book to market value stocks and portfolio of the lowest book to market value stocks.

The Fama and French three factor model is as follows

$$E(r_j) = r_f + \beta_{i,m}(E(r_m) - r_f) + \beta_{i,S}\,SIZE + \beta_{i,D}\,DIST$$

where $\beta_{i,m}$ is the stock's beta

$\beta_{i,S}$ is beta with respect to size

$\beta_{i,D}$ is the stock's beta with respect to distress

Unlike the CAPM, the APT leaves the factors to be determined empirically.

4.7.3 Bond-yield-plus premium approach

The bond yield-plus model is based on the empirical observation that the return on equity is higher than the yield on bonds. Since equities are riskier than bonds, the difference between the two is a reward the investor requires in order to invest in the riskier asset. Now if this equity market premium was constant, then the required rate of return for equity could simply be calculated by looking at the bond yields and then adding the fixed premium.

4.7.4 Market implied method

The market-implied method is based on a particular assumption about the growth rate or earnings or dividends of a company. For example, if we were to assume a constant rate of growth for dividends at the rate of g per annum, the shareholders' required rate of return is r_e per annum, and the next period's dividend payment is d_1 then the market value of the share will be

$$V_{\text{ex-div}} = \frac{d_0(1+g)}{r_e - g}$$

where $V_{\text{ex-div}}$ = the ex-div market value of the shares that may need to be calculated using

$V_{\text{ex-div}}$ = $V_{\text{cum div}} - d_0$

$V_{\text{cum div}}$ is the cum div market value of the shares

d_0 is the dividend about to be paid now if we are cum dividend

d_0 = the current dividend

r_e = the investors' required rate of return

g = the expected annual growth rate of the dividends

The formula can be rearranged as follows $k_e - g = \dfrac{d_0(1+g)}{V_{\text{ex-div}}}$

to produce the cost of equity

$$k_e = \frac{d_0(1+g)}{V_{\text{ex-div}}} + g$$

where d_0 = the current dividend

$V_{\text{ex-div}}$ = the market value determined by the investor

g = the expected annual growth rate of the dividends

Growth Rates

The cost of capital we have derived is based on the current market price of shares but also on the growth rate assumptions we have made. If the constant growth assumption in the implied method is not appropriate, then the estimates we have derived will not be accurate.

Question	Cost of retained earnings

A company is about to pay a dividend of $1 on its common stock. The shares are currently quoted at $23.00. The dividend is expected to grow at the rate of 10% per annum. Calculate the cost of retained earnings for the company.

Since we are about to pay the dividend, we will assume that the share is currently cum div. Hence, since we need the ex-div value, we must use the expression

$$V_{ex\text{-}div} = V_{cum\text{-}div} - d_0$$

to calculate the ex-div price as

$$V_{ex\text{-}div} = \$23.00 - \$1.00 = \$22.00$$

Then using the above formula for the cost of equity, we get

$$k_e = \frac{d_0(1+g)}{E_{ex\text{-}div}} + g$$

$$k_e = \frac{\$1 \times 1.1}{\$22.00} + 0.1$$

$$k_e = \frac{1.10}{\$22.00} + 0.1$$

$$k_e = 0.05 + 0.1 = 0.15 \text{ or } 15\% \text{ per annum}$$

Note that k_e is calculated as dividend yield plus growth rate here.

4.8 New share issues by quoted companies

FAST FORWARD

> New shares can be issued either to existing shareholders or to new shareholders.

A new issue of shares might be made in a variety of different circumstances.

- The company might want to **raise more cash**, for example for expansion of its operations.
- The company might want to issue new shares partly to raise cash but more importantly to obtain a **stock market listing**. When a UK company is floated, for example on the main stock market, it is a requirement of the Stock Exchange that at least a minimum proportion of its shares should be made available to the general investing public if the shares are not already widely held.
- The company might issue new shares to the shareholders of another company, in order to **take it over**.

4.8.1 Practicalities for issuing new shares

A lot of the practicalities involved are specific to the type of issue. However, general factors apply to all types.

- **Costs.** There will be administrative costs, but how great these are will vary enormously.
- **Income to investors.** In Britain and other jurisdictions, companies are not obliged to pay dividends to shareholders in a particular year. However in the long-term shareholders will expect dividends and/or capital appreciation.
- **Tax.** Unlike loan finance interest or charges, dividends paid are **not normally tax-deductible**.
- **Effect on control.** Unless shares are issued to **existing shareholders** in proportion to their **current holdings**, the balance of voting power will change and there may ultimately be an impact on the **control** of the firm.

4.8.2 Timing of new share issue

New equity issues in general will be more common when share prices are high than when share prices are low.

- When **share price are high**, **investors' confidence** will probably be **high**, and investors will be more willing to put money into companies with the potential for growth.
- By issuing shares at a high price, a company will **reduce** the **number of shares** it must issue to raise the amount of capital it wants. This will reduce the dilution of earnings for existing shareholders.
- Following on from (b), the company's **total dividend commitment** on the new shares, to meet shareholders' expectations, will be **lower**.
- If **share prices are low**, business **confidence** is likely to be **low** too. Companies may not want to raise capital for new investments until expectations begin to improve.

4.8.3 A rights issue

A **rights issue** is an offer to existing shareholders for them to buy more shares, usually at lower than the current share price.

A **rights issue** is the raising of new capital by giving existing shareholders the right to subscribe to new shares in proportion to their current holdings. These shares are usually issued at a discount to market price. A shareholder not wishing to take up a rights issue may sell the rights.

A **dilution** is the reduction in the earnings and voting power per share caused by an increase or potential increase in the number of shares in issue.

Existing shareholders have **pre-emption rights** when new shares are issued. So that existing shareholders' rights are not diluted by the issue of new shares, legislation in many countries requires that before any equity shares are allotted for cash, they must first be offered to existing shareholders.

Rights issues are **cheaper** than offers for sale to the general public. This is partly because no **prospectus** is generally required (provided that the issue is for less than 10% of the class of shares concerned), partly because the **administration** is **simpler** and partly because the cost of underwriting will be less.

Rights issues are **more beneficial** to **existing shareholders** than issues to the general public. New shares are issued at a **discount** to the current market price, to make them attractive to investors. A rights issue secures the discount on the market price for existing shareholders, who may either keep the shares or sell them if they wish.

Relative voting rights are **unaffected** if shareholders all take up their rights.

The finance raised may be used to **reduce gearing** in book value terms by increasing share capital and/or to pay off long-term debt which will reduce gearing in market value terms.

A company making a rights issue must set a price which is low enough to **secure the acceptance** of shareholders, who are being asked to provide extra funds, but not so low that earnings per share are excessively diluted. Other possible problems include getting the issue **underwritten** and an excessive **fall** in the **share price.**

Example: rights issue (1)

Seagull can achieve a profit after tax of 20% on the capital employed. At present its capital structure is as follows.

	$
200,000 ordinary shares of $1 each	200,000
Retained earnings	100,000
	300,000

The directors propose to raise an additional $126,000 from a rights issue. The current market price is $1.80.

Required

(a)   Calculate the number of shares that must be issued if the rights price is: $1.60; $1.50; $1.40; $1.20.

(b)   Calculate the dilution in earnings per share in each case.

Solution

The earnings at present are 20% of $300,000 = $60,000. This gives earnings per share of 30c. The earnings after the rights issue will be 20% of $426,000 = $85,200.

Rights price $	No of new share ($126,000 ÷ rights price)	EPS ($85,200 ÷ total no of shares) Cents	Dilution Cents
1.60	78,750	30.6	+ 0.6
1.50	84,000	30.0	–
1.40	90,000	29.4	– 0.6
1.20	105,000	27.9	– 2.1

Note that at a high rights price the earnings per share are increased, not diluted. The breakeven point (zero dilution) occurs when the rights price is equal to the capital employed per share: $300,000 ÷ 200,000 = $1.50.

A right issue is effectively a call option on the firm's equity and even if issued at the current price – that is, a zero intrinsic value – it may still have time value . The value of the call is effectively a deduction from the existing shareholder value. We will cover call options in more detail in Chapter 8.

4.8.4 Scrip dividends

Scrip dividends, **scrip issues** and **stock splits** are not methods of raising new equity funds, but they *are* methods of altering the share capital structure of a company, or in the case of scrip dividends and scrip issues, increasing the issued share capital of the company.

Scrip dividend is a dividend paid by the issue of additional company shares, rather than by cash.

A scrip dividend effectively converts profit and loss reserves into **issued share capital**. When the directors of a company would prefer to retain funds within the business but consider that they must pay at least a certain amount of dividend, they might offer equity shareholders the choice of a **cash dividend** or a **scrip dividend**. Each shareholder would decide separately which to take.

Recently **enhanced scrip dividends** have been offered by many companies. With enhanced scrip dividends, the value of the shares offered is much greater than the cash alternative, giving investors an incentive to choose the shares.

Advantages of scrip dividends

They can **preserve** a company's **cash position** if a substantial number of shareholders take up the share option.

Investors may be able to obtain **tax advantages** if dividends are in the form of shares.

Investors looking to **expand their holding** can do so **without incurring** the **transaction costs** of buying more shares.

A small scrip issue will **not dilute the share price significantly.** If however cash is not offered as an alternative, empirical evidence suggests that the share price will tend to fall.

A share issue will **decrease** the company's **gearing**, and may therefore **enhance** its **borrowing capacity.**

4.8.5 Bonus issues

A **bonus/scrip/capitalisation issue** is the capitalisation of the reserves of a company by the issue of additional shares to existing shareholders, in proportion to their holdings. Such shares are normally fully paid-up with no cash called for from the shareholders.

For example, if a company with issued share capital of 100,000 ordinary shares of $1 each made a one for five scrip issue, 20,000 new shares would be issued to existing shareholders, one new share for every five old shares held. Issued share capital would be increased by $20,000, and reserves (probably share premium account, if there is one) reduced by this amount.

By creating more shares in this way, a scrip issue does not raise new funds, but does have the advantage of making shares **cheaper** and therefore (perhaps) **more easily marketable** on the Stock Exchange. For example, if a company's shares are priced at $6 on the Stock Exchange, and the company makes a one for two scrip issue, we should expect the share price after the issue to fall to $4 each. Shares at $4 each might be more easily marketable than shares at $6 each.

4.8.6 Stock splits

The advantage of a scrip issue is also the reason for a **stock split** which we discussed earlier.

4.9 Methods for obtaining a listing

An unquoted company can obtain a listing on the stock market by means of:

- Direct **offer by subscription** to the public
- **Offer for sale**
- **Placing**
- **Introduction**

Of these an offer for sale or a placing are the most common.

4.9.1 Direct offer by subscription to general public

Issues where the issuing firm sells shares directly to the general public tend to be quite rare on many stock exchanges, and the issues that are made tend to be quite large. These issues are sometimes known as **offers by prospectus**. This type of issue is very risky, because of the lack of guarantees that all shares will be taken up.

4.9.2 Offer for sale

Offer for sale is an invitation to apply for shares in a company based on information contained in a prospectus. It is a means of selling the shares of a company to the public at large. When companies 'go public' for the first time, a **large** issue will probably take the form of an offer for sale. Subsequent issues are likely to be **placings** or **rights issues**, described later.

An offer for sale entails the **acquisition by an issuing house** of a large block of shares of a company, with a view to offering them for sale to the public. An issuing house is usually a merchant bank (or sometimes a firm of stockbrokers). It may acquire the shares either as a direct allotment from the company or by purchase from existing members. In either case, the issuing house publishes an invitation to the public to apply for shares, either at a fixed price or on a tender basis.

The advantage of an offer for sale over a direct offer by the company to the public is that the issuing house **accepts responsibility** to the public, and gives to the issue the support of its own standing.

An issuing house has the job of trying to ensure a successful issue for the company's shares, by advising on an issue price for the shares, and trying to interest institutional investors in buying some of the shares.

The offer price must be **advertised a short time in advance**, so it is fixed without certain knowledge of the condition of the market at the time applications are invited. In order to ensure the success of an issue, share prices are often set **lower** than they might otherwise be. An issuing house normally tries to ensure that a share price rises to a **premium** above its issue price soon after trading begins. A target premium of 20% above the issue price would be fairly typical.

4.9.3 Offers for sale by tender

It is often very difficult to decide upon the price at which the shares should be offered to the general public. One way of trying to ensure that the issue price reflects the value of the shares as perceived by the market is to make an **offer for sale by tender**. A **minimum price** will be fixed and subscribers will be invited to tender for shares at prices equal to or above the minimum. The shares will be **allotted at the highest price** at which they will **all be taken up**. This is known as the **striking price**.

Example: offer for sale by tender

Byte Henderson is a new company that is making its first public issue of shares. It has decided to make the issue by means of an offer for sale by tender. The intention is to issue up to 4,000,000 shares (the full amount of authorised share capital) at a minimum price of 300 cents. The money raised, net of issue costs of $1,000,000, would be invested in projects which would earn benefits with a present value equal to 130% of the net amount invested.

The following tenders have been received. (Each applicant has made only one offer.)

Price tendered per share	Number of shares applied for at this price
$	
6.00	50,000
5.50	100,000
5.00	300,000
4.50	450,000
4.00	1,100,000
3.50	1,500,000
3.00	2,500,000

(a) How many shares would be issued, and how much in total would be raised, if Byte Henderson Inc chooses:

(i) To maximise the total amount raised?
(ii) To issue exactly 4,000,000 shares?

(b) Harvey Goldfinger, a private investor, has applied for 12,000 shares at a price of $5.50 and has sent a cheque for $66,000 to the issuing house that is handling the issue. In both cases (a)(i) and (ii), how many shares would be issued to Mr Goldfinger, assuming that any partial acceptance of offers would mean allotting shares to each accepted applicant in proportion to the number of shares applied for? How much will Mr Goldfinger receive back out of the $66,000 he has paid?

(c) Estimate the likely market value of shares in the company after the issue, assuming that the market price fully reflects the investment information given above and that exactly 4,000,000 shares are issued.

Solution

(a) We begin by looking at the cumulative tenders.

Price	Cumulative number of shares applied for	Amount raised if price is selected, before deducting issue costs
$		$
6.00	50,000	300,000
5.50	150,000	825,000
5.00	450,000	2,250,000
4.50	900,000	4,050,000
4.00	2,000,000	8,000,000
3.50	3,500,000	12,250,000
3.00	6,000,000 (4,000,000 max)	12,000,000

(i) To maximise the total amount raised, the issue price should be $3.50. The total raised before deducting issue costs would be $12,250,000.

(ii) To issue exactly 4,000,000 shares, the issue price must be $3.00. The total raised would be $12,000,000, before deducting issue costs.

(b) (i) Harvey Goldfinger would be allotted 12,000 shares at $3.50 per share. He would receive a refund of 12,000 × $2 = $24,000 out of the $66,000 he has paid.

(ii) If 4,000,000 shares are issued, applicants would receive two thirds of the shares they tendered for. Harvey Goldfinger would be allotted 8,000 shares at $3 per share and would receive a refund of $42,000 out of the $66,000 he has paid.

(c) The net amount raised would be $12,000,000 minus issue costs of $1,000,000 which equals $11,000,000.

The present value of the benefits from investment would be 130% of $11,000,000 which equals $14,300,000. If the market price reflects this information, the price per share would rise to $$\frac{£14,300,000}{4,000,000} = \$3.575 \text{ per share.}$$

4.9.4 A placing

A **placing** is an arrangement whereby the shares are not all offered to the public, but instead, the sponsoring market maker arranges for most of the issue to be bought by a **small number of investors**, usually institutional investors such as pension funds and insurance companies.

The choice between an offer for sale and a placing

When a company is planning a flotation, is it likely to prefer an offer for sale of its shares, or a placing?

- **Placings** are much **cheaper**. Approaching institutional investors privately is a much cheaper way of obtaining finance, and thus placings are often used for smaller issues.
- Placings are likely to be **quicker**.
- Placings are likely to involve **less disclosure** of **information.**
- However, most of the shares will be placed with a **relatively small number of (institutional) shareholders**, which means that most of the shares are unlikely to be available for trading after the flotation, and that institutional shareholders will have control of the company.

4.9.5 A Stock Exchange introduction

By this method of obtaining a quotation, no shares are made available to the market, neither existing nor newly created shares; nevertheless, the stock market grants a quotation. This will only happen where shares in a large company are already widely held, so that a market can be seen to exist. A company might want an **introduction** to obtain **greater marketability** for the shares, a known share valuation for inheritance tax purposes and easier access in the future to additional capital.

4.9.6 Underwriting

A company about to issue new securities in order to raise finance might decide to have the issue underwritten. **Underwriters** are financial institutions which agree (in exchange for a fixed fee, perhaps 2.25% of the finance to be raised) to buy at the issue price any securities which are **not subscribed** for by the investing public.

Underwriters **remove** the **risk** of a share issue's being under-subscribed, but at a cost to the company issuing the shares. It is not compulsory to have an issue underwritten. Ordinary offers for sale are most likely to be underwritten although rights issues may be as well.

Because of the costs of underwriting, there has been a trend in recent years for companies whose securities are marketable to adopt the practice known as the **'bought deal'**, whereby an investment bank buys the whole of a new issue at a small discount to the market.

4.9.7 Costs of share issue on the stock market

Companies may incur the following costs when issuing shares.

- Underwriting costs
- Stock market listing fee (the initial charge) for the new securities
- Fees of the issuing house, solicitors, auditors and public relations consultant
- Charges for printing and distributing the prospectus
- Advertising in national newspapers

4.9.8 Costs of equity for new share issue on the stock market

When we are dealing with newly issued equity, the company needs to take into account the flotation cost involved with the new stock. We need to adapt the formula used for retained earnings to allow for the additional cash outflow that the company suffers at time 0, being the **flotation costs**, f. Therefore the cost of equity for the company becomes

$$k_e = \frac{d_0(1+g)}{P_0(1-f)} + g$$

Example

Assume that there were flotation costs of 8% and $d_0 = \$1.00$, $P_0 = \$22$, $g = 10\%$. What is the cost of new shares issued?

Solution

$$k_e = \frac{\$1.10}{\$22.00(1-0.08)} + 0.1 = 15.4\%$$

Note that the formula for new shares issued could be learned as a general formula for the cost of equity, with retained earnings being a special case where issue costs are zero (f = 0).

The optimal capital structure is also considered further in Chapter 7a Sections 8 and 9.

5 Dividend policy

FAST FORWARD >>

> Dividend decisions determine the amount of and the way that a company's profits are distributed to its shareholders.

5.1 Is dividend policy irrelevant?

Shareholders who hold the shares of a company are entitled to a portion of the income that the company generates and of the assets that it owns. The dividend policy of a company refers to the decision taken by the management of the company with regard to how much of a company's earnings will be distributed to shareholders and how much will be retained within the firm.

In reaching this decision, the management of the company should try, as in all financial management decisions, to maximise the wealth of the company's shareholders. However there is little agreement as to the impact of dividend policy on shareholder wealth, and the interaction between dividend payments, financing decision and the value of a company has been the subject of theoretical analysis and empirical investigation.

At one end of the debate Modigliani and Miller have maintained that the dividend policy of a corporation is irrelevant because the value of a company is not affected by its financial policy.

Suppose a company pays dividends without changing investment and financing policies. The money that the company will pay as dividends has to come from somewhere else. If the company maintains the amount of debt (does not borrow to pay the dividend), the company needs to issue new shares to finance the dividend. The new shareholders will pay only what the shares are worth, and the old shareholders will receive the money paid by the new shareholders as dividends. After the dividend is paid, the value per-share should be equal to the old price minus the dividend paid by the new shareholders. The value of the firm remains the same, but money changed hands from new to old shareholders. Dividend policies are therefore irrelevant.

5.2 Ways of paying dividend

Companies have many ways of returning money to the shareholders. The main ones are:

(a) **Cash dividends**. This the most common way of paying dividends by corporations. These dividends are paid in cash, usually quarterly. Companies can declare both regular and 'extra' dividends. Regular dividends usually remain unchanged in the future, but 'extraordinary' or 'special' dividends are unlikely to be repeated.

(b) **Dividends in the form of shares** are paid instead of cash dividends by allocating to existing shareholders shares of equivalent value. Shareholders receive new shares in the corporation as a form of a dividend. Like a 'share split', the number of shares increases, but no cash changes hands

(c) **Share repurchases** is an alternative to distribute cash to its shareholders. The firm buys back its own shares. This can be done **on the open market, by tender offer or by buying stock from major shareholders.**

A **major difference** between dividends and share repurchases is their **tax treatment. Cash dividends** are **taxed as income** but **share repurchases** are subject to capital gains tax **only if a capital gain has been realised.**

Both cash and stock dividends reduce the value per share.

5.3 Dividend capacity

The **dividend capacity** of a corporation determines how much of a company's income can be paid out as dividend. The dividend capacity of the company is also known as the **free cash-flow** to equity (FCFE).

The estimation of dividend capacity of a firm is dealt with in Chapter 18. Here we simply give the definition of the **free cash flow to equity**.

Free Cash Flow to Equity = Net income (EBIT – Net Interest – Tax paid)

add	Depreciation
less	Total net investment (change in capital investment + change in working capital)
add	Net debt issued (new borrowings less any repayments)
add	Net equity issued (new issues less any equity repurchases)

The FCFE represents the cash available to the company which could be paid out to shareholders as dividends.

The FCFE is usually not the same as actual dividends in a given year because normally the management of a company deliberately smoothes dividend payments across time. There are also rules which restrict the payment of distributable profits only as dividends.

5.4 Theories of dividend policy

The **Modigliani and Miller** argument that dividend policy is irrelevant should have led to a random pattern of dividend payments. In practice, dividend payments tend to be smoothed over time. In this section we review some of the reasons that have been put forward as explanation for the payment of dividends.

5.4.1 The residual theory of dividend payments

According to this theory, firms will only pay dividends if all the profitable investment opportunities have been funded. This theory assumes that internal funds are the cheapest source of financing, and the company will resort to external financing only if the available internal funds, current and retained earnings have been exhausted.

5.4.2 Target payout ratio

According to the target payout theory, companies pay out as dividends a fixed proportion of their earnings. Firms have long-run target dividend payout ratios.

(a)   Mature companies with stable earnings usually have a higher dividend pay-out ratio than growth companies.

(b)   Managers focus more on dividend changes than in absolute amounts.

(c)   Transitory changes in earnings usually do not affect dividend pay-outs.

(d)   Only long-term shifts in earnings can be followed by changes in dividends.

(e)   Managers are reluctant to change dividend pay-out ratios due to the potential signals that such changes may send to the markets (see below).

5.4.3 Dividends as signals

Dividends can be used to convey good (or bad) information. A firm that increases its dividend payout ratio may be signalling that it expects future cash flows to increase as this ratio tends to remain steady over time. Bad firms can also increase dividends to try to convince the markets that they too are expecting increased future cash flows. However this increase may be unsustainable if the promised increases do not occur and the inevitable reduction in dividend payout ratio will mean heavy penalities from the markets.

5.4.4 Agency theory

Dividend payments can be an instrument to monitor managers. When firms pay dividends they often need to subsequently go to the capital markets to fund the projects. When firms go to the financial markets they will be scrutinised by different market participants. For instance, investors will require an analysis of the creditworthiness of the firm. Companies often announce dividend payments in conjunction with trying to raise new capital.

5.4.5 Dividends and taxes

A final theory explaining dividend payments is based on the presence of different corporate and personal taxes on one hand and of different income and capital gains taxes on the other. Modigliani and Miller assume that there are no personal taxes. Taxes on dividends (ordinary income) are higher than taxes on capital gains. Thus, under the presence of personal taxes, companies should not pay dividends because investors require a higher return to companies that pay dividends. If payments are to be made to shareholders, the company should opt for other alternatives, such as share repurchases. This is true if taxes on dividend income are higher than taxes on capital gains.

However, different investors have different tax rates. High tax rate individuals will prefer that the firm invest more, whereas low tax individuals may prefer that the firm does not invest and instead pay dividends. Investors try to select companies with dividend policies that approximate their requirements.

Dividend capacity and dividend policy were also covered in Chapter 1 Section 4 and are considered further in Chapter 18.

6 Risk management

Exposure to risk by corporations should be rewarded and **risk management** is the process through which the company determines the risk-return combination that is consistent with the company's risk appetite. Risk management requires the **identification**, **measurement** and **transfer** of risks. The decision whether to transfer any of the risks to which the company is exposed will depend on the cost of transfer and the risk aversion of the company.

The transfer of risk can take place through the financial or insurance markets, or through product markets. It should be clarified that risk management does not necessarily imply a reduction in risk. If the expected rewards for undertaking risks warrant it, a company may increase its exposure to risk. **Risk mitigation** on the other hand is the process through which a company reduces its exposure to risk.

6.1 The rationale for risk management

Exam focus point

The examiner has written an article entitled 'Risk Management – understanding why is as important as understanding how' in the September 2010 issue of *Student Accountant*. Make sure you read this article.

6.1.1 The theoretical rationale

There has been substantial volumes of literature published on the theoretical rationale for risk management. Throughout the literature the over-riding rationale tends to be the **maximisation of shareholder value**.

Companies should be looking to **limit uncertainty** and to **manage speculative risks and opportunities** in order to **maximise positive outcomes and hence shareholder value**.

Boards should consider the factors that determine **shareholder valuations** of the company, the **risks** associated with these and the ways in which shareholders would like the **risks to be managed**.

Most risks must be managed to some extent, and some should be sought to be eliminated as being outside the scope of the remit of the management of a business. For example, a business in a high-tech industry, such as computing, which evolves rapidly within ever-changing markets and technologies, has to accept high risks in its research and development activities; but should it also be speculating on interest and exchange rates within its treasury activities?

Risk management under this view is an integral part of strategy, and involves analysing what the key value drivers are in the organisation's activities, and the risks tied up with those value drivers. In its Risk Management Standard, the Institute of Risk Management linked in key value drivers with major risk categories

6.1.2 The practical rationale

From a practical point of view, companies must be seen to be managing risk to maintain **confidence** in their business operations. Companies that are cavalier with their shareholders' funds may enjoy higher than average returns in the short-term but are unlikely to sustain this favourable position for long. Whilst shareholders like to enjoy high returns, most of them will prefer to know that some care is being taken with how their funds are being handled.

6.1.3 Management's attitude towards risk management

Managers that have **large equity stakes** (as opposed to equity options) in an organisation are more likely to take positive steps to manage risk. This is due to the fact that such managers will face both systematic and unsystematic risk (whilst external equity shareholders face only systematic risk). However managers may not increase shareholder value by managing unsystematic risk as external investors should have already diversified away this risk themselves.

If managers holding large equity stakes can concentrate on risks that they can do something about, it is more likely that they will be able to increase the value of the organisation.

What about managers who hold **share options** rather than actual shares? These managers are more likely to try to increase the risk of an organisation as they are trying to maximise future profits and share price. Managers may actively seek more risky investments which are not necessarily in the best interests of the organisation in their pursuit of higher profits and share price.

You only need to glance at the business pages of a newspaper on any day to find out why risk management is a key issue in today's business world.

As the effects of the global financial crisis are still being felt, companies face greater pressures to demonstrate the effectiveness of their risk management strategies. Without such strategies in an uncertain and still extremely risk world, confidence in these companies' operations would diminish, leading to fewer investors willing to risk their funds to finance them.

6.2 Risk mitigation

FAST FORWARD

Risk mitigation is the process of minimising the probability of a risk's occurrence or the impact of the risk should it occur.

Risk mitigation is the process through which a corporation reduces its risk exposure. Risk mitigation is therefore closely linked with the process of risk transferring.

The following risk assessment matrix – known as the severity/frequency matrix or the likelihood/consequences matrix – can be used to set **priorities** for **risk mitigation**.

		Severity	
		Low	*High*
Frequency	*Low*	Loss of small suppliers	Loss of senior or specialist staff Loss of sales to competitor Loss of sales due to macroeconomic factors
	High	Loss of lower-level staff	Loss of key customers Failure of computer systems

A company's risk mitigation strategy can be linked into the matrix above and also the company's **appetite** for risk-taking.

		Severity	
		Low	*High*
Frequency	*Low*	**Accept** Risks are not significant. Keep under view, but costs of dealing with risks unlikely to be worth the benefits.	**Transfer** Insure risk or implement contingency plans. Reduction of severity of risk will minimise insurance premiums.
	High	**Control or reduce** Take some action, eg enhanced control systems to detect problems or contingency plans to reduce impact.	**Abandon or avoid** Take immediate action, eg changing major suppliers or abandoning activities.

Case Study

Consider a company such as **Virgin**. It has many stable and successful brands, and healthy cash flows and profits: little need, you would have thought, to consider risky new ventures.

Yet Virgin operates a subsidiary called **Virgin Galactic** to own and operate privately-built spaceships, and to offer 'affordable' sub-orbital **space tourism to everybody** – or everybody willing to pay US$200,000 for the pleasure. The risks are enormous: developing the project will involve investing very large amounts of money, there is no guarantee that the service is wanted by sufficient numbers of people to make it viable, and the risks of catastrophic accidents are self-evident. In 2012 it was reported that almost 500 bookings have already been taken.

There is little doubt that Virgin's risk appetite derives directly from the **risk appetite** of its chief executive, Richard Branson – a self-confessed adrenaline junkie – who also happens to own most parts of the Virgin Group privately, and so faces little pressure from shareholders.

The most common risk mitigation strategies are **hedging** and **diversification**.

6.3 Hedging

Hedging involves the creation of offsetting or counterbalancing flows so that the exposure of a company to risk is either eliminated or reduced. Depending of the instrument that is employed by the company, the hedging strategy can be classified as **financial** or **operational** hedging.

6.3.1 Financial hedging

Financial hedging involves the use of financial instruments, mainly derivatives to reduce or eliminate exposure to risks. A company that imports raw materials, for example, may worry about an increase in the price of raw materials due to a depreciation of the home currency, and may want to use forwards, futures or options to hedge such a risk. Financial hedging is considered in detail in Chapters 16 and 17.

6.3.2 Operational hedging

Operational hedging is the course of action that **hedges a firm's risk exposure** through operational activities using **non-financial instruments**, The main way of implementing an operational hedging strategy is through **real options**. Real options give the possibility of delaying, abandoning, enhancing or switching activities and are covered in more detail in Chapter 6.

Consider a manufacturing firm, for example, which decides to expand its scale of activity in an overseas subsidiary. The parent company is exposed to both demand and exchange rate risks. The exposure to foreign exchange risk can be hedged using financial instruments e.g. forward contracts. However financial tools cannot be used to alter the demand risk exposure. This risk can be managed by postponing the production decision until after more accurate information about the demand is acquired. This kind of operational hedging is achieved by exercising the real option to postpone the extra investment.

6.4 Diversification strategies

Diversification strategies seek to reduce the volatility of earnings of a company. This can be achieved through **product** or **geographical** diversification.

6.4.1 Product diversification

Diversification into new products is considered one of the main strategies of reducing the volatility of earnings and the main motivation of conglomerate mergers which are examined in Chapter 12. Examples of conglomerate mergers include the acquisition for example of hotels and holiday resorts by a car manufacturer. The main idea of diversification is that earnings in various industries are subject to different risk factors, which are offset against each other when companied, resulting in aggregate earnings with less volatility.

6.4.2 Geographical diversification

Geographical diversification is achieved when the costs and revenues of a firm are aligned in such a way that they are exposed to the same risks. For example domestic firms selling to overseas markets can ensure that their production costs and sales revenues are exposed to the same exchange rate risk by opening a production facility in the overseas markets.

To demonstrate how controls are an important part of managing risks, we list below a number of the important risks that a business may well face. See if you can suggest some appropriate controls.

Risks		Example controls
Investor	Investors losing confidence in the way the company is run and selling their shares	
Investment	Loss-making investments being made	
Foreign exchange transaction	Having to pay more on a future transaction because of adverse exchange rate movements	
Political	Operations or revenues being disrupted by political activity	
Information	Taking the wrong decisions due to inadequate information	

Answer

Risks		Example controls
Investor	Investors losing confidence in the way the company is run and selling their shares	**Corporate governance** arrangements ensuring board exercises proper stewardship over the company and communicates effectively with shareholders
Investment	Loss-making investments being made	Use of **different financial measures** to provide extra perspectives on the investment
Foreign exchange transaction	Having to pay more on a future transaction because of adverse exchange rate movements	**Purchase an instrument** fixing the exchange rate used in the transaction
Political	Operations or revenues being disrupted by political activity	**Monitor** political situation; **negotiate with key stakeholders** (political parties)
Information	Taking the wrong decisions due to inadequate information	**Information systems** the organisation chooses providing quality of information needed for decision-making

7 Different types of risk

7.1 Systematic and unsystematic risk

Knowledge brought forward from earlier studies

Key terms

Market or **systematic risk** is risk that cannot be diversified away. **Non-systematic** or **unsystematic risk** applies to a single investment or class of investments, and can be reduced or eliminated by diversification.

See section 7.2 of this chapter for more on systematic and unsystematic risk.

7.2 Business risk and non-business risk

Key terms

Business risks are threats to the net profits of an organisation and are borne by both debt and equity holders. The level of business risk depends on the decisions an organisation makes in relation to its products or services.

Non-business risks are threats to profits that are not influenced by the products or services the organisation supplies.

As the name suggests, **business risk** arises from the type of business an organisation is involved in and relates to uncertainty about the future and the organisation's **business prospects**. The cost of capital of any organisation will include a premium for business risk. Business risk will be higher for some firms than for others – for example, you would expect the business risk of a large retail chain such as Walmart to be lower than that of a technological firm such as Microsoft.

(a) Examples of **business risks** include:

    (i) Threats of long-term **product obsolescence**

    (ii) **Changes in technology** changing the production process

    (iii) Long-term **macroeconomic changes**, for example a worsening of a country's exchange rate

(b) Examples of **non-business risks** include:

    (i) Risks arising from the long-term **sources of finance** chosen

    (ii) Risks from a collapse in trade because of an **adverse event**, an accident or natural disaster

Business risk is a mixture of **systematic** and **unsystematic risk** (see section 6.1 above for definitions). The systematic risk comes from such factors as revenue sensitivity and the mix of fixed and variable costs within the total cost structure. Unsystematic risk is determined by such company-specific factors as management ability and labour relations.

7.2.1 Degree of operating gearing

One way of measuring business risk is by calculating a company's **operating gearing** or 'operational gearing'.

$$\text{Operating gearing or leverage} = \frac{\text{Contribution}}{\text{Profit before interest and tax (PBIT)}}$$

Contribution is sales minus variable cost of sales.

The significance of operating gearing is as follows.

(a) **If contribution is high but PBIT is low**, fixed costs will be high, and only just covered by contribution. Business risk, as measured by operating gearing, will be high.

(b) **If contribution is not much bigger than PBIT**, fixed costs will be low, and fairly easily covered. Business risk, as measured by operating gearing, will be low.

7.3 Financial risk

Key term

Financial risk is the systematic risk borne by the equity shareholders. It is the risk that equity shareholders will receive a reduced or zero dividend and increases as the company increases its level of gearing. The ultimate financial risk is that the organisation will be unable to continue to function as a going concern.

Financial risks include the risks relating to the **structure of finance** the organisation has. In particular the risks include those relating to the mix of equity and debt capital, the risk of not being able to access funding, also whether the organisation has an insufficient long-term capital base for the amount of trading it is doing (overtrading).

The higher the gearing of an organisation's capital structure, the greater will be the risk to ordinary shareholders. This will be reflected in a higher risk premium and therefore a higher cost of capital.

Organisations also must consider the risks of **fraud and misuse** of financial resources.

Other shorter-term financial risks include:

- **Credit risk** – the possibility of payment default by the customer

- **Liquidity risk** – the risk of being unable to finance the credit, arising from cash restrictions or the need for more cash

- **Cash management risk** – risks relating to the security of cash, risks arising from unpredictable cash flows

Longer-term risks include currency and interest rate risks, and risks arising from other changes in the **macroeconomic environment**. Currency risk and how to deal with it is dealt with in Chapter 16. Interest rate risk is covered in Chapter 17.

7.4 Relationship between business and financial risk

In order to increase its share price, a company should aim to achieve higher profits without taking excessive business risk or financial risk.

Most shareholders are willing to accept a certain level of risk in order to earn returns on their investment. Directors and managers are expected to act within these risk parameters in pursuit of the maximisation of shareholders' wealth.

A business with high business risk may be **restricted** in the amount of financial risk it can sustain. Shareholders' acceptable level of risk may be made up mainly of the high level of business risk which means that the organisation cannot take on too much financial risk. The organisation will be unable to add too much debt to its capital structure as this would increase financial risk and potentially push total risk beyond the shareholders' acceptable level.

7.5 Political risk

Key term

> **Political risk** is the risk that political action will affect the position and value of a company.

When a multinational company invests in another country, either by setting up a subsidiary or by entering into a joint venture, it may face a political risk of action by that country's government which may affect the operation of the company. The ultimate political risk is the expropriation of the company's investment by the government of the host country. Although expropriation or nationalisation is not very common today, a multinational company is still exposed to political risk in the form of various restrictions.

(a) Import quotas could be used to limit the quantities of goods that a subsidiary can buy from its parent company and import for resale in its domestic markets.

(b) Exchange control regulations could be applied that may affect the ability of the subsidiary to remit profits to the parent company.

(c) Government actions that could restrict the ability of foreign companies to buy domestic companies, especially those that operate in politically sensitive industries such as defence contracting, communications, energy supply and so on.

(d) Government legislation that may specify minimum shareholding in companies by residents. This would force a multinational to offer some of the equity in a subsidiary to investors in the country where the subsidiary operates.

There are a large number of factors that can be considered to assess political risk, for example government stability, remittance restrictions and product boycotting as a result of deterioration in the relationships between the host country and the country where the parent company is based. Measurement is often by subjective weighting of these factors. Industry specific factors are also important.

7.6 Economic risk

Key term

> **Economic risk** arises from changes in economic policy in the host country that affect the macroeconomic environment in which the multinational company operates.

Examples of political risk include:

- A highly restricted monetary policy may lead to high interest rates and a recession affecting aggregate demand and the demand for the products of the multinational in the host country. On the other hand a inflation in the host country may lead to a devaluation of the currency and it may decrease the value of remittances to the parent company.
- Currency inconvertibility for a limited period of time.
- The host country may also be subjected to economic shocks, e.g. falling commodity prices which may also affect its exchange rate of fiscal and monetary policy which may affect again the state of the economy and the exchange rate.

7.7 Fiscal risk

Key term

> **Fiscal risk** is the risk that a multinational company is exposed to that the tax arrangements in the host country may change after the investment in the host country is undertaken.

Fiscal risks include:

- The imposition of indirect taxes such as VAT on the products of the company, raising the price of its products and potentially reducing demand.
- The imposition of excise duties on imported goods and services that are used by the subsidiary.
- An increase in the corporate tax rate
- The abolition of the accelerated tax depreciation allowances for new investments
- Changes in the tax law regarding admissibility of expenses for tax deductibility

7.8 Regulatory risk

Key term

> **Regulatory risk** is the risk that arises from the change in the legal and regulatory environment which determines the operation of a company.

For example a change in employment legislation making the firing of workers more difficult may increase costs of production and may affect the profitability of a company. Anti-monopoly laws may also restrict the capacity of a company to expand and it may restrict its profitability. Disclosure requirements or stricter corporate governance may also affect the freedom of a company to operate in the host country. Also legal standards of safety or quality (non-tariff barriers) could be imposed on imported goods to prevent multinationals from selling goods through a subsidiary which have been banned as dangerous in other countries.

7.9 Operational risk

Key term

> **Operational risk** is the risk arising from the execution (operation) of an organisation's business functions.

Operational risk includes such risks as human error, breakdowns in internal procedures and systems or external events.

It is difficult to identify and assess the extent of operational risk – many organisations historically accepted this risk as an inevitable cost of doing business. However, it is becoming more common for organisations to collect and analyse data relating to losses arising from, for example, systems failures or fraud

The **Basel II regulations** define specific types of operational risk as follows.

Specific types of operational risk	Examples
Internal fraud	Terrorism, vandalism, natural disasters
External fraud	Hacking, forgery, theft of information
Damage to physical assets	Terrorism, natural disasters, vandalism
Business disruption and systems failure	Failure of hardware or software, disruption to services
Employment practices, workplace safety	Health and safety requirements, employee compensation payments
Clients, products, business practices	Market manipulation, product defects
Process management	Errors in data entry, accounting or reporting

Operational risk does not include such strategic risks as losses arising from poor strategic business decisions.

7.10 Reputational risk

Key term

> **Reputational risk** is the risk related to the way in which a business is viewed by others.

Damage to an organisation's reputation can result in lost revenues or significant reductions (permanent or temporary) in shareholder value.

Reputational risk can be seen as one of the consequences of operational risk. Damage to an organisation's reputation can arise from **operational failures** and the way in which stakeholders react to such events.

 Case Study

In April 2010, the exploratory offshore drilling rig Deepwater Horizon exploded and sank, with the loss of 11 lives. This led to extensive oil spillage in the Gulf of Mexico, covering over 2,500 square miles.

The rig was owned and operated by Transocean Ltd on behalf of British Petroleum (BP). The US government named BP as the responsible party and the company spent at least $7 million per day trying to contain and eventually halt the oil spillage (at that time, BP's daily profits were approximately $61 million).

The damage to BP's reputation resulted in its share price falling by 52% in 50 days on the New York Stock Exchange (from $60.57 on 20 April 2010 to $29.20 on 9 June 2010), the share price has recovered since then but has not reached above $50 and in April 2012 was trading around $43.

7.11 Strategies to deal with risks

There are various strategies that multinational companies can adopt to limit the effects of political and other risks.

Negotiations with host government

The aim of these negotiations is generally to obtain a **concession agreement**. This would cover matters such as the transfer of capital, remittances and products, access to local finance, government intervention and taxation, and transfer pricing. The main problem with concession agreements can be that the initial terms of the agreement may not prove to be satisfactory subsequently. Companies may have different reasons for choosing to set up initially and choosing to stay, whilst the local government may be concerned if profits are too high.

Insurance

In the UK the Export Credits Guarantee Department (ECGD) provides protection against various threats including nationalisation, currency conversion problems, war and revolution.

Production strategies

It may be necessary to strike a balance between contracting out to local sources (thus losing control) and producing directly (which increases the investment and hence increases the potential loss.) Alternatively it may be better to locate key parts of the production process or the distribution channels abroad. Control of patents is another possibility, since these can be enforced internationally.

Contacts with markets

Multinationals may have contacts with customers which interventionist governments cannot obtain.

Financial management

If a multinational obtains funds in local investment markets, these may be on terms that are less favourable than on markets abroad, but would mean that local institutions suffered if the local government intervened. However governments often do limit the ability of multinationals to obtain funds locally.

Alternatively guarantees can be obtained from the government for the investment that can be enforced by the multinational if the government takes action.

Management structure

Possible methods include joint ventures or ceding control to local investors and obtaining profits by a management contract.

If governments do intervene, multinationals may have to make use of the advantages they hold or threaten withdrawal. The threat of expropriation may be reduced by negotiation or legal threats.

8 Capital investment monitoring

Capital investment projects require appraisal, and implementation monitoring.

8.1 The need for investment monitoring

Capital investment projects require a large proportion of a company's monetary and human resources and its implementation is crucial for a company's performance. Implementation is one of the stages of the capital investment process which consist of the appraisal stage, the budgeting stage, the authorisation stage, the implementation stage and the post audit report.

The monitoring functions of the implementation stage seek to ensure

- That the project expenses are within the budgeted limits
- That any revenues budgeted are achieved.
- That the completion time schedule is adhered to.
- That the risk factors identified during the appraisal stage remain valid.

8.2 Aspects of the monitoring process

Monitoring is a multifaceted function which requires clearly delineated roles and planning as well as recommendations for responding to any violations of the planned targets. Monitoring sets milestones for the assessment of the implementation process and the assessment of the various risks associated with the project implementation. Such risks may stem from industrial action, from changes in raw material prices, from changes in interest and exchange rates or from changes in tastes which may affect the demand for the company's products and therefore its revenues. The monitoring process is therefore closely linked to periodic risk assessment of the project   Below is a list of key activities in the monitoring process, which includes planning, execution and strategic reassessment.

8.2.1 Monitoring and risk management planning

(a)   Organisation of the monitoring function and roles and responsibilities assigned and communicated to individual members of the monitoring committee.

(b)   Milestones and risk tracking methods selected.

(c)   Determination of the critical path in the implementation phase. The critical path is a series of linked activities which make up the entire project.

8.2.2 Monitoring and risk management execution

(a)   Project risk factor database created and risk assessment against the deliverables at each time point to take place.

(b)   System of revenue and cost evaluation to be used along the critical path to verify compliance with budgets and time scheduling.

(c)   Project risks assigned impact and probability values eg risks could be classified as

<table>
<tr><td></td><td colspan="2" align="center">Probability</td></tr>
<tr><td rowspan="2">Impact</td><td align="center">Low probability
High impact</td><td align="center">High probability
High impact</td></tr>
<tr><td align="center">Low probability
Low Impact</td><td align="center">High probability
Low Impact</td></tr>
</table>

(d)   Risk mitigation actions decided and implemented.

8.2.3 Project reassessment

Produce final monitoring and risk management report on whether project requires revision of time schedules and financial assumptions and viability reassessed.

8.3 Post-completion auditing

Once a project has been completed, an audit should take place to compare the income, costs and timing with the corresponding budgeted items. A valuable aspect of the post-completion audit is the attribution to specific and identifiable factors of any deviations between budgeted items and actual outcomes. Such attribution will be valuable for a company that may undertake similar projects. However such attribution is not easy and it may be costly. It may not be easy to identify the causes of a delay for example in the execution of a project as there may several related and contingent factors. The usefulness of an audit may also be limited especially for projects that are unique.

Chapter Roundup

- Corporate performance can be measured using such means as ratios, trends and specialised techniques including Economic Value Added(EVA^{TM}) and Market Value Added (MVA).

- Market Value Added (MVA) is the difference between current total market value of the firm and the capital contributed by investors (debt and equity).

- As well as ratios, other information can be used to analyse a company's performance and identify possible problem areas. This will include information relating to non-current assets and financial obligations, contingencies and post balance sheet events.

- Decisions on how to finance the acquisition of assets are based on the cost of the various sources of finance.

- Debt capital takes various forms such as **loan capital**, **debentures**, **zero coupon bonds** and the interest on debt is tax-deductible.

- Preference shares have priority over ordinary shares in divided payments and capital repayment.

- **Retained earnings** are the **cumulative undistributed earnings** of the company and can be used to finance the **capital expenditure** programme of the company.

- New shares can be issued either to existing shareholders or to new shareholders.

- Dividend decisions determine the amount of and the way that a company's profits are distributed to its shareholders.

- Risk mitigation is the process of minimising the probability of a risk's occurrence or the impact of the risk should it occur.

- Capital investment projects require appraisal, and implementation monitoring.

Quick Quiz

1   Name three advantages and three disadvantages of debt as a source of finance

2   What is the main difference between operational and financial hedging?

3   Complete the severity/frequency matrix in relation to methods of dealing with risk.

1   Advantages – any three from

- Debt holders rank above shareholders in the case of liquidation
- Debt is generally cheaper than equity, as interest is tax deductible in most tax regimes
- Debt is secured against assets ∴ should be more attractive to investors
- Issue costs are normally lower for debt than for equity
- No immediate change in control when debt is issued, but this may change over time if debt is converted into shares
- Lenders do not participate in high profits – payout is restricted to interest and principal
- No immediate dilution in earnings and dividends per share

Disadvantages – any three from

- There is a legal obligation to pay interest, regardless of the size of annual profit, but there is no such obligation to pay dividends
- The increased burden of interest may cause shareholders to demand a higher return, as the greater burden increases the risk that dividends won't be paid
- The financial risks of ordinary shareholders is increased by heavy borrowing
- There may be restrictions on a company's power to borrow, either from a company's constitution or the trust deeds of existing stock
- Money has to be made available for redemption or repayment of debt

2   Financial hedging involves the use of financial instruments, usually derivatives, whereas operational hedging uses non-financial instruments usually real options

3

Severity

		Low	High
Frequency	Low	Accept	Transfer
	High	Control	Abandon

Now try the questions below from the Exam Question Bank

Number	Level	Marks	Time
2	Introductory	15	27 mins

Conflicting stakeholder interests

Topic list	Syllabus reference
1 Potential sources of stakeholder conflict	A (3) (a)
2 Strategies for the resolution of stakeholder conflict	A (3) (b)
3 Emerging governance structures	A (3) (c)

Introduction

The purpose of this chapter is to look at the ways in which a modern organisation is governed and more specifically at the possible conflicts between the various stakeholders of the organisation and the ways in which these conflicts can be resolved.

We first assess the possible sources of conflicts which may arise amongst stakeholders and review these in the light of alternative theories of managerial behaviour such as agency theory and transaction cost theory.

We then analyse alternative strategies for the resolution of conflict. Finally we compare the emerging governance structures of the European and UK/US models with respect to the role of the financial manager. A useful appendix to the chapter includes details of the UK Corporate Governance Code, Sarbanes-Oxley and the King report.

Study guide

		Intellectual level
A3	**Conflicting stakeholder interests**	
(a)	Assess the potential sources of the conflict within a given corporate governance/stakeholder framework informed by an understanding of the alternative theories of managerial behaviour. Relevant underpinning theory for this assessment would be: (i) The Separation of Ownership and Control (ii) Transaction cost economics and comparative governance structures (iii) Agency Theory	3
(b)	Recommend, within specified problem domains, appropriate strategies for the resolution of stakeholder conflict and advise on alternative approaches that may be adopted	3
(c)	Compare the different governance structures and policies (with particular emphasis upon the European stakeholder and the US/UK shareholder model) and with respect to the role of the financial manager	3

Exam guide

You must be prepared to answer questions on key concepts such as agency theory or goal congruence, or developments in corporate governance and emerging governance structures. Questions are likely to be of a practical nature and are likely to require you to advise the board on the resolution of stakeholder conflict and alternative approaches that may be adopted.

1 Potential sources of stakeholder conflict

FAST FORWARD

> The central source of shareholder conflict is the difference between the interests of managers and those of owners.

1.1 Stakeholders' objectives

Here is a checklist of stakeholders' objectives. It is not comprehensive.

(a) **Employees and managers**

    (i)   Job security (over and above legal protection)
    (ii)   Good conditions of work (above minimum safety standards)
    (iii)   Job satisfaction
    (iv)   Career development and relevant training

(b) **Customers**

    (i)   Products of a certain quality at a reasonable price
    (ii)   Products that should last a certain number of years
    (iii)   A product or service that meets customer needs.

(c) **Suppliers**: regular orders in return for reliable delivery and good service

(d) **Shareholders**: long-term wealth

(e) **Providers of loan capital (stock holders):** reliable payment of interest due and maintenance of the value of any security.

(f)   **Society as a whole**

    (i)   Control pollution

    (ii)   Financial assistance to charities, sports and community activities

    (iii)   Co-operate with government in identifying and preventing health hazards

An organisation might accept the **legitimacy of the expectations of stakeholders other than shareholders** and build those expectations into its stated purposes. This would be because without appropriate relationships with groups such as suppliers, employers and customers, the organisation would not be able to function.

Clearly, organisations have a duty to respect the **legal rights** of stakeholders other than shareholders. These are extensive in the UK, including wide-ranging **employment law** and **consumer protection law**, as well as the more basic legislation relating to such matters as contract and property. Where **moral entitlements** are concerned, organisations need to be practical: they should take care to establish just what *expectations* they are prepared to treat as *obligations*, bearing in mind their general ethical stance and degree of concern about bad publicity.

1.2 Stakeholder theory

Stakeholder theory proposes **corporate accountability** to a broad range of stakeholders. It is based on companies being so large, and their impact on society being so significant that they cannot just be responsible to their shareholders. There is a moral case for a business knowing how its decisions affect people both inside and outside the organisation. Stakeholders should also be seen not as just existing, but as **making legitimate demands** upon an organisation. The relationship should be seen as a **two-way** relationship.

1.3 Objectives of the organisation

The fundamental objective of any organisation should be the maximisation of shareholders' wealth. In its purest sense this means squeezing every last cent of profits out of the organisation's operations. This objective has its origins in the owner-manager set-up, where the owners actually managed their own businesses and paid little or no attention to other stakeholders such as the wider community and the government.

1.3.1 Separation of ownership from control

In most modern organisations the owners do not actually manage the company. Whilst the **equity shareholders** own the company, the day to day operations are managed on their behalf by the **board of directors**. The directors and managers within the organisation have their own personal goals that may **conflict** with those of the shareholders. The problem that shareholders have is that they are seen as being **passive** stakeholders – that is, they do not (and are not expected to) contribute to business decisions that affect the company. Whilst managers are privy to privileged information about the company, shareholders have to rely on publicly available details such as annual reports and press articles, a situation known as **information asymmetry**.   As a result managers are very much left to their own devices when making business decisions

1.4 Examples of conflicts of interest between managers and shareholders

As mentioned in above, the fact that the managers of a company are not necessarily the owners of the company leaves open the possibility that managers may not act in the interests of the owners. Some examples are given below.

1.4.1 Short-termism

There is evidence that in many companies the primary driver of decision-making has been to **increase share prices** and hence **managerial rewards** in the short-term. The longer-term benefits of investment in

research and development may be ignored in the short-term drive to cut costs and increase profits thus jeopardising the long term prospects of the company.

1.4.2 Sales maximisation

This strategy is often employed by managers to increase market share and therefore the importance of the company within its sector. An increase in importance for the company will mean greater status for management but will not necessarily be in the best interests of the shareholders.

1.4.3 Overpriced acquisitions

Takeovers is another manifestation of the non-alignment of the interests of shareholders and managers. In Chapter 10 we explore in more depth the issue of why so many takeovers or mergers fail to increase shareholder value. In brief, the explanation lies in the fact that managers have motives other than shareholder value maximisation.

1.4.4 Resistance to takeovers

The management of a company may tend to resist takeovers if they feel that their position is threatened even if in doing so shareholder value is also reduced.

1.4.5 Relationships

Many companies' pursuit of short-term cost reduction may lead to difficult relationships with their wider stakeholders. Relationships with **suppliers** may be disrupted by demands for major improvements in terms and in reduction of prices. **Employees** may be made redundant in a drive to reduce costs and **customers** may be able to buy fewer product lines and have to face less favourable terms. These policies may aid short-term profits, but in the long-term suppliers and employees are able to take full advantage of market conditions and move to other companies, and customers can shop elsewhere or over the internet.

1.5 Conflict between stakeholders

What stakeholders want from an organisation will vary. Some will actively seek to influence what the organisation does and others may be concerned with limiting the effects of the organisation's activities upon themselves.

Relations with stakeholders can also vary. Possible relationships can include conflict, support, regular dialogue or joint enterprise.

There is considerable dispute about whose interests should be taken into account. The **legitimacy of each stakeholder's claim** will depend on your ethical and political perspective on whether certain groups should be considered as stakeholders. Should for example distant communities, other species, or future generations be considered as legitimate stakeholders?

Although we discussed the **conflict** between **managers** and **owners**, there are other areas of potential conflict between managers, owners and **other stakeholders** who provide **capital**, namely the **debt holders**. The relationship between the long-term creditors of a company, the management and the shareholders of a company encompasses the following factors:

(a) Management may decide to raise finance for a company by taking out **long-term** or **medium-term loans**.

(b) Investors who provide debt finance will rely on the company's management to generate enough net cash inflows to make **interest payments** on time, and eventually to repay loans. Long-term creditors will often take **security** for their loan, perhaps in the form of a fixed charge over an asset (such as a mortgage on a building). Debentures are also often subject to certain **restrictive covenants**, which restrict the company's rights to borrow more money until the debentures have been repaid.

(c) The money that is provided by long-term creditors will be invested to **earn profits**, and the profits (in excess of what is needed to pay interest on the borrowing) will provide extra dividends or retained profits for the shareholders of the company. In other words, shareholders will expect to increase their wealth using creditors' money.

Sometimes the needs of shareholders and debtholders may conflict:

(a) Managers may be tempted to take **risky decisions** using debtholders' money to finance them, knowing that the benefits of these decisions will accrue to the shareholders. If the projects go badly and the company fails, the debtholders may suffer a greater loss than the equity shareholders.

(b) In many jurisdictions there are rules limiting the proportion of company assets that can be paid out as dividends. However, it may still be possible to pay out lawfully **considerable sums** as dividends, enough to jeopardise the company's future and hence the amounts that the debtholders have advanced, should trading results turn bad in the near future.

(c) Shareholders and managers may wish to **prolong the company's life** as long as possible, whereas debtholders may wish to safeguard the amount loaned and realise their security as soon as the company appears to be getting into difficulties.

(d) Managers may attempt to undermine the position of debtholders by seeking further loan capital, committing the company to an **increased interest burden** and hence greater risk of insolvency. The additional loan capital may also have superior claims on the company's assets to the original amounts borrowed.

Exam focus point

You may be asked about the differing interests of share and bond holders.

1.6 Conflict between headquarters and divisions

We have so far examined potential conflicts between managers and outside investors. However, there is another potential conflict between divisional managers and corporate headquarters. Example of this type of conflict usually arises over the allocation of capital to the various subdivisions by headquarters. If there are too many divisions competing for funds, then the allocation of capital may not be efficient. It is quite common for corporate headquarters to allocate capital in an equitable way which may not maximise the return on capital for the organisation as a whole.

1.7 Agency theory

FAST FORWARD

The **agency problem** arises when agents do not act in the best interests of their principals. **Agency theory** seeks to give insight in the relationship between the owners and the management of a firm.

The relationship between management and shareholders is sometimes referred to as an **agency relationship**, in which managers act as agents for the shareholders.

Key term

Agency theory proposes that, although individual members of the business team act in their own self-interest, the well-being of each individual depends on the well-being of other team members and on the performance of the team in competition with other teams.

1.7.1 The agency problem

Classical microeconomic theory views a firm as an homogenous entity which decides on profit maximisation and production levels according to market conditions. In this framework there is no distinction between ownership and management. However when such a distinction exists and managers are the agents of the shareholders, then the separation of ownership from management is sometimes characterised as the '**agency problem**'. For example, if managers hold none or very little of the equity shares of the company they work for, what is to stop them from working inefficiently, not bothering to look for profitable new investment opportunities, or giving themselves high salaries and perks?

We have already examined some manifestations of the **agency problem**. The costs of the agency problem include auditing systems to limit ill behaviour of the managers, various kinds of bonding assurances by the managers to ensure that such abuses will not be practised and changes in organisation systems that limit the ability of managers to engage in undesirable practices.

The goal of agency theory is to find **governance structures** and **control mechanisms** that minimise the problem caused by the separation of ownership and control. In that sense agency theory is the cornerstone of the theory of corporate governance. More specifically agency theory tries to find means for the owners to control the managers in such a way that the managers will operate in the interest of the owners. **Moral hazard problems** are related to the **agency problems** in that the managers, once appointed as representatives for the owner, do not always act in the interest of the owners although they should.

Whereas in the **classical microeconomic setting** a firm employs **labour** and **capital** to produce **output**, the starting point of the agency theory is that there are many more factors of production including management as well as the capital providers and that the firm is a nexus of contracts among these individual factors of productions. The contracts between these individual factors of productions are constantly negotiated, each factor of production maximising in the process their own utility function.

In the **agency theory** set up, shareholders as the main providers of capital, enter into contractual agreements with managers so as the managers manage the assets of the company in a way that maximises the utility of shareholders. Thus the shareholders are the principals and the managers the agents. For the contracts that are negotiated between the principal and the agent to lead to the utility maximisation of both parties, it requires the existence of efficient markets for corporate control, managers and corporate information.

The **agency theory** suggests that the existence of the efficient markets for corporate control, managers and information ensures that management bears the cost of possible misconduct. It is in the interest of management to align its interest with the interest of the principals. One power that shareholders possess is the right to **remove the directors** from office. But shareholders have to take the initiative to do this, and in many companies the shareholders lack the energy and organisation to take such a step. Even so, directors will want the **company's report and accounts**, and the **proposed final dividend**, to meet with **shareholders' approval** at the AGM.

The agency theory implies heavy **monitoring costs** of the agents by the principals as well as high costs of enforcing the **negotiated contracts**. The resulting corporate structure is designed to monitor and control.

This view of the corporate world by the agency theory is, however, not universally accepted. The **stewardship theory** for example maintains that the interests of managers and shareholders are not always at variance, and management may have incentives such as **responsibility**, **altruism** or **recognition** that do not conflict with the interests of the shareholders. According to this theory, the managers of a company are the **stewards** of the company.

1.8 Transaction cost economics

FAST FORWARD

> The **transaction cost economics** theory postulates that the **governance structure** of a corporation is determined by **transaction costs**.

The theory of **transaction cost economics** explains the organisational structure of a firm and its behaviour as a result of the costs that are incurred when the owners of the firm are making transactions. These transaction costs include **search** and **information costs**, **bargaining costs** and **policing** and **enforcement costs**. Bargaining costs arise from the process of agreeing (bargaining) on a contract, and the enforcement costs, are the costs of ensuring that every party complies with the contract.

Transaction costs imply limited liability for shareholders and limited liability enables investors to diversify. Diversification allows investors to ignore the idiosyncratic risks of individual companies. This implies that investors require relatively little direct monitoring of the operations of individual business firms.

Exam focus point

> Although the detail of the theories is not examinable, you need to be aware of them in so far as they give insight into managerial behaviour and the development of corporate governance.

2 Strategies for the resolution of stakeholder conflict

FAST FORWARD

The **resolution** of the **agency problem** arising when agents do not act in the best interests of their principals is to bring about **goal congruence** between the objectives of the shareholders and those of management by devising **appropriate mechanisms**. Alternatively, the relevant authorities should enforce good **corporate governance** practice.

2.1 Assessing the relative importance of stakeholder interests

Apart from the problem of taking different stakeholder interests into account, an organisation also faces the problem of **weighing shareholder interests** when considering future strategy. How for example do you compare the interest of a major shareholder with the interest of a local resident coping with the noise and smell from the company's factory?

2.2 Agency theory resolution strategy

Agency theory analyses the problems that can arise when ownership and control are separated and how they might be mitigated by negotiating contracts that allow the principal to control the agent in such a way that the agent will operate in the interests of the principal. These contractual ways of resolving the problem include a variety of strategies some of which are discussed below.

2.3 Firm induced strategies

Agency theory sees employees of businesses, including managers, as individuals, each with his or her own objectives. Within a department of a business, there are departmental objectives. If achieving these various objectives leads also to the achievement of the objectives of the organisation as a whole, there is said to be **goal congruence**.

Key term

> **Goal congruence** is accordance between the objectives of agents acting within an organisation and the objectives of the organisation as a whole.

Goal congruence may be better achieved and the 'agency problem' better dealt with by giving managers some profit-related pay, or by providing incentives which are related to profits or share price. Examples of such remuneration incentives are:

(a) **Profit-related/economic value-added pay**

Pay or bonuses related to the size of profits or economic value-added.

(b) **Rewarding managers with shares**

This might be done when a private company 'goes public' and managers are invited to subscribe for shares in the company at an attractive offer price. In a **management buy-out** or buy-in (the latter involving purchase of the business by new managers; the former by existing managers), managers become owner-managers.

(c) **Executive Share Options Plans (ESOPs)**

In a share option scheme, selected employees are given a number of share options, each of which gives the holder the right after a certain date to subscribe for shares in the company at a fixed price. The value of an option will increase if the company is successful and its share price goes up.

Exam focus point

> Discussion of managerial priorities may be part of a longer question in the exam. The integrated approach to the syllabus may mean that a question on the effect on management motivation of the introduction of a share option scheme may be examined as part of a question on general option theory.

Such measures might merely encourage management to adopt **'creative accounting'** methods which will distort the reported performance of the company in the service of the managers' own ends.

2.4 Separation of roles

The agency theory suggests that not too much power should accrue to a single individual within an organisation. The role of the Chairman and the Chief executive for example should be split.

2.5 Accounting standards

The financial statements of a company are the main vehicle of corporate information to the shareholders. Agency theory suggests that **audited accounts** of limited companies are an important source of 'post-decision' information minimising investors' agency costs.

2.6 Corporate governance

An alternative approach to attempt to monitor managers' behaviour is through the adoption of a corporate framework of decision making that restricts the power of managers and increases the role of independent external parties in the monitoring of their duties. This can be achieved for example by establishing 'management audit' procedures, by introducing additional reporting requirements, or by seeking assurances from managers that shareholders' interests will be foremost in their priorities.

3 Emerging governance structures

You should be familiar with corporate governance from your P1 – *Governance, risk and ethics* studies. However you should read this section and the appendix to this chapter carefully to familiarise yourself with the different corporate governance structures. You should also read the **Appendix** to this chapter which covers the UK Corporate Governance Code, Sarbanes-Oxley and the King Report in more detail.

3.1 Corporate governance in the UK

FAST FORWARD

> Three UK reports – Cadbury, Greenbury and Hampel – recommend best practice in **corporate governance**, **financial reporting** and **accountability.** The Combined Code merges the recommendations of the three reports into best practice that should be followed by listed companies. The Combined Code was replaced by the UK Corporate Governance Code in 2010.

Key term

> The Cadbury Report defines **corporate governance** as 'the system by which companies are directed and controlled'.

There were three significant corporate governance reports in the United Kingdom during the 1990s. The **Cadbury and Hampel reports** covered general corporate governance issues, whilst the **Greenbury report** concentrated on remuneration of directors.

The recommendations of these three reports were merged into a **Combined Code** in 1998, with which companies listed on the London Stock Exchange are required to comply.

Since the publication of the Combined Code a number of reports in the UK have been published about specific aspects of corporate governance.

- The **Turnbull report** focused on risk management and internal control
- The **Smith report** discussed the role of audit committees
- The **Higgs report** focused on the role of the non-executive director

The Combined Code was renamed as **the UK Corporate Governance Code** when a new version was published in 2010. Details of the UK Corporate Governance Code can be found in the appendix to this chapter.

3.2 Comparison between UK and USA models

FAST FORWARD

> The voluntary code-based UK approach can be contrasted with the American approach, very much founded in **regulation** and **legislation**.

Corporate scandals in the United States, particularly the Enron and Worldcom scandals, led to the Sarbanes-Oxley Act 2002 and consequent changes to the listing rules that companies quoted on Wall Street have to fulfil.

The following is a comparison of the main points of UK and US guidance.

	UK guidance (UK Corporate Governance Code and Turnbull report except where indicated)	US guidance (Sarbanes-Oxley)
Scope	All types of internal control including financial, operational and compliance	Internal control over financial reporting
Audit committee	Smith report states should consist of independent non-executive directors, at least one having relevant and recent financial experience	Should consist of independent directors, one of whom should be a financial expert
Audit rotation	Ethical guidance states lead audit partner should be rotated at least every five years, other key audit partners at least every seven years	Rotation of lead partner required every five years
Non-audit services	Audit committee should review non-audit services provided by auditor to ensure auditor objectivity and independence is safeguarded. Accountancy bodies state that executing transactions or acting in a management role not compatible with being an objective auditor; other services (custody, preparing accounting records) cast doubts on objectivity	Auditors forbidden by law from carrying out a number of non-audit services including internal audit, bookkeeping, systems design/implementation, valuation, actuarial, management, expert services
Reports on internal control	Accounts include statement of responsibility of management for internal controls; also disclosure that there is a process for identifying, evaluating and managing risks and the process board has applied to review this	Accounts include statement of responsibility of management for internal controls and financial reporting; accounts should also include audited assessment of effectiveness of financial reporting controls
Code of ethics	No equivalent guidance	Companies should adopt a code of ethics for senior financial officers
Certification by directors	Under UK legislation directors required to state in directors' report that there is no relevant audit information that they know and that auditors are unaware of	Certification of appropriateness and fair presentation of accounts by chief executive and chief finance officer
Sanctions	No equivalent UK provision	If accounts have to be restated, chief executive and chief finance officer forfeit their bonuses

The appendix to this chapter provides a detailed summary of the UK Corporate Governance Code and the Sarbanes-Oxley Act 2002.

3.3 Corporate governance internationally: comparisons with other countries

FAST FORWARD

Other examples of corporate governance models include Germany (**supervisory board**) and Japan (three boards, low level of regulation, **stakeholder collaboration** stressed).

The establishment of a voluntary code of practice on corporate governance in the UK characterises a different approach to that adopted in many other countries.

(a) In continental Europe, **reporting requirements** tend to be more statutorily based in tax law, although all EU members are subject to EU company law directives.

(b) **Japanese** companies are characterised by what is sometimes called a flexible approach to corporate governance, with a low level of regulation. All stakeholders are supposed to collaborate in the company's best interests.

(c) The **South African** regime relies heavily on disclosure as a regulatory measure.

(d) The Organisation for Economic Co-operation and Development (OECD) has issued a set of non-binding principles that are intended to provide guidance to governments, stock exchanges, investors and companies in various countries.

3.3.1 Germany: institutional differences

A significant difference between companies in the UK and many German companies is the **distribution of power** between **workers and managers,** and **shareholders and managers**.

In the UK, ownership is something which can be easily traded on the Stock Exchange in the form of shares. Buyers of shares seek the best combination of risk and return. While managers have most power for practical purposes, in theory they are acting in the shareholders' interests. From the company's point of view, the **stock market** is the **principal source of** investment capital, especially for large companies. Banks generally provide credit, not capital.

In Germany the role of stock markets in company finance and management is not so important. **German banks** specialising in lending to industry and commercial enterprises have a relatively long-term interest in a company, and might even have an equity investment in it, as the sign of a long-term business relationship. It is argued that this makes them more sympathetic to a company's problems.

Institutional arrangements in German companies, typified by the **two-tiered board**, allow employees to have a formal say in the running of the company. A **supervisory board** has workers' representatives, and perhaps shareholders' representatives including banks' representatives, in equal numbers. The board has no executive function, although it does review the company's direction and strategy and is responsible for safeguarding **stakeholders**' interests. An **executive board**, composed entirely of managers, will be responsible for the **running** of the business.

3.3.2 Japan: cross shareholdings

The main emphasis of Japanese corporate governance is on **management** by **consensus** rather than directors following voluntary codes or statutory regulations.

In Japan, the stock market does have an important role to play, particularly in savings. However, the separation between investment and management is in practice drawn differently to the UK. The stock market is less 'open'. The corporate sector has close links with the banks, who are often represented on boards of directors.

There are three different types of board of director.

- **Policy boards** – concerned with long-term strategic issues
- **Functional boards** – made up of the main senior executives with a functional role
- **Monocratic boards** – with few responsibilities and having a more symbolic role

Japanese companies generally set up **long-term business relationships** with banks, suppliers and customers, even to the extent of buying each other's shares as a symbol of the relationship. When share prices fall, friendly companies do not sell shares in each other. If the web of interrelated companies is large enough, it may possibly include a bank which provides credit to participants in the group.

In Japan the long-term interests of the company are stressed rather than the short-term preferences of shareholders. These arrangements have enabled some companies to be protected from the rigours of profit-performance, so that long-term objectives such as market share have been traditionally favoured instead. There is evidence, however, that this system is gradually coming to an end.

3.3.3 South Africa

South Africa's major contribution to the corporate governance debate has been the **King report**, first published in 1994 and updated in 2002 to take account of developments in South Africa and elsewhere in the world.

The King report differs in emphasis from other guidance by advocating an integrated approach to corporate governance in the interest of a wide range of stakeholders – embracing the social, environmental and economic activities of a company's activities. The report encourages activism by shareholders, business and the financial press and relies heavily on disclosure as a regulatory measure.

The appendix to this chapter contains further details on the contents of the King Report.

3.3.4 OECD guidance

The Organisation for Economic Co-operation and Development (OECD) has developed a **set of principles of corporate governance** that countries and companies should work towards achieving. The OECD has stated that its interest in corporate governance arises from its concern for **global investment**. Corporate governance arrangements should be credible and should be understood across national borders. Having a common set of accepted principles is a step towards achieving this aim.

The OECD developed its Principles of Corporate Governance in 1998 and issued a revised version in April 2004. They are non-binding principles, intended to assist governments in their efforts to evaluate and improve the legal, institutional and regulatory framework for corporate governance in their countries. They are also intended to provide guidance to stock exchanges, investors and companies.

The OECD principles deal mainly with governance problems that result from the **separation of ownership and management** of a company. Issues of ethical concern and environmental issues are also relevant, although not central, to the problems of governance.

The OECD principles are grouped into five broad areas:

(a) **The rights of shareholders**

Shareholders should have the right to **participate and vote in general meetings** of the company, **elect** and **remove members of the board** and **obtain relevant and material information** on a timely basis. Capital markets for corporate control should function in an **efficient and timely manner**.

(b) **The equitable treatment of shareholders**

All shareholders of the same class of shares should be treated equally, including **minority shareholders** and **overseas shareholders**. **Impediments** to **cross-border shareholdings** should be **eliminated**.

(c) **The role of stakeholders**

Rights of stakeholders should be **protected**. All stakeholders should have **access to relevant information** on a regular and timely basis. **Performance-enhancing mechanisms** for employee participation should be **permitted to develop**. Stakeholders, including employees, should be able to **freely communicate their concerns** about illegal or unethical relationships to the board.

(d) **Disclosure and transparency**

Timely and accurate disclosure must be made of all material matters regarding the company, including the financial situation, foreseeable risk factors, issues regarding employees and other stakeholders and governance structures and policies. The company's approach to disclosure should promote the provision of analysis or advice that is relevant to decisions by investors.

(e)   **The responsibilities of the board**

The board is responsible for the **strategic guidance** of the company and for the **effective monitoring** of management. Board members should act on a fully informed basis, in good faith, with due diligence and care and in the **best interests of the company and its shareholders**. They should treat **all shareholders fairly**. The board should be able to exercise **independent judgement**; this includes assigning independent non-executive directors to appropriate tasks.

Question

Corporate governance

Briefly explain what is meant by corporate governance and discuss how the main measures recommended by the corporate governance codes should contribute towards better corporate governance.

Answer

Definition of corporate governance

Corporate governance can be defined broadly as the **system** by which an **organisation** is **directed and controlled**. It is concerned with systems, processes, controls, accountability and decision making at the heart of and at the highest level of an organisation. It is therefore concerned with the way in which top managers **execute their responsibilities** and authority and how they **account** for that authority to those who have entrusted them with assets and resources. In particular it is concerned with the potential abuse of power and the need for openness, integrity and accountability in corporate decision making.

Recommendations of corporate governance codes

Clearly, a company must have senior executives. The problem is how to ensure as far as possible that the actions and decisions of the executives will be for the benefit of shareholders. Measures that have been recommended by various corporate governance codes include the following.

Directors

(a)   A listed company is required by the 'voluntary' UK Corporate Governance Code to appoint **non-executive directors**, most of whom should be **independent.** The non-executives are intended to provide a check or balance against the power of the chairman and chief executive.

(b)   The posts of **chairman and chief executive** should not be held by the same person, to prevent excessive executive power being held by one individual.

(c)   Non-executive directors should **make up** the **membership** of the remuneration committee of the board, and should determine the remuneration of executive directors. This is partly to prevent the executives deciding their own pay, and rewarding themselves excessively. Another purpose is to try to devise incentive schemes for executives that will motivate them to **achieve results** for the company that will also be in the best interests of the shareholders.

Risk assessment

The requirement in many codes for a risk audit should ensure that the board of directors is **aware** of the **risks** facing the company, and have **systems** in place for managing them. In theory, this should provide some protection against risk for the company's shareholders.

Dialogue with shareholders

The UK Corporate Governance Code encourages **greater dialogue** between a **company** and its **shareholders**. Institutional investor organisations are also encouraging greater participation by shareholders, for example in voting.

Audits

The **audit committee** of the board is seen as having a **major role** to play, in promoting dialogue between the external auditors and the board. Corporate governance should be improved if the views of the **external auditors** are given greater consideration.

Chapter Roundup

- The central source of shareholder conflict is the difference in the interest of managers and owners.

- The **agency problem** arises when agents do not act in the best interests of their principals. The **agency theory** tries to give insight in the relationship between the owners and the management of a firm.

- The **transaction cost economics** theory postulates that the governance structure of a corporation is determined by transaction costs.

- The **resolution** of the **agency problem** which arises when agents do not act in the best interests of their principals is to bring about **goal congruence** between the objectives of the shareholders and management by devising appropriate mechanisms. Alternatively, the relevant authorities should enforce good **corporate governance** practice.

- Three UK reports – Cadbury, Greenbury and Hampel – recommend best practice in **corporate governance**, **financial reporting** and **accountability.** The Combined Code merges the recommendations of the three reports into best practice that should be followed by listed companies. The Combined Code was replaced by the UK Corporate Governance Code in 2010.

- The voluntary code-based UK approach can be contrasted with the American approach, very much founded in **regulation** and **legislation**.

- Other examples of corporate governance models include Germany (**supervisory board**) and Japan (three boards, low level of regulation, **stakeholder collaboration** stressed).

Quick Quiz

1 What is the key proposition of agency theory?

2 **Fill in the blank**

.... is accordance between the objectives of agents acting within an organisation.

3 To which code have the Cadbury, Greenbury and Hampel reports contributed?

4 **Fill in the blank**

The Cadbury report defines corporate governance as ....

5 What is the best way to achieve a division of responsibilities at the head of a company?

6 What target length of time for directors' service contracts was suggested by the Greenbury report?

7 Which two boards go to make up the German system of two-tiered boards?

Answers to Quick Quiz

1   Although individual members of the business team act in their own self-interest, the well-being of each individual depends on the well-being of other team members and on the performance of the team in competition with other teams.

2   Goal congruence

3   The combined corporate governance code

4   The system by which companies are directed and controlled

5   Separation of the posts of Chairman and Chief Executive

6   One year or less

7   A supervisory board (workers and shareholders)
    An executive board (management)

Now try the question below from the Exam Question Bank

Number	Level	Marks	Time
3	Introductory	12	22 mins

APPENDIX

1 UK Corporate Governance Code

A Leadership

A1 Role of the board

All listed companies should be led by an **effective board**, responsible for providing **entrepreneurial leadership**, within a **framework of prudent** and **effective controls**, enabling **risk to be assessed** and **managed**. The board is responsible for setting strategic aims, ensuring sufficient resources are available, setting values and standards and ensuring obligations to shareholders. The board should **meet regularly**, with a **formal schedule of matters** reserved for it. The annual report should explain how the board operates, and give details of members and attendance.

A2 Division of responsibilities

A **clear division of responsibilities** should exist so that there is a balance of power, and no one person has unfettered powers of decision. The roles of **chairman** and **chief executive** should not be exercised by one person.

A3 The chairman

The chairman is responsible for leading the board and ensuring its effectiveness. The chairman should establish the board's agenda, and ensure there is **adequate time for discussion**, particularly of strategic matters. The chairman should promote **openness and debate**, help non-executive directors contribute effectively and promote constructive relations between executives and non-executives. The chairman should ensure that the board receives **accurate, timely and clear information** and should ensure communication with shareholders is effective. The chairman should meet the independence criteria for non-executive directors. A chief executive should not go on to become chairman.

A4 Non-executive directors

Non-executive directors should scrutinise management's performance and constructively challenge strategy. They should obtain assurance about the integrity of financial information and that financial controls and risk management systems are **robust** and **defensible**. Other important tasks include **determining executive remuneration** and playing a significant role in decisions about **board changes**. One of the independent non-executives should be appointed as senior independent director, to act as an intermediary with other directors and shareholders. The chairman should hold meetings with the non-executives without the executives being there, and the non-executives should meet without the chairman to appraise the chairman's performance. Directors should ensure that concerns they have that cannot be resolved are formally recorded.

B Effectiveness

B1 Composition of the board

The board and its committees should have a balance of **skills, experience, independence and knowledge** of the company. The board should be of sufficient size to **operate effectively**, but not so large as to be **unwieldy.** The board should have a **balance** of **executive and non-executive directors** so that no individual or small group is dominant. Decisions on committee membership should take into account the need to avoid undue reliance on particular individuals. At least half the board of FTSE 350 companies should be **independent non-executive directors**. Smaller listed companies should have at least **two independent non-executive directors.**

B2 Appointments to the board

There should be a **clear, formal procedure** for appointing new directors. A nomination committee should make recommendations about all new board appointments. The majority of members of this committee should be independent non-executives. Directors should be appointed **on merit,** against objective criteria, and considering the value of diversity, including gender diversity. There should be an **orderly succession process** in place.

B3 Commitment

Directors should allocate sufficient time to the company to **discharge their duties effectively**. In particular the nomination committee should assess the **time commitment expected** of the chairman, and the chairman's other commitments should be disclosed to the board and shareholders. Non-executives' letters of appointment should set out the expected time commitment and non-executives should undertake to have sufficient time to fulfil their responsibilities. Their other significant commitments should be disclosed to the board. A full time executive director should not take on more than one non-executive directorship of a FTSE 100 company, nor the chairmanship of a FTSE 100 company.

B4 Development

All directors should be properly inducted when they join the board and regularly update their skills and knowledge. The chairman should **agree training and development needs** with each director.

B5 Information and support

The board should be **promptly supplied** with **enough information** to enable it to carry out its duties. Information volunteered by management will sometimes need to be supplemented by information from other sources. The chairman and secretary should ensure good information flows. Directors should be able to obtain independent professional advice and have access to the services of the company secretary. The company secretary is responsible for **advising the chairman** on **all governance matters.** The whole board should be responsible for appointing and removing the company secretary.

B6 Evaluation

There should be a **vigorous annual performance evaluation** of the board as a whole, individual directors (effective contribution and commitment) and board committees. Evaluation of the board of FTSE 350 companies should be externally facilitated at **least once every three years.** The chairman should take action as a result of the review, if necessary proposing new board members or seeking the **resignation of directors.**

B7 Re-election

All directors should submit themselves for **re-election regularly**, and at least once every three years. Directors of FTSE 350 companies should be subject to **annual election by shareholders.**

C Accountability

C1 Financial and business reporting

The board should present a **balanced and understandable assessment** of the **company's position and prospects** in the annual accounts and other reports such as interim reports and reports to regulators. The directors should explain their responsibility for the accounts, and the auditors should state their reporting responsibilities. The directors should explain the basis on which the company **generates or preserves**

value and the **strategy for delivering the company's longer-term objectives**. The directors should also report on the going concern status of the business.

C2 Risk management and internal control

The board is responsible for determining the **nature and extent of the significant risks** it is willing to take to achieve objectives. Good systems of **risk management and control** should be maintained. The directors should **review effectiveness** annually and report to shareholders that they have done so. The review should cover all controls including financial, operational and compliance controls and risk management.

C3 Audit committee and auditors

There should be **formal and clear arrangements** with the **company's auditors**, and for applying the financial reporting and internal control principles. Companies should have an **audit committee** consisting of independent non-executive directors. One member should have **recent and relevant financial experience**. The committee should **monitor the accounts**, review **internal financial controls** and also other **internal controls and risk management systems** if there is no risk committee. The audit committee should make recommendations for the **appointment and remuneration of the external auditor**, and consider the auditor's **independence and objectivity,** the **effectiveness of the audit process** and whether the external auditor should **provide non-audit services.** The audit committee should also **review internal audit's work.** If there is no internal audit function, the audit committee should consider annually whether it is needed. The audit committee should also review 'whistleblowing' arrangements for staff who have **concerns about improprieties.**

D Directors' remuneration

D1 Level and components of remuneration

Remuneration levels should be sufficient to attract directors of **sufficient calibre** to run the company effectively, but companies should not pay more than is necessary. A proportion of remuneration should be based on **corporate and individual performance.** Comparisons with other companies should be used with caution. When designing performance-related elements of remuneration, the remuneration committee should consider annual bonuses and different kinds of long-term incentive schemes. Targets should be stretching. Levels of remuneration for non-executive directors should reflect **time commitment and responsibilities**, and should not include share options or performance-related options.

Boards' ultimate objectives should be to set **notice periods at one year or less**. The remuneration committee should consider the appropriateness of compensation commitments included in the contracts of service.

D2 Procedure

Companies should establish a formal and clear procedure for **developing policy** on **executive remuneration** and for fixing the remuneration package of individual directors. **Directors should not be involved** in **setting their own remuneration**. A **remuneration committee**, staffed by independent non-executive directors, should make **recommendations** about the framework of executive remuneration, and should determine remuneration packages of executive directors and the chairman. The board or shareholders should determine the remuneration of non-executive directors.

E Relations with shareholders

E1 Dialogue with shareholders

The board should keep up a dialogue with shareholders, particularly **major (institutional) shareholders**. The board should try to understand issues and concerns, and discuss governance and strategy with major shareholders.

E2 Constructive use of the AGM

The AGM should be a **means of communication** with **investors.** Companies should count all proxies and announce proxy votes for and against on all votes on a show of hands, except when a poll is taken. Companies should propose a **separate resolution** on each substantially separate issue, and there should be a resolution covering the **report and accounts**. The chairmen of the audit, nomination and remuneration committees should be available to answer questions at the AGM. Papers should be sent to members at least 20 working days before the AGM.

Compliance with the Code

The UK Corporate Governance Code requires listed companies to include in their accounts:

(a)   A narrative statement of how they **applied** the **principles** set out in the UK Corporate Governance Code. This should provide explanations which enable their shareholders to assess how the principles have been applied.

(b)   A statement as to whether or not they **complied throughout** the **accounting period** with the provisions set out in the UK Corporate Governance Code. Listed companies that did not comply throughout the accounting period with all the provisions must specify the provisions with which they did not comply, and give **reasons** for **non-compliance**.

2 Revised guidance for directors on the Combined Code (Turnbull report)

Note: The Turnbull report was published before the Combined Code became the UK Corporate Governance Code. Hence references below are to the Combined Code that was in place when Turnbull was published.

2.1 Introduction

The importance of internal control and risk management

The internal control systems have a key role in **managing the risks linked with a company's business objectives, helping to safeguard assets and the shareholders' investment**. The control system also aids the **efficiency and effectiveness of operations**, the **reliability of reporting and compliance with laws** and **regulations**. Effective financial records, including proper accounting records, are an important element of internal control.

A company's environment is constantly evolving and the risks it faces are constantly changing. To maintain an effective system of internal control, the company should regularly carry out a **thorough review of the risks** it faces.

As profits are partly the reward for risk-taking in business, the purpose of internal control is to help **manage risk** rather than eliminate it.

Objectives of guidance

The guidance is designed to reflect good business practice by **embedding internal control in a company's business processes**, remaining relevant in the evolving business environment and enabling each company to apply it to its own circumstances. Directors must exercise judgement in determining how the Combined Code has been implemented. The guidance is based on a **risk-based approach**, which should be incorporated within the normal management and governance processes, and not be treated as a separate exercise.

Internal control requirements of the Combined Code

This guidance aims to provide guidance for the directors on the requirements of the Combined Code relating to:

- Maintaining a sound system of internal control
- Conducting an annual review of internal control
- Reporting on this review in the annual report

2.2 Maintaining a sound system of internal control

Responsibilities

The board is responsible for the system of internal control, for setting policies and seeking assurance that will enable it to satisfy itself that the system is functioning effectively, in particular managing risks.

In determining what the system of controls should be, the board should take account of the following:

- The nature and extent of risks facing the company
- The extent and categories of acceptable risks
- The likelihood of the risks materialising
- The company's ability to reduce the impact of risks
- The costs versus the benefits of internal controls

Management is responsible for implementing board policies on risk and control. Management should **identify and evaluate the risks faced** by the company for board consideration, and **design, implement** and **monitor a suitable internal control system**. All employees have some responsibility for internal control as part of their accountability for achieving business objectives. They should have the knowledge, skills, information and authority to operate the system of internal control effectively.

Elements of internal control systems

The control system should **facilitate a company's effective and efficient operation** by enabling it to respond to risks effectively. It should help ensure the quality of reporting by ensuring the company maintains proper accounting records and processes that generate the necessary information. The system should also help **ensure compliance with laws and regulations**, and internal policies.

Control systems reflect the **control environment and organisational structure**. They include control activities, information and control processes and monitoring the continuing effectiveness of internal control systems. The systems should be **embedded in the company's operations** and form part of its **culture**, be able to **respond quickly to evolving risks** and include procedures for **reporting immediately to management**.

Control systems reduce rather than eliminate the possibility of poor judgement in decision-making, human error, control processes being circumvented, management override of controls and unforeseeable circumstances. They provide reasonable but not absolute assurance against risks failing to materialise.

2.3 Reviewing the effectiveness of internal controls

Reviewing control effectiveness is an essential part of the board's responsibilities. Management is responsible for **monitoring the system of internal control and providing assurance to the board that it has done so**. Board committees may have a significant role in the review process. The board has responsibility for disclosures on internal control in the annual report accounts.

A reliable system of internal control requires **effective monitoring**, but the board cannot just rely on monitoring taking place automatically. The board should regularly **review and receive reports on internal control** and should undertake **an annual assessment for** the purposes of making its report on internal controls.

The reports from management should provide a balanced assessment of the **significant risks and the effectiveness of the internal controls in managing those risks**. Reports should include details of control failings and weaknesses, including their impact and the action taken to rectify them.

When reviewing reports during the year, the board should consider what the risks are and how they have been identified, evaluated and managed. It should **assess the effectiveness of the internal controls**, consider whether any actions are being taken to remedy weaknesses and consider whether more effective monitoring is required.

The board should also carry out an **annual assessment**, considering what has been reported during the year plus any other relevant information. The annual assessment should consider the **changes in the significant risks** and the company's **ability to respond to changes in its environment**. It should also cover the monitoring of risks, the internal control and audit systems, the reports regularly given to the board, the significance of control failings and weaknesses, and the effectiveness of reporting.

2.4 The board's statement on internal control

The annual report and accounts should include **appropriate high-level information** to aid shareholders' understanding of the main features of the company's risk management and internal control processes. The minimum disclosure should be that a process of risk management exists, it has been in place for the whole period, the board has reviewed it and it accords with the provisions in the Turnbull report. The board should acknowledge its responsibility for internal controls and that the system is designed to manage rather than eliminate the risk of failure. It should disclose details of its review process and what actions have been taken to deal with weaknesses and related internal control aspects.

3 Sarbanes-Oxley Act 2002

3.1 Public Oversight Board

A **Public Oversight Board** has been established to register and regulate accounting firms.

3.2 Auditing standards

Audit firms should **retain working papers** for several years, have **quality control standards** in place, and as part of the audit review internal control systems to ensure that they **reflect the transactions** of the client and provide **reasonable assurance** that the transactions are recorded in a manner that will **permit preparation** of the **financial statements.**

3.3 Non-audit services

Auditors are expressly prohibited from carrying out a number of services including internal audit, bookkeeping, systems design and implementation, appraisal or valuation services, actuarial services, management functions and human resources, investment management, legal and expert services. **Provision of other non-audit services** is only allowed with the **prior approval** of the **audit committee**.

3.4 Partner rotation

There should be **rotation** of lead or reviewing audit partners every five years.

3.5 Auditors and audit committee

Auditors should discuss **critical accounting policies** and **alternative treatments** with the audit committee.

3.6 Audit committees

All members of audit committees should be **independent.** At least one member should be a financial expert. Audit committees should be responsible for the **appointment, compensation** and **oversight** of auditors. Audit committees should establish mechanisms for dealing with complaints about accounting, internal controls and audit.

3.7 Corporate responsibility

The **chief executive officer** and **chief finance officer** should certify the **appropriateness** of the **financial statements** and that those **financial statements fairly present** the **operations and financial condition** of the issuer. If the company has to prepare a restatement of accounts due to material non-compliance with standards, the **chief finance officer** and **chief executive officer** should **forfeit their bonuses.**

3.8 Transactions not included in accounts

There should be **appropriate disclosure** of **material transactions** and other relationships.

3.9 Internal control reporting

Annual reports should contain **internal control reports** that state the responsibility of management for establishing and maintaining an **adequate internal control structure** and **procedures for financial reporting.** Annual reports should also contain an **assessment** of the **effectiveness** of the **internal control structure** and **procedures** for **financial reporting.** Auditors should report on this assessment.

Companies should also report whether they have adopted a **code of conduct** for senior financial officers and the content of that code.

3.10 Whistleblowing provisions

Employees of **listed companies** and **auditors** will be granted whistleblower protection against their employers if they **disclose private employer information** to parties involved in a fraud claim.

4 The King report

4.1 The seven characteristics of good corporate governance

(a) **Discipline**, adherence to correct and proper behaviour including the underlying principles of good corporate governance

(b) **Transparency**, ease with which analysis can be made of actions, economic fundamentals, and non-financial matters. This reflects how good management is at making necessary information available

(c) **Independence**, reflecting mechanisms to minimise or avoid conflicts of interest such as composition of board, appointments to board committees and relations with auditors

(d) **Accountability,** mechanisms allowing investors to query and assess actions of board

(e) **Responsibility,** including responsibility to stakeholders. Governance should permit corrective action and penalising of mismanagement

(f) **Fairness,** balanced systems that take into account everyone having an interest in the company

(g) **Social responsibility**, in particular ethical standards, but also laying stress on being non-discriminatory and non-exploitative

4.2 Boards and directors

4.2.1 The board

A **unitary board** ensures positive interaction and diversity of views. The board must give **strategic direction**, retain **full and effective control** over the company, **monitor management, ensure** that the company **complies** with all relevant laws, regulations and codes of practice and **communicate** with shareholders and relevant stakeholders openly and promptly. The board should consider whether its **size,** diversity and **demographics** make it effective. The board should consider developing a **code of conduct**, covering conflicts of interest of management. The board should **identify key risk areas** and **key performance indicators**, and **identify and monitor non-financial aspects** of these.

4.2.2 Board composition

The board should comprise a mix of executive and non-executive directors, particularly **independent non-executives**, to protect shareholder interests. **Formal appointment procedures**, including a nomination committee, should be in place. **Board continuity** should be ensured by a director rotation programme.

4.2.3 Chairperson and chief executive

There should be a clear **division of responsibilities**, with preferably **separation of the roles of chairperson and chief executive** and the **chairperson** being an **independent non-executive director.** The chairperson's performance should be **appraised** regularly, the chief executive's at least annually.

4.2.4 Directors

No one individual or **block of individuals** should dominate the board's decision-taking.

Non-executive directors should have **calibre** and **credibility** and have the necessary skill and experience to assess all strategic, operational and conduct issues.

4.2.5 Remuneration

Remuneration should be sufficient to **attract**, **retain** and **motivate** executives of the required quality. A **remuneration policy** should be established and a remuneration committee should make **recommendations**; the **chief executive** can be **consulted** but should not fix his own remuneration. Full disclosure should be made in the accounts. **Performance-related elements** should constitute a substantial part of **executives' total remuneration packages.** Executive directors' **fixed term service contracts** should **not exceed three years**.

4.2.6 Board meetings

Boards should meet at **least once a quarter. Non-executive directors** should have **access to management**. Boards should regularly review **processes** and **procedures** to ensure the **effectiveness** of the company's **system of internal controls**. The board should receive **relevant non-financial information**, going beyond assessing the financial and quantitative performance of the company, looking at **qualitative measures** that involve **broader stakeholder interests**.

4.2.7 Board committees

Boards should not shelter behind board committees, but there should be a **formal procedure** for **certain functions** of the board to be **delegated.** At a minimum boards should have **audit** and **remuneration committees.** All board committees should preferably be chaired by an independent non-executive director.

4.2.8 Company secretary

The company secretary has a pivotal role in corporate governance, in providing detailed guidance on responsibilities, inducting new directors and assisting the chairperson.

4.3 Risk management

The board is responsible for the total process of **risk management** and for forming its opinion on the **effectiveness** of the process. Management is responsible for integrating the **risk management process** into the activities of the company. **Risk strategy policies** should be **communicated** to **all employees.**

The board should make use of **generally accepted models** to assess whether **organisational objectives** are being **achieved.** The board should **at a minimum** assess the following risks:

- Physical and operational
- Human resource
- Technology
- Business continuity
- Credit and markets
- Compliance

A board committee should aid the board in risk assessment. Boards should consider the need for a **whistle-blowing** process.

A comprehensive system of control should be established to **ensure risks are mitigated and objectives obtained. Risks** should be assessed on an on-going basis and control activities respond to risks, with relevant information about risks being **identified**, **captured** and **communicated**. Management should report on significant risks, system effectiveness and weaknesses found.

Boards should acknowledge their accountability for risk management and state that there is an **ongoing process** for **identifying, evaluating and managing risks** and there is an **adequate system of internal control** in place to mitigate risks.

4.4 Internal audit

Companies should have an **effective internal audit function,** with **access** to the **chief executive, chairman** and **audit committee.** There should be **adequate segregation of duties** if internal and external audit are carried out by the same firm.

Internal audit should **seek assurance** that **management processes** are **adequate** to **identify and monitor significant risks, confirm the effective operation** of **control systems, review processes** for **feedback** on **risk management** and **assurance,** and **confirm** that the board **receives** the **right quality of information**. The audit plan should be risk-based and **linked** to the **board's risk assessment**.

4.5 Sustainability reporting

Companies should report at least annually on the nature and extent of its **social, transformation, ethical, safety, health** and **environmental management policies** and practices. These include concerns such as workplace accidents, impact of HIV/AIDS, environmental concerns, black economic empowerment, human capital development and equal opportunities policies.

Each company should introduce a **code of ethics** and **disclose adherence** to it.

4.6 Accounting and auditing

The audit committee should recommend the **appointment of external auditors** and should **encourage consultation** between external and internal auditors. The audit committee should set out principles for whether non-audit services should also be supplied by auditors.

The majority of members of the audit committee should be independent non-executive directors and should be **financially literate**. It should be chaired by an independent non-executive director who is not the chairperson of the board. The committee should have formal terms of reference.

4.7 Relations with shareowners

Companies should maintain a **dialogue** with **institutional shareholders.** They should explain each item of special business and consider using **polls** to approve special business.

4.8 Accounts

Boards should present a **balanced and understandable assessment** of the company's position and a **comprehensive and objective assessment** of the activities of the company. Reports must be made in the context of society demanding **greater transparency and accountability** from companies regarding their non-financial matters.

Ethical issues in financial management

Topic list	Syllabus reference
1 The ethical dimension in business	A (4) (a)
2 Ethical aspects and functional areas of the firm	A (4) (b)
3 The elements of an ethical financial policy	A (4) (c),(d),(e)

Introduction

In this chapter we discuss the ethical dimension to the financial manager's role. The chapter provides a framework to enable the student to identify with reasons where ethical issues might arise in given scenarios in an examination.

Study guide

		Intellectual level
A4	**Ethical issues in financial management**	
(a)	Assess the ethical dimension within business issues and decisions and advise on best practice in the financial management of the organisation	3
(b)	Demonstrate an understanding of the interconnectedness of the ethics of good business practice between all of the functional areas of the organisation	2
(c)	Establish an ethical financial policy for the financial management of the organisation which is grounded in good governance, the highest standards of probity and is fully aligned with the ethical principals of the Association	3
(d)	Recommend an ethical framework for the development of an organisation's financial policies and a system for the assessment of their ethical impact upon the financial management of the organisation	3
(e)	Explore the areas within the ethical framework of the organisation which may be undermined by agency effects and/or stakeholder conflicts and establish strategies for dealing with them	3

Exam guide

The ethical dimension to the financial manager's job is very important and will be a consistent issue in examinations. The concern with ethics is a practical one and the examiner will be concerned to see that candidates can identify with reasons where ethical issues might emerge in given scenarios. The student should be able to put forward soundly based arguments to support their views.

1 The ethical dimension in business   12/08, 6/11

FAST FORWARD

In the **financial management** of businesses, the key objective is the **maximisation of shareholders' wealth**.

Ethical considerations are part of the **non-financial objectives** of a company and influence the decisions of management.

Exam focus point

Ethics as a topic appears regularly in the exam, most recently in Question 5 of the June 2011 paper where you were required to discuss issues (including ethical issues) surrounding the commercialisation of a product in an overseas country.

1.1 The prime financial objective of a company

The theory of company finance is based on the assumption that the objective of management is to **maximise the market value of the company's shares**. Specifically, the main objective of a company should be to maximise the wealth of its ordinary shareholders.

A company is financed by ordinary shareholders, preference shareholders, loan stock holders and other long-term and short-term payables. All surplus funds, however, belong to the legal owners of the company, its ordinary shareholders. Any retained profits are undistributed wealth of these equity shareholders.

1.2 Non-financial objectives

The goal of **maximising shareholder wealth** implies that shareholders are the only stakeholders of a company. In fact the stakeholders of a company include employees, customers, suppliers and the wider community. The formulation of the financial policy of the firm takes into account the interests of the shareholders as a stakeholder group and the formulation of non-financial objectives addresses the concerns of other stakeholders. We will discuss in Chapter 3c, the measures that companies adopt in order to address issues related to **sustainability** and **environmental reporting**. Here we provide some other examples of non-financial objectives. Note that these **non-financial objectives**, could potentially limit the achievement of **financial objectives**.

Non-financial objectives	
Ethical considerations	**Actions and strategies**
Welfare of employees	Competitive wages and salaries, comfortable and safe working conditions, good training and career development
Welfare of management	High salaries, company cars, perks
Welfare of society	Concern for environment
Provision of service to minimum standard	For example regulations affecting utility (water, electricity providers)
Responsibilities to customers	Providing quality products or services, fair dealing
Responsibilities to suppliers	Not exploiting power as buyer
Leadership in research and development	Failure to innovate may have adverse long-term financial consequences

Most of these non-financial objectives reflect an **ethical dimension** of business activity.

1.3 Ethical dimensions in business

Businesses play an important role in the economic and social life of a nation. They provide **employment, tax revenues** and have been responsible through **research** and **development** for some of the greatest technological breakthroughs which have changed our everyday life. The **downside** of this **dominant role is abuse of power** in the market place, **disregard for the environment**, irresponsible use of **depletable resources**, adverse effect on local culture and customs. Companies like Coca Cola, Imperial Tobacco and Mc Donald's have had an impact on developing countries that transcended the economic sphere and affected dietary habits and ways of life.

Given the power that companies exercise how do we measure their impact on society? How do we assess their behaviour against some ethical norm as opposed to mere financial norms? The answer to this question is provided by the development of **business ethics**, as a branch of **applied morality** that deals specifically with the behaviour of firms and the norms they should follow so that their behaviour is judged as ethical.

It should be stressed that **business ethics** does not invoke a universally acceptable framework of principles that all companies should adhere to. Hence the requirement for a corporate governance framework that would ensure a minimum degree of **ethical commitment** by firms became apparent. These movements towards the adoption of **corporate governance norms** have been discussed in Chapter 1.

Ethical considerations are sometimes easy to be incorporated into the policy of a company. For example, during the apartheid years many companies were boycotting South Africa, without any governmental coercion. In this case the ethical aspect was clear and easily identifiable. However, for a multinational company in a developing country not to pay wages to its employees that would render a project uneconomical, may not be seen as unethical, as the employees of that country may have remained unemployed without the multinational company's presence.

2 Ethical aspects and functional areas of the firm

Business ethics should govern the conduct of corporate policy in all functional areas of a company such as:

- Human resources management
- Marketing
- Market behaviour
- Product development

Maximising the wealth of shareholders generally implies maximising profits consistent with long-term stability. It is often found that short-term gains must be sacrificed in the interests of the company's long-term prospects. In the context of this overall objective of financial management, there are five main types of decisions facing financial managers:

- Investment decisions,
- Financing decisions,
- Dividend decisions,
- Financial planning and control decisions
- Risk management decisions.

In practice, these areas are interconnected and should not be viewed in isolation. An equally important function of the financial manager is to **communicate the financial policy and corporate goals to internal and external stakeholders**.

2.1 Human resources management

Employees in a modern corporation are not simply a factor of production which is used in a production process. Employees as human beings have feelings and are entitled to be treated by their employers with respect and dignity. In most advanced countries there are employment laws that determine the **rights** of employees and provide protection against the abuses of their employers.

Ethical problems arise when there is a conflict between the financial objectives of the firm and the rights of the employees. These ethical problems arise in relation to minimum wages, and discrimination.

2.1.1 Minimum wage

Companies are obliged to pay their employees at least the minimum wage. However when multinational companies operate in countries where there are no minimum wage requirements then the companies may try to take advantage of the lack of protection and offer low wages. Business ethics would require that companies should not exploit workers and pay lower than the warranted wages.

2.1.2 Discrimination

Discrimination on the basis of **race, gender, age, marital status, disability or nationality** is prohibited in most advanced economies, through **equal opportunity legislation**. However, companies may have the power in some instances to circumvent many of the provisions. Companies for example may be able to discriminate against black applicants for certain positions for which they may feel that they are appropriate.

Employers may also wish to discriminate against mothers in certain jobs for which overtime is required. In other circumstances a company may want to restrict applicants from a certain ethnic background when they deal with people of similar ethnic backgrounds. In all the cases of potential discrimination the company wishing to behave ethically should be aware of the risk of breaking the rules.

2.2 Marketing

Marketing decisions by the firm are also very important in terms of the impact on firm performance. Marketing is one of the main ways of communicating with its customers and this communication should be **truthful** and sensitive to the **social** and **cultural impact** on society. The marketing strategy should not target vulnerable groups, create artificial wants or reinforce consumerism. It should also avoid creating stereotypes or creating insecurity and dissatisfaction.

2.3 Market behaviour

Companies should not take advantage of their **dominant position** in the market to **exploit suppliers** or **customers**.

Ethical behaviour in this context refers to the exercise of restraint in their pricing policies. Companies which are dominant in the product market and enjoy monopolistic power may charge a price which will result in abnormally high profits. For example a water company may charge high prices for water in order to increase its profits because the remuneration of managers may be linked to profitability. Similarly a company which in the input markets may be able to pay too low a price to their suppliers. For example in many developing countries multinational companies are the only buyers of raw materials and they determine the price they pay to their suppliers.

3 The elements of an ethical financial policy

Ethical policy can be implemented through measures that ensure that the company takes into account the concerns of its stakeholders.

3.1 The ethical framework

The company should develop an ethical corporate philosophy and should make the enhancement of corporate governance as one of its most important management issues. The aim is to have customers and society, as well as shareholders and investors, place even greater trust in the company and to ensure that the company is one that society wants to exist. The ethical framework should be developed as part of the overall company's social responsibility which according to Carroll includes

(a)   Economic responsibility
(b)   Legal responsibility
(c)   Ethical responsibility
(d)   Philanthropic responsibility

The **four responsibilities** have been classified in terms of priority for the firm. **Economic responsibility** is the first and **philanthropic responsibility** the last. **Carroll's framework** is considered a useful way of integrating the various aspects of a company's activities and helpful as a means for management to set social responsibility targets within an organisation.

The only problem with the framework is the lack of an **explicit mechanism** for addressing **conflicting corporate responsibilities**, when for example **legal** and **regulatory** compliance may limit the **economic return** that a company can achieve. The resolution of conflict between stakeholder groups is considered in Chapter 3a Section 2.

3.2 Economic responsibility

The first responsibility of a company is to its shareholders. Shareholders have invested their money in the company and require a return. The company has therefore a responsibility to manage the funds of outside investors in such a way that the required return is generated. The main aspects of the economic responsibility were analysed in Chapter 1 and include the various decisions that the financial manager is responsible for, such as financing, investment, risk management and dividend.

3.3 Legal responsibility

Companies operate within a legal framework as defined by company law, the various accounting and environmental standards, labour law etc. It is a duty of the company to comply with all the legal and regulatory provisions, and to ensure that employees are aware of this policy.

As we have already said, ethical responsibilities arise in situations where there is no explicit legal or regulatory provision and the company needs to exercise its judgement as to what is right and fair.

3.4 Ethical responsibility

Ethical responsibilities arise not as a result of legal requirements but as a result of a moral imperative for companies to operate in an ethical and fair manner. We have already discussed examples where issues of business ethics arise. How does a company ensure that an ethical approach to the various aspects of a company's activities is adopted? The following are deemed to be the elements of a business ethics management in a European or US corporation:

(a) **Mission or value statement.** A corporation has a mission statement in which some social goal is included.

(b) **Codes of ethics** to be followed by the employees, and which specify their attitude and response to ethical dilemmas. The code of ethics should reflect **corporate values** but it should also incorporate **professional codes** of ethics, which individual employees as members of professional bodies need to observe.

(c) **Reporting/advice channels** for employees to notify unethical behaviour or to seek advice on specific situations.

(d) **Ethics managers**, officers and committees to coordinate or assume responsibility for the implementation of ethics in the corporation.

(e) **Ethics consultants** should be consulted by corporations on specific issues of business ethics on which the corporation needs advice as to the appropriate course of action or policy formulation.

(f) **Ethics education and training** should be provided to the managers and employees of a corporation to ensure that ethical problems are recognised and dealt with according to the ethics code of the corporation.

(g) **Auditing, accounting and reporting** are necessary aspects of a business ethics programme since the corporation needs to be able to measure and report its economic and social impact to its stakeholders.

3.5 Philanthropic responsibility

Philanthropy is the last of the responsibilities of a company and includes all those actions that the company needs to take in order improve the life of its employees, to contribute to the local community and to make a difference to society as a whole. Philanthropic activities include **charitable donations**, the provision of **recreation facilities** to **employees**, the support to **educational institutions**, the **sponsoring of athletic** and **cultural events** and so on.

Chapter Roundup

- In the **financial management** of businesses, the key objective is the **maximisation of shareholders' wealth**.

- **Ethical considerations** are part of the **non-financial objectives** of a company and influence the decisions of management.

- **Business ethics** should govern the conduct of corporate policy in all functional areas of a company such as:

  - Human resources management
  - Marketing
  - Market behaviour
  - Product development

- Companies should not take advantage of their **dominant position** in the market to **exploit suppliers** or **customers**.

- **Ethical policy** can be implemented through measures that ensure that the company takes into account the concerns of its stakeholders.

Quick Quiz

1   On what management objective is the theory of company finance primarily based?

2   To which areas might non-financial objectives of a company relate?

3   List two areas of a company's activity where ethical issues may arise.

4   What are the main corporate social responsibilities of a firm?

5   What are the main elements through which the ethical responsibility of a company is discharged?

Answers to Quick Quiz

1   The objective of management is to maximise the market value of the enterprise.

2   (1) Welfare of employees   (2) Welfare of management
    (3) Welfare of society   (4) Quality of service provision
    (5) Responsibilities to customers and suppliers   (6) Leadership in research and development

3   Human resources management and marketing

4   Economic responsibility, legal responsibility, ethical responsibility, philanthropic responsibility

5   (a)   Mission or value statement.
    (b)   Codes of ethics.
    (c)   Reporting/advice channels.
    (d)   Ethics managers.
    (e)   Ethics consultants.
    (f)   Ethics education and training.
    (g)   Auditing, accounting and reporting.

Now try the questions below from the Exam Question Bank

Number	Level	Marks	Time
4	Introductory	20	36 mins

Impact of environmental issues on corporate objectives and governance

3C

Topic list	Syllabus reference
1 Sustainability and environmental risk	A (5) (a)
2 The carbon trading economy and emissions	A (5) (a)
3 The role of the environment agency	A (5) (a)
4 Environmental audits	A (5) (a)
5 Triple bottom line (TBL) reporting	A (5) (a)
6 Wider reading	–

Introduction

In this chapter we discuss the impact of environmental issues on corporate objectives and governance.

Sustainability and environmental concerns are closely related to the ethical issues facing the financial manager.

Study guide

		Intellectual level
A5	**Impact of environmental issues on organisational objectives and on governance**	
(a)	Assess the issues which may impact upon organisational objectives and governance from	3
	(i) Sustainability and environmental risk	
	(ii) The carbon-trading economy and emissions	
	(iii) The role of the environment agency	
	(iv) Environmental audits and the triple bottom line approach	

Exam guide

You may be asked to discuss how the financial manager needs to take into account environmental issues when formulating corporate policy.

1 Sustainability and environmental risk 6/11

FAST FORWARD

> **Environmental** and **social** factors contribute to **sustainable** business.

1.1 Sustainability

The extensive use of exhaustible resources and the adoption of production processes which are potentially harmful to the environment have jeopardised the welfare of future generations. There is a growing realisation and pressure from the wider stakeholders that companies need to take into account the long-term sustainability of their activities.

Although there is no single agreed or precise definition of sustainability a broad definition is given below based on the common understanding about its underlying principles.

Key term

> **Sustainability** refers to the concept of balancing growth with environmental, social and economic concerns.

1.2 Environmental concerns

Business activities in general were formerly regarded as problems for the environmental movement, but the two are now increasingly complementary. There has been an increase in the use of the 'green' approach to market products. 'Dolphin friendly' tuna and paper products from 'managed forests' are examples.

1.3 The impact of green issues on business practice

Environmental impacts on business may be **direct**.

- Changes affecting costs or resource availability
- Impact on demand
- Effect on power balances between competitors in a market

They may also be **indirect**, as legislative change may affect the environment within which businesses operate. Finally, pressure may come from customers or staff as a consequence of concern over environmental problems.

1.4 Ecology and strategic planning

Physical environmental conditions are important.

(a) **Resource inputs**

Managing physical resources successfully (eg oil companies, mining companies) is a good source of profits.

The physical environment presents logistical problems or opportunities to organisations. Proximity to road and rail links can be a reason for siting a warehouse in a particular area.

(b) **Government**

The physical environment is under the control of other organisations.

(i) Local authority town planning departments can influence where a building and necessary infrastructure can be sited.

(ii) Governments can set regulations about some of the organisation's environmental interactions.

(c) **Disasters**

In some countries, the physical environment can pose a major 'threat' to organisations – for example the tsunami that hit Japan in March 2011 caused catastrophic damage to entire towns.

Issues relating to the effect of an organisation's activities on the physical environment (which, to avoid confusion, we shall refer to as 'ecology'), have come to the fore in recent years.

1.5 Environmental reporting

More companies are now producing an external report for external stakeholders, covering:

(a) What the **business does** and how it impacts on the environment
(b) An **environmental objective** (eg use of 100% recyclable materials within x years)
(c) The **company's approach** to achieving and monitoring these objectives
(d) An **assessment of its success** towards achieving the objectives
(e) An **independent verification** of **claims made**

1.6 Environmental policy

FAST FORWARD

Companies are acknowledging the advantages of having an **environmental policy**. These include **reduction/management of risk to the business, motivating staff** and enhancement of corporate reputation.

Many believe that development of a policy will mean a **long term improvement in profitability**. According to Shell plc 'we believe long-term competitive success depends on being trusted to meet society's expectations.'

Pressure is increasing on companies to widen their scope of corporate public accountability. This pressure stems from **increasing expectations of stakeholders** and knowledge about the consequences of ignoring such pressures. There is an increasing expectation on companies to follow **social policies** of their business in addition to **economic** and **environmental policies**.

The corporate world is responding to these pressures. Environmental and social factors are seen to **contribute** to a **sustainable business** that will enhance long-term shareholder value by addressing the needs of its stakeholders – employees, customers, suppliers, the community and the environment.

2 The carbon trading economy and emissions

FAST FORWARD

Carbon trading allows companies which emit **less** than their **allowance** to **sell** the **right** to **emit** CO_2 to another company.

2.1 Background to emissions trading

The first world summit on the environment was convened in Stockholm in 1972, at which time world leaders declared the intention of having regular assessments of **global environmental issues**. In 1987, the Intergovernmental Panel on Climate Change was formed by the United Nations Environmental Programme (UNEP) together with the World Meteorological Organisation (WMO).

In 1992 the UN general assembly proposed a treaty now known as the United Nations Framework Convention on Climate Change (UNFCCC), which was subsequently accepted and signed by more than 150 nations represented at the second summit which was held in 1992 in Rio de Janeiro.

Countries ratifying the convention agreed:

(a)   To develop programs to slow climate change
(b)   To share technology and cooperate to reduce greenhouse gas emissions
(c)   To develop a greenhouse gas inventory listing national sources and sinks

At the summit, it was also agreed that the responsibility falls upon the **developed nations** to lead the fight against **climate change**, as they are largely responsible for the current concentrations of **greenhouse gases** in the atmosphere. The original target for emission reductions that was generally accepted in 1992 was that the developed nations should, at a minimum, seek to return to 1990 levels of emissions by the year 2000. Additionally, developed nations should provide financial and technological aid and assistance to the developing nations to produce inventories and work toward more **efficient energy use**.

2.1.1 The Kyoto protocol

In December 1997 the countries which met in Rio in 1992 re-convened in Kyoto to develop a set of legally binding agreements on the reduction of greenhouse gas emissions.

The Kyoto Protocol to the UNFCCC could only come into force after two conditions had been fulfilled.

It had been ratified by at least 55 countries.

It had been ratified by nations accounting for at least 55% of emissions from what the Treaty calls 'Annex 1' countries – that is, 38 industrialised countries given targets for reducing emissions, plus Belarus, Turkey and Kazakhstan.

The Kyoto Protocol came into force on 16 February 2005 - 90 days after Russia ratified. As at October 2009, 187 countries had ratified the Treaty.

During the period 2008-2012 industrialised countries have to reduce their GHG emissions by on average 5% below their 1990 levels. For EU-15 the reduction target is 8%.

2.2 The European Union trading

FAST FORWARD

Emissions trading is emerging as a key part of the strategy both within the EU and globally to reduce the emission of greenhouse gases.

2.2.1 The EU gas emissions allowance scheme

As part of their policy towards implementation of the Kyoto Protocol, the EU set the total amount of CO_2 emissions to be produced in the EU as a whole to no more than 2.2 billion tonnes per annum. This total amount was then allocated to member states based primarily on the historical emission of CO_2. Each member state was therefore allocated a European Union Allowance to emit CO_2 for a specific compliance period.

2.2.2 The EU emissions trading scheme

EU governments are addressing the challenge of reducing carbon emissions through a combination of increased regulation and market mechanisms.

The European Union Emissions Trading Scheme (ETS) commenced on 1 January 2005, creating the world's first multi-country emissions trading system and the largest scheme ever implemented. The EU ETS runs in two phases: 2005-2007 (Phase I) and 2008-2012 (Phase II, coinciding with the first commitment period of the Kyoto Protocol).

The EU allowance given to a company represents their target or 'cap' for a compliance period. If at the end of the period their total emissions during the period are below their cap then they have allowances to sell; if not, they must purchase allowances from companies which have exceeded their emissions reductions targets.

Thus the underlying commodity being traded are EU allowances (EUAs) as issued under the EU ETS. One EUA equals one tonne of CO_2 (right-to-emit). These allowances are traded on a special exchange, the ECX.

Emissions trading is using a **market-based mechanism** for **environment protection**. The rationale behind emission trading is to ensure that the required **overall emission** reductions take place where the cost of the reduction is lowest, thus lowering the overall costs of combating climate change. It does not impose a particular type of technology or set rigid limitations on how much can be emitted.

3 The role of the environment agency

The role of an **environmental agency** is to protect the environment and promote sustainable development.

This section gives an example of good practice. Different countries have their own approaches to regulating the environment which are equally relevant to this syllabus.

3.1 The goal of the Environment Agency

The **Environment Agency** of England and Wales and the Scottish Environment Protection Agency were created in 1996.

The stated mission of the newly created agencies was *'to protect or enhance the environment, taken as a whole'* so as to promote *'the objective of achieving sustainable development'*.

3.2 The responsibilities of the environment agency

3.2.1 Flood risk management

The agency is the main body responsible for creating and maintaining flood defences and providing flood warning systems. Control of water levels is usually by systems of sluices, weirs and locks. The agency issues regular flood warnings and maintains maps of areas liable to flooding.

3.2.2 Waste regulation

The agency is the regulatory authority for all waste management activities including the licensing of sites such as landfill and incineration facilities. It also grants licenses for handling special waste such as radioactive, chemical or medical materials. The agency monitors waste management sites and any individuals or companies found to have caused pollution or have infringed their licence conditions can be prosecuted and potentially have waste handling licenses revoked by the Courts.

3.2.3 Pollution control

Under the provisions of a series of Acts of Parliament, the Agency is the main regulator of discharges to the aquatic environment, to air and to land. It does this through the issue of formal consents to discharge or, in the case of large, complex or potentially damaging industries, by means of a permit. Failure to comply with such a consent or permit or making a discharge without the benefit of a consent or permit can lead to criminal prosecution. Under recent legislation changes enforcement action regarding a pollution event can, through the Magistrates courts system, result in a fine of up to £50,000 or 5 years imprisonment, or unlimited fines and up to 5 years' imprisonment through the Crown courts.

3.2.4 Air quality management

The Agency regulates the release of air pollutants into the atmosphere from large, complex industrial processes. This will soon include emissions from some large-scale agricultural activities, but air pollutant releases from many agricultural activities will continue to be unregulated.

Emissions from major sources of pollution, such as transport, are subject to various measures at the European, national and local level. Local authorities control air pollution from smaller industrial processes.

The Agency works with local authorities, the Highways Agency and others to implement the UK government's air quality strategy in England and Wales as mandated in the Environment Act 1995.

4 Environmental audits

FAST FORWARD

Environmental audits attempt to measure the economic, social and environmental impacts of a business.

4.1 A framework for social reporting

The provision of a framework for social reporting is being addressed in various ways. A green paper has been issued by the European Union to encourage companies to (voluntarily) 'contribute to a better society and a cleaner environment'. The current company law review in the UK sets out social and environmental reporting requirements. The Financial Times FTSE has launched a new index - **FTSE4good** - exclusively for companies who are deemed to be socially responsible. In the six months to March 2008 there were 41 new entrants to this index, including the Big Yellow Group (UK), Bank of Kyoto (Japan) and Google (USA).

The United Nations has backed a Global Reporting Initiative (GRI). This Initiative sets out a framework for reporting, including a **statement of vision and strategy** from the CEO together with **performance indicators** divided into economic, environmental and social performance indicators against which performance can be **measured** and **independently verified**.

The development of measurement and independent verification techniques are important, as in the past companies' own valuation of their contribution to the environment has sometimes been accepted uncritically. Enron was awarded six environmental awards in 2000, voted the best company to work for three years in a row and boasted its achievements in a report on its economic, environmental and social performance.

Exam focus point

> Look out in investment appraisal questions for details of non-financial objectives. If a company is for example aiming to respect the interests of stakeholders and operate to the highest ethical standards, this could have an impact on the investments it undertakes.

4.2 Environmental accounting

In their capacity as information providers, accountants may be required to report on a firm's environmental impact and possible consequences.

106   **3c: Impact of environmental issues on corporate objectives and governance** | Part A Role and responsibility towards stakeholders

BPP
LEARNING MEDIA

Examples of environmental management accounting objectives are as follows.

(a) **Eco-balance**

The firm identifies the raw materials it uses and outputs such as waste, noise etc, which it gives a notional value. The firm can identify these outputs as a social 'cost'.

(b) **Cleaner technology**

This can be used in the manufacturing process to avoid waste. Simple waste-minimisation measures can increase profit on purely economic grounds.

(c) **Corporate liabilities**

Firms are being sued for environmental damage, and this might need to be recorded as a liability, with a suitable risk assessment. This might have to be factored into the project appraisal and risk.

(d) **Performance appraisal**

This can include reducing pollution.

(e) **Life cycle assessments**

The total environmental impact of a product is measured, from the resources it consumes, the energy it requires in use, and how it is disposed of, if not recycled. It may be that a product's poor ecological impact (and consequent liability or poor publicity) can be traced back to one component or material, which can be replaced.

(f) **Budgetary planning and control system**

These can be used to develop variances analysing environmental issues.

4.3 Environmental audits and reporting

4.3.1 Environmental audits

Key term

An **environmental audit** is an audit that seeks to assess the environmental impact of a company's policies.

The starting point for assessing the impact of management decisions and company policies on the environment is for the auditor to obtain and review the company's environmental policy, where such a policy is formulated and documented.

The auditor will need to check whether the policy

- satisfies key stakeholder criteria
- meets legal requirements
- complies with British Standards or other local regulations

4.3.2 Impact of environmental issues on company reporting

Environmental issues are reflected in the financial accounts in the form of **contingent environmental liabilities**.

Potential environmental liabilities that are unrecorded in the financial statements can jeopardise the future profitability of the company.

As shown from asbestos claims, the number of environmental issues giving rise to liabilities is potentially quite large and increasing with enhanced environmental awareness and technological advances.

Examples of environmental exposures giving rise to liabilities include:

(a) soil contamination

(b) surface and ground water contamination

(c) site restructuring and rehabilitation

(d) removal of asbestos

(e) removal of controlled chemicals following new regulations eg recent international regulations on polychlorinated biphenyls (PCBs)

(f) air emissions

Certain industries, by the nature of their operations tend to be more exposed to environmental liabilities than others.

These industries include:

- chemical industries
- oil and gas industries
- pharmaceutical industries
- metallurgical and mining industries
- utility industries

4.3.3 The European eco-management and audit scheme (EMAS)

The main elements of the eco-management and audit scheme which was adopted in 1993 as a voluntary scheme are:

(a)   Transparency of environmental statements

(b)   Employee involvement in the implementation of the scheme

(c)   Examination of the environmental effects of capital investments, planning decisions and procurement decisions.

Participating companies commit themselves to follow an environmental policy which will:

(a)   Comply with environmental legislation

(b)   Try to prevent pollution

(c)   Strive to improve environmental improvements.

5 Triple bottom line (TBL) reporting   12/11

5.1 The main elements of TBL

Key term

> **Triple bottom line (TBL) reporting** is external reporting that gives consideration to financial outcomes, environmental quality and social equity.

The term **triple bottom line** originated among investors seeking investments in enterprises that were socially just, economically profitable and environmentally sound.

The underlying principle is that in order to evaluate a company's true performance and assess the risk to the investor, one must look at a corporation's social, financial and environmental performance.

The triple bottom approach is often conceptualised as a pyramid or a triangle. An example of how this approach has been represented diagrammatically are given below:

The triple bottom approach to decision making

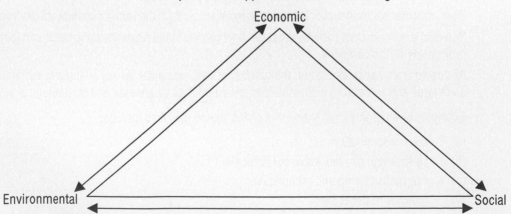

(Source: The Triple Bottom Line: A Viable Strategy for Rural Development? *Cornelia Butler Flord)*

Under the triple bottom approach decision making should ensure that each perspective is growing but not at the expense of the other. That is economic performance should not come at the expense of the environment or society.

The triple bottom line can be defined conceptually as **economic prosperity**, **environmental quality** and **social justice**. Triple bottom line reporting is the latest evolution of what is often reported as corporate sustainable development, or corporate social responsibility (sustainable development reporting). **Corporate sustainable development** tends to be very much **forward looking** and **qualitative**. By comparison, **triple bottom line reporting** is a more **quantitative summary** of a company's **economic**, **environmental** and **social performance** over the previous year.

However, more specific methods of measurement are still being defined, making management and reporting difficult. Many companies, thinking it is just a matter of **pollution control**, are missing the bigger picture that meeting the needs of the current generation will destroy the ability of future generations to meet theirs.

5.2 Reasons for triple bottom line

The concept of **triple bottom line** developed as a response to an increasing demand by community and business groups for reporting the environmental and social impacts as well as the economic impact of a company on the life of a community. Investors, taxpayers, consumers and other stakeholders are demanding that reporting extends beyond economic return or 'output' to cover issues of equity, justice and responsibility. Demands are being made to report on corporate performance in areas such as:

(a) assurances of food safety after highly public problems such as food recalls and food contamination.

(b) assurances of long-term sustainable production systems and environmental stewardship; eg. investments in renewable resources, recycling, waste reduction, or reducing green house gas emissions. Demands are on a global basis so that pollution problems are not exported offshore.

(c) looking after human rights, equity and equality; e.g. not using child labour, minimum working standards, no human rights violations, work/life balance, social equity for aboriginal communities.

(d) looking after the welfare of animals such as no testing on animals (Body Shop), humane transportation, feeding etc.

(e) ethical corporate conduct such as demonstrated due diligence and disclosure of conflicts of interest after the public spectacles of Enron, HIH, One Tel, Nippon Meat Packers and others.

(f) ethical business investments

The supporters of the TBL approach advocate that a corporation's (whether private or public) ultimate success is measured not just by the financial bottom line but by the corporation's social and ethical environmental performance.

Triple Bottom Line provides a framework for measuring and reporting **corporate performance** against **economic, social and environmental** benchmarks. Reporting on Triple Bottom Line makes transparent the organisation's decisions that explicitly take into consideration impacts on the environment and people, as well as on financial capital.

5.3 The advantages of triple bottom line reporting

- **Better risk management** through

    - identifying stakeholder concerns
    - employee involvement
    - good governance
    - performance monitoring

- **Improved decision making** through

    - stakeholder consultation
    - better information gathering
    - better reporting processes

- **Attracting and retaining higher calibre employees** through practising sustainability and ethical values

The critics of the triple bottom line argue that whereas the aspirations of the TBL movement are sound, on both practical and conceptual grounds, the TBL is an unhelpful addition to the corporate social responsibility debate and it promises more than it can deliver.

Some critics go so far as to argue that the rhetoric behind TBL can 'in fact provide a smokescreen behind which firms can avoid truly effecting social and environmental reporting and performance.'

(Source: Getting to the Bottom of 'Triple Bottom Line' *Wayne Normal and Chris MacDonald)*

5.4 Triple bottom line indicators

Triple bottom line reporting requires proxies to indicate the economic, environmental and social impact of doing business. Examples of useful proxies are given below.

An indication of **economic impact** can be gained from such items as:

(a)   gross operating surplus
(b)   dependence on imports
(c)   stimulus to the domestic economy by purchasing of locally produced goods and services.

An indication of **social impact** can be gained from, for example:

(a)   the organisation's tax contribution
(b)   employment.

An indication of **environmental impact** can be gained from such measures as:

(a)   the ecological footprint
(b)   emissions to soil, water and air
(c)   water and energy use.

Such indicators can distil complex information into a form that is accessible to stakeholders. Organisations report on indicators that reflect their objectives and are relevant to stakeholders. One difficulty in identifying and using indicators is to ensure consistency within an organisation, over time, and between organisations. This is important for benchmarking and comparisons.

6 Wider reading

This is an extremely topical chapter and there are considerable amounts of information available in quality newspapers and websites. Make sure you keep up to date with latest developments by reading such materials and mention relevant real-life examples where appropriate in exam answers.

Chapter Roundup

- **Environmental** and **social** factors contribute to **sustainable** business.

- Companies are acknowledging the advantages of having an **environmental policy**. These include **reduction/management of risk to the business, motivating staff** and enhancement of corporate reputation.

- **Carbon trading** allows companies which emit **less** than their **allowance** to **sell** the **right** to **emit** CO_2 to another company.

- Emissions trading is emerging as a key part of the strategy both within the EU and globally to reduce the emission of greenhouse gases.

- EU governments are addressing the challenge of reducing carbon emissions through a combination of increased regulation and market mechanisms.

- The role of **environmental agency** is to protect the environment and promote sustainable development.

- **Environmental audits** attempt to measure the economic, social and environmental impacts of a business.

Quick Quiz

1. What does a company's external environmental report cover?

2. How can the triple bottom line be defined conceptually, and what are the differences between the triple bottom line accounting and corporate sustainable development?

3. Give two examples of triple bottom line indicators for each of the following impacts of doing business:

   (a) economic
   (b) social
   (c) environmental

BPP
LEARNING MEDIA

Part A Role and responsibility towards stakeholders | **3c: Impact of environmental issues on corporate objectives and governance**   111

Answers to Quick Quiz

1
- What the business does and how it impacts on the environment
- The company's environmental objective(s)
- The company's approach to achieving and monitoring these objectives
- Assessment of success towards achieving objectives
- Independent verification of claims made

2   TBL can be defined conceptually as:

- Economic prosperity
- Environmental quality
- Social justice

Differences between TBL and Corporate Sustainable Development:

- CSD is forward looking and qualitative

- TBL is a quantitative summary of economic, environmental and social performance over the previous year, ie backward looking

3   Any two from:

(a)   Gross operating surplus
Dependence on imports
Purchase of locally produced goods
Services

(b)   Tax contribution
Employment
'Giving back' to the community, eg Tesco's 'Computers for Schools' scheme

(c)   Water and energy use
Emissions to air, soil and water
Ecological footprint

Now try the questions below from the Exam Question Bank

Number	Level	Marks	Time
5	Introductory	15	27 mins

Economic environment for multinationals

Trading and planning in a multinational environment

4

Topic list	Syllabus reference
1 Corporate strategy in multinational enterprises	B (1) and (2)
2 Theory and practice of international trade	B(1) (a)
3 Trade agreements	B (1) (b)
4 The World Trade Organisation (WTO)	B (1) (c)
5 International monetary institutions	B (1) (d)
6 International financial markets and global financial stability	B (1) (e)
7 Framework for financial planning in multinationals	B (2) (a)
8 International debt finance	B (2) (a)
9 Compliance with listing requirements	B (2) (a) (i)
10 Capital mobility and blocked funds	B (2) (a) (ii)
11 Risk exposure	B (2) (a) (iii)
12 Litigation issues	B (2) (a) (iv)
13 Cultural risks	B (2) (a) (iii)
14 Agency issues	B (2) (a) (iv)

Introduction

In this chapter we look at the international environment within which companies need to make financial decisions. We discuss the various aspects of international trade and the benefits and risks for the company. We also look at strategic decision-making in a multinational company and the agency issues arising between subsidiaries and the parent company.

Study guide

		Intellectual level
B1	**Management of international trade and finance**	
(a)	Advise on the theory and practice of free trade and the management of barriers to trade	3
(b)	Demonstrate an up to date understanding of the major trade agreements and common markets and, on the basis of contemporary circumstances, advise on their policy and strategic implications for a given business	3
(c)	Discuss the objectives of the World Trade Organisation	2
(d)	Discuss the role of international financial institutions within the context of a globalised economy, with particular attention to the International Monetary Fund, the Bank of International Settlements, The World Bank and the principal Central Banks (the Fed, Bank of England, European Central Bank and the Bank of Japan)	2
(e)	Assess the role of the international financial markets with respect to the management of global debt, the financial development of the emerging economies and the maintenance of global financial stability	2
B2	**Strategic business and financial planning for multinationals**	
(a)	Advise on the development of a financial planning framework for a multinational taking into account:	3
	(i) Compliance with national governance requirements (for example, the London Stock Exchange admission requirements)	
	(ii) The mobility of capital across borders and national limitations on remittances and transfer pricing	
	(iii) The pattern of economic and other risk exposures in the different national markets	
	(iv) Agency issues in the central coordination of overseas operations and the balancing of local financial autonomy with effective central control	

1 Corporate strategy in multinational enterprises

FAST FORWARD

Multinational enterprises undertake **foreign direct investment (FDI)** for reasons including obtaining **cost and revenue advantages**, **tax considerations** and **process specialisation**.

FDI can stimulate economic activity in the host country, but it can also lead to a **loss of political and economic sovereignty**.

1.1 The nature of multinational enterprises

A company does not become 'multinational' simply by virtue of exporting or importing products: ownership and the control of facilities abroad are involved.

Key term

A **multinational enterprise** is one which owns or controls production facilities or subsidiaries or service facilities outside the country in which it is based.

Multinational enterprises range from medium-sized companies having only a few facilities (or 'affiliates') abroad to giant companies having an annual turnover larger than the gross national product (GNP) of some smaller countries of the world. Indeed, the largest – such as the US multinationals Ford, General Motors and Exxon – each have a turnover similar to the GNP a medium-sized national economy.

The **size and significance of multinationals** is increasing. Many companies in 'middle-income' countries such as Singapore are now becoming multinationals, and the annual growth in output of existing multinationals is in the range 10-15%.

The extensive activities of multinational enterprises, particularly the larger ones, raises questions about the problems of controlling them. Individual governments may be largely powerless if multinationals are able to exploit the tax regimes of **'tax haven'** countries through **transfer pricing** policies or if the multinationals' production is switched from one country to another.

Key term

> **Tax havens** are countries with lenient tax rules or relatively low tax rates, which are often designed to attract foreign investment.

The empirical evidence on the growth of multinational companies shows that companies become multinational in a gradual way. First companies expand their operations into overseas markets by exporting. Then they create overseas sale subsidiaries and enter into licensing agreements. And finally they invest and create production facilities in overseas locations. The key element of the process of expansion is the creation of competitive advantages

1.2 Competitive advantages of multinationals

FAST FORWARD

> There are many strategic reasons for engaging in foreign investment which include seeking **new markets** for goods, **new sources** of **raw materials**, **production efficiency**, expertise and **political safety**.

The main strategic reasons for engaging in foreign direct investment (FDI) include:

1.2.1 Market seeking

'Market seeking' firms engage in FDI either to meet **local demand** or as a way of exporting to markets other than the home market. Examples of this are the manufacturing operations of US and Japanese car producers in Europe. Some FDI is undertaken to provide a sales and market organisation in the overseas economy for the exporter's goods.

1.2.2 Raw material seeking

Firms in industries such as oil, mining, plantation and forestry will extract raw materials in the **places where they can be found**, whether for export or for further processing and sale in the host country.

1.2.3 Production efficiency seeking

The labour-intensive manufacture of electronic components in Taiwan, Malaysia and Mexico is an example of locating production where one or more **factors of production** are **cheap** relative to their productivity.

1.2.4 Knowledge seeking

Knowledge seeking firms choose to set up operations in countries in which they can **gain access to technology or management expertise**. For example, German, Japanese and Dutch companies have acquired technology by buying US-based electronics companies.

1.2.5 Political safety seekers

Firms which are seeking 'political safety' will acquire or set up new operations in those countries which are thought to be **unlikely to expropriate or interfere** with **private enterprise or impose import controls**. More positively these companies may offer grants and tax concessions.

1.2.6 Economies of scale

There are advantages to be gained in production, marketing, finance, research and development, transport and purchasing by virtue of firms being large. **Production economies** can arise from use of large-scale plant or from the possibility of rationalising production by adopting worldwide specialisation. Multinational car manufacturers produce engines in one country, transmissions in another, bodies in another, and assemble cars in yet another country.

1.2.7 Managerial and marketing expertise

Managerial expertise may be fostered in the environment of the larger multinational enterprise, and can be developed from previous knowledge of foreign markets. Empirical studies show that multinationals tend to **export to markets** before **establishing production operations** there, thus partly overcoming the possibly superior local knowledge of firms based in the host country.

1.2.8 Technology

Empirical studies suggest a link between **research and development (R & D)** work, which enhances technological, scientific and engineering skills and the larger multinationals engaged in FDI. Vernon's **product cycle theory** is based on the idea that multinational firms originate much new technology as a result of R&D activities on new products initially launched in their home markets. Host nations are often interested in FDI for the reason that technology transfer may result from it.

1.2.9 Financial economies

Multinationals enjoy considerable cost advantages in relation to finance. They have the advantage of access to the **full range of financial instruments** such as Eurocurrency and Eurobonds, which reduces their borrowing costs. Multinationals' financial strength is also achieved through their ability to **reduce risk** by **diversifying their operations** and their sources of borrowing.

1.2.10 Differentiated products

Firms create their own firm-specific advantages by **producing** and **marketing differentiated products**, which are similar products differentiated mainly by branding. Once the firm has developed differentiated products for the home market, it can maximise return on the heavy marketing costs by marketing them worldwide. Competitors will find it expensive and possibly difficult to imitate such products.

1.3 Issues in overseas production decisions   12/10

FAST FORWARD

Commonly used means to establish an **interest abroad** include:

- Joint ventures
- Licensing agreements
- Management contracts
- Subsidiary
- Branches

Most of the two-way traffic in investment by multinational companies (**foreign direct investment** or **FDI**) is between the developed countries of the world. While the present pattern of FDI can be traced back to the initial wave of investment in Europe by the USA following the Second World War, more recently Europe and Japan have become substantial overseas investors.

Developments in international capital markets have provided an environment conducive to FDI.

Key term

Globalisation describes the process by which the capital markets of each country have become internationally integrated.

The process of integration is facilitated by improved telecommunications and the deregulation of markets in many countries.

There have been significant changes affecting the pattern of multinationals' activities over the last twenty years or so.

1.3.1 Destination countries

The focus has shifted from Canada and Latin America in the days when the USA was the major source of FDI to other areas, including the countries of South East Asia which receive significant direct investment from Japanese companies in particular.

1.3.2 Centralised control

Centralised control of production activities within multinationals has increased, prompted partly by the need for **strategic management of production planning** and worldwide resource allocation. This process of centralisation has been facilitated by the development of sophisticated worldwide computer and telecommunications links.

1.3.3 Type of integration

A firm might develop **horizontally** in different countries, replicating its existing operations on a global basis. **Vertical integration** might have an international dimension through FDI to acquire raw material or component sources overseas (**backwards integration**) or to establish final production and distribution in other countries (**forward integration**). **Diversification** might alternatively provide the impetus to developing international interests.

Different forms of expansion overseas are available to meet various strategic objectives.

(a) Firms may expand by means of **new 'start-up' investments**, for example in manufacturing plants. This does allow flexibility, although it may be slow to achieve, expensive to maintain and slow to yield satisfactory results.

(b) A firm might **take over or merge** with established firms abroad. This provides a means of **purchasing market information**, **market share** and **distribution channels**. If speed of entry into the overseas market is a high priority, then acquisition may be preferred to start-up. However, the better acquisitions may only be available at a **premium**.

(c) **A joint venture with a local overseas partner** might be entered into. A joint venture may be defined as 'the commitment, for more than a very short duration, of funds, facilities and services by two or more legally separate interests to an enterprise for their mutual benefit.' Different forms of joint venture are distinguished below.

1.3.4 Joint ventures   12/10

The two distinct types of joint venture are **industrial co-operation (contractual)** and **joint-equity**. A **contractual joint venture** is for a fixed period and the duties and responsibility of the parties are contractually defined. A **joint-equity venture** involves investment, is of no fixed duration and continually evolves. Depending on government regulations, joint ventures may be the **only** means of access to a particular market.

The main advantages of joint ventures are:

(a) Relatively **low cost access** to new markets

(b) **Easier access** to **local capital markets**, possibly with accompanying tax incentives or grants

(c) **Use of joint venture partner's existing management expertise**, local knowledge, distribution network, technology, brands, patents and marketing or other skills

(d) **Sharing of risks**

(e) **Sharing of costs**, providing economies of scale

The main disadvantages of joint ventures are:

(a) **Managerial freedom** may be **restricted** by the need to take account of the views of all the joint venture partners.

(b) There may be **problems** in **agreeing on partners' percentage ownership**, transfer prices, reinvestment decisions, nationality of key personnel, remuneration and sourcing of raw materials and components.

(c) Finding a **reliable joint venture partner** may take a long time.

(d) Joint ventures are **difficult to value**, particularly where one or more partners have made intangible contributions.

1.3.5 Exploiting and licensing

Exporting and **licensing** stand as alternatives to FDI. **Exporting** may be direct selling by the firm's own export division into the overseas markets, or it may be indirect through agents, distributors, trading companies and various other such channels. **Licensing** involves conferring rights to make use of the licensor company's production process on producers located in the overseas market.

> **Licensing** is an alternative to foreign direct investment by which overseas producers are given rights to use the licensor's production process in return for royalty payments.
>
> **Exporting** may be unattractive because of tariffs, quotas or other import restrictions in overseas markets, and local production may be the only feasible option in the case of bulky products such as cement and flat glass.

The main advantages of licensing are:

(a) It can allow fairly **rapid penetration of** overseas markets.

(b) It does **not require substantial financial resources**.

(c) **Political risks** are **reduced** since the licensee is likely to be a local company.

(d) **Licensing** may be a **possibility** where direct investment is restricted or prevented by a country.

(e) For a multinational company, licensing agreements provide a way for **funds** to be **remitted** to the parent company in the form of licence fees.

The main disadvantages of licensing are:

(a) The arrangement may give to the licensee **know-how** and **technology** which it can use in competing with the licensor after the license agreement has expired.

(b) It may be more **difficult to maintain quality standards**, and lower quality might affect the standing of a brand name in international markets.

(c) It might be possible for the licensee to **compete** with the licensor by exporting the produce to markets outside the licensee's area.

(d) Although relatively insubstantial financial resources are required, on the other hand **relatively small cash inflows** will be **generated**.

1.3.6 Management contracts

Management contracts whereby a firm agrees to sell management skills are sometimes used in combination with licensing. Such contracts can serve as a means of obtaining funds from subsidiaries, and may be a useful way of maintaining cash flows where other remittance restrictions apply. Many multinationals use a **combination** of various methods of servicing international markets, depending on the particular circumstances.

1.3.7 Overseas subsidiaries

The basic structure of many multinationals consists of a parent company (a holding company) with subsidiaries in several countries. The subsidiaries may be wholly owned or just partly owned, and some may be owned through other subsidiaries. Whatever the reason for setting up subsidiaries abroad, the aim is to increase the profits of the multinational's parent company. However there are different approaches to increasing profits that the multinational might take. At one extreme, the parent company might choose **to get as much money as it can** from the subsidiary, and **as quickly as it can**. This would involve the transfer of all or most of the subsidiary's profits to the parent company.

At the other extreme, the parent company might encourage a foreign subsidiary to **develop its business gradually**, to achieve long-term growth in sales and profits. To encourage growth, the subsidiary would be allowed to retain a large proportion of its profits, instead of remitting the profits to the parent company.

1.3.8 Branches

Firms who want to establish a definite presence in an overseas country may choose to establish a **branch** rather than a subsidiary. Key elements in this choice are as follows.

Taxation

In many countries the remitted profits of a subsidiary will be taxed at a higher rate than those of a branch, as profits paid in the form of dividends are likely to be subject to a withholding tax. How much impact the withholding tax has however, is questionable, particularly as a double tax treaty can reduce its import. In many instances a multinational will establish a branch and utilise its initial losses against other profits, and then turn the branch into a subsidiary when it starts making profits.

Formalities

As a separate entity, a subsidiary may be subject to more legal and accounting formalities than a branch. However, as a separate legal entity, a subsidiary may be able to claim more reliefs and grants than a branch.

Marketing

A local subsidiary may have a greater profile for sales and marketing purposes than a branch.

2 Theory and practice of international trade

FAST FORWARD

World output of **goods** and **services** will increase if countries specialise in the production of goods/services in which they have a **comparative advantage** and **trade** to obtain other goods and services.

Business enterprises are now also becoming increasingly 'internationalised' by the development of **multinational activities** beyond pure import and export trade.

2.1 Theory of international trade

In the modern economy, production is based on a high degree of **specialisation**. Within a country individuals specialise, factories specialise and whole regions specialise. Specialisation increases productivity and raises the standard of living. International trade extends the principle of the division of labour and specialisation to countries. International trade originated on the basis of nations exchanging their products for others which they could not produce for themselves.

International trade arises for a number of reasons.

- Different goods require **different proportions** of **factor inputs** in their production.
- Economic resources are **unevenly distributed** throughout the world.
- The **international mobility** of **resources** is extremely **limited.**

Since it is difficult to move resources between nations, the goods which 'embody' the resources must move. The main reason for trade therefore is that there are differences in the relative efficiency with which different countries can produce different goods and services.

2.2 The law of comparative advantage

The significance of the law of comparative advantage is that it provides a justification for the following beliefs.

(a)   Countries should **specialise** in what they produce, even when they are less efficient (in absolute terms) in producing every type of good. They should specialise in the goods where they have a **comparative advantage** (they are **relatively** more efficient in producing).

(b)   **International trade** should be allowed to take place **without restrictions** on imports or exports – ie there should be **free trade**.

2.2.1 Does the law apply in practice?

The law of **comparative advantage** does apply in practice, and countries do specialise in the production of certain goods. However, there are certain limitations or restrictions on how it operates.

(a)   **Free trade does not always exist**. Some countries take action to protect domestic industries and discourage imports. This means that a country might produce goods in which it does not have a comparative advantage.

(b)   **Transport costs** (assumed to be nil in the examples above) can be **very high** in international trade so that it is cheaper to produce goods in the home country rather than to import them.

2.3 The advantages of international trade

The law of comparative advantage is perhaps the major advantage of encouraging international trade. However, there are other advantages to the countries of the world from encouraging international trade. These are as follows.

(a)   Some countries have a **surplus** of **raw materials** to their needs, and others have a deficit. A country with a surplus (eg of oil) can take advantage of its resources to export them. A country with a deficit of a raw material must either import it, or accept restrictions on its economic prosperity and standard of living.

(b)   International trade **increases competition** amongst suppliers in the world's markets. Greater competition reduces the likelihood of a market for a good in a country being dominated by a monopolist. The greater competition will force firms to be competitive and so will increase the pressures on them to be **efficient**, and also perhaps to produce goods of a high quality.

(c)   International trade creates larger markets for a firm's output, and so some firms can benefit from **economies of scale** by engaging in export activities.

(d)   There may be **political advantages** to international trade, because the development of **trading links** provides a foundation for **closer political links**. An example is the development of political links based on trade is the **European Union**.

2.4 Barriers to entry

Key term

> **Barriers to entry** are factors which make it difficult for suppliers to enter a market.

Multinationals may face various entry barriers. All of these barriers may be more difficult to overcome if a multinational is investing abroad because of factors such as unfamiliarity with local consumers or government favouring local firms.

Strategies of expansion and diversification imply some logic in carrying on operations. It might be a better decision, although a much harder one, to cease operations or to pull out of a market completely. There are likely to be **exit barriers** making it difficult to pull out of a market.

2.4.1 Product differentiation barriers

An **existing major supplier** would be able to exploit its position as supplier of an established product that the consumer/ customer can be persuaded to believe is better. A new entrant to the market would have to design a better product, or convince customers of the product's qualities, and this might involve spending substantial sums of money on research and development, advertising and sales promotion.

2.4.2 Absolute cost barriers

These exist where an existing supplier has access to **cheaper raw material sources** or to know-how that the new entrant would not have. This gives the existing supplier an advantage because its input costs would be cheaper in absolute terms than those of a new entrant.

2.4.3 Economy of scale barriers

These exist where the **minimum level of production** needed to achieve the greatest economies of scale is at a high level. New entrants to the market would have to be able to achieve a substantial market share before they could gain full advantage of potential scale economies, and so the existing firms would be able to produce their output more cheaply.

2.4.4 Fixed costs

The amount of **fixed costs** that a firm would have to sustain, regardless of its market share, could be a significant entry barrier.

2.4.5 Legal barriers

These are barriers where a supplier is fully or partially protected by law. For example, there are some **legal monopolies** (nationalised industries perhaps) and a company's products might be protected by **patent** (for example computer hardware or software).

3 Trade agreements

FAST FORWARD

Justifications for **protection** include prevention of the import of cheap goods and dumping, and protection of infant or declining industries.

Free trade can lead to greater competition and efficiency, and achieve better economic growth worldwide.

3.1 Free trade

Free trade exists where there is no restriction on imports from other countries or exports to other countries. The **European Union** (EU) is a free trade area for trade between its member countries. In practice, however, there exist many barriers to free trade because governments wish to protect home industries against foreign competition. **Protectionism** would in effect be intended to hinder the operation of the law of comparative advantage.

3.2 Protectionist measures

Protectionist measures may be implemented by a government, but **popular demand** for protection commonly exceeds what governments are prepared to allow. In the UK, for example, some protectionist measures have been taken against Japanese imports (eg a voluntary restriction on car imports by Japanese manufacturers) although more severe measures are called for from time to time by popular demand or lobbying interests.

Protection can be applied in several ways, including the following.

- Tariffs or customs duties
- Import quotas
- Embargoes
- Hidden subsidies for exporters and domestic producers
- Import restrictions
- Deliberately restrictive bureaucratic procedures ('red tape') or product standards
- Government action to devalue the domestic currency

3.2.1 Tariffs or customs duties

Tariffs or customs duties are taxes on imported goods. The effect of a tariff is to raise the price paid for the imported goods by domestic consumers, while leaving the price paid to foreign producers the same, or even lower. The difference is transferred to the government sector.

For example, if goods imported to the UK are bought for £100 per unit, which is paid to the foreign supplier, and a tariff of £20 is imposed, the full cost to the UK buyer will be £120, with £20 going to the government.

An **ad valorem** tariff is one which is applied as a percentage of the value of goods imported. A **specific** tariff is a fixed tax per unit of goods.

3.2.2 Import quotas

Import quotas are restrictions on the **quantity** of a product that is allowed to be imported into the country. The quota has a similar effect on consumer welfare to that of import tariffs, but the overall effects are more complicated.

- Both domestic and foreign suppliers enjoy a higher price, while consumers buy less.
- Domestic producers supply more.
- There are fewer imports (in volume).
- The government collects no revenue.

An **embargo** on imports from one particular country is a total ban, ie effectively a zero quota.

3.2.3 Hidden export subsidies and import restrictions

An enormous range of government subsidies and assistance for exports and deterrents against imports have been practised, such as:

(a)   **For exports** – export credit guarantees (government-backed insurance against bad debts for overseas sales), financial help (such as government grants to the aircraft or shipbuilding industry) and state assistance via the Foreign Office

(b)   **For imports** – complex import regulations and documentation, or special safety standards demanded from imported goods and so on

3.2.4 Government action to devalue the currency

If a government allows its currency to fall in value, imports will become more expensive to buy. This will reduce imports by means of the price mechanism, especially if the demand and supply curves for the products are elastic.

3.3 Arguments against protection

Arguments against protection are as follows:

Reduced international trade

Because protectionist measures taken by one country will almost inevitably provoke retaliation by others, protection will reduce the volume of international trade. This means that the following benefits of international trade will be reduced.

(a)   **Specialisation**

(b)   **Greater competition**, and so greater efficiency amongst producers

(c)   The advantages of **economies of scale** amongst producers who need world markets to achieve their economies and so produce at lower costs

Retaliation

Obviously it is to a nation's advantage if it can apply protectionist measures while other nations do not. But because of **retaliation by other countries**, protectionist measures to reverse a balance of trade deficit are unlikely to succeed. Imports might be reduced, but so too would exports.

Effect on economic growth

It is generally argued that widespread protection will damage the **prospects for economic growth** amongst the countries of the world, and protectionist measures ought to be restricted to 'special cases' which might be discussed and negotiated with other countries.

Political consequences

Although from a nation's own point of view, protection may improve its position, protectionism leads to a **worse outcome for all**. Protection also creates political ill-will amongst countries of the world and so there are **political disadvantages** in a policy of protection.

3.4 Arguments in favour of protection

Imports of cheap goods

Measures can be taken against imports of cheap goods that compete with higher priced domestically produced goods, and so **preserve output and employment** in domestic industries. In the UK, advocates of protection have argued that UK industries are declining because of competition from overseas, especially the Far East, and the advantages of more employment at a reasonably high wage for UK labour are greater than the disadvantages that protectionist measures would bring.

Dumping

Measures might be necessary to counter **'dumping'** of surplus production by other countries at an uneconomically low price. Although dumping has short-term benefits for the countries receiving the cheap goods, the longer term consequences would be a **reduction** in **domestic output** and **employment**, even when domestic industries in the longer term might be more efficient.

Retaliation

This is why protection tends to spiral once it has begun. Any country that does not take protectionist measures when other countries are doing so is likely to find that it suffers all of the disadvantages and none of the advantages of protection.

Infant industries

Protectionism can protect a country's **'infant industries'** that have not yet developed to the size where they can compete in international markets. **Less developed countries** in particular might need to protect industries against competition from advanced or developing countries.

Declining industries

Without protection, the industries might collapse and there would be severe problems of sudden mass unemployment amongst workers in the industry.

Reduction in balance of trade deficit

However, because of retaliation by other countries, the success of such measures by one country would depend on the demand by other countries for its exports being inelastic with regard to price and its demand for imports being fairly elastic.

3.5 The 'optimal tariff' argument

In each of the above cases, tariffs and other protectionist measures are being advocated instead of alternative policies specifically targeted on the objectives sought.

Another argument in favour of tariffs targets directly the problem of a divergence between social and private marginal costs arising from trade itself. This **optimal tariff argument** provides a clearer demonstration of the possibility of gains in welfare from a tariff.

If a country's imports make up a significant share of the world market for a particular good, an increase in imports is likely to result in the world price of the good rising. The economic agents in the country collectively 'bid up' the price of imports. In a free market, each individual will buy imports up to the point at which the benefit to the individual equals the world price. Because of the price-raising effect referred to above, the cost to the economy as a whole of the last import exceeds the world price, and therefore exceeds its benefit.

In such a case, society can gain by restricting imports up to the point at which the **benefit of the last import equals its cost to society as a whole**. A tariff set to achieve this result is called an 'optimal tariff'.

Tariffs would decrease the welfare of a country in circumstances in which the optimal tariff is zero and there is no longer a need to discourage imports. This is when a country does not 'bid up' the world price of imports, as with a relatively small country in a large world market for a good.

3.6 Other measures

As an alternative to protection, a country can try to stimulate its export competitiveness by making efforts to improve the productivity and lower the costs of domestic industries, thus making them more competitive against foreign producers. **Hidden subsidies** and **exchange rate devaluation** are examples of indirect protectionist measures, but other measures, such as **funding industrial training schemes and educational policies**, might in the longer term result in improvements in domestic productivity.

3.7 The European Union

The **EU** is one of several international economic associations. It dates back to 1957 (the Treaty of Rome) and now consists of twenty-seven countries including formerly communist Eastern European countries.

The EU incorporates a **common market** combining different aspects.

(a)   A **free trade area exists** when there is no restriction on the movement of goods and services between countries. This has been extended into a **customs union** (see below).

(b)   A **common market** encompasses the idea of a customs union but has a number of additional features. In addition to free trade among member countries there is also **complete mobility** of the **factors of production**. A British citizen has the freedom to work in any other country of the European Union, for example. A common market will also aim to achieve stronger links between member countries, for example by harmonising government economic policies and by establishing a closer political confederation.

(c)   The **single European currency**, the **euro**, was adopted by eleven countries of the EU from the inception of the currency at the beginning of 1999.

3.8 The customs union

The customs union of the EU **establishes a free trade area between member states**, and also erects **common external tariffs** to charge on imports from non-member countries. The EU thus promotes free trade among member states, while acting as a **protectionist bloc** against the rest of the world. It is accordingly consistent that the EU negotiates in GATT talks as a single body.

3.9 The single European market

The EU set the end of 1992 as the target date for the removal of all existing physical, technical and fiscal barriers among member states, thus creating a large multinational **European Single Market**. In practice, these changes have not occurred 'overnight', and many of them are still in progress.

3.9.1 Elimination of trade restrictions

(a) **Physical barriers** (eg customs inspection) on good and services have been removed for most products. Companies have had to adjust to a new VAT regime as a consequence.

(b) **Technical standards** (eg for quality and safety) should be harmonised.

(c) Governments should not **discriminate** between EU companies in awarding public works contracts.

(d) **Telecommunications** should be subject to greater competition.

(e) It should be possible to provide **financial services** in any country.

(f) There should be **free movement of capital** within the community.

(g) **Professional qualifications** awarded in one member state should be recognised in the others.

(h) The EU is taking a **co-ordinated stand** on matters related to consumer protection.

3.9.2 Remaining barriers

There are many areas where harmonisation is a long way from being achieved. Here are some examples.

(a) **Company tax rates**, which can affect the viability of investment plans, vary from country to country within the EU.

(b) Whilst there have been moves to harmonisation, there are still differences between **indirect tax** rates imposed by member states.

(c) There are considerable **differences in prosperity** between the wealthiest EU economies (eg Germany), and the poorest (eg Greece). This has meant that grants are sometimes available to depressed regions, which might affect investment decisions; and that different marketing strategies are appropriate for different markets.

(d) **Differences in workforce skills** can have a significant effect on investment decisions. The workforce in Germany is perhaps the most highly trained, but also the most highly paid, and so might be suitable for products of a high added value.

(e) Some countries are better provided with road and rail infrastructure than others. Where accessibility to a market is an important issue, **infrastructure** can mean significant variations in distribution costs.

3.10 The European Free Trade Area (EFTA)

The European Free Trade Area (EFTA) was established in 1959, with seven member countries, one of which was the UK. The UK, Denmark and Portugal have since transferred to the EU, while Finland and Iceland joined the other original member states, Sweden, Norway, Austria and Switzerland. More recently, Finland, Sweden and Austria have also joined the EU. There is free trade between EFTA member countries but there is no harmonisation of tariffs with non-EFTA countries.

3.11 North American Free Trade Agreement (NAFTA)

Canada, the USA and Mexico formed the North American Free Trade Agreement (NAFTA) which came into force in 1994. This free trade area covering a population of 360 million and accounting for economic output of US$6,000 billion annually is almost as large as the European Economic Area, and is thus the second largest free trade area after the EEA.

Under NAFTA, virtually all tariff and other (non-tariff) barriers to trade and investment between the NAFTA members are to be eliminated over a 15-year period. In the case of trade with non-NAFTA members, each NAFTA member will continue to set its own external tariffs, subject to obligations under GATT. The NAFTA agreement covers most business sectors, with special rules applying to especially sensitive sectors, including agriculture, the automotive industry, financial services and textiles and clothing.

4 The World Trade Organisation (WTO)

The **World Trade Organisation** (WTO) is a global international organisation dealing with the rules of trade between nations.

4.1 The World Trade Organisation (WTO)

The **World Trade Organisation (WTO)** was formed in 1995 to continue to implement the General Agreement on Tariffs and Trade (GATT). The WTO has well over 100 members including the entire European Union. Its aims include:

(a) To **reduce existing barriers** to free trade

(b) To **eliminate discrimination** in international trade such as tariffs and subsidies

(c) To **prevent the growth of protection** by getting member countries to consult with others before taking any protectionist measures

(d) To act as a **forum** for assisting free trade, by for example administering agreements, helping countries negotiate and **offering a disputes settlement process**

(e) Establishing **rules and guidelines** to make **world trade more predictable**

4.1.1 The most favoured nation principle

Key term

> **Most favoured nation**: a principle in the GATT international trade agreement binding the parties to grant to each other treatment which is as favourable as that offered to any other GATT member in respect of tariffs and other trading conditions.

The WTO encourages free trade by applying the **'most favoured nation'** principle where one country (which is a member of GATT) that offers a reduction in tariffs to another country must offer the same reduction to all other member countries of GATT.

4.1.2 Impact on protectionist measures

Although the WTO has helped reduce the level of protection, some problems still remain:

(a) Special circumstances (for example economic crises, the protection of an infant industry, the rules of the EU) have to be **admitted** when protection or special low tariffs between a group of countries are allowed.

(b) A country in the WTO may **prefer not to offer a tariff reduction** to another country because it would have to offer the same reduction to all other GATT members.

(c) In spite of much success in reducing tariffs, the WTO has had **less effect** in dealing with **many non-tariff barriers** to trade that countries may set up. Some such barriers, for example those in the guise of health and safety requirements, can be very difficult to identify.

(d) New agreements are **not always accepted initially** by all members.

Nevertheless the WTO exists to help business, and ultimately businesses should be able to benefit from the **expanded opportunities** a freer global market brings, even if in certain countries some businesses may suffer through losing the benefits of protection.

5 International monetary institutions

FAST FORWARD

The IMF was set up partly with the role of providing finance for any countries with temporary balance of payments deficits.

The World Bank and the IDA have tried to provide long-term finance for **developing countries**, to help them to continue developing.

5.1 The International Monetary Fund

Most countries of the world have membership of the IMF. The three broad aims of the IMF are:

- To **promote international monetary** co-operation, and to establish a code of conduct for making international payments
- To **provide financial support** to countries with **temporary balance of payments deficits**
- To provide for the **orderly growth** of international liquidity, through its Special Drawing Rights (SDR) scheme (launched in 1970).

5.2 The IMF and financial support for countries with balance of payment difficulties

If a country has a balance of payments deficit on current account, it must **either borrow capital** or use up official reserves to offset this deficit. Since a country's official reserves will be insufficient to support a balance of payments deficit on current account for very long, it must borrow to offset the deficit.

The IMF can provide financial support to member countries. Most IMF loans are repayable in 3 to 5 years.

Of course, to lend money, the IMF must also have funds. Funds are made available from subscriptions or 'quotas' of member countries. The IMF uses these subscriptions to lend foreign currencies to countries which apply to the IMF for help.

5.3 IMF loan conditions

The pre-conditions that the IMF places on its loans to debtor countries vary according to the individual situation of each country, but the general position is as follows.

(a) The IMF wants countries which borrow from the IMF to get into a position to start **repaying the loans fairly quickly**. To do this, the countries must take effective action to improve their balance of payments position.

(b) To make this improvement, the IMF generally believes that a country should take action to **reduce the demand for goods and services** in the economy (eg by increasing taxes and cutting government spending). This will reduce imports and help to put a brake on any price rises. The country's industries should then also be able to divert more resources into export markets and hence exports should improve in the longer-term.

(c) With 'deflationary' measures along these lines, **standards of living will fall** (at least in the short term) and unemployment may rise. The IMF regards these short-term hardships to be necessary if a country is to succeed in sorting out its balance of payments and international debt problems.

5.4 Borrowing to supplement liquidity

Countries which have balance of payments deficits can borrow their way out of trouble, at least temporarily. There are various sources of borrowing:

(a) The IMF (IMF lending has already been described)

(b) Other institutions, such as the World Bank, the International Development Association (IDA), and the Bank for International Settlements (BIS)

(c) Borrowing from private banks (in the eurocurrency markets)

5.5 The World Bank (IBRD)

The **World Bank** (more properly called the **International Bank for Reconstruction and Development** or **IBRD**) began operations in 1946. Its chief aim now is to **supplement private finance** and lend money on a commercial basis for capital projects. Loans are usually direct to governments or government agencies, for a long-term period of over 10 years (typically 20 years). Lending is usually tied to specific projects, although the Bank's lending policy has been more flexible in recent years.

The World Bank's funds are obtained from **capital subscriptions** by member countries of the IMF, its profits, and borrowing. The major source of funds is borrowing, and the World Bank makes bond issues on the world's capital markets (eg New York).

5.6 The IDA

World Bank lending is for projects concerned with the development of agriculture, electricity, transport and so on. The cost of World Bank loans was (and still is) high to developing countries, and in 1960, the **International Development Association (IDA)** was set up to provide 'soft' loans – ie loans at a low cost with easy repayment terms – to less developed countries, for similar types of projects financed by the World Bank. The IDA is a subsidiary of the World Bank and member countries of the IDA are also members of the World Bank.

5.7 The BIS

The **Bank for International Settlements (BIS)** is the banker for the central banks of other countries. It is situated in Basle, where it was founded in 1930. Most of its deposits are from the central banks of various countries and some are shareholders and represented on its board. It is a profit making institution, and lends money at commercial rates. The Bank of England, for example, has a 10% stake in the BIS.

The main functions of the BIS are to

- Promote co-operation between central banks
- Provide facilities for international co-operation

5.8 European Central Bank

The European Central Bank (ECB) was established in 1998 and is based in Frankfurt. It is responsible for administering the monetary policy of the 17 EU Eurozone member states and is thus one of the world's most powerful central banks.

The main objective of the ECB is to maintain price stability within the Eurozone (keep inflation low). Its key tasks are to define and implement monetary policy for the Eurozone member states and to conduct foreign exchange operations.

Unlike the US style of central banking (where the economy remains liquid via the purchase of Treasury bonds by the Federal Bank), the ECB operates a different system. Individual eligible banks may bid for short-term repo contracts (2 weeks to 3 months' duration) – that is the banks are effectively borrowing cash and pay it back. An increase in the quantity of notes offered at auction will increase the economy's liquidity whilst the opposite effect is true if the quantity of notes offered decreases.

The European Sovereign Debt crisis in 2011 highlighted the problems inherent in a banking system whereby the primary assets were issued by state entities, not all of which had the desire or the ability to repay what they had borrowed. The credit-worthiness of the ECB's statement of financial position therefore depends on a group of member states with extremely different taxation systems and economic conditions.

The European Sovereign Debt crisis will be dealt with in further detail in Chapter 19.

5.9 Bank of England

The Bank of England is the central bank of the UK. It was founded in 1694 and in 1997 it became an independent public organisation (wholly owned by the Treasury Solicitor on behalf of the Government) with independence on setting monetary policy.

The Bank of England performs all the functions of a Central Bank. The most important of these functions is the maintenance of price stability and support of British economic policies (thus promoting economic growth).

Stable prices and market confidence in sterling are the two main criteria for **monetary stability**. The Bank aims to meet inflation targets set by the Government by adjusting interest rates (determined by the Monetary Policy Committee which meets on a monthly basis).

Financial stability is maintained by protecting against threats to the overall financial system. Such threats are detected through the Bank's surveillance and market intelligence functions and are dealt with through domestic and international financial operations.

The Bank of England works with other institutions to ensure both monetary and financial stability, including HM Treasury, the Financial Services Authority (FSA) and other central banks and international organisations.

The Bank can also operate as a **'lender of last resort'** – that is, it will extend credit when no other institution will. There are several examples of this function during the global financial crisis, for example Northern Rock in 2007. This function is now performed by UK Financial Investments Ltd (set up by the Government) but the Bank of England still remains 'lender of last resort' in the event of any further major shocks to the UK financial system.

5.10 US Federal Reserve System

The Federal Reserve System (known as the Fed) is the central banking system of the United States. Created in 1913, its responsibilities and powers have evolved significantly over time. Its current main duties include conducting the US monetary policy, maintaining stability of the financial system and supervising and regulating banking institutions.

Whilst the Board of Governors states that the Fed can make decisions without ratification by the President or any other member of government, its authority is derived from US Congress and subject to its oversight.

The Fed also acts as the 'lender of last resort' to those institutions that cannot obtain credit elsewhere and the collapse of which would have serious repercussions for the economy. However the Fed's role as lender of last resort has been criticised as it shifts risk and responsibility from the lenders and borrowers to the general public in the form of inflation.

The Fed sets monetary policy by influencing the Federal funds rate (the rate of interbank lending of excess reserves) using the three 'tools' of monetary policy:

(1) **Open market operations** – the purchase and sale of US Treasury and federal agency securities. Such operations allow the Fed to increase or decrease the amount of money in the banking system.

(2) **Discount rate** – the interest rate charged to commercial banks on loans they receive from the Fed. This rate is generally set at a rate close to 100 base points above the target federal funds rate in an attempt to encourage banks to seek alternative funding before approaching the Fed.

(3) **Reserve requirements** (required reserve ratio) – the amount of funds that a depository institution must hold in reserve against specified deposit liabilities

5.11 Bank of Japan

The Bank of Japan is Japan's central bank and is based in Tokyo. Following several restructures in the 1940s, the bank's operating environment evolved during the 1970s whereby the closed economy and fixed foreign currency exchange rate was replaced with a large open economy and variable exchange rate.

Until 1991, the Bank of Japan's monetary policy has been largely conducted via its 'window guidance' credit controls, where the central bank imposes credit growth quotas on the commercial banks. This tool significantly contributed to the creation of the 'bubble economy' of the 1980s.

In 1997, a major revision of the Bank of Japan Act was intended to give the bank greater independence from the government, although the bank had already been criticised for having excessive independence and lack of accountability before these revisions were introduced. However the Act has tried to ensure a certain degree of dependence by stating that the bank should always maintain in close contact with the government to ensure harmony between their currency and monetary policies and those of the government.

Despite these safeguards, the bank has persistently ignored or rebuffed government requests to stimulate the Japanese economy. As a result the Japanese economy remains in a critical state. However in August 2011, the Bank of Japan announced a scheme to offer 3 trillion yen (approximately $35 billion) in low-interest loans in an attempt to stimulate the ailing economy.

6 International financial markets and global financial stability

The globalisation of the financial markets has facilitated the transfer of funds to emerging markets but it has contributed to financial instability.

6.1 The rise of global financial markets.

One of the main developments of the last decades has been the globalisation of the financial markets. This globalisation has been buoyed by the expansion of the European Union, the rise of China and India as important trading players in the world economy and the creation of the World Trade Organisation. The globalisation in financial markets is manifested in developments in international equity markets, in international bond markets and in international money markets.

6.2 International capital markets and emerging economies development

Private capital flows are important for emerging economies, and the transfer of flows has increased significantly as a result of the development in international capital markets. The capital flows to emerging markets take three forms:

(a)   **Foreign direct investment** by multinational companies .

(b)   **Borrowing from international banks.** Borrowing from international banks is becoming more important. There are several advantages in borrowing from international banks. It is possible to obtain better terms and in currencies which may be more appropriate in term of the overall risk exposure of the company.

(c)   **Portfolio investment** in emerging markets capital markets. Emerging markets equity has become a distinct area for investment, with many specialist investment managers dedicated to emerging markets.

6.3 The European Monetary System (EMS)

European Monetary System (EMS) reduces exchange dealing costs and enhances economic policies, but limits the ability of governments to pursue independent economic policies.

The purposes of the EMS are:

(a)   To **stabilise exchange rates** between the currencies of the member countries

(b)   To promote **economic convergence** in Europe, pushing inflation rates down by forcing economic policies on partner governments similar to the policies of the more successful members

(c)   To develop **European Economic and Monetary Union (EMU)**

6.4 International capital markets and financial stability

The globalisation of the financial markets has created more liquid, efficient and transparent market, but it has also created volatility in the capital flows especially in emerging markets. One important feature of the second half of the 1990s has been the phenomenon of financial contagion which creates global instability. Financial contagion occurs when crisis in one country spills to other countries. The phenomenon started when the collapse of Thailand's currency triggered the crises in other Asian emerging markets.

The experience of the Asian crisis shows that globalisation also needs a series of measures to improve financial stability in emerging-market economies and thus to reduce the frequency and intensity of future crises. These measures include both an improved framework for macroeconomic policy and improved corporate governance.

6.5 The global debt crisis

A **global debt crisis** arose as governments in **less developed countries (LDCs)** took on levels of debt to fund their development programmes which are beyond their ability to finance. As a result, the level of debt rose and their ability to repay decreased, as increasing amounts of GDP were absorbed in servicing the debt rather in financing development. A further factor was that, in some countries with substantial oil reserves, banks were keen to lend against the fact of these reserves combined with high world oil prices. Examples of such countries include Nigeria and Venezuela. As the oil price fell, the fall in oil revenues to the LDCs precipitated a debt crisis.

6.6 Resolving the global debt crisis

Various approaches have been taken in attempts to overcome these problems. Where the situation has arisen due to a sudden (and hopefully temporary) fall in commodity prices, one solution may be for the country to take on **additional short-term debt** to cover the temporary shortfall.

Where the problem is of a longer term nature, approaches include the following.

(a)   The **debt** may be **restructured** and/or rescheduled in order to allow the government a longer time to repay the loan.

(b)   Restructuring is often linked to a **package of economic reforms** which are aimed at improving the balance of trade and stimulating growth. Some countries may initiate such reforms themselves as a way out of their problem – in other cases, reforms are linked to the rescheduling package and are approved and monitored by the IMF.

(c)   Some of the debt may be **written off** by the lending governments and banks thereby reducing the interest burden and enhancing the prospects of eventual payment.

(d)   Some of the debt may be **converted to equity**, giving foreign companies a stake in local industries and reducing the level of interest payments.

The debt crisis is also covered in Chapter 19 of this text.

6.7 Negative impacts on multinational firms

The debt crisis has a number of adverse consequences for multinational firms which undertake FDI in less developed countries. Many of these adverse consequences result from the policies of 'economic adjustment' which are imposed on debtor countries by the IMF.

6.7.1 Effects of deflationary policies

Deflationary policies imposed on LDCs by the IMF are likely to **damage** the **profitability of multinationals' subsidiaries** by reducing their sales in the local market. These deflationary policies are designed to improve the balance of payments position of the debtor countries by reducing their imports and boosting exports. Higher interest rates are likely to be introduced to suppress domestic consumer's demand for imports. However, higher interest rates will tend to dampen domestic investment and could result in increased unemployment and loss of business confidence.

6.7.2 Effects of devaluation

Devaluation of the domestic currency is a policy which the debtor country may **adopt** to try to **boost exports**. The country will be able to sell its exports more cheaply in foreign currency terms – while imports to the country will become more expensive. This will adversely affect the level of operating costs for multinational firms which make use of imported inputs to their production process.

6.7.3 Sourcing of imports

Debtor countries' **lack of foreign currency** (arising from the need to service their debt) means that **less can be imported**. Host countries may require that multinationals increase their use of local inputs which may be of higher cost or lower quality than the same goods obtained from elsewhere.

6.7.4 Lack of capital inflows

Measures such as the Baker Plan were intended to increase the level of lending available to debtor countries. Nevertheless, as already indicated, the international banks have **not been willing** to provide these **increased capital inflows** to the less developed countries. As a result, multinational firms operating in these countries have been forced to rely more heavily on **host country funding** for their activities in those countries, which they may have preferred not to do.

6.8 Dealing with currency risk

To reduce or to eliminate the currency risk of an overseas investment, a company might **finance** it with **funds** in the **same currency** as the investment. The advantages of borrowing in the same currency as an investment are as follows.

(a)   Assets and liabilities in the same currency can be **matched**, thus avoiding exchange losses on conversion in the group's annual accounts.

(b)   **Revenues** in the foreign currency can be used to **repay borrowings** in the same currency, thus eliminating losses due to fluctuating exchange rates.

7 Framework for financial planning in multinationals

As part of the fulfilment of the performance objective 'evaluate potential business/investment opportunities and the required finance options' you are expected to be able to identify and apply different finance options to single and combined entities in domestic and multinational business markets. This section looks at the financing options available to multinationals which you can put to good use if you work in such an environment.

Multinational companies need to develop a **financial planning framework** in order to make sure that the strategic objectives and competitive advantages are realised. Such a financial **planning framework** will include ways of raising **capital** and **risks** related to overseas operations and the **repatriation of profits**.

7.1 Financing an overseas subsidiary

Once the decision is taken by a multinational company to start overseas operations in any of the forms that have been discussed in the previous section, there is a need to decide on the source of funds for the proposed expansion. There are some differences in methods of financing the **parent company** itself, and the **foreign subsidiaries**. The parent company itself is more likely than companies which have no foreign interests to raise finance in a foreign currency, or in its home currency from foreign sources.

The **need to finance a foreign subsidiary** raises the following questions.

(a) How much **equity capital** should the parent company put into the subsidiary?

(b) Should the subsidiary be allowed to **retain a large proportion** of its profits, to build up its equity reserves, or not?

(c) Should the parent company hold **100% of the equity** of the subsidiary, or should it try to create a minority shareholding, perhaps by floating the subsidiary on the country's domestic stock exchange?

(d) Should the subsidiary be encouraged to **borrow** as much **long-term debt** as it can, for example by raising large bank loans? If so, should the loans be in the domestic currency of the subsidiary's country, or should it try to raise a foreign currency loan?

(e) Should the subsidiary be listed on the local stock exchange, raising funds from the local equity markets?

(f) Should the subsidiary be encouraged to minimise its working capital investment by relying heavily on trade credit?

The **method of financing** a subsidiary will give some indication of the **nature and length of time** of the investment that the parent company is prepared to make. A sizeable equity investment (or long-term loans from the parent company to the subsidiary) would indicate a long-term investment by the parent company.

7.2 Choice of finance for an overseas investment

The choice of the source of funds will depend on:

(a) The **local finance costs**, and any subsidies which may be available

(b) **Taxation systems** of the countries in which the subsidiary is operating. Different tax rates can favour borrowing in high tax regimes, and no borrowing elsewhere.

(c) Any **restrictions on dividend remittances**

(d) The possibility of **flexibility in repayments** which may arise from the parent/subsidiary relationship

Tax-saving opportunities may be maximised by **structuring the group** and its subsidiaries in such a way as to **take the best advantage** of the different local tax systems.

Because subsidiaries may be operating with a guarantee from the parent company, different gearing structures may be possible. Thus, a subsidiary may be able to operate with a higher level of debt that would be acceptable for the group as a whole.

Parent companies should also consider the following factors.

(a) **Reduced systematic risk.** There may be a small incremental reduction in systematic risk from investing abroad due to the segmentation of capital markets.

(b) **Access to capital.** Obtaining capital from foreign markets may increase liquidity, lower costs and make it easier to maintain optimum gearing.

(c) **Agency costs.** These may be higher due to political risk, market imperfections and complexity, leading to a higher cost of capital.

7.3 Dealing with currency risk

To reduce or to eliminate the currency risk of an overseas investment, a company might **finance** it with **funds** in the **same currency** as the investment. The advantages of borrowing in the same currency as an investment are as follows.

(a) Assets and liabilities in the same currency can be **matched**, thus avoiding exchange losses on conversion in the group's annual accounts.

(b) **Revenues** in the foreign currency can be used to **repay borrowings** in the same currency, thus eliminating losses due to fluctuating exchange rates.

Exam focus point

> You must be prepared to answer questions about various methods of financing an overseas subsidiary.

8 International debt finance

 FAST FORWARD

Multinational companies will have access to international debt, such as **Eurobonds**.

PER alert

As part of the fulfilment of the performance objective 'evaluate potential business/investment opportunities and the required finance options' you are expected to be able to identify and apply different finance options to single and combined entities in domestic and multinational business markets. This section looks at the financing options available to multinationals which you can put to good use if you work in such an environment.

8.1 International borrowing

Borrowing markets are becoming increasingly internationalised, particularly for larger companies. Companies are able to borrow long-term funds on the **eurocurrency (money) markets** and on the markets for **eurobonds**. These markets are collectively called '**euromarkets**'. Large companies can also borrow on the **syndicated loan market** where a syndicate of banks provides medium to long-term currency loans.

If a company is receiving income in a foreign currency or has a long-term investment overseas, it can try to **limit the risk** of adverse exchange rate movements by **matching**. It can take out a long-term loan and use the foreign currency receipts to repay the loan.

8.2 Eurocurrency markets

Key terms

Eurocurrency is currency which is held by individuals and institutions outside the country of issue of that currency.

Eurodollars are US dollars deposited with, or borrowed from, a bank outside the USA.   *(OT 2005)*

A UK company might borrow money from a bank or from the investing public, in sterling. However it might also borrow in a foreign currency, especially if it trades abroad, or if it already has assets or liabilities abroad denominated in a foreign currency. When a company borrows in a foreign currency, the loan is known as a **eurocurrency loan**. (As with euro-equity, it is not only the euro that is involved, and so the 'euro-' prefix is a misnomer.) Banks involved in the euro currency market are **not subject to central bank reserve requirements** or regulations in respect of their involvement.

The eurocurrency markets involve the **depositing of funds** with a **bank outside the country** of the currency in which the funds are denominated and **re-lending these funds for a fairly short term**, typically three months, normally at a floating rate of interest. **Eurocredits** are medium to long-term international bank loans which may be arranged by individual banks or by **syndicates of banks**. Syndication of loans increases the amounts available to hundreds of millions, while reducing the exposure of individual banks.

8.3 Eurobonds

Key term

A **eurobond** is a bond sold outside the jurisdiction of the country in whose currency the bond is denominated.   *(OT 2005)*

In recent years, a strong market has built up which allows very large companies to borrow in this way, long-term or short-term. Again, the market is not subject to national regulations.

Eurobonds are **long-term loans raised by international companies** or other institutions and **sold to investors in several countries** at the same time. Eurobonds are normally repaid after 5-15 years, and are for major amounts of capital ie $10m or more.

Exam focus point

Don't make the common mistake of thinking that eurobonds are issued in Europe or only denominated in euros.

8.3.1 How are Eurobonds issued?

Step 1 A lead manager is appointed from a major merchant bank; the lead manager liaises with the credit rating agencies and organises a **credit rating** of the Eurobond.

Step 2 The lead manager organises an **underwriting syndicate** (of other merchant banks) who agree the terms of the bond (eg interest rate, maturity date) and buy the bond.

Step 3 The underwriting syndicate then organise the sale of the bond; this normally involves **placing** the bond with **institutional investors**.

8.3.2 Advantages of Eurobonds

(a) Eurobonds are '**bearer instruments**', which means that the owner does not have to declare his identity.

(b) Interest is paid gross and this has meant that Eurobonds have been used by investors to avoid tax.

(c) Eurobonds create a liability in a foreign currency to **match** against a foreign currency asset.

(d) They are often **cheaper** than a foreign currency bank loan because they can be sold on by the investor, who will therefore accept a lower yield in return for this greater liquidity.

(e) They are also extremely **flexible**. Most eurobonds are fixed rate but they can be floating rate or linked to the financial success of the company.

(f) They are typically issued by companies with excellent credit ratings and are normally **unsecured**, which makes it easier for companies to raise debt finance in the future.

(g) Eurobond issues are not normally advertised because they are **placed** with institutional investors and this reduces issue costs.

8.3.3 Disadvantages of Eurobonds

Like any form of debt finance there will be **issue costs** to consider (approximately 2% of funds raised in the case of Eurobonds) and there may also be problems if gearing levels are too high.

A borrower contemplating a eurobond issue must consider the **foreign exchange risk** of a long-term foreign currency loan. If the money is to be used to purchase assets which will earn revenue in a currency different to that of the bond issue, the borrower will run the risk of exchange losses if the currency of the loan strengthens against the currency of the revenues out of which the bond (and interest) must be repaid.

9 Compliance with listing requirements

FAST FORWARD

When a company decides to raise funds from the local equity markets, the company must comply with the requirements of the local exchanges for listing.

9.1 Listing requirements for the London Stock Exchange

The listing requirements for the London Stock Exchange are:

9.1.1 Track record requirements

The track record requirements are:

(a) At least 75 percent of the entity's business must be supported by a revenue earnings record for the three years period. The UK listing authority has the discretion to allow a shorter period in certain circumstances.

(b) Must report significant acquisitions in the three year running up to the flotation.

9.1.2 Market capitalisation

Market capitalisation and share in public hands:

(a)   At least £700,000 for shares at the time of listing.
(b)   At least 25% of shares should be in public hands.

9.1.3 Future prospects

The company must show that it has enough working capital for its current needs and for at least the next 12 months.

The company must be able to carry on its business independently and at arm's length from any shareholders with economic interest.

A general description of the future plans and prospects must be given.

If the company gives n optional profit forecast in the document or has already given one publicly, a report will be required from the sponsor and the Reporting Accountant.

9.1.4 Audited historical financial information

Cover latest three full years and any published later interim period.

If latest audited financial data is more than 6 months old, interim audited financial information is required.

9.1.5 Corporate governance

Although the UK corporate governance rules do not apply to the non-UK companies, investors would expect similar standard, and an explanation for any differences. UK companies are expected to:

(a)   Splitting the roles of Chairman and CEO.
(b)   Except for smaller companies (below FTSE 350), at least half of the board, excluding the chairman, should comprise independent non-executive directors. Smaller companies should have at least two independent non-executive directors.
(c)   Have an independent audit committee, a remuneration committee and a nomination committee.
(d)   Provide evidence of a high standard of financial controls and accounting systems.

9.1.6 Acceptable jurisdiction and accounting standards

The company must be properly incorporated

IFRS and equivalent accounting standards are acceptable.

9.1.7 Other considerations

Sponsors/Underwriters usually recommend that existing shareholders should be barred form selling their shares for a period after initial listing offering of their shares.

The sponsor will need to make sure through due and careful enquiry, that the applicant has established procedures that enable it to comply with the listing rules and disclosure rules, as well having established procedures which provide a reasonable basis for the applicant to make proper judgements on an ongoing basis as to its financial position and prospects.

10 Capital mobility and blocked funds

FAST FORWARD

Multinationals can take various measures to combat the risks of political **interference** or **turbulence** including agreements with governments, insurance, and location elsewhere of key parts of the production process.

Multinationals can **counter exchange controls** by management charges or royalties.

10.1 Blocked funds

Exchange controls block the flow of foreign exchange into and out of a country, usually to defend the local currency or to protect reserves of foreign currencies. Exchange controls are generally more restrictive in developing and less developed countries although some still exist in developed countries. Typically, a government might enforce regulations:

(a) **Rationing the supply of foreign exchange**. Anyone wishing to make payments abroad in a foreign currency will be restricted by the limited supply, which stops them from buying as much as they want from abroad.

(b) **Restricting the types of transaction** for which payments abroad are allowed, for example by suspending or banning the payment of dividends to foreign shareholders, such as parent companies in multinationals, who will then have the problem of **blocked funds**.

10.2 Dealing with blocked funds

Ways of overcoming blocked funds include the following.

(a) The parent company could **sell goods or services** to the subsidiary and obtain payment. The amount of this payment will depend on the volume of sales and also on the transfer price for the sales.

(b) A parent company which grants a subsidiary the right to make goods protected by patents can charge a **royalty** on any goods that the subsidiary sells. The size of any royalty can be adjusted to suit the wishes of the parent company's management.

(c) If the parent company makes a **loan** to a subsidiary, it can set the interest rate high or low, thereby affecting the profits of both companies. A high rate of interest on a loan, for example, would improve the parent company's profits to the detriment of the subsidiary's profits.

(d) **Management charges** may be levied by the parent company for costs Incurred in the management of international operations.

Refer also to Chapter 18 on Dividend Policy for further details on issues with blocked funds.

11 Risk exposure

FAST FORWARD

The methods of financing overseas subsidiaries will depend on the **length of investment period** envisaged, also the **local finance costs, taxation systems** and **restrictions on dividend remittances**.

11.1 Political risks for multinationals

Key term

> **Political risk** is the risk that political action will affect the position and value of a company.

When a multinational company invests in another country, by setting up a subsidiary, it may face a **political risk** of action by that country's government which restricts the multinational's freedom.

If a government tries to prevent the exploitation of its country by multinationals, it may take various measures.

(a) Import **quotas** could be used to limit the quantities of goods that a subsidiary can buy from its parent company and import for resale in its domestic markets.

(b) Import **tariffs** could make imports (such as from parent companies) more expensive and domestically produced goods therefore more competitive.

(c) Legal standards of safety or quality (**non-tariff barriers**) could be imposed on imported goods to prevent multinationals from selling goods through a subsidiary which have been banned as dangerous in other countries.

(d) **Exchange control regulations** could be applied (see below).

(e) A government could **restrict** the ability of foreign companies to buy domestic companies, especially those that operate in politically sensitive industries such as defence contracting, communications, energy supply and so on.

(f) A government could **nationalise** foreign-owned companies and their assets (with or without compensation to the parent company).

(g) A government could insist on a **minimum shareholding** in companies by residents. This would force a multinational to offer some of the equity in a subsidiary to investors in the country where the subsidiary operates.

11.2 Assessment of political risk

There are a large number of factors that can be taken into account when assessing political risk, for example:

- Government stability
- Political and business ethics
- Economic stability/inflation
- Degree of international indebtedness
- Financial infrastructure
- Level of import restrictions
- Remittance restrictions
- Assets seized
- Existence of special taxes and regulations on overseas investors, or investment incentives

In addition **micro factors**, factors only affecting the company or the industry in which it invests, may be more significant than macro factors, particularly in companies such as hi-tech organisations.

Measurement is often by **subjective weighting** of these factors. Macro analysis may involve use of measures such as those developed by Euromoney or the Economist Intelligence Unit. Micro analysis may be more problematic; specially tailored consultancy reports may be needed, also visits to the country or drawing on the experience of those who know the country

11.3 Dealing with political risks

There are various strategies that multinational companies can adopt to limit the effects of political risk.

11.3.1 Negotiations with host government

The aim of these negotiations is generally to obtain a **concession agreement**. This would cover matters such as the transfer of capital, remittances and products, access to local finance, government intervention and taxation, and transfer pricing.

11.3.2 Insurance

In the UK the Export Credits Guarantee Department (ECGD) provides **protection against various threats** including nationalisation, currency conversion problems, war and revolution.

11.3.3 Production strategies

It may be necessary to strike a balance between **contracting out to local sources** (thus losing control) and **producing directly** (which increases the investment and hence increases the potential loss). Alternatively it may be better to locate key parts of the production process or the distribution channels abroad. Control of patents is another possibility, since these can be enforced internationally.

11.3.4 Contacts with markets

Multinationals may have **contacts with customers** which interventionist governments cannot obtain.

11.3.5 Financial management

If a multinational obtains funds in local investment markets, these may be on terms that are **less favourable** than on markets abroad, but would mean that local institutions suffered if the local government intervened. However governments often do limit the ability of multinationals to obtain funds locally.

Alternatively guarantees can be obtained from the government for the investment that can be enforced by the multinational if the government takes action.

11.3.6 Management structure

Possible methods include **joint ventures** or **ceding control** to local investors and obtaining profits by a management contract.

If governments do intervene, multinationals may have to make use of the advantages they hold or threaten withdrawal. The threat of expropriation may be reduced by negotiation or legal threats.

<table>
<tr>
<td>Exam focus point</td>
<td>The political risks of investing overseas may be examined in a number of ways. Discussion of the risks may be part of a longer question involving a numerical analysis of an overseas investment. Alternatively political risks may be examined as a shorter optional question or part of one.</td>
</tr>
</table>

12 Litigation risks

Litigation risks can be reduced by keeping abreast of changes, acting as a good corporate citizen and lobbying.

12.1 Legal impacts

Companies may face government legislation or action in any jurisdiction that extend over its whole range of activities. Important areas may include:

(a) **Export and import controls** for political, environmental, or health and safety reasons. Such controls may not be overt but instead take the form of bureaucratic procedures designed to discourage international trade or protect home producers.

(b) **Favourable trade status** for particular countries, eg EU membership, former Commonwealth countries.

(c) **Monopolies and mergers legislation**, which may be interpreted not only within a country but also across nations. Thus the acquisition of a company in country A, by company B, which both sell in country C may be seen as a monopolistic restraint of trade.

(d) **Law of ownership.** Especially in developing countries, there may be legislation requiring local majority ownership of a firm or its subsidiary in that country, for example.

(e) **Acceptance of international trademark, copyright and patent conventions.** Not all countries recognise such international conventions.

(f) Determination of minimum **technical standards** that the goods must meet eg noise levels, contents and so on.

(g) **Standardisation measures** such as packaging sizes.

(h) **Pricing regulations**, including credit (eg, some countries require importers to deposit payment in advance and may require the price to be no lower than those of domestic competitors).

(i) **Restrictions on promotional messages**, methods and media.

(j) **Product liability.** Different countries have different rules regarding product liability (ie the manufacturer's/retailer's responsibility for defects in the product sold and/or injury caused). US juries are notoriously generous in this respect.

Bear in mind that organisations may also face legal risks from lack of legislation (or lack of enforcement of legislation) designed to protect them.

12.2 Dealing with legal risks

12.2.1 Consequences of non-compliance

Businesses that fail to comply with the law run the risk of **legal penalties** and accompanying **bad publicity**. Companies may also be forced into legal action to counter claims of allegedly bad practice that is not actually illegal.

The issues of legal standards and costs have very significant implications for companies that trade internationally. Companies that meet a strict set of standards in one country may face accusations of **hypocrisy** if their practices are laxer elsewhere. Ultimately higher costs of compliance, as well as costs of labour may mean that companies **relocate** to countries where costs and regulatory burdens are lower.

12.2.2 The legislative process

Policy in many areas only changes slowly over time. Industries and organisations must however be alert for **likely changes in policy.**

Businesses also need to consider the impact of changes in how powers are **devolved** outside central government. In America state legislatures have been described as 'the forum for the ideas of the nation'. Directly elected mayors also wield considerable power in major cities.

12.2.3 Good citizenship

One aspect of minimising problems from governmental intervention is social and commercial good citizenship, **complying with best practice** and being responsive to **ethical concerns**. Often what is considered good practice at present is likely to acquire some regulatory force in the future. In addition, compliance with voluntary codes, particularly those relating to best practice or relations with consumers, can be **marketed positively**.

12.2.4 Other steps

Companies may wish to take all possible steps to avoid the bad publicity resulting from a court action. This includes implementing systems to make sure that the company **keeps abreast** of **changes in the law**, and staff are kept fully informed. Internal procedures may be designed to minimise the risks from legal action, for example **human resource policies** that minimise the chances of the company suffering an adverse judgement in a case brought by a disgruntled ex-employee. Contracts may be drawn up requiring **binding arbitration** in the case of disputes.

Of course compliance with legislation may involve **extra costs**, including the extra procedures and investment necessary to conform to safety standards, staff training costs and legal costs. However these costs may also act as a **significant barrier to entry**, benefiting companies that are already in the industry.

13 Cultural risks

FAST FORWARD

> **Cultural risks** affect the products and services produced and the way organisations are managed and staffed. Businesses should take cultural issues into account when deciding where to sell abroad, and how much to **centralise** activities.

13.1 Challenges of different cultures

Where a business trades with, or invests in, a foreign country additional uncertainty is introduced by the existence of different customs, laws and language. Communication between parties can be hindered, and potential deals put into jeopardy by ignorance of the expected manner in which such transactions should be conducted.

The following areas may be particularly important.

(a) The **cultures and practices of customers** and consumers in individual markets

(b) The **media and distribution systems** in overseas markets

(c) The **different ways of doing business** (eg it is reputed that Japanese companies are concerned to avoid excessive legalism) in overseas markets

(d) The degree to which **national cultural differences matter** for the product concerned (a great deal for some consumer products, eg washing machines where some countries prefer front-loading machines and others prefer top-loading machines, but less so for products such as gas turbines)

(e) The degree to which a firm can use its own '**national culture'** as a selling point

13.2 Dealing with cultural risk

13.2.1 Deciding which markets to enter

Making the right choices about which markets to enter is a key element in dealing with cultural risk. When deciding what types of country it should enter (in terms of environmental factors, economic development, language used, cultural similarities and so on), the major criteria for this decision should be as follows.

(a) **Market attractiveness**. This concerns such indicators as GNP/head and forecast demand.

(b) **Competitive advantage**. This is principally dependent on prior experience in similar markets, language and cultural understanding.

(c) **Risk**. This involves an analysis of political stability, the possibility of government intervention and similar external influences.

Some products are extremely sensitive to the **environmental differences**, which bring about the need for adaptation; others are not at all sensitive to these differences, in which case standardisation is possible.

Environmentally sensitive	Environmentally insensitive
Adaptation necessary	Standardisation possible
• Fashion clothes	• Industrial and agricultural products
• Convenience foods	• World market products, eg jeans

13.2.2 Use of control systems

Local conditions and the scale of operations will influence the organisation structure of companies trading internationally. Conglomerates with widely differing product groups may organise globally by product, with each operating division having its own geographic structure suited to its own needs.

Companies with more integrated operations may prefer their top-level structure to be broken down **geographically** with product management conducted locally.

Very large and complex companies may be organised as a **heterarchy,** an organic structure with significant local control.

(a) **Some headquarters functions are diffused geographically**. For example, R&D might be in the UK, marketing in the US. Some central functions might be split up: many firms are experimenting with having several centres for R&D.

(b) **Subsidiary managers have a strategic role for the corporation as a whole** (eg through bargaining and coalition forming).

(c) **Co-ordination is achieved through corporate culture and shared values** rather than a formal hierarchy. Employees with long experience might have worked in a number of different product divisions.

(d) **Alliances** can be formed with other company parts and other firms, perhaps in joint ventures or consortia.

13.2.3 Management of human resources

The balance between local and expatriate staff must be managed. There are a number of influences.

- The availability of technical skills such as financial management
- The need for control
- The importance of product and company experience
- The need to provide promotion opportunities
- Costs associated with expatriates such as travel and higher salaries
- Cultural factors

For an international company, which has to think globally as well as act locally, there are a number of problems.

- Do you employ mainly **expatriate staff** to control local operations?
- Do you employ **local managers**, with the possible loss of central control?
- Is there such a thing as the **global manager**, equally at home in different cultures?

Expatriate staff are sometimes favoured over local staff.

(a) Poor **educational opportunities** in the market may require the import of skilled technicians and managers. For example, expatriates have been needed in many western firms' operations in Russia and Eastern Europe, simply because they understand the importance of profit.

(b) Some senior managers believe that a business run by expatriates is easier to **control** than one run by local staff.

(c) Expatriates might be better able than locals to **communicate** with the corporate centre.

(d) The expatriate may **know more about the firm** overall, which is especially important if he or she is fronting a sales office.

The use of expatriates in overseas markets has certain disadvantages.

(a) They **cost** more (eg subsidised housing, school fees).

(b) **Culture shock**. The expatriate may fail to adjust to the culture (eg by associating only with other expatriates). This is likely to lead to poor management effectiveness, especially if the business requires personal contact.

(c) A substantial training programme might be needed.

    (i) **Basic facts** about the country will be given with basic language training, and some briefings about cultural differences.

    (ii) **Immersion training** involves detailed language and cultural training and simulation of field social and business experiences. This is necessary to obtain an intellectual understanding and practical awareness of the culture.

Employing local managers raises the following issues.

(a) A **glass ceiling** might exist in some companies. Talented local managers may not make it to board level if, most members of the board are drawn from one country.

(b) In some cases, it may be hard for locals to **assimilate** into the **corporate culture**, and this might led to communication problems.

(c) Locals will **have greater knowledge of the country**, but may find it difficult to understand the wider corporate picture.

The following issues may also be important.

(a) **Recruitment and training**. In countries with low levels of literacy, more effort might need to be spent on basic training.

(b) **Career management**. Can overseas staff realistically expect promotion to the firm's highest levels if they do well?

(c) **Appraisal schemes**. These can be a minefield at the best of times, and the possibilities for communications failure are endless. For example, in some cultures, an appraisal is a two way discussion whereas in others arguing back might be considered a sign of insubordination.

(d)   Problems associated with the **status of women**.

(e)   **Communications**. Human resources management tries to mobilise employees' commitment to the goals of the organisation. In far-flung global firms, the normal panoply of staff newsletters and team briefings may be hard to institute but are vital. Time differences also make communication difficult.

14 Agency issues

Agency issues can be observed in all types and at all levels of organisations for example between managers at headquarters and managers of subsidiaries. These issues can be addressed by a bundle of corporate governance mechanisms.

14.1 Agency problems in multinational companies

We have already studied in Chapter 3a of this text the **agency problem** between **shareholders** and **managers**. However, these are not the only kinds of dyadic agency relationships. In fact, agency relationships are fairly general and can be observed in all types and levels of organisations. For example, **agency relationships** exist between the CEOs of conglomerates (the principals) and the strategic business unit (SBU) managers that report to these CEOs (agents). The interests of the individual SBU managers may be **incongruent** not only with the interests of the CEOs, but also with those of the other SBU managers. Each SBU manager may try to make sure his or her unit gets access to **critical resources** and achieves the **best performance** at the expense of the performance of other SBUs and the whole organization.

Similarly, **agency relationships** exist between the **managers** at the **headquarters** of **multinational corporations (principals)** and the managers that run the **subsidiaries** of **multinational corporations (agents)**. The **agency relationships** are created between the headquarters and subsidiaries of multinational corporations because, the interests of the managers at the headquarters who are responsible for the performance of the whole organization can be considerably different from the interests of the managers that run the subsidiaries.

The incongruence of interests between the multinationals' headquarters and subsidiaries can arise, not only due to concerns that can be seen in any parent-subsidiary relationship, but also due to the fact that the multinationals' headquarters and subsidiaries operate in different cultures and have divergent backgrounds.

Finally, similar to what we observe in shareholder-manager relationships, the subsidiary managers in the headquarters-subsidiary relationships are monitored and bonded via bundles of **subsidiary specific corporate governance mechanisms**, so that the **agency costs** are **minimised**. These **subsidiary specific bundles** of **monitoring** and **bonding contracts** represent the **headquarters-subsidiary corporate governance relationships**.

It is also possible that the **corporate governance** mechanisms that make-up the bundles that represent corporate governance relationships are institutions that are **internal** to the firm, such as

- The board of directors
- Large outside shareholders
- Mutual monitoring among managers
- Managerial share ownership
- Managerial compensation packages
- Financial leverage

Other mechanisms involve institutions that are external to the firm, such as

- Capital market
- Market for corporate control
- External managerial labour market
- Product market

14.2 Solutions to the agency problems in multinational companies

14.2.1 Board of directors

One way of reducing **agency costs** is to separate the **ratification** and **monitoring** of managerial decisions from their **initiation** and **implementation**. Boards of directors, which consist of top level executives of firms and non-executive outside members, are institutions that carry out the role of **ratifying** and **monitoring** the managerial decisions with the help of their **non-executive** outside members.

As is the case with all **corporate governance** mechanisms, monitoring by boards of directors is not without costs. Outsiders on the board may lack the expertise about the firm that the managers of the firm have, therefore, the outsiders may accept unsound managerial proposals and reject sound ones. The outsiders may also lack the incentives to challenge managerial decisions. **Subsidiary boards** of directors have similar characteristics to the **corporate boards** of directors. However, it must be noted that in subsidiary boards the role of outsiders may be played not only by directors that are not affiliated with the parent company or the subsidiary in any way, but also by **directors** that are **employees** of the **parent** but not of the **subsidiary**.

14.2.2 Managerial compensation packages

FAST FORWARD

> **Managerial compensation packages** can be used to reduce **agency costs** in aligning the interests of top executives with shareholders and the interests of subsidiary managers to those of head office.

Top executive incentive systems can reduce **agency costs** and align the interests of the managers to those of the shareholders by making top **executives' pay contingent** upon the **value** they **create** for the **shareholders**. **Value** created for the **shareholders** can be measured by various criteria such as the **growth** in the **firm's market value**, **accounting returns**, **cash flows**, and even **subjective measures**.

Tying managerial compensation to firm value is not without costs. As managers' exposure to firm specific risk increases, the risk averse managers may ask to be compensated at higher levels to make up for the risk they are undertaking.

Managerial compensation packages can be used to align the interests of the **subsidiary managers** to those of the headquarters, too. An additional friction that makes using contingent compensation more costly in subsidiaries is that most subsidiaries of multinational corporations are not publicly traded companies. As a result, market value based standards and rewards can not be used in subsidiary contingent compensation schemes.

14.2.3 Bundles of corporate governance mechanisms as the nexus of contracts

As we have emphasized in our review of each **corporate governance mechanism**, none of the mechanisms operates without costs or frictions. As a result, any single mechanism cannot mitigate the agency problem completely. In order to address the agency problem a firm faces, a **multiple of** these **mechanisms** need to work in **unison**. Another important characteristic of corporate governance mechanisms is that they substitute for and complement each other. The frictions related to each mechanism and substitution effects between mechanisms suggest that the mechanisms do not operate independently (i.e., their effects are not additive), rather the mechanisms work as **bundles of mechanisms** in reducing the **agency costs**.

Finally, we can say that the bundles of corporate governance mechanisms are the **nexus of contracts**, which align the interests of the shareholders and the managers in the public corporation and the interests of the headquarters and the subsidiaries in the multinational corporation. Therefore, the bundles of corporate governance mechanisms represent **shareholder-manager** and **parent-subsidiary corporate governance relationships**.

Chapter Roundup

- Multinational enterprises undertake foreign direct investment (FDI) for reasons including obtaining cost and revenue advantages, tax considerations and process specialisation.

- FDI can stimulate economic activity in the host country, but it can also lead to a loss of political and economic sovereignty.

- There are many strategic reasons for engaging in foreign investment which include seeking new markets for goods, new sources of raw materials, production efficiency, expertise and political safety.

- Commonly used means to establish an **interest abroad** include:

    - Joint ventures
    - Licensing agreements
    - Management contracts
    - Branches

    - Subsidiaries

- World output of goods and services will increase if countries specialise in the production of goods/services in which they have a comparative advantage and trade to obtain other goods and services.

- Business enterprises are now also becoming increasingly 'internationalised' by the development of multinational activities beyond pure import and export trade.

- Justifications for protection include prevention of the import of cheap goods and dumping, and protection of infant or declining industries.

- Free trade can lead to greater competition and efficiency, and achieve better economic growth worldwide.

- The World Trade Organisation (WTO) is a global international organisation dealing with the rules of trade between nations.

- The IMF was set up partly with the role of providing finance for any countries with temporary balance of payments deficits.

- The World Bank and the IDA have tried to provide long-term finance for developing countries, to help them to continue developing.

- The globalisation of the financial markets has facilitated the transfer of funds to emerging markets but it has contributed to financial instability.

- European Monetary System (EMS) reduces exchange dealing costs and enhances economic policies, but limits the ability of governments to pursue independent economic policies.

- **Multinational companies** need to develop a **financial planning framework** in order to make sure that the strategic objectives and competitive advantages are realised. Such a financial **planning framework** will include ways of raising **capital** and **risks** related to overseas operations and the **repatriation of profits**.

- Multinational companies will have access to international debt, such as **Eurobonds**.

- When a company decides to raise funds from the local equity markets, the company must comply with the requirements of the local exchanges for listing.

- Multinationals can take various measures to combat the risks of political **interference** or **turbulence** including agreements with governments, insurance, and location elsewhere of key parts of the production process.

- Multinationals can **counter exchange controls** by management charges or royalties.

- The methods of financing overseas subsidiaries will depend on the **length of investment period** envisaged, also the **local finance costs**, **taxation systems** and **restrictions on dividend remittances**.

- **Litigation risks** can be reduced by keeping abreast of changes, acting as a good corporate citizen and lobbying.

- **Cultural risks** affect the products and services produced and the way organisations are managed and staffed. Businesses should take cultural issues into account when deciding where to sell abroad, and how much to **centralise** activities.

- **Agency issues** can be observed in all types and at all levels of organisations for example between managers at headquarters and managers of subsidiaries. These issues can be addressed by a bundle of corporate governance mechanisms.

- **Managerial compensation packages** can be used to reduce **agency costs** in aligning the interests of top executives with shareholders and the interests of subsidiary managers to those of head office.

Quick Quiz

1   Define a multinational enterprise.

2   What is meant by the law of comparative advantage?

3   What is meant by:
    (a)   a free trade area
    (b)   a customs union
    (c)   a common market

4   Assume that two small countries, X and Y, produce two commodities P and Q, and that there are no transport costs. One unit of resource in Country X produces 4 units of P or 8 units of Q. One unit of resource is Country Y produces 1 unit of P or 3 units of Q. Which of the following statements is true?

    A   Country X has an absolute advantage over Country Y in producing P and Q, and so will not trade.
    B   Country X does not have an absolute advantage over Country Y in producing P and Q.
    C   Country Y has a comparative advantage over Country X in producing Q.
    D   Country X has a comparative advantage over Country Y in producing both P and Q.

5   How do deflationary measures help to eliminate a balance of payments deficit?

6   **Fill in the blank.** _____ are countries with lenient tax rules or low tax rates, often designed to attract foreign investment.

7   What according to Eiteman, Stonehill and Moffett are the five main strategic reasons for undertaking foreign direct investment?

8   Give three examples of barriers to entry that multinationals might face.

9   Forward integration would involve acquiring final production and distribution facilities in other countries.
    True   ☐
    False ☐

10 What principal characteristics is a tax haven most likely to have?

11 Why might a firm looking to establish an overseas presence choose to set up a branch rather than a subsidiary?

12 What are the main differences between a contractual joint venture and a joint-equity venture?

Answers to Quick Quiz

1   A multinational enterprise is one which has a physical presence or property interests in more than one country.

2   The law of comparative advantage or comparative costs states that two countries can gain from trade when each specialises in the industries in which it has the lowest opportunity costs.

3   A free trade area exists when there is no restriction on trade between countries. This is extended into a customs union when common external tariffs are levied on imports from non-member countries. A common market adds free movement of the factors of production, including labour and may harmonise economic policy.

4   C. Country Y has a comparative advantage over country X in producing Q.

5   Domestic deflation cuts demand including demand for imports. Industry is therefore encouraged to switch to export markets.

6   Tax havens

7   Market; Raw material; Production efficiency; Knowledge; Political safety

8   Any three of: Product differentiation barriers; Absolute cost barriers; Economy of scale barriers; Fixed costs; Legal barriers

9   True

10   (a)   Tax on foreign investment or sales income earned by resident companies, and withholding tax on dividends paid to parent should be low

       (b)   Stable government and stable currency

       (c)   Adequate financial service support facilities

11   (a)   More favourable tax (not subject to withholding tax)
       (b)   Fewer legal formalities

12   A contractual joint venture is for a fixed period, duties and responsibilities are defined in a contract
       A joint-equity venture involves investment, is of no fixed duration and continually evolves.

> Now try the question below from the Exam Question Bank

Number	Level	Marks	Time
6	Introductory	12	20 mins
7	Examination	19	34 mins

Advanced investment appraisal

5

Discounted cash flow techniques

Topic list	Syllabus reference
1 Net present value	C (1) (a)
2 Monte Carlo simulation and investment appraisal	C (1) (b)
3 Internal rate of return	C (1) (c)
4 Comparison of NPV and IRR	C (1) (c)
5 Modified internal rate of return (MIRR)	C (1) (c)

Introduction

In this chapter we discuss two criteria for investment appraisal, the net present value (NPV) and the internal rate of return (IRR). A number of issues related to the two criteria are explored, such as inflation and taxation effects and Monte Carlo simulation.

Study guide

		Intellectual level
C1	**Discounted cash flow techniques**	
(a)	Evaluate the potential value added to an organisation arising from a specified capital investment project or portfolio using the net present value (NPV) model. Project modelling should include explicit treatment of:	3
	(i) Inflation and specific price variation	
	(ii) Taxation including capital allowances and tax exhaustion	
	(iii) Single period capital rationing and multi-period capital rationing. Multi-period capital rationing to include the formulation of programming methods and the interpretation of their output	
	(iv) Probability analysis and sensitivity analysis when adjusting for risk and uncertainty in investment appraisal	
	(v) Risk adjusted discount rates	
(b)	Outline the application of Monte Carlo simulation to investment appraisal. Candidates will not be expected to undertake simulations in an examination context but will be expected to demonstrate an understanding of:	2
	(i) Simple model design	
	(ii) The different types of distribution controlling the key variables within the simulation	
	(iii) The significance of the simulation output and the assessment of the likelihood of project success.	
	(iv) The measurement and interpretation of project value at risk	
(c)	Establish the potential economic return (using internal rate of return and modified internal rate of return) and advise on a project's return margin. Discuss the relative merits of NPV and IRR	3

Exam Guide

Discounted cash flow techniques may arise as a means of solving part of a larger problem in the exam. A previous question required candidates to recommend procedures for the appraisal of capital investment projects from the point of view of a senior financial manager, including the provision of advice on a project and its likely impact on the company.

One of the optional performance objectives in your PER is the evaluation of potential business/investment opportunities. This chapter covers some of the most popular methods of investment appraisal – NPV, IRR and MIRR – which you can regularly put into practice in the real world.

1 Net present value   12/10, 6/12

This section covers material that should be familiar to you from previous studies. It is however important that you revise this section as net present value is a fundamental investment appraisal technique.

FAST FORWARD

> Projects with a positive net present value should be undertaken.

The **net present value (NPV)** of a project is the sum of the discounted cash flows less the initial investment.

Question

NPV calculations

Project X requires an immediate investment of $150,000 and will generate net cash inflows of $60,000 for the next three years. The project's discount rate is 7%. If net present value is used to appraise the project, should Project X be undertaken?

Answer

Time	Cash Flow	Discount Factor	Present Value
0	−150,000	1	−150,000
1	60,000	0.935	56,100
2	60,000	0.873	52,380
3	60,000	0.816	48,960
			7,440

The NPV of this project is $7,440. As NPV is positive, Project X should be undertaken as it will increase shareholders' wealth.

Exam focus point

NPV with taxation and foreign currency complications was examined as part of a 30-mark compulsory question in December 2008. Deciding on a cost of capital to use for NPV calculations was examined in June 2012.

1.1 NPV and shareholder wealth maximisation

The main advantage of the NPV method is that it evaluates projects in the same way as shareholders would do – that is, it focuses on how individual projects would affect shareholders' wealth. Only those projects with a **positive** NPV are accepted, meaning that only those projects that will **increase** shareholders' wealth will be undertaken.

1.2 The effect of inflation

FAST FORWARD

Inflation is present in all economies and must be accounted for when evaluating projects.

Key terms

Real cash flows have had the effects of inflation removed and should be discounted using the **real discount rate**. **Nominal cash flows** include the effects of inflation and should be discounted using the **nominal discount rate**.

The above example (*NPV calculations*) assumes that net cash flows do not change from year to year. This is unrealistic, given the existence of inflation. It is important to take proper account of inflation when undertaking investment appraisal as it could change the NPV of the project and ultimately the decision as to whether the project should be accepted.

NPV calculations can be carried out using either **real** or **nominal** cash flows.

1.2.1 Real and nominal interest rates

The **real interest rate** has removed the effects of inflation and represents purchasing power (it is really the nominal interest rate 'deflated' to take out the effects of inflation). When the nominal rate of interest **exceeds** the rate of inflation, the real interest rate will be **positive**. If the nominal rate of interest **is less than** the rate of inflation, the real interest rate will be **negative**.

$(1 + i) = (1 + r)(1 + h)$

Where   i = nominal (money) rate
      r = real rate
      h = inflation rate

This is known as the **Fisher equation**.

Question
Nominal discount factor

If the real rate of interest is 5% and the expected inflation is 3% what is the nominal return?

Answer

$(1 + i) = (1 + 0.05)(1 + 0.03) = 1.0815$

The nominal rate is therefore 8.15%.

1.2.2 Real rate or nominal rate?

The rule is as follows.

(a)   We use the **nominal** rate if cash flows are expressed in **actual numbers of dollars** that will be received or paid at various future dates (remember: 'money at money').

(b)   We use the real rate if cash flows are expressed in **constant price terms** (that is, in terms of their value at time 0). Remember: 'real at real'.

1.2.3 Advantages and misuses of real values and a real rate of return

Although generally companies should discount money values at the nominal cost of capital, there are some advantages of using real values discounted at a real cost of capital.

(a)   When all costs and benefits rise at the same rate of price inflation, **real values** are the **same as current day values**, so that **no further adjustments** need be made to cash flows before discounting. In contrast, when nominal values are discounted at the nominal cost of capital, the **prices** in **future years** must be **calculated** before discounting can begin.

(b)   The government might prefer to set a real return as a target for investments, as being more suitable than a commercial money rate of return.

Question
Effect of inflation

Rice is considering a project which would cost $5,000 now. The annual benefits, for four years, would be a fixed income of $2,500 a year, plus other savings of $500 a year in year 1, rising by 5% each year because of inflation. Running costs will be $1,000 in the first year, but would increase at 10% each year because of inflating labour costs. The general rate of inflation is expected to be 7½% and the company's required money rate of return is 16%. Is the project worthwhile? (Ignore taxation.)

Answer

The cash flows at inflated values are as follows.

Year	Fixed income	Other savings	Running costs	Net cash flow
	$	$	$	$
1	2,500	500	1,000	2,000
2	2,500	525	1,100	1,925
3	2,500	551	1,210	1,841
4	2,500	579	1,331	1,748

The NPV of the project is as follows.

Year	Cash flow	Discount factor	PV
	$	16%	$
0	(5,000)	1.000	(5,000)
1	2,000	0.862	1,724
2	1,925	0.743	1,430
3	1,841	0.641	1,180
4	1,748	0.552	965
			+ 299

The NPV is positive and the project would appear to be worthwhile.

1.2.4 Expectations of inflation and the effects of inflation

When managers evaluate a particular project, or when shareholders evaluate their investments, they can only guess at what the rate of inflation is going to be. Their expectations will probably be wrong, at least to some extent, because it is extremely difficult to forecast the rate of inflation accurately. The only way in which uncertainty about inflation can be allowed for in project evaluation is by risk and uncertainty analysis.

Costs and benefits may rise at levels different from the general rate of inflation: inflation may be **general,** affecting prices of all kinds, or **specific** to particular prices. Generalised inflation has the following effects.

(a) Since **non-current assets, inventories** and **other working capital** will **increase in money value**, the same quantities of assets or working capital must be financed by **increasing amounts of capital**.

(b) Inflation means higher costs and higher selling prices. The effect of higher prices on demand is not necessarily easy to predict. A company that raises its prices by 10% because the general rate of inflation is running at 10% might suffer a serious fall in demand.

(c) Inflation, because it affects financing needs, is also likely to affect gearing, and so the cost of capital.

1.3 Allowing for taxation

FAST FORWARD

In investment appraisal, tax is often assumed to be payable **one year in arrears,** but you should read the question details carefully.

Tax allowable depreciation details should be checked in any question you attempt.

Typical assumptions which may be stated in questions are as follows.

(a) An assumption about the timing of payments will have to be made.

    (i) Half the tax is **payable** in the **same year** in which the **profits are earned** and **half in the following year.** This reflects the fact that large companies have to pay tax **quarterly** in some regimes.

(ii)   Tax is payable in the **year following** the one in which the taxable profits are made. Thus, if a project increases taxable profits by $10,000 in year 2, there will be a tax payment, assuming tax at (say) 30%, of $3,000 in year 3.

(iii)   Tax is payable in the **same year** that the **profits arise.**

The question should make clear what assumptions you should use.

(b)   Net cash flows from a project should be considered as the taxable profits arising from the project (unless an indication is given to the contrary).

1.3.1 Tax-allowable depreciation

Tax allowable depreciation is used to reduce taxable profits, and the consequent reduction in a tax payment should be treated as a cash saving arising from the acceptance of a project.

For example, suppose tax-allowable depreciation is allowed on the cost of **plant and machinery** at the rate of 25% on a **reducing balance** basis. Thus if a company purchases plant costing $80,000, the subsequent writing down allowances would be as follows.

Year		Tax-allowable depreciation	Reducing balance
		$	$
1	(25% of cost)	20,000	60,000
2	(25% of RB)	15,000	45,000
3	(25% of RB)	11,250	33,750
4	(25% of RB)	8,438	25,312

When the plant is eventually sold, the difference between the sale price and the reducing balance amount at the time of sale will be treated as:

(a)   A taxable profit if the sale price exceeds the reducing balance, and

(b)   A tax-allowable loss if the reducing balance exceeds the sale price

The cash saving on the tax-allowable depreciation (or the cash payment for the charge) is calculated by multiplying the depreciation (or charge) by the tax rate.

Assumptions about tax-allowable depreciation could be simplified in an exam question. For example, you might be told that tax-allowable depreciation can be claimed at the rate of 25% of cost on a straight line basis (that is, over four years).

There are two possible assumptions about the time when tax-allowable depreciation start to be claimed.

(a)   It can be assumed that the **first claim** occurs at the **start of the project** (at year 0).

(b)   Alternatively it can be assumed that the **first claim** occurs **later in the first year**.

You should state clearly which assumption you have made. Assumption (b) is more prudent, but assumption (a) is also perfectly feasible. It is very likely, however that an examination question will indicate which of the two assumptions is required.

1.3.2 Example: taxation

A company is considering whether or not to purchase an item of machinery costing $40,000 in 20X5. It would have a life of four years, after which it would be sold for $5,000. The machinery would create annual cost savings of $14,000.

The machinery would attract tax-allowable depreciation of 25% on the reducing balance basis which could be claimed against taxable profits of the current year, which is soon to end. A balancing allowance or charge would arise on disposal. The tax rate is 30%. Tax is payable half in the current year, half one year in arrears. The after-tax cost of capital is 8%.

Should the machinery be purchased?

Solution

Tax-allowable depreciation is first claimed against year 0 profits.

Cost: $40,000

Year	Tax-allowable depreciation $	Reducing balance (RB) $	
(0) 20X5 (25% of cost)	10,000	30,000	(40,000 – 10,000)
(1) 20X6 (25% of RB)	7,500	22,500	(30,000 – 7,500)
(2) 20X7 (25% of RB)	5,625	16,875	(22,500 – 5,625)
(3) 20X8 (25% of RB)	4,219	12,656	(16,875 – 4,219)
(4) 20X9 (25% of RB)	3,164	9,492	(12,656 – 3,164)

	$
Sale proceeds, end of fourth year	5,000
Less reducing balance, end of fourth year	9,492
Balancing allowance	4,492

Having calculated the depreciation each year, the tax savings can be computed. The year of the cash flow is one year after the year for which the allowance is claimed.

Year of claim	Tax-allowable depreciation $	Tax saved $	Year of tax payment/saving (50% in each)
0	10,000	3,000	0/1
1	7,500	2,250	1/2
2	5,625	1,688	2/3
3	4,219	1,266	3/4
4	7,656	2,297	4/5
	35,000 *		

* Net cost $(40,000 – 5,000) = $35,000

These tax savings relate to tax-allowable depreciation. We must also calculate the extra tax payments on annual savings of $14,000.

The net cash flows and the NPV are now calculated as follows.

Year	Equip-ment $	Savings $	Tax on savings $	Tax saved on tax-allowable depreciation $	Net cash flow $	Discount factor 8%	Present value of cash flow $
0	(40,000)			1,500	(38,500)	1.000	(38,500)
1		14,000	(2,100)	2,625	14,525	0.926	13,450
2		14,000	(4,200)	1,969	11,769	0.857	10,086
3		14,000	(4,200)	1,477	11,277	0.794	8,954
4	5,000	14,000	(4,200)	1,782	16,582	0.735	12,188
5			(2,100)	1,148	(952)	0.681	(648)
							5,530

The NPV is positive and so the purchase appears to be worthwhile.

1.3.3 An alternative and quicker method of calculating tax payments or savings

In the above example, the tax computations could have been combined, as follows.

Year	0	1	2	3	4
	$	$	$	$	$
Cost savings	0	14,000	14,000	14,000	14,000
Tax-allowable depreciation	10,000	7,500	5,625	4,219	7,656
Taxable profits	(10,000)	6,500	8,375	9,781	6,344
Tax at 30%	3,000	(1,950)	(2,512)	(2,934)	(1,903)

The net cash flows would then be as follows.

Year	Equipment	Savings	Tax	Net cash flow
	$	$	$	$
0	(40,000)		1,500	(38,500)
1		14,000	525	14,525
2		14,000	(2,231)	11,769
3		14,000	(2,723)	11,277
4	5,000	14,000	(2,418)	16,582
5			(952)	(952)

The net cash flows are exactly the same as calculated previously.

1.3.4 Taxation and DCF

The effect of taxation on capital budgeting is theoretically quite simple. Organisations must pay tax, and the effect of undertaking a project will be to increase or decrease tax payments each year. These incremental tax cash flows should be included in the cash flows of the project for discounting to arrive at the project's NPV.

When **taxation is ignored** in the DCF calculations, the discount rate will **reflect the pre-tax rate of return** required on capital investments. When taxation is included in the cash flows, a **post-tax required rate of return** should be used.

If there is inflation and tax in a question, remember that tax flows do not get inflated by an extra year even though they may be paid one year later.

Question	Effect of taxation

A project requires an initial investment in machinery of $300,000. Additional cash inflows of $120,000 at current price levels are expected for three years, at the end of which time the machinery will be scrapped. The machinery will attract tax-allowable depreciation of 25% on the reducing balance basis, which can be claimed against taxable profits of the current year, which is soon to end. A balancing charge or allowance will arise on disposal.

The tax rate is 50% and tax is payable 50% in the current year, 50% one year in arrears. The pre-tax cost of capital is 22% and the rate of inflation is 10%. Assume that the project is 100% debt financed.

Required

Assess whether the project should be undertaken.

Answer

Post-tax: Year	Purchase $	Inflation factor	Cash flow after inflation $	Tax on cash inflow $	(W1-3) Tax saved on tax-allowable depreciation $	Net cash flow $	Discount factor 11%	Present value $
0	(300,000)	1.000	(300,000)		18,750	(281,250)	1.000	(281,250)
1		1.100	132,000	(33,000)	32,813	131,813	0.901	118,764
2		1.210	145,200	(69,300)	24,609	100,509	0.812	81,613
3		1.331	159,720	(76,230)	42,187	125,677	0.731	91,870
4				(39,930)	31,640	(8,290)	0.659	(5,463)
							NPV =	5,534

The project should be undertaken at least from the financial viewpoint.

Workings

1   *Tax-allowable depreciation* (Initial cost $300,000)

Year		Tax-allowable depreciation $	Reducing balance (RB) $
0	(25% at cost)	75,000	225,000
1	(25% of RB)	56,250	168,750
2	(25% of RB)	42,188	126,562
3	(25% of RB)	31,641	94,921

2   *Balancing allowance*

	$
Sale proceeds, end of third year	–
RB, end of third year	94,921
Balancing allowance	94,921

3   *Tax saved on tax-allowable depreciation*

Year of claim	Tax-allowable depreciation claimed $	Tax saved $	Year of tax saving
0	75,000	37,500	0/1
1	56,250	28,125	1/2
2	42,188	21,094	2/3
3	126,562	63,281	3/4
	300,000		

1.4 Tax exhaustion

FAST FORWARD

Capital allowances in the form of **first-year allowances** or **writing down allowances** determine the tax liabilities and after tax earnings.

In most tax systems, capital expenditure is set off against tax liabilities so as to reduce the taxes a company pays and to encourage investment. These **capital allowances** take two forms; **first year allowances** which are set off against tax liabilities in the year the investment takes place and **writing down allowances** which are set off against tax liabilities in subsequent years.

The effect of capital allowances can be from the definition of after-tax – earnings

After tax earnings = Earnings before tax – Tax liability

Where tax liability = tax rate × (Earnings before tax – capital allowances)

There will be circumstances when the capital allowances in a particular year will equal or exceed before tax earnings. In such a case the company will pay no tax. In most tax systems unused capital allowances can be carried forward indefinitely, so that the capital allowance that is set off against the tax liability in any one year includes not only the writing down allowance for the particular year but also any unused allowances from previous years.

Question

Capital allowances

Suppose that a company has invested $10 million in a plant. The first year allowance is 40 percent, whereas the remaining amount is written down over a period of four years. The tax rate is 30 percent. Earnings before tax over a five year period are as follows:

Year 1	Year 2	Year 3	Year 4	Year 5
$m	$m	$m	$m	$m
3	2.5	3.5	3.8	4.2

(a)   Calculate the tax liability every year and the after-tax earnings.
(b)   Calculate the impact on earnings if the first year allowance is 60 percent

Answer

(a)   The first year allowance is 0.4 x $10 = $4m

Since the capital allowance exceeds the earnings before tax, the tax liability is 0 and the unused capital allowance of $1m will be added to the second year writing down allowance of 0.6 x$10m/4 = $1.5m to yield a capital allowance for year 2 of $2.5m. The capital allowance is the same as the before tax earnings and the tax liability is again zero. However this time there is no unused capital allowance to be carried forward.

Capital allowance in each year are shown below

	Year 1	Year 2	Year 3	Year 4	Year 5
	$m	$m	$m	$m	$m
Earnings before tax	3	2.5	3.5	3.8	4.2
First year allowance	4				
Unused capital allowance brought forward		1.0	0		
Writing down allowance		1.5	1.5	1.5	1.5
Total allowance	$4m	$2.5m	$1.5m	$1.5m	$1.5m

The tax liability for every year and the after tax earnings are shown in the table below

	Year 1	Year 2	Year 3	Year 4	Year 5
	$m	$m	$m	$m	$m
Tax liability	0	0.0	0.600	0.690	0.810
After-tax-earnings	3	2.5	2.900	3.110	3.390

(b)   When the first year allowance is 60 percent, the capital allowances are larger in the first three years but lower in the subsequent two years.

	Year 1	Year 2	Year 3	Year 4	Year 5
	$m	$m	$m	$m	$m
Earnings before tax	3	2.5	3.5	3.8	4.2
First year allowance	6				
Unused capital allowance brought forward		3.0	1.5	0.0	0
Writing down allowance		1.0	1.0	1.0	1
Total allowance	6	4.0	2.5	1.0	1

The tax liability for every year and the after tax earnings are shown in the table below

	Year 1 $m	Year 2 $m	Year 3 $m	Year 4 $m	Year 5 $m
Tax liability	0	0.0	0.300	0.840	0.960
After-tax earnings	3	2.5	3.200	2.960	3.240

After tax earnings are affected by the pattern of writing down allowances.

1.5 Multi-period capital rationing

FAST FORWARD

Capital rationing problems exist when there are insufficient funds available to finance all available profitable projects.

Capital rationing may occur due to internal factors (**soft** capital rationing) or external factors (**hard** capital rationing).

When capital rationing is present across **multiple periods**, linear programming may be used to solve the problem of **which projects** to undertake.

Knowledge brought forward from earlier studies

Hard and soft capital rationing

Soft capital rationing may arise for such reasons as:

(a) Management may be **reluctant** to **issue additional share capital** because of concerns that this may lead to **outsiders** gaining control of the business.

(b) **Capital expenditure budgets** may restrict spending.

(c) Management may wish to **limit investment** to a level that can be financed solely from retained earnings.

Hard capital rationing may arise for one of the following reasons.

(a) There may be restrictions on bank lending due to government control.

(b) The costs associated with making small **issues** of capital may be too great.

(c) Lending institutions may consider an organisation to be **too risky** to be granted further loan facilities.

For **single period** capital rationing problems, projects are ranked according to the **profitability index**. This gives the shadow price of capital or the maximum rate a company should be prepared to pay to obtain short term funds to release the capital constraint.

Single period capital rationing was recapped in Chapter 1 Section 3.4, refer to this section if you are unsure of the technique.

1.5.1 Introduction

Companies do not have inexhaustible resources therefore it is likely that only limited funds will be available for capital investment in each period. The problem facing financial managers is how best to spend the money in order to meet their objective of maximising shareholders' wealth. This problem can be solved using **linear programming**.

1.5.2 An example

The board of Bazza Inc has approved the following investment expenditure over the next three years.

Year 1	Year 2	Year 3
$16,000	$14,000	$17,000

You have identified four investment opportunities which require different amounts of investment each year, details of which are given below.

		Required investment		Project
Project	Year 1	Year 2	Year 3	NPV
Project 1	7,000	10,000	4,000	8,000
Project 2	9,000	0	12,000	11,000
Project 3	0	6,000	8,000	6,000
Project 4	5,000	6,000	7,000	4,000

Which combination of projects will result in the highest overall NPV whilst remaining within the annual investment constraints?

The problem can be formulated as a linear programming problem as follows.

Let Y1 be investment in project 1
Y2 be investment in project 2
Y3 be investment in project 3
Y4 be investment in project 4

Objective function

Maximise $Y_1 \times 8,000 + Y_2 \times 11,000 + Y_3 \times 6,000 + Y_4 \times 4,000$

Subject to the three annual investment constraints:

$Y_1 \times 7,000 + Y_2 \times 9,000 + Y_3 \times 0 + Y_4 \times 5,000 \leq 16,000$ (Year 1 constraint)
$Y_1 \times 10,000 + Y_2 \times 0 + Y_3 \times 6,000 + Y_4 \times 6,000 \leq 14,000$ (Year 2 constraint)
$Y_1 \times 4,000 + Y_2 \times 12,000 + Y_3 \times 8,000 + Y_4 \times 7,000 \leq 17,000$ (Year 3 constraint)

When the objective function and constraints are fed into a computer programme, the results are:

$Y_1 = 1, Y_2 = 1, Y_3 = 0, Y_4 = 0$

This means that Project 1 and Project 2 will be selected and Project 3 and Project 4 will not. The NPV of the investment scheme will be equal to $19,000.

Note that the solution:

$Y_1 = 0, Y_2 = 0, Y_3 = 1, Y_4 = 1$

also satisfies the constraints. However this is not the optimal solution since the combined NPV of projects 3 and 4 is $10,000 which is lower than the value derived above.

1.6 Risk and uncertainty

Before deciding whether or not to undertake a project, financial managers will want to assess the project's **risk** (which can be predicted), and **uncertainty** (which is unpredictable).

Risk can be built into project appraisal using such tools as **expected values** and different **costs of capital**.

Project duration is a measure of how long it takes to recover approximately **half** of the value of the investment.

1.6.1 Risk

You should already be familiar with how financial managers incorporate risk into project appraisal. The **cost of capital** of a project gives an indication of its risk – the **higher** the cost of capital, the **greater** the risk.

Investors want higher returns for higher risk investments. The greater the risk attached to future returns, the greater the risk premium required. Investors also prefer cash now to later and require a higher return for longer time periods.

In investment appraisal, a **risk-adjusted discount rate** can be used for particular types or **risk classes** of investment projects to reflect their relative risks. For example, a **high discount rate** can be used so that a cash flow which occurs quite some time in the future will have less effect on the decision. Alternatively, with the launch of a new product, a higher **initial** risk premium may be used with a decrease in the discount rate as the product becomes established.

Risk can also be incorporated into project appraisal using **expected values**, whereby each possible outcome is given a probability. The expected value is obtained by multiplying each present value by its probability and adding the results together. The **lower** the expected value, the **higher** the risk.

Question
Expected values

A project has the following possible outcomes, each of which is assigned a probability of occurrence.

	Probability	Present value
		$
Low demand	0.3	20,000
Medium demand	0.6	30,000
High demand	0.1	50,000

What is the expected value of the project?

Answer

The expected value is the sum of each present value multiplied by its probability.

Expected value = (20,000 × 0.3) + (30,000 × 0.6) + (50,000 × 0.1) = $29,000

Question
Expected values 2

What would happen to the expected value of the project if the probability of medium demand fell to 0.4 and the probability of low demand increased to 0.5?

Answer

Expected value = (20,000 × 0.5) + (30,000 × 0.4) + (50,000 × 0.1) = $27,000

The project is more risky than before as there is a greater probability of demand being low, which results in a lower expected value.

1.6.2 Uncertainty

Uncertainty is more difficult to plan, for obvious reasons. There are several ways in which uncertainty can be dealt with in project appraisal. Three of them – **payback period, sensitivity analysis** and **discounted payback** will be familiar to you from earlier studies. Make sure you understand how each of them works.

Example – sensitivity analysis

Nevers Ure has a cost of capital of 8% and is considering a project with the following 'most-likely' cash flows.

Year	Purchase of plant	Running costs	Savings
	$	$	$
0	(7,000)		
1		2,000	6,000
2		2,500	7,000

Required

Measure the sensitivity (in percentages) of the project to changes in the levels of expected costs and savings.

Solution

The PVs of the cash flows are as follows.

Year	Discount factor @ 8%	PV of plant cost $	PV of running costs $	PV of savings $	PV of net cash flow $
0	1.000	(7,000)			(7,000)
1	0.926		(1,852)	5,556	3,704
2	0.857		(2,143)	5,999	3,856
		(7,000)	(3,995)	11,555	560

The project has a positive NPV and would appear to be worthwhile. The changes in cash flows which would need to occur for the project to break even (NPV = 0) are as follows.

(a) Plant costs would need to increase by a PV of $560, that is by:

$$\frac{560}{7,000} \times 100\% = 8\%$$

(b) Running costs would need to increase by a PV of $560, that is by:

$$\frac{560}{3,995} \times 100\% = 14\%$$

(c) Savings would need to fall by a PV of $560, that is by:

$$\frac{560}{11,555} \times 100\% = 4.8\%$$

Weaknesses of sensitivity analysis

These are as follows.

(a) The method requires that **changes** in each key variable are **isolated.** However management is more interested in the combination of the effects of changes in two or more key variables.

(b) Looking at factors in isolation is unrealistic since they are often **interdependent**.

(c) Sensitivity analysis does not examine the **probability** that any particular variation in costs or revenues might occur.

(d) **Critical factors** may be those over which managers have no control.

(e) In itself it does not provide a decision rule. Parameters defining **acceptability** must be laid down by managers.

1.6.3 Project duration

By calculating the project duration, the financial manager will be able to determine how long it will be before approximately 50% of the value of the investment is recovered.

Project duration is calculated by **weighting** each year of the project by the **percentage** of the present value of the cash flows **recovered** in that year.

Question

Monty Inc is considering a project which requires an initial investment of $100,000. Projected cash flows discounted at Monty's cost of capital of 10% are as follows.

Year	0	1	2	3	4	5
Present value	(100,000)	45,455	36,364	26,296	13,660	6,209

Calculate the project duration.

Answer

The first thing we have to do is determine the total cash inflows over the life of the project, which is the sum of the present values of the cash inflows for years 1 to 5.

Total present value of cash inflows = $127,984

The second step is to calculate each present value as a percentage of $127,984.

Year	1	2	3	4	5
Present value	45,455	36,364	26,296	13,660	6,209
Percentage of total PV	36%	28%	21%	11%	4%

Project duration is the sum of the year number multiplied by the relevant percentage

$$= (1 \times 0.36) + (2 \times 0.28) + (3 \times 0.21) + (4 \times 0.11) + (5 \times 0.04)$$
$$= 2.19$$

This means that it takes **approximately** 2.19 years to recover half of the present value of the project. Unlike the payback period, this method looks at the cash flows earned in **every year** of the project, rather than just up to the point where the initial investment is paid back.

2 Monte Carlo simulation and investment appraisal

FAST FORWARD

The Monte Carlo method of estimating a project's NPV assumes that the key factors affecting NPV can be modelled as a probability distribution.

2.1 Monte Carlo method

This section provides a brief outline of the Monte Carlo method in investment appraisal. The method appeared in 1949 and is widely used in situations involving uncertainty. The method amounts to adopting a particular probability distribution for the uncertain (random) variables that affect the NPV and then using simulations to generate values of the random variables.

To deal with uncertainty the Monte Carlo method assumes that the uncertain parameters (such as the growth rate or the cost of capital k) or variables (such as the free cash flow) follow a specific probability distribution.

The basic idea is to generate through simulation thousands of values for the parameters or variables of interest and use those variables to derive the net present value for each possible simulated outcome.

From the resulting values we can derive the distribution of the NPV.

To illustrate the method, assume that a company has a project with an expected cash flow of $2 million after the first year of operation. Cash flows will increase by 5% annually in perpetuity. The cost of capital is 10% and initial investment is $18 million.

The present value of the project can be calculated using the constant growth model covered in section 7.1 above.

$$NPV = \frac{2 \times (1+g)}{(0.1-g)} - 18$$

In our simple example, since the only source of uncertainty is the growth rate, we can assume that the growth rate follows a particular probability distribution. For the sake of simplicity we shall assume that the growth rate follows a normal distribution with a mean of 5 percent and a standard deviation of 3 percent. Our model is thus $g \sim N(5, 3^2)$

The probability distribution of the growth rate is shown in the figure below. The Monte Carlo method works as follows. From the normal distribution we sample 1,000 random values of g. This can be done easily in EXCEL using the random number generator to generate 1,000 random numbers coming from a normal distribution with a mean of 5 and a standard deviation of 3. For each value of g we calculate the NPV from our model.

$$NPV = \frac{2 \times (1+g)}{(0.1-g)} - 18$$

Probability Distribution of Growth Rates

Calculating the NPV for all 1000 random values of g and plotting the resulting values for the NPV we obtain the following distribution of values for the NPV. Whilst the probability distribution of g is normal the distribution of the NPV is not normal. The empirical distribution can be constructed from the table below which shows the cumulative frequency distribution of the NPV

NPV	Cumulative Frequency
<−5.7	1
<−5.1	2
<−4.5	3
<−3.9	4
<−3.4	11
<−2.8	16
<−2.2	29
<−1.6	40
<−1.0	50
<−0.4	76
<0.0	100
<0.7	172
<1.3	217
<1.9	279
<2.5	351
<3.1	417
<3.6	480
<4.2	563
<4.8	628

NPV	Cumulative Frequency
<5.4	689
<6.0	756
<6.5	805
<7.1	846
<7.7	875
<8.3	899
<8.9	929
<9.5	951
<10.0	971
<10.6	981
<11.2	990
<11.8	996
<17.0	1,000
	1,000

The table provide a complete description of the distribution of the NPV of the model we have employed. For example the probability of getting a negative NPV is 10 percent since

Probability (NPV < 0) = $\dfrac{100}{1,000}$ = 0.1.

Similarly the probability of getting a NPV of less than 3.6 is equal to:

$\dfrac{480}{1,000}$ or 48%

The frequency distribution of the net present values resulting from the simulation are shown in the following diagram. The distribution shows that most of the values for the NPV are around 2 and 6 with a mean value of about 4. Statistical measures such as the standard deviation can be calculated to describe the dispersion of prices. The overwhelming conclusion from the analysis is that the NPV of the project under a wide range of assumptions for the growth rate is most likely to be positive.

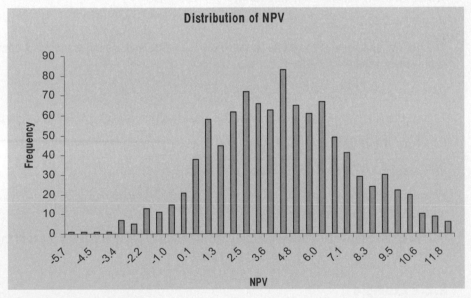

2.2 Project Value at Risk

6/12

The project value at risk is the potential loss of a project with a given probability.

The empirical distribution of the NPV leads naturally to the concept of the project value at risk.

Value at Risk (VAR) is the minimum amount by which the value of an investment or portfolio will fall over a given period of time at a given level of probability. Alternatively it is defined as the maximum amount that it may lose at a given level of confidence. For example we may say that the Value at Risk is $100,000 at 5 percent probability, or that it is $100,000 at 95 percent confidence level. The first definition implies that there is a 5 percent chance that the loss will exceed $100,000, or that we are 95 percent sure that it will not exceed $100,000. VAR can be defined at any level of probability or confidence, but the most common probability levels are 1, 5 and 10 percent.

A formal definition of the VAR of a position where the value of the position is denoted by V is the value V* such that values of V less than V* have a chance of only p to appear. Formally this can be written as Probability (V < V*) =p and is shown below. The probability level is the area under the curve and it can be calculated as the value of the random variable that determines the desired area under the curve.

When the random variable follows the normal distribution, the value at risk at specific probability levels is easily calculated as a multiple of the standard deviation. For example the 5 percent VAR is simply 1.645σ, the 1 percent VAR is 2.33σ.

For example the annual standard deviation of a position is $200,000. The value at risk is 200,000 × 1.645) = $329,000. Only in 5 percent of the cases will the value fall by a larger amount within a year.

The value at risk can be calculated over more that one period by using the standard deviation for the entire period. For example if we assume the life of a project is two years we may calculate the value at risk for a year, or we may calculate the value at risk over two years.

$$V = V_1 + V_2$$

and both V_1 and V_2 have the same variance σ = $200,000 and are independent of each other, then the value at risk will be:

$$VAR = 1.645 \times \$200,000 \times \sqrt{2} = \$465,276$$

That is, there is only a 5 percent chance that losses will exceed the $465,276 over a two year period.

In general the value at risk will be given by:

$$VAR = k\sigma\sqrt{N}$$

Where k is determined by the probability level, σ is the standard deviation and N is the periods over which we want to calculate the value at risk.

Having defined the value at risk, we can define the project value at risk, as the loss that may occur at a given level of probability over the life of the project.

2.2.1 Example

The annual cash flows from a project are expected to follow the normal distribution with a mean of $50,000 and standard deviation of $10,000. The project has a 10 year life. What is the project value at risk?

The project value at risk for a year is:

PVAR = 1.645 × $10,000 = $16,450

The project value at risk that takes into account the entire project life is:

PVAR = 1.645 × $10,000 × $\sqrt{10}$ = $52019, this is the maximum amount by which the value of the project will fall at a confidence level of 95%.

So far we have used the normal distribution to calculate the value at risk. The assumption that project cash flows or values follow the normal distribution may not be plausible. An alternative way is to use the distribution from a Monte Carlo simulation. For example using the previous table we see that the probability of getting a net present value less or lower than −$1 million is 5 percent. So the project value at risk at 5 percent probability is −$1 million for the specific example. According to our notation V* = − 1 million. That means that the chance of losing more than $1 million in the above project is only 5 percent.

The project value at risk can be calculated at different probability levels. The project value at risk at 1 percent probability level is −5.7 million. That means that the chance of losses exceeding $5.7 million is only 1 percent.

3 Internal rate of return

FAST FORWARD

A project will only be selected if its internal rate of return **exceeds** the cost of capital or target rate of return.

Key term

The **internal rate of return** of any investment is the discount rate at which the NPV is equal to zero.

Knowledge brought forward from earlier studies

The IRR is used to calculate the exact discount rate at which NPV is equal to zero.

If calculating IRR manually we use the interpolation method as follows.

(a) Calculate a net present value using a discount rate that gives **a whole number** and gives an NPV **close to zero**.

(b) Calculate a second NPV using another discount rate. If the first NPV was **positive**, use a rate that is **higher** than the first rate; if it was **negative**, use a rate that is **lower** than the first rate.

(c) Use the two NPVs to calculate the IRR. The formula to apply is:

$$IRR = a + \left(\left(\frac{NPV_a}{NPV_a - NPV_b} \right)(b-a) \right) \%$$ This formula is not given in the exam.

where a = the lower of the two rates of return used
       b = the higher of the two rates of return used
   NPV_a = the NPV obtained using rate a
   NPV_b = the NPV obtained using rate b

The project should be accepted if the IRR is **greater** than the **cost of capital** or **target rate of return**.

3.1 Example of IRR calculation

A company is considering the purchase of a piece of equipment costing $120,000 that would save $30,000 each year for five years. The equipment could be sold at the end of its useful life for $15,000. The company requires every project to yield a return of 10% or more otherwise they will be rejected. Should this equipment be purchased?

Solution

Annual depreciation will be $\frac{\$(120,000 - 15,000)}{5}$ = $21,000

Step 1   Calculate the first NPV, using a rate that is two thirds of the return on investment.

The return on investment would be:

$$\frac{30,000 - \text{depreciation of } 21,000}{0.5 \times (120,000 + 15,000)} = \frac{9,000}{67,500} = 13.3\%$$

Two thirds of this is 8.9% and so we can start by trying 9%.

The IRR is the rate for the cost of capital at which the NPV = 0.

Year	Cash flow	PV factor 9%	PV of cash flow
	$		$
0	(120,000)	1.000	(120,000)
1–5	30,000	3.890	116,700
5	15,000	0.650	9,750
		NPV =	6,450

This is fairly close to zero. It is also **positive**, which means that the actual **rate of return** is **more than 9%**. We can use 9% as one of our two NPVs close to zero.

Step 2   Calculate the second NPV, using a rate that is **greater** than the first rate, as the first rate gave a positive answer.

Suppose we try 12%.

Year	Cash flow	PV factor 12%	PV of cash flow
	$		$
0	(120,000)	1.000	(120,000)
1–5	30,000	3.605	108,150
5	15,000	0.567	8,505
		NPV =	(3,345)

This is fairly close to zero and **negative**. The real rate of return is therefore greater than 9% (positive NPV of $6,450) but less than 12% (negative NPV of $3,345).

Step 3   Use the two NPV values to estimate the IRR.

The interpolation method assumes that the NPV rises in linear fashion between the two NPVs close to 0. The real rate of return is therefore assumed to be on a straight line between NPV = $4,300 at 9% and NPV = –$2,230 at 12%.

Using the formula

$$IRR \approx a + \left(\left(\frac{NPV_a}{NPV_a - NPV_b} \right)(b - a) \right)\%$$

$$IRR \approx 9 + \frac{6,450}{(6,450 + 3,345)} \times (12 - 9)\% = 10.98\%, \text{ say } 11\%$$

If it is company policy to undertake investments which are expected to yield 10% or more, this project would be undertaken.

3.2 The multiple IRR problem

FAST FORWARD

A project being accepted based on IRR may be misleading if the cash flows from the project are not positive.

The example employed to calculate the IRR indicates that the IRR and the NPV produce the same result, ie a positive NPV implies $IRR \geq k$ and a negative NPV implies $IRR < k$. However, this is true only when the project has normal cash flows, i.e. a negative initial cash flow followed by a series of positive cash flows. If the cash flows change signs then the IRR may not be unique. This is the multiple **IRR problem**.

Key term

The **multiple IRR** occurs when cash flows change sign and result in more than one value for the IRR.

3.2.1 Example

Consider the following example, where the cash flow for the second year is negative. Note that in this case the NPV is equated to zero for two values of IRR, when IRR = 5.1% and when IRR = 39.8%.

Time	Cash Flow	Discount Factor	Present Value
0	− 245,000	1	− 245,000
1	600,000	0.909	545,455
2	− 360,000	0.826	− 297,521
			2,934

If we plot the NPV for this project at various different discount rates, we find the following:

Multiple IRR problem

The NPV is initially negative, increases and becomes positive, reaches a maximum value and then declines and becomes negative again. According to the decision rule, we should accept projects for which IRR > k. However, the IRR takes two values.

4 Comparison of NPV and IRR

The rule for making investments under the NPV method is that where investments are mutually exclusive, the one with the higher NPV should be preferred. Where investments are independent, all investments should be accepted if they have positive NPVs. The reason for this is that they are generating sufficient cash flows to give an acceptable return to providers of debt and equity finance. This is known as the NPV rule.

The IRR rule states that, where an investment has cash outflows followed by cash inflows, it should be accepted if its IRR exceeds the cost of capital. This is because such investments will have positive NPVs.

4.1 Limitations of the IRR technique

Where we are dealing with independent investments, the IRR should usually come to the same decision as the NPV approach. However, it cannot be used to distinguish between mutually exclusive investments. This is because it merely indicates whether or not a project has a positive NPV. It does not tell us the magnitude of the NPV. Hence, it cannot decide which is the superior project.

4.2 Mutually exclusive projects

Question	Mutually exclusive projects

We have two projects that both require an initial investment of $10,000. Project A has an IRR of 25% per annum, project B has an IRR of 20% per annum. Which project should we select?

The answer may appear fairly clear cut, i.e. that we select the project with the higher IRR. However, we are also told that the company's cost of capital is 10% and are provided with the following data.

Time	Project A	Project B
0	(10,000)	(10,000)
1	12,000	1,000
2	625	13,200

Answer

It is incorrect to decide between these alternatives based on IRRs. If we were to work out the NPVs of these two projects, we could then summarize the findings as follows:

	Project A	Project B
NPV @ 10%	1,426	1,818
IRR	25%	20%

What we can see is that project A has the higher IRR of 25%, but it has a lower NPV at the company's cost of capital. This means that at a 10% cost of capital, project B is preferable, even though it has the lower IRR.

However, when the cost of capital is 20% project A would be preferred since project B would then have a NPV of zero while project A must still have a positive NPV. It can be seen that the decision depends not on the IRR but on the cost of capital being used.

Question	NPV profile

Considering this example more fully, if we calculate the NPVs at various costs of capital we find the following.

Rate %	Project A NPV	Project B NPV
	$	$
5.0	1,995	2,925
7.5	1,704	2,353
10.0	1,426	1,818
12.5	1,160	1,319
15.0	907	851
17.5	665	412
20.0	434	0
22.5	212	(387)
25.0	0	(752)
27.5	(204)	(1,096)
30.0	(399)	(1,420)

Plotting these on a graph we get the following.

What we can see is that up to a cost of capital of just over 14%, project B has the highest NPV. Above that cost of capital, project A has the greater NPV and would, therefore, be preferable. For both the above projects, the NPV profile is that the NPV falls as the discount rate increases.

4.3 Reasons why the NPV profiles differ

The NPV profiles cross over at a discount rate of approximately 14%. There are two reasons why this may occur.

- Differences in the timing of the cash flows for each project
- Differences in the project sizes (or project scales)

In this case, there is no difference in project size, with both projects having an initial investment of $10,000. However, there are differences in the timing of the cash flows, with project B having high cash flows in Year 2 and project A having high cash flows in Year 1.

The NPV profile for project B shows a far steeper line. This is because it has higher cash inflows in the more distant year. Therefore, it is much more affected by an increasing discount rate. In contrast, project A has higher value cash flows in the earlier year. This means that it is less affected by the increase in discount rate.

4.4 Conflicting rankings using the NPV and IRR methods

Note that, where the discount rate is greater than 15% (the **changeover** or **crossover rate**), selecting an investment based on either the higher NPV or the higher IRR will give the same answer. In this case, for discount rates between 15% and 20%, project A has the higher NPV and it also has the higher IRR.

For discount rates of less than 15%, selecting an investment based on the higher IRR gives an answer which conflicts with the NPV method, since it will select project A, although project B has the higher NPV.

4.4.1 Re-investment rate

The problem with selecting investments based on the **higher IRR** is that it makes an assumption that **cash flows** can be **reinvested** at the **IRR** over the **life of the project**.

In contrast, the **NPV method** assumes that cash flows can be **reinvested** at the **cost of capital** over the life of the project.

If the assumption that the IRR as a reinvestment rate is valid, then the IRR technique will be superior. However, it is unlikely that this will be the case and therefore the NPV method is likely to be superior. The better reinvestment rate assumption will be the cost of capital used for the NPV method.

4.5 Other factors

For projects with **non-normal cash flows**, e.g. flows where the sign changes more than once, there may be more than one IRR. This means that the IRR method cannot be used.

The NPV method gives no indication as to the **sensitivity** of the project to changes in forecast figures or the amount of capital at risk, unlike the IRR method.

5 Modified internal rate of return (MIRR)   6/12

FAST FORWARD

> The modified internal rate of return is the IRR that would result if it was **not assumed that project proceeds were reinvested at the IRR.**

The MIRR overcomes the problem of the **reinvestment assumption** and the fact that **changes in the cost of capital over the life of the project** cannot be incorporated in the IRR method.

Exam formula

$$\left(\frac{PV_R}{PV_I}\right)^{\frac{1}{n}} \times (1+r_e) - 1$$

Where PV_R = is the present value of the return phase (the phase of the project with cash inflows)
  PV_I = is the present value of the investment phase (the phase of the project with cash outflows)
  r_e = the cost of capital

This topic was examined as part of a 30-mark compulsory question in December 2008 – calculations and appreciation of the advantages and disadvantages of the method relative to NPV were required. It was also examined in June 2012 where IRR and IRR calculations were required.

5.1 Example of MIRR calculations

Consider a project requiring an initial investment of $24,500, with cash inflows of $15,000 in years 1 and 2 and cash inflows of $3,000 in years 3 and 4. The cost of capital is 10%.

Solution

Calculate **present value** of the investment phase and the return phase:

Year	Cash flow	Discount factor	Present value
	$	10%	$
0	(24,500)	1.000	(24,500)
1	15,000	0.909	13,635
2	15,000	0.826	12,390
3	3,000	0.751	2,253
4	3,000	0.683	2,049

PV_R = Total PV for years 1 – 4 = $30,327

PV_I = Cost of investment = $24,500

$$MIRR = \left[\frac{30,327}{24,500}\right]^{\frac{1}{4}} \times (1 + 0.1) - 1 = 16\%$$

The MIRR is calculated on the basis of **investing the inflows** at the **cost of capital**.

5.2 Alternative method

An alternative way of calculating MIRR would be to calculate the terminal value of the return phase (assuming that the cash flows are reinvested at the firm's cost of capital).

The MIRR formula to use in this case would be:

$$\text{MIRR} = \sqrt[n]{\frac{\text{Terminal value of return phase}}{\text{PV of investment phase}}} - 1$$

The table below shows the **values of the inflows if they were immediately reinvested at 10%**. For example the $15,000 received at the end of year 1 could be reinvested for three years at 10% pa (multiply by $1.1 \times 1.1 \times 1.1 = 1.331$).

Year	Cash inflows $	Interest rate Multiplier	Amount when reinvested $
1	15,000	1.331	19,965
2	15,000	1.21	18,150
3	3,000	1.1	3,300
4	3,000	1.0	3,000
			44,415

MIRR can be calculated as follows:

$$\text{Total return} = \frac{44,415}{24,500} = 1.813$$

$$\text{MIRR} = \sqrt[4]{1.813} - 1$$
$$= 1.16 - 1$$
$$= 16\%$$

Exam focus point

> Make sure you read the article entitled 'A better measure?' in the April 2008 issue of *Student Accountant* which deals with MIRR and how to calculate it.

5.3 Advantages of MIRR

MIRR has the advantage of IRR that it assumes the **reinvestment rate** is the **company's cost of capital**. IRR assumes that the reinvestment rate is the IRR itself, which is usually untrue.

In many cases where there is conflict between the NPV and IRR methods, the MIRR will give the same indication as NPV, which is the **correct theoretical method**. This helps when explaining the appraisal of a project to managers, who often find the concept of rate of return easier to understand than that of net present value.

5.4 Disadvantages of MIRR

However, MIRR, like all rate of return methods, suffers from the problem that it may lead an investor tor eject a project which has a **lower rate of return** but, because of its size, generates a **larger increase in wealth**.

In the same way, a **high-return** project with a **short life** may be preferred over a **lower-return** project with a longer life.

Chapter Roundup

- Projects with a positive net present value should be undertaken

- Inflation is present in all economies and must be accounted for when evaluating projects.

- In investment appraisal, tax is often assumed to be payable **one year in arrears,** but you should read the question details carefully.

  Tax allowable depreciation details should be checked in any question you attempt.

- **Capital** allowances in the form of first year allowances or writing down allowances determine the tax liabilities and after tax earnings.

- Capital rationing problems exist when there are insufficient funds available to finance all available profitable projects.

- **Capital rationing** may occur due to internal factors (**soft** capital rationing) or external factors (**hard** capital rationing).

- When capital rationing is present across **multiple periods**, linear programming may be used to solve the problem of **which projects** to undertake.

- Before deciding whether or not to undertake a project, financial managers will want to assess the project's risk (which can be predicted) and uncertainty (which is unpredictable).

- Risk can be built into project appraisal using such tools as expected values and different costs of capital.

- Project duration is a measure of how long it takes to recover approximately half of the value of the investment.

- The Monte Carlo method of estimating a project's NPV assumes that the key factors affecting NPV can be modelled as a probability distribution.

- The project value at risk is the potential loss of a project with a given probability.

- A project will only be selected if its internal rate of return **exceeds** the cost of capital or target rate of return.

- A project being accepted based on IRR may be misleading if the cash flows from the project are not positive.

- The modified internal rate of return is the IRR that would result if it was **not assumed that project proceeds were reinvested at the IRR.**

Quick quiz

1 Why is NPV preferable to IRR as a project selection criterion?

2 When does the multiple value IRR normally occur?

3 What is the appropriate criterion for ranking projects when there is a constraint of funds?

4 What is the main difference between modified IRR and IRR?

5 If Project A had a duration of 3.5 years and Project B had a duration of 2.6 years, which project would be preferable and why?

6 What is the advantage of the Monte Carlo calculation of the NPV?

Answers to quick quiz

1   The NPV criterion is consistent with the shareholder wealth maximisation whereas the IRR criterion is not

2   The multiple value of IRR occurs when there is a negative cash flow

3   The appropriate criterion is the profitability index

4   The IRR implies that the profits from a project are re-invested at the IRR whereas the modified IRR allows the re-investment rate to change

5   Project B would be preferable as it takes less time to recoup approximately half of the investment, which makes it appear less risky.

6   The Monte Carlo calculation of the NPV derives the NPV under a wide range of assumptions

Now try the questions below from the Exam Question Bank

Number	Level	Marks	Time
8	Examination	20	36 mins
9	Examination	20	36 mins

6

Application of option pricing theory in investment decisions

Topic list	Syllabus reference
1 Overview	C (2)
2 Basic concepts	C (2) (a)
3 Determinants of option values	C (2) (a)
4 Real options	C (2) (b)
5 Valuation of real options	C (2) (c)

Introduction

In this chapter we look at how option valuation techniques can be applied to capital budgeting. First we review the basic theory underlying the pricing of financial options and then we examine a number of options embedded in projects, such as the option to delay, the option to abandon, the option to expand and the option to redeploy productive resources.

Study guide

		Intellectual level
C2	**Application of option pricing theory in investment decisions**	
(a)	Apply the Black-Scholes Option Pricing (BSOP) model to financial product valuation and to asset valuation	3
	(i) Determine, using published data, the five principal drivers of option value (value of the underlying, exercise price, time to expiry, volatility and the risk free rate).	
	(ii) Discuss the underlying assumptions, structure, application and limitations of the Black-Scholes model	
(b)	Evaluate embedded real options within a project, classifying them into one of the real option archetypes	3
(c)	Assess, calculate and advise on the value of options to delay, expand, redeploy and withdraw using the Black-Scholes model	3

1 Overview

The topic of real options applies the option valuation techniques to capital budgeting exercises in which a project is coupled with a put or call option. For example, the firm may have the option to abandon a project during its life. This amounts to a put option on the remaining cash flows associated with the project. Ignoring the value of these real options (as in standard discounted cash flow techniques) can lead to incorrect investment evaluation decisions.

2 Basic concepts

FAST FORWARD

Options are contracts that give to one party the right to enter into a transaction but not the obligation to do so.

2.1 Types of options

2.1.1 Definition

An option is a contract that gives one party the option to enter into a transaction either at a specific time in the future or within a specific future period at a price that is agreed when the contract is issued.

2.1.2 Exercise price

The exercise or strike price is the price at which the future transaction will take place

2.1.3 Premium

Premium is the price paid by the option buyer to the seller, or writer, for the right to buy or sell the underlying shares.

2.1.4 Call and put options

The buyer of a call option acquires the right, but not the obligation, to buy the underlying at a fixed price. The buyer of a put option acquires the right, but not the obligation, to sell the underlying shares at a fixed price.

2.1.5 European, American and Bermudan options

A European option can only be exercised at expiration, whereas an American option can be exercised any time prior to expiration. A Bermudan option is an option where early exercise is restricted to certain dates during the life of the option. It derives its name from the fact that its exercise characteristics are somewhere between those of the American and the European style of options and the island of Bermuda lies between America and Europe.

2.1.6 Long and short positions

When an investor buys an option the investor is long, and when the investor sells an option the investor has a short position.

2.1.7 Price quotations

It should be noted that, for simplicity, only one price is quoted for each option in the national newspapers. In practice, there will always be two prices quoted for each option, ie a bid and an offer price. For example, the January option could be quoted as 500/550. This can be interpreted to mean that it would cost an investor 550 to buy those options and that he would receive 500 for selling it.

Underlying Share — Type of Option

Option		Calls			Puts		
		Apr	Jul	Oct	Apr	Jul	Oct
BP	500	$29\frac{1}{2}$	40	$44\frac{1}{2}$	$9\frac{1}{2}$	15	$19\frac{1}{2}$
(*519)	550	$6\frac{1}{2}$	16	21	38	42	46

Underlying Share Price (@4.10 pm) — Exercise Price (in pence) — Premium (pence/share) — Expiry date (3 cycles)

2.2 Profiles of call options at expiration

FAST FORWARD

A long call option position at expiration may lead to unlimited profits, and a short option position may lead to unlimited losses.

2.2.1 Long Call

A call option will be exercised at expiration only if the price of the underlying is higher than the exercise price. Otherwise the option will not be exercised. The value of a call option at expiration is the higher of

The difference between the value of the underlying security at expiration and the exercise price (if the value of the underlying security > exercise price)

Or

Zero, if value of the underlying security is equal to or less than the exercise price.

Since the buyer of a call option has paid a premium to buy the option, the profit from the purchase of the call option is the value of the option minus the premium paid. ie

Profit = value of call option – premium paid for the purchase of the option

Question _____ **Call option profile at expiration**

Suppose that you buy the October call option with an exercise price of 550. The premium is 21 cents. Calculate the potential profit/loss at expiration.

The profit loss/loss will be calculated for possible values of the underlying at expiration. Here we examine the profit/loss profile for prices ranging from 500 to 600.

Value of underlying at expiration	Value of underlying – exercise price	Value of option	Profit/loss
500	−50	0	−21
530	−20	0	−21
540	−10	0	−21
550	0	0	−21
560	10	10	−11
570	20	20	−1
600	50	50	29

The profit or loss at expiration is shown below:

2.2.2 Short Call

The seller of a call loses money when the option is exercised and gains the premium if the option is not exercised. The value of the call option for a seller is exactly the opposite of the value of the call option for the buyer. The value of the short call at expiration is the negative of the long position. That is, the negative of

The greater of the difference between the value of the underlying and the exercise price

And

Zero.

The profit of the short position at expiration is:

Profit = premium received − value of call option

A short call option has a maximum profit, which is the premium, but unlimited losses.

Question

Suppose that you sell the October call option with an exercise price of 550. The premium is 21c. Calculate the potential profit/loss at expiration for the writer of the option

Answer

Column A Value of the underlying at expiration	Column B Value of the underlying at expiration – exercise price	Column C – Maximum of zero and the difference between the value of the underlying and the exercise price	Negative Column C + premium
500	−50	0	21
530	−20	0	21
540	−10	0	21
550	0	0	21
560	10	−10	11
570	20	−20	−1
600	50	−50	−29

The profit or loss at expiration is shown below:

2.3 Profiles of put options at expiration

FAST FORWARD

The maximum profit from a long put position and the maximum loss from a short put position occurs when the price of the underlying becomes zero.

2.3.1 Long Put

A put will be exercised at expiration only if the price of the underlying asset is lower than the exercise price of the option. The **value** of the option when exercised is the **difference** between the **exercise price** and the **value of the underlying**.

The **profit** from a long position is the **difference** between the **value of the option** at expiration and the **premium paid**.

As in the case of the long call option, the buyer of the option has limited losses, that is the premium if the option is not exercised, but unlike the long call which has unlimited upside, the maximum value of the put option is X, which is attained when the price of the underlying is zero.

Question

Suppose that you buy the October put option with an exercise price of 550. The premium is 46c. Calculate the potential profit/loss at expiration.

Answer

Column A Value of underlying at expiration	Column B Exercise price – value of underlying	Column C Maximum of Column B and zero	Column C – premium
500	50	50	4
530	20	20	–26
540	–10	10	–36
550	0	0	–46
560	–10	0	–46
570	–20	0	–46
600	–50	0	–46

The profit or loss at expiration is shown below

2.3.2 Short Put

Value of put option at expiration is the maximum of

The difference between the exercise price and the value of the underlying at expiration

And

Zero

Profit = Premium received – value of put option

The **maximum profit** for the writer of a put option is the **premium paid** which occurs when the put option is **not exercised** (that is, when the value at expiration = 0). This happens when the value of the underlying at expiration **is greater than** the exercise price.

The profit will be **zero** when the value of the underlying at expiration is **equal to** the sum of the exercise price and the premium paid.

The **highest loss** occurs when the value of the underlying = 0. The maximum loss will be equal to the **exercise price**.

Question | Short put at expiration

Suppose that you buy the October call option with an exercise price of 550. The premium is 46c. Calculate the potential profit/loss at expiration.

Answer

Column A Value of underlying at expiration	Column B Exercise price – value of underlying	Column C (Maximum of column B and zero)	Column C + premium
500	50	−50	−4
530	20	−20	26
540	−10	−10	36
550	0	0	46
560	−10	0	46
570	−20	0	46
600	−50	0	46

The profit or loss at expiration is shown below

3 Determinants of option values

FAST FORWARD

The value of an option is determined by the exercise price, the price of the underlying, the time to expiration, the volatility of the underlying and the interest rate.

3.1 Introduction

Options are financial instruments whose value changes all the time. The value of a call or a put option at expiration was derived earlier. In this section we shall identify the factors that affect the price of an option prior to expiration.

3.1.1 The exercise price

The higher the exercise price, the lower the probability that a call will be exercised. So call prices will decrease as the exercise prices increase. For the put, the effect runs in the opposite direction. A higher exercise price means that there is higher probability that the put will be exercised. So the put price increases as the exercise price increases.

3.1.2 The price of the underlying

As the current stock price goes up, the higher the probability that the call will be in the money. As a result, the call price will increase. The effect will be in the opposite direction for a put. As the stock price goes up, there is a lower probability that the put will be in the money. So the put price will decrease.

3.1.3 The volatility of the underlying

Both the call and put will increase in price as the underlying asset becomes more volatile. The buyer of the option receives full benefit of favourable outcomes but avoids the unfavourable ones (option price value has zero value).

3.1.4 The time to expiration

Both calls and puts will benefit from increased time to expiration. The reason is that there is more time for a big move in the stock price. But there are some effects that work in the opposite direction. As the time to expiration increase, the present value of the exercise price decreases. This will increase the value of the call and decrease the value of the put. Also, as the time to expiration increase, there is a greater amount of time for the stock price to be reduced by a cash dividend. This reduces the call value but increases the put value.

3.1.5 The interest rate

The higher the interest rate, the lower the present value of the exercise price. As a result, the value of the call will increase. The opposite is true for puts. The decrease in the present value of the exercise price will adversely affect the price of the put option.

3.1.6 The intrinsic and time value

The price of an option has two components; Intrinsic value and time value. Intrinsic value is the value of the option if it was exercised now.

Call Options: Intrinsic value (at time t) = Underlying Stock's Current Price – Call Strike Price
Put Options: Intrinsic value (at time t) = Put Strike Price – Underlying Stock's Current Price

If the intrinsic value is positive the option is in the money (ITM). If the intrinsic value is zero, the option is at the money (ATM) and if the intrinsic value is negative the option is out of the money (OTM)

The difference between the market price of an option and its intrinsic value is the time value of the option. Buyers of ATM or OTM options are simply buying time value, which decreases as an option approaches expiration. The more time an option has until expiration, the greater the option's chance of ending up in-the-money and the larger its time value. On the expiration day the time value of an option is zero and all an option is worth is its intrinsic value. It's either in-the-money, or it isn't.

3.2 The Black Scholes pricing model   12/10, 6/11

FAST FORWARD
> The Black Scholes model predicts the value of an option for given values of its determinants.

The payoffs at expiration for a call option were derived earlier as

The difference between the value of the underlying at expiration and the exercise price (where value of underlying > exercise price)

Or

Zero (where value of underlying $\leq$ exercise price)

The expected value of the payoff will depend on the probability that the option will be on the money, which we do not know. The value of the call option today will be the present value of the expected payoff at expiration. Apart from the probability to be in the money we also need to specify a discount factor, which will reflect the risk of the option. The problem of option valuation concerned financial specialists for a long time until Black, Scholes and Merton resolved the problem.

3.2.1 The Black Scholes Formula

The Black Scholes formula for the value of a **European call option** is given by:

$$c = P_a \, N(d_1) - P_e \, N(d_2) e^{-rt}$$

where P_a is the current price of the underlying asset

$\quad P_e$ is the exercise price

$\quad\quad r$ is the continuously compounded risk-free rate

$\quad\quad t$ is the time to expiration measured as a fraction of one year, for example $t = 0.5$ means that the time to expiration is six months.

$\quad\quad e$ is the base of the natural logarithms

$$d_1 = \frac{\ln\left(\dfrac{P_a}{P_e}\right) + \left(r + 0.5s^2\right)t}{s\sqrt{t}}$$

$$d_2 = d_1 - s\sqrt{t}$$

where s is the standard deviation of S

$\ln\left(\dfrac{P_a}{P_e}\right)$ is the natural logarithm of the spot price over the exercise price

3.2.2 Value of European put options

The value of a **European put option** can be calculated by using the Put Call Parity relationship which is given to you in the exam formulae sheet.

$$p = c - P_a + P_e \, e^{-rt}$$

where p is the value of the put option

$\quad\quad c$ is the value of the call option

3.2.3 Value of American call options

Although American options can be exercised any time during their lifetime it is **never optimal** to exercise an option earlier. The value of an American option will therefore be the same as the value of an equivalent European option and the Black-Scholes model can be used to calculate its price.

3.2.4 Value of American put options

Unfortunately, no exact analytic formula for the value of an American put option on a non-dividend-paying stock has been produced. Numerical procedures and analytic approximations for calculating American put values are used instead.

Question

Consider the situation where the stock price 6 months from the expiration of an option is $42, the exercise price of the option is $40, the risk-free interest rate is 10% p.a. and the volatility is 20% p.a. This means $P_a = 42$, $P_e = 40$, r = 0.1s = 0.2, t = 0.5.

Answer

$$d_1 = \frac{\ln(42/40) + (0.1 + \frac{0.2^2}{2})0.5}{0.2\sqrt{0.5}} = 0.7693 = 0.77$$

$$d_2 = 0.7693 - 0.2 \times \sqrt{0.5} = 0.6279 = 0.63$$

and

$$P_e{}^{-rt} = 40e^{-0.1 \times 0.5} = 40e^{-0.05} = 38.049$$

The values of the standard normal cumulative probability distribution can be found from the tables and are:

$N(0.77) = 0.7794$
$N(0.63) = 0.7357$

Hence if the option is a European call, its value, is given by:

c = (42 x 0.7794) − (38.049 x 0.7357) = 4.76

If the option is a European put, its value is given by:

p = 4.76 − 42 + 38.049 = 0.81

The stock price has to rise by $2.76 for the purchaser of the call to break even. Similarly, the stock price has to fall by $2.81 for the purchaser of the put to break even.

3.2.5 Assumptions of the Black-Scholes model

Assumptions of the model will be discussed in Section 5.3 of this chapter.

4 Real options

6/11, 6/12

FAST FORWARD

Real options are alternatives or choices that may be available with a business investment opportunity.

Exam focus point

Real options are highly examinable. An optional question in the June 2011 paper focused on the option to delay. The option to follow-on was examined in June 2012.

An option exists when the decision-maker has the right, but not the obligation, to take a particular action. They add value as they provide opportunities to take advantage of an uncertain situation as the uncertainty resolves itself over time.

Real options are known as such as they usually relate to **tangible assets**. Options that were discussed earlier in this chapter – and will be discussed further in Chapters 16 and 17 – are financial instruments that relate to such intangibles as exchange rates or interest rates.

A real option embodies flexibility in the development of a project. It gives the company the right but not the obligation to take some course of action that may be desirable if there is an unfortunate turn of events or a new opportunity presents itself. A real option represents either a **form of insurance** or a **means to take advantage** of a favourable situation.

Real options are '**actual options**' – that is, actual choices that a business can make in relation to investment opportunities. For example, a natural resource company may decide to suspend extraction of copper at its mine if the price of copper falls below the extraction cost. Conversely, a company with the right to mine in a particular area may decide to begin operations if the price rises above the cost of extraction. Such options can be extremely important when valuing potential investments but are often overlooked by traditional investment appraisal techniques (eg NPV). They can significantly increase the value of an investment by eliminating potentially unfavourable outcomes.

For a real option to exist, there must be uncertainty in terms of future cash flows *and* management must have the flexibility to respond to the uncertainty as it evolves.

In this section we describe the various options embedded in projects and provide examples. In the following section we illustrate how to estimate the value of real options using the Black Scholes method.

Firstly however we look at the shortcomings of the NPV investment appraisal technique.

4.1 Limitations of the NPV rule

You should be very familiar with the NPV technique by now (refer to Chapter 5 for examples). However despite its widespread use in real life, the technique does have several shortcomings.

4.1.1 Dealing with uncertainty

Although the cash flows are discounted at an appropriate cost of capital, NPV does not explicitly deal with uncertainty when valuing the project. A risk-adjusted discount rate reduces the present value of the cash flows (the higher the discount rate, the lower the present value) rather than giving the decision-maker an indication of the range of cash flows that a project may deliver. The use of a single discount rate means that risk is defined in one measure. This does not allow for the many sources of uncertainty that may surround the project and its cash flows.

4.1.2 Flexibility in responding to uncertainty

NPV fails to consider the extent of management's flexibility to respond to uncertainties surrounding the project. Such flexibility can be an extremely valuable part of the project and by failing to account for it, NPV may significantly underestimate the project's value.

Take mining as an example. When a new mining project is being considered, management usually produces a 'life of mine' plan which forms the basis for an NPV evaluation. It includes the information you might expect in an NPV calculation such as costs of extraction, recovery rates of the mined item, together with the amount, quality and distribution of the item. All of these will affect the estimated cash flows of the project.

However in practice management will have some degree of flexibility depending on the actual rate at which the item is mined. If external or internal conditions change, they can decided to increase or decrease the rate of mining – or even stop it altogether. When the NPV of the mine is calculated, such flexibilities (or options) are not incorporated. NPV will be based on an assumption that the item will be mined at a predetermined rate. This means that NPV will only provide an accurate estimate of the mine's value if there is no flexibility or no uncertainty (that is, flexibility will have no value as management knows exactly what is going to happen).

In order to correct the shortcomings of the NPV technique, real options can be incorporated into the calculations. The four different types of real options are discussed below.

4.2 Option to delay   6/11

Exam focus point

A 20 mark optional question in the December 2007 paper focused on the valuation of an option to delay. An optional question in the June 2011 paper also focused on an option to delay.

When a firm has exclusive rights to a project or product for a specific period, it can delay taking this project or product until a later date. A traditional investment analysis just answers the question of whether the project is a "good" one if taken today. Thus, the fact that a project is not selected today either because its NPV is negative, or its IRR is less than its cost of capital, does not mean that the rights to this project are not valuable.

Consider a situation where a company considers paying an amount C to acquire a licence to mine copper. The company needs to invest an extra amount I in order to start operations. The company has three years over which to develop the mine, otherwise it will lose the licence. Suppose that today copper prices are low and the NPV from developing the mine is negative. The company may decide not to start the operation today, but it has the option to start any time over the next three years provided that the NPV is positive. Thus the company has paid a premium C to acquire an American option on the present value of the cash flows from operation, with an exercise price equal to the additional investment (I.) The value of the option to delay is therefore:

NPV = PV − I if PV > I
NPV = 0 otherwise

The payoff of the option to delay is shown below and it is the same as the payoff of a **call option**, the only difference being that the underlying is the present value (that is in this case S = PV) and the exercise price is the additional investment (X = I)

4.3 Option to expand

The option to expand exists when firms invest in projects which allow them to make further investments in the future or to enter new markets. The initial project may be found in terms of its NPV as not worth undertaking. However when the option to expand is taken into account, the NPV may become positive and the project worthwhile. The initial investment may be seen as the premium required to acquire the option to expand.

Expansion will normally require an additional investment, call it I. The extra investment will be undertaken only if the present value from the expansion will be higher than the additional investment, ie when PV > I. If PV ≤ I, the expansion will not take place. Thus the option to expand is again a call option of the present value of the firm with an exercise equal to the value of the additional investment.

4.4 Option to abandon/withdraw

Whereas traditional capital budgeting analysis assumes that a project will operate in each year of its lifetime, the firm may have the option to cease a project during its life. This option is known as an abandonment option. Abandonment options, which are the right to sell the cash flows over the remainder of the project's life for some salvage value, are like American put options. When the present value of the remaining cash flows (PV) falls below the liquidation value (L) , the asset may be sold. Abandonment is effectively the exercising of a put option. These options are particularly important for large capital intensive projects such as nuclear plants, airlines, and railroads. They are also important for projects involving new products where their acceptance in the market is uncertain and companies would like to switch to more alternative uses.

Case Study

In June 2011 it was announced that the troubled and over-budget Edinburgh tram scheme in Scotland's capital city would cost approximately £750m to abandon. This would include the costs of cancelling all contracts, winding up the council's tram company and dismantling the parts of the network that have already been built. This being the case, the decision was made to continue with the project although plans have been scaled down from the original proposed route

4.5 Option to redeploy

The option to redeploy exists when the company can use its productive assets for activities other than the original one. The switch from one activity to another will happen if the PV of cash flows from the new activity will exceed the costs of switching. The option to abandon is a special case of an option to redeploy.

These options are particularly important in agricultural settings. For example, a beef producer will value the option to switch between various feed sources, preferring to use the cheapest acceptable alternative.

These options are also valuable in the utility industry. An electric utility, for example, may have the option to switch between various fuel sources to produce electricity. In particular, consider an electric utility that has the choice of building a coal-fired plant or a plant that burns either coal or gas.

Naïve implementation of discounted cash flow analysis might suggest that the coal-fired plant be constructed since it is considerably cheaper. Whereas the dual plant costs more, it provides greater flexibility. Management has the ability to select which fuel to use and can switch back and forth depending on energy conditions and the relative prices of coal and gas. The value of this operating option should be taken into account.

5 Valuation of real options

12/07, 6/11

FAST FORWARD

Real options can be valued using the Black-Scholes model, but certain adjustments need to be made since the underlying is not traded.

Exam focus point

Part of a 20 mark optional question in December 2007 asked students to discuss the limitations of the Black-Scholes model in valuing a real option. In June 2011, students were asked in an optional Section B question to value an option to delay production and marketing of a project.

5.1 Black-Scholes option analysis

Since American call options can be valued using the Black Scholes model, one could use in principle the Black Scholes model to estimate the value of the real options we have identified in the previous section. However there are certain differences between the application of the Black-Scholes model to financial options and real options. The main practical problem is the estimation of volatility. As the underlying asset is not traded, it is very difficult to established the volatility of the value. The main method to overcome this problem is to use simulation methods to estimate the volatility. Since the option to expand is a call option its value will be given by:

$c = P_a N(d_1) - P_e N(d_2)e^{-rt}$

In this case

P_a is the value of the project

P_e is the additional investment involved in expansion

$$d_1 = \frac{\ln(P_a/P_e) + \left(r + 0.5s^2\right)t}{s\sqrt{t}}$$

$d_2 = d_1 - s\sqrt{t}$

Similarly the option to abandon is a put option and its value is given by:

Put option $= P_e N(-d_2) e^{-rt} - P_a N(-d_1)$

Question

Valuation of option to abandon

Assume that Four Seasons International is considering taking a 20-year project which requires an initial investment of $ 250 million in an real estate partnership to develop time share properties with a Spanish real estate developer, and where the present value of expected cash flows is $ 254 million. While the net present value of $ 4 million is small, assume that Four Seasons International has the option to abandon this project anytime by selling its share back to the developer in the next 5 years for $ 150 million. A simulation of the cash flows on this time share investment yields a variance in the present value of the cash flows from being in the partnership of 0.09. The 5 year risk-free rate is 7%.

Calculate the total NPV of the project, including the option to abandon.

Answer

The value of the abandonment option can be estimated by determining the value of the put option using the Black-Scholes formula.

Put option = $P_e N(-d_2)e^{-rt} - P_a N(-d_1)$

Where Value of the underlying asset (P_a) = PV of cash flows from Project = $ 254 million

Strike Price (P_e) = Salvage value from abandonment = $ 150 million
Variance in underlying asset's value = 0.09 (standard deviation = $\sqrt{0.09}$ = 0.3)
Time to expiration = Life of the Project = 5 years

$$d_1 = \frac{\ln\left(\dfrac{P_a}{P_e}\right) + \left(r + 0.5s^2\right)t}{s\sqrt{t}}$$

$$d_1 = \frac{\ln\left(\dfrac{254}{150}\right) + \left(0.07 + 0.5 \times 0.3^2\right) \times 5}{0.3 \times \sqrt{5}}$$

$$= \frac{0.5267 + 0.115 \times 5}{0.6708}$$

$$= 1.6424$$

$$d_2 = d_1 - s\sqrt{t}$$

$$= 1.6424 - 0.3 \times \sqrt{5}$$

$$= 0.9716$$

Using normal distribution tables:

$N(d_1)$ = 0.9495

$N(-d_1)$ = 1 − $N(d_1)$ = 1 − 0.9495 = 0.0505

$N(d_2)$ = 0.8340

$N(-d_2)$ = 1 − 0.8340 = 0.166

The value of the put option can be calculated as follows:

Put option = ($150m x $0.166e^{-0.07 \times 5}$) − ($254m x 0.0505)

$$= \$17.55m - \$12.83m$$

$$= \$ 4.72m$$

The value of this abandonment option is added to the project's NPV of $4m, which gives a total NPV with abandonment option of $8.72m

Pandy Inc is considering a project that currently has an NPV of $(3.5m). However as part of this project, Pandy Inc will be developing technology that it will be able to use in five years' time to break into the Asian market. The expected cost of the investment at year 5 is $20m. The Asian project is currently valued with an NPV of 0 but management believes that NPV could be positive in five years' time due to changes in economic conditions.

The standard deviation is 0.25, risk free rate is 5% and Pandy's cost of capital is 12%.

Required

Evaluate the value of the option to expand.

Answer

The value of the project (P_a) is $20m at year 5. We therefore have to discount this back to Year 0 to obtain the present value.

P_a = $20m x 0.567 = $11.34m

The other variables are as follows.

P_e = $20m $\qquad$ t = 5 $\qquad$ s = 0.25 $\qquad$ r = 0.05 $\qquad$ e^{-rt} = 0.779

d_1 $\quad$ = [ln(11.34/20) + (0.05 + 0.5 x 0.25^2) x 5] / (0.25 x $\sqrt{5}$)

$\qquad$ = [-0.5674 + 0.40625] / 0.5590

$\qquad$ = -0.288

d_2 $\quad$ = -0.288 - 0.5590

$\qquad$ = -0.847

$N(d_1)$ = 0.5 - 0.1141 = 0.3859

$N(d_2)$ = 0.5 - 0.3023 = 0.1977

Option to expand $\quad$ = ($11.34m x 0.3859) - ($20m x 0.1977 x 0.779)

$\qquad\qquad\qquad$ = $4.376m - $3.080m

$\qquad\qquad\qquad$ = $1.296m

NPV of the project is now $1.296m - $3.5m = $(2.204m)

The project still has a negative NPV and should not be undertaken.

5.2 What does the real option valuation mean?

The valuation of a real option – and its inclusion in the NPV calculations – takes into account the **uncertainty** of the project. In the Four Seasons question above, for example, the abandonment option increases the attractiveness of the project by increasing its NPV. However the company **does not actually receive the value of the real option**. What it means is that the project could be abandoned for $150 million in the next five years and the value attached to this choice is $4.72 million. In the ensuing period before the abandonment option can be exercised, Four Seasons can take steps to promote the properties and create a larger potential market. By doing so, Four Seasons can reduce the uncertainty surrounding the project. The time that the company has before it has to make the abandonment decision is reflected in the value of project via the inclusion of real options.

A company may have a project with a negative NPV, which becomes feasible due to the value placed on the real option to expand the project. Again the company will not receive the value of the real option but the value attached to the option should be used in investment appraisal.

Remember that interpretation of results is at least as important as being able to calculate the numbers. Make sure you appreciate the meaning of the value of real options and be prepared to discuss this in exam questions.

5.3 Assumptions of the Black-Scholes model

The Black-Scholes model makes a number of assumptions which are discussed below.

(a) **Lognormality**. The model assumes that the return on the underlying asset follows a normal distribution which means the return itself follows a lognormal distribution.

(b) **Perfect markets**. This suggests that the direction of the market cannot be consistently predicted and thus the returns on the underlying asset can go up or down at any given moment in time.

(c) **Constant interest rates**. The risk-free rate is used in the Black-Scholes model and this rate is assumed to be constant and known.

(d) **Constant volatility**. The model assumes that the volatility of the project is known and remains constant throughout its life.

(e) **Tradability of asset**. The model assumes that there is a market for the underlying asset and it can therefore be traded.

The two latter assumptions do not necessarily apply to real options. Whilst volatility can be relatively constant in the very short term, it is never constant in the long term. It is not always the case that the underlying asset can be traded therefore this assumption limits the usefulness of the model for valuing real options.

These assumptions can form part of a critique of the Black-Scholes model for option valuation in an exam question. A number of the assumptions are unrealistic and can therefore at best lead to an approximation of the value of options.

An optional question in June 2011 required you to comment on the implications of the value of a real option for a company – knowledge of the above assumptions would have been useful when answering this question.

5.4 Implications of real options for capital budgeting

Real options provide a more accurate estimate of a project's value but this greater accuracy comes at a cost. The analysis of real options is a much more complex approach to valuation than NPV and therefore requires a greater investment in time and effort.

However real options shift the focus away from trying to predict the future 'perfectly' to identifying what can (or should) be done about responding to uncertainty. In addition, this focus on responding in the best possible way to uncertainty promotes a discipline that extends over the entire life of the project (not just when the decision is originally made). Finally, real options give decision-makers the ability to identify the **optimal levels of flexibility** by providing estimates of the additional value that increased flexibility can bring.

Chapter Roundup

- Options are contracts that give to one party the right to enter into a transaction but not the obligation to do so.

- A long call option position at expiration may lead to unlimited profits, and a short option position may lead to unlimited losses.

- The maximum profit from a long put position and the maximum loss from a short put position occurs when the price of the underlying becomes zero.

- The value of an option is determined by an exercise price, the price of the underlying, the time to expiration, the volatility of the underlying and the interest rate.

- The Black Scholes model predicts the value of an option for given values of its determinants.

- Real options are alternatives or choices that may be available with a business investment opportunity.

- Real options can be valued using the Black Scholes model, but certain adjustments need to be made since the underlying is not traded.

Quick Quiz

1   A call option with an exercise price of $60 is bought for $3. On expiry day the underlying is $61. Should the call option be exercised?

2   You have bought a put option, which expires in 3 months. The day after you bought the put option, the volatility of the underlying asset increased. What would happen to the value of the put options?

3   You have bought an out-of-the-money call option, with an exercise price of $40. The option cost $2 and it expires in 6 months. What would you expect the value of the call option to be in 5 months if the price and volatility of the underlying remain unchanged?

Answers to Quick Quiz

1   The option should be exercise since the price of the underlying is higher than the exercise price. The value of the option at expiration is $61 − $60 = $1.

   The overall result is a loss of $2 since the option was bought for $3.

2   The value of the put option will increase as the volatility increases, because it makes it more likely for the price of the underlying to fall below the exercise price.

3   As an option nears its expiration date its time value goes down. The value of the out-of-the-money option one month before expiration will be lower than the price 6 months before expiration since there is less time for the price of the underlying to exceed the exercise price.

Now try the question below from the Exam Question Bank

Number	Level	Marks	Time
10	Examination	20	36 mins

Impact of financing on investment decisions and adjusted present values

7a

Topic list	Syllabus reference
1 Sources of finance – appropriateness	C (3) (a)
2 Cost of capital	C (3) (b)
3 CAPM and portfolios	C (3) (c)
4 Project specific cost of capital	C (3) (c)
5 Duration	C (3) (d)
6 Credit risk	C (3) (e)
7 Credit spreads and cost of debt capital	C (3) (f)
8 Theories of capital structure – traditional and Modigliani and Miller (MM)	C (3) (g)
9 Alternative theories of capital structure	C (3) (g)
10 The adjusted present value method	C (3) (h)
11 Effect of alternative financing strategies on financial reporting	C (3) (i)

Introduction

The purpose of this chapter is to review some of the theories that seek to explain capital structure and the role of capital structure in investment appraisal. We look at the appropriateness of various available sources of finance and then consider the extent of a company's debt exposure to interest rate changes. Exposure to credit risk and credit spreads are followed by a discussion of different theories of capital structure. We will then look at the adjusted present value approach to valuing a firm and conclude the chapter with an assessment of how alternative financing strategies impact on reported financial position.

Study guide

		Intellectual level
C3	**Impact of financing on investment decisions and adjusted present values**	
(a)	Identify and assess the appropriateness of the range of sources of finance available to an organisation including equity, debt, hybrids, lease finance, venture capital, business angel finance, private equity, asset securitisation and sale	3
(b)	Calculate the cost of capital of an organisation, including the cost of equity and cost of debt, based on the range of equity and debt sources of finance. Discuss the appropriateness of using the cost of capital to establish project and organisational value, and discuss its relationship to such value.	3
(c)	Calculate and evaluate project specific cost of equity and cost of capital, including their impact on the overall cost of capital of an organisation. Demonstrate detailed knowledge of business and financial risk, the capital asset pricing model and the relationship between equity and asset betas.	3
(d)	Assess an organisation's debt exposure to interest rate changes using the simple Macaulay duration method	3
(e)	Discuss the benefits and limitations of duration, including the impact of convexity	3
(f)	Assess the organisation's exposure to credit risk, including	2
	(i) Explain the role of, and the risk assessment models used by the principal rating agencies (ii) Estimate the likely credit spread over risk free (iii) Estimate the organisation's current cost of debt capital using the appropriate term structure of interest rates and the credit spread	
(g)	Assess the impact of financing upon investment decisions of	3
	(i) Modigliani and Miller proposition before and after tax	
	(ii) Static trade-off theory	
	(iii) Pecking order propositions	
	(iv) Agency effects	
(h)	Apply the adjusted value technique to the appraisal of investment decisions that entail significant alterations in the financial structure of the organisation, including their fiscal and transactions cost implications	3
(i)	Assess the impact of a significant capital investment project upon the reported financial position and performance of the organisation taking into account alternative financing strategies	3

1 **The relationship between risk and return**

Risk averse investors prefer less risk than more. In order to be persuaded to take on more risk, they must be 'compensated' in the form of higher returns.

2 **Diversifiable and non-diversifiable risk**

Diversifiable risk (also known as **unsystematic risk)** arises due to **random** and unpredicted factors. It can be diversified away by holding a portfolio of investments.

Non-diversifiable risk (also known as **systematic risk)** is caused by factors that **affect all firms** and therefore **cannot** be eliminated by diversification.

3 **The capital asset pricing model (CAPM)**

The following formula is given in the exam.

$$E(r_i) = R_f + \beta(E(R_m - R_f))$$

4 **Weighted average cost of capital (WACC)**

The formula for the WACC which is given in the exam is

$$WACC = \left[\frac{V_e}{V_e + V_d}\right] k_e + \left[\frac{V_d}{V_e + V_d}\right] k_d (1 - T)$$

This formula can be used to calculate the cost of capital at which potential investment projects should be discounted.

1 Sources of finance – appropriateness   6/12

You should be familiar with the various sources of finance available to businesses from Paper F9 – *Financial Management*. This section revisits these sources of finance, considering their appropriateness for different organisations and relative cost.

1.1 Short-term debt

Short-term debt consists mainly of overdrafts and short-term loans.

The advantage of overdrafts is that they can be arranged relatively quickly and offer the company a degree of flexibility with regard to the amount borrowed. Interest is only paid when the account is overdrawn. However if the account is overdrawn beyond the authorised amount, penalties can be severe.

Overdrafts are usually most appropriate when a company wants help to finance 'day to day' trading and cash flow requirements. The company is unlikely to be short of cash all the time therefore an informal overdraft agreement that can be called on where necessary would be the best choice of funding.

Short-term loans are more formal than overdrafts in that they are for fixed amounts for a specified period of time. The company knows how much it has to pay back at regular intervals and does not have to worry about the bank withdrawing or reducing an overdraft facility. However interest has to be paid for the duration of the loan, rather than just when the account is overdrawn.

It may be that a mixture of short-term loans and overdrafts is the most appropriate method of funding. For example, if you are purchasing a shop with inventory, the shop premises might be financed by a loan whilst the inventory could be funded by an overdraft.

1.2 Long-term debt finance

Make sure you read the article written by the examiner entitled 'Bond valuation and bond yields' in the September 2011 issue of *Student Accountant*. This article deals with how bonds are valued and the relationship between bond value or price, the yield to maturity and the spot yield curve.

Long-term finance is most appropriate for major investments. It tends to be more expensive and less flexible than short-term finance.

Long-term debt comes in various forms – redeemable and irredeemable, fixed and floating rates, convertibles – and the price will vary according to the product and prevailing market conditions. For example, where the coupon rate is fixed at the time of issue, it will be set after considering the credit rating of the company issuing the debt. Although subsequent changes in market and company conditions may cause the market value of the debt to fluctuate, the interest charged (the price of the debt) will remain at the fixed percentage of the nominal value.

Long-term debt tends to be most appropriate for long-term investments. One of the main advantages of long-term debt is that interest is tax deductible, making it cheaper than equity finance.

1.2.1 Valuing redeemable bonds

Bonds are usually **redeemable**. They are issued for a term of ten years or more, and perhaps 25 to 30 years. At the end of this period, they will 'mature' and become redeemable (at par or possibly at a value above par).

Some redeemable bonds have an earliest and a latest redemption date. For example, 12% Loan Notes 2010/12 are redeemable at any time between the earliest specified date (in 2010) and the latest date (in 2012). The issuing company can choose the date. The decision by a company when to redeem a debt will depend on **how much cash** is available to the company to repay the debt, and on the **nominal rate of interest** on the debt.

Some bonds do not have a redemption date, and are **'irredeemable'** or **'undated'**. Undated bonds might be redeemed by a company that wishes to pay off the debt, but there is no obligation on the company to do so.

Value of debt = (Interest earnings × Annuity factor) + (Redemption value × Discounted cash flow factor)

Example

Furry has in issue 12% bonds with par value $100,000 and redemption value $110,000, with interest payable quarterly. The redemption yield on the bonds is 8% annually and 2% quarterly. The bonds are redeemable on 30 June 20X4 and it is now 31 December 20X0.

Required

Calculate the market value of the bonds.

Solution

You need to use the redemption yield cost of debt as the discount rate, and remember to use an annuity factor for the interest. We are discounting over 14 periods using the quarterly discount rate (8%/4).

Period		Cash flow	Discount factor	Present value
		$	2%	$
1–14	Interest	3,000	12.106	36,318
14	Redemption	110,000	0.758	83,380
				119,698

Market value is $119,698

1.2.2 The term structure of interest rates

Interest rates depend on the **term to maturity** of the asset. For example, government bonds might be short-dated, medium-dated, or long-dated depending on when the bonds are to be redeemed and the investor repaid.

The **term structure of interest rates** refers to the way in which the yield on a security varies according to the term of the borrowing, as shown by the **yield curve**.

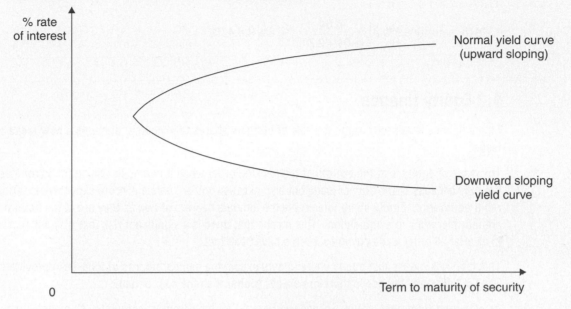

The reasons why, in theory, the yield curve will normally be upward sloping, so that long-term financial assets offer a higher yield than short-term assets, are as follows.

(a) **The investor must be compensated for tying up his money in the asset for a longer period of time**. The only way to overcome this **liquidity preference** of investors is to compensate them for the loss of liquidity; in other words, to offer a higher rate of interest on longer dated bonds.

(b) **There is a greater risk in lending long-term than in lending short-term**. To compensate investors for this risk, they might require a higher yield on longer dated investments.

A yield curve might **slope downwards**, with short-term rates higher than longer term rates for a number of reasons.

(a) **Expectations**. When interest rates are expected to fall, short-term rates might be higher than long-term rates, and the yield curve would be downward sloping.

(b) **Government policy**. A policy of keeping interest rates relatively high might have the effect of forcing short-term interest rates higher than long-term rates.

(c) The **market segmentation theory**. The slope of the yield curve will reflect conditions in different segments of the market. This theory holds that the major investors are confined to a particular segment of the market and will not switch segment even if the forecast of likely future interest rates changes.

1.2.3 Yield to maturity

The yield to maturity (or **redemption yield**) is the effective yield on a redeemable bond which allows for the time value of money and is effectively the **internal rate of return** of the cash flows.

For example, a five year unsecured bond with a coupon of 5% per annum, redeemable at par and issued at a 6% discount to par will have a yield to maturity of 6.47%. This is calculated by assuming a nominal value of $100 and calculating NPVs at 5% and 7% discount rates.

Year	Cash flow $m	Discount factor @ 5%	Present value $m	Discount factor @ 7%	Present value $m
0	(94)	1.000	(94.00)	1.000	(94.00)
1–5	5	4.329	21.64	4.100	20.50
5	100	0.784	78.40	0.713	71.30
NPV			6.04		(2.20)

Yield to maturity = $5\% + \left(\dfrac{6.04}{(6.04 + 2.20)} \right) \times 2\% = 6.47\%$

1.3 Equity finance

Equity finance is raised through the sale of ordinary shares to investors, either as a **new issue** or a **rights issue**.

The issue of equity is at the bottom of the pecking order when it comes to raising funds for investments, not only because of the cost of issue but also because equity finance is more expensive in terms of required returns. Equity shareholders are the ultimate bearers of risk as they are at the bottom of the creditor hierarchy in a liquidation. This means that there is a significant risk that they will receive nothing at all after all other trade payables' claims have been met.

This high risk means that equity shareholders expect the highest returns of long-term providers of finance. The cost of equity finance is therefore always **higher** than the cost of debt.

As with long-term debt, equity finance will be used for long-term investments. Companies may choose to raise equity rather than debt finance if

(a)   their gearing ratios are approaching the maximum allowable
(b)   any further increases in gearing will be perceived as a significant increase in risk by investors.

1.4 Venture capital

Venture capital is risk capital which is generally provided in return for an equity stake in the business. They are most suited to private companies with high growth potential. Venture capitalists seek a high return (usually at least 20%), although their principal return is achieved through an **exit strategy**.

Venture capitalists generally like to have a predetermined target exit date (usually 3 – 7 years). At the outset of their investment, they will have established various exit routes, including the sale of shares to the public or to institutional investors following a flotation of the company's shares.

As well as providing funding to start-up businesses, venture capital is an important source of finance for **management buyouts** (these are discussed further in Chapter 14).

1.5 Business angels

Business angels are wealthy individuals who invest in start-up and growth businesses in return for an equity stake. The investment can involve both time and money depending on the investor. These individuals are prepared to take **high risks** in the hope of **high returns**. As a result, business angel finance can be expensive for the business.

Investments made by business angels can vary but, in the UK, most investments are in the region of £25,000.

Business angels are a very useful tool to fill the gap between venture capital and debt finance, particularly for start-up businesses. One of the main advantages of business angels is that they often follow up their initial investment with later rounds of financing as the business grows. New businesses benefit from their expertise in the difficult early stages of trying to establish themselves.

1.6 Lease finance

From your Paper F9 – *Financial Management* studies you should remember that there are two types of leases.

(a) **Finance lease** – transfers substantially all the risks and rewards of ownership of the asset to the lessee

(b) **Operating lease** – the lessor retains most of the risks and rewards of ownership

Case Study

The aircraft leasing industry has come to the fore after several aviation downturns in recent years. Lessors' ownership of the world's civil aircraft fleet has increased from 12 per cent in 1990 to 36 per cent in 2010, according to Boeing, the plane maker.

Some aircraft lessors are predicting their share of the global fleet will rise to as much as 50 per cent by 2015, partly because some airlines may find it harder to secure financing for their jets due to economic circumstances. Lessors make most of their money through the charges paid by airlines that use their jets.

Source Financial Times 17 January 2012

1.7 Private equity

Private equity consists of equity securities in companies that are not publicly traded on a stock exchange.

In Europe, private equity represents the entire spectrum of the investment sector that includes venture capital and management buy-ins and buy-outs (therefore venture capital is a specific type of private equity). In the United States, private equity and venture capital are treated as different types of investment.

In Europe, private equity funds tend to invest in more mature companies with the aim of eliminating inefficiencies and driving growth. Venture capitalists, as we have seen above, are more likely to invest in start-ups and companies in the early stages of development.

Private equity funds might require

- A 20 – 30% shareholding
- Special rights to appoint a number of directors
- The company to seek their prior approval for new issues or acquisitions

1.8 Asset securitisation

Asset securitisation involves the aggregation of assets into a pool then issuing new securities backed by these assets and their cash flows. The securities are then sold to investors who share the risk and reward from these assets.

Securitisation is similar to 'spinning off' part of a business, whereby the holding company 'sells' its right to future profits in that part of the business for immediate cash. The new investors receive a premium (usually in the form of interest) for investing in the success or failure of the segment.

Most securitisation pools consist of 'tranches'. Higher tranches carry less risk of default (and therefore lower returns) whereas junior tranches offer higher returns but greater risk.

The main reason for securitising a cash flow is that it allows companies with a credit rating of (for example) BB but with AAA-rated cash flows to possibly borrow at AAA rates. This will lead to greatly reduced interest payments as the difference between BB rates and AAA rates can be hundreds of basis points.

However securitisation is expensive due to management costs, legal fees and continuing administration fees.

1.9 Islamic finance

Islamic finance products may be suitable for an organisation, either for cultural reasons or because it offers an a commercial advantage over conventional financing.

From your Paper F9 – *Financial Management* studies you should remember the following Islamic finance transactions:

Islamic finance transaction	Similar to	Differences
Murabaha	Trade credit / loan	There is a pre-agreed mark-up to be paid, in recognition of the convenience of paying later, for an asset that is transferred immediately. There is no interest charged.
Musharaka	Venture capital	Profits are shared according to a pre-agreed contract. There are no dividends paid. Losses are shared according to capital contribution.
Mudaraba	Equity	Profits are shared according to a pre-agreed contract. There are no dividends paid. Losses are solely attributable to the provider of capital.
Ijara	Leasing	Whether an operating or finance transaction, in Ijara the lessor is still the owner of the asset and incurs the risk of ownership. This means that the lessor will be responsible for major maintenance and insurance which is different from a conventional finance lease.
Sukuk	Bonds	There is an underlying tangible asset in which the Sukuk holder shares in the risk and rewards of ownership. This gives the Sukuk properties of equity finance as well as debt finance.

Islamic finance is a growth are in finance, this is covered in more detail in Chapter 19.

1.10 Hybrids

Hybrids are means of finance that combine debt and equity. Such securities pay a fixed or floating rate of return up to a certain date, after which the holder has such options as converting the securities into the underlying equity.

Examples of hybrids include convertible bonds, debt with attached warrants and preference shares.

Most companies that issue convertible bonds expect them to be converted to equity and view the funds as 'delayed equity'. They are often used either because the company's ordinary share price is considered to be particularly depressed at the time of issue or because the issue of equity shares would result in an immediate and significant drop in earnings per share. The main risk to the company is that there is no guarantee that the security holders will choose to convert to equity. If they do not then the bonds may have to run their full term and need to be redeemed.

| Question | New business financing |

The following two new businesses are trying to raise finance to fund development.

(a) Nick Payne, a trained sports physiotherapist and personal trainer, is setting up a sports consultancy business where amateur and professional athletes can come for advice on prevention and treatment of injuries. Nick is also considering offering consultancy services on sports kits and training regimes. He is planning to rent small premises until his business becomes established. The location of the business is in a town with excellent sports facilities but with little if any sports consultancy services. He is looking for approximately $30,000 to develop his business, recruit two members of staff and set up a consultancy web site. He is hoping that the funds will also help him to go round sports centres and gyms to give presentations on the services his business can offer. Research carried out so far has shown that there is an encouraging number of interested parties in the area.

206   7a: Impact of financing on investment decisions and adjusted present values | Part C Advanced investment appraisal

BPP
LEARNING MEDIA

Nick has invested $5,000 of his own money so far on market research and initial advertising but does not have a great deal of previous business knowledge.

(b) Paula Donnelly is setting up a small hat shop, selling both formal and casual hats. She has considerable experience of making these goods herself and has produced a number of 'one off' hats for private clients. She now wants to expand her expertise into business and has been busy producing inventory for the shop. She has already invested $20,000 of her own money in obtaining and fitting out suitable premises, buying materials, building up inventory and marketing. There are no such shops in the area and research has shown Paula that ladies looking for hats have to travel a considerable distance. She has made contact with two shops in the area that specialise in formal ladies' wear for weddings, race meetings, balls etc and the owners have agreed to recommend her shop based on their existing knowledge of the quality of her 'one off' creations.

Required

Using the information above, which type(s) of finance do you think will be most suitable for each of the new businesses? Give reasons for your recommendations.

Answer

(a) Whilst Nick is a trained physiotherapist and personal trainer, the fact that he has no assets or a 'tangible' product to sell makes his business a more risky investment than Paula's. He does not have a great deal of previous business knowledge which increases the risk, although he has done some market research to determine likely customer base.

Finance for Nick's business is likely to come from sources where risk is not so much of an issue. Business angel finance is a possibility as such finance providers are prepared to take high risks in the hope of high returns. The amount of investment that Nick is looking for is also typical of what business angels are likely to provide.

Venture capital is another possibility for Nick as the business is quite unique in an area with a strong sports background. As a personal trainer, Nick is likely to have an understanding of the private health club market and the needs of members. The main problem is that Nick does not have much previous business experience – an attribute that venture capitalists look for in potential investments.

Nick has not invested a great deal of his own money in the business so far and has no assets that could act as collateral for a bank loan. It is likely that any loan that a bank might offer to Nick will come with very high interest rates to reflect the perceived risk therefore this method of financing is not a good option. If he wanted to pursue the possibility of a bank loan he might be advised to apply to the Enterprise Fund Guarantee Scheme or the Small Firms Loan Guarantee Scheme in order to obtain a guarantee for a percentage of the loan amount.

(b) Paula is in a different position to Nick. She has invested a considerable amount of her own money and has built up an asset base already (premises and inventory). Her business has a tangible product (hats) and she has established contacts with complimentary businesses to help build up her customer base. Paula has already had some business experience in that she has produced 'one off' designs for private clients that have apparently built up her good reputation (the fashion shops have agreed to recommend her based on these designs).

Paula is in a better position to obtain a bank loan at a reasonable rate. She has assets to support the loan and has already invested a considerable amount of her own cash. Tangible products are usually seen as being less risky than consultancy businesses therefore banks are more likely to grant her a loan.

Business angels and venture capitalists are also available to Paula, although business angels might be less interested due to the lower levels of risk involved. Paula might not be willing to give away a proportion of her business to business angels, in which case a bank loan might be a more favourable option.

1.11 Financial position, financial risk and value

The sources of finance available to an organisation depend on several factors, including the **financial position** of the company, the **financial risk** and the **value** of the organisation.

Unless an organisation has a good financial position, several sources of finance may be unavailable. It is difficult to imagine a loss making organisation which also has net liabilities being able to raise debt or equity finance successfully.

Similarly, a company with a high level of financial gearing may not be able to raise additional debt finance due to the high level of financial risk.

The value of an organisation will also make a difference to the types of finance that are available. An organisation that has a higher value is more likely to attract providers of finance and be able to raise equity or debt finance. Listed companies (which typically are worth more than other organisations) will also have access to international capital markets, in which they will be able to raise funds.

2 Cost of capital

You should remember the following material from your studies of F9 *Financial Management*.

There are two ways of calculating the cost of equity for an organisation – the dividend growth model and the CAPM.

2.1 The dividend growth model

Formula to learn

Cost of ordinary (equity) share capital, having a current ex div price, P_0, having just paid a dividend, d_0, with the dividend growing in perpetuity by a constant g% per annum:

$$k_e = \frac{d_0(1+g)}{P_0} + g \text{ or } k_e = \frac{d_1}{P_0} + g$$

Question

Cost of equity

A share has a current market value of 96c, and the last dividend was 12c. If the expected annual growth rate of dividends is 4%, calculate the cost of equity capital.

Answer

$$
\begin{aligned}
\text{Cost of capital} \quad &= \quad \frac{12(1 + 0.04)}{96} + 0.04 \\
&= \quad 0.13 + 0.04 \\
&= \quad 0.17 \\
&= \quad 17\%
\end{aligned}
$$

2.1.1 Estimating the growth rate

There are two methods for estimating the growth rate that you need to be familiar with.

Firstly, the future growth rate can be predicted from an **analysis of the growth in dividends** over the past few years using the formula

$$g = \sqrt[x-n]{\frac{\text{Dividend in year } x}{\text{Dividend in year } n}}$$

Alternatively the growth rate can be estimated using **Gordon's growth approximation**. The **rate of growth in dividends** is sometimes expressed, theoretically, as:

Formula to learn

> $g = br$
>
> where g   is the annual growth rate in dividends
>   b   is the proportion of profits that are retained
>   r   is the rate of return on new investments

So, if a company retains 65% of its earnings for capital investment projects it has identified and these projects are expected to have an average return of 8%:

$g = br = 65\% \times 8 = 5.2\%$

2.2 The CAPM formula

The capital asset pricing model can be stated as follows.

Exam Formula

> $E(r_i) = R_f + \beta_i(E(r_m) - R_f)$
>
> where $E(r_i)$ is the cost of equity capital
> R_f is the risk-free rate of return
> $E(r_m)$ is the return from the market as a whole
> β_i is the beta factor of the individual security

Question   Returns

The risk-free rate of return is 7%. The average market return is 11%.

(a)   What will be the return expected from a share whose β factor is 0.9?

(b)   What would be the share's expected value if it is expected to earn an annual dividend of 5.3c, with no capital growth?

Answer

(a) $7\% + 0.9 (11\% - 7\%) = 10.6\%$

(b) $\dfrac{5.3c}{10.6\%} = 50c$

2.2.1 Problems with applying the CAPM in practice

(a)   The need to **determine** the **excess return** $(E(r_m) - R_f)$. Expected, rather than historical, returns should be used, although historical returns are often used in practice.

(b)   The need to **determine** the **risk-free rate**. A risk-free investment might be a government security. However, interest rates vary with the term of the lending.

(c)   **Errors** in the **statistical analysis used** to calculate β values. Betas may also **change over** time.

(d)   The CAPM is also **unable to forecast accurately returns** for companies with **low price/earnings** ratios and to take account of seasonal 'month-of-the-year' effects and 'day-of-the-week' effects that appear to influence returns on shares.

✎ Question

(a) What does beta measure, and what do betas of 0.5, 1 and 1.5 mean?

(b) What factors determine the level of beta which a company may have?

Answer

(a) **Beta measures** the systematic risk of a risky investment such as a share in a company. The total risk of the share can be sub-divided into two parts, known as **systematic (or market) risk** and **unsystematic (or unique) risk**. The systematic risk depends on the sensitivity of the return of the share to general economic and market factors such as periods of boom and recession. The capital asset pricing model shows how the return which investors expect from shares should depend only on systematic risk, not on unsystematic risk, which can be eliminated by holding a well-diversified portfolio.

The average risk of stock market investments has a **beta of 1**. Thus shares with betas of 0.5 or 1.5 would have half or 1½ times the average sensitivity to market variations respectively.

This is reflected by higher volatility of share prices for shares with a beta of 1.5 than for those with a beta of 0.5. For example, a 10% increase in general stock market prices would be expected to be reflected as a 5% increase for a share with a beta of 0.5 and a 15% increase for a share with a beta of 1.5, with a similar effect for price reductions.

(b) The beta of a company will be the **weighted average** of the beta of its shares and the beta of its debt. The beta of debt is very low, but not zero, because corporate debt bears default risk, which in turn is dependent on the volatility of the company's cash flows.

Factors determining the beta of a company's equity shares include:

(i) **Sensitivity** of the company's **cash flows** to economic factors, as stated above. For example sales of new cars are more sensitive than sales of basic foods and necessities.

(ii) The company's **operating gearing**. A high level of fixed costs in the company's cost structure will cause high variations in operating profit compared with variations in sales.

(iii) The company's **financial gearing**. High borrowing and interest costs will cause high variations in equity earnings compared with variations in operating profit, increasing the equity beta as equity returns become more variable in relation to the market as a whole. This effect will be countered by the low beta of debt when computing the weighted average beta of the whole company.

2.3 Cost of debt

2.3.1 Irredeemable debt

Formula to learn

Cost of irredeemable debt capital, paying interest i in perpetuity, and having a current ex-interest price P_0:

$$k_d = \frac{i(1-T)}{P_0}$$

2.3.2 Redeemable debt

If the debt is **redeemable** then in the year of redemption the interest payment will be received by the holder as well as the amount payable on redemption, so:

$$P_0 = \frac{i(1-T)}{(1+k_{d\,net})} + \frac{i(1-T)}{(1+k_{d\,net})^2} + \ldots + \frac{i(1-T) + p_n}{(1+k_{d\,net})^n}$$

where p_n = the amount payable on redemption in year n.

The above equation cannot be simplified, so 'r' will have to be calculated by trial and error, as an **internal rate of return (IRR)**.

2.3.3 Example: cost of debt capital

Owen Allot has in issue 10% bonds of a nominal value of $100. The market price is $90 ex interest. Calculate the cost of this capital if the bond is:

(a) Irredeemable
(b) Redeemable at par after 10 years

Taxation is 30%.

Solution

(a) **The cost of irredeemable debt capital** is $\dfrac{i(1-T)}{P_0} = \dfrac{\$7}{\$90} \times 100\% = 7.8\%$

(b) **The cost of redeemable debt capital**.

Year		Cash flow	Discount factor	PV	Discount factor	PV
		$	10%	$	5%	$
0	Market value	(90)	1.000	(90.00)	1.000	(90.00)
1–10	Interest	7	6.145	43.02	7.722	54.05
10	Capital repayment	100	0.386	38.60	0.614	61.40
				(8.38)		25.45

The approximate cost of redeemable debt capital is, therefore:

$$\left(5 + \frac{25.45}{(25.45 - -8.38)} \times (10 - 5)\right) = 8.76\%$$

2.3.4 The cost of convertible debt

The cost of capital of convertible to debt is harder to determine. The calculation will depend on whether or not conversion is likely to happen.

(a) If conversion is **not** expected, the conversion value is ignored and the bond is treated as **redeemable debt**, using the IRR method.

(b) If conversion **is** expected, the IRR method for calculating the cost of redeemable debt is used, but the number of years to redemption is replaced by the **number of years to conversion** and the redemption value is replaced by the **conversion value** ie the market value of the shares into which the debt is to be converted.

Formula to learn

Conversion value = $P_0 (1 + g)^n R$

where
- P_0 is the current ex-dividend ordinary share price
- g is the expected annual growth of the ordinary share price
- n is the number of years to conversion
- R is the number of shares received on conversion

BPP LEARNING MEDIA

Part C Advanced investment appraisal | **7a: Impact of financing on investment decisions and adjusted present values**   211

2.3.5 Example: Cost of convertible debt

A company has issued 8% convertible bonds which are due to be redeemed in five years' time. They are currently quoted at $82 per $100 nominal. The bonds can be converted into 25 shares in five years' time. The share price is currently $3.50 and is expected to grow at a rate of 3% pa. Assume a 30% rate of tax.

Calculate the cost of the convertible debt.

Solution

$$\text{Conversion value} = P_0(1+g)^n R$$
$$= 3.50 \times (1+0.03)^5 \times 25$$
$$= \$101.44$$

As the redemption value is $100, investors would **choose to convert** the bonds so the **conversion value** is used in the IRR calculation.

Year	Cash flow		Discount factor 8%	PV $	Discount factor 12%	PV $
0	Market value	(82.00)	1.000	(82.00)	1.000	(82.00)
1 – 5	Interest (8 ×(1 – 0.3))	5.60	3.993	22.36	3.605	20.19
5	Conversion value	101.44	0.681	69.08	0.567	57.52
				9.44		(4.29)

$$\text{Cost of debt} = 8\% + \frac{9.44}{9.44 + 4.29}(12\% - 8\%) = 10.75\%$$

2.4 The cost of preference shares

For preference shares the future cash flows are the dividend payments in perpetuity so that:

The cost of preference shares can be calculated as $k_{pref} = \dfrac{d}{P_0}$.

2.5 General formula for the WACC

A general formula for the weighted average cost of capital (WACC) k_0 is as follows.

$$\text{WACC} = \left[\frac{V_e}{V_e + V_d} \right] k_e + \left[\frac{V_d}{V_e + V_d} \right] k_d (1 - T)$$

where
k_e is the cost of equity
k_d is the cost of debt
V_e is the market value of equity in the firm
V_d is the market value of debt in the firm
T is the rate of company tax

2.6 The relationship between company value and cost of capital

The market value of a company depends on its cost of capital. The lower a company's WACC, the higher will be the net present value of its future cash flows and therefore the higher will be its market value.

212 **7a: Impact of financing on investment decisions and adjusted present values** | Part C Advanced investment appraisal

BPP
LEARNING MEDIA

2.7 Using the WACC in investment appraisal

The weighted average cost of capital can be used in investment appraisal if:

(a) The project being appraised is **small relative** to the company.
(b) The **existing capital structure** will be maintained (same financial risk).
(c) The project has the same **business risk** as the company.

2.8 Arguments against using the WACC

(a) New investments undertaken by a company might have different **business risk** characteristics from the company's existing operations. As a consequence, the return required by investors might go up (or down) if the investments are undertaken, because their business risk is perceived to be higher (or lower).

(b) The finance that is raised to fund a new investment might substantially change the capital structure and the perceived **financial risk** of investing in the company. Depending on whether the project is financed by equity or by debt capital, the perceived financial risk of the entire company might change. This must be taken into account when appraising investments.

(c) Many companies raise **floating rate** debt capital as well as fixed interest debt capital. With floating rate debt capital, the interest rate is variable, and is altered every three or six months or so in line with changes in current market interest rates. The cost of debt capital will therefore fluctuate as market conditions vary. Floating rate debt is difficult to incorporate into a WACC computation, and the best that can be done is to substitute an 'equivalent' fixed interest debt capital cost in place of the floating rate debt cost.

3 CAPM and portfolios

FAST FORWARD

> The **expected return** of a portfolio of shares can be calculated by calculating the weighted beta of the portfolio and using CAPM.

3.1 Beta factors of portfolios

Just as an individual security has a beta factor, so too does a portfolio of securities.

(a) A portfolio consisting of all the **securities** on the **stock market** (in the same proportions as the market as a whole), excluding risk-free securities, will have an expected return equal to the expected return for the market as a whole, and so will have a **beta factor of 1**.

(b) A portfolio consisting entirely of **risk-free securities** will have a beta factor of **0**.

(c) The beta factor of an investor's portfolio is the **weighted average** of the **beta factors** of the securities in the **portfolio**.

3.1.1 Example: Beta factors and portfolios

A portfolio consisting of five securities could have its beta factor computed as follows.

Security	Percentage of portfolio %	Beta factor of security	Weighted beta factor
A Inc	20	0.90	0.180
B Inc	10	1.25	0.125
C Inc	15	1.10	0.165
D Inc	20	1.15	0.230
E Inc	35	0.70	0.245
	100	Portfolio beta =	0.945

If the risk-free rate of return is 12% and the average market return is 20%, the required return from the portfolio using the CAPM equation would be 12% + (20 − 12) × 0.945% = 19.56%

The calculation could have been made as follows.

Security	Beta factor	Expected return $E(r_i)$	Weighting %	Weighted return %
A Inc	0.90	19.2	20	3.84
B Inc	1.25	22.0	10	2.20
C Inc	1.10	20.8	15	3.12
D Inc	1.15	21.2	20	4.24
E Inc	0.70	17.6	35	6.16
			100	19.56

3.2 CAPM and portfolio management

Practical implications of CAPM theory for an investor are as follows.

(a) He should decide what **beta factor** he would **like to have** for his portfolio. He might prefer a portfolio beta factor of greater than 1, in order to expect above-average returns when market returns exceed the risk-free rate, but he would then expect to lose heavily if market returns fall. On the other hand, he might prefer a portfolio beta factor of 1 or even less.

(b) He should seek to invest in shares with **low beta factors** in a **bear market**, when average market returns are falling. He should then also sell shares with high beta factors.

(c) He should seek to invest in shares with **high beta factors** in a **bull market**, when average market returns are rising.

3.3 International CAPM

The possibility of international portfolio diversification increases the opportunities available to investors.

If we assume that the international capital market is a **fully integrated market** like an enlarged domestic market, then we have an international CAPM formula as follows.

$$E(r_i) = r_f + [E(r_w) - r_f]\beta_w$$

where $E(r_w)$ is the expected return from the world market portfolio and β_w is a measure of the world systematic risk.

This analysis implies that the risk premium is proportional to the world systematic risk, β_w, and that investors can benefit from maximum diversification by investing in the world market portfolio consisting of all securities in the world economy. New risk and return combinations may be available.

In practice, such complete diversification will of course not be practicable. However, significant international diversification can be achieved by the following methods:

- Direct investment in companies in different countries
- Investments in multinational enterprises
- Holdings in unit trusts or investment trusts which are diversified internationally

3.4 Segmentation and integration

The international picture may be complicated by market segmentation. Segmentation is usually caused by government-imposed restrictions on the movement of capital, leading to restricted capital availability within a country or other geographical segment. Therefore:

- Returns on the same security may differ in different markets
- Some investments may only be available in certain markets

In a segmented market the parent company of a international group would use its own country's risk-free rate and market return in CAPM calculations.

In practice the situation that a multinational company faces will often not be completely integrated nor completely segmented. In this situation a multinational can use CAPM to estimate a local cost of equity and a world cost of equity, and use a cost of equity that is somewhere in between the two.

3.5 Limitations of the CAPM for the selection of a portfolio

Under the CAPM, the return required from a security is related to its systematic risk rather than its total risk. If we relax some of the assumptions upon which the model is based, then the total risk may be important. In particular, the following points should be considered.

(a) The model assumes that the **costs of insolvency** are **zero**, or in other words, that all **assets** can be **sold** at **going concern prices** and that there are no selling, legal or other costs. In practice, the costs of insolvency cannot be ignored. Furthermore, the risk of insolvency is related to a firm's total risk rather than just its systematic risk.

(b) The model assumes that the **investment market** is **efficient**. If it is not, this will limit the extent to which investors are able to eliminate unsystematic risk from their portfolios.

(c) The model also assumes that **portfolios are well diversified** and so need only be concerned with systematic risk. However, this is not necessarily the case, and undiversified or partly-diversified shareholders should also be concerned with unsystematic risk and will seek a total return appropriate to the total risk that they face.

4 Project specific cost of capital

CAPM can also be used to calculate a **project-specific cost of capital**.

The CAPM produces a required return based on the expected return of the market $E(r_m)$, the risk-free interest rate (R_f) and the variability of project returns relative to the market returns (β). Its main advantage when used for investment appraisal is that it produces a discount rate which is based on the **systematic** risk of the individual investment.

It can be used to **compare projects of all different risk classes** and is therefore superior to an NPV approach which uses only one discount rate for all projects, regardless of their risk.

The model was developed with respect to securities; by applying it to an investment within the firm, the company is assuming that the shareholder wishes investments to be evaluated as if they were securities in the capital market and thus assumes that all shareholders will hold **diversified portfolios** and will not look to the company to achieve diversification for them.

4.1 Limitations of using CAPM in investment decisions

The greatest practical problems with the use of the CAPM in capital investment decisions are as follows.

(a) It is **hard to estimate** returns on projects under different economic environments, market returns under different economic environments and the probabilities of the various environments.

(b) The CAPM is really just a **single period model**. Few investment projects last for one year only and to extend the use of the return estimated from the model to more than one time period would require both project performance relative to the market and the economic environment to be reasonably stable.

In theory, it should be possible to apply the CAPM for each time period, thus arriving at successive discount rates, one for each year of the project's life. In practice, this would exacerbate the estimation problems mentioned above and also make the discounting process much more cumbersome.

(c) It may be **hard to determine the risk-free rate of return**. Government securities are usually taken to be risk-free, but the return on these securities varies according to their term to maturity.

(d) Some experts have argued that betas calculated using complicated statistical techniques often overestimate high betas, and underestimate low betas, particularly for small companies.

4.1.1 Beta values and the effect of gearing

The gearing of a company will affect the risk of its equity. If a company is geared and its **financial risk is therefore higher** than the risk of an all-equity company, then the β value of the geared company's equity will be higher than the β value of a similar ungeared company's equity.

The CAPM is consistent with the propositions of Modigliani and Miller. MM argue that as gearing rises, the cost of equity rises to compensate shareholders for the extra financial risk of investing in a geared company. This financial risk is an aspect of systematic risk, and ought to be reflected in a company's beta factor.

4.1.2 Geared betas and ungeared betas

The connection between MM theory and the CAPM means that it is possible to establish a mathematical relationship between the β value of an ungeared company and the β value of a similar, but geared, company. The β value of a geared company will be higher than the β value of a company identical in every respect except that it is all-equity financed. This is because of the extra financial risk. The mathematical relationship between the 'ungeared' (or asset) and 'geared' betas is as follows.

Exam Formulae

$$\beta_a = \left[\frac{V_e}{(V_e + V_d(1-T))}\beta_e \right] + \left[\frac{V_d(1-T)}{(V_e + V_d(1-T))}\beta_d \right]$$

This is the **asset beta formula** on the exam formula sheet.

where β_a is the asset or ungeared beta

β_e is the equity or geared beta

β_d is the beta factor of debt in the geared company

V_D is the market value of the debt capital in the geared company

V_E is the market value of the equity capital in the geared company

T is the rate of corporate tax

Debt is often assumed to be risk-free and its beta (β_d) is then taken as zero, in which case the formula above reduces to the following form.

$$\beta_a = \beta_e \times \frac{V_e}{V_e + V_d(1-T)} \quad \text{or, without tax,} \quad \beta_a = \beta_e \times \frac{V_e}{V_e + V_d}$$

4.1.3 Example: CAPM and geared betas

Two companies are identical in every respect except for their capital structure. Their market values are in equilibrium, as follows.

	Geared	Ungeared
	$'000	$'000
Annual profit before interest and tax	1,000	1,000
Less interest (4,000 × 8%)	320	0
	680	1,000
Less tax at 30%	204	300
Profit after tax = dividends	476	700
Market value of equity	3,900	6,600
Market value of debt	4,180	0
Total market value of company	8,080	6,600

The total value of Geared is higher than the total value of Ungeared, which is consistent with MM.

All profits after tax are paid out as dividends, and so there is no dividend growth. The beta value of Ungeared has been calculated as 1.0. The debt capital of Geared can be regarded as risk-free.

Calculate:

(a) The cost of equity in Geared

(b) The market return R_m

(c) The beta value of Geared

Solution

(a) Since its market value (MV) is in equilibrium, the cost of equity in Geared can be calculated as:

$$\frac{d}{MV} = \frac{476}{3,900} = 12.20\%$$

(b) The beta value of Ungeared is 1.0, which means that the expected returns from Ungeared are exactly the same as the market returns, and $R_m = 700/6,600 = 10.6\%$.

(c) $\beta_e = \beta_a \times \dfrac{V_e + V_d(1-T)}{V_e}$

$= 1.0 \times \dfrac{3,900 + (4,180 \times 0.70)}{3,900} = 1.75$

The beta of Geared, as we should expect, is higher than the beta of Ungeared.

4.1.4 Using the geared and ungeared beta formula to estimate a beta factor

Another way of estimating a beta factor for a company's equity is to use data about the returns of other quoted companies which have similar operating characteristics: that is, to use the beta values of other companies' equity to estimate a beta value for the company under consideration. The beta values estimated for the firm under consideration must be **adjusted to allow for differences in gearing** from the firms whose equity beta values are known. The formula for geared and ungeared beta values can be applied.

If a company plans to invest in a project which involves diversification into a new business, the investment will involve a different level of systematic risk from that applying to the company's existing business. A discount rate should be calculated which is specific to the project, and which takes account of both the project's systematic risk and the company's gearing level. The discount rate can be found using the CAPM.

Step 1 Get an estimate of the systematic risk characteristics of the project's operating cash flows by obtaining published beta values for companies in the industry into which the company is planning to diversify.

Step 2 Adjust these beta values to allow for the company's capital gearing level. This adjustment is done in two stages.

(a) Convert the beta values of other companies in the industry to ungeared betas, using the formula:

$$\beta_a = \beta_e \left(\frac{V_e}{V_e + V_d(1-T)} \right)$$

(b) Having obtained an ungeared beta value β_a, convert it back to a geared beta β_e, which reflects the company's own gearing ratio, using the formula:

$$\beta_e = \beta_a \left(\frac{V_e + V_d(1-T)}{V_e} \right)$$

Step 3 Having estimated a project-specific geared beta, use the CAPM to estimate a project-specific cost of equity.

4.1.5 Weaknesses in the formula

The problems with using the geared and ungeared beta formula for calculating a firm's equity beta from data about other firms are as follows.

(a) It is **difficult to identify other firms with identical operating characteristics**.

(b) **Estimates of beta values** from **share price information are not wholly accurate**. They are based on statistical analysis of historical data, and as the previous example shows, estimates using one firm's data will differ from estimates using another firm's data.

(c) There may be **differences in beta values** between firms caused by:
   (i) Different cost structures (eg, the ratio of fixed costs to variable costs)
   (ii) Size differences between firms
   (iii) Debt capital not being risk-free

(d) If the firm for which an equity beta is being estimated has **opportunities for growth** that are recognised by investors, and which will affect its equity beta, estimates of the equity beta based on other firms' data will be inaccurate, because the opportunities for growth will not be allowed for.

Perhaps the most significant simplifying assumption is that to link MM theory to the CAPM, it must be assumed that the **cost of debt** is a **risk-free rate of return**. This could obviously be unrealistic. Companies may default on interest payments or capital repayments on their loans. It has been estimated that corporate debt has a beta value of 0.2 or 0.3.

The consequence of making the assumption that debt is risk-free is that the formulae tend to **overstate** the financial risk in a geared company and to **understate** the business risk in geared and ungeared companies by a compensating amount.

Question	Gearing and ungearing betas

Backwoods is a major international company with its head office in the UK, wanting to raise £150 million to establish a new production plant in the eastern region of Germany. Backwoods evaluates its investments using NPV, but is not sure what cost of capital to use in the discounting process for this project evaluation.

The company is also proposing to increase its equity finance in the near future for UK expansion, resulting overall in little change in the company's market-weighted capital gearing.

The summarised financial data for the company before the expansion are shown below.

INCOME STATEMENT (EXTRACTS) FOR THE YEAR ENDED 31 DECEMBER 20X1

	£m
Revenue	1,984
Gross profit	432
Profit after tax	81
Dividends	37
Retained earnings	44

STATEMENT OF FINANCIAL POSITION (EXTRACTS) AS AT 31 DECEMBER 20X1

	£m
Non-current assets	846
Working capital	350
	1,196
Medium term and long term loans (see note below)	210
	986
Shareholders' funds	
Issued ordinary shares of £0.50 each nominal value	225
Reserves	761
	986

218   **7a: Impact of financing on investment decisions and adjusted present values** | Part C Advanced investment appraisal

BPP
LEARNING MEDIA

Note on borrowings

These include £75m 14% fixed rate bonds due to mature in five years time and redeemable at par. The current market price of these bonds is £120.00 and they have an after-tax cost of debt of 9%. Other medium and long-term loans are floating rate UK bank loans at LIBOR plus 1%, with an after-tax cost of debt of 7%.

Company rate of tax may be assumed to be at the rate of 30%. The company's ordinary shares are currently trading at 376 pence.

The equity beta of Backwoods is estimated to be 1.18. The systematic risk of debt may be assumed to be zero. The risk free rate is 7.75% and market return 14.5%.

The estimated equity beta of the main German competitor in the same industry as the new proposed plant in the eastern region of Germany is 1.5, and the competitor's capital gearing is 35% equity and 65% debt by book values, and 60% equity and 40% debt by market values.

Required

Estimate the cost of capital that the company should use as the discount rate for its proposed investment in eastern Germany. State clearly any assumptions that you make.

Answer

The discount rate that should be used is the weighted average cost of capital (WACC), with weightings based on market values. The cost of capital should take into account the systematic risk of the new investment, and therefore it will not be appropriate to use the company's existing equity beta. Instead, the estimated equity beta of the main German competitor in the same industry as the new proposed plant will be ungeared, and then the capital structure of Backwoods applied to find the WACC to be used for the discount rate.

Since the systematic risk of debt can be assumed to be zero, the German equity beta can be 'ungeared' using the following expression.

$$\beta_a = \beta_e \, \frac{V_e}{V_e + V_d\,(1-T)}$$

where: β_a = asset beta
β_e = equity beta
V_e = proportion of equity in capital structure
V_d = proportion of debt in capital structure
T = tax rate

For the German company:

$$\beta_a = 1.5 \left(\frac{60}{60 + 40(1 - 0.30)} \right) = 1.023$$

The next step is to calculate the debt and equity of Backwoods based on market values.

		£m
Equity	450m shares at 376p	1,692.0
Debt: bank loans	(210 – 75)	135.0
Debt: bonds	(75 million × 1.20)	90.0
Total debt		225.0
Total market value		1,917.0

The beta can now be re-geared

$$\beta_e = \frac{1.023(1,692 + 225\,(1 - 0.3))}{1,692} = 1.118$$

This can now be substituted into the capital asset pricing model (CAPM) to find the cost of equity.

$$E(r_i) = R_f + \beta (E(r_m) - R_f)$$

where: $E(r_i)$ = cost of equity
  R_f = risk free rate of return
  $E(r_m)$ = market rate of return
  $E(r_i)$ = 7.75% + (14.5% − 7.75%) × 1.118 = 15.30%

The WACC can now be calculated:

$$\left[15.3 \times \frac{1,692}{1,917} \right] + \left[7 \times \frac{135}{1,917} \right] + \left[9 \times \frac{90}{1,917} \right] = 14.4\%$$

5 Duration

FAST FORWARD

> Duration (also known as Macaulay duration) is the weighted average length of time to the receipt of a bond's benefits (coupon and redemption value), the weights being the present value of the benefits involved.

Exam focus point

Macaulay duration was examined as a 17 mark Section B optional question in June 2011. As well as performing calculations, students were required to discuss how useful duration is as a measure of the sensitivity of a bond price to changes in interest rates.

5.1 What is duration?

The average time taken to recover the cash flow from an investment is not only affected by the maturity date of the investment but also by the coupon rate (which determines the interest payments). We want to be able to compare bonds quickly – this is where duration is useful.

Duration gives each bond an overall **risk weighting** that allows two bonds to be compared. In simple terms, it is a **composite** measure of the risk expressed in years.

Duration is the **weighted average** length of time to the receipt of a bond's **benefits** (coupon and redemption value), the weights being the **present value** of the benefits involved.

5.2 Calculating duration

Formula to learn

Step 1 Add the present value of the cash flows in each time period together.

Step 2 Multiply the present value of cash flows for each time period by the time period and add together.

Step 3 Divide the result of step 2 by the result of step 1

Example

Magic Inc has a bond (Bond X) in issue which has a nominal value of $1,000 and is redeemable at par.

Bond X is a 6% bond maturing in three years' time and has a gross redemption yield (GRY) of 3.5%. The current price of the bond is $1,070.12.

Required

Calculate the duration of the bond.

Solution

Bond X

	1	2	3	Total
Cash flow	60	60	1,060	
Discount factor (3.5%)	0.966	0.934	0.902	
Present value	57.96	56.04	956.12	1,070.12
× by year	57.96	112.08	2,868.36	3,038.40

Duration = 3,038.40/1,070.12 = 2.84 years

Note that the total present value of the cash flows from the bond is equal to the current market price, which is what we expect. We could therefore simplify the duration calculation to

> Duration = Sum of PV of cash flows multiplied by respective years/Market price of bond

5.3 Properties of duration

The basic features of sensitivity to interest rate risk will all be mirrored in the duration calculation.

- **Longer-dated bonds** will have longer durations
- **Lower-coupon bonds** will have longer durations. The ultimate low-coupon bond is a zero-coupon bond where the duration will be the maturity
- **Lower yields** will give longer durations. In this case, the present value of flows in the future will rise if the yield falls, extending the point of balance, therefore lengthening the duration

The duration of a bond will shorten as the life span of the bond decays. However, the rate of decay will not be at the same rate. In our example above, a three-year bond has a duration of 2.84 years. In a year's time the bond will have a remaining life of two years and a duration based on the same GRY of 1.94 years. The life span has decayed by a full year, but the duration by only 0.9 years.

5.4 Modified duration

> **Modified duration** is a measure of the sensitivity of the price of a bond to a change in interest rates.

Rather than looking at the weighted average time it takes to receive the bond's benefits, modified duration measures how sensitive the price of the bond is to a change in the interest rate.

> $$\text{Modified duration} = \frac{\text{Macaulay duration}}{1 + \text{GRY}}$$

Using the above example on duration, the modified duration of the bond is

2.84/(1 + 0.035) = 2.74

This can be used to determine the proportionate change in bond price for a given change in yield as follows.

$$\frac{\Delta P}{P} = -\text{Modified duration} \times \Delta Y$$

which can also be expressed as:

> $\Delta P = -\text{Modified duration} \times \Delta Y \times P$
>
> Where:
>
> ΔP = change in bond price $\quad$ P = current market price of the bond
>
> ΔY = change in yield

Remember there is an **inverse relationship** between yield and bond price, therefore the modified duration figure is expressed as a negative number.

If, in the above example, the yield increased by 0.5%, the change in price can be calculated as follows.

$\Delta P = -2.74 \times 0.005 \times \$1,070.12 = \$(14.66)$

Thus for a 0.5% increase in yield, the bond price will fall by $14.66.

5.4.1 Properties of modified duration

As the modified duration is derived from the Macaulay duration, it shares the same properties.

- **Longer dated bonds** will have higher modified durations – that is, bonds which are due to be redeemed at a later date are more price-sensitive to changes in interest rates and are therefore more risky
- **Lower coupon bonds** will have higher modified durations
- **Lower yields** will give higher modified durations

The higher the modified duration, then the greater the sensitivity of that bond to a change in the yield.

5.5 The benefits and limitations of duration   6/11

5.5.1 Benefits

The main **benefits** of duration are as follows.

(a) Duration allows bonds of **different maturities** and **coupon rates** to be directly compared. This makes decision-making regarding bond finance easier and more effective.

(b) If a bond portfolio is constructed based on weighted average duration, it is possible to determine portfolio value changes based on estimated changes in interest rates.

(c) Managers may be able to modify interest rate risk by changing the duration of the bond portfolio – for example, by adding shorter maturity bonds or those with higher coupons (which will reduce duration), or by adding longer maturity bonds or those with lower coupons (which will increase duration).

5.5.2 Limitations

The main limitation of duration is that it **assumes a linear relationship** between interest rates and price – that is, it assumes that for a certain percentage change in interest rates there will be an equal percentage change in price.

However as interest rates change the bond price is unlikely to change in a linear fashion. Rather, it will have some kind of convex relationship with interest rates (see below).

Relationship Between Bond Price and Yield

222   **7a: Impact of financing on investment decisions and adjusted present values** | Part C Advanced investment appraisal

BPP
LEARNING MEDIA

As you can see from the diagram above, the more convex the relationship the more inaccurate duration is for measuring interest rate sensitivity. Therefore duration should be treated with caution in your predictions of interest rate/price relationships.

Duration can only be applied to measure the approximate change in bond price due to changes in interest rates if the interest rate change does not lead to a change in the shape of the yield curve. This is because it is an average measure based on the GRY (yield to maturity).

However used in conjunction with each other, convexity and duration can provide a more accurate approximation of the percentage change in price resulting from a percentage change in interest rates. It can also be used to compare bonds with the same duration but different levels of convexity. For example, if Bond X has a higher convexity than Bond Y, its price would fall by a lower percentage in the event of rising interest rates.

6 Credit risk   12/08, 12/11

Key term

> **Credit risk**, also referred to as **default risk**, is the risk undertaken by the lender that the borrower will default either on **interest payments** or on the **repayment of principal** on the due date, or on both.

Exam focus point

> In an optional question in December 2008, you were asked to estimate the probability of default. One of the features of the question was the reliance on basic financial maths skills.
>
> The issues and techniques involved in the question were covered in an article in the August 2008 issue of Student Accountant.
>
> In December 2011, credit ratings were examined in an optional question.

6.1 Credit risk aspects

Credit risk arises from the inability of a party to fulfil its obligation under the terms of a contract. We have already discussed credit risk in relation to the OTC derivatives and how exchanges deal with it through the introduction of margins. Creditors to companies such as corporate bondholders and banks are also exposed to credit risk. The credit risk of an individual loan or bond is determined by the following two factors:

The probability of default

This is the probability that the borrower or counterparty will default on its contractual obligations to repay its debt.

The recovery rate

This is the fraction of the face value of an obligation that can be recovered once the borrower has defaulted. When an company defaults, bond holders do not necessarily lose their entire investment. Part of the investment may be recovered depending on the **recovery rate**.

Key term

> The **loss given default** (LGD) is the difference between the **amount of money owed** by the borrower less the **amount of money recovered**.

For example, a bond has a face value of $100 and the recovery rate is 80 percent. The **loss given default** in this case is:

Loss given default = $100 − $80 = $20

Key term

> The **expected loss** (EL) from credit risk shows the amount of money the lender should expect to lose from the investment in a bond or loan with credit risk.

The **expected loss** (EL) is the product of the **loss given default** (LGD) and the **probability of default** (PD).

EL = PD × LGD

If the probability of default is, say, 10 percent, the expected loss form investing in the above bond is:

EL = 0.10 × 20 = $2

6.2 Credit risk measurement

We have already discussed how to measure **market risk**, using measures such as the **standard deviation** or the **beta**. The measurement of **credit risk** is slightly more complex. All the approaches concentrate on the estimation of the **default probability** and the **recovery rate**.

The oldest and most common approach is to assess the probability of default using financial and other information on the borrowers and assign a rating that reflects the expected loss from investing in the particular bond. This assignment of **credit risk ratings** is done by **credit rating companies** such Standard & Poor, Moody's Investor Services or Fitch. These ratings are widely accepted as indicators of the credit risk of a bond. The table below shows the credit rating used by Moody's and Standard and Poor..

Credit Risk Rating

Standard & Poor	Moody's	Description of Category
AAA	Aaa	Highest quality, lowest default risk
AA	Aa	High quality
A	A	Upper medium grade quality
BBB	Baa	Medium grade quality
BB	Ba	Lower medium grade quality
B	B	Speculative
CCC	Caa	Poor quality (high default risk)
CC	Ca	Highly speculative
C	C	Lowest grade quality

For Standard and Poor's ratings, those ratings from 'AA' to 'CCC' may be modified by the addition of a plus (+) or minus (-) sign to show relative standing within the major rating categories. For example, a company with BB+ rating is considered to have a better credit rating than a company with a BB rating, although they are in the same major rating category.

With Moody's, numerical modifiers 1, 2 and 3 are added to each ratings category from Aa to Caa, with 1 indicating a higher ranking within the category. For example, a rating of Baa1 is higher than Baa2.

Both credit rating agencies estimate default probabilities from the **empirical performance** of issued **corporate bonds** of each category. The table below shows the probability of default for certain credit categories over different investment horizons. The probability of default within a year for AAA, AA,or A bonds is practically zero whereas for a CCC bond is 19.79%. However, although the probability of default for a AAA company is **practically zero** over a single year, it becomes 1.40% over a fifteen year period (this is consistent with the theory that, the longer the time horizon, the riskier the investment).

Standard and Poor's cumulative default probabilities

Initial Rating Term	Years							
	1	2	3	4	5	7	10	15
AAA	0.00%	0.00	0.07	0.15	0.24	0.66	1.40	1.40
AA	0.00%	0.02	0.12	0.25	0.43	0.89	1.29	1.48
A	0.06%	0.16	0.27	0.44	0.67	1.12	2.17	3.00
BBB	0.18%	0.44	0.72	1.27	1.78	2.99	4.34	4.70
BB	1.06%	3.48	6.12	8.68	10.97	14.46	17.73	19.91
B	5.20%	11.00	15.95	19.40	21.88	25.14	29.02	30.65
CCC	19.79%	26.92	31.63	35.97	40.15	42.64	45.10	45.10

6.3 Criteria for establishing credit ratings

The criteria for rating international organisations encompasses the following.

Country risk	No issuer's debt will be rated higher than the country of origin of the issuer (the 'Sovereign Ceiling' concept)
Universal/Country Importance	The company's standing relative to other companies in the country of domicile and globally (measured in terms of sales, profits, relationship with government, importance of the industry to the country, etc)
Industry risk	The strength of the industry within the country, measured by the impact of economic forces, cyclical nature of the industry, demand factors, etc.
Industry position	Issuer's position in the relevant industry compared with competitors in terms of operating efficiency.
Management evaluation	The company's planning, controls, financing policies and strategies, overall quality of management and succession, merger and acquisition performance and record of achievement in financial results.
Accounting quality	Auditor's qualifications (if any) of the accounts, and accounting policies for inventory, goodwill, depreciation policies and so on.
Earnings protection	Earnings power including return on capital, pre-tax and net profit margins, sources of future earnings growth.
Financial gearing	Long-term debt and total debt in relation to capital, gearing, nature of assets, off-balance sheet commitments, working capital, management, etc.
Cash flow adequacy	Relationship of cash flow to gearing and ability to finance all business cash needs.
Financial flexibility	Evaluation of financing needs, plans and alternatives under stress (ability to attract capital), banking relationships, debt covenants.

Case Study

In August 2011, Standard and Poor's downgraded the USA's long-term credit rating from AAA to AA+. Speaking after the financial markets closed on 5 August 2011, the agency said
'*The downgrade reflects our opinion that the fiscal consolidation plan that Congress and the administration recently agreed to falls short of what, in our view, would be necessary to stabilise the government's medium-term debt dynamics*'.

Moody's did not downgrade the credit rating but lowered its outlook on US debt to 'negative', which indicates a possibility that the agency will downgrade the rating within the next year or two.

In January 2012 Standard and Poor's also downgraded France from AAA to AA+.

6.4 Credit migration

FAST FORWARD

The credit rating of a borrower may change after a bond is issued. This is referred to as credit migration.

There is another aspect of **credit risk** which should be taken into account when investors are investing in **corporate bonds**, beyond the **probability of default** .

A borrower may not default, but due to changing economic conditions or management actions the borrower may be become more or less risky than at the time the bond was issued and as a result, the bond issuer will be assigned by the credit agency a different credit rating. This is called **credit migration**. The significance of credit migration lies in the fact that the assignment of **lower credit rating** will

decrease the market value of the corporate bond. This is discussed in the next section in the context of credit spreads.

6.5 Reducing credit risk – credit enhancement

FAST FORWARD

Credit enhancement is the process of reducing credit risk by requiring collateral, insurance, or other agreements to provide the lender with reassurance that it will be compensated if the borrower defaulted.

Credit enhancement is a key part of the securitisation transaction in structured finance and is important for credit rating agencies when raising a securitisation.

6.5.1 Internal credit enhancement

FAST FORWARD

There are two main types of internal credit enhancement – excess spread and over-collateralisation.

Excess spread

Another name for excess spread is 'excess interest cash flow'. It is the difference between interest received by issuers of asset-based securities (such as mortgages) on the securities sold and the interest paid to the holders of these securities. One example is sub-prime mortgages. Such mortgages are sold at a higher rate of interest than prime mortgages, resulting in higher interest receipts for the mortgage providers. This surplus interest – usually deposited into reserve accounts – can be used as a 'first line of protection' against

Over-collateralisation

Over-collateralisation is a common form of credit enhancement. In simple terms, it is the **ratio of assets to liabilities**. Over-collateralisation occurs when the value of the assets held to support a security is actually greater than the security itself (the ratio of assets to liabilities is greater than 1). This gives the holder of the assets a 'cushion' in the event of late or non-payment from the security

How the level of over-collateralisation is determined can be illustrated using an example from Standard and Poor's. A cash flow transaction involves the issue of $80 million of senior debt which is supported (backed) by a collateral pool of assets which has a par value of $100 million (known as an 80/20 liability structure). The level of over-collateralisation is the ratio of assets to liabilities – that is, $100 million/$80 million or 125%.

6.5.2 External credit enhancement

FAST FORWARD

External credit enhancement tools include surety bonds, letters of credit and cash collateral accounts.

Surety bond

A **surety bond** is a guarantee to pay a loss sustained as a result of a breach of contractual or legal obligations. Strictly speaking, a surety bond is a **contract of guarantee**, not of insurance and involves three persons: the **contractor**, who puts the bond in place, the **employer**, who is contracting with the contractor and requires the surety bond to be provided, and the **guarantor**, who may be an insurer. In the event of the contractor's default, the guarantor compensates the employer for any losses incurred. Often the guarantor provides its guarantees only to securities already of at least investment-grade quality (that is, BBB/Baa or equivalent).

Letter of credit

A financial institution (typically a bank) which issues a letter of credit is **obliged** to reimburse any losses incurred up to the required credit-enhancement amount, in return for a fee.

Letters of credit are **often used in international trade** to protect both the importer and exporter. A letter of credit represents a written undertaking given by a bank on behalf of an importer to pay a specified sum of money to the exporter within a certain time. In order to be entitled to the payment however the exporter must be able to produce necessary documentation that complies with the terms stated in the letter of credit.

In the early 1990s, the long-term debt of some of the banks responsible for issuing letters of credit was **downgraded**, which lessened the appeal of these tools.

Cash collateral account

A **cash collateral account** is an account that is used to secure and service a loan. Deposits are made into this account but no sums can be withdrawn. When funds are paid in and have cleared, this reduces the loan which is served by this account. As no sums can be withdrawn it is viewed as a zero-balance account – any money that is paid in goes immediately towards reducing the extent of the loan being served.

As a cash collateral account is an actual deposit of cash, a downgrade of the account provider would not result in a similar downgrade of the security (unlike letters of credit and surety bonds).

7 Credit spreads and the cost of debt capital

FAST FORWARD

> The cost of debt capital and the market price of corporate bonds depend on the credit risk of the bond.

7.1 Credit spreads

Key term

> The **credit spread** is the premium required by an Investor in a corporate bond to compensate for the **credit risk** of the bond.

The yield to a government bond holder is the compensation to the investor for foregoing consumption today and saving. However, corporate bond holders should require compensation not only for foregoing consumption, but also for the credit risk that they are exposed to. As we discussed in the previous section, this is a function of the probability of default, the recovery rate and the probability of migration. Assuming that a government bond such as the one issued by the US or an EU government is **free** of **credit risk**, the yield on a corporate bond will be

Formula to Learn

> Yield on corporate bond = risk free rate + credit spread

Since **credit spreads** reflect the **credit risk** of a bond, they will be inversely related to the credit quality of the bond. **Low credit quality** bonds will be characterised by **large spreads** and **high credit quality** bonds will be characterised by **low spreads**. An example of credit spreads by type of bond and maturity is given below.

Reuters Corporate Spreads for Industrials (in basis points)

Rating	1 year	2 year	3 year	5 year	7 year	10 year	30 year
AAA	5	10	15	20	25	33	60
AA	15	25	30	35	44	52	71
A	35	44	55	60	65	73	90
BBB	60	75	100	105	112	122	143
BB	140	180	210	205	210	250	300
B	215	220	260	300	315	350	450
CCC	1,125	1,225	1,250	1,200	1,200	1,275	1,400

Source: www.bondsonline.com, 10th August 2011

Example (1)

The current return on a 10 year government bond is 4.2%. Roger Inc, a company rated AA, has 10 year bonds in issue. Using the credit spread table above, calculate the expected yield on Roger Inc's bonds.

Solution

The credit spread on a 10 year AA bond is 52, which means that 0.52% should be added to the return on the government bond.

Expected yield on Roger Inc's bonds = 4.2% + 0.52% = 4.72%

Example (2)

A 15 year government bond has a current yield of 5%. Dibble Inc, a B rated company, has equivalent bonds in issue. What is the expected yield on Dibble Inc's bonds?

Solution

The table does not include credit spreads for 15 year bonds therefore some adjustment is required to the figures we have available.

The credit spread on a 10 year B rated bond is 350 and a 30 year B rated bond is 450. The adjustment can be calculated as follows.

$$350 + \frac{(450 - 350)}{(30 - 10)} \times 5 = 375$$

This means that 3.75% must be added to the yield on government bonds.

The expected yield on Dibble's bonds is therefore 5% + 3.75% = 8.75%

7.2 The cost of debt capital

The cost of debt capital for a company is determined by the following:

(a)   its credit rating
(b)   the maturity of the debt.
(c)   the risk-free rate at the appropriate maturity
(d)   the corporate tax rate

Formula to learn

Cost of debt capital = (1 – tax rate)(risk free rate + credit spread)

Question

Cost of Capital

Jolly Inc, a BBB rated company, has 5 year bonds in issue. The current yield on equivalent government bonds is 3.7% and the current rate of tax is 28%.

Required

Using the information in the credit spread table above, calculate

(a) the expected yield on Jolly Inc's bonds

(b) Jolly Inc's post-tax cost of debt associated with these 5 year bonds

Answer

(a) Expected yield on 5 year bonds = 3.7% + 1.05% = 4.75%

(b) Post-tax cost of debt = (1 – 0.28) x 4.75 = 3.42%

7.3 Impact of credit spreads on bond values

FAST FOARD

> The deterioration in the credit quality of a bond, referred to as credit migration, will affect the market value of the bond.

We have already mentioned that credit risk is affected by the probability of migration of a certain debt or loan to another credit category. In markets where loans or corporate bonds are traded this migration is reflected in increased spreads. Using only the probability of default and ignoring the probability of migration from one category to another may give a misleading estimate of the risk exposure. Thus a company that has a very low or even zero probability of default but a high probability of being downgraded will have its credit risk significantly underestimated.

To explain how credit migration may impact on bond values consider a bond which is currently rated as BBB. In a year's time the bond may still be rated BBB, or it may have a higher or lower credit rating. The probability of being at the same or a different rating in a year's time is reproduced in the table below.

Value of BBB bond for different credit ratings

Year-end rating	Probability of migration
AAA	0.02%
AA	0.33%
A	5.95%
BBB	86.93%
BB	5.30%
B	1.17%
CCC	0.12%
Default	0.18%

As we have discussed, each credit category implies a different credit spread which in turn implies a different cost of debt capital. The table below is an example of the cost of debt capital for bonds of different credit ratings and different maturities. The cost of debt capital for a AAA bond with a maturity of one year is 3.6% , whereas the cost of capital for a CCC bond with a maturity of 4 years is 13.52%.

Yields by credit category (%)

Category	Year 1	Year 2	Year 3	Year 4
AAA	3.60	4.17	4.73	5.12
AA	3.65	4.22	4.78	5.17
A	3.72	4.32	4.93	5.32
BBB	4.10	4.67	5.25	5.63
BB	5.55	6.02	6.78	7.27
B	6.05	7.02	8.03	8.52
CCC	15.05	15.02	14.03	13.52

Source: CreditMetrics Manual

The value of a bond is the **present value** of the coupons and the redemption value, **discounted** using the appropriate cost of debt capital.

For the BBB bond of our example we need to assume a coupon rate and a face value. Suppose the bond has a face value of $100 and pays an annual coupon of 6%. Using the discount factors from Table 6 we calculate the value of the bond at the end of a year if it remained rated BBB using:

$$P_{BBB} = \frac{6}{1.041} + \frac{6}{(1.0467)^2} + \frac{6}{(1.0525)^3} + \frac{106}{(1.0563)^4} = 101.53$$

If it is upgraded to A, it will be worth $102.64.

$$P_A = \frac{6}{1.0372} + \frac{6}{(1.0432)^2} + \frac{6}{(1.0493)^3} + \frac{106}{(1.0532)^4} = 102.64$$

If it is downgraded to CCC, it will be worth .$77.63

$$P_{CCC} = \frac{6}{1.1505} + \frac{6}{(1.1502)^2} + \frac{6}{(1.1403)^3} + \frac{106}{(1.1352)^4} = 77.63$$

Calculating the values of the BBB bond for all possible ratings results in the values that are shown in the table below.

Value of BBB bond for different credit ratings

Year-end rating	bond value
AAA	$103.35
AA	$103.17
A	$102.64
BBB	$101.53
BB	$96.01
B	$92.09
CCC	$77.63

The value of the bond when it defaults will not be zero, as the issuing firm will have some assets. The available empirical evidence from credit rating agencies shows that about 51 percent of the value of a BBB bond is recovered when the issuing firm defaults.

If bondholders expect to recover in case of bankruptcy, the non-recoverable amount is $49 per $100 of face value. The Loss Given Default for a BBB bond will therefore be:

LGD = 0.49 × 100 = $49

The expected loss for the BBB bond in the example is:

EL = 0.0018 × $49 = $0.0882

The low probability of default reduces the credit risk of a BBB bond despite the fact that it loses nearly 50 percent of its value in the case of a default.

7.4 Predicting credit ratings

Credit rating companies use financial ratios and other information in order to arrive at the credit score of a company. Many researchers have tried to 'guess' the models that are employed by credit rating agencies and have estimated models which link the observed credit rating to financial characteristics of a company. One of these models is the Karlan Urwitz model. This model calculates a numerical value for a company based on certain characteristics which is then used to assign a credit rating to that company.

Exam focus point

If a question on the Kaplan-Urwitz model comes up in an exam, the formula will be given.

7.4.1 Quoted companies

Key term

> **Unsubordinated debt** is the debt that has priority claim.

In contrast, subordinated debt has no priority claim as it is subordinated to other debt.

The Kaplan Urwitz model for **quoted companies** is as follows.

$$Y = 5.67 + 0.011F + 5.13\pi - 2.36S - 2.85L + 0.007C - 0.87\beta - 2.90\sigma$$

Where

Y is the score that the model produces.

F is the size of a firm measured in total assets.

π is net income/total assets.

S is debt status (subordinated debt = 1, otherwise 0)

L is gearing (measured as long term debt/total assets)

C is interest cover (PBIT/Interest payment)

β is beta of the company estimated using CAPM

σ is the variance of the residuals from the CAPM regression equation (calculated as $\sqrt{(\sigma^2 - \beta^2 \cdot \sigma_m^2)}$, where σ_m^2 is the variance of the market)

7.4.2 Classification into credit rating categories

The classification of companies into credit rating categories is done in the following way

Score (Y)	Rating category
Y > 6.76	AAA
Y > 5.19	AA
Y > 3.28	A
Y > 1.57	BBB
Y > 0	BB

Question	Kaplan-Urwitz Model – quoted company

The following information is available for Trench Inc, a quoted company.

Total assets = $650m

Net Income = $250m

TYPE OF DEBT = unsubordinated

Long-term debt (unsubordinated) = $200m

Profit before interest and tax = $500m

Interest payments = $40m

In addition, the following CAPM model was estimated:

R_{Trench} = 0.045 + 0.800 x market risk premium

Trench's volatility (σ) and the volatility of the market are 22% and 20% respectively.

Required

What is the predicted credit rating for Trench Inc, using the Kaplan Urwitz model which is expressed as

$$Y = 5.67 + 0.011F + 5.13\pi - 2.36S - 2.85L + 0.007C - 0.87\beta - 2.90\sigma \ ?$$

The inputs to the model are as follows (note that we have removed the 'm' from the figures – this is always the case otherwise the results will be distorted).

F = $650

π = ($250/$650) = 0.385

S = 0 (unsubordinated debt)

L = ($200/$650) = 0.308

C = ($500/$40) = 12.5 times

β = 0.800

$\sigma = \sqrt{(0.22^2 - 0.8^2 \times 0.20^2)} = 0.151$

Y =   5.67 + (0.011 x 650) + (5.13 x 0.385) – (2.36 x 0) – (2.85 x 0.308) + (0.007 x 12.5) – (0.87 x 0.800) – (2.90 x 0.151)

Y =   12.87

The credit rating for Trench Inc = AAA

7.4.3 Unquoted companies

The second Kaplan-Urwitz model was estimated using data on unquoted companies:

$Y = 4.41 + 0.0014F + 6.4\pi - 2.56S - 2.72L + 0.006C - 0.53\sigma$

You will notice that there is no beta factor in the above equation – this is because we are dealing with unquoted companies.

In this case σ is the standard deviation of earnings. All the other variables remain the same.

8 Theories of capital structure – traditional and Modigliani and Miller (MM)

8.1 The traditional view of WACC

The **traditional view** is as follows:

(a)   As the **level of gearing increases**, the **cost of debt** remains **unchanged** up to a certain level of gearing. Beyond this level, the cost of debt will increase as interest cover falls, the amount of assets available for security falls and the risk of bankruptcy increases.

(b)   The **cost of equity** rises as the level of **gearing increases** and **financial risk increases**.

(c)   The **weighted average cost of capital** does **not remain constant**, but rather falls initially as the proportion of debt capital increases, and then begins to increase as the rising cost of equity (and possibly of debt) becomes more significant.

(d)   The **optimum level of gearing** is where the **company's weighted average cost of capital is minimised**.

The traditional view about the cost of capital is illustrated in the following figure. It shows that the weighted average cost of capital will be minimised at a particular level of gearing P.

232   **7a: Impact of financing on investment decisions and adjusted present values** | Part C Advanced investment appraisal

BPP
LEARNING MEDIA

Where k_e is the cost of equity in the geared company

k_d is the cost of debt

k_0 is the weighted average cost of capital.

The traditional view is that the weighted average cost of capital, when plotted against the level of gearing, is saucer shaped. The optimum capital structure is where the weighted average cost of capital is lowest, at point P.

8.2 The net operating income (Modigliani-Miller (MM)) view of WACC

The MM theory predicts that the financial structure has no impact on the cost of capital and therefore the way a project is financed has no impact on the value of the project.

Exam focus point

The examiner has stated that you will only need to know the key issues of the MM theory – you will not be asked to enter into any lengthy proofs.

The net operating income approach takes a different view of the effect of gearing on WACC. In their 1958 theory, Modigliani and Miller (MM) proposed that the total market value of a company, in the absence of tax, will be determined only by two factors:

- The **total earnings** of the company
- The **level of operating (business) risk** attached to those earnings

The total market value would be computed by discounting the total earnings at a rate that is appropriate to the level of operating risk. This rate would represent the WACC of the company.

Thus Modigliani and Miller concluded that **the capital structure of a company would have no effect on its overall value or WACC**.

8.2.1 Assumptions of net operating income approach

Modigliani and Miller made various assumptions in arriving at this conclusion, including:

(a) A **perfect capital market** exists, in which investors have the same information, upon which they act rationally, to arrive at the same expectations about future earnings and risks.

(b) There are no **tax or transaction costs**.

(c) **Debt is risk-free** and freely available at the same cost to investors and companies alike.

Modigliani and Miller justified their approach by the use of **arbitrage**.

Key term

Arbitrage is the simultaneous purchase and sale of a security in different markets, with the aim of making a risk-free profit through the exploitation of any price difference between the markets.

Arbitrage can be used to show that once all opportunities for profit have been exploited, the market values of two companies with the same earnings in equivalent business risk classes will have moved to an equal value.

If Modigliani and Miller's theory holds, it implies:

(a) The **cost of debt remains unchanged** as the level of gearing increases.

(b) The **cost of equity rises** in such a way as to keep the **weighted average cost of capital constant**.

This would be represented on a graph as shown below.

8.3 Modigliani-Miller theory adjusted for taxation

Having argued that debt has no benefit in the absence of taxation, MM then went on to demonstrate that debt can be beneficial where tax relief applies.

Allowing for **taxation reduces the cost of debt capital** by multiplying it by a factor $(1 - t)$ where t is the rate of tax (assuming the debt to be irredeemable).

MM modified their theory to admit that tax relief on interest payments does makes debt capital cheaper to a company, and therefore **reduces the weighted average cost of capital** where a company has debt in its capital structure. They claimed that the weighted average cost of capital will continue to fall, up to gearing of 100%.

BPP LEARNING MEDIA

8.4 Formula for cost of equity

The principles of the MM theory with tax gave rise to the following formula for cost of equity.

Exam formula

$$k_e = k_e^i + (1-T)(k_e^i - k_d)\frac{V_d}{V_e}$$

Where k_e is the cost of equity in a geared company

k_e^i is the cost of equity in an ungeared company

V_d, V_e are the market values of debt and equity respectively

k_d is the cost of debt pre-tax

8.5 Example of MM cost of equity calculation

Shiny Inc is an ungeared company with a cost of equity of 10%. Shiny is considering introducing debt to its capital structure as it is tempted by a loan with a rate of 5%, which could be used to repurchase shares. Once the equity is repurchased, the ratio of debt to equity will be 1:4. Assume that corporation tax is 30%.

(a)   What will be the revised cost of equity if Shiny takes out the loan?

(b)   At what discount rate will Shiny now appraise its projects? Comment on your results.

Solution

(a) $k_e = 0.10 + (1 - 0.3)(0.10 - 0.05) \times 0.25 = 10.9\%$

(b)   WACC = $(0.2 \times 0.7 \times 0.05) + (0.8 \times 0.109) = 9.42\%$

The new WACC figure is lower than that for the ungeared company. This means that future investments will be able to bring greater wealth to the shareholders. More projects will become acceptable to management, given that they are being discounted at a lower discount rate.

8.6 Weaknesses in MM theory

MM theory has been criticised as follows.

(a)   MM theory assumes that **capital markets are perfect**. For example, a company will always be able to raise finance to fund worthwhile projects. This ignores the danger that higher gearing can lead to **financial distress costs** and **agency problems** (see Section 1.3).

(b)   **Transaction costs** will restrict the arbitrage process.

(c)   Investors are **assumed to act rationally** which may not be the case in practice.

8.7 Capital structure conclusions

The practical implications of these capital structure theories can be generalised as follows.

Level of gearing

Low ←————————————————————————————→ High

Young company	Mature company
Volatile cash flows	Stable cash flows
Tax benefits < financial distress costs	Tax benefits > financial distress costs

9 Alternative theories of capital structure

9.1 Static trade-off theory

Static trade-off theory states that firms in a static position will seek to achieve a target level of gearing by adjusting their current gearing levels.

We know that a firm enjoys an increase in tax savings with an increase in debt financing due to the tax deductibility of interest. However, an increase in debt financing will also result in an increase in the chances of the firm going bankrupt because of its increased commitment in interest payments. This is the effect of financial leverage. It is important to remember that a firm can skip its dividend payments but not its interest payments. Failure to meet those interest payments because of inadequate cash on hand will cause the firm some financial distress, and the ultimate form of financial distress is bankruptcy.

What are some of the financial distress costs faced by a firm? We can classify them into two categories:

(a)   Direct financial distress costs
(b)   Indirect financial distress costs

9.1.1 Direct financial distress costs

The direct financial distress costs faced by a firm are the legal and administrative costs associated with the bankruptcy or reorganisation of the firm. Studies have shown that such costs range from less than 1% to approximately 4-5% of the value of the firm.

9.1.2 Indirect financial distress costs

There are different types of cost (mostly implicit) that a firm faces when it is in a financially stressful situation (but not bankruptcy). The following are some of those costs:

• A higher cost of capital (either for debt or equity) due to its financial situation.

• Lost sales due to fear of impaired services and loss of trust.

• Managers and employees will try drastic actions to save the firm that might result in some long-term problems. Such actions include closing down plants, downsizing, drastic cost cuts, and selling off valuable assets. These actions will ultimately dilute the value of the firm.

• Firms might have trouble keeping highly skilled managers and employees, which is bad for the firms in the long run.

As a result of these costs the **gearing-adjusted** value of the firm should be decreased. The value of the company in this case will be:

Value of the ungeared firm + (tax rate × interest payments) – present value of the bankruptcy costs

This effect can be seen in the figure below. As the figure shows, when the present value of the bankruptcy costs increases with gearing, there is an optimal capital structure for the firm.

Starting from the empirical observation that firms do not have 100 percent gearing ratios, it is plausible to argue that a firm's WACC will start to increase and its value will start to decrease after a certain value of the gearing ratio, to reflect the increasing costs of gearing. Such as possible explanation is depicted in the graph below.

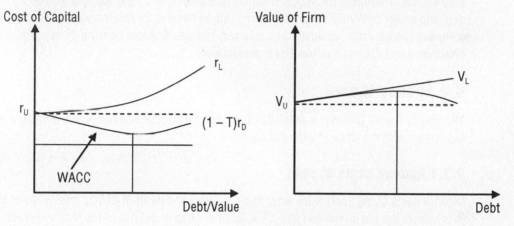

Where:

r_U is the cost of capital of the ungeared firm V_U is the value of the ungeared firm

r_L is the cost of capital of the geared firm V_L is the value of the geared firm

r_D is the cost of debt   T is the tax rate

From the above graph, it is plausible that there exists a certain combination of **debt** and **equity financing** that will enable a firm to **minimise** its **cost of capital** and to **maximise** its **value**. The issue a financial manager is most concerned with is identifying the firm's **optimal capital structure** that will allow it to **minimise firm's WACC** and **maximise its value**.

In MM's propositions, debt was considered to be **risk-free** and the company was considered not to have any risk of failing. In addition, it was assumed that EBIT will not be affected by capital structure. However, corporate failure is an unfortunate and expensive reality.

If a company actually becomes insolvent and has to be liquidated, there are many administrative and other costs to be borne (such as liquidators' fees) which would not otherwise have been suffered. As a result, the expected EBIT will fall.

Even if a company does not become insolvent, but merely has a rough ride for several years, there will be additional costs. These will arise because, among other factors, the management will need to spend extra time speaking to debt and equity investors and will be restricted in their actions due to loan covenants that prescribe various courses of action.

These additional costs of financial distress will reduce payouts to investors. As a company borrows more money, the probability that these cash outflows will occur increases, reducing the value of the company.

The conclusion is that a company should gear up to take advantage of any tax benefits available, but only to the extent that the **marginal benefits exceed** the **marginal costs** of **financial distress**. After this point, the market value of the firm will start to fall and its WACC will start to rise. This is known as the static trade-off theory of capital structure.

9.1.3 The implications of financial distress on the value of the firm and on WACC

The value of the firm will reach a **maximum** point where the **marginal benefits of tax relief equal the marginal costs of financial distress**. At the same point, the WACC will reach a minimum point.

Remember that the firm's **weighted average cost of capital** is the weighted sum of debt and equity costs or the minimum overall return that is required on existing operations to satisfy the demands of all stakeholders. The theory is based on the assumption that debt is generally cheaper than equity as a source of investment finance. Hence, a firm can lower its average cost of capital by increasing its debt relative to equity (ie. its gearing), provided the firm's cost of debt and equity remain constant.

However, this process cannot be extended indefinitely because, in reality, higher levels of debt **increase the likelihood of default** resulting in debtholders and shareholders each demanding greater returns on their capital. Therefore, the WACC schedule is U-shaped when plotted against gearing, with the cost of debt and equity both rising at an increasing rate as bankruptcy risk increases. The corresponding company market value schedule is an inverted U-shape. **Optimal gearing** occurs where WACC is **minimised** and the value of the firm is **maximised**.

9.2 Agency theory

The agency theory provides a rationale for an optimal structure based on the existence of agency costs associated with the issue of debt and equity.

9.2.1 Agency costs of debt

Agency costs of debt only arise when there is a **risk of default**. If debt is totally free of default risk, debtholders are not concerned about the income, value or the risk of the firm. However, as **gearing increases**, the **probability of default also increases** and with this comes the likelihood of substantial bankruptcy costs.

If the possibility of default exists, **shareholders can gain at the expense of debtholders**. For instance, after issuing debt, a firm may decide to restructure its assets, selling off those with low business risk and acquiring assets that are more risky and thus have a higher possibility of default but also have higher expected returns. If things work out well, then the **shareholders** will get most of the benefit, but if not, then much of the loss will fall on the **bondholders**, who will have already agreed to be anticipated with a lower interest rate than the risk level of the firm presupposes.

9.2.2 Agency costs of equity

Agency costs also exist in relation to the **new share issues**. The cause of agency costs in this case is the potential conflict between **old shareholders** and **new shareholders**. New shareholders will want to monitor the management of the company to make sure that the original shareholders do not benefit at the expense of new shareholders. These monitoring mechanisms are expensive and the agency costs associated with the issue of new equity is increased with the amount of new equity issued.

The **optimal capital structure** of the firm will be formed at the particular level of debt and equity where the **benefits of the debt** that can be received by the shareholders balance **equal the costs of debt** imposed by the debt holders.

9.3 Pecking order theory

Pecking order theory is based on the idea that shareholders have less information about the firm than directors do.

Shareholders and other investors will use directors' actions as signals to indicate what directors believe about the firm, given their superior information.

9.3.1 Debt or equity?

When deciding how to finance a project, managers will consider such issues as tax relief on debt and risk of default on debt. However trying to get the timing right is another consideration.

Managers will prefer to **issue equity** when the **share price is** high (even to the point of being overvalued). They will prefer not to issue equity when the share price is considered to be low (or undervalued). In other words, managers will **issue debt** (increase gearing) when the **share price is low** and issue equity when the share price is high.

As a result, investors will use the issue of debt or equity as a **signal** from managers as to the true worth of the company's shares. Managers typically have better information than investors that can be used to value the shares (**information asymmetry**).

9.3.2 Market signals

As mentioned above, investors may use the issue of debt or equity as a signal as to the likely true worth of the company's shares.

If equity is issued, the market will take this as a signal that shares are overvalued. This may result in investors selling their shares (thus making substantial gains) which will lead to a fall in the share price. If this happens, the cost of equity may rise which will result in a higher marginal cost of finance. To avoid this possibility, managers may decide to issue debt even if shares are seen as being overvalued.

An issue of debt may be interpreted as an undervaluation of the shares. Investors will want to 'get a bargain' and will thus start to buy the shares, leading to an increase in share price.

9.3.3 So what is the 'pecking order'?

The preferred 'pecking order' for financing instruments is as follows:

(a) **Retained earnings**. To avoid any unwanted signals, managers will try to finance as much as possible through internal funds.

(b) **Debt**. When internal funds have been exhausted and there are still positive NPV opportunities, managers will use debt to finance any further projects until the company's debt capacity has been reached. **Secured debt** (which is less risky) should be **issued first**, followed by unsecured (risky) debt.

(c) **Equity**. The 'finance of last resort' is the issue of equity.

10 The adjusted present value method   12/10

The **APV** method suggests that it is possible to calculate an **adjusted** cost of capital for use in project appraisal, as well as indicating how the net present value of a project can be increased or decreased by project financing effects.

- Evaluate the project as if it was all equity financed
- Make adjustments to allow for the effects of the financing method

10.1 NPV and APV

We have seen that a company's gearing level has implications for both the value of its equity shares and its WACC. The viability of an investment project will depend partly on how the investment is financed, and how the method of finance affects gearing.

The net present value method of investment appraisal is to **discount** the **cash flows** of a project at a **cost of capital**. This cost of capital might be the WACC, but it could also be another cost of capital, perhaps one which allows for the risk characteristics of the individual project.

An alternative method of carrying out project appraisal is to use the **adjusted present value (APV) method**.

APV was examined in June 2008 as part of an optional question. The examiner reported that, whilst many candidates demonstrated a good understanding of the mechanics, they showed less understanding of the underlying principles and rationale.

10.2 Carrying out an APV calculation

The APV method involves two stages.

Step 1   **Evaluate** the **project** first of all as if it was **all equity financed**, and so as if the company were an all equity company to find the 'base case NPV'

Step 2   **Make adjustments** to allow for the effects of the method of financing that has been used

10.3 Example: APV method

A company is considering a project that would cost $100,000 to be financed 50% by equity (cost 21.6%) and 50% by debt (pre-tax cost 12%). The financing method would maintain the company's WACC unchanged. The cash flows from the project would be $36,000 a year in perpetuity, before interest charges. Tax is at 30%.

Appraise the project using firstly the NPV method and secondly the APV method.

Solution

We can use the **NPV method** because the company's WACC will be unchanged.

	Cost %	Weighting	Product %
Equity	21.6	0.5	10.8
Debt (70% of 12%)	8.4	0.5	4.2
WACC			15.0

Annual cash flows in perpetuity from the project are as follows.

	$
Before tax	36,000
Less tax (30%)	10,800
After tax	25,200

NPV of project = −$100,000 + (25,200 ÷ 0.15)
    = −$100,000 + £168,000
    = $68,000

Note that the tax relief that will be obtained on debt interest is taken account of **in the WACC *not* in the project cash flows.**

Since £100,000 of new investment is being created, the value of the company will increase by £100,000 + $68,000 = $168,000, of which 50% must be debt capital.

The company must raise 50% × $168,000 = $84,000 of 12% debt capital, and (the balance) $16,000 of equity. The NPV of the project will raise the value of this equity from $16,000 to $84,000 thus leaving the gearing ratio at 50:50.

The **APV approach** to this example is as follows.

(a) First, we need to know the cost of equity in an equivalent ungeared company. The MM formula we can use to establish this is as follows.

Cost of ordinary (equity) share capital in a geared firm (with tax):

$$k_e = k_e^i + (1+T)(k_e^i - k_d)\frac{V_d}{V_e}$$

Remember:

k_d = the **pre-tax** cost of debt. Using the information from the question:

$$21.6\% = k_e^i + (k_e^i - 12\%) \times \left[\frac{50 \times 0.7}{50}\right]$$

$$21.6\% = k_e + 0.70k_e - 8.4\%$$

$$1.70k_e = 30\%$$

$$k_e = 17.647\%$$

(b) Next, we calculate the **NPV of the project as if it were all equity financed**. The cost of equity would be 17.647%

$$NPV = \frac{\$25,200}{0.17647} - \$100,000 = \$42,800$$

(c) Next, we can use an MM formula for the relationship between the value of geared and ungeared companies, to establish **the effect of gearing on the value of the project**. £84,000 will be financed by debt.

$$V_g \text{ (APV)} = V_u + \text{(value of debt} \times \text{corporate tax rate)}$$
$$= \$42,800 + (\$84,000 \times 0.30)$$
$$= \$42,800 + \$25,200$$
$$= \$68,000$$

The value of debt × corporate tax rate represents the **present value of the tax shield on debt interest,** that is the present value of the savings arising from tax relief on debt interest.

This can be proved as follows.

Annual interest charge = 12% of $84,000 = $10,080

Tax saving (30% × $10,080) = $3,024.00

Cost of debt (pre-tax) = 12%

PV of tax savings in perpetuity = $\dfrac{\$3,024}{0.12}$ (by coincidence only this equals the project net of tax cash flows)

$$= \$25,200$$

10.4 Example: APV method and limited cash flows

Suppose in the above example the cash flows only lasted for five years, and tax was payable one year in arrears. Calculate the present value of the tax shield.

Solution

The tax saving will now only last for years 2 to 6. (Remember interest will be paid in years 1 to 5, but the tax benefits will be felt a year in arrears).

PV of tax savings = 3,024 × Annuity factor years 2 to 6
$$= 3,024 \times (\text{Annuity factors years 1 to 6} - \text{Annuity factor year 1})$$
$$= 3,024 \times (4.111 - 0.893)$$
$$= \$9,731$$

The APV and NPV approaches produce the same conclusion.

10.5 APV and changes in gearing

However, the APV method can also be adapted to allow for financing which **changes the gearing structure** and the WACC.

In this respect, it is superior to the NPV method. Suppose, for example, that in the previous example, the **entire project were to be financed by debt**. The APV of the project would be calculated as follows.

(a)   The NPV of project if all equity financed is:

$$\frac{\$25,200}{0.17647} - \$100,000 = + \$42,800 \text{ (as before)}$$

(b)   The adjustment to allow for the method of financing is the present value of the tax relief on debt interest in perpetuity.

$$DT_c = \$100,000 \times 0.30 = \$30,000$$

(c)   APV = $42,800 + $30,000 = +$72,800

The project would increase the value of equity by $72,800.

Question   APV

A project costing $100,000 is to be financed by $60,000 of irredeemable 12% loan stock and $40,000 of new equity. The project will yield an after-tax annual cash flow of $21,000 in perpetuity. If it were all equity financed, an appropriate cost of capital would be 15%. The tax rate is 30%. What is the project's APV?

Answer

	$
NPV if all equity financed: $21,000/0.15 − $100,000	40,000
PV of the tax shield: $60,000 × 12% × 30%/0.12	18,000
APV	58,000

10.6 Discounting tax relief at the risk-free rate

Often in exams you will be given the risk-free rate of return. As tax relief is allowed by the government and is almost certain, there is an argument for saying that **all tax relief** should be discounted at the **risk-free rate**. However there is the opposing argument that the **risk of the tax relief** is the same as the **risk of the debt** to which it relates, and therefore the tax relief should be discounted at the cost of debt. The risk-free rate would also not be used if the company was unlikely to be in a taxpaying position for some years.

In the exam we suggest that you make clear the reasons for choosing the discount rate that you have chosen to discount the tax relief, and add a comment that an alternative rate might be used.

10.7 Other elements in APV calculation

The tax shield may not be the only complication introduced into APV calculations.

10.7.1 Issue costs

The costs of issuing the finance needed for the project may also be brought into APV calculations.

10.7.2 Example: issue costs

Edted is about to start a project with an initial investment of $20 million, which will generate cash flow over four years. The project will be financed with a $10 million 10 year bank loan and a rights issue. Issue costs are 5% of the amount raised.

Calculate the issue costs that will be used in the APV calculation.

Solution

Issue costs will not equal 5% of $10 million ($20 million – $10 million). The $10 million will be the figure left after the issue costs have been paid. Therefore $10 million must be 95%, not 100% of the amount raised, and the

$$\text{Issue costs} = \frac{5}{95} \times \$10 \text{ million} = \$526,316$$

In the above example, the issue costs do not need to be discounted as they are assumed to be paid at time 0. The complication comes if issue costs are allowable for tax purposes.

10.7.3 Example: the tax implications of issue costs

Assume in the example above that issue costs are allowable for tax purposes, the tax is assumed to be 30% payable one year in arrears and the risk-free rate of return is assumed to be 8%.

Calculate the tax effect of the issuing costs to be included in the APV calculation.

Solution

Tax effect = Tax rate × Issue costs × Discount rate
= 0.3 × 526,316 × 0.926
= $146,211

10.7.4 Spare debt capacity

Projects may yield other incremental benefits, for example increased borrowing or debt capacity. These benefits should be included in the APV calculations, even if the debt capacity is utilised elsewhere.

10.7.5 Example: spare debt capacity

Continuing with the Edted example, suppose the project increased the borrowing capacity of the company by $6 million, at the risk-free rate of return of 8%. Calculate the effect on the APV calculation.

Solution

Remember that we are concerned with the incremental benefit which is the **tax shield effect** of the increased debt finance.

Present value of tax shield effect	=	Increased debt capacity		Interest rate		Tax rate		Discount factor Years 2 to 5
	=	$6million	×	8%	×	30%	×	3.067
	=	$441,648						

10.7.6 Subsidy

You may face a situation where a company can obtain finance at a lower interest rate than its normal cost of borrowing. In this situation you have to include in the APV calculation the tax shield effect of the cheaper finance and the effect of the saving in interest.

10.7.7 Example: subsidy

Gordonbear is about to start a project requiring $6 million of initial investment. The company normally borrows at 12% but a government loan will be available to finance all of the project at 10%. The risk-free rate of interest is 6%.

Tax is payable at 30% one year in arrears. The project is scheduled to last for four years.

Calculate the effect on the APV calculation if Gordonbear finances the project by means of the government loan.

Solution

(a)   The tax shield is as follows.

We assume that the loan is for the duration of the project (four years) only.

Annual interest = $6 million × 10%
                           = $600,000

Tax relief   = $600,000 × 0.3
                           = $180,000

This needs to be discounted over years 2 to 5 (remember the one year time lag). We do not however use the 10% to discount the loan and the tax effect; instead we assume that the government loan is risk-free and the tax effect is also risk-free. Hence we use the 6% factor in discounting.

NPV tax relief = $180,000 × Discount factor Years 2 to 5
                        = $180,000 × 3.269
                        = $588,420

(b)   We also need to take into account the benefits of **being able** to pay a **lower interest rate**.

Benefits = $6 million × (12% – 10%) × 6% Discount factor Years 1 to 4
                = $6 million × 2% × 3.465
                = $415,800

(c)   Total effect = $588,420 + $415,800 = $1,004,220.

10.8 The advantages and disadvantages of the APV method

The main advantages of the APV are as follows.

(a)   APV can be used to **evaluate** all the **effects of financing** a product including:

   (i)   Tax shield
   (ii)   Changing capital structure
   (iii)   Any other relevant cost

(b)   When using APV you do not have to adjust the WACC using assumptions of perpetual risk-free debt.

The main difficulties with the APV technique are:

(a)   **Establishing** a **suitable cost of equity**, for the initial DCF computation as if the project were all-equity financed, and also establishing the all-equity β

(b)   **Identifying all the costs** associated with the method of financing

(c)   Choosing the correct discount rates used to discount the costs

244   **7a: Impact of financing on investment decisions and adjusted present values** | Part C Advanced investment appraisal

BPP
LEARNING MEDIA

Exam focus point

Always be prepared to discuss the limitations of a technique.

11 Effect of alternative financing strategies on financial reporting

Gearing affects the volatility of **earnings per share**. The higher the level of gearing the higher the **volatility of EPS**.

11.1 Financial gearing and debt

Fixed income securities issued by corporations to fund capital projects include **debt** and **preferred stock**.

Debt is **less risky** than **equity** for investors and therefore requires a **lower rate** of **return**. In addition, interest payments attract tax relief, hence the cost of debt will be lower than the cost of equity. The effect of this on the company's WACC is that as a company gears up, its WACC will be reduced due to the higher proportion of the cheaper debt financing in the company's overall financial structure.

The return on debt is not directly linked to the underlying performance of the business. The same predetermined amount is paid whether the profits are high or low and this in turn makes any residual claims that shareholders have on the income of a company more volatile.

11.2 Impact of gearing on earnings per share, EBIT and return on equity

To appreciate the impact of financial gearing we shall explain and calculate the effects of changes in earnings before interest and taxes (EBIT) on **earnings per share** for a company with differing amounts of **debt financing**.

Assume that a company has the following statement of financial position structure.

	Current	Proposed
Asset	500	500
Debt	–	300
Equity	500	200

The company currently has 100 shares in issue with a price of $5. It is proposing to buy back 60 shares for a total cost of $300, financing this by issuing debt at a cost of 10%. This will leave 40 shares in issue.

The earnings per share for the company when it has no debt is:

$$EPS(U) = \frac{EBIT}{100}$$

Whereas the earnings per share for the company under the proposed borrowing is:

$$EPS(G) = \frac{EBIT}{100}$$

The values of the ungeared earnings per share for different values of EBIT are shown in the table below:

	Scenario 1	Scenario 2	Scenario 3	Scenario 4	Scenario 5	Scenario 6	Scenario 7
EBIT	0	10	30	50	70	90	110
Interest payments	0	0	0	0	0	0	0
Net income	0	10	30	50	70	90	110
EPS(U)	0	0.1	0.3	0.5	0.7	0.9	1.1

Similarly, the values of the geared earnings per share for different values of EBIT are shown in the table below:

	Scenario 1	Scenario 2	Scenario 3	Scenario 4	Scenario 5	Scenario 6	Scenario 7
EBIT	0	10	30	50	70	90	110
Interest payments	30	30	30	30	30	30	30
Net income	−30	−20	0	20	40	60	80
EPS(L)	−0.75	−0.5	0	0.5	1	1.5	2

As it can be seen from the two tables, the earnings for the geared company are more volatile. When the values of EPS are plotted against the values of EBIT, this is reflected in the gradient of the line showing the values of the geared earnings per share, which will be steeper than the line plotting showing the values of unleveraged earnings per share.

The breakeven level of EBIT where the two alternative financing schemes give the same earnings per share, ie when:

EPS(U) = EPS(G)

EBIT = $50. This can be seen from the fact that:

$$\frac{EBIT-30}{40} = \frac{EBIT}{100}$$

Implies EBIT = $50

This breakeven point can be checked as follows.

Original all equity structure $\dfrac{50}{100}$ = $0.50

Revised structure $\dfrac{50-30}{40}$ = $0.50

Above an EBIT of $50, the geared structure gives a higher earnings per share. In addition, the company's return on equity will exceed the interest cost of 10%. Below $50, it gives a lower earnings per share and the return on equity is less than the cost of debt of 10%.

At the break-even point, the return on equity is equal to the interest rate on the debt, ie:

$$ROE = \frac{EBIT}{500} = \frac{50}{500} = 10\%.$$

At an EBIT of zero, the original ungeared earnings per share will also be zero. However, with debt, there will be a loss per share of $\dfrac{-30}{40}$ = −$0.75.

Note that, although the earnings per share and return on equity are more volatile for the geared company, the mean return is higher. This can be demonstrated by calculating the mean returns for the above two capital structures, assuming that each scenario has an equal likelihood of arising.

Ungeared Company

Mean net income for ungeared company = $\dfrac{0+10+30+50+70+90+110}{7}$ = \$51.43

Earnings per share = $\dfrac{51.43}{100}$ = \$0.5143

Return on equity = $\dfrac{51.43}{500}$ = 10.286%

Geared Company

Mean net income for geared company = $\dfrac{-30-20+0+20+40+60+80}{7}$ = \$21.429

Earnings per share = $\dfrac{21.429}{40}$ = \$0.5357

Return on equity = $\dfrac{21.429}{200}$ = 10.714%

11.3 Degree of financial gearing

The degree of financial gearing measures the sensitivity of EPS to changes in EBIT.

Key term

> The **degree of financial gearing** (DFG) is defined as the change in earnings per share (EPS) over the change in earnings before interest and tax (EBIT) or
>
> $\dfrac{\% \text{ Change in EPS}}{\% \text{ Change in EBIT}}$

The degree of financial gearing can be calculated from the formula:

$$\dfrac{\text{EBIT}}{\text{EBIT} - \text{Interest}}$$

For the ungeared company in the example above, the degree of financial gearing can be calculated as follows, for a particular value of EBIT, say EBIT = \$75. For the ungeared company we have:

$$\dfrac{75}{75 - 0} = 1$$

Whereas for the geared company, we have:

$$\dfrac{75}{75 - 30} = 1.67$$

The degree of gearing confirms our earlier finding that the geared EPS is more sensitive to changes in EBIT.

We have thus established that the relationship between the EPS and EBIT depends on the degree of **financial gearing**. The relationship can be expressed as follows:

$$\dfrac{\Delta \text{ EPS}}{\text{EPS}} = \text{degree of financial gearing} \times \dfrac{\Delta \text{ EBIT}}{\text{EBIT}}$$

That is the relationship between earnings per share (EPS) and earnings before interest and tax in linear and is affected by the degree of financial gearing.

The higher the degree of financial gearing, the higher the impact of changes of EBIT on EPS.

When there is no debt DFG = 1 and EBIT changes are equal to EPS changes in percentage terms.

When there is debt DFG > 1 and EPS changes by more than the changes in EBIT due to the effect of DFG, the 'multiplier'.

Suppose for example that there is a 33% increase in EBIT from $75 to $100. There is a 55% increase in EPS from $45 to $70.The link between the two percentage increases is the degree of financial gearing – that is $1.67 \times 33\% = 55\%$.

Chapter Roundup

- The **expected return** of a portfolio of shares can be calculated by calculating the weighted beta of the portfolio and using CAPM.

- Duration (also known as Macaulay duration) is the weighted average length of time to the receipt of a bond's benefits (coupon and redemption value), the weights being the present value of the benefits involved.

- **Modified duration** is a measure of the sensitivity of a bond's price to a change in interest rates.

- The credit rating of a borrower may change after a bond is issued. This is referred to as credit migration.

- Credit enhancement is the process of reducing credit risk by requiring collateral, insurance, or other agreements to provide the lender with reassurance that it will be compensated if the borrower defaulted.

- Credit enhancement is a key part of the securitisation transaction in structured finance and is important for credit rating agencies when raising a securitisation.

- There are two main types of internal credit enhancement – excess spread and over-collateralisation.

- External credit enhancement tools include surety bonds, letters of credit and cash collateral accounts.

- The cost of debt capital and the market price of corporate bonds depend on the credit risk of the bond.

- The deterioration in the credit quality of a bond, referred to as credit migration, will affect the market value of the bond.

- The MM theory predicts that the financial structure has no impact on the cost of capital and therefore the way a project is financed has no impact on the value of the project.

- Static trade-off theory states that firms in a static position will seek to achieve a target level of gearing by adjusting their current gearing levels.

- Pecking order theory is based on the idea that shareholders have less information about the firm than directors do.

- Shareholders and other investors will use directors' actions as signals to indicate what directors believe about the firm, given their superior information.

- The **APV** method suggests that it is possible to calculate an **adjusted** cost of capital for use in project appraisal, as well as indicating how the net present value of a project can be increased or decreased by project financing effects.

    - Evaluate the project as if it was all equity financed

    - Make adjustments to allow for the effects of the financing method

- Gearing affects the volatility of **earnings per share**. The higher the level of gearing the higher the **volatility of EPS**.

Quick Quiz

1   Using the beta values for the following companies calculate the cost of equity if the market risk premium is 5% and the return on a risk-free investment is 4 percent.

Company	Beta
Company	*Beta*
Boeing	0.73
Hewlett-Packard	1.76
Intel	2.06

2   You have invested in a bond with a default probability of 10 percent. In the event of default you hold collateral that amount to about 70 percent of the value of the bond. What is your expected loss?

3   What is the relationship between credit rating and the cost of debt capital?

4   What is the most likely rating next year of a BBB bond?

5   What will happen to the value of a corporate bond if its credit rating is downgraded?

Answers to Quick Quiz

1   **Boeing**

$r = 0.04 + 0.73 \times 0.05 = 0.0765$ or 7.65%

Hewlett-Packard

$r = 0.04 + 1.76 \times 0.05 = 0.128$ or 12.8%

Intel

$r = 0.04 + 2.06 \times 0.05 = 0.143$ or 14.3%

2   The expected loss is equal to $0.10 \times (1-0.70) = 0.03$ or 3 percent.

3   The lower the credit rating the higher the credit spread and consequently the higher the cost of capital.

4   From the historical migration tables the most likely rating for a BBB bond will be a BBB rating.

5   The value of the bond will fall.

Now try the questions below from the Exam Question Bank

Number	Level	Marks	Time
11	Introductory	15	27 mins
12	Introductory	15	27 mins
13	Examination	10	18 mins

Valuation and the use of free cash flows

Topic list	Syllabus reference
1 Yield curve and bond price	C (4) (a)
2 Forecasting a firm's free cash flow	C (4) (b)
3 Free cash flow to equity	C (4) (c)
4 Valuations of equity	C (4) (a)
5 Valuing an organisation using free cash flow	C (4) (c)
6 Assessing default risk using option pricing models	C (4) (d),(e)

Introduction

The purpose of this chapter is to look at different methods of valuing both debt and equity, including the use of free cash flows. It considers how the yield curve can be used to estimate the value of a bond before moving on to look at how an organisation can forecast its free cash flow. Section 4 recaps methods of valuing equity that should be brought forward knowledge from *F9 Financial Management* and Section 5 looks at valuations using free cash flow and the final section looks at the use of option pricing models and assessment of default risk.

Study guide

		Intellectual level
C4	**Valuation and the use of free cash flows**	
(a)	Apply asset based, income based and cashflow based models to value equity. Apply appropriate models, including term structure of interest rates, the yield curve and credit spreads to value corporate debt	3
(b)	Forecast an organisation's free cash flow and its free cash flow to equity (pre and post capital reinvestment)	2
(c)	Advise on the value of a firm using its free cash flow and free cash flow to equity under alternative horizon and growth assumptions	3
(d)	Explain the use of the BSOP model to estimate the value of equity of an organisation and discuss the implications of the model for a change in the value of equity	2
(e)	Explain the role of BSOP model in the assessment of default risk, the value of debt and its potential recoverability	2

1 Yield curve and bond price   6/12

The yield curve can be used to estimate the value of a bond, which in turn can be used to estimate an issue price. This can be done by splitting up the payments associated with one bond into separate bonds and discounting by the relevant rate according to the yield curve.

Yield curve rates are published by the financial press and by central banks.

Question   Yield curve

YZ Co wants to issue a five year redeemable bond with an annual coupon of 4%. The bond is redeemable at par ($100). Tax can be ignored.

The annual spot yield curve for this risk class of bond in the financial press is given as

One-year	3.3%
Two-year	3.8%
Three-year	4.2%
Four-year	4.8%
Five-year	5.5%

Required

Using the information above, calculate

(a) the expected price at which the bond can be issued

(b) the yield to maturity of the bond

Answer

(a)   The five year bond can be split into separate bonds as follows

Year	1	2	3	4	5
Bond 1	4				
Bond 2		4			
Bond 3			4		
Bond 4				4	
Bond 5					104

Each bond can then be discounted as follows using the yield curve rates

Bond 1	$4 \times 1/1.033$	$3.87
Bond 2	$4 \times 1/1.038^2$	$3.71
Bond 3	$4 \times 1/1.042^3$	$3.54
Bond 4	$4 \times 1/1.048^4$	$3.32
Bond 5	$104 \times 1/1.055^5$	$79.57

The total of the discounted cash flows is $94.01 which represents the price at which the bond can be issued.

(b)   An IRR style calculation is needed to calculate the yield to maturity

Since the current price is below par, the YTM is more than 4%. Therefore we will try 5% and 8%

Year		5% discount factor	PV	8% discount factor	PV
0	(94.01)	1.000	(94.01)	1.000	(94.01)
1-5	4	4.329	17.32	3.993	15.97
5	100	0.784	78.40	0.681	68.10
			1.71		(9.94)

The YTM is therefore

$5 + 1.71 \times (8 - 5)/(1.71 + 9.94) = 5.44\%$

Note that the yield to maturity is lower than the 5 year bond yield rate because the bond returns are not all in the fifth year, but in earlier years when the interest rates are lower.

In general the bond price for n time periods can be calculated by the following formula

$$\text{Price} = \text{Coupon} \times \frac{1}{(1+r_1)^1} + \text{coupon} \times \frac{1}{(1+r_2)^2} + \dots + \text{coupon} \times \frac{1}{(1+r_n)^n} + \text{redemption value} \times \frac{1}{(1+r_n)^n}$$

Where r_n is the spot rate based on the yield curve.

Note that coupons may be made more frequently than annually and this should be taken into account as each coupon payment needs to be discounted by an appropriate time period related bond yield rate.

2 Forecasting a firm's free cash flow

A firm's free cash flow is the actual amount of cash that a company has left from its operations that could be used to pursue opportunities that enhance shareholder value.

So far we have dealt with the two main decision rules for accepting investment projects. Both decision rules require estimates of the cash flows and the required rate of return. The issue of the required rate of return was dealt with extensively in Chapter 7a. In this section we shall discuss the estimation of free cash flows.

2.1 Definition of free cash flow

Key term

The **free cash flow** is the cash flow derived from the operations of a company after subtracting working capital, investment and taxes and represents the funds available for distribution to the capital contributors, ie shareholders and debt holders.

The idea is to provide a measure of what is available to the owners of a firm, after providing for capital expenditures to maintain existing assets and to create new assets for future growth and is measured as follows:

Free Cash Flow = Earnings before Interest and Taxes (EBIT)

Less tax on EBIT
Plus non cash charges (eg depreciation)
Less capital expenditures
Less net working capital increases
Plus net working capital decreases
Plus salvage value received

Question

Albion Inc needs to invest $9,000 to increase productive capacity and also to increase its working capital by $1,000. Earnings before taxes are $90,000 and it sets off against tax $6,000 of depreciation. Profits are taxed at 40 percent. What is the free cash flow?

Answer

The calculations for the free cash are given below:

	$
Earnings before interest and taxes (EBIT)	90,000
Less taxes	36,000
Operating income after taxes	54,000
Plus depreciation (non cash item)	6,000
Less capital expenditures	9,000
Less changes to working capital	1,000
Free Cash Flow	50,000

2.2 Forecasting Free Cash Flows

Free cash flows can be forecast in similar ways to such other items as expenses, sales and capital expenditure. We must consider the likely behaviour of each of the elements that make up the free cash flow figure – such as movements in future tax rates, potential spending on capital projects and the associated working capital requirements.

2.2.1 Constant growth

One approach to forecasting free cash flows is to assume that they will grow at a constant rate. The calculation of free cash flows is therefore quite straightforward.

$FCF_t = FCF_{t-1}(1 + g)$

Where FCF_t = the free cash flow at time t

FCF_{t-1} = the free cash flow in the previous period

g = growth rate

If you wish to forecast the total free cash flow over a number of periods where the growth rate is assumed to be constant the following formula can be used.

$FCF = FCF_0(1 + g)^n$

Where FCF is the total forecast free cash flow

FCF_0 is the free cash flow at the beginning of the forecast period

n is the number of years for which the free cash flow is being forecast

Question

The current value of the free cash flow is $6 million and it is estimated that the free cash flows will grow at a constant rate of 10 percent for the next seven years. What is the total FCF predicted for year 7?

$$FCF_7 = (1 + 0.1)^7 \times \$6 = \$11.7 \, m$$

2.2.2 Differing growth rates

When the elements of free cash flow are expected to grow at different rates each element must be forecast separately using the appropriate rate. Free cash flow can then be estimated using the revised figures for each year.

Question   **Definite variables**

Pokey Inc is trying to forecast its free cash flow for the next three years. Current free cash flow is as follows.

	Expected annual increase	
	%	$
EBIT	4	500,000
Tax	30% of EBIT	150,000
Depreciation	5	85,000
Capital expenditure	2	150,000
Working capital requirements	3	60,000

By what percentage will free cash flow have increased between now and the end of year 3?

Answer

	Year 0	Year 3
	$	$
EBIT ($EBIT_0 \times (1 + 0.04)^3$)	500,000	562,432
Tax	(150,000)	(168,730)
Depreciation ($Depreciation_0 \times (1 + 0.05)^3$)	85,000	98,398
Capital expenditure ($Cap \, Ex_0 \times (1 + 0.02)^3$)	(150,000)	(159,181)
Working capital requirements ($WC_0 \times (1 + 0.03)^3$)	(60,000)	(65,564)
Free cash flow	225,000	267,355

$$\text{Percentage increase} = \frac{267,355 - 225,000}{225,000} = 18.8\%$$

3 Free cash flow to equity

Exam focus point

Students were asked to produce a cash flow statement as part of a compulsory 30 mark question in the December 2007 exam. An appreciation of the free cash flow to equity concept was expected, although the examiner commented that only a small number of students made reasonable adjustments for net investment.

The free cash flow derived in the previous section is the amount of money that is available for distribution to the capital contributors. If the project is financed by equity only, then these funds could be potentially distributed to the shareholders of the company.

However, if the company is financing the project by issuing debt, then the shareholders are entitled to the residual cash flow left over after meeting interest and principal payments. This residual cash flow is called free cash flow to equity (FCFE).

3.1 Direct method of calculation

Free Cash Flow to Equity = Net income (EBIT – Net Interest – Tax paid)
Add depreciation
Less total net investment (change in capital investment + change in working capital)
Add net debt issued (new borrowings less any repayments)

Question   Free cash flow to equity

The following information is available for ABC Co:

Capital expenditure $20 million
Corporate tax rate 35%
Debt repayment $23 million
Depreciation charges $10 million

	20X8
	$m
Sales	650.00
Less: cost of goods sold	(438.00)
Gross profit	212.00
Operating expenses	(107.50)
EBIT	104.50
Less: interest expense	(8.00)
Earnings before tax	96.50
Less: taxes	(33.77)
Net Income	62.73

What is the FCFE?

Answer

The free cash flow to equity is calculated as follows:

	20X8
	$m
Net Income	62.73
Plus: depreciation	10.00
Less: capital expenditures	(20.00)
Less: debt repayment	(23.00)
Free Cash Flow to Equity	29.73

3.2 Indirect method of calculation

Using the indirect method, FCFE is calculated as follows.

Free Cash Flow (calculated using the formula in section 3.1 above)
Less (net interest + net debt paid)
Add tax benefit from debt (net interest × tax rate)

Question   Free cash flow to equity – indirect method

Using the information in the question 'Free cash flow to equity' above, calculate the FCFE using the indirect method.

The free cash flow is given by:

EBIT(1 – Tax rate)	67.93
Plus: depreciation expense	10.00
Less: CAPEX	(20.00)
Free cash flow	57.93

FCFE $= \$57.93 - (8 + 23) + 0.35 \times 8 = \$29.73$

Free cash flow to equity is also covered later in Chapter 18 as part of dividend capacity.

4 Valuations of equity

Before we move on to look at valuing equity using free cash flow, we will briefly cover methods of valuing equity which should be familiar to you from Paper F9 *Financial Management*.

4.1 Market capitalisation

Market capitalisation is the market value of a company's shares multiplied by the number of issued shares.

4.2 The net assets method of share valuation

Using this method of valuation, the value of a share in a particular class is equal to the **net tangible assets** divided by the **number of shares. Intangible assets** (including goodwill) should be excluded, unless they have a market value (for example patents and copyrights, which could be sold).

(a)   **Goodwill**, if shown in the accounts, is unlikely to be shown at a true figure for purposes of valuation, and the value of goodwill should be reflected in another method of valuation (for example the earnings basis)

(b)   **Development expenditure**, if shown in the accounts, would also have a value which is related to future profits rather than to the worth of the company's physical assets.

4.2.1 Advantages and disadvantages of asset based valuations

Advantages

*   Valuations can be made relatively simply
*   They provide a base value for the organisation

Disadvantages

*   They do not incorporate future earnings potential

*   If based on historic cost, then they are subject to accounting conventions and may not represent market value

*   They exclude the value of intangible assets

4.3 The P/E ratio (earnings) method of valuation

This is a common method of valuing a **controlling interest** in a company, where the owner can decide on **dividend** and **retentions policy**. The P/E ratio relates earnings per share to a share's value.

Since P/E ratio $= \dfrac{\text{Market value}}{\text{EPS}}$,

then market value per share = EPS × P/E ratio

Remember that earnings per share (EPS) = $\dfrac{\text{Profit/loss attributable to ordinary shareholders}}{\text{Weighted average number of ordinary shares}}$

Examiners have commented in the past that students often calculate earnings per share incorrectly.

The P/E ratio produces an **earnings-based** valuation of shares by deciding a suitable P/E ratio and multiplying this by the EPS for the shares which are being valued.

Market valuation or capitalisation = P/E ratio × Earnings per share or **P/E ratio × Total earnings**

Depending on whether the market value per share, or total market value of the company is being calculated.

The EPS could be a historical EPS or a prospective future EPS. For a given EPS figure, a higher P/E ratio will result in a higher price.

4.4 The earnings yield valuation method

Another income based valuation model is the earnings yield method.

Earnings yield (EY) = $\dfrac{\text{EPS}}{\text{Market price per share}} \times 100\%$

This method is effectively a variation on the P/E method (the EY being the reciprocal of the P/E ratio), using an appropriate earnings yield effectively as a discount rate to value the earnings:

Market value = $\dfrac{\text{Earnings}}{\text{EY}}$

4.4.1 Advantages and disadvantages of earnings based valuations

Advantages

- They can be used to value a controlling stake in an organisation
- They are easily understood methods

Disadvantages

- It can be difficult to identify a suitable P/E ratio for an unlisted entity
- Valuation is based on accounting profits rather than cash flows
- It can be difficult to establish a realistic sustainable level of earnings

4.5 The dividend growth model

Using the **dividend growth model** we have:

$$P_0 = \frac{D_0(1+g)}{(1+k_e)} + \frac{D_0(1+g)^2}{(1+k_e)^2} + \dots = \frac{D_0(1+g)}{(k_e-g)} = \frac{D_1}{k_e-g}$$

where
D_0 = Current year's dividend
g = Growth rate in earnings and dividends
$D_0(1+g)$ = Expected dividend in one year's time (D_1)
k_e = Shareholders' required rate of return
P_0 = Market value excluding any dividend currently payable

4.5.1 Advantages and disadvantages of dividend based valuations

Advantages

- Based on expected future income
- Useful for valuing a minority stake in an organisation

Disadvantages

- Growth rate can be difficult to estimate

- It can be difficult to estimate a cost of equity for an unlisted company

- Companies that don't pay and are not expected to pay dividends do not have a zero value

5 Valuing an organisation using free cash flow   6/12

In Section 6 above we saw that free cash flow could be calculated in two ways, either by calculating it directly or by calculating the free cash flow to equity and adding the **cash flows** to **debt holders**. Similarly we can value an organisation using free cash flows by either using the predicted free cash flows or by adding together all the cash flows payable to the different claimants of the organisation (equity and debt holders).

5.1 Valuation using free cash flows

The valuation using free cash flows is very similar to carrying out a net present value calculation. The value of the organisation is simply the **sum of the discounted free cash flows** over the appropriate horizon.

If we assume that free cash flows remain **constant** (that is, with no growth) over the appropriate horizon, then the value of the organisation is the **free cash flow divided by the cost of capital**.

Alternatively if the free cash flows are growing at a **constant rate** every year, the value can be calculated using the *Gordon Model* (also known as the *Constant Growth Model*).

$$PV_0 = \frac{FCF_0(1+g)}{k-g}$$

Where g is the growth rate
      k is the cost of capital

5.1.1 Example

Rick Inc currently has free cash flows of $5 million per year and a cost of capital of 12%. Calculate the value of Rick Inc if

(a)   The free cash flows are expected to remain constant
(b)   The free cash flows are expected to grow at a constant rate of 4% per annum

Solution

(a)   Value of Rick Inc = $\frac{\text{Free cash flow}}{\text{Cost of capital}} = \frac{\$5\text{ million}}{0.12\text{ million}}$ = $41.67 million

(b)   Use the *Gordon Model*

       Value of Rick Inc = $\frac{(\$5\text{ million} \times 1.04)}{(0.12 - 0.04)}$ = $65 million

5.2 Terminal values

Key term

> The **terminal value** of a project or a stream of cash flows is the value of all the cash flows occurring from period N + 1 onwards ie beyond the normal prediction horizon of periods 1 to N.

These flows are subject to a greater degree of uncertainty as they are beyond the horizon 1 to N where normal forecasts are acceptable. As such simplifying assumptions need to be made for any flows occurring after period N.

BPP
LEARNING MEDIA

When we refer to a project, the terminal value is equivalent to the **salvage value** remaining at the end of the expected project horizon.

5.2.1 Terminal values and company valuation

Terminal values can be used in valuing an organisation. The value of the organisation will be calculated as **the sum of the discounted free cash flows plus the discounted terminal value**.

5.2.2 Calculating terminal values

Assume that free cash flows are constant

When calculating the terminal value, we can assume that the free cash flows after the 'normal' time horizon (period N) will be constant. Terminal value is determined by dividing the free cash flow at time (N + 1) by the cost of capital (required rate of return).

Question   Terminal value

Consider the following information on a project

Cash flow in period N+1 = $2 million
Required rate of return = 10%

Assuming that the free cash flow will remain at $2 million indefinitely and the initial investment is $18 million what is the terminal value?

Answer

The terminal value of the project is:

$$TV_N = \frac{2}{0.1} = \$20 \text{ million}$$

Assume that cash flows increase at a constant rate

An alternative assumption is to assume that cash flows increase from year to year at a constant rate g, ie:

$$FCF_{N+1} = (1 + g)\, FCF_N$$

and the terminal value will be:

$$TV_N = \frac{FCF_N (1 + g)}{k - g}$$

Provided that $k > g$

Question   Terminal value

Assume the following values for the expected growth, current cash flows and required return:

$$\begin{aligned} g &= 0.05 \\ FCF_N &= \$2 \text{ million} \\ k &= 0.10 \end{aligned}$$

What is the terminal value?

The terminal value according to the constant growth model will then be:

$$TV = \frac{2 \times (1 + 0.05)}{0.10 - 0.05} = \$42 \text{ million}$$

Question

You have completed the following forecast of free cash flows for an eight year period, capturing the normal business cycle of Marathon Inc:

Year	FCF
20X8	1,860.0
20X9	1,887.6
20Y0	1,917.6
20Y1	1,951.2
20Y2	1,987.2
20Y3	2,016.0
20Y4	2,043.6
20Y5	2,070.0

Free cash flows are expected to grow at 3% beyond 20Y5. The cost of capital is assumed to be 12%. What is Marathon's value?

Answer

Year	FCF	Discount factor @ 12%	Present Value
20X8	1,860.0	0.893	1,661
20X9	1,887.6	0.797	1,504
20Y0	1,917.6	0.712	1,365
20Y1	1,951.2	0.636	1,241
20Y2	1,987.2	0.567	1,127
20Y3	2,016.0	0.507	1,022
20Y4	2,043.6	0.452	924
20Y5	2,070.0	0.404	836

Total present value for forecast period = $9,680

Terminal value = $\dfrac{(\$2,070 \times 1.03)}{(0.12 - 0.03)}$ = $23,690

Discount terminal value back to year 0 = $23,690 x 0.404 = $9,571

Total value of Marathon = $19,431

5.3 Organisation valuation using FCFE

The techniques used for the valuation of a company using the FCFE can also be applied for the value of equity. The value of equity is simply the present value of the free cash flow to equity, discounted at the cost of equity (k_e), plus the terminal value discounted at the cost of equity.

Once the value of equity is calculated, the value of debt needs to be calculated next. The value of the organisation is then simply the value of equity and the value of debt.

6 Assessing default risk using option pricing models

Option pricing models can be used to calculate the expected loss associated with a corporate bond.

6.1 Options and default probability

The role of **option pricing models** in the assessment of **default risk** is based on the **limited liability property** of **equity investments**.

The **equity** of a company can be seen as **a call option** on the **assets** of the company with an **exercise price** equal to the **outstanding debt.**

The role of **option pricing models** in the assessment of **default risk** is based on the **limited liability property** of **equity investments**. Whereas shareholders can participate in a increase in the profits of a company, their losses are limited to the values of their holding. To see how this property is exploited, consider a firm with assets whose market value is denoted by V. Furthermore the firm is assumed to have a very simple capital structure where the acquisition of assets is funded by equity whose market value is denoted by E and by debt with market value D. The statement of financial position of this firm is given by

Assets	Liabilities
V	Equity E
	Debt D

The **debt** issued by the firm is a **one year zero coupon bond** with **one year maturity** and **face value F**. The **market value** of **debt** is:

$$D = \frac{F}{1+y}$$

Note that y is not the risk-free return but includes a risk premium over the risk-free rate to reflect the fact that bondholders are exposed to credit risk and they may not receive the promised payment F. This can happen when on the date the debt matures, the value of the assets V_1 are not sufficient to pay the bondholders. The company will default on its debt if $V_1 < F$ in which case bond holders will receive not F but V_1, suffering a loss of $F - V_1$. The lower the value of the assets on maturity the higher the loss suffered by the bond holders.

Equity is a residual claim on the assets of the company and the value of equity on maturity date will be the difference between the value of the assets and the face value of debt. It will be positive if the value of the assets is higher than the outstanding debt, and zero if the value of the assets is lower than the outstanding debt. In summary the value of the equity E_1 will be:

$E_1 = V_1 - F$ if $V_1 > F$

$E_1 = 0$ if $V_1 \leq F$

The value of equity on maturity date is shown in Figure 1 below. The value of equity is positive when $V_1 > F$ and zero when $V_1 \leq F$. Because of the limited liability feature of equity, the lowest value it can reach is zero.

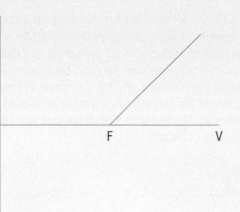

Figure 1

As we have already discussed in Chapter 6, this is the payoff of a call option on the assets of a company with an exercise price equal to the face value of debt F.

The value of the firm's equity can therefore be estimated using a variation of the **Black-Scholes model** for the valuation of a European call option.

Exam formula

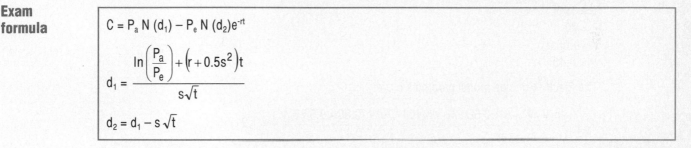

$$C = P_a \, N\,(d_1) - P_e \, N\,(d_2)e^{-rt}$$

$$d_1 = \frac{\ln\left(\dfrac{P_a}{P_e}\right) + \left(r + 0.5s^2\right)t}{s\sqrt{t}}$$

$$d_2 = d_1 - s\sqrt{t}$$

The value of $N(d_1)$ shows how the value of equity changes when the value of the assets change. This is the delta of the call option (delta is covered in more detail in Chapter 17). The value of $N(d_2)$ is the probability that a call option will be in the money at expiration. In this case it is the probability that the value of the asset will exceed the outstanding debt, i.e. $V_1 > F$. The probability of default is therefore given by $1 - N(d_2)$. This is shown as the shaded part in Figure 2 below.

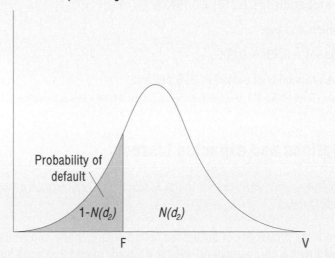

Figure 2

The option pricing model provides useful insights on what determines the probability of default of a bond and it can therefore be used to asses the impact of its determinants on credit risk and the cost of debt capital. From the Black –Scholes formula, it can be seen that the probability of default depends on three factors.

- The debt/asset ratio, F/V
- The volatility of the company assets (σ).
- The maturity of debt (t).

The effect of the debt/asset ratio or level of leverage is unambiguous. A **higher F/V ratio increases** the **probability of default**. Similarly, an **increase** in **volatility** will also **increase** the **probability of default**. Remember that effect of maturity on the probability of default depends on whether F>V or whether F<V. If F>V, the firm is technically insolvent. To avoid bankruptcy, it will need to have increasing earnings. As maturity increases, there is more time for the increase in earnings to occur and for the risk to be reduced. In this case the longer the maturity the lower the probability of default. If F<V and the loan has only a short time to go before maturity, it is unlikely that the loan will default. In this case the longer the maturity the higher the probability of default.

Question
Default Probability

The market value of the assets is $100, and the face value of the 1-year debt is 70. The risk free rate is 5% and the volatility of asset value is 40%. Find the value of the default probability using the Black-Scholes model.

Answer

For this problem we have

$V = 100$
$F = 70$
$r = 0.05$
$\sigma = 0.40$

The Black –Scholes model parameters are:

$$d_1 = \frac{\ln(V/F) + (r + 0.5\sigma^2)t}{\sigma\sqrt{t}} = \frac{\ln(100/70) + (0.05 + 0.5 \times 0.4^2)}{0.4} = 1.217$$

$d_2 = 1.217 - 0.4 = 0.817$

The delta of the option is:

$N(d_1) = $ Probability $(z \le 1.217) = 0.889$

$N(d_2) = $ Probability $(z \le 0.817) = 0.794$

From which we have:

$1 - N(d_2) = 1 - 0.794 = 0.206$

Thus the probability of default is 20.6 percent.

6.2 Options and expected losses

FAST FORWARD

Expected losses are a put option on the assets of the firm with an exercise price equal to the value of the outstanding debt.

Apart from the probability of default the option pricing model can be used to measure the expected loss associated with a corporate bond. We have already stated that bond holders are exposed to credit risk and to losses. The expected loss for the bondholder is

Loss = 0 if $V_1 > F$
Loss = $F - V_1$ if $V_1 < F$

The expected losses can be seen in Figure 3 below

Figure 3

This is the **payoff** of a **put option** written on the **assets** of the **company** V, with **exercise price** F. The expected losses at expiration can be estimated from the **value** of the **put option**. Using the **Black Scholes** model the value of the put option and consequently the expected losses is given by the formula for a European put option with exercise price F and underlying value V:

Put Option = Losses = $(1 - N(d_2))Fe^{-rt} - (1 - N(-d_1))V$

Using the fact that:

$N(-d_1) = 1 - N(d_1)$ and $N(-d_2) = 1 - N(d_2)$, the formula for a European put option can be written as:

Put Option = Losses = $N(-d_2)Fe^{-rt} - N(-d_1)V$

The expected losses are represented by the difference between the face value of the bond and the value of the assets which is unknown prior to maturity date. This can be seen by rewriting the formula for the put option as:

Put Option = Expected Loss = $N(-d_2)\left(Fe^{-rt} - \dfrac{N(-d_1)}{N(-d_2)}V \right)$

The term $\dfrac{N(-d_1)}{N(-d_2)}V$ shows the recovery value of the asset.

Question

The market value of the assets is $100, and the face value of the 1-year debt is 70. The risk free rate is 5% and the volatility of asset value is 40%. What is the recovery value and the expected loss?

Answer

We have already found from the previous question that for V=100, F=70, r = 0.05, and s = 0.40 the Black-Scholes formula yields d_1 =1.217

$d_2 = 0.817$

$N(d_1) = 0.889$

$N(d_2) = 0.794$

$N(-d_1) = 0.111$

$N(-d_2) = 0.206$

The discounted recovery amount is:

$$\frac{N(-d_1)}{N(-d_2)}V = \frac{0.111}{0.206} \times 100 = 53.883$$

The discounted loss given default is given by

$$\left(Fe^{-rt} - \frac{N(-d_1)}{N(-d_2)}V\right) = \left(70e^{-0.05} - 53.883\right) = 12.703$$

The expected loss is given by:

$$\text{Expected Loss} = N(-d_2)\left(Fe^{-rt} - \frac{N(-d_1)}{N(-d_2)}V\right) = 0.206 \times 12.703 = \$2.617$$

Question

Equity Value

The market value of the assets of a company is \$100, and the face value of the 1-year debt is 70. The risk free rate is 5% and the volatility of asset value is 40%. What is the market value of equity?

Answer

We have already found from the previous questions that for $V = 100$, $F = 70$, $r = 0.05$, and $s = 0.40$ the Black-Scholes formula yields $d_1 = 1.217$

$d_2 = 0.817$

$N(d_1) = 0.889$

$N(d_2) = 0.794$

$N(-d_1) = 0.111$

$N(-d_2) = 0.206$

Using the Black-Scholes formula for the value of a European call option yields

$$E = N(d_1)V - N(d_2)Fe^{-rt} = 0.889 \times 100 - 0.794 \times 70 \times e^{-0.05} = \$36.031$$

Question

The market value of the assets of a company is $100, and the face value of the 1-year debt is 70. The risk free rate is 5% and the volatility of asset value is 40%. What is the credit spread of the bond?

Answer

We have already found from the previous questions that for V = 100, F = 70, r = 0.05, and s = 0.40 the Black-Scholes formula yields E = $36.031

The market value of debt is the discounted present value of the face value, discounted at the interest rate that includes a credit spread:

$$D = \frac{F}{1 + r + s}$$

The credit spread can be calculated by rearranging the above formula:

$$s = \frac{F}{D} - 1 - r$$

The market value of debt is calculated as the difference between the market value of assets and the market value of equity, where the latter is calculated using the Black Scholes model.

The market value of debt is therefore given by:

D = V − E = 100 − 36.031 = $63.969

The credit spread is given by:

$$s = \frac{70}{63.969} - 1 - 0.05 = 0.044 = 4.4\%$$

Chapter Roundup

- A firm's free cash flow is the actual amount of cash that a company has left from its operations that could be used to pursue opportunities that enhance shareholder value.

- Option pricing models can be used to calculate the expected loss associated with a corporate bond.

- The role of **option pricing models** in the assessment of **default risk** is based on the **limited liability property** of **equity investments**.

- The equity of a company can be seen as a call option on the assets of the company with an exercise price equal to the outstanding debt.

- Expected losses are a put option on the assets of the firm with an exercise price equal to the value of the outstanding debt.

BPP
LEARNING MEDIA

Quick Quiz

1   The following information is available for XYZ Co:

Capital expenditure $50 million
Corporate tax rate 25%
Debt repayment $27 million
Depreciation charges $13 million
Shareholders required return 13%

	20X8 $m
Sales	725.00
Less: cost of goods sold	(517.00)
Gross profit	208.00
Operating expenses	(91.75)
EBIT	116.25
Less: interest expense	(11.00)
Earnings before tax	105.25
Less: taxes	(26.31)
Net Income	78.94

What is the FCFE (using the direct method of calculation)?

2   Using the information above, what is the FCFE using the indirect method of calculation?

3   Using the information above and assuming the free cash flow is expected to grow at a constant rate of 3% per year, what is the valuation of XYZ Co?

4   A company has assets with a market value of $500,000, and 2-year debt with a face value of $280,000. The risk free rate is 3% and the volatility of asset value is 35%. Find the value of the default probability using the Black-Scholes model.

Answers to Quick Quiz

1

	20X8 $m
Net Income	78.94
Plus: depreciation	13.00
Less: capital expenditures	(50.00)
Less: debt repayment	(27.00)
Free Cash Flow to Equity	14.94

2

EBIT(1 – Tax rate)	87.19
Plus: depreciation expense	13.00
Less: CAPEX	(50.00)
Free cash flow	50.19

FCFE = $50.19 – (11 + 27) + (0.25 × 11) = $14.94m

3   Value of XYZ Co = $\dfrac{(\$14.94 \text{ million} \times 1.03)}{(0.13 - 0.03)}$ = $153.9 million

4   For this problem we have

V = 500,000
F = 280,000
t = 2
r = 0.03
σ = 0.35

The Black–Scholes model parameters are:

$$d_1 = \frac{\ln(V/F) + (r + 0.5\sigma^2)t}{\sigma\sqrt{t}} = \frac{\ln(500,000/280,000) + (0.03 + 0.5 \times 0.35^2)2}{0.35\sqrt{2}} = 1.540$$

$d_2 = 1.540 - 0.35\sqrt{2} = 1.045$ say 1.05

$N(d_2) = 0.8531$

From which we have:

$1 - N(d_2) = 1 - 0.8531 = 0.1469$

Thus the probability of default is 14.7 percent.

8

International investment and financing decisions

Topic list	Syllabus reference
1 Overview	C (5)
2 Effects of exchange rate assumptions on project values	C (5) (a)
3 Forecasting cash flows from overseas projects	C (5) (b)
4 The impact of exchange controls	C (5) (c), F (2) (a)
5 Transaction, translation and economic risks	C (5) (d)
6 Issues in choosing finance for overseas investment	C (5) (e)
7 Costs and benefits of alternative sources of finance for MNCs	C (5) (e)

Introduction

In this chapter we look at the international dimension of project appraisal.

Companies that undertake overseas projects are exposed to exchange rate risks as well as other risks such as exchange control, taxation and political risks.

In this chapter we look at capital budgeting techniques for multinational companies that incorporate these additional complexities in the decision-making process.

Study guide

		Intellectual level
C5	**International investment and financing decisions**	
(a)	Assess the impact upon the value of a project of alternative exchange rate assumptions	3
(b)	Forecast project or organisation free cash flows in any specific currency and determine the project's net present value or organisation value under differing exchange rate, fiscal and transaction cost assumptions	2
(c)	Evaluate the significance of exchange controls for a given investment decision and strategies for dealing with restricted remittance	3
(d)	Assess the impact of a project upon an organisation's exposure to translation, transaction and economic risk	3
(e)	Assess and advise upon the costs and benefits of alternative sources of finance available within the international equity and bond markets	3
F2	**The use of financial derivatives to hedge against forex risk**	
(a)	Assess the impact on an organisation to exposure in translation, transaction and economic risks and how these can be managed	3

1 Overview

Many of the projects that companies are appraising may have an international dimension. For example, the assumption can be made that part of the production from a project may be exported. In appraising a tourist development, a company may be making assumptions about the number of tourists from abroad who may be visiting. Imported goods and materials could be a factor in the determination of cash flows. All these examples show that exchange rates will have an influence on the cash flows of the company.

Companies that undertake overseas projects are exposed, in addition to exchange rate risks, to other types of risk such as exchange control, taxation or political risks. The latter is particularly true in countries with undemocratic regimes that may be subject to changes in a rather disorderly fashion.

Capital budgeting techniques for multinational companies therefore need to incorporate these additional complexities in the decision making process. These can be based on similar concepts to those used in the purely domestic case which we have examined. Special considerations, examples of which were given above, may apply.

2 Effects of exchange rate assumptions on project values

Changes in exchange rates are as important as the underlying profitability in selecting an overseas project.

In a domestic project the NPV is the sum of the discounted cash flows plus the terminal value (discounted at the WACC) less the initial investment.

When a project in a foreign country is assessed we must take into account some specific considerations such as **local taxes, double taxation agreements, and political risk** that affect the present value of the project. The main consideration of course in an international project is the exchange rate risk, that is the risk that arises from the fact that the cash flows are denominated in a foreign currency. An appraisal of an international project requires estimates of the exchange rate. In the rest of this section we discuss some fundamental relationships that help the financial manager form views about exchange rates.

2.1 Purchasing power parity

Purchasing power parity theory states that the exchange rate between two currencies is the same in equilibrium when the purchasing power of currency is the same in each country.

Purchasing power parity theory predicts that the exchange value of foreign currency depends on the relative purchasing power of each currency in its own country and that **spot exchange rates will vary over time according to relative price changes.**

Formally, purchasing power parity can be expressed in the following formula.

Exam formula

$$S_1 = S_0 \times \frac{(1+h_c)}{(1+h_b)}$$

Where S_1 = expected spot rate
S_0 = current spot rate
h_c = expected inflation rate in country c
h_b = expected inflation rate in country b

Note that the expected future spot rate will not necessarily coincide with the 'forward exchange rate' currently quoted.

2.1.1 Example: Purchasing power parity

The spot exchange rate between UK sterling and the Danish kroner is £1 = 8.00 kroners. Assuming that there is now purchasing parity, an amount of a commodity costing £110 in the UK will cost 880 kroners in Denmark. Over the next year, price inflation in Denmark is expected to be 5% while inflation in the UK is expected to be 8%. What is the 'expected spot exchange rate' at the end of the year?

Using the formula above:

Future (forward) rate, $S_1 = 8 \times \dfrac{1.05}{1.08} = 7.78$

This is the same figure as we get if we compare the inflated prices for the commodity. At the end of the year:

UK price = £110 × 1.08 = £118.80

Denmark price = Kr880 × 1.05 = Kr924

S_t = 924 ÷ 118.80 = 7.78

In the real world, exchange rates move towards purchasing power parity only over the **long term**. However, the theory is sometimes used to predict future exchange rates in **investment appraisal problems** where forecasts of relative inflation rates are available.

Case Study

An amusing example of purchasing power parity is the Economist's Big Mac index. Under PPP movements in countries' exchange rates should in the long-term mean that the prices of an identical basket of goods or services are equalised. The McDonalds Big Mac represents this basket.

The index compares local Big Mac prices with the price of Big Macs in America. This comparison is used to forecast what exchange rates should be, and this is then compared with the actual exchange rates to decide which currencies are over and under-valued.

2.2 Interest rate parity

FAST FORWARD

Under interest rate parity the difference between spot and forward rates reflects differences in interest rates.

Key term

Interest rate parity predicts foreign exchange rates based on the hypothesis that the difference between two countries' interest rates should offset the difference between the spot rates and the forward exchange rates over the same period.

Under interest rate parity the difference between spot and forward rates reflects differences in interest rates. If this was not the case then investors holding the currency with the lower interest rate would switch to the other currency, ensuring that they would not lose on returning to the original currency by fixing the exchange rate in advance at the forward rate. If enough investors acted in this way, forces of supply and demand would lead to a change in the forward rate to prevent such risk-free profit making.

The principle of interest rate parity links the foreign exchange markets and the international money markets. The principle can be stated using the following formula which is given in the exam formula sheet.

Exam formula

$$F_0 = S_0 \frac{(1+i_c)}{(1+i_b)}$$

where F_0 is the forward rate

S_0 is the spot rate

i_c is the interest rate in the country overseas

i_b is the interest rate in the base country

This equation links the spot and forward rates to the difference between the interest rates.

Example

A US company is expecting to receive Zambian kwacha in one year's time. The spot rate is US$1 = ZMK4,819. The company could borrow in kwacha at 7% or in dollars at 9%. There is no forward rate for one year's time.

Estimate the forward rate in one year's time.

Solution

The base currency is dollars therefore the dollar interest rate will be on the bottom of the fraction.

$$F_0 = 4,819 \frac{(1+0.07)}{(1+0.09)} = 4,730.58$$

However this prediction is subject to considerable inaccuracy as future events can result in large unexpected currency rate swings that were not predicted by interest rate parity. In general interest rate parity is regarded as **less accurate** than purchasing power parity for predicting future exchange rates.

2.2.1 Use of interest rate parity to compute the effective cost of foreign currency loans

Loans in some currencies are cheaper than in others. However when the likely strengthening of the exchange rate is taken into consideration, the cost of apparently cheap international loans becomes much more expensive.

Example

Cato, a Polish company, needs a one year loan of about 50 million zlotys. It can borrow in zlotys at 10.80% pa but is considering taking out a sterling loan which would cost only 6.56% pa. The current spot exchange rate is zloty/£ 5.1503. The company decides to borrow £10 million at 6.56% per annum. Converting at the spot rate, this will provide zloty51.503 million. Interest will be paid at the end of one year along with the repayment of the loan principal.

Assuming the exchange rate moves in line with interest rate parity, you are required to show the zloty values of the interest paid and the repayment of the loan principal. Compute the effective interest rate paid on the loan.

Solution

By interest rate parity, the zloty will have weakened in one year to:

$$5.1503 \times \frac{1.1080}{1.0656} = 5.3552$$

Time		£'000	Exchange rate	Zloty '000
Now	Borrows	10,000	5.1503	51,503
In 1 year	6.56% interest	(656)		
	Repayment	(10,000)	5.3552	
		(10,656)		(57,065)

The effective interest rate paid is $\frac{57,065}{51,503} - 1 = 10.80\%$, the same as it would have paid in £.

This rate would have to be incorporated into the discount rate for any Investment projects financed by this loan. As the discount rate would now be higher than originally anticipated, the NPV of the project will be lower (which may result in the project being unviable).

2.3 International Fisher effect

The International Fisher effect states that currencies with high interest rates are expected to depreciate relative to currencies with low interest rates.

According to the **International Fisher effect**, interest rate differentials between countries provide an unbiased predictor of future changes in spot exchange rates. The currency of countries with relatively high interest rates is expected to depreciate against currencies with lower interest rates, because the higher interest rates are considered necessary to compensate for the anticipated currency depreciation. Given free movement of capital internationally, this idea suggests that the real rate of return in different countries will equalise as a result of adjustments to spot exchange rates.

The International Fisher effect can be expressed as:

Formula to learn

$$\frac{1 + i_c}{1 + i_b} = \frac{1 + h_c}{1 + h_b}$$

Where i_a is the nominal interest rate in country c
             i_b is the nominal interest rate in country b
             h_a is the inflation rate in country c
             h_b is the inflation rate in country b

Example

The nominal interest rate in the US is 5% and inflation is currently 3%. If inflation in the UK is currently 4.5% what is its nominal interest rate? Would the dollar be expected to appreciate or depreciate against sterling?

Solution

The dollar is the base currency.

$$\frac{1+i_c}{1+0.05} = \frac{1+0.045}{1+0.03}$$

$$1 + i_c = (1 + 0.05) \times \frac{1+0.045}{1+0.03}$$

$1 + i_c = 1.065$ therefore $i_c = 6.5\%$

The dollar would be expected to depreciate against sterling as it has a lower interest rate. According to the International Fisher effect, the currency of a country with a lower interest rate will depreciate against the currency of a country with a higher interest rate.

Question	Forecasting exchange rates

Suppose that the nominal interest rate in the UK is 6 percent and the nominal interest rate in the US is 7 percent. What is the expected change in the dollar/sterling exchange rate?

Answer

Since

$$r_\$ - r_\pounds = 0.01$$

It means that

$$\frac{e_1 - e_0}{e_0} = 1\%$$

And the implication is that the dollar will depreciate by 1 percent.

2.4 Expectations theory

Expectations theory looks at the relationship between differences in forward and spot rates and the expected changes in spot rates.

The formula for expectations theory is:

$$\frac{Spot}{Forward} = \frac{Spot}{Expected\ future\ spot}$$

> The NPV of an international project can be calculated either by converting the cash flows or the NPV.

There are **two alternative approaches** for calculating the NPV from a overseas project.

1st approach

(a)   Forecast **foreign currency** cash flows including inflation

(b)   **Forecast exchange rates** and therefore the home currency cash flows

(c)   Discount home currency cash flows at the **domestic cost of capital**

2nd approach-

(a)   Forecast **foreign currency** cash flows including inflation

(b)   Discount at **foreign currency cost of capital** and calculate the foreign currency NPV

(c)   Convert into a **home currency NPV** at the spot exchange rate

Question

Overseas investment appraisal

Bromwich Inc, a US company, is considering undertaking a new project in the UK. This will require initial capital expenditure of £1,250 million, with no scrap value envisaged at the end of the five year lifespan of the project. There will also be an initial working capital requirement of £500 million, which will be recovered at the end of the project. The initial capital will therefore be £1,750 million. Pre-tax net cash inflows of £800 million are expected to be generated each year from the project.

Company tax will be charged in the UK at a rate of 40%, with depreciation on a straight-line basis being an allowable deduction for tax purposes. Portuguese tax is paid at the end of the year following that in which the taxable profits arise.

There is a double taxation agreement between the US and the UK, which means that no US tax will be payable on the project profits.

The current $/£ spot rate is $1 = £0.625. Inflation rates are 3% in the US and 4.5% in the UK. A project of similar risk recently undertaken by Bromwich Inc in the US had a required post-tax rate of return of 10%.

Required

Calculate the present value of the project using each of the two alternative approaches.

Answer

Method 1 – convert sterling cash flows into $ and discount at $ cost of capital

Firstly we have to estimate the exchange rate for each of years 1 – 6. **This can be done using purchasing power parity**.

$$S_1 = S_0 \times \frac{(1+h_c)}{(1+h_b)}$$

Year		$/£ expected spot rate
0		0.625
1	0.625 x (1.045/1.03)	0.634
2	0.634 x (1.045/1.03)	0.643
3	0.643 x (1.045/1.03)	0.652
4	0.652 x (1.045/1.03)	0.661
5	0.661 x (1.045/1.03)	0.671
6	0.671 x (1.045/1.03)	0.681

	0 £m	1 £m	2 £m	3 £m	4 £m	5 £m	6 £m
Capital	−1,750					500	
Net Cash flows		800	800	800	800	800	
Depreciation		250	250	250	250	250	
Tax			(220)	(220)	(220)	(220)	(220)
	(1,750)	800	580	580	580	1080	(220)
Exchange rate $/£	0.625	0.634	0.643	0.652	0.661	0.671	0.681
Cash flows in $m	(2,800)	1,261.83	902.02	889.57	877.46	1,609.54	(323.05)
Discount factor	1	0.909	0.826	0.751	0.683	0.621	0.564
PV	(2,800)	1,147.00	745.07	668.07	599.31	999.52	(182.20)
NPV in $m	1,176.77						

Method 2 – discount sterling cash flows at adjusted cost of capital

When we use the this method we need to find the cost of capital for the project in the host country. If we are to keep the cash flows in £ they need to be discounted at a rate that takes account of both the US discount rate (10%) and different rates of inflation in the two countries. This is an application of the **International Fisher effect**.

$$\frac{1+i_c}{1+i_b} = \frac{1+h_c}{1+h_b}$$

$$\frac{1+i_c}{1+0.10} = \frac{1+0.045}{1+0.03} \quad \text{where } i_c \text{ is the UK discount rate}$$

$1 + i_c = 1.116$, therefore i_c is approximately 12%

Sterling cash flows should be discounted at this rate.

	0 £m	1 £m	2 £m	3 £m	4 £m	5 £m	6 £m
Capital	(1,750)					500	
Net Cash flows		800	800	800	800	800	
Depreciation		250	250	250	250	250	
Tax			(220)	(220)	(220)	(220)	(220)
Net Cash Flows	(1,750)	800	580	580	580	1080	(220)
Discount factor	1	0.893	0.797	0.712	0.636	0.567	0.507
PV	(1,750.00)	714.40	462.26	412.96	368.88	612.36	(111.54)
NPV in £m	709.32						

Translating this present value at the spot rate gives

$$NPV = \frac{£709.32}{0.625} = \$1,134.91$$

Note that the two answers are almost identical (with differences being due to rounding). In the first approach the dollar is appreciating due to the relatively low inflation rate in the US (not good news when converting sterling to $). In the second approach the UK discount rate is higher due to the relatively high inflation rate in the UK (again this is bad news as the NPV of the project will be lower).

2.6 The effect of exchange rates on NPV

Now that we have created a framework for the analysis of the effects of exchange rate changes on the net present value from an overseas project we can use the NPV equation to calculate the impact of exchange rate changes on the sterling denominated NPV of a project.

NPV = the sum of the discounted domestic cash flows

Add: discounted domestic terminal value
Less: initial domestic investment (converted at spot rate)

When there is a devaluation of the domestic currency relative to a foreign currency, then the domestic currency value of the net cash flows increases and thus the NPV increases. The opposite happens when the domestic currency appreciates. In this case the domestic currency value of the cash flows decline and the NPV of the project in sterling declines. The relationship between NPV in sterling and the exchange rate is shown in the diagram below

Question

Effect of changes in the exchange rate

Calculate the NPV for the UK project of Bromwich Inc under three different scenarios.

(a)   The exchange rate remains constant at $1 = £0.625 for the duration of the project
(b)   The dollar appreciates by 1.5% per year (as per the original question)
(c)   The dollar depreciates by 1.5% per year

Answer

If the dollar depreciates by 1.5% each year the exchange rates are as follows:

Year		Exchange rate ($/£)
0		0.625
1	0.625/1.015	0.616
2	0.616/1.015	0.607
3	0.607/1.015	0.598
4	0.598/1.015	0.589
5	0.589/1.015	0.580
6	0.580/1.015	0.571

The NPV under the three scenarios is given in the table below.   Cash flows are discounted at 10%.

Cash flows in dollars

Period	Cash flows in £	Constant Exchange rate ($1 = £0.625)	Dollar appreciates 1.5% per year	Dollar depreciates 1.5% per year
0	(1,750)	(2,800.00)	(2,800)	(2,800)
1	800	1,280	1,261.83	1,298.70
2	580	928	902.02	955.52
3	580	928	889.57	969.90
4	580	928	877.46	984.72
5	580	1,728	1,609.54	1,862.07
6	(220)	(352)	(323.05)	(385.29)
NPV (discounted at 10%)		1,336	1,065.24	1,509.78

3 Forecasting cash flows from overseas projects

3.1 Forecasting project cash flows and APV

In Chapter 5 we computed the cash flows that are required for the valuation of a project. The calculation of cash flows for the appraisal of overseas projects requires a number of other factors to be taken into account.

3.2 Effect on exports

When a multinational company sets up a subsidiary in another country, to which it already exports, the relevant cash flows for the evaluation of the project should take into account the loss of export earnings in the particular country. The NPV of the project should take explicit account of this potential loss and it should be written as

Sum of discounted (net cash flows – exports) + discounted terminal value – initial investment

The appropriate discount rate will be WACC.

3.3 Taxes

Taxes play an important role in the investment appraisal as it can affect the viability of a project. The main aspects of taxation in an international context are:

- Corporate taxes in the host country.
- Investment allowances in the host country
- Withholding taxes in the host country
- Double taxation relief in the home country
- Foreign tax credits in the home country

The importance of taxation in corporate decision making is demonstrated by the use of **tax havens** by some multinationals as a means of deferring tax on funds prior to their repatriation or reinvestment. A tax haven is likely to have the following characteristics.

(a)   Tax on foreign investment or sales income earned by resident companies, and withholding tax on dividends paid to the parent, should be low.

(b)   There should be a stable government and a stable currency.

(c)   There should be adequate financial services support facilities.

For example suppose that the tax rate on profits in the Federal West Asian Republic is 20% and the UK corporation tax is 30%, and there is a double taxation agreement between the two countries. A subsidiary of a UK firm operating in the Federal West Asian Republic earns the equivalent of £1 million in profit, and therefore pays £200,000 in tax on profits. When the profits are remitted to the UK, the UK parent can claim a credit of £200,000 against the full UK tax charge of £300,000, and hence will only pay £100,000.

Flagwaver Inc is considering whether to establish a subsidiary in Slovenia at a cost of €20,000,000. The subsidiary will run for four years and the net cash flows from the project are shown below.

	Net Cash Flow
	€
Project 1	3,600,000
Project 2	4,560,000
Project 3	8,400,000
Project 4	8,480,000

There is a withholding tax of 10 percent on remitted profits and the exchange rate is expected to remain constant at $1 = €1.50. At the end of the four year period the Slovenian government will buy the plant for €12,000,000. The latter amount can be repatriated free of withholding taxes.

If the required rate of return is 15 percent what is the present value of the project?

Answer

	Remittance	Discount factor (15%)	Discounted
€	$		$
3,240,000	2,160,000	0.870	1,879,200
4,104,000	2,736,000	0.756	2,068,416
7,560,000	5,040,000	0.658	3,316,320
19,632,000	13,088,000	0.572	7,486,336
			14,750,272

The NPV is $14,750,272 - $\dfrac{EUR20,000,000}{1.50}$ = \$1,416,939

Goody plc is considering whether to establish a subsidiary in the USA, at a cost of $2,400,000. This would be represented by non-current assets of $2,000,000 and working capital of $400,000. The subsidiary would produce a product which would achieve annual sales of $1,600,000 and incur cash expenditures of $1,000,000 a year.

The company has a planning horizon of four years, at the end of which it expects the realisable value of the subsidiary's fixed assets to be $800,000.

It is the company's policy to remit the maximum funds possible to the parent company at the end of each year.

Tax is payable at the rate of 35% in the USA and is payable one year in arrears. A double taxation treaty exists between the UK and the USA and so no UK taxation is expected to arise.

Tax allowable depreciation is at a rate of 25% on a straight line basis on all non-current assets. The tax allowable depreciation can first be claimed one year after the investment ie at t_1.

Because of the fluctuations in the exchange rate between the US dollar and sterling, the company would protect itself against the risk by raising a eurodollar loan to finance the investment. The company's cost of capital for the project is 16%.

Calculate the NPV of the project.

The annual writing down allowance (WDA) is 25% of US$2,000,000 = $500,000, from which the annual tax saving would be (at 35%) $175,000.

Year	Investment $m	Contribution $m	Tax on contribution $m	Tax saving on WDA and tax on realisable value $m	Net cash flow $m	Discount factor @ 16%	Present value $m
0	(2.4)				(2.400)	1.000	(2.400)
1		0.6		0.175	0.775	0.862	0.668
2		0.6	(0.21)	0.175	0.565	0.743	0.420
3		0.6	(0.21)	0.175	0.565	0.641	0.362
4	1.2*	0.6	(0.21)	0.175	1.765	0.552	0.974
5			(0.21)	(0.280)**	(0.490)	0.476	(0.233)
							(0.209)

* Non-current assets realisable value $800,000 plus working capital $400,000

** It is assumed that tax would be payable on the realisable value of the non-current assets, since the tax written down value of the assets would be zero. 35% of $800,000 is $280,000.

The NPV is negative and so the project would not be viable at a discount rate of 16%.

3.4 Subsidies

Many countries offer concessionary loans to multinational companies in order to entice them to invest in the country. The benefit from such concessionary loans should be included in the NPV calculation. The benefit of a concessionary loan is the difference between the repayment when borrowing under market conditions and the repayment under the concessionary loan.

For a UK company this benefit is calculated as

$$\text{Benefit} = \frac{L_0}{e_0} - \sum_{t=1}^{N} \frac{LP_t / e_t}{(1+i)^t}$$

Where
- L_0 is the amount of concessionary loan in foreign currency
- LP is the periodic loan repayment in foreign currency
- $i_£$ is the borrowing rate in the UK
- e_0 is the foreign currency exchange rate
- e_t is the foreign currency exchange rate at time t

3.5 Exchange restrictions

In calculating the NPV of an overseas project only the proportion of cash flows that are expected to be repatriated should be included in the calculation of the NPV.

3.6 Impact of transaction costs on NPV for international projects

Transaction costs are incurred when companies invest abroad due to currency conversion or other administrative expenses. These should also be taken into account.

3.7 A general model using adjusted present value

3.7.1 A recap of the APV approach

The APV method of investment appraisal was introduced in Chapter 7a in the context of domestic investments. Just to recap, there are three steps.

Step 1   Estimate NPV assuming that the project is financed entirely by equity.

Step 2   Estimate the effects of the actual structure of finance (for example, tax effects of borrowing)

Step 3   Add the values from steps 1 and 2 to obtain the APV.

3.7.2 APV in the international context

You should follow the normal procedure of estimating the relevant cash flows and discounting them at an appropriate cost of capital. However you must also take account of the international dimension of the project, so that the steps become as follows.

Step 1   As the initial NPV assumes that the project is financed entirely by equity, the appropriate cost of capital is the cost of equity (allowing for project risk but excluding financial risk).

Step 2   Make adjustments for:

- Tax effects of debt and debt issue costs
- Any finance raised in the local markets
- Restrictions on remittances
- Subsidies from overseas governments

Step 3   Add the values from the first two steps to obtain the APV

The steps for calculating the APV of an international project are essentially the same as for domestic projects, although more care has to taken with the extra adjustments

4 The impact of exchange controls

4.1 The nature of exchange controls

Exchange controls restrict the flow of foreign exchange into and out of a country, usually to defend the local currency or to protect reserves of foreign currencies. Exchange controls are generally more restrictive in developing and less developed countries although some still exist in developed countries. These controls take the following forms:

Rationing the supply of foreign exchange. Anyone wishing to make payments abroad in a foreign currency will be restricted by the limited supply, which stops them from buying as much as they want from abroad.

Restricting the types of transaction for which payments abroad are allowed, for example by suspending or banning the payment of dividends to foreign shareholders, such as parent companies in multinationals, who will then have the problem of **blocked funds**.

4.2 Impact of exchange controls on investment decisions

In order to investigate the impact of exchange rate controls we can use the basic equation for the NPV.

Step 1   Convert net cash flows to home currency and discount at WACC

Step 2   Convert terminal value to home currency and discount at WACC

Step 3   Add the values from Steps 1 and 2 and deduct the initial investment (converted to home currency)

Assuming that **no repatriation** is possible until period N, when the life of the project will have been completed then the NPV will be calculated as follows.

Step 1   Add all net cash flows together and then add the terminal value

Step 2   Convert the value from Step 1 to home currency

Step 3   Discount the value from Step 2 at WACC

Step 4   Convert initial investment to home currency

Step 5   Deduct the value from Step 4 from the value in Step 3 to obtain NPV

The above formula assumes that non repatriated funds are not invested. If in fact we assume that the cash flow is invested each period and earns a return equal to i, then the NPV will be calculated as follows.

Step 1   Convert terminal value to home currency and discount at WACC

Step 2   Convert net cash flows to home currency, gross up for interest and add together, before discounting the total using WACC

Step 3   Convert initial investment to home currency and deduct from the sum of the values in Steps 1 and 2

The impact will depend on the interest rate earned and the cost of capital. An example will illustrate how this may be calculated.

Question   Exchange controls

Consider again the case of Flagwaver Inc, and its proposed subsidiary in Slovenia in question *International Investment 1*.

Now assume that no funds can be repatriated for the first three years, but all the funds are allowed to be remitted to the home market in year 4. The funds can be invested at a rate of 5 percent per year.

Is the project still financially viable?

Answer

Year	1st payment	2nd payment	3rd payment	4th payment
1	€3,600,000			
2		€4,560,000		
3			€8,400,000	
4[1]	4,167,450	5,027,400	8,820,000	€8,480,000
Withholding tax	(416,745)	(502,740)	(882,000)	(848,000)
Net cash flow	3,750,705	4,524,660	7,938,000	7,632,000
Exchange rate ($/€)	1.50	1.50	1.50	1.50
Cash flow ($)	2,500,470	3,016,440	5,292,000	5,088,000

[1] The first payment represents the initial profit of €3,600,000 + 3 years' investment interest of 5% - that is:

$€3,600,000 \times 1.05^3 = €4,167,150$

The second payment includes 2 years' investment interest and the 3rd payment one year's investment interest.

Total net cash flow receivable in Year 4 is $15,896,910. When the salvage value of $8,000,000 (€20,000,000/1,50) is included, total cash receivable is $23,896,910. Discounted at 15% (discount factor at year 4 = 0.572), the present value is $13,669,033.

Net present value = $13,669,033 – (€20,000,000/1.5) = $335,700

Note that the exchange controls have reduced the NPV of the project by 76% (original NPV = $1,416,939) but the project is still financially viable.

4.3 Strategies for dealing with exchange controls

Multinational companies have used many different strategies to overcome exchange controls the most common of which are

- **Transfer pricing** where the parent company sells goods or services to the subsidiary and obtain payment. The amount of this payment will depend on the volume of sales and also on the transfer price for the sales.
- **Royalty payments** when a parent company grants a subsidiary the right to make goods protected by patents. The size of any royalty can be adjusted to suit the wishes of the parent company's management.
- Loans by the parent company to the subsidiary. If the parent company makes a **loan** to a subsidiary, it can set the interest rate high or low, thereby affecting the profits of both companies. A high rate of interest on a loan, for example, would improve the parent company's profits to the detriment of the subsidiary's profits.
- **Management charges** may be levied by the parent company for costs incurred in the management of international operations.

5 Transaction, translation and economic risks

The main risks faced by companies dealing with foreign currencies are transaction, translation and economic risks.

Exposure to foreign exchange risk can occur in a variety of ways. Most companies and certainly multinational corporations are affected by movements in exchange rates. Generally, exposure to foreign exchange risk can be categorised as **transaction** exposure, **translation** exposure and **economic** exposure.

5.1 Transaction exposure

Key term

Transaction risk is the risk of adverse exchange rate movements occurring in the course of **normal international trading transactions**.

Transaction exposure occurs when a company has a future transaction that will be settled in a foreign currency. Such exposure could arise for example as the result of a US company operating a foreign subsidiary. Operations in foreign countries encounter a variety of transactions for example, purchases or sales or financial transactions that are denominated in a foreign currency. Under these circumstances it is often necessary for the parent company to convert the home currency in order to provide the necessary currency to meet foreign obligations. This necessity gives rise to a foreign exchange exposure. The cost of foreign obligations could rise as a result of a domestic currency or the domestic value of foreign revenues could depreciate as a result of a stronger home currency. Even when foreign subsidiaries operate independently of the parent company, without relying on the parent company as a source of cash, they will ultimately remit dividends to the parent in the home currency. Once again, this will require a conversion from foreign to home currency.

Transaction risk and its management will be covered in greater detail in Chapter 16 when we look at hedging foreign currency exposure.

5.2 Translation exposure

Key term

Translation risk is the risk that the organisation will make **exchange losses** when the **accounting results** of its foreign branches or subsidiaries are **translated** into the **home currency**.

Translation exposure occurs in multinational corporations that have foreign subsidiaries with assets and liabilities denominated in foreign currency. Translation exposure occurs because the value of these accounts must eventually be stated in domestic currency for reporting purposes in the company's financial statements. In general, as exchange rates change, the home currency value of the foreign subsidiaries' assets and liabilities will change. Such changes can result in translation losses or gains, which will be recognised in financial statements. The nature and structure of the subsidiaries' assets and liabilities determine the extent of translation exposure to the parent company.

Translation losses can also result from, for example, restatingthe book value of a foreign subsidiary's assets at the exchange rate on the date of the statement of financial position. Such losses will not have an impact on the firm's cash flow unless the assets are sold. This could influence investors' and lenders' attitudes to the financial worth and creditworthiness of the company. Such risk can be reduced if assets and liabilities denominated in particular currencies can be held in balanced accounts.

For example, suppose a UK firm has a European subsidiary that has a European bank deposit of €1 million and payable of €1 million. Also, suppose the exchange rate between the € and sterling is €1.10 per £. The sterling value of the subsidiary's position in these two accounts is £909,090 in both cases. If sterling was to suddenly appreciate against the €, say to €1.15/£ the asset and the liability accounts would lose sterling value in the same amount. Both would be revalued in sterling at £869,565. However, there would be no loss to the UK parent, since the sterling loss on the bank deposit is exactly offset by the sterling gain on the payable. In essence, these two accounts hedged each other from translation exposure to exchange rate changes.

Case Study

In 2011, Coca Cola used 73 functional currencies in addition to the US dollar. As Coca Cola's consolidated financial statements are presented in US dollars, revenues, income and expenses, together with assets and liabilities, must be translated into US dollars at the prevailing exchange rates at the end of the financial year. Increases or decreases in the value of the US dollar against other major currencies will affect reported figures in the financial statements.

Although Coca Cola hedges against currency fluctuations it states in its annual 10K return that it cannot guarantee that currency fluctuations will not have a material effect on its reported figures. In 2011 Coca Cola made a foreign exchange loss of $73 million.

In 2010, Coca Cola made a loss of $103 million as a result of the Venezuelan government devaluing the bolivar as a response to hyperinflation. This loss was based on the carrying value of Coca Cola's assets and liabilities that were denominated in Venezuelan bolivar.

5.3 Economic exposure

Key term

> **Economic risk** is the risk that exchange rate movements might reduce the international competitiveness of a company. It is the risk that the present value of a company's future cash flows might be reduced by adverse exchange rate movements.

Economic exposure is the degree to which a firm's present value of future cash flows is affected by fluctuations in exchange rates.

Economic exposure differs from transaction exposure in that exchange rate changes may affect the value of the firm even though the firm is not involved in foreign currency transactions.

Example

Trends in exchange rates

Suppose a US company sets up a subsidiary in an Eastern European country. The Eastern European country's currency depreciates continuously over a five year period. The cash flows remitted back to the US are worth less in dollar terms each year, causing a reduction in the investment project.

Another US company buys raw materials which are priced in euros. It converts these materials into finished products which it exports mainly to Singapore. Over a period of several years the US dollar depreciates against the euro but strengthens against the Singapore dollar. The US dollar value of the company's income declines whilst the US dollar value of its materials increases, resulting in a drop in the value of the company's net cash flows.

The value of a company depends on the **present value** of its **expected future cash flows**. If there are fears that a company is exposed to the type of exchange rate movements described above, theis may reduce the company's value. Protecting against economic exposure is therefore necessary to protect the company's share price.

A company need not even engage in any foreign activities to be subject to economic exposure. For example, if a company trades only in the UK but sterling strengthens significantly against other world currencies, it may find that it loses UK sales to an overseas competitor who can now afford to charge cheaper sterling prices.

One-off events

As well as trends in exchange rates, one-off events such as a major stock market crash or disaster such as the attacks on 9/11 may administer a 'shock' to exchange rate levels.

Assessing the impact of economic risks

None of the above examples are as simple as they seem however due to the compensating actions of economic forces. For example, if the exchange rate of an Eastern European depreciates significantly it is probably because of its high inflation rates.

So if the Eastern European subsidiary of a US company **increases its prices** in line with inflation, its cash flows in the local currency will increase each year. These will be converted at the depreciating exchange rate to produce a fairly constant US dollar value of cash flows. Therefore what is significant for companies is the effect on **real cash flows**, after the effects of inflation have been removed. In order for there to be real operating risk there must be relative price changes between countries.

5.3.1 Hedging economic risks

Various actions can reduce economic exposure, including the following.

(a) **Matching assets and liabilities**

A foreign subsidiary can be financed, as far as possible, with a loan in the currency of the country in which the subsidiary operates. A depreciating currency results in reduced income but also reduced loan service costs. A multinational will try to match assets and liabilities in each country as far as possible. Matching will be discussed further in Chapter 16.

(b) **Diversifying the supplier and customer base**

For example, if the currency of one of the supplier countries strengthens, purchasing can be switched to a cheaper source.

(c) **Diversifying operations world-wide**

On the principle that companies which confine themselves to one country suffer from economic exposure, international diversification is a method of reducing such exposure.

(d) **Change prices**

The amount of scope a company has to change its prices in response to exchange movements will depend on its competitive position. If there are numerous domestic and overseas competitors, an increase in prices may lead to a significant fall in demand.

6 Issues in choosing finance for overseas investment

As part of the fulfilment of the performance objective 'evaluate potential business/investment opportunities and the required finance options' you are expected to be able to identify and apply different finance options to single and combined entities in domestic and multinational business markets. This section and Section 7 look at the financing options available to multinationals which you can put to good use if you work in such an environment.

6.1 Financing an overseas subsidiary

Once the decision is taken by a multinational company to start overseas operations in any of the forms that have been discussed in the previous section, there is a need to decide on the source of funds for the proposed expansion. There are some differences in methods of financing the **parent company** itself, and the **foreign subsidiaries**. The parent company itself is more likely than companies which have no foreign interests to raise finance in a foreign currency, or in its home currency from foreign sources.

The **need to finance a foreign subsidiary** raises the following questions.

(a) How much **equity capital** should the parent company put into the subsidiary?

(b) Should the subsidiary be allowed to **retain a large proportion** of its profits, to build up its equity reserves, or not?

(c) Should the parent company hold **100% of the equity** of the subsidiary, or should it try to create a minority shareholding, perhaps by floating the subsidiary on the country's domestic stock exchange?

(d) Should the subsidiary be encouraged to **borrow** as much **long-term debt** as it can, for example by raising large bank loans? If so, should the loans be in the domestic currency of the subsidiary's country, or should it try to raise a foreign currency loan?

(e) Should the subsidiary be listed on the local stock exchange, raising funds from the local equity markets?

(f) Should the subsidiary be encouraged to minimise its working capital investment by relying heavily on trade credit?

The **method of financing** a subsidiary will give some indication of the **nature and length of time** of the investment that the parent company is prepared to make. A sizeable equity investment (or long-term loans from the parent company to the subsidiary) would indicate a long-term investment by the parent company.

6.2 Choice of finance for an overseas investment

The choice of the source of funds will depend on:

(a) The **local finance costs**, and any subsidies which may be available

(b) **Taxation systems** of the countries in which the subsidiary is operating. Different tax rates can favour borrowing in high tax regimes, and no borrowing elsewhere.

(c) Any **restrictions on dividend remittances**

(d) The possibility of **flexibility in repayments** which may arise from the parent/subsidiary relationship

Tax-saving opportunities may be maximised by **structuring the group** and its subsidiaries in such a way as to **take the best advantage** of the different local tax systems.

Because subsidiaries may be operating with a guarantee from the parent company, different gearing structures may be possible. Thus, a subsidiary may be able to operate with a higher level of debt that would be acceptable for the group as a whole.

Parent companies should also consider the following factors.

(a) **Reduced systematic risk.** There may be a small incremental reduction in systematic risk from investing abroad due to the segmentation of capital markets.

(b) **Access to capital.** Obtaining capital from foreign markets may increase liquidity, lower costs and make it easier to maintain optimum gearing.

(c) **Agency costs.** These may be higher due to political risk, market imperfections and complexity, leading to a higher cost of capital.

Exam focus point

You must be prepared to answer questions about various methods of financing an overseas subsidiary.

7 Costs and benefits of alternative sources of finance for MNCs

FAST FORWARD

Multinational companies will have access to international debt facilities, such as Eurobonds and syndicated loans.

Multinational companies (MNCs) fund their investments from retained earnings, the issue of new equity or the issue of new debt. Equity and debt funding can be secured by accessing both domestic and overseas capital markets. Thus multinational companies have to make decisions not only about their capital structure as measured by the debt/equity ratio and which was discussed extensively in Chapter 7a, but also about the source of funding, that is whether the funds should be drawn from the domestic or the international markets.

7.1 International borrowing

Borrowing markets are becoming increasingly internationalised, particularly for larger companies. Companies are able to borrow long-term funds on the **eurocurrency (money) markets** and on the markets for **eurobonds**. These markets are collectively called 'euromarkets'. Large companies can also borrow on the **syndicated loan market** where a syndicate of banks provides medium to long-term currency loans.

If a company is receiving income in a foreign currency or has a long-term investment overseas, it can try to **limit the risk** of adverse exchange rate movements by **matching**. It can take out a long-term loan and use the foreign currency receipts to repay the loan.

7.2 Eurocurrency markets

Eurocurrency markets were dealt with in Chapter 4 Section 8 in the context of international debt finance.

7.3 Syndicated loans

Key term

A **syndicated loan** is a loan offered by a group of lenders (a 'syndicate') to a single borrower.

A syndicated loan is a loan put together by a group of lenders (a 'syndicate') for a single borrower. Banks or other institutional lenders may be unwilling (due to excessive risk) or unable to provide the total amount individually but may be willing to work as part of a syndicate to supply the requested funds. Given that many syndicated loans are for very large amounts, the risk of even one single borrower defaulting could be disastrous for an individual lender. Sharing the risk is likely to be more attractive for investors.

Each syndicate member will contribute an agreed percentage of the total funds and receive the same percentage of the repayments.

Originally syndicated loans were limited to international organisations for acquisitions and other investments of similar importance and amounts. This was mainly due to the following:

(a) **Elimination of foreign exchange risk** – borrowers may be able to reduce exchange rate risk by spreading the supply of funds between a number of different international lenders.

(b) **Speed** – in normal circumstances it may take some time to raise very large amounts of money. The efficiency of the syndicated loans market means that large loans can be put together very quickly.

Syndicated loans are now much more widely available, with small and medium sized organisations now making use of such provision of funds. These loans can also be made on a 'best efforts' basis – that is, if a sufficient number of investors cannot be found the amount the borrower receives will be lower than originally anticipated.

7.4 The advantages of borrowing internationally

There are three main advantages from borrowing for international capital markets, as opposed to domestic capital markets

(a) **Availability**. Domestic financial markets, with the exception of the large countries and the Euro zone, lack the depth and liquidity to accommodate either large debt issues or issues with long maturities.

(b) **Lower cost of borrowing.** In Eurobond markets interest rates are normally lower than borrowing rates in national markets

(c) **Lower issue costs**. The cost of debt issuance is normally lower than the cost of debt issue in domestic markets.

7.5 The risks of borrowing internationally

A multinational company has three options when financing an overseas project by borrowing. The first is to borrow in the same currency as the inflows from the project. The second option is borrowing in a currency other than the currency of the inflows but with a hedge in place and the third option is borrowing in a currency other than the currency of the inflows but without hedging the currency risk. The last case exposes the company to **exchange rate risk** which can substantially change the profitability of a project.

Question	International investment 3

Donegal plc manufactures Irish souvenirs. These souvenirs are exported in vast quantities to the USA to the extent that Donegal is considering setting up a manufacturing and commercial subsidiary there. After undertaking research, it has been found that it would cost $6m, comprising $5m in non-current assets and $1m in working capital. Annual sales of the souvenirs have been estimated as $4m and they would cost $2.5m per annum to produce. Other costs are likely to be $300,000 per annum.

Tax rates are as follows.

Ireland   23%   USA   25%

Tax is payable in the year of occurrence in both countries. Assume there is no double tax relief.

Capital allowances at a rate of 20% reducing balance are available. Balancing allowances or balancing charges should also be accounted for at the end of the project's life.

The maximum possible funds will be remitted to the home country (Ireland) at the end of each year. The exchange rate is $1 = €0.71. It is assumed that this rate will remain constant over the project's life.

The project is being appraised on a five year time span. The non-current assets will be sold for an expected $2.5m at the end of the project's life.

Donegal uses a cost of capital of 12% on all capital investment projects.

Required

Calculate the NPV of the proposed project and recommend to the Board of Directors of Donegal whether the US subsidiary should be set up.

Answer

	Time 0	1	2	3	4	5
	$m	$m	$m	$m	$m	$m
Cash inflows - sales		4.0	4.0	4.0	4.0	4.0
Cash outflows		(2.8)	(2.8)	(2.8)	(2.8)	(2.8)
Taxable cash flows		1.2	1.2	1.2	1.2	1.2
Tax at 25%		(0.30)	(0.30)	(0.30)	(0.30)	(0.30)
Capital allowances (W1)		0.25	0.20	0.16	0.13	
Initial expenditure	(5.0)					
Residual value						2.5
Balancing charge (W1)						(0.11)
Working capital	(1.0)					1.0
Net cash flow	(6.0)	1.15	1.10	1.06	1.01	4.29
Exchange rates	0.71	0.71	0.71	0.71	0.71	0.71
€ cash flows						
From/(to) USA	(4.26)	0.82	0.78	0.75	0.72	3.05
Additional Irish tax (W2)		(0.20)	(0.20)	(0.20)	(0.20)	(0.60)
Net cash flows	(4.26)	0.62	0.58	0.55	0.52	2.45
Irish discount factors	1.00	0.893	0.797	0.712	0.636	0.567
Present values	(4.26)	0.55	0.46	0.39	0.33	1.39

NPV = €(1.14)m, therefore the company should not proceed.

Workings

(1)   *Capital allowances*

	Cost/WDA $m	Tax saving at 25%
Year 0 - Cost	5.00	
Year 1 - WDA	(1.00)	0.25
	4.00	
Year 2 - WDA	(0.80)	0.20
	3.20	
Year 3 - WDA	(0.64)	0.16
	2.56	
Year 4 - WDA	(0.51)	0.13
	2.05	
Year 5 – residual value	2.50	
Balancing charge	0.45	(0.11)

(2)   *Years 1–4*

$ taxable cash flows = $1.2m
Taxable cash flows in € = $1.2m x 0.71 = €0.85m
Tax at 23% = €0.20m

Year 5

$ taxable profit = $1.2m + $2.5m = $3.7m

In € = $3.7m x 0.71 = €2.63m
Tax at 23% = €0.60m

Chapter Roundup

- Changes in exchange rates are as important as the underlying profitability in selecting an overseas project.

- **Purchasing power parity** theory states that the exchange rate between two currencies is the same in equilibrium when the purchasing power of currency is the same in each country.

- Under interest rate parity the difference between spot and forward rates reflects differences in interest rates.

- The International Fisher Effect states that currencies with high interest rates are expected to depreciate relative to currencies with low interest rates.

- The NPV of an international project can be calculated either by converting the cash flows or the NPV.

- The main risks faced by companies dealing with foreign currencies are transaction, translation and economic risks.

- Multinational companies will have access to international debt facilities, such as Eurobonds and syndicated loans.

Quick Quiz

1 What does the absolute purchasing parity relationship state?

2 Suppose that the annual interest rate is 5 percent in the United states and 6 percent in the United Kingdom, and that the spot exchange rate is £1 = $1.756 and the forward exchange rate, with one-year maturity, is £1 = $1.749. Does interest rate parity hold?

3 Using the data in question 2 how can you profit?

4 What are the two ways NPV can be calculated for an overseas project?

5 What is the impact of exchange controls on the decisions to invest in an international project?

6 What is the difference between transaction and translation exposure?

7 What are the implications of the following on the potential purchasing power of the dollar?

   (a) High $ interest rate

   (b) High $ inflation rate

8 Give four examples of ways in which a company could hedge economic exposure.

9 Give three reasons why a multinational might establish an overseas subsidiary.

10 Give three factors that might influence the choice of finance for an overseas subsidiary.

11 By what methods do governments impose exchange controls?

12 Give four examples of ways companies can overcome exchange controls.

Answers to Quick Quiz

1   The absolute purchasing parity relationship states that prices in different countries will be the same when expressed in the same currency.

2   Interest rate parity means that

$$\frac{1+i_{US}}{1+i_{uk}} = \frac{\text{Forward rate}}{\text{Spot rate}}$$

However

$$\frac{1+0.05}{1+0.06} < (1.749/1.756)$$

so interest rate parity does not hold.

3   Borrow $1,000,000 at 5 percent – amount to be repaid $1,050,000

Buy £569,476 spot using $1,000,000

Invest £569,476 in the UK for a year. The value of the investment in a year's time will be £603,645

Sell £603,645 forward in exchange for $1,055,775 (= £603,645 x $1.749/£)

Resulting profit = $1,055,774 – $1,050,000 = $5,774

4   The first way is to translate the overseas cash flows into domestic currency and use a domestic discount factor.

The second way is to use an appropriate overseas discount factor and calculate the NPV in foreign currency. The NPV can then be converted into domestic currency.

5   Exchange controls will normally lower the NPV from an overseas investment unless they earn a sufficient return from reinvestment in the country of origin until repatriation is allowed.

6   Transaction exposure occurs when a company has a future transaction that will be settled as a foreign currency. Translation exposure occurs when a company has overseas subsidiaries whose assets are denominated in foreign currency. Unlike transaction exposure, translation exposure does not affect the company's cash flows.

7   (a) High $ interest rate will lead to a reduction in the purchasing power of the $ (International Fisher effect)

(b) A high $ inflation rate means that the purchasing power of the $ will decrease (purchasing power parity).

8   Managing assets and liabilities

Diversifying supplier and customer base

Diversifying operations worldwide

Changing prices in response to exchange rate movements

9   Any three of:

(a)   Location of markets
(b)   Need for a sales organisation
(c)   Opportunity to produce goods more cheaply
(d)   Need to avoid import controls
(e)   Need to obtain access for raw materials
(f)   Availability of grants and tax concessions

10   Any three of:

(a)   Local finance costs
(b)   Taxation systems
(c)   Restrictions on dividend remittances
(d)   Flexibility in repayments

11   (a)   Rationing the supply of foreign exchange
       (b)   Restricting the types of transaction for which payments abroad are allowed

12   (a)   Selling goods or services to subsidiary
       (b)   Charging a royalty on goods sold by subsidiary
       (c)   Interest rate manipulation
       (d)   Management charges

Now try the question below from the Exam Question Bank

Number	Level	Marks	Time
14	Introductory	15	27 mins

Acquisition and mergers

9

Acquisitions and mergers versus other growth strategies

Topic list	Syllabus reference
1 Mergers and acquisitions as a method of corporate expansion	D(1) (a)
2 Evaluating the corporate and competitive nature of a given acquisition proposal	D(1) (b)
3 Developing an acquisition strategy	D(1) (b)
4 Criteria for choosing an appropriate target for acquisition	D(1) (c)
5 Creating synergies	D(1) (e)
6 Explaining high failure rate of acquisitions in enhancing shareholder value	D(1)(d)

Introduction

In this chapter we discuss the advantages and disadvantages of mergers and acquisitions as forms of expanding the scale of operations of an organisation. We look at the types of mergers and their purpose illustrating these with real life examples. We evaluate the merits of a given acquisition proposal and set out the criteria for choosing an appropriate target. The evaluation of synergy in the context of two real life examples is also considered.

Study guide

		Intellectual level
D1	**Acquisitions and mergers versus other growth strategies**	
(a)	Discuss the arguments for and against the use of acquisitions and mergers as a method of corporate expansion	2
(b)	Evaluate the corporate and competitive nature of a given acquisition proposal	3
(c)	Advise upon the criteria for choosing an appropriate target for acquisition	3
(d)	Compare the various explanations for the high failure rate of acquisitions in enhancing shareholder value	3
(e)	Evaluate, from a given context, the potential for synergy separately classified as: (i) Revenue synergy (ii) Cost synergy (iii) Financial synergy	3

One of the ways in which you can demonstrate competence in the performance objective 'evaluate potential business/investment opportunities and the required finance options' is to identify the advantages and disadvantages of potential corporate action (such as buyouts, mergers or takeovers). This chapter evaluates mergers and acquisitions as a method of corporate expansion and also looks at the potential corporate consequences of such activity. This information will be invaluable in practice as it gives you an idea of the issues that might arise when considering the viability of mergers and acquisitions.

1 Mergers and acquisitions as a method of corporate expansion

FAST FORWARD

> Although **growth strategy through acquisition** requires high premiums, it is widely used by corporations as an alternative to **internal organic growth**.

Exam focus point

> The wholly written optional question in the June 2008 paper dealt with the regulatory, financial and ethical issues of a particular takeover.

Companies may decide to increase the scale of their operations through a strategy of **internal organic growth** by **investing money** to **purchase** or **create assets** and product lines **internally**.

Alternatively, companies may decide to grow by **buying** other **companies** in the market thus acquiring ready made tangible and intangible assets and product lines. Which is the right strategy? The decision is one of the most difficult the financial manager has to face.

The right answer is not easy to arrive at. **Organic growth** in areas where the company has been successful and has expertise may present **few risks** but it can be **slow**, **expensive** or sometimes **impossible**. On the other hand **acquisitions** require **high premiums** that make the **creation** of **value** difficult. Irrespective of the merits of a **growth strategy** by acquisition or not, the fact remains that this is used by corporations extensively.

Case Study

In June 2010, Deutsche Bank predicted that mergers and acquisitions volumes will be either flat or lower than 2009. Global mergers and acquisitions volume in 2009 was $2.4 trillion, the lowest since 2004. The global economic crisis hit merger and acquisition activity hard.

Steve Krouskos, Americas Markets leader for Ernst &Young's transactions advisory ser vice, said that merger and acquisition activity was all about 'the three Cs – cash, confidence and credit'. All three have been lacking since the global economic collapse, although 57% of respondents to Ernst & Young's 2010 mid-year mergers and acquisitions report stated that they were 'highly likely' or 'likely' to undertake acquisitions in the next 12 months.

Source: Deutsche Bank predicts flat year for M & A, *www.efinancialnews.com*, 23rd June 2010

When companies decide to expand their scale of operations by merging with or acquiring another company, there are many ways that this strategy can be implemented and many possible target companies.

In this section we will look at the each type of merger that companies have used for growth and present the arguments for and against each particular case. As a general rule, expansion either by building new plants or by acquisition should not be undertaken unless the expansion results in increased profitability for the company and enhances shareholder wealth.

1.1 Advantages of mergers as an expansion strategy

FAST FORWARD

As an **expansion strategy** mergers are thought to provide a quicker way of acquiring productive capacity and **intangible assets** and accessing **overseas markets**.

There are four main advantages that have been put forward in the literature and these are summarised below:

Speed

The acquisition of another company is a quicker way of implementing a business plan, as the company acquires another organization that is already in operation. An acquisition also allows a company to reach a certain optimal level of production much quicker than through organic growth. Acquisition as a strategy for expansion is particularly suitable for management with rather short time horizons.

Lower cost

An acquisition may be a cheaper way of acquiring productive capacity than through organic growth. An acquisition can take place for instance through an exchange of shares which does not have an impact on the financial resources of the firm.

Acquisition of intangible assets

A firm through an acquisition will acquire not only tangible assets but also intangible assets, such as brand recognition, reputation, customer loyalty and intellectual property which are more difficult to achieve with organic growth.

Access to overseas markets

When a company wants to expand its operations in an overseas market, acquiring a local firm may be the only option of breaking into the overseas market.

1.2 Disadvantages of mergers as an expansion strategy

FAST FORWARD

An **expansion strategy** through acquisition is associated with exposure to a higher level of **business and financial risk**.

The risks associated with expansion through acquisitions are:

Exposure to business risk

Acquisitions normally represent large investments by the bidding company and account for a large proportion of their financial resources. If the acquired company does not perform as well as it was envisaged, then the effect on the acquiring firm may be catastrophic.

Exposure to financial risk

During the acquisition process, the acquiring firm may have less than complete information on the target company, and there may exist aspects that have been kept hidden from outsiders.

Acquisition premium

When a company acquires another company, it normally pays a premium over its present market value. This premium is normally justified by the management of the bidding company as necessary for the benefits that will accrue from the acquisition. However, too large a premium may render the acquisition unprofitable.

Managerial competence

When a firm is acquired, which is large relative to the acquiring firm, the management of the acquiring firm may not have the experience or ability to deal with operations on the new larger scale, even if the acquired company retains its own management.

Integration problems

Most acquisitions are beset with problems of integration as each company has its own culture, history and ways of operation.

1.3 Types of mergers

Mergers can be classified as **horizontal, vertical or conglomerate**, depending on the type of company that is acquired.

A merger generally involves two companies pooling their interests and having common ownership of the new company's assets.

An acquisition usually involves a stronger company (the 'predator') taking over the assets of a smaller company (the 'target') and assuming ownership of these assets.

Mergers and acquisitions can be classified in terms of the company that is acquired or merged with, as **horizontal**, **vertical** or **conglomerate**. Each type of merger represents a **different way** of **expansion** with **different benefits** and **risks**.

Horizontal mergers

A **horizontal merger** is one in which one company acquires another company in the **same line of business**. A horizontal merger happens between firms which were formerly competitors and who produce products that are considered **substitutes** by their buyers. The main impact of a horizontal merger is therefore to **reduce competition** in the market in which both firms operate. These firms are also likely to purchase the same or substitute products in the input market. A **horizontal merger** is said to achieve **horizontal integration**.

 Case Study

The airline industry provides good examples of horizontal mergers. In 2008, the US carriers Delta and Northwest merged in a $3.1 billion deal whilst in 2010 British Airways and Iberia (the Spanish national carrier) merged operations. The latter was given the go-ahead by the European Commission in July 2010 after concerns that the merger would breach EU rules on fair competition.

Such mergers made it easier for the individual airlines to gain access to routes that would otherwise have been expensive and difficult to obtain.

Vertical mergers

Vertical mergers are mergers between firms that operate at different stages of the same production chain, or between firms that produce complementary goods such as a newspaper acquiring a paper manufacturer. Vertical mergers are either backward when the firm merges with a supplier or forward when the firm merges with a customer.

Conglomerate mergers

Conglomerate mergers are mergers which are neither vertical nor horizontal. In a conglomerate merger a company acquires another company in an unrelated line of business, for example a newspaper company acquiring an airline.

2 Evaluating the corporate and competitive nature of a given acquisition proposal

FAST FORWARD

> Expansion by **organic growth** or by acquisition should only be undertaken if it leads to an **increase** in the **wealth** of the **shareholders**.

We have discussed so far the reasons why a company may opt for growth by acquisition instead of organic growth and the three main types of mergers. We should not of course lose sight of the fact that expansion either by organic growth or by acquisitions is only undertaken if it leads to an increase in the wealth of the shareholders. This happens when the merger or acquisition creates **synergies** which either **increase revenues** or **reduce costs**, or when the management of the acquiring company can manage the assets of the target company better than the incumbent management, thus **creating additional** value for the new owners over and above the current market value of the company. We look at some of the aspects that will have an impact on the competitive position of the firm and its profitability in a given acquisition proposal.

Market power

The impact on **market power** is one of the most important aspects of an acquisition. By acquiring another firm, in a horizontal merger, the competition in the industry is reduced and the company may be able to charge higher prices for its products. Competition regulation however may prevent this type of acquisition. To the extent that both companies purchase for the same suppliers, the merged company will have greater bargaining power when it deals with its suppliers.

Barriers to entry

A second aspect of an acquisition proposal and related to the previous one is the possibility of creating **barriers to entry** through **vertical acquisitions** of production inputs.

Aspects of a merger that will have an impact on the firm's **competitive position** include **increased market power**, the **creation of barriers to entry**, **supply chain security** and **economies of scope** and **scale**.

Supply chain security

A third aspect that has an impact on the competitive position of a firm is the acquisition of a firm which has an important role in the **supply chain**. Companies acquire suppliers to ensure that there is no disruption in the supply of the inputs that will threaten the ability of the company to produce, sell and retain its competitive position. Although the risk of disruption can be eliminated by long-term contracts, acquisition is still considered an important option.

Economies of scale

The merged company will be bigger in size than the individual companies and it will have a larger scale of operations. The larger scale of operations may give rise to what is called economies of scale from a reduction in the cost per unit resulting from increased production, realized through operational efficiencies. Economies of scale can be accomplished because as production increases, the cost of producing each additional unit falls.

Economies of scope

Scope economies or changes in product mix are another potential way in which mergers might help improve the performance of the acquiring company. Economies of scope occur when it is more economical to produce two or more products jointly in a single production unit than to produce the products in separate specializing firms. Scope economies can arise from two sources:

(a)   the spreading of fixed costs over an expanded product mix; and
(b)   cost complementarities in producing the different products.

Economies of scope have been invoked as the main reason driving mergers in the financial sector. The fixed capital of a bank branch for example, or its computer systems are more fully utilized when they issue not just banking products such as deposits and loans but also insurance products and investment services. These additional services allow the spreading of fixed costs over a larger number of activities reducing the unit cost of each activity.

2.1 Financial synergy: tax and debt benefits

The final aspect in an acquisition proposal has to do with the existence of financial synergies which take the form of diversification, tax and debt benefit synergies. This will be discussed in detail in **section five** of this chapter.

3 Developing an acquisition strategy

The main reasons behind a strategy for acquiring a target firm includes the target being undervalued or to diversify operations in order to reduce risk.

Not all firms considering the acquisition of a target firm have acquisition strategies, and even if they do, they do not always stick to them. We are going to look at a number of different motives for acquisition in this section. A coherent acquisition strategy should be based on one of these motives.

3.1 Acquire undervalued firms

This is one of the main reasons for firms becoming targets for acquisition. If a predator recognises that a firm has been **undervalued** by the market it can take advantage of this discrepancy by purchasing the firm at a '**bargain**' price. The difference between the real value of the target firm and the price paid can then be seen as a '**surplus**'.

For this strategy to work, the predator firm must be able to fulfil three things.

3.1.1 Find firms that are undervalued

This might seem to be an obvious point but in practice it is not easy to have such **superior knowledge** ahead of other predators. The predator would either have to have access to **better information** than that available to other market players, or have **superior analytical tools** to those used by competitors.

3.1.2 Access to necessary funds

It is one thing being able to identify firms that are undervalued – it is quite another **obtaining** the funds to acquire them. Traditionally, **larger firms** tend to have **better access** to capital markets and internal funds than smaller firms. A history of success in **identifying** and **acquiring** undervalued firms will also make funds more accessible and future acquisitions easier.

3.1.3 Skills in executing the acquisition

There are **no gains** to be made from driving the share price up in the process of acquiring an undervalued firm. For example, suppose the estimated value of a target firm is $500 million and the current market price is $400 million. In acquiring this firm, the predator will have to pay a **premium**. If this premium exceeds 25% of the current market price (the difference between estimated value and current market price divided by current market price) then the price paid will actually **exceed** the estimated value. **No value** would thus be created by the predator.

3.2 Diversify to reduce risk

Firm-specific risk (**unsystematic risk**) can be reduced by holding a diversified portfolio. This is another potential acquisition strategy. Predator firms' managers believe that they may reduce earnings volatility and risk – and increase potential value – by acquiring firms in other industries.

3.2.1 Diversifying by acquisition versus diversifying across traded shares

Can diversification be achieved more efficiently at **company** level or at **individual investor** level? Obviously **individual investors** can diversify much more **cheaply** than companies can. All they have to do is buy shares in companies in different industries, whereas companies have to go through long, complicated and expensive processes in order to acquire other companies.

There are **two exceptions** to this.

(a) Owners of private firms with all or most of their wealth invested in the firm. The owner is exposed to all the risk therefore there is a greater case for diversification.

(b) Incumbent managers who have large amounts of their wealth invested in the firm. If these managers diversify through acquisition, they will reduce their exposure to total risk. This opens up other arguments as to whether these managers are acting in the best interests of the other shareholders, if the other shareholders do hold well diversified portfolios of other shares.

4 Criteria for choosing an appropriate target for acquisition

There are a number of different aspects to successful target identification. One important emerging need is to identify acquisitions in overseas markets. Acquirers must be able to assess the acquisition from the target's point of view, as well as from their own. But understanding the regulatory and competitive environment in another country can be complex and time-consuming.

Case Study

Microsoft uses the enormous resources of its extended enterprise to identify potential acquisitions. The business groups take the lead, looking within their own and related markets for opportunities. Ideas also come from venture capital relationships in both the United States and Europe, as well as through the company's alliance and partner community.

Acquirers must also be able to identify and capture new skills in the companies they buy.

Case Study

Cisco Systems, often known as the 'acquirer of choice' by target companies, is an outstanding example of success in this regard. The maker of Internet networking equipment emphasizes that it acquires people and ideas, not just technologies. The leadership and talent of the acquired company must be committed to seeing the acquisition and the integration of the company work. It is not the first version of a product that becomes a billion-dollar market, Cisco argues, but the subsequent versions. Cisco needs the acquired company's talent to stay and build those next versions.

The criteria that should be used to assess whether a target is appropriate will depend on the motive for the acquisition. The main criteria that are consistent with the underlying motive are:

Benefit for acquiring undervalued company

The target firm should trade at a price below the estimated value of the company when acquired. This is true of companies which have assets that are not exploited.

Diversification

The target firm should be in a business which is different from the acquiring firm's business and the correlation in earnings should be low.

Operating synergy

The target firm should have the characteristics that create the operating synergy. Thus the target firm should be in the same business in order to create cost savings through economies of scale. Or it should be able to create a higher growth rate through increased monopoly power.

Tax savings

The target company should have large claims to be set off against taxes and not sufficient profits. The acquisition of the target firm should provide a tax benefit to acquirer.

Increase the debt capacity

This happens when the target firm is unable to borrow money or is forced to pay high rates. The target firm should have capital structure such that its acquisition will reduce bankruptcy risk and will result in increasing its debt capacity.

Disposal of cash slack

This is where a cash rich company seeks a development target. The target company should have great projects but no funds. This happens when for example the target company has some exclusive right to product or use of asset but no funds to start activities.

Access to cash resources

A company with a number of cash intensive projects or products in their pipeline, or heavy investment in R&D might seek a company that has significant cash resources or highly cash generative product lines to support their own needs.

Control of the company

In this case the objective is to find a target firm which is badly managed and whose stock has underperformed the market. The management of an existing company is not able to fully utilize the potential of the assets of the company and the bidding company feels that it has greater expertise or better management methods. The bidding company therefore believes that the assets of the target company will generate for them a greater return than for their current owners. The criterion in this case is a market valuation of the company which is lower than for example the value of its assets.

Access to key technology

Some companies do not invest significantly in R&D but acquire their enabling technologies by acquisition. Pharmaceutical companies who take over smaller biotechs in order to get hold of the technology are a good example of this type of strategy.

5 Creating synergies

The three main types of synergy to be gained from acquisitions or mergers are **revenue**, **cost** and **financial** synergies.

The existence of synergies has been presented as one of the two main explanations that may increase shareholder value in an acquisition. Indeed the identification, quantification and announcement of these synergies are an essential part of the process as shareholders of the companies need to be persuaded to back the merger.

Case Study

In April 2010, Delta (the US airline that merged with Northwest in 2008) announced that it had realised more than $200 million in incremental synergy benefits in 2009 from the merger. Merger-related costs were reported to be only $36 million.

Case Study

In March 2010 it was announced that Kraft was looking to find at least $675 million in cost synergies following its takeover of Cadbury, the UK confectioner. Cadbury's staff were reported to be concerned that such synergies might result in jobs being lost at the company's UK manufacturing sites and Head Office.

In this section we consider ways, through a series of examples, of identifying revenue, cost and financial synergies when a target company is evaluated for acquisition.

5.1 Revenue synergy

Revenue synergy exists when the acquisition of the target company will result in **higher revenues** for the acquiring company, **higher return on equity** or a **longer period of growth**. Revenue synergies arise from:

(a) Increased market power
(b) Marketing synergies
(c) Strategic synergies

Revenue synergies are more difficult to quantify relative to **financial** and **cost synergies**. When companies merge, cost synergies are relatively easy to assess pre-deal and to implement post-deal. But revenue synergies are more difficult. It is hard to be sure how customers will react to the new (in financial services mergers, massive customer defection is quite common),whether customers will actually buy the new, expanded 'total systems capabilities,' and how much of the company's declared cost savings they will demand in price concessions (this is common in automotive supplier M&A where the customers have huge purchasing power over the suppliers). Nevertheless, revenue synergies must be identified and delivered. The stock markets will be content with cost synergies for the first year after the deal, but thereafter they will want to see growth. Customer Relationship Management and Product Technology Management are the two core business processes that will enable the delivery of revenue.

5.2 Cost synergy

A **cost synergy** results primarily from the existence of **economies of scale**. As the level of operation increases, the marginal cost falls and this will be manifested in greater operating margins for the combined entity. The resulting **costs** from **economies of scale** are normally estimated to be substantial.

5.3 Sources of financial synergy

Diversification

Acquiring another firm as a way of reducing risk cannot create wealth for two publicly traded firms, with diversified stockholders, but it could create wealth for private firms or closely held publicly traded firms. A takeover, motivated only by diversification considerations, has no effect on the combined value of the two firms involved in the takeover. The value of the combined firms will always be the sum of the values of the independent firms. In the case of private firms or closely held firms, where the owners may not be diversified personally, there might be a potential value gain from diversification.

Cash slack

When a firm with significant excess cash acquires a firm, with great projects but insufficient capital, the combination can create value. Managers may reject profitable investment opportunities if they have to raise new capital to finance them. It may therefore make sense for a company with excess cash and no investment opportunities to take over a cash-poor firm with good investment opportunities, or vice versa. The additional value of combining these two firms lies in the present value of the projects that would not have been taken if they had stayed apart, but can now be taken because of the availability of cash.

Case Study

Assume that Softscape Inc, a hypothetical company, has a severe capital rationing problem, that results in approximately $500 million of investments, with a cumulative net present value of $100 million, being rejected. IBM has far more cash than promising projects, and has accumulated $4 billion in cash that it is trying to invest. It is under pressure to return the cash to the owners. If IBM takes over Softscape Inc, it can be argued that the value of the combined firm will increase by the synergy benefit of $100 million, which is the net present value of the projects possessed by the latter that can now be taken with the excess cash from the former.

Tax benefits

The tax paid by two firms combined together may be lower than the taxes paid by them as individual firms. If one of the firms has tax deductions that it cannot use because it is losing money, while the other firm has income on which it pays significant taxes, the combining of the two firms can lead to tax benefits that can be shared by the two firms. The value of this synergy is the present value of the tax savings that accrue because of this merger. The assets of the firm being taken over can be written up to reflect new market value, in some forms of mergers, leading to higher tax savings from depreciation in future years.

Debt capacity

By combining two firms, each of which has little or no capacity to carry debt, it is possible to create a firm that may have the capacity to borrow money and create value. Diversification will lead to an increase in debt capacity and an increase in the value of the firm. Has to be weighed against the immediate transfer of wealth that occurs to existing bondholders in both firms from the stockholders. When two firms in different businesses merge, the combined firm will have less variable earnings, and may be able to borrow more (have a higher debt ratio) than the individual firms.

6 Explaining high failure rate of acquisitions in enhancing shareholder value

A number of theories have been put forward to explain the **high failure rate** of **acquisitions** in **enhancing shareholder value**. These include **agency theory**, **errors in valuing a target firm**, the **pre-emptive theory** and **market irrationality**.

The purpose of this section is to assess the various explanations put forward for the high failure rate of acquisitions in enhancing shareholder value.

One of the most common empirical findings is that in an acquisition the shareholders of the **acquiring company** seldom enjoy any benefits, whereas the shareholders of the **target company** do. What is the reason for the failure to enhance shareholder value? We said earlier that there must be some evidence of synergies or concrete proof of managerial superiority in the acquiring firm to produce an acquisition that would enhance shareholder value. A number of alternative theories explain the phenomenon of failure by postulating that the main motive of the management of a company when they bid for another company is not maximisation of the shareholder value but other motives which have been found to be consistent with empirical evidence.

6.1 Agency theory

Agency theory suggests that takeovers are primarily motivated by the **self-interest** of the acquirer's management. Reasons that have been advanced to explain the divergence in the interests of the management and the shareholder of a company include:

- Diversification of management's own portfolio
- Use of free cash flow to increase the size of the firm
- Acquiring assets that increase the firm's dependence on management

The common idea of these explanations is that acquisitions is a process that results in value being transferred from the shareholder of the acquiring firm to the managers of the acquiring firm.

The implication of agency theory is that, because the target firm knows that a bid is in the interest of the management rather than the shareholders of the acquiring firm, it sees this bid opportunity to extract some of the value that would have gone to acquiring firm management. How much value the target firm can extract depends on the bargaining power they have.

6.2 Errors in valuing a target firm

Managers of the bidding firm may advise their company to bid too much as they do not know how to value an essentially recursive problem. A risk-changing acquisition cannot be valued without revaluing your own company on the presupposition that the acquisition has gone ahead. The value of an acquisition cannot be measured independently. As a result the merger fails as the subsequent performance cannot compensate for the high price paid.

6.3 Market irrationality

If a **rational manager** observes that his firm's stocks are overvalued in the short run, he has an incentive to exchange the overvalued stocks to real assets before the market corrects the overvaluation. A merger therefore occurs in order to take advantage of market irrationality and it is not related to either synergies or better management. The lack of the latter may in the end lead to a failing merger even though the acquired firm was bought cheaply through the exchange of over-valued shares.

6.4 Pre-emptive theory

This theory explains why acquiring firms pursue value-decreasing horizontal mergers even if managers are rational and are trying to maximize shareholders' value. If large cost savings can be achieved through the merger by several potential acquiring firms, these firms will compete for the opportunity to merge with the target. The winning firm who acquires the target could become a lower cost producer, improve its product market position and gain market share from the rivals. Intuitively, if a firm fears that one of its rivals will gain large cost savings or synergies from taking over some other firm, then it can be rational for the first firm to pre-empt this merger with a takeover attempt of its own.

6.5 Window dressing

Another reason for the high failure rate is that companies are not acquired because of the synergies that they may create, but in order to present a better financial picture in the short term.

6.6 Poor integration management

In order to integrate two or more organisations effectively there must be effective integration management and a recognition that successful integration takes time. Where management is poor or there is an attempt to do too much too soon, potentially successful mergers can actually fail.

Inflexibility in the application of integration plans drawn up prior to the event can be damaging. Once the merger has taken place, management must be prepared to adapt plans in the light of changed circumstances or inaccurate prior information.

Poor man-management can be detrimental to successful integration. Keeping staff informed in what may be a very unsettling period is important. Lack of communication of goals and future prospects of employees, and failure to recognise and deal with their uncertainties and anxieties can lead to employees being unclear of what is expected of them. Hostilities may develop between the two groups of staff, with a unwillingness to adapt to new procedures and practices.

Chapter Roundup

- Although **growth strategy through acquisition** requires high premiums, it is widely used by corporations as an alternative to **internal organic growth**.

- As an **expansion strategy** mergers are thought to provide a quicker way of acquiring productive capacity and **intangible assets** and accessing **overseas markets**.

- An **expansion strategy** through acquisition is associated with exposure to a higher level of **business and financial risk**.

- Mergers can be classified as **horizontal, vertical or conglomerate**, depending on the type of company that is acquired.

  A merger generally involves two companies pooling their interests and having common ownership of the new company's assets.

  An acquisition usually involves a stronger company (the 'predator') taking over the assets of a smaller company (the 'target') and assuming ownership of these assets.

- Expansion by **organic growth** or by acquisition should only be undertaken if it leads to an **increase** in the **wealth** of the **shareholders**.

- Aspects of a merger that will have an impact on the firm's **competitive position** include **increased market power**, the **creation of barriers to entry, supply chain security** and **economies of scope** and **scale**.

- The main reasons behind a strategy for acquiring a target firm includes the target being undervalued or to diversify operations in order to reduce risk.

- The three main types of synergy to be gained from acquisitions or mergers are **revenue**, **cost** and **financial** synergies.

- A number of theories have been put forward to explain the **high failure rate** of **acquisitions** in **enhancing shareholder value**. These include **agency theory**, **errors in valuing a target firm**, the **pre-emptive theory** and **market irrationality**.

Quick Quiz

1   State at least five criteria for choosing an appropriate target.

2   Provide three explanations for the failure of acquisitions to enhance shareholder value.

3   What are the sources of financial synergy?

4   What are the main advantages of mergers as an expansion strategy?

5   What are the main disadvantages of mergers as an expansion strategy?

Answers to Quick Quiz

1   Undervaluation of target
    Diversification
    Operating synergy
    Tax Savings
    Debt Capacity
    Use of Cash slack
    Control of company

2   Any three of the following

    Hubris hypothesis
    Market irrationality
    Pre-emptive action
    Window dressing

3   Diversification and reduction in volatility
    Cash slack
    Tax benefits
    Debt capacity

4   Speed of growth
    Lower cost
    Acquisition of intangible assets
    Access to overseas markets

5   Exposure to business risk
    Exposure to financial risk
    Acquisition premium
    Managerial incompetence

Now try the questions below from the Exam Question Bank

Number	Level	Marks	Time
15	Introductory	8	15 mins
16	Examination	20	36 mins
17	Examination	20	36 mins

Valuation of acquisitions and mergers

Introduction

In this chapter we discuss ways of estimating the value of a target company. First we examine the various methods of predicting earnings growth for a company, using external and internal measures. We analyse the impact of an acquisition on the risk of the acquiring company and its cost of capital. We then examine the three possible types of impact of an acquisition on the risk of the acquiring company.

Study guide

		Intellectual level
D2	**Valuation for acquisitions and mergers**	
(a)	Discuss the problem of overvaluation.	2
(b)	Estimate the potential near-term and continuing growth levels of a corporation's earnings using both internal and external measures.	3
(c)	Assess the impact of an acquisition or merger upon the risk profile of the acquirer distinguishing: (i) Type I acquisitions that do not disturb the acquirer's exposure to financial or business risk (ii) Type II acquisitions that impact upon the acquirer's exposure to financial risk (iii) Type III acquisitions that impact upon the acquirer's exposure to both financial and business risk	3
(d)	Advise on the valuation of a type I acquisition of both quoted and unquoted entities using: (i) 'Book value-plus' models (ii) Market based models (iii) Cash flow models, including EVA™, MVA	3
(e)	Advise on the valuation of type II acquisitions using the adjusted net present value model	3
(f)	Advise on the valuation of type III acquisitions using iterative revaluation procedures.	2
(g)	Demonstrate an understanding of the procedure for valuing high growth start-ups	2

Exam focus point

A compulsory question in the June 2008 exam focused on the valuation of a business for a potential flotation or outright sale. One of the complications was the effect of taxation on both the cost of debt and its weighting in the calculation of asset betas.

1 The overvaluation problem

FAST FORWARD

When a company acquires another company, it always pays above its current market value. This is known as the overvaluation problem.

1.1 What gives rise to the overvaluation problem?

We have already discussed the reasons why so many mergers fail to enhance shareholder value in Chapter 9.

Economic theory suggests that mergers only enhance shareholders' value if there are

(a) **Synergies** which can be exploited

(b) **Significant improvements** in the **management** of the **assets** of the **target** company that could be realised by an acquisition

In Chapter 9 we proposed a number of theories that could explain the **incidence** of **mergers** in the **absence** of the **two conditions** mentioned above.

Most of the theories were based on the existence of **agency problems** and the pursuit by management of takeovers that satisfied **management's goals** rather than those of the shareholders.

A reflection of these managerial motives is the control premium that management is prepared to pay in order to acquire the target company.

The larger the agency problem within the **acquiring** company, the larger the premium the **acquiring** company will be willing to pay.

Moreover, if the management/shareholders of the target company are aware that the merger will benefit the **management** of the **acquirer** rather than the **shareholders** of the **acquiring company**, then they will try to extract as much of the benefit as possible resulting in a high bid price.

Empirical studies have shown that during an acquisition, there is **normally** a **fall** in the **price** of the **bidder** and an **increase** in the **price** of the **target**.

The consensus of empirical studies is that the target company shareholders enjoy the benefit of the premium as they are paid more than the market value whereas the shareholders of the acquirer do not always benefit and sometimes even lose value as the result of the bidding.

In a sense there is a **transfer of value** from the **acquirer** to the **target**. This is reflected in the **premium** that is paid and is determined by the degree of the **agency problem** prevalent in the acquirer and the ability of the **target's shareholders** to **extract this premium**.

The overvaluation problem may of course arise as a miscalculation of the potential synergies or the overestimation of the ability of the acquiring firm's management to improve performance. Both errors will lead to a higher price being paid as compared to the current market price.

2 Estimation of the growth levels of a firm's earnings

FAST FORWARD

The growth rate of a company's earnings is the most important determinant of a company's value. The growth rate may be based on historical estimates, analyst's forecasts or company fundamentals.

The **growth rate** of a company's **earnings** is the most important factor in the **value** of the **company**. We have already considered this in the valuation formula derived from the Gordon constant growth model in Chapter 7b.

$$PV = \frac{FCF_0(1+g)}{k-g}$$

There are three ways to estimate the **growth rate** of earnings of a company. One is by extrapolating past values, the second is by relying on analysts' forecasts and a third is by looking at the fundamentals of the company.

2.1 Historical estimate

Historical estimates of the growth rate are estimated by observing the realised growth rates over a specific period.

Example

The historical EPS for Megatera Inc is shown below

Year	EPS
20X6	0.53
20X5	0.43
20X4	0.37
20X3	0.26
20X2	0.25
20X1	0.18

The rate of growth is given by the formula

$$g = \left(\frac{53}{18}\right)^{1/5} - 1 = 24.1$$

There are several problems associated with historical estimates.

- First of all a decision needs to be made regarding the length of the estimation period. Too long a period may reflect conditions that are no longer relevant for the future.
- Secondly, even if the same conditions prevail, the average value estimated may not be relevant for the near term especially if growth rates are volatile. An average value may be close to the expected future growth rate over the medium term.

2.2 Analyst forecasts

The second way of estimating the growth in earnings is by using the forecasts of analysts. Analysts regularly produced forecasts on the growth of a company and these estimates can be the base for forming a view of the possible growth prospects for the company.

2.3 Company fundamentals

The determinants of the **rate of growth** of a company are the **return on equity** and the **retention rate of earnings** (that is, the proportion of earnings that are not distributed to shareholders as dividends).

The **retention rate** can be calculated as follows.

Formula to learn

> $$\text{Retention rate} = \frac{\text{Retained earnings}}{\text{Total earnings}}$$
>
> The **growth** rate = Return on equity x retention rate

Question   Implied retention rate

On 21 December 20X6, Jinky Inc had a dividend yield of 3.8% and a price-earnings ratio (PE) of 15.3. What is the implied retention rate of Jinky Inc?

Answer

The retention rate was defined above as: $\frac{\text{Retained earnings}}{\text{Total earnings}}$

Retained earnings can be defined as the difference between total earnings and dividends.

$$\text{Dividend yield} = \frac{\text{Dividend per share}}{\text{Market price per share}}$$

By substituting retained earnings = Total earnings – dividends into the retention rate equation, we can find that:

Retention rate = 1 – dividend yield × P/E ratio
Retention rate = 1 – 0.038 × 15.3 = 0.4186 or 41.86%

3 The impact of an acquisition or merger upon the risk profile of the acquirer 6/08

An acquisition may have an impact on the financial and business risk exposure of the acquirer.

A Type I acquisition does not affect the acquiring firm's exposure to financial or business risk.

A Type II acquisition affects the acquiring firm's exposure to financial risk only – it does not affect exposure to business risk.

A Type III acquisition affects both the financial and business risk exposure of the acquiring firm.

We have already discussed in Chapter 2 that the total risk of the company can be divided into business risk and financial risk.

An acquisition may have an impact on both the financial and the business risk. There are three possibilities which also characterise the type of acquisitions.

(1) **Type I acquisition**

These are acquisitions that do not disturb the acquirer's exposure to financial or business risk.

(2) **Type II acquisition**

These are acquisitions that affect the acquirer's exposure to financial risk but it does not affect the exposure of the firm to business risk.

(3) **Type III acquisition**

These are acquisitions that affect the acquirer's exposure to both financial and business risk.

3.1 The business risk of the combined entity

The business risk of the combined entity will be affected by the betas of the target and predator firms and the beta of the synergy that results from the acquisition.

3.1.1 The asset beta

The asset beta of the combined firm is the weighted average of the betas of the target firm, the predator firm and the synergy generated from the acquisition.

3.1.2 The equity beta

To obtain the equity beta for the combined entity you should follow these steps.

Step 1 Calculate the value of debt after tax and add the value of equity.

Step 2 Divide the value from Step 1 by the value of equity.

Step 3 Multiply the value from Step 2 by the combined asset beta.

3.1.3 WACC

The WACC of the combined beta is the weighted average of the cost of equity and the cost of debt for the combined entity.

This section links to Chapter 7a sections 2 and 3 where we looked at costs of capital.

4 Valuation of a type I acquisition of both quoted and unquoted entities

6/08, 6/11

FAST FORWARD

A type I acquisition does not affect the acquiring company's exposure to business or financial risk.

Type I acquisitions may be valued using one of the following valuation methods:

- Book value-plus models
- Market relative models
- Cash flow models, including EVA™, MVA

We defined earlier as **Type I acquisitions**, acquisitions that do not disturb the acquirer's exposure to financial or business risk.

4.1 Book value-plus models

FAST FORWARD

Book value or asset-based methods of company valuation are based on the statement of financial position as the starting point in the valuation process.

Book value or asset-based methods of **company valuation** use the **statement of financial position** as the starting point in the valuation process.

The statement of financial position records the company's non-current assets (both tangible and intangible), current assets and liabilities to payables, both short and long-term. After deducting long-term and short-term payables from the total asset value, we arrive at the company's net asset value, (NAV). The book value of net assets is also referred to as 'equity shareholders' funds' as this represents the owners' stake in the company.

Question
Book value model

The summary statement of financial position of Cactus Co is as follows.

	$	$	$
Non-current assets			
Land and buildings			160,000
Plant and machinery			80,000
Motor vehicles			20,000
			260,000
Goodwill			20,000
Current assets			
Inventory		80,000	
Receivables		60,000	
Short-term investments		15,000	
Cash		5,000	
		160,000	
Current liabilities			
Payables	60,000		
Taxation	20,000		
Proposed ordinary dividend	20,000		
		(100,000)	
			60,000
			340,000
12% debentures			(60,000)
Deferred taxation			(10,000)
			270,000

		$
Ordinary shares of $1		80,000
Reserves		140,000
		220,000
4.9% preference shares of $1		50,000
		270,000

What is the value of an ordinary share using the net assets basis of valuation?

Answer

If the figures given for asset values are not questioned, the valuation would be as follows.

	$	$
Total value of net assets		340,000
Less: intangible asset (goodwill)		20,000
Total value of tangible assets (net)		320,000
Less: preference shares	50,000	
Debentures	60,000	
deferred taxation	10,000	
		120,000
Net asset value of equity		200,000
Number of ordinary shares		80,000
Value per share		$2.50

4.2 Market relative models (P/E ratio)

FAST FORWARD

Market relative models may be based on the P/E ratio which produces an earnings based valuation of shares.

The P/E ratio is a very popular approach to share valuation. The P/E ratio compares a share's value to its latest earnings (profits).

Since P/E ratio = $\dfrac{\text{Market value}}{\text{EPS}}$, then **market value per share = EPS × P/E ratio**

If you are given total earnings rather than EPS, you will be calculating the total market value of equity rather than market value per share.

The P/E ratio produces an **earnings-based** valuation of shares. A higher P/E ratio will result in a higher price (or total value). **A high P/E ratio may indicate:**

Optimistic expectations

Expectations that the EPS will grow rapidly in the years to come, so that a **high price is being paid for future profit prospects.** Many small but successful and fast-growing companies are valued on the stock market on a high P/E ratio. Some stocks (for example those of some internet companies in the late 1990s) have reached high valuations before making any profits at all, on the strength of expected future earnings.

Security of earnings

A well-established low-risk company would be valued on a higher P/E ratio than a similar company whose earnings are subject to greater uncertainty.

Status

If a quoted company (the predator) made a share-for-share takeover bid for an unquoted company (the target), it would normally expect its own shares to be valued on a higher P/E ratio than the target company's shares. A quoted company ought to be a lower-risk company; but in addition, there is an advantage in having shares which are quoted on a stock market: the shares can be readily sold. **The P/E ratio of an unquoted company's shares might be around 50% to 60% of the P/E ratio of a similar public company with a full Stock Exchange listing** (and perhaps 70% of that of a company whose shares are traded on the AIM).

 Case Study

Some sample P/E ratios taken from the *Financial Times* on 26 April 2012:

Market indices

FTSE 100	9.80
FTSE all-share	10.59
FTSE all-small	22.31
FTSE fledgling	Negative
FTSE AIM	Negative

Industry sector averages (main market)

Chemicals	18.14
Construction	39.59
Food producers and processors	8.90
General retailers	10.79
Health care	11.70
Telecommunications	7.42

 Question   **Minimum and maximum bid values**

Macleanstein Inc is considering making a bid for 100% of Thomasina Inc's equity capital. Thomasina has a P/E ratio of 14 and earnings of $500m.

It is expected that $150m in synergy savings will be made as a result of the takeover and the P/E ratio of the combined company is estimated to be 16.

Macleanstein currently has a P/E ratio of 17 and earnings of $750m.

Required

(a)   What is the maximum amount that Macleanstein should pay for Thomasina?

(b)   What is the minimum bid that Thomasina's shareholders should be prepared to accept?

Answer

(a)   Maximum amount to be paid

Macleanstein must consider the synergies to be made from the combination when determining the maximum amount to pay.

Value of Thomasina to Macleanstein = value of combined company – current value of Macleanstein

Value of combined company   = new P/E ratio x combined earnings

= 16 x (500m + 750m + 150m) = $22,400m

Current value of Macleanstein   = 17 x $750m = $12,750m

Value of Thomasina to Macleanstein = $22,400 - $12,750m = $9,650m

Therefore the maximum amount that Macleanstein should pay for Thomasina is $9,650m.

(b)   Minimum amount that Thomasina's shareholders should accept

= current value of Thomasina's equity

= 14 x $500m = $7,000m

The final amount paid will probably fall between these two extremes.

4.3 Market to book ratio – based on Tobin's Q ratio

FAST FORWARD

> Market value of a target company = market to book ratio x the book value of assets of target company.

Market to book ratio = market capitalisation/book value of assets for a similar company
An industry average could also be used in the absence of a similar company.

Key term

> The **Q ratio itself** is defined as the market value of a firm/total asset value of the firm

As a guideline for valuing a potential target, a firm with a Q <1 is vulnerable since the assets of a company can be acquired at a cheaper price than they were bought on their own as assets. So, high-Q firms usually buy low Q-firms. In fact empirical studies have shown that in more than two thirds of all mergers the acquirer's Q exceeded the target's Q.

4.4 Free cash flow models   6/11

Exam focus point

> There was a 30 mark compulsory question on acquisitions in the December 2007 exam. Part of the question focused on the validity of the use of the free cash flow model for valuing acquisitions so make sure you can critically evaluate the valuation methods in particular scenarios.
>
> The free cash flow to firm method was examined as part of a compulsory Section A question in 2011 where students were required to estimate the values of a predator company and the combined company following an acquisition. A discussion of the limitations of the valuations was also required.

The free cash flow approach has been explained in detail in Chapter 7b in the context of project appraisal. The procedure for valuing a target company on the basis of its predicted cash flow is the same.

Formula to learn

> Free cash flow (FCF) = after-tax operating (pre-interest) cash flows – net investment in assets
>
> Free cash flow to equity (FCFE) – FCF – net interest paid

Note: free cash flow to equity is sometimes called **dividend capacity**.

There are **two approaches** to valuing a company using the free cash flow basis.

Approach 1	Approach 2
1 Identify the free cash flows of the target company (**before interest**)	1 Identify the free cash flow **to equity** of the target company (**after interest**)
2 Discount FCF at **WACC** to obtain NPV	2 Discount FCFE at **cost of equity** Ke to obtain NPV

3 NPV of company – **debt**
 	
   = value of the target
	3 NPV
	
	   = value of the target

Make sure you do not mix the two approaches –for example, it would be wrong to discount free cash flows before interest at the cost of equity.

A similar approach is used for the dividend valuation model, see section 4.7 of this chapter.

Question

Aquisition

Chunky Trot Inc is planning on making a bid to take over Turkey Lurkey Inc which is in the same industry. Both companies have similar gearing levels of 18% (where gearing is debt as a % of total finance).

Chunky Trot has estimated that the takeover will increase its annual cash flows over the next few years by the following amounts.

Year	After-tax (but before interest) cash flows
	$m
20X1	14.00
20X2	18.50
20X3	20.75
20X4 onwards	30.25

Turkey Lurkey Inc has 6.5% irredeemable debentures of $37.5 million trading at par.

The risk-free rate is 6.5% and the market rate is 12%. Chunky Trot's equity beta is 2.450 and the corporation tax rate is 28%.

Required

If Chunky Trot was prepared to bid $100 million for the entire share capital of Turkey Lurkey, would the acquisition increase shareholder wealth? Use both approaches given above to illustrate your answer.

Answer

K_e (using CAPM) = 6.5 + 2.45(12 − 6.5) = 19.98% (say 20%)

$K_d = [i/P_0] \times (1 − T) = [6.5/100] \times 0.72 = 4.68\%$

WACC = (20 x 0.82) + (4.68 x 0.18) = 17.2% say 17%

Approach 1

Year	20X1	20X2	20X3	20X4 onwards
	$m	$m	$m	$m
Cash flow (after tax, before int)	14.00	18.50	20.75	30.25
Perpetuity (1/0.17)				5.882
Value at 20X3				177.94
Discount factor (17%)	0.855	0.731	0.624	0.624
Present value	11.97	13.52	12.95	111.03

Total present value	149.47
Less debt	(37.50)
Value of equity	111.97

As value of equity > the proposed bid, the shareholders' wealth would increase if the target was acquired.

Approach 2

Annual interest after tax = (6.5% of $37.5 million) x 0.72 = $1.76 million

Year	20X1	20X2	20X3	20X4
	$m	$m	$m	$m
Cash flow	14.00	18.50	20.75	30.25
Less interest	(1.76)	(1.76)	(1.76)	(1.76)
Cash flow after interest and tax	12.24	16.74	18.99	28.49
Perpetuity (1/0.2)				5.0
Value at 20X3				142.45
Discount factor (20%)	0.833	0.694	0.579	0.579
Present value	10.20	11.62	11.00	82.48
Total present value	115.3			

4.5 Economic Value Added (EVA®) approach

Exam focus point

EVA® was examined as part of a 30 mark compulsory question in December 2007, in the context of analysing potential performance. The examiner commented that relatively few candidates were able to complete the EVA® calculation and only a minority could explain the significance of the measure. Make sure you can do both.

Economic Value Added (EVA®) gives the economic value or profit added per year. It can be used as a means of **measuring managerial performance**, by assessing the net present value of revenues (profits) less resources used (capital employed). We use EVA® here to estimate the value of a company. EVA® is calculated as follows:

Formula to learn

EVA® = Net operating profit after tax (NOPAT) − (WACC × book value of capital employed)

EVA® can also be calculated as:

Formula to learn

Book value of capital employed × (Return on invested capital − WACC)

Note that NOPAT cannot simply be lifted from the financial statements. There are numerous adjustments that may have to be made such as

(a) **Intangibles** (for example, advertising, research and development, training). These are viewed as investments and are added to the statement of financial position.

(b) **Goodwill** written off and **accounting depreciation**. These are replaced by **economic depreciation**, which is a measure of the actual **decline** in the **market value** of the assets.

(c) **Net interest on debt capital** – debt is included in capital employed and the cost of debt is included in the WACC.

4.5.1 Example

Summary financial statements for Wobbly Inc are as follows.

SUMMARY INCOME STATEMENT	20X8
	$m
Sales	1,520
Pre-tax accounting profit (after economic depreciation)	335
Tax at 28%	(94)
Profit after tax	241
Dividends	(73)
Retained earnings	168

SUMMARY STATEMENT OF FINANCIAL POSITION

	$m
Non-current assets	625
Net current assets	
	1,265
Financed by:	
Shareholders' funds	950
Medium and long-term loans	315
	1,265

Notes

1   Tax rate is 28%

2   Interest payable in 20X8 was $20 million

3   Economic depreciation for the year was $180 million. This was equal to tax depreciation and the amount charged in the income statement.

4   Capital employed at the end of 20X7 was $800 million

5   Pre-tax cost of debt in 20X8 was 12%

6   Cost of equity in 20X8 was 18%

7   Target capital structure is 80% equity 20% debt

8   Non-cash expenses (excluding depreciation) were $50 million

Required

Calculate Wobbly's EVA®.

Solution

	$m	
Capital employed	800	
Adjusted profit	305.4	$241 + 50 + (20 \times 0.72)$

WACC is based on the target capital structure (80% equity 20% debt).

WACC = $(0.8 \times 18) + (0.2 \times 12) = 16.8\%$

EVA = $\$305.4m - (16.8\% \times \$800m) = \$171m$

4.5.2 Using EVA® to calculate the value of a firm

The value of a firm can be calculated as

Value of invested capital + sum of discounted EVA®

To arrive at the value of the **equity** as in the case of the free cash flow valuation, we need to **subtract** the **value of debt** from the value of the company. An example of how to calculate the value of a company using EVA® is shown in the following example.

4.5.3 Example

Year	0	1	2	3	4	5
Invested capital	2,000	1,600	1,200	800	400	–
NOPAT	–	88	160	400	440	200
Less change in invested capital	(2,000)	400	400	400	400	400
Free cash flow	(2,000)	488	560	800	840	600
PV factor (WACC 10%)	1	0.91	0.83	0.75	0.68	0.62
PV of cash flow	(2,000)	444	463	601	574	373
Cumulative PV	(2,000)	(1,556)	(1,094)	(493)	81	454
NPV	454					
ROIC		4%	10%	33%	55%	50%
EVA® =(ROIC – WACC) x BV of capital employed)		(112)	–	280	360	160
PV factor	1	0.91	0.83	0.75	0.68	0.62
PV of EVA®	–	(102)	–	210	246	99
Cumulative PV	–	(102)	(102)	109	354	454
Total PV of EVA®	454					

4.6 Market value added approach

The Market Value Added (MVA) of a company is defined as:

Formula to learn

> MVA = Market Value of Debt + Market Value of Equity – Book Value of Equity – Book Value of Debt

The MVA shows how much the management of a company has added to the value of the capital contributed by the capital providers.

The MVA is related to EVA® because MVA is simply the present value of the future EVA®s of the company.

In terms of the notation used in the previous section:

MVA = PV of EVA® = 454

If the market value and the book value of debt is the same, then the MVA simply measures the difference between the market value of common stock and the equity capital of the firm.

A firm's equity MVA is sometimes expressed as a market to book ratio:

$$\frac{MVA}{Book\ value}$$

4.7 Dividend valuation basis

4.7.1 Using the dividend growth model

The dividend valuation model is based on the theory that an equilibrium price for any share (or bond) on a stock market is the **future expected stream of income** from the security **discounted** at a suitable cost of capital.

Exam formula

> $$P_0 = \frac{D_0(1+g)}{K_e - g}$$

Where D_0=dividend paid now
  K_e=cost of equity **of the target**
  g=growth rate in dividends

Note:

If D_0 is given as dividend per share, then P_0 will refer to the value of the share.

If D_0 is given as total dividend, then P_0 will refer to the value of the company.

Example: dividend growth (1)

Hibby Inc has declared a dividend of 35 cents per share. Dividends are expected to grow at 5% in the future in line with previous growth rates. The current cost of equity is 8%.

What is the estimated value of one share in Hibby Inc?

Solution

Exam formula

$$P_0 = \frac{D_0\,(1+g)}{K_e - g}$$

$P_0 = (35 \times 1.05)/(0.08 - 0.05) = \$12.25$

Example: dividend growth (2)

Janster Inc has declared a dividend of 20 cents per share and has a cost of equity of 15%.

What is the estimated value of one share in Janster Inc in each of the following situations?

(a)   No growth in dividends
(b)   A constant growth in dividends of 6% per annum
(c)   A constant dividend for four years and then 7% per annum in perpetuity thereafter.

Solution

(a) $P_0 = 20/0.15 = \$1.33$ per share

(b) $P_0 = (20 \times 1.06)/(0.15 - 0.06) = \$2.36$ per share

(c)   (i)   Present value of four years' dividends with no growth

$\$0.20 \times 2.855 = \$0.57$

    (ii)   Present value at year 5 of growing dividend in perpetuity

$(\$0.20 \times 1.07)/(0.15 - 0.07) = \$2.68$

Discount back to year 0 = $\$2.68 \times 0.572 = \$1.53$

Total value of each share = $\$0.57 + \$1.53 = \$2.10$

 Question

Dividend valuation model

Target paid a dividend of $250,000 this year. The current return to shareholders of companies in the same industry as Target is 12%, although it is expected that an additional risk premium of 2% will be applicable to Target, being a smaller and unquoted company. Compute the expected valuation of Target, if:

(a)   The current level of dividend is expected to continue into the foreseeable future, or
(b)   The dividend is expected to grow at a rate of 4% pa into the foreseeable future

$k_e = 12\% + 2\% = 14\%\ (0.14)$ $d_0 = \$250,000$ $g\ (\text{in (b)}) = 4\%$ or 0.04

(a) $P_0 = \dfrac{d_0}{k_e} = \dfrac{\$250,000}{0.14} = \$1,785,714$

(b) $P_0 = \dfrac{D_0(1+g)}{K_e - g} = \dfrac{\$250,000(1.04)}{0.14 - 0.04} = \$2,600,000$

5 Valuation of type II acquisitions using the adjusted present value model

FAST FORWARD

A type II acquisition affect the acquiring company's exposure to financial risk only – it does not affect exposure to business risk.

The theory behind the Adjusted Present Value (APV) has been explained in Chapter 7a. An acquisition is valued by discounting the Free Cash Flows to the firm by the ungeared cost of equity and then adding the present value of the tax shield. The net present value is given by

APV = Value of acquired company if all–equity financed + Present Value of Debt Tax Shields – Initial investment

If the APV is positive then the acquisition should be undertaken.

Steps for the calculation of APV

Step 1   Calculate the NPV as if ungeared – that is, $K_e^{\ 1}$

Step 2   Add the PV of the tax saved as a result of the debt used in the project

Step 3   Deduct the debt of the target company to obtain the value of equity and then deduct the proposed cost of the acquisition)

Example

The management of XERON Inc is considering the acquisition of NERON Inc. an unquoted company. The owners of NERON want $500 million for the business. The analysis of the prospects of NERON by XERON is reflected in the following financial statements

INCOME STATEMENT

	Current Year 20X7	20X8	20X9	20Y0	20Y1	20Y2	20Y3
				Years			
Sales	620.00	682.00	750.20	825.22	907.74	998.52	998.52
Less: cost of goods sold	(410.00)	(441.00)	(475.10)	(512.61)	(553.87)	(599.26)	(599.26)
Gross profit	210.00	241.00	275.10	312.61	353.87	399.26	399.26
Operating expenses	(133.00)	(144.30)	(156.53)	(169.78)	(184.16)	(199.78)	(199.78)
EBIT	77.00	96.70	118.57	142.83	169.71	199.48	199.48
Less interest expense	–	(32.00)	(26.88)	(20.19)	(11.73)	(1.27)	–
Earnings before tax	77.00	64.70	91.69	122.64	157.98	198.21	199.48
Less taxes	(21.56)	(18.12)	(25.67)	(34.34)	(44.23)	(55.50)	(55.85)
Net Income	55.44	46.58	66.02	88.30	113.75	142.71	143.63

	Current Year 20X7	20X8	20X9	20Y0	20Y1	20Y2	20Y3
STATEMENT OF FINANCIAL POSITION							
Current assets	100.00	100.00	100.00	100.00	100.00	242.90	404.55
Non-current assets	400.00	378.00	354.00	328.00	300.00	270.00	238.00
Total assets	500.00	478.00	454.00	428.00	400.00	512.90	642.55
Debt	400.00	335.95	252.35	146.63	15.94	–	–
Equity	100.00	142.05	201.65	281.37	384.06	512.90	642.55
Total assets	500.00	478.00	454.00	428.00	400.00	512.90	642.55

Other information

Growth rate for sales	10%
Depreciation expense (20X7)	$40m
Interest rate on debt (all debt is interest-bearing)	8%
Tax rate	28%
Capital expenditures/year (depreciation charged at 10% per annum)	$20m
All available cash flow is applied to repaying debt until repaid in full	
Ungeared beta	1.1
Terminal value reflects level perpetuity equal to year 6 cash flow	
Risk free rate	6.0%
Market risk premium	7.5%

There are no disposals of non-current assets for the duration of the project

XERON proposes to take over NERON in 20X8

Step 1 Calculation of NPV as if ungeared

Tutorial note

> Don't forget to include the terminal value before calculating the final NPV in this step.

	20X8	20X9	20Y0	20Y1	20Y2	20Y3
EBIT(1 – Tax rate)						
Plus: Depreciation Expense	42.00	44.00	46.00	48.00	50.00	52.00
Less: CAPEX	(20.00)	(20.00)	(20.00)	(20.00)	(20.00)	(20.00)
Firm free cash flow	91.62	109.37	128.84	150.19	173.63	175.63
Discount factor (14%) (W1)						
Net present value	80.35	84.11	86.97	88.91	90.11	80.09
Total NPV before terminal value	510.54					

Terminal value = $\dfrac{\$175.63}{0.14}$ = $1,254.5m

The present value of the terminal value is:

$\dfrac{\$1,254.5m}{(1.14)^6}$ = $571.53m

Total NPV = $510.54m + $571.53m = $1,082.07m

The discount factor can be calculated using CAPM

$$E(r_i) = R_f + \beta (E(R_m - R_f))$$

$$E(r_i) = 6 + 1.1 \times 7.5$$

$$E(r_i) = 14.25\% \text{ (say 14\%)}$$

Step 2 PV of tax saved on debt interest

The tax shield is discounted at the gross cost of debt (8%).

	20X7	20X8	20X9	20Y0	20Y1	20Y2	20Y3
	$m	$m	$m	$m	$m	$m	$m
Interest tax savings	–	8.960	7.530	5.650	3.280	0.360	–
Discount factor at 8%	–	0.926	0.857	0.794	0.735	0.681	–
Present value	–	8.300	6.450	4.490	2.410	0.250	–

Total PV of tax shield	21.9
Add PV from Step 1	1,082.07
Total PV	1,103.97

Step 3 Deduct current debt and cost of acquisition to obtain equity value

Equity value = $1,103.97m - $500m - $400m = $203.97m

Conclusion – as NERON's equity value exceeds the price paid and the debt, XERON should proceed with the acquisition.

6 Valuation of type III acquisitions using iterative revaluation procedures

FAST FORWARD

A type III acquisition affects both the financial and business risk exposure of the acquiring company.

6.1 Steps for valuing a type III acquisition

In a type III valuation both the **business** and the **financial risk** of the acquiring company change. The following steps are followed in order to value an acquisition.

Step 1 Calculate the asset beta of both companies

Step 2 Calculate the average asset beta for the group post-acquisition

Step 3 Regear the beta to reflect the group's post-acquisition gearing

Step 4 Calculate the group's new WACC

Step 5 Discount the group's post-acquisition free cash flows using the new WACC

Step 6 Calculate the group's revised NPV and subtract debt to calculate the value of the equity

Example

Omnivore Inc is considering the acquisition of Sweet Meals Co. The management of Omnivore have estimated that the cash flows of Sweet Meals will grow much faster than theirs over the next 10 years, and that considerable savings will be realised by integrating their distribution networks and marketing operations. The estimated cash flows for Omnivore, Sweet Meals and the synergies in the case of a merger are shown below. It is estimated that on acquisition Omnivore will be able to sell one of its storage sites realising an instant income of $5 million.

Year	Sweet Meals $m	Synergies $m	Omnivore $m	Cash flows of combined entity $m
20X5		5		5.00
20X6	12.00	6	42	60.00
20X7	14.40	6	45	65.40
20X8	17.28	6	48.01	71.29
20X9	20.74	6	50.97	77.71
20Y0	24.88	6	53.81	84.69
20Y1	29.86	6	56.46	92.32
20Y2	35.83	6	58.79	100.62
20Y3	39.41	6	64.27	109.68
20Y4	43.36	6	70.20	119.56
20Y5	45.52	6	78.79	130.31
Terminal value	682.86	50	1,663.97	2,396.84

The following information is available.

	Omnivore $m	Sweet Meals $m
Debt	100	20
Equity	900	280
Asset beta	0.9	2.4

Omnivore has decided to make a cash offer of $380 million to the shareholders of Sweet Meals for the purchase of 100 percent of their shares. The cash offer will be funded by additional borrowing.

The tax rate is 30%. Risk-free rate is 5% and the required rate of return for the combined company is 9%. Cost of debt for the combined company is expected to be 7%.

Calculate the change in equity for Omnivore's shareholders that would result from the acquisition.

Solution

The **asset beta of the combined company** is:

$$\frac{\text{Total value of Omnivore}}{\text{Total combined value}} \times \text{Beta (Omnivore)} + \frac{\text{Total value of Sweet Meals}}{\text{Total combined value}} \times \text{Beta (Sweet Meals)}$$

$$= \frac{1,000}{1,300} \times 0.9 + \frac{300}{1,300} \times 2.4 = 1.25$$

Geared beta of combined company

$$\text{Asset beta} \times \left(1 + (1-T) \times \frac{\text{Total debt}}{\text{Total equity}}\right) = 1.25 \times \left(1 + 0.7 \times \frac{500}{1,180}\right) \quad \text{(Total debt includes \$380m for 100\%}$$

$$\text{of Sweet Meals shares)}$$

$$= 1.62$$

Cost of equity (using CAPM)

$$K_e = 5 + 1.62 \times 4 = 11.48\%$$

$$\text{WACC} = \frac{1,180}{1,680} \times 11.48 + \frac{500}{1,680} \times 7 \times 0.7 = 9.52\%$$

Discount cash flows at WACC to find the value of the combined firm = $1,422.76 million

Value of equity = Value of firm − value of debt
 = $1,422.76 − 500
 = $922.76 million

Omnivore's shareholders' value has increased by ($922.76 − 900) million = $22.76 million

Question

Nessie Inc is considering making a bid for 100% of Patsy Inc, a company in a completely different industry. The bid of $200 million, which is expected to be accepted, will be financed entirely by new debt with a post-tax cost of debt of 7%.

Pre-acquisition information

Nessie

Nessie has debt finance totalling $60 million at a pre-tax rate of 7.5%. There are 50 million equity shares with a current market value of $22 each and an equity beta of 1.37.

Post-tax operating cash flows are as follows.

Year 1	Year 2	Year 3	Year 4	Year 5
$m	$m	$m	$m	$m
60.3	63.9	67.8	71.8	76.1

Patsy

Patsy has an equity beta of 2.5 and 65 million shares with a total current market value of $156 million. Current debt – which will also be taken over by Nessie – is $12.5 million.

Post-acquisition information

Land with a value of $14 million will be sold.

Post-tax operating cash flows of Patsy's current business will be

Year 1	Year 2	Year 3	Year 4	Year 5
$m	$m	$m	$m	$m
15.2	15.8	16.4	17.1	17.8

If the acquisition goes ahead, Nessie will experience an improvement in its credit rating and all **existing** debt will be charged at a rate of 7%.

Cash flows after year 5 will grow at a rate of 1.5% per annum.

General information

The risk-free rate is 5.2% and the market risk premium is 3%. Corporation tax rate is 28%. Debt beta is 0.

Required

Should Nessie go ahead with the acquisition of Patsy? Give reasons for your answer.

Answer

(1) **Calculate asset betas of both companies**

Assuming a debt beta of 0, asset beta can be calculated using the following formula.

$$\beta_a = \left(\frac{Ve}{(Ve + Vd(1-T))} \right) be$$

Nessie = (1,100m/[1,100m +(60m x 0.72)]) x 1.37 = 1.32

Patsy = (156m/[156m + (12.5m x 0.72)]) x 2.5 = 2.36

(2) **Combined asset beta**

Combined beta = 1.32 x (1,100/[1,100 + 156]) + 2.36 x (156/[1,100 + 156]) = 1.45

(3) Regear beta to reflect group post-acquisition gearing

Using pre-acquisition debt and equity weightings

Equity beta = 1.45 / (1,256/[1,256 + [(60 + 12.5 + 200) x 0.72]]) = 1.68

(4) **Calculate the group's new WACC**

Ke = 5.2 + (1.68 x 3) = 10.24%

WACC = (10.24 x 1,256/[1,256 + 272.5]) + (7 x 272.5/[1,256 +272.5])

= 8.4144 + 1.2480

= 9.66%

(5) Discount group's post-acquisition cash flows using this WACC

Post-acquisition NPV

Year	1 $m	2 $m	3 $m	4 $m	5 $m	Year 6 onwards $m
Combined cash flow	75.5	79.7	84.2	88.9	93.9	95.3
Annuity (1/r-g))						12.3
Value as at time 5						1,172.2
at 9.66%	0.912	0.832	0.758	0.692	0.631	0.631
PV	68.9	66.3	63.8	61.5	59.3	739.7

Total PV	1,059.5
Sale of land	14.0
Nessie's debt	(60.0)
Patsy's debt	(12.5)
New debt to fund acquisition	(200.0)
Net value	**801.0**

The net value of the combined companies is less than Nessie's individual value (50 million shares x $11 = $1,100m) therefore the acquisition of Patsy should not go ahead.

6.2 A problem with the WACC

In the first example above, however, we have introduced an inconsistency in the calculation of the WACC because we have assumed that equity represents 70 percent of the value of the firm (1180/1680) and debt represents 30 percent of the value of the firm (500/1680).

In the values we have derived the value of the equity represents 65 percent of the value of the firm (922.76/1422.76) and debt represents 35 percent of the value of the firm. That is, the WACC weights are not consistent with the values derived.

If the two sets of weights differ significantly, the valuation is **internally inconsistent**. In such circumstances, we need to adopt **an iterative procedure** that takes into account the interrelation between the market value of the firm and the WACC. In the iterative procedure we must go back and re-compute the beta using a revised set of weights that are closer to the weights derived from the valuation. This process is then repeated until the assumed weights and the weights calculated from the derived values are approximately equal. Because the value of the debt is assumed to be equal to its book values, the interrelation involves the WACC and the market value of the equity. A **change in the WACC affects the market value of the equity**, which alters the equity weight, and thereby affects the WACC.

The iteration proceeds as follows.

(a) The market value of FCF is initially set equal to its book value and the capital structure weights are computed.

(b) Then, given the capital structure weights, the WACC is calculated and used to discount the forecast cash flows to present value.

(c) Finally, the market value of the firm calculated from the discounting process is used to compute a revised value of the equity by subtracting the value of the debt. Based on this revised value, the initial assumption for the value of the equity is set equal to the original equity value plus one-half of the difference between the original value and the revised value and the program is rerun. This procedure is repeated until the change in the market value of the equity is less than a specified small value.

Fortunately this iterative procedure need not be done manually. It can be calculated in EXCEL using the Tools/Options/Calculation commands. The iteration box needs to be ticked and the maximum number of iterations to be set to a large number, 10,000 to ensure convergence. In practice since the iteration requires recalculation of the equity values, if the book values do not differ too much from the market values a few iterations will suffice for convergence.

The internally consistent results of the iterative procedure are presented below.

Value of the firm	$1,395.45 million
Value of equity	$1,395.45– 500 = $895.45 million
Geared beta	1.73
Cost of equity	11.93%
Weighted average cost of capital	9.41

The value of equity is reduced now to $895.45 million below pre-acquisition value of Omnivore. The increased debt has increased the leveraged beta and the cost of equity, but it has slightly reduced the WACC as a result of the larger proportion of debt.

The iterative procedure has shown that at this price, the acquisition of Sweet Meals is not in the interest of the Omnivore shareholders.

7 Valuation of high growth start-ups

7.1 Characteristics of high growth start-ups

Due to their unique characteristics high growth start-ups presents a number of challenges.

The valuation of **start-ups** presents a number of challenges for the methods that we have considered so far due to their unique characteristics which are summarised below:

(1) Most start-ups typically have no track record
(2) Ongoing losses
(3) Few revenues, untested products
(4) Unknown market acceptance, unknown product demand
(5) Unknown competition
(6) Unknown cost structures, unknown implementation timing
(7) High development or infrastructure costs
(8) Inexperienced management

7.2 Projecting economic performance

All valuation methods require reasonable projections to be made with regard to the key drivers of the business. The following steps should be undertaken with respect to the valuation of a high-growth start up company.

Identifying the drivers

Any market-based approach or discounted cash flow analysis depends on the reasonableness of financial projections. Projections must be analyzed in light of the market potential, resources of the business, management team, financial characteristics of the guideline public companies, and other factors.

Period of projection

One characteristic of high growth start-ups is that in order to survive they need to grow very quickly. Start-ups that do grow quickly usually have operating expenses and investment needs in excess of their revenues in the first years and experience losses until the growth starts to slow down (and the resource needs begin to stabilise). This means that long-term projections, all the way out to the time when the business has sustainable positive operating margins and cash flows, need to be prepared. These projections will depend on the assumptions made about growth. However, rarely is the forecast period less than seven years.

Forecasting Growth

Forecasting growth in earnings can be accommodated in the framework we have already explained for the prediction of earnings. The growth in earnings will be:

g = retention rate × ROIC

For most high growth start-ups retention rate = 1 as the company in order to achieve a high growth rate need to invest in research and development, expansion of distribution and manufacturing capacity, human resource development to attract new talent, and development of new markets, products, or techniques.

With a b =1, it means that the sole determinant of growth is the return on invested capital (ROIC). The ROIC can be estimated from industry projections from securities analysts or from an evaluation of the company's management, marketing strengths, and level of investment.

Estimation of the ROIC is possible by decomposing it further to get an insight:

$$ROIC = \frac{EBIT}{IC} = \frac{EBIT}{Sales} \times \frac{Sales}{IC} \quad \text{(where IC = invested capital)}$$

That is the ROIC is determined by the profit margin and by revenue growth.

7.3 Valuation methods

Once growth rates have been estimated, the next step is to consider which is the most appropriate of the valuation approaches we have considered so far: net-assets, market or discounted cash flows.

Asset-based method

The asset based method is not appropriate because the value of capital in terms of tangible assets may not be high. Most of the investment of a start-up is in people, marketing and /or intellectual rights that are treated as expenses rather than as capital.

Market-based methods

The market approach to valuation also presents special problems for start-ups. This valuation process involves finding other companies, usually sold through private transactions, that are at a similar stage of development and that focus on existing or proposed products similar to those of the company being valued. Complicating factors include comparability problems, differences in fair market value from value paid by strategic acquirers, lack of disclosed information, and the fact that there usually are no earnings with which to calculate price-to-earnings ratios (in this case price-to-revenue ratios may be helpful).

Discounted cash flows

Using the DCF methodology, free cash flows are first projected and are then discounted to the present using a risk-adjusted cost of capital. For example, one could use the constant growth model which specifies that:

$$V = \frac{FCF}{r - g}$$

Our discussion of the high growth start-up indicates that the growth rates of revenues and costs may vary. Since FCF = Revenue – Costs = R – C, the value of company will be given by:

$$V = \frac{R - C}{r - g}$$

Now assuming that the growth rate of revenues g_R is different than the growth rate of costs g_C:

$$V = \frac{R}{r - g_R} - \frac{C}{r - g_C}$$

Question   Valuation of start-ups

QuickLeg is an internet legal services provider which next year expects revenue of $100 m and costs of $500 m. The revenues of the firm are expected to rise by 21 percent every year but costs will remain at the same level. The required rate of return is assumed to 22 percent. What is the value of QuickLeg?

Answer

$$V = \frac{\$100m}{0.22 - 0.21} - \frac{\$500m}{0.22 - 0} = \$7,727.27 \text{ million.}$$

The above model seems to capture the phenomenon observed in many start-ups of high losses in the first year of operations with high values of the company. The predicted profits for QuickLeg are shown in the diagram

QuickLeg Profits

A very important problem with the discounted flow approach is the sensitivity of the valuation model to the underlying assumptions. Changes in the growth rate induced by changes in demand, technology, and management of other causes can have a dramatic effect on the value of the start-up. For example suppose that the growth rate of revenues falls from 21 percent to 20 percent. The value of the company now is:

$$V = \frac{\$100}{0.22 - 0.20} - \frac{\$500}{0.22 - 0} = \$2,727.27 \text{ million}$$

That is the company has lost $5 billion.

Another problem with the discounted cash flow is that it cannot reflect managerial flexibilities and the strategic options to expand, delay, abandon, or switch investments at various decision points. The best way of incorporating uncertainty into the discounted cash flow analysis for a new company, technology, or product is to assign probabilities of success to each of the various possibilities.

7.4 Probabilistic valuation methods (expected values)

In a probabilistic cash flow model, we assume a number of scenarios for the drivers of value and derive a value under each scenario. The next step is to assign probabilities to each scenario and arrive at a weighted average value. The procedure to be followed is similar to the Monte Carlo methodology described in Chapter 5.

Example

Suppose you have calculated three valuations of QuickLeg over a 10 year forecast period. Based on your analysis of value drivers, strategies, competition, and other variables, you have assigned the following values to each scenario:

Scenario	Probability	Value Derived from Scenario	Expected value
Conservative	0.2	1,000	200
Normal	0.7	1,600	1,120
High Growth	0.1	2,200	220
	Overall value		1,540

Assigning the above values and respective probabilities to each scenario, the expected overall value of Quickleg is $1,540 million.

8 Intangible assets

The valuation of **intangible assets** and **intellectual capital** presents special problems. Various methods can be used to value them including the relief from royalties, premium profits and capitalisation of earnings methods.

8.1 Valuation of intangibles

The book value-plus method discussed earlier specifically excluded most intangible assets from the computation. This rendered this method unsuitable for the valuation of most established businesses, particularly those in the service industry. Here we consider the various types of intangible assets that a business may benefit from and how they might be valued.

8.1.1 Intangible assets and goodwill

Key terms

> **Intangible assets** are identifiable non-monetary assets without physical substance which must be controlled by the entity as the result of past events and from which the entity expects a flow of future economic benefits. *(IAS 38)*
>
> **Goodwill** (acquired)is future economic benefits arising from assets that are not capable of being individually identified and separately recognised. *(IFRS 3)*

The above definition of intangible assets distinguishes:

(a)   Intangible assets from tangible assets, by the phrase 'do not have physical substance'.

(b)   Intangible assets from goodwill, by the word 'identifiable', an identifiable asset is legally defined as one that can be disposed of separately without disposing of a business of the entity.

The strict accounting distinctions do not need to concern us here. We are interested in any element of business that may have some value.

Certain intangible assets can be recorded at their **historical cost**. Examples include patents and trademarks being recorded at **registration value** and franchises being recorded at **contract cost**. However over time these historical values may become poor reflections of the assets' value in use or of their market value.

8.1.2 Intellectual capital

Key terms

> **Intellectual capital** is knowledge which can be used to create value. Intellectual capital includes:
>
> (a) **Human resources**: the collective skills, experience and knowledge of employees
>
> (b) **Intellectual assets**: knowledge which is defined and codified such as a drawing, computer program or collection of data
>
> (c) **Intellectual property**: intellectual assets which can be legally protected, such as patents and copyrights
>
> *(OT 2005)*

As the demand for knowledge-based products grows with the changing structure of the global economy, knowledge plays an expanding role in achieving competitive advantage. Employees may thus be extremely valuable to a business, and they should be included in a full assets based valuation.

The principles of valuation discussed below should be taken as applying to all assets, resources or property that are defined as intangible assets or intellectual capital, which will include

- Patents, trademarks and copyrights
- Franchises and licensing agreements
- Research and development
- Brands
- Technology, management and consulting processes
- Know-how, education, vocational qualification
- Customer loyalty
- Distribution channels
- Management philosophy

8.2 Measurement of intangible assets of an enterprise

The expanding intellectual capital of firms accentuates the need for methods of valuation for comparative purposes, for example when an acquisition or buy-out is being considered.

Ramona Dzinkowski (*The measurement and management of intellectual capital*, Management Accounting) identifies the following three indicators, which are derived from audited financial statements and are independent of the definitions of intellectual capital adopted by the firm.

- **Market-to-book values**
- **Tobin's 'Q'**
- **Calculated intangible value**

8.2.1 Market-to-book values

We covered this method earlier in the chapter. The value of a firm's intellectual capital is defined as **the difference between the book value of tangible assets and the market value of the firm**. Thus, if a company's market value is $8 million and its book value is $5 million, the $3 million difference is taken to represent the value of the firm's **intangible** (or intellectual) assets.

Although obviously **simple**, this method's simplicity merely serves to indicate that it fails to take account of **real world complexities.** There may be imperfections in the market valuation, and book values are subject to accounting standards which reflect historic cost and amortisation policies rather than true market values of tangible non-current assets.

In addition, the accounting valuation does not attempt to value a company as a whole, but rather as a sum of separate asset values computed under particular accounting conventions. The market, on the other hand, values the entire company as a going concern, following its defined strategy.

8.2.2 Tobin's 'Q'

The Nobel prize-winning economist James Tobin developed the 'Q' method initially as a way of predicting investment behaviour.

'Q' is the ratio of the **market capitalisation of the firm** (share price × number of shares) to the **replacement cost** of its assets.

If the replacement cost of assets is **lower** than the market capitalisation, **'Q' is greater than 1** and the company is enjoying higher than average returns on its investment ('monopoly rents'). Technology and so-called 'human-capital' assets are likely to lead to high 'Q' values.

Tobin's 'Q' is affected by the **same variables** influencing market capitalisation as the **market-to-book** method. In common with that method, it is used most appropriately to make comparisons of the value of intangible assets of companies within an industry which serve the same markets and have similar tangible non-current assets. As such, these methods could serve as performance benchmarks by which to appraise management or corporate strategy.

8.2.3 Calculated intangible values (CIV)

CIV calculates an 'excess return' on tangible assets. This figure is then used in determining the proportion of return attributable to intangible assets.

A step-by-step approach would be as follows.

Step 1   Calculate average pre-tax earnings over a time period.

Step 2   Calculate average year end tangible assets over the time period using statement of financial position figures.

Step 3   Divide earnings by average assets to get the return on assets.

Step 4   Find the industry's return on assets.

Step 5   Multiply the industry's return on asset percentage by the entity's average tangible asset. Subtract this from the entity's pre-tax earnings to calculate the excess return.

Step 6   Calculate the average tax rate over the time period and multiply this by the excess return. Subtract this from the excess return to give the after-tax premium attributable to intangible assets.

Step 7   Calculate the NPV of the premium by dividing it by the entity's cost of capital.

8.2.4 Example of CIV method

Jools Inc is trying to value its intangible assets and has decided to use the CIV method. Details for Jools over the last three years are as follows.

	20X6 $m	20X7 $m	20X8 $m
Pre-tax earnings	350.0	359.8	370.6
Tangible assets	1,507.5	1,528.9	1,555.9

The current return on assets ratio for the industry as a whole is 21%. Jools' WACC is 8%.

Calculate the fair value of Jools Inc's intangible assets, assuming an average tax rate of 30%.

Solution

Average pre-tax earnings $= \dfrac{350 + 359.8 + 370.6}{3}$ $= \$360.13$ million

Average tangible assets $= \dfrac{1{,}507.5 + 1{,}528.9 + 1{,}555.9}{3}$ $= \$1{,}530.77$ million

Return on assets $= \dfrac{360.13}{1{,}530.77} = 23.5\%$

Excess return $= 360.13 - (0.21 \times 1{,}530.77) = \$38.67$ million

After-tax premium $= 38.67 - (0.3 \times 38.67) = \$27.07$ million

NPV of premium $= \dfrac{27.07}{0.08} = \$338.38$ million

8.2.5 Problems with the CIV approach

Whilst this seemingly straightforward approach, using readily available information, seems attractive, it does have two problems.

(a)   It uses average industry ROA as a basis for computing excess returns, which may be distorted by extreme values.

(b)   The choice of discount rate to apply to the excess returns to value the intangible asset needs to be made with care. To ensure comparability between companies and industries, some sort of average cost of capital should perhaps be applied. This again has the potential problems of distortion.

8.2.6 Lev's knowledge earnings method

Lev's knowledge earnings method involves separating the earnings that are deemed to come from intangible assets and capitalise these earnings.

This method involves separating the earnings that are deemed to come from intangible assets and capitalise them. This model does produce results that are very close to the quoted share price, suggesting that it is a good method of valuation.

The main problem with this technique is that it can be very complicated and in the end unrealistic. In practice most valuations come from intense negotiations between the interested parties rather than complex calculations.

8.3 Valuation of individual intangible assets

8.3.1 Relief from royalties method

This method involves trying to determine:

(a)   The value obtainable from licensing out the right to exploit the intangible asset to a third party, or

(b)   The royalties that the owner of the intangible asset is relieved from paying through being the owner rather than the licensee

A **notional royalty rate** is estimated as a percentage of revenue expected to be generated by the intangible asset. The estimated royalty stream can then be **capitalised**, for example by discounting at a risk-free market rate, to find an estimated market value.

This relatively simple valuation method is easiest to apply if the intangible asset is already subject to licensing agreements. If they are not, the valuer might reach an appropriate figure from other comparable licensing arrangements.

8.3.2 Premium profits method

The premium profits method is often used for **brands**. It bases the valuation on capitalisation of the **extra profits generated** by the brand or other intangible asset in excess of profits made by businesses lacking the intangible asset or brand.

The premium profits specifically attributable to the brand or other intangible asset may be estimated (for example) by comparing the price of branded products and unbranded products. The estimated premium profits can then be capitalised by discounting at a risk-adjusted market rate.

8.3.3 Capitalisation of earnings method

With the capitalised earnings method, the **maintainable earnings accruing to the intangible asset** are estimated. An **earnings multiple** is then applied to the earnings, taking account of expected risks and rewards, including the prospects for future earnings growth and the risks involved. This method of valuation is often used to value **publishing titles**.

8.3.4 Comparison with market transactions method

This method looks at **actual market transactions** in similar intangible assets. A multiple of revenue or earnings from the intangible asset might then be derived from a similar market transaction. A problem with this method is that many **intangible assets are unique** and it may therefore be difficult to identify 'similar' market transactions, although this might be done by examining acquisitions and disposals of businesses that include similar intangible assets.

The method might be used alongside other valuation methods, to provide a comparison.

9 Firms with product options

FAST FORWARD

> A product option is where a firm has the option to sell a product in the future but does not have the obligation to do so.
>
> Traditional valuation techniques may not be suitable for valuing firms with product options – the option-based approach may be more suitable.

Examples of product options are patents and copyrights, and firms owning natural resources. Firms that have product options are often research and technology-based.

When a firm has a product option that is not currently generating cash flow, there is a risk that a discounted cash flow approach to valuation will not fully reflect that full value of the option. This is because a DCF approach may not incorporate all the possible future cash flows of the company.

9.1 Problems with traditional DCF techniques

The value of a firm usually comes from two different sources, as follows.

- The current assets of the business. Typically, the value of the current assets can be captured in the current cash flows of the firm.
- The present value of any future growth opportunities. Typically, the value of future growth opportunities is captured by the growth in cash flows in the future.

In the context of a product option, this approach is not fully appropriate, for the following reasons.

- The options represent a current asset of the business, but are not generating any cash flows.
- Any cash flows expected to be generated by the product could be outside of the detailed forecasting period.

9.2 Possible solutions to the valuation problem

There are three possible methods of valuing product options.

- **Value the option on the open market**. This is only possible if there is a traded market in such options. If there is no active market or if the option is difficult to separate from the other operations of the firm, this approach is probably not feasible.
- Use a traditional **DCF framework** and factor in a higher growth rate than would be justified given the existing assets of the firm. The problem with this is that any growth rate used will be subjective. In addition, it expresses contingent cash flows as expected cash flows.
- Use an **option-based approach** to valuation. This is considered below.

9.3 Use of option pricing models

Option pricing models for real options were covered in detail in Chapter 6.

9.3.1 Benefits and problems of option pricing models

The benefit of using option pricing models is that the approach is based on **contingent claim valuation**, which reflects the situation more precisely than a DCF approach.

The problems of using option pricing models, such as Black-Scholes, are as follows.

(a) **They need the underlying asset to be traded**. This is because the model is based on the principle of arbitrage, which means that the underlying asset must be easy to buy and sell. This is not a problem when valuing options on quoted shares. However, the underlying asset in the context of product options will not be traded, meaning that arbitrage is not possible.

(b) **They assume that the price of the underlying asset follows a continuous pattern**. While this may be a reasonable approximation most of the time for quoted shares, it is clearly inappropriate in the context of product options. The impact of this is that the model will undervalue deeply out-of-the-money options, since it will underestimate the probability of a sudden large increase in the value of the underlying asset.

(c) **They assume that the standard deviation of price of the underlying asset is known** and does not vary over the life of the option. While this may be a reasonable assumption in the context of short-dated equity options, it is not appropriate for long-term product options.

(d) **They assume that exercise occurs at a precise point in time**. In the case of product options, exercise may occur over a long period of time. For example, if a firm has the right to mine natural resources, it will take time to extract the resources. This will reduce the present value of the asset.

9.4 Using option pricing models to value product patents

When valuing product patents as options, the key inputs for an option pricing will need to be identified, being the underlying asset price, the strike price, the expected volatility of the underlying asset price and the time to expiry. The following approach could be adopted.

Step 1   **Identify the value of the underlying asset**. This will be based on the expected cash flows that the asset can generate. Given the uncertain nature of the cash flows and the distant time periods in which they may arise, it clearly will be difficult to value the underlying asset precisely.

Step 2   **Identify the standard deviation of the cash flows above**. Again this will be difficult to identify, owing to changes in the potential market for the product, changes in technology and so on. It would, however, be possible to use techniques such as scenario analysis. The higher the standard deviation, the more valuable the asset.

Step 3   **Identify the** exercise price of the option. This is the cost of investing in the resources needed to produce the asset. It is typically assumed that this remains constant in present value terms, with any uncertainty being reflected in the cash flows of the asset.

Step 4   Identify the expiry date of the option. This is when the patent expires. Any cash flows after this date are expected to have an NPV of zero, since there will be generic competition after patent protection ends.

Step 5   **Identify the cost of delay.** If the product is not implemented immediately, this will reduce the value of the cash flows from the project as competing products will enter the market in future years.

A similar approach could be adopted to valuing other product options, such as **natural resources**. Where a company is investing in research and development, but has no patents developed, the same approach will apply, but the value of the option is clearly even more uncertain due to the greater uncertainty of the inputs.

Chapter Roundup

- When a company acquires another company, it always pays above its current market value. This is known as the overvaluation problem.

- The growth rate of a company's earnings is the most important determinant of a company's value. The growth rate may be based on historical estimates, analyst's forecasts or company fundamentals.

- An acquisition may have an impact on the financial and business risk exposure of the acquirer.

  A Type I acquisition does not affect the acquiring firm's exposure to financial or business risk.

  A Type II acquisition affects the acquiring firm's exposure to financial risk only – it does not affect exposure to business risk.

  A Type III acquisition affects both the financial and business risk exposure of the acquiring firm.

- The business risk of the combined entity will be affected by the betas of the target and predator firs and the beta of the synergy that results from the acquisition.

- Type I acquisitions may be valued using one of the following valuation methods:

  - Book value-plus models
  - Market relative models
  - Cash flow models, including EVA^{TM}, MVA

- Book value or asset-based methods of company valuation are based on the statement of financial position as the starting point in the valuation process.

- Market relative models may be based on the P/E ratio which produces an earnings based valuation of shares.

- Market value of a target company = market to book ratio x the book vale of assets of target company.

- A type II acquisition affects the acquiring company's exposure to financial risk only – it does not affect exposure to business risk.

- A type III acquisition affects both the financial and business risk exposure of the acquiring company.

- Due to their unique characteristics high growth start-ups presents a number of challenges.

- The valuation of **intangible assets** and **intellectual capital** presents special problems. Various methods can be used to value them including the relief from royalties, premium profits and capitalisation of earnings methods.

- Lev's knowledge earnings method involves separating the earnings that are deemed to come from intangible assets and capitalise these earnings.

- A product option is where a firm has the option to sell a product in the future but does not have the obligation to do so.

  Traditional valuation techniques may not be suitable for valuing firms with product options – the option-based approach may be more suitable.

Quick Quiz

1   Give three ways in which the growth rate of a firm's earnings can be estimated.

2   What is the relationship between earnings growth and retained profits?

3   If the return on equity is 12 percent and the retention rate is 0.4 what is the growth rate of earnings?

4   What is a type I acquisition?

5   What is a type II acquisition?

6   What is a type III acquisition?

7   What is EVA®?

8   If the Q ratio is less than one, what does this tell you about the management of the company?

9   What is the most appropriate method for the valuation of type II acquisition?

10   What is the main problem with the WACC when valuing a type III acquisition?

Answers to Quick Quiz

1   Historical estimates
Analysts forecasts
Company fundamentals

2   The higher the percentage of earnings retained the higher the earnings growth

3   Earnings growth = return on equity × retention rate = 0.12 × 0.4 = 0.048 or 4.8 percent

4   A type I acquisition is an acquisition that affects neither the business risk nor the financial risk of the acquiring company.

5   A type II acquisition is an acquisition that doesn't affect the business risk but does affect the financial risk of the acquiring company.

6   A type III acquisition is an acquisition that affects both the business risk and the financial risk of the acquiring company.

7   EVA® is the difference between the dollar return on invested capital minus the capital charge the company needs to pay to the capital contributors.

8   A Q ratio of less than 1 means that management destroys value.

9   The Adjusted Present Value approach (APV).

10   The calculation of the WACC requires knowledge of the market value of debt and equity for which calculations we need knowledge of the WACC.

Now try the question below from the Exam Question Bank

Number	Level	Marks	Time
18	Introductory	15	27 mins
19	Examination	30	54 mins
20	Examination	40	72 mins
21	Examination	40	72 mins
22	Introductory	15	27 mins
23	Examination	25	45 mins
24	Examination	20	36 mins

11

Regulatory framework and processes

Topic list	Syllabus reference
1 The global regulatory framework	D(3) (a)
2 Key aspects of takeover regulation	D(3) (a)
3 Regulation in the UK	D(3) (b)
4 Defensive tactics in a hostile takeover	D(3) (b)

Introduction

In this chapter we discuss the main factors that have influenced the development of the regulatory framework for mergers and acquisitions globally and compare the two different models of regulation used in the UK and continental Europe respectively. We explain the convergence sought by the implementation of the EU Directive and discuss issues that are likely to arise in a given offer as well as defensive measures available to management in a hostile bid.

Study guide

		Intellectual level
D3	**Regulatory framework and processes**	
(a)	Demonstrate an understanding of the principal factors influencing the development of the regulatory framework for mergers and acquisitions globally and, in particular, be able to compare and contrast the shareholder versus the stakeholder models of regulation.	2
(b)	Identify the main regulatory issues which are likely to arise in the context of a given offer and (i) assess whether the offer is likely to be in the shareholders' best interests (ii) advise the directors of a target entity on the most appropriate defence if a specific offer is to be treated as hostile.	3

1 The global regulatory framework

1.1 Introduction

FAST FORWARD

Takeover regulation is an important corporate governance device in protecting the interests of all stakeholders as the agency problem can have a significant potential impact on mergers and acquisitions.

The **agency problem** (discussed in Part A) and the issues arising from the separation of ownership and control have a significant potential impact on mergers and acquisitions.

Merger booms and a succession of corporate scandals have contributed to the need for adequate regulation both from the point of view of the shareholders and the wider group of stakeholders.

Takeover regulation is an important **corporate governance device** that seeks to protect the interests of **minority shareholders** and other types of **stakeholders** and ensure a **well-functioning market** for corporate control.

1.2 Potential conflicts of interest

Takeover regulation seeks to regulate the conflicts of interest between the management and shareholders of both the **target** and the **bidder**.

There are **two main agency problems** that emerge in the context of a takeover that regulation seeks to address.

(a) The first is the **protection of minority shareholders**. In addition to existing minority shareholders, transfers of control may turn existing majority shareholders of the target into minority shareholders.

(b) The second is the possibility that the management of the target company may implement **measures** to **prevent the takeover** even if these are **against stakeholder interests**.

1.3 Background and brief history of regulation in the UK and continental Europe

1.3.1 The City Code on Takeovers and Mergers and UK legislation

FAST FORWARD

The City Code on Takeovers and Mergers is a voluntary set of principles governing takeovers and mergers of UK companies. It is issued and administered by the Takeover Panel, an independent body of representatives from UK financial institutions with key members appointed by the Bank of England.

Takeover regulation in the UK goes back to 1968 when a **voluntary code**, the **City Code on Takeovers and Mergers** (known as the City Code) was introduced. Since then the Code, a set of general principles and rules governing takeovers and mergers of UK companies, has been frequently amended.

Mergers and acquisitions in the UK are also regulated by legislation through the **1985 Companies Act**, the **Financial Services and Markets Act 2000** (the FSMA) and the insider dealing provisions of the **Criminal Justice Act 1993**. The Companies Act 2006 (CA 2006) will repeat almost all of the provisions of CA 1985 and will re-state the law in plain English. Most of the provisions of CA 2006 will come into force in October 2008. However, provisions relating to public company takeovers and disclosure of major shareholding come into force in January 2007 under the new Financial Services Authority (FSA) Disclosure and Transparency rules, with FSA enforcement (see section 3.3.1).

In continental Europe, takeover regulation was put in place in the late 1980s based largely on voluntary codes following the UK City Code. However, these were soon replaced by legislation in the mid-1990s.

1.3.2 The Takeover Panel

The City Code is issued and administered by the Takeover Panel, an independent body made up of representatives from UK financial institutions and professional associations with key members currently appointed by the Bank of England.

1.3.3 Legal status of the City Code

Although the City Code (before the implementation of the EU Directive) was not legally binding, it was in practice mandatory for both UK and non-UK bidders. If a party to a takeover failed to comply with the Code they run the risk that facilities of the London Markets would be withdrawn.

In addition, the Panel could ask the Financial Services Authority under the FSMA to take action if a party's behaviour amounts to market abuse, with sanctions involving unlimited fines.

1.3.4 Scope and application of the City Code

The City Code applies to any offer where the target or offeree is a listed or unlisted public company resident in the UK, the Channel Islands or the Isle of Man.

The nature or country of residence of the company or entity making the offer, ie the bidder or offeror, does not affect the application of the City Code.

The main principles of the City Code are detailed in Section 3 below where the principal issues of which a bidder should be aware when making an offer are also discussed.

1.4 The two models of regulation

FAST FORWARD

Takeover regulation in the UK is centred around the City Code and is referred to as a 'market-based' model designed to protect a dispersed shareholder base.

Takeover regulation in the UK, centred around the City Code, is based upon what is often referred to as a **'market-based model'**[1] designed to protect a wide and dispersed shareholder base. This system which also prevails in the Commonwealth countries and the US is based on case law and the legal rules resulting from it. These seek to a great extent the protection of shareholder rights.

FAST FORWARD

The system prevalent in continental Europe is referred to as the block-holder or stakeholder system and relies on codified civil law designed to protect a broader group of stakeholders.

The second system, prevalent in continental Europe, is referred to as the **'block-holder'**[1] or **stakeholder system** and relies on codified or civil law seeking to protect a broader group of stakeholders such as creditors, employees and the wider national interest.

The two systems differ not only in terms of their regulatory framework (civil versus common law) but also in terms of the underlying structure of ownership and control that they seek to address.

In the UK and the US the system is characterised by wider share ownership than in continental Europe where companies tend to be owned by majority or near-majority stakes held by a small number of investors.

In the Anglo-American model, the emphasis is on the agency problem and the protection of the widely distributed shareholder base.

The civil law countries rely via **legislation** on the monitoring by large shareholders, **creditors** and **employees**.

[1] *Georgen, Martynova and Renneboog (2005) Corporate governance convergence: evidence from takeover regulations reforms in Europe Oxford Review of Economic Policy*

1.5 Towards European harmonisation – the EU Takeovers Directive

FAST FORWARD

The Takeovers Directive was introduced by the EU in 2002 and its principles became effective from May 2006 in order to achieve harmonisation and convergence of the market based and stakeholder systems.

The **Takeovers Directive** lays down for the first time minimum EU rules concerning the regulation of takeovers of companies whose shares are traded on regulated markets. It is one of the measures adopted under the EU Financial Services Action Plan and aims to strengthen the single market in financial services.

The **Takeover Directive** requires that certain of the activities of the **Takeover Panel** are placed within a legal framework bringing an end to the non-statutory approach to regulation in the UK. In terms of approach, the new regulatory model leads to the **convergence** of the **European system** to the **UK-US** one by adopting many of the elements of the **City Code**.

The **European Commission**, seeking to harmonise European takeover regulation presented a draft Takeover Directive in 2002. This draft introduced the following five main regulatory devices (the rationale of which is explained in Section 2 below).

(a) Mandatory-bid rule
(b) The principle of equal treatment of shareholders
(c) A squeeze-out rule and sell-out rights
(d) The principle of board neutrality
(e) A break-through rule

The break-through rule, described below, faced much resistance and the directive allowed individual countries to opt out of it.

2 Key aspects of takeover regulation

Goergen, Martynova and Renneboog [1] *(2005) in their investigation of takeover reforms in Europe and the trend towards harmonisation, identify the following seven regulatory devices available to regulators and aimed at the protection of shareholders.*

[1] Georgen, Martynova and Renneboog (2005). Corporate governance convergence: evidence from takeover regulations reforms in Europe *Oxford Review of Economic Policy*

The mandatory-bid rule

The aim of this rule is to protect minority shareholders by providing them with the opportunity to exit the company at a fair price once the bidder has accumulated a certain percentage of the shares.

National thresholds vary between countries but the trend has been for these to decrease over the years.

In the UK, this threshold is specified by the City Code for Takeovers and Mergers and is at 30%.

The mandatory-bid rule is based on the grounds that once the bidder obtains control he may exploit his position at the expense of minority shareholders. This is why the mandatory-bid rule normally also specifies the price that is to be paid for the shares.

The bidder is normally required to offer to the remaining shareholders a price not lower than the highest price for the shares already acquired during a specified period prior to the bid.

The principle of equal treatment

The principle of treating all shareholders equally is fundamental in all western European countries.

In general terms, the principle of equal treatment requires the bidder to offer to minority shareholders the same terms as those offered to earlier shareholders from whom the controlling block was acquired.

Transparency of ownership and control

The disclosure of information about major shareholdings is an important element of investor protection and a well-functioning corporate market. The transparency enables the regulator to monitor large shareholders, minimise potential agency problems and investigate insider dealing. It also enables both minority shareholders and the market to monitor large shareholders who may be able to exercise undue influence or exact benefits at the expense of other shareholdings.

The squeeze-out and sell-out rights

Squeeze-out rights gives the bidder who has acquired a specific percentage of the equity (usually 90%) the right to force minority shareholders to sell their shares.

The threshold in the UK and in most European countries is 90%, although in Belgium, France, Germany and the Netherlands the threshold is 95% and in Ireland it is the lowest at 80%. The rule enables the bidder to acquire 100% of the equity once the threshold percentage has been reached and eliminates potential problems that could be caused by minority shareholders.

Sell-out rights enable minority shareholders to require the majority shareholder to purchase their shares.

The one share-one vote principle

Where the one share-one vote principle is upheld, arrangements restricting voting rights are forbidden.

Differentiated voting rights, such as non-voting shares and dual-clan shares with multiple voting rights, enable some shareholders to accumulate control at the expense of other shareholders and could provide a significant barrier to potential takeovers.

The break-through rule

The effect of the break-through rule, where this is allowed by corporate law, is to enable a bidder with a specified proportion of the company's equity to break-through the company's multiple voting rights and exercise control as if one share-one vote existed.

Board neutrality and anti-takeover measures

Seeking to address the agency issue where management may be tempted to act in their own interests at the expense of the interests of the shareholders, several regulatory devices propose board neutrality. For instance the board would not be permitted to carry out post-bid aggressive defensive tactics (such as selling the company's main assets, known as crown jewels defence, or entering into special arrangements giving rights to existing shareholders to buy shares at a low price, known as poison pill defence), without the prior authority of the shareholders.

3 Regulation in the UK

3.1 The City Code: general principles

The City Code is divided into general principles and detailed rules which must be observed by persons involved in a merger or takeover transaction. The ten principles of the City Code are the following.

1 **All the shareholders of the target company must be treated similarly**

'All shareholders of the same class of an offeree company must be **treated similarly** by an offeror.' In other words, a company making a takeover bid cannot offer one set of purchase terms to some shareholders in the target company, and a different set of terms to other shareholders holding shares of the same class in that company.

2   **All information disclosed to one or more shareholders of the target company must be disclosed to all**

'During the course of a takeover, or when such is in contemplation, neither the offeror nor the offeree company ... may furnish information to some shareholders which is **not made available to all shareholders.**'

3   **An offer should only be made if it can be implemented in full**

Individuals or firms should not make an offer unless they have reason to believe that they will be able to implement this in full.

4   **Sufficient information, advice and time to be given for a properly informed decision**

'Shareholders must be given **sufficient information and advice** to enable them to reach a properly informed decision and must have sufficient time to do so. No relevant information should be withheld from them.'

5   **All documentation should be of the highest standards of accuracy**

All documentation produced by the bidding company or the directors of the target should be produced to the highest standards of accuracy.

6   **All parties must do everything to ensure that a false market is not created in the shares of the target company**

A false market is created when a deliberate attempt is made to distort the market in the offeror's or target's shares. An example would be where false information is either given or withheld in such a way as to prevent the free negotiation of prices.

7   **Shareholder approval**

'At no time after a *bona fide* offer has been communicated to the board of an offeree company ... may any action be taken by the board of the offeree company in relation to the affairs of the company, **without the approval of the shareholders** in general meeting, which could effectively result in any *bona fide* offer being frustrated or in the shareholders being denied an opportunity to decide on its merits.' In other words, directors of a target company are not permitted to frustrate a takeover bid, nor to prevent the shareholders from having a chance to decide for themselves.

8   **'Rights of control must be exercised in good faith and the oppression of a minority is wholly unacceptable**'

For example, a holding company cannot take decisions about a takeover bid for one of its subsidiaries in such a way that minority shareholders would be unfairly treated.

9   **The directors of both target and bidder must act in the interest of their respective companies**

The directors of both companies in the acquisition must act in the interest of their companies with no regard for their own holding or any of that of their family or any other special interest.

10 **'Where control of a company is acquired ... a general offer to all other shareholders is normally required'**

Control is defined as a 'holding, or aggregate holdings, of shares carrying 30% of the voting rights of a company, irrespective of whether that holding or holdings gives *de facto* control'.

3.2 Timetable for compliance with City Code

The City Code lays down time limits governing the overall period of an offer. The aim of the timetable is to minimise disruption of the normal activities of the target.

3.2.1 Outline timetable for a takeover offer

Day	Action Required	Note	Rule
−28	Announcement of intention to bid.	The offer document must be posted to the shareholders within 28 days of the notice of intention to make the offer.	30.1
0	Last day for posting offer document.		
+14	Last day for target's written response to offer.	The target company's board should advise its shareholders of its views on the offer. The target board's views may already be contained in the offer document if this is an offer which the board recommend.	30.2
+21	Earliest day for offer to close.	The offer cannot close before 21 days have passed from the day the intention to bid was announced.	31.1
+39	Last day for target to announce material new information including trading results, profit or dividend forecasts and any other relevant information.		
+42	Target shareholders may withdraw their acceptance if offer is not unconditional.		
+46	Last day for offeror to revise its offer.	Any subsequent revised offer must be kept open for at least 14 days after the revised offer document is posted. Therefore, because the acceptance condition (see 3.3.2 below) must be met within 50 days, no revised document may be posted after day 46.	32.1
+60	Last day for offer to be declared unconditional as to acceptances.	If the acceptance condition (see 3.3.2 below) is not satisfied by day 60 then the offer will lapse.	31.6
+81	Last day for offer to be made wholly unconditional.		
+95	Last day for paying the offer consideration to the target shareholders who accepted by day 81.		

3.2.2 The acceptance condition

Whether an offer is successful or not depends on whether the offeror has sufficient acceptances to give it the required degree of control over the target. Therefore the offeror makes the offer subject to the condition that a minimum level of acceptance is achieved. The minimum acceptance condition permitted is 50% of the target's voting rights. Normally, however, a 90% condition will be specified because this is the level that will enable the offeror to force the remaining minority shareholders to sell their shares under the compulsory acquisition per the Companies Act 1985.

If the specified level of acceptances is not reached within 60 days from posting the offer document, the offer will lapse.

3.3 Stake building and the relevant thresholds

Normally, a potential offeror will wish to build a stake prior to making an offer. The City Code places a number of restrictions to regulate the substantial acquisition of shares (SARs) where the resulting holding would represent between 15 and 30 percent of the voting rights. These rules were intended to make the market and the offeree board and shareholders aware of the potential offeror's interest and give them more time to decide how to proceed. However, these were abolished in May 2006. Following the abolition of SARS, any person can acquire a stake of up to 29.9 percent in a listed or AIM (Alternative Investment Market) company without being subject to any timing restrictions. Some of the important share stakes and their consequences are outlined below:

%	Consequence	Source of regulation
Any	Ability of the company to enquire as to the ultimate ownership under s212 CA 1985.	CA 1985
3%	Requirement to disclose interest in the company under ss198-199 CA 1985 (the material interests rules)	CA 1985
10%	Shareholders controlling not less than 10% of the voting rights may requisition the company to serve notices, under s212 CA 1985 to identify another shareholder. Notifiable interests rules of CA 1985 become operative for institutional investors and non-beneficial stakes.	CA 1985
30%	City Code definition of effective control. Mandatory bid triggered and takeover offer becomes compulsory. If the bidder holds between 30% and 50% (normally due to earlier attempts at a takeover) a mandatory offer is triggered with any additional purchase.	City Code rule 9 City Code rule 5
50%+	CA 1985 definition of control (since at this level the holder will have the ability to pass ordinary resolutions). First point at which a full offer could be declared unconditional with regard to acceptances. Minimum acceptance condition (see 3.2.2 above).	CA 1985 City Code
75%	Major control boundary since at this level the holder will be able to pass special resolutions.	
90%	Minorities may be able to force the majority to buy out their stake. Equally, the majority may, subject to the way in which the stake has been acquired, require the minority to sell out their position. Compulsory acquisition of remaining 10% is now possible.	CA 1985

3.3.1 Disclosure and Transparency Rules (DTR)

The relevant sections of CA 1985 relating to disclosure were repealed with effect from January 2007. These were replaced by the **Disclosure and Transparency Rules (DTR)** enforced by the FSA and introduced as part of the process of implementation of the **Transparency Directive**. Under these rules, the FSA retains the notification threshold of a 3% holding, and every 1% thereafter.

Instead of disclosure of 'interests' in shares as under the Companies Act 1985, the Transparency Directive requires the disclosure of **holdings of shares to which voting rights are attached**.

3.4 The Competition Commission

A UK company might have to consider whether its proposed takeover would be drawn to the attention of the Competition Commission (formerly called the Monopolies and Mergers Commission). Under the terms of the Monopolies and Mergers Act, the Office of Fair Trading (OFT) is entitled to scrutinise and possibly reject all major mergers and takeovers. If the OFT thinks that a merger or takeover might be against the public interest, it can refer it to the **Competition Commission** (formerly called the Monopolies and Mergers Commission).

If a transaction is referred to the Competition Commission and the Commission finds that it results in a substantial lessening of competition in the defined market, it will specify action to remedy or prevent the adverse effects identified, or it may decide that the merger does not take place (or, in the case of a completed merger, is reversed).

Any person aggrieved by a decision of the OFT, the Secretary of State or the Competition Commission in connection with a reference or possible reference, may apply to the Competition Appeal Tribunal (CAT) for a review of that decision.

A number of tests may be used to decide whether there has been a **substantial lessening** of **competition** (SLC). These normally include:

The turnover test

No investigation will normally be conducted if the target's turnover is less than £70 million.

The share of supply test

An investigation will not normally be conducted unless, following the merger, the combined entity supplies 25%. The 25% share will be assessed by the commission.

The substantial lessening of competition test

Even if the thresholds in (a) and (b) above are met, the Competition Commission will only be involved if there has been a substantial lessening of competition (SLC) in the market.

3.5 The European Union

Mergers fall within the exclusive jurisdiction of the European Union where, following the merger, the following two tests are met.

(a) **Worldwide turnover** of more than **€5 billion per annum**
(b) **European Union** turnover of more than **€250 million per annum**

The European Union will assess the merger in a similar way as the Competition Commission in the UK by considering the effect on competition in the market.

The merger will be blocked if the merged company results in a market oligopoly or results in such a dominant position in the market, that consumer choice and prices will be affected.

4 Defensive tactics in a hostile takeover 6/11

FAST FORWARD

There are a number of defensive measures that can be taken where the management of the takeover target perceives the bid to be hostile. Takeover defences can be categorised into **pre-offer** and **post-offer** defences.

Most takeovers may be referred to as **friendly** and take place when the management of the two firms negotiate an agreement that is **beneficial** to both sides.

However, not all takeovers are negotiated in this way and some are perceived as hostile and resisted by the directors.

There are a number of **defensive** measures that can be taken where the management of the takeover target perceives the bid as **hostile**.

Takeover defences can be categorised into **pre-offer defences** and **post-offer defences**. Both types of defence have developed over the years, mainly in the US during the wave of takeover bids of the 1980s.

The more **aggressive tactics** which often **risk shareholders' interests** in favour of those of management. The EU Takeover Directive seeks to override certain of the more aggressive tactics that may be taken by management to frustrate a bid and which may be at the expense of the shareholders.

Both **pre-offer** and **post-offer defences** are set out below, together with an explanation of what can be appropriately used in the UK following the implementation of the Takeover Directive.

(a) **Pre-bid defences** normally include provisions in the company's articles of association whereby **differential share structures** are set up under which **minority shareholders** exercise **disproportionate voting rights**, thus enabling the target to frustrate a takeover bid.

The Takeover Directive, now being implemented in the UK, gives companies with voting shares traded on a regulated market to opt for the breakthrough provisions should they wish to do so, thereby breaking the restrictions on voting rights.

(b) **Post-bid defences** include actions such as selling the major assets of the company (crown jewels) in an attempt to make the target less attractive and setting up schemes where existing shareholders can but shares at very low prices (poison pill). The Takeover directive now incorporated into the **City Code** requires that the management of the company does not take any such defensive action unless this is authorised by the shareholders.

Summary of defensive tactics

Tactic	Explanation
Golden parachute	Large compensation payments made to the top management of the target firm if their positions are eliminated due to hostile takeover. This may include cash or bonus payments, stock options or a combination of these.
Poison pill	This is an attempt to make a company unattractive normally by giving the right to existing shareholders to buy shares at a very low price. Poison pills have many variants.
White knights and white squires	This would involve inviting a firm that would rescue the target from the unwanted bidder. The white knight would act as a friendly counter-bidder. A white squire is similar to a white knight but the former does not take control of the target firm.
Crown jewels	The firm's most valuable assets may be the main reason that the firm became a takeover target in the first place. By selling these or entering into arrangements such as sale and leaseback, the firm is making itself less attractive as a target.
Pacman defence	This defence is carried out by mounting a counter-bid for the attacker. The Pacman defence is an aggressive rather than defensive tactic and will only work where the original acquirer is a public company with diverse shareholdings. This tactic also appears to suggest that the company's management are in favour of the acquisition but they disagree about which company should be in control.
Litigation or regulatory defence	The target company can challenge the acquisition by inviting an investigation by the regulatory authorities or though the courts. The target may be able to sue for a temporary order to stop the predator from buying any more of its shares.

Chapter Roundup

- Takeover regulation is an important corporate governance device in protecting the interests of all stakeholders as the agency problem can have a significant potential impact on mergers and acquisitions.

- The City Code on Takeovers and Mergers is a voluntary set of principles governing takeovers and mergers of UK companies. It is issued and administered by the Takeover Panel, an independent body of representatives from UK financial institutions with key members appointed by the Bank of England.

- Takeover regulation in the UK is centred around the City Code and is referred to as a 'market-based' model designed to protect a dispersed shareholder base.

- The system prevalent in continental Europe is referred to as the block-holder or stakeholder system and relies on codified civil law designed to protect a broader group of stakeholders.

- The Takeovers Directive was introduced by the EU in 2002 and its principles became effective from May 2006 in order to achieve harmonisation and convergence of the market based and stakeholder systems.

- There are a number of defensive measures that can be taken where the management of the takeover target perceives the bid to be hostile. Takeover defences can be categorised into **pre-offer** and **post-offer** defences.

Quick Quiz

1   What are the two models of takeover regulation?

2   What are the key points of the takeover regulation?

3   What are the ten principles of the City Code?

4   Which mergers fall within the jurisdiction of the European Union?

5   What are the main defensive tactics in a takeover?

Answers to Quick Quiz

1   The market-based model
     The stakeholder system

2   The mandatory-bid rule
     The principle of equal treatment
     Transparency of ownership and control
     The squeeze-out and sell-out rights
     The one share-one vote principle
     The break through rule
     Board neutrality and anti-takeover measures

3   All the shareholders of the target company must be treated similarly

     All information disclosed to one or more shareholders of the target company must be disclosed

     An offer should only be made if it can be implemented in full

     Sufficient information, advice and time to be given for a properly informed decision

     All documents should be of the highest standards of accuracy

     All parties must do everything to ensure that false market is not created in the shares of the target company

     Shareholder approval

     Rights of control must be exercised in good faith and the oppression of a minority is wholly unacceptable

     The directors of both target and bidder must act in the interest of their respective companies

     Where control of a company is acquired a general offer to all other shareholders is normally required.

4   Mergers where the resulting combined company will have worldwide turnover of more than €5 billion per annum.

     Mergers where the resulting combined company will have a European Union turnover in excess of €250 million per annum.

5   Golden parachute
     Poison Pill
     White knights and white squires
     Crown jewels
     Pacman Defence
     Litigation or regulatory defence

Now try the question below from the Exam Question Bank

Number	Level	Marks	Time
25	Examination	20	36

12

Financing mergers and acquisitions

Topic list	Syllabus reference
1 Methods of financing mergers	D(4) (a)
2 Assessing a given offer	D(4) (b)
3 Effect of an offer on financial position and performance	D(4) (c)

Introduction

In this chapter we deal with three issues. First we discuss how a bidding firm can finance an acquisition, either by cash or by a share offer or a combination of the two, and discuss the funding of cash offers. Second we discuss ways to evaluate a financial offer in terms of the impact on the acquiring company and criteria for acceptance or rejection. Finally we discuss ways of estimating the possible impact of an offer on the performance and the financial position of the acquiring firm.

Study guide

Exam guide

Questions in this area are likely to involve some calculations so you will need to bring in your knowledge of company valuation. However, questions will not be purely numerical. Topics you might be asked to discuss include why companies might choose to make an offer in a particular form, takeover tactics, the effect on shareholder wealth, and what happens after the takeover including post-audits. Questions on the subjects discussed in this chapter will be **regularly** set in the compulsory section of this paper.

You will be expected to demonstrate competence in the analysis of various finance options when fulfilling the performance objective 'evaluate potential business/investment opportunities and the required finance options'. This chapter focuses on the various ways in which mergers could be financed and assesses the costs and benefits of each option – knowledge which you can put into practice if your organisation is involved in merger and acquisition activity.

1 Methods of financing mergers   6/11

FAST FORWARD

Payment can be in the form of **cash**, a **share exchange** or **convertible loan stock**. The choice will depend on available cash, desired levels of gearing, shareholders' taxation position and changes in control.

1.1 Methods of payment

The terms of a takeover will involve a purchase of the shares of the target company for **cash** or for **'paper'** (shares, or possibly loan stock). A purchase of a target company's shares with shares of the predator company is referred to as a **share exchange**.

1.2 Cash purchases

If the purchase consideration is in **cash**, the shareholders of the target company will simply be bought out. For example, suppose that there are two companies.

	Big Co	Small Co
Net assets (book value)	$1,500,000	$200,000
Number of shares	100,000	10,000
Earnings	$2,000,000	$40,000

Big Co negotiates a takeover of Small Co for $400,000 in cash.

As a result, Big Co will end up with:

(a)   Net assets (book value) of

$1,500,000 + $200,000 − $400,000 cash = $1,300,000

(b)   100,000 shares (no change)

(c) Expected earnings of $2,040,000, minus the loss of interest (net of tax) which would have been obtained from the investment of the $400,000 in cash which was given up to acquire Small Co

1.3 Funding cash offers

A cash offer can be financed from:

(a) **Cash retained from earnings.** This is a common way when the firm to be acquired is small compared to the acquiring firm, but not very common if the target firm is large relative to the acquiring firm. A company occasionally may divest of some of its own assets to accumulate cash prior to bidding for another company.

(b) **The proceeds of a debt issue.** That is the company may raise money by issuing bonds. This is not an approach that is normally taken, because the act of issuing bonds will alert the markets to the intentions of the company to bid for another company and it may lead investors to buy the shares of potential targets, raising their prices.

(c) **A loan facility from a bank.** This can be done as a short term funding strategy, until the bid is accepted and then the company is free to make a bond issue.

(d) **Mezzanine finance**. This may be the only route for companies that do not have access to the bond markets in order to issue bonds.

1.4 Purchases by share exchange

One company can acquire another company by **issuing shares** to pay for the acquisition. The new shares might be issued:

(a) **In exchange** for shares in the target company. Thus, if A Inc acquires B Co, A Inc might issue shares which it gives to B Co's shareholders in exchange for their shares. The B Co shareholders therefore become new shareholders of A Inc. This is a takeover for a 'paper' consideration. Paper offers will often be accompanied by a **cash alternative.**

(b) **To raise cash** on the stock market, which will then be used to buy the target company's shares. To the target company shareholders, this is a cash bid.

Sometimes, a company might acquire another in a share exchange, but the shares are then **sold immediately** on a stock market to raise cash for the seller.

Whatever the detailed arrangements of a takeover with paper, the end result will be an **increase in the issued share capital of the predator company**.

1.5 Use of convertible loan stock

Alternative forms of paper consideration, including debentures, loan stock and preference shares, are not so commonly used, due to

- Difficulties in establishing a rate of return that will be attractive to target shareholders
- The effects on the gearing levels of the acquiring company
- The change in the structure of the target shareholders' portfolios
- The securities being potentially less marketable, and possibly lacking voting rights

Issuing **convertible loan stock** will overcome some of these drawbacks, by offering the target shareholders the option of partaking in the future profits of the company if they wish.

Key term

> **Convertible loan stock** is a loan which gives the holder the right to convert to other securities, normally ordinary shares, at a predetermined price/rate and time.

1.6 The choice between a cash offer and a paper offer

The choice between cash and paper offers (or a combination of both) will depend on how the different methods are viewed by the company and its existing shareholders, and on the attitudes of the shareholders of the target company. Generally speaking, firms which believe that their stock is under valued will not use stock to do acquisitions. Conversely, firms which believe that their stock is over or correctly valued will use stock to do acquisitions. Not surprisingly, the premium paid is larger when an acquisition is financed with stock rather than cash. There might be an accounting rationale for using stock as opposed to cash. You are allowed to use pooling instead of purchase. There might also be a tax rationale for using stock. Cash acquisitions create tax liabilities to the selling firm's stockholders.

The use of stock to finance a merger may be a sign of an agency problem – that is, trying to exploit the information advantage the acquirer has over the target firm's shareholders. There is also the possibility that mergers may reflect agency problems between the acquiring firm's managers and its shareholders. There is evidence that mergers increase the private benefits of managers even when they do not benefit a firm's shareholders. A declining stock price may indicate that management is pursuing its own goals rather than solely attempting to maximize shareholder value.

The factors that the directors of the bidding company must consider include the following.

COMPANY AND ITS EXISTING SHAREHOLDERS	
Dilution of EPS	Fall in EPS attributable to existing shareholders may occur if purchase consideration is in equity shares
Cost to the company	Use of loan stock to back cash offer will attract tax relief on interest and have lower cost than equity. Convertible loan stock can have lower coupon rate than ordinary stock
Gearing	Highly geared company may not be able to issue further loan stock to obtain cash for cash offer
Control	Control could change considerably if large number of new shares issued
Authorised share capital increase	May be required if consideration is in form of shares. This will involve calling a general meeting to pass the necessary resolution
Borrowing limits increase	General meeting resolution also required if borrowing limits have to change

SHAREHOLDERS IN TARGET COMPANY	
Taxation	If consideration is cash, many investors may suffer immediate liability to tax on capital gain
Income	If consideration is not cash, arrangement must mean existing income is maintained, or be compensated by suitable capital gain or reasonable growth expectations
Future investments	Shareholders who want to retain stake in target business may prefer shares
Share price	If consideration is shares, recipients will want to be sure that the shares retain their values

1.7 Mezzanine finance and takeover bids

When the purchase consideration in a takeover bid is cash, the cash must be obtained somehow by the bidding company, in order to pay for the shares that it buys. Occasionally, the company will have sufficient cash in hand to pay for the target company's shares. More frequently, the cash will have to be raised, possibly from existing shareholders, by means of **a rights issue** or, more probably, by **borrowing from banks** or other financial institutions.

When cash for a takeover is raised by borrowing, the loans would normally be **medium-term** and **secured**.

However, there have been many takeover bids, with a cash purchase option for the target company's shareholders, where the bidding company has arranged loans that:

(a) Are **short-to-medium term**

(b) Are **unsecured** (that is, 'junior' debt, low in the priority list for repayment in the event of liquidation of the borrower)

(c) Because they are unsecured, attract a **much higher rate of interest** than secured debt (typically 4% or 5% above LIBOR)

(d) Often, give the lender the **option to exchange** the loan for shares after the takeover

This type of borrowing is called **mezzanine finance** (because it lies between equity and debt financing) – a form of finance which is also often used in **management buyouts** (which are discussed later in this chapter).

1.8 Earn-out arrangements

The purchase consideration may not all be paid at the time of acquisition. Part of it may be deferred, payable upon the target company reaching certain performance targets. You should refer back to Chapter 6.

2 Assessing a given offer

FAST FORWARD

Shareholders of both the companies involved in a merger will be sensitive to the effect of the merger on **share prices** and **earnings per share**.

2.1 The market values of the companies' shares during a takeover bid

Market share prices can be very important during a takeover bid. Suppose that Velvet Inc decides to make a takeover bid for the shares of Noggin Inc. Noggin Inc shares are currently quoted on the market at $2 each. Velvet shares are quoted at $4.50 and Velvet offers one of its shares for every two shares in Noggin, thus making an offer at current market values worth $2.25 per share in Noggin. This is only the value of the bid so long as Velvet's shares remain valued at $4.50. If their value falls, the bid will become less attractive.

This is why companies that make takeover bids with a share exchange offer are always concerned that the market value of their shares should not fall during the takeover negotiations, before the target company's shareholders have decided whether to accept the bid.

If the market price of the target company's shares rises above the offer price during the course of a takeover bid, the bid price will seem too low, and the takeover is then likely to fail, with shareholders in the target company refusing to sell their shares to the bidder.

2.2 EPS before and after a takeover

If one company acquires another by issuing shares, its EPS will **go up or down** according to the P/E ratio at which the target company has been bought.

(a) If the **target company's shares** are **bought** at a **higher P/E** ratio than the predator company's shares, the predator company's shareholders will suffer a **fall in EPS**.

(b) If the target company's shares are valued at a lower **P/E ratio**, the **predator company's shareholders** will benefit from a **rise in EPS**.

2.3 Example: Mergers and takeovers (1)

Giant Inc takes over Tiddler Co by offering two shares in Giant for one share in Tiddler. Details about each company are as follows.

	Giant Inc	Tiddler Co
Number of shares	2,800,000	100,000
Market value per share	$4	–
Annual earnings	$560,000	$50,000
EPS	20p	50p
P/E ratio	20	

By offering two shares in Giant worth $4 each for one share in Tiddler, the valuation placed on each Tiddler share is $8, and with Tiddler's EPS of 50c, this implies that Tiddler would be acquired on a P/E ratio of 16. This is lower than the P/E ratio of Giant, which is 20.

If the acquisition produces no synergy, and there is no growth in the earnings of either Giant or its new subsidiary Tiddler, then the EPS of Giant would still be higher than before, because Tiddler was bought on a lower P/E ratio. The combined group's results would be as follows.

	Giant group
Number of shares (2,800,000 + 200,000)	3,000,000
Annual earnings (560,000 + 50,000)	610,000
EPS	20.33c

If the P/E ratio is still 20, the market value per share would be $4.07 (20.33 × 20), which is 7c more than the pre-takeover price.

2.4 Example: Mergers and takeovers (2)

Redwood Inc agrees to acquire the shares of Hawthorn Co in a share exchange arrangement. The agreed P/E ratio for Hawthorn's shares is 15.

	Redwood Inc	Hawthorn Co
Number of shares	3,000,000	100,000
Market price per share	$2	–
Earnings	$600,000	$120,000
P/E ratio	10	

The EPS of Hawthorn Co is $1.20, and so the agreed price per share will be $1.20 × 15 = $18. In a share exchange agreement, Redwood would have to issue nine new shares (valued at $2 each) to acquire each share in Hawthorn, and so a total of 900,000 new shares must be issued to complete the takeover.

After the takeover, the enlarged company would have 3,900,000 shares in issue and, assuming no earnings growth, total earnings of $720,000. This would give an EPS of:

$$\frac{\$720,000}{3,900,000} = 18.5c$$

The pre-takeover EPS of Redwood was 20c, and so the EPS would fall. This is because Hawthorn has been bought on a higher P/E ratio (15 compared with Redwood's 10).

The process of buying a company with a lower P/E ratio and looking to boost its P/E ratio to the predator company P/E ratio is known as **bootstrapping**. Whether the stock market is fooled by this process is debatable. The P/E ratio is likely to fall after the takeover in the absence of synergistic or other gains.

2.5 Buying companies on a higher P/E ratio, but with profit growth

Buying companies with a higher P/E ratio will result in a fall in EPS unless there is profit growth to offset this fall. For example, suppose that Starving Inc acquires Bigmeal Inc, by offering two shares in Starving for three shares in Bigmeal. Details of each company are as follows:

	Starving Inc	Bigmeal Inc
Number of shares	5,000,000	3,000,000
Value per share	$6	$4
Annual earnings		
Current	$2,000,000	$600,000
Next year	$2,200,000	$950,000
EPS	40c	20c
P/E ratio	15	20

Starving Inc is acquiring Bigmeal Inc on a higher P/E ratio, and it is only the profit growth in the acquired subsidiary that gives the enlarged Starving group its growth in EPS.

	Starving group
Number of shares (5,000,000 + 3,000,000 × 2/3)	7,000,000

Earnings

If no profit growth (2,000,000 + 600,000) $2,600,000   EPS would have been 37.14c
With profit growth (2,200,000 + 950,000) $3,150,000   EPS will be 45c

If an acquisition strategy involves buying companies on a higher P/E ratio, it is therefore essential for continuing EPS growth that the acquired companies offer prospects of strong profit growth.

2.6 Further points to consider: net assets per share and the quality of earnings

There are circumstances where a dilution of earnings is acceptable if any of the following benefits arise as a result:

- Earnings growth
- Quality of earnings acquired is superior
- Dilution of earnings compensated by an increase in net asset backing

You might think that **dilution of earnings** must be avoided at all costs. However, there are **three** cases where a dilution of earnings might be accepted on an acquisition if there were other advantages to be gained.

(a)   **Earnings growth** may hide the dilution in EPS as above

(b)   A company might be willing to accept earnings dilution if the **quality of the acquired company's earnings** is superior to that of the acquiring company

(c)   A trading company with high earnings, but with few assets, may want to increase its assets base by acquiring a company which is strong in assets but weak in earnings so that assets and earnings get more into line with each other. In this case, **dilution in earnings is compensated for by an increase in net asset backing.**

Question
Effect of acquisition

Intangible Inc has an issued capital of 2,000,000 $1 ordinary shares. Net assets (excluding goodwill) are $2,500,000 and annual earnings average $1,500,000. The company is valued by the stock market on a P/E ratio of 8. Tangible Co has an issued capital of 1,000,000 ordinary shares. Net assets (excluding goodwill) are $3,500,000 and annual earnings average $400,000. The shareholders of Tangible Co accept an all-equity offer from Intangible Inc valuing each share in Tangible Co at $4. Calculate Intangible Inc's earnings and assets per share before and after the acquisition of Tangible Co.

(a) Before the acquisition of Tangible Co, the position is as follows.

Earnings per share (EPS) = $\dfrac{\$1,500,000}{2,000,000}$ = 75c

Assets per share (APS) = $\dfrac{\$2,500,000}{2,000,000}$ = $1.25

(b) Tangible Co's EPS figure is 40c ($400,000 ÷ 1,000,000), and the company is being bought on a multiple of 10 at $4 per share. As the takeover consideration is being satisfied by shares, Intangible Inc's earnings will be diluted because Intangible Inc is valuing Tangible Co on a higher multiple of earnings than itself. Intangible Inc will have to issue 666,667 (4,000,000/6) shares valued at $6 each (earnings of 75c per share at a multiple of 8) to satisfy the $4,000,000 consideration. The results for Intangible Inc will be as follows.

EPS = $\dfrac{\$1,900,000}{2,666,667}$ = 71.25c (3.75c lower than the previous 75c)

APS = $\dfrac{\$6,000,000}{2,666,667}$ = $2.25 ($1 higher than the previous $1.25)

If Intangible Inc is still valued on the stock market on a P/E ratio of 8, the share price should fall by approximately 30c (8 × 3.75c, the fall in EPS) but because the asset backing

$\left(\dfrac{\text{Net assets exc goodwill}}{\text{Shares}}\right)$ has been increased substantially the company will probably now be

valued on a higher P/E ratio than 8.

The shareholders in Tangible Co would receive 666,667 shares in Intangible Inc in exchange for their current 1,000,000 shares, that is, two shares in Intangible for every three shares currently held.

(a) **Earnings**

	$
Three shares in Tangible earn (3 × 40c)	1.200
Two shares in Intangible will earn (2 × 71.25c)	1.425
Increase in earnings, per three shares held in Tangible	0.225

(b) **Assets**

	$
Three shares in Tangible have an asset backing of (3 × $3.5)	10.50
Two shares in Intangible will have an asset backing of (2 × $2.25)	4.50
Loss in asset backing, per three shares held in Tangible	6.00

The shareholders in Tangible Co would be trading asset backing for an increase in earnings.

3 Effect of an offer on financial position and performance

6/11

Often takeovers fail to achieve their full potential because of lack of attention paid to **post-acquisition integration**. A clear programme should be in place, designed to re-define objectives and strategy, and take appropriate care of the human element.

3.1 Effects on earnings

Failures of takeovers often result from **inadequate integration** of the companies after the takeover has taken place. There is a tendency for senior management to devote their energies to the next acquisition rather than to the newly-acquired firm. The particular approach adopted will depend upon the **culture** of the organisation as well as the **nature** of the company acquired and **how it fits** into the amalgamated organisation (eg horizontally, vertically, or as part of a diversified conglomerate).

One obvious place to start is to assess how the merger will affect earnings. P/E ratios (price to earnings per share) can be used as a rough indicator for assessing the impact on earnings. The higher the P/E Ratio of the acquiring firm compared to the target company, the greater the increase in Earnings per Share (EPS) to the acquiring firm. Dilution of EPS occurs when the P/E ratio paid for the target exceeds the P/E ratio of the acquiring company. The size of the target's earnings is also important; the larger the target's earnings are relative to the acquirer, the greater the increase to EPS for the combined company. The following examples will illustrate these points.

Question

Greer Company has plans to acquire Holt Company by exchanging stock. Greer will issue 1.5 shares of its stock for each share of Holt. Financial information for the two companies is as follows:

	Greer	Holt
Net income	$400,000	$100,000
Shares outstanding	200,000	25,000
Earnings per share	$2.00	$4.00
Market price of stock	$40.00	$48.00

Greer expects the P/E Ratio for the combined company to be 15. What is the expected share price after the acquisition?

Answer

Combined earnings = $400,000 + $100,000 = $500,000
Combined shares = 200,000 shares + (25,000 x 1.5) = 237,500
Combined EPS = $500,000/237,500 = $2.11
Expected price of stock = expected P/E ratio × combined EPS = 15 × $2.11 = $31.65

Question

Romer Company will acquire all of the outstanding stock of Dayton Company through an exchange of stock. Romer is offering $65.00 per share for Dayton. Financial information for the two companies is as follows.

	Romer	Dayton
Net income	$50,000	$10,000
Shares outstanding	5,000	2,000
Earnings per share	$10.00	$5.00
Market price of stock	$150.00	
P/E ratio	15	

Required

(a) Calculate the shares to be issued by Romer
(b) Calculate the combined EPS
(c) Calculate P/E ratio paid: price offered/EPS of target
(d) Compare P/E ratio paid to current P/E ratio
(e) Calculate maximum price before dilution of EPS

(a) Shares to be issued by Romer: $65/$150 × 2,000 shares = 867 shares to be issued.

(b) Combined EPS: ($50,000 + $10,000)/(5,000 + 867) = $10.23

(c) Calculate P/E ratio paid: price offered/EPS of target or $65.00/$5.00 = 13

(d) P/E ratio paid to current P/E ratio: since 13 is less than the current ratio of 15, there should be no dilution of EPS for the combined company.

(e) Maximum price before dilution of EPS: 15 = price/$5.00 or $75.00 per share. $75.00 is the maximum price that Romer should pay before EPS are diluted.

3.2 Effects on the statement of financial position

In this example we investigate the effects of a takeover of the financial position of a company by looking at the statement of financial position sheet of the company. ABC Co is planning to bid for DEZ Co. The acquisition will be funded by cash which ABC will borrow.

STATEMENT OF FINANCIAL POSITION OF ABC

Assets	$m	Liabilities	$m
Non-current assets	600	Short-term liabilities	30
Equity investments	20	Long-term liabilities	100
Receivables	15	Equity capital	15
Cash	45	Share premium	35
		Earnings	500
	680		680

STATEMENT OF FINANCIAL POSITION OF DEZ CO

Assets	$m	Liabilities	$m
Non-current assets	80	Short-term liabilities	10
Equity investments	5	Long-term liabilities	10
Receivables	25	Equity capital	20
Cash	10	Share premium	30
		Earnings	50
	120		120

This is a cash offer funded entirely by the issue of debt. The company makes an offer of $120m which is raised by issuing corporate bonds worth $120m.

STATEMENT OF FINANCIAL POSITION OF ABC AFTER THE OFFER

Assets	$m	Liabilities	$m
Non-current assets	600	Short-term liabilities	30
Equity Investments	20	Long-term liabilities	220
Receivables	15	Equity capital	15
Cash	45	Share premium	35
Investment	120	Earnings	500
	800		800

CONSOLIDATED STATEMENT OF FINANCIAL POSITION

Assets	$m	Liabilities	$m
Non-current assets	680	Short –term liabilities	40
Equity Investments	25	Long – term liabilities	230
Receivables	40	Equity Capital	15
Cash	55	Share premium	35
Goodwill	20	Earnings	500
	820		820

Chapter Roundup

- Payment can be in the form of **cash**, a **share exchange** or **convertible loan stock**. The choice will depend on available cash, desired levels of gearing, shareholders' taxation position and changes in control.

- Shareholders of both the companies involved in a merger will be sensitive to the effect of the merger on **share prices** and **earnings per share**.

- There are circumstances where a dilution of earnings is acceptable if any of the following benefits arise as a result:

  - Earnings growth
  - Quality of earnings acquired is superior
  - Dilution of earnings compensated by an increase in net asset backing

- Often takeovers fail to achieve their full potential because of lack of attention paid to **post-acquisition integration**. A clear programme should be in place, designed to re-define objectives and strategy, and take appropriate care of the human element.

Quick Quiz

1   What are the main factors a bidding company needs to consider in order to decide between a paper and a cash offer?

2   What are the main factors the shareholders of a target company need to consider in order to decide between a cash or a paper offer?

3   Yellow Company has plans to acquire Brown Company by exchanging stock. Yellow will issue 2 shares of its stock for each share of Brown. Financial information for the two companies is as follows:

	Yellow	Brown
Net income	500	200
Shares outstanding	300	50
Earnings per share $	2.5	3.8
Market price of stock	38	50

Yellow expects the P/E Ratio for the combined company to be 12. Produce an estimate of the value of the shares of the combined company.

Answers to Quick Quiz

1   Dilution of EPS
    Cost of the company
    Gearing
    Control
    Authorised share capital increase
    Borrowing limits increase

2   Taxation
    Income
    Future investments
    Share price

3   Combined earnings = $500,000 + $200,000 = $700,000
    Combined shares = 300,000 shares + (50,000 x 2) = 400,000
    Combined EPS = $700,000/400,000 = $1.75

    Expected price of stock   = expected P/E ratio × combined EPS
                              = 12 × $1.75 = $21.00

Now try the question below from the Exam Question Bank

Number	Level	Marks	Time
26	Introductory	15	27 mins

BPP
LEARNING MEDIA

Corporate reconstruction and reorganisation

Financial reconstruction

Topic list	Syllabus reference
1 Reconstruction schemes	E 1(a)
2 Financial reconstructions	E 1(a)
3 Financial reconstruction and firm value	E 1(b), 1(c)
4 Leveraged buy-outs (LBOs)	E 1(a), (b), (c)
5 Market response to financial reconstruction	E 1 (b)
6 Case study in financial reconstruction	E 1 (c)

Introduction

In this chapter we discuss financial restructuring in companies. Financial restructuring and other means of corporate re-shaping can take place when companies are in difficulties or seeking to change their focus.

Study guide

		Intellectual level
E1	**Financial reconstruction**	
(a)	Assess an organisational situation and determine whether a financial reconstruction is the most appropriate strategy for dealing with the problem as presented.	3
(b)	Assess the likely response of the capital market and/or individual suppliers of capital to any reconstruction scheme and the impact their response is likely to have upon the value of the organisation.	3
(c)	Recommend a reconstruction scheme from a given business situation, justifying the proposal in terms of its impact upon the reported, performance and financial position of the organisation.	3

Exam guide

As with mergers and acquisitions, most questions in this area are likely to be a mixture of calculations (for example assessing the financing mix for a management buy-out) and narrative (discussing the implications of a scheme of reconstruction on various interested parties). You may be asked to consider a reconstruction scheme and various alternatives (liquidation, selling off part or all of the company).

1 Reconstruction schemes

FAST FORWARD

Reconstruction schemes are undertaken when companies have got into difficulties or as part of a strategy to enhance the value of the firm for its owners.

1.1 Reconstruction schemes to prevent business failure

Not all businesses are profitable. Some incur losses in one or more years, but eventually achieve profitability. Others remain unprofitable, or earn only very small and unsatisfactory profits. Other companies are profitable, but run out of cash.

(a) A poorly performing company which is unprofitable, but has enough cash to keep going, might eventually decide to **go into liquidation**, because it is not worth carrying on in business. Alternatively, it might become the target of a successful takeover bid.

(b) A company which runs out of cash, even if it is profitable, might be forced into liquidation by **unpaid creditors**, who want payment and think that applying to the court to wind up the company is the best way of getting some or all of their money.

However, a company might be on the brink of going into liquidation, but hold out good promise of profits in the future. In such a situation, the company might be able to attract fresh capital and to persuade its creditors to accept some securities in the company as 'payment', and achieve a **capital reconstruction** which allows the company to carry on in business.

1.2 Reconstruction schemes for value creation

Reconstruction schemes may also be undertaken by companies which are not in difficulties as part of a strategy to create value for the owners of the company. The management of a company can improve operations and increase the value of the company by

(a) Reducing costs through the sale of a poorly performing division or subsidiary

(b) increasing revenue or reducing costs through the acquisition of a company to exploit revenue or cost economies

(c) improving the financial structure of the company.

1.3 Types of reconstruction

Depending on the actions that a company needs to take as part of its reconstruction plans, these schemes are usually classified in three categories

(a) **Financial reconstruction** which involves changing the capital structure of the firm

(b) **Portfolio reconstruction**, which involves making additions to or disposals from companies' businesses eg through acquisitions or spin-offs.

(c) **Organisational restructuring**, which involves changing the organisational structure of the firm.

1.4 Step-by-step approach to designing reconstructions

You can use the following approach to designing reconstructions.

Step 1 **Estimate** the **position** of each party if **liquidation** is to go ahead. This will represent the minimum acceptable payment for each group.

Step 2 **Assess additional sources of finance**, for example selling assets, issuing shares, raising loans. The company will most likely need more finance to keep going.

Step 3 **Design the reconstruction**. Often the question will give you details of how to do it.

Step 4 **Calculate** and **assess** the new position, and also how each group has fared, and compare with Step 1 position.

Step 5 Check that the company is **financially viable** after the reconstruction.

In addition you should remember the following points when designing the reconstruction.

(a) Anyone providing extra finance for an ailing company must be persuaded that the expected return from the extra finance is attractive. A **profit forecast** and a **cash forecast** or a **funds flow forecast** will be needed to provide reassurance about the company's future, to creditors and to any financial institution that is asked to put new capital into the company. The reconstruction must indicate that the company has a **good chance** of being **financially viable**.

(b) The actual reconstruction might involve the **creation of new share capital** of a **different nominal value** than existing share capital, or the cancellation of existing share capital.

It can also involve the conversion of equity to debt, debt to equity, and debt of one type to debt of another.

(c) For a scheme of reconstruction to be acceptable it needs to **treat all parties fairly** (for example, preference shareholders must not be treated with disproportionate favour in comparison with equity shareholders), and it needs to offer creditors a better deal than if the company went into liquidation. If it did not, the creditors would press for a winding up of the company. A reconstruction might therefore include an arrangement to pay off the company's existing debts in full.

Exam focus point

> Although assumptions may sometimes need to be made (and should be stated), you would not be expected to 'invent' basic financial data.

2 Financial reconstructions 12/10

Key term

> A **financial reconstruction scheme** is a scheme whereby a company reorganises its capital structure, including leveraged buyouts, leveraged recapitalisations and debt for equity swaps.

There are many possible reasons why management would wish to restructure a company's finances. A reconstruction scheme might be agreed when a company is in danger of being put into liquidation, owing debts that it cannot repay, and so the creditors of the company agree to accept securities in the company, perhaps including equity shares, in settlement of their debts. On the other hand a company may be willing to undergo some financial restructuring to better position itself for long term success.

2.1 Leveraged recapitalisations

In leveraged recapitalisation a firm replaces the majority of its equity with a package of debt securities consisting of both senior and subordinated debt. Leveraged capitalisations are employed by firms as defence mechanisms to protect them from takeovers. The high level of debt in the company discourages corporate raiders who will not be able to borrow against the assets of the target firm in order to finance the acquisition.

In order to avoid the possible financial distress arising from the high level of debt, companies that engage in leveraged recapitalisation should be relatively debt free, they should have stable cash flows and they should not require substantial ongoing capital expenditure in order to retain their competitive position.

2.2 Debt-equity swaps

A second way of changing its capital is to issue a debt/equity or an equity/debt swap. In the case of an equity/debt swap, all specified shareholders are given the right to exchange their stock for a predetermined amount of debt (ie bonds) in the same company. A debt/equity swap works the opposite way: debt is exchanged for a predetermined amount of equity (or stock). The value of the swap is determined usually at current market rates, but management may offer higher exchange values to entice share and debt holders to participate in the swap. After the swap takes place, the preceding asset class is cancelled for the newly acquired asset class.

One possible reason that the company may engage in debt-equity swaps is because the company must meet certain contractual obligations, such as a maintaining a debt/equity ratio below a certain number. Also a company may issue equity to avoid making coupon and face value payments because they feel they will be unable to do so in the future. The contractual obligations mentioned can be a result of financing requirements imposed by a lending institution, such as a bank, or may be self-imposed by the company, as detailed in the company's prospectus. A company may self-impose certain valuation requirements to entice investors to purchase its stock. Debt/equity swaps may also be carried out to rebalance a firm's WACC.

Question

Financing policy

For illustration, assume there is an investor who owns a total of $2,000 in ABC Inc stock. ABC has offered all shareholders the option to swap their stock for debt at a rate of 1.5. What is the amount worth of debt that the investor will receive?

Answer

The investor would receive, if he or she elected to take the swap, $3,000 (1.5 * $2,000) worth of debt, gaining $1,000 for switching asset classes. However, the investor would lose all rights as a shareholder, such as voting rights, if he swapped his equity for debt.

2.3 Leveraged buy-outs

A leveraged buy out is a transaction in which a group of private investors uses debt financing to purchase a company or part of a company. In a leveraged buy out, like a leveraged capitalisation, the company increases its level of leverage, but unlike the case of leveraged capitalisations, the company does not have access to equity markets any more. This is covered in more detail in section 4 of this chapter.

2.4 Dividend policy

A company may change its dividend policy as part of financial restructuring and increase retained earnings and therefore its equity base.

3 Financial reconstruction and firm value

The impact of a financial reconstruction scheme on the **value** of the firm can be assessed in terms of its impact on the **growth rate** of the company, its **risk**, and its **required rate of return**.

3.1 Effect on growth rate

The impact of changes in financial policy on the value of the firm can be assessed through one of the valuation models that we have considered in previous chapters. For example the growth rate following a financial restructuring can be calculated from the formula

Formula to learn

$$g = b\left(ROA + \frac{V_D}{V_E}\left(ROA - r(1-T)\right)\right)$$

Where ROA is the return on the net assets of the company
   b is the retention rate
   V_D is the book value of debt
   V_E is the book value of equity
   r is the cost of debt
   T is the corporate tax rate

Changes in the level of debt will be reflected in the growth rate through its impact on the debt ratio D/E. Similarly, changes in dividend policy can be reflected in the earnings growth rate. Changes in the dividend policy will change the value of b. Decreasing dividends (a higher b) will increase the growth rate, and increasing dividends will decrease the growth rate.

Question
Financing policy

A firm currently has a debt-equity ratio of 0.12 and a return on assets (ROA) equal to 15 percent. The optimal debt ratio is however much lower than the optimal level, since it can raise the debt-equity ratio up to 0.30 without increasing the risk of bankruptcy. The firm plans to borrow and repurchase stock to get to this optimal ratio. The interest rate is expected to increase from 7 percent to 8 percent. The tax rate is 25 percent and the retention rate is 50 percent. Find the impact of the increase in debt on the growth rate.

Answer

Before the increase in the debt ratio we have:

ROA = 0.15
b = 0.50
D/E = 0.12
r = 0.07
T = 0.25

$$g = b\left(ROA + \frac{V_D}{V_E}\left(ROA - r(1-T)\right)\right) = 0.5\left(0.15 + 0.12\left(0.15 - 0.07(1-0.25)\right)\right) = 0.08085$$

After the increase in the debt ratio we have:

ROA = 0.15
b   = 0.50
D/E = 0.30
r   = 0.08
T   = 0.25

$$g = b\left(ROA + \frac{V_D}{V_E}(ROA - r(1-T))\right) = 0.5\left(0.15 + 0.30(0.15 - 0.08(1 - 0.25))\right) = 0.0885$$

The increase in the debt-equity ratio will raise the growth rate from 8.085 percent to 8.85 percent, that is by nearly one percentage point.

Question

Dividend policy

Continuing the previous example suppose that the firm plans to reduce its dividend payout to 30 percent instead of increasing the debt ratio. What is the impact on the growth rate?

Answer

The growth rate before the reduction in the dividend payout ratio is 0.08085. The growth rate after the decrease in the payout rate (ie increase in b) is:

$$g = b\left(ROA + \frac{V_D}{V_E}(ROA - r(1-T))\right) = 0.7\left(0.15 + 0.12(0.15 - 0.07(1 - 0.25))\right) = 0.1132$$

The increase in the retention rate will raise the growth rate from 8.085 percent to 11.32 percent, that is over three percentage points.

3.2 Effect on systematic risk

The impact of changes in financial policy on the value of the firm can be assessed through one of the valuation models that we have considered in previous chapters. For example the growth rate following a financial restructuring can be calculated from the formula

$$\beta_e = \beta_a\left(1 + \frac{V_D}{V_E}(1-T)\right)$$

Where β_a = is the asset beta and
        β_e = is the geared beta

A higher level of debt relative will increase the geared beta of the company, and a lower level of debt will reduce it.

Question

Effect on risk

A firm currently has a debt equity ratio of 0.12 and an asset beta of 0.9. The optimal debt ratio is however much lower than the optimal level, since it can raise the debt/equity ratio up to 0.30 without increasing the risk of bankruptcy. The firm plans to borrow and repurchase stock to get to this optimal ratio. The tax rate is 25%. Find the impact of the increase in debt on the geared beta.

Before the increase in the debt ratio we have:

$D/E = 0.12$
$T = 0.25$
$\beta_a = 0.9$

$$\beta_e = \beta_a\left(1+\frac{V_D}{V_E}(1-T)\right) = 0.9\left(1+0.12\left(1-0.25\right)\right) = 0.981$$

After the increase in the debt ratio we have:

$D/E = 0.30$
$T = 0.25$
$\beta_a = 0.9$

The new beta following the change in the level of debt will be

$$\beta_e = \beta_a\left(1+\frac{V_D}{V_E}(1-T)\right) = 0.9\left(1+0.30\left(1-0.25\right)\right) = 1.1025$$

4 Leveraged buy-outs (LBOs)

FAST FORWARD

In an LBO a publicly quoted company is **acquired** by a specially established **private company.** The private company funds the acquisition by substantial borrowing.

4.1 Procedures for going private

A public company **'goes private'** when a **small group of individuals**, possibly including existing shareholders and/or managers and with or without support from a financial institution, **buys all of the company's shares.** This form of restructuring is relatively common in the USA and may involve the shares in the company ceasing to be listed on a stock exchange.

4.2 Advantages of leveraged buy-outs

(a)   The **costs of meeting listing requirements** can be saved.

(b)   The **company is protected** from **volatility** in share prices which financial problems may create.

(c)   The company will be **less vulnerable** to hostile takeover bids.

(d)   Management can **concentrate** on the **long-term needs** of the business rather than the short-term expectations of shareholders.

(e)   Shareholders are likely to be **closer to management** in a private company, reducing costs arising from the separation of ownership and control (the 'agency problem').

4.3 Disadvantages of leveraged buy-outs

The main disadvantage with leveraged buy outs is that the company loses its ability to have its shares publicly traded. If a share cannot be **traded** it may **lose some of its value**. However, one reason for seeking private company status is that the company has had difficulties as a quoted company, and the prices of its shares may be low anyway.

5 Market response to financial reconstruction

FAST FORWARD

The **market response** to financial reconstruction has been estimated from **empirical studies** of the **behaviour** of **share prices**.

The empirical evidence shows that the market responds positively to financial restructuring. The available empirical evidence shows that the market reacts positively to firms raising their level of debt up to a certain level, since the constraint that debt imposes on future cash flows makes companies choosier when selecting investment opportunities.

A number of studies have dealt with the performance of **leveraged buyouts**. Since the company becomes private as a result of the leveraged buyout we cannot assess the impact of the market. However most studies show that a company does significantly better after the leveraged buyout. More specifically leveraged buy-outs result in increases in free cash flow, improved operational efficiency and a greater focus on the company's core business. The causes of the improvement following financial restructuring are reportedly benign and cannot be attributed to lay-offs of employees – rather the increased efficiency of operations coupled with improved control of capital expenditure seem to account for much of the difference.

The empirical evidence also shows that leveraged buy-outs which involve divisions of companies seem to display larger improvement gains than corporate leveraged buy-outs. On the other hand, the authors do enter a caveat, as the risk of bankruptcy and financial disaster with leveraged buy-outs seems to be greater. Moreover, leveraged buy-outs would appear to under-invest in long-term assets where the risk is greater.

The market reaction to dividend changes has been studied extensively. Most studies show abnormally high returns for dividend increases and abnormally low returns for dividend decreases around the announcement days.

6 Case study in financial reconstruction

FAST FORWARD

A company **goes private** when a small group of individuals buys all the company's shares. Going private may **decrease costs** and make the company **less vulnerable** to hostile takeover bids.

6.1 Example: Financial reconstruction schemes

Crosby and Dawson Co is a private company that has for many years been making mechanical timing mechanisms for washing machines. The management was slow to appreciate the impact that new technology would have and the company is now faced with rapidly falling sales.

In July 20X1, the directors decided that the best way to exploit their company's expertise in the future was to diversify into the high precision field of control linkages for aircraft, rockets, satellites and space probes. By January 20X2, some sales had been made to European companies and sufficient progress had been made to arouse considerable interest from the major aircraft manufacturers and from NASA in the USA. The cost, however, had been heavy. The company had borrowed $2,500,000 from the Vencap Merchant Bank plc and a further $500,000 from other sources. Its bank overdraft was at its limit of $750,000 and the dividend on its cumulative preference shares, which was due in December, had been unpaid for the fourth year in succession. On 1 February 20X2, the company has just lost another two major customers for its washing machine timers. The financial director presents the following information.

If the company remains in operation, the expected cash flows for the next five periods are as follows.

	9 months to 31.12.X2	20X3	20X4	20X5	20X6
	$'000	$'000	$'000	$'000	$'000
Receipts from sales	8,000	12,000	15,000	20,000	30,000
Payments to suppliers	6,000	6,700	7,500	10,800	18,000
Purchase of equipment	1,000	800	1,600	2,700	2,500
Other expenses	1,800	4,100	4,200	4,600	6,400
Interest charges	800	900	700	400	100
	9,600	12,500	14,000	18,500	27,000
Net cash flow	(1,600)	(500)	1,000	1,500	3,000

Years ending 31 December (header spanning 20X3–20X6)

The above figures are based on the assumption that the present capital structure is maintained by further borrowings as necessary.

STATEMENTS OF FINANCIAL POSITION

	31.12.X0	31.12.X1	31.3.X2 Projected
	$'000	$'000	$'000
Assets employed			
Non-current assets			
Freehold property	2,780	2,770	2,760
Plant and machinery	3,070	1,810	1,920
Motor vehicles	250	205	200
Deferred development expenditure	–	700	790
Current assets			
Inventory	890	970	1,015
Receivables	780	795	725
	1,670	1,765	1,740
Current liabilities			
Trade payables	1,220	1,100	1,960
Bank overdraft (unsecured)	650	750	750
	1,870	1,850	2,710
	(200)	(85)	(970)
	5,900	5,400	4,700
Long-term liabilities			
10% debentures 20X8 (secured on Freehold property)	(1,000)	(1,000)	(1,000)
Other loans (floating charges)	–	(3,000)	(3,000)
	4,900	1,400	700
	$'000	$'000	$'000
Ordinary shares of $1	3,500	3,500	3,500
8% Cumulative preference shares	1,000	1,000	1,000
Accumulated reserves/(accumulated deficit)	400	(3,100)	(3,800)
	4,900	1,400	700

Other information

1   The freehold property was revalued on 31 December 20X0. It is believed that its net disposal value at 31 March 20X2 will be about $3,000,000.

2   A substantial quantity of old plant was sold during the second six months of 20X1 to help pay for the new machinery needed. It is estimated that the break up value of the plant at 31 March 20X2 will be about $1,400,000.

3   The motor vehicles owned at 31 March 20X2 could be sold for $120,000.

4   Much of the work done on the new control linkages has been patented. It is believed that these patents could be sold for about $800,000, which can be considered as the break-up value of development expenditure incurred to 31 March 20X2.

5   On liquidation, it is expected that the current assets at 31 March 20X2 would realise $1,050,000. Liquidation costs would be approximately $300,000.

Suggest a scheme of reconstruction that is likely to be acceptable to all the parties involved. The ordinary shareholders would be prepared to invest a further $1,200,000 if the scheme were considered by them to be reasonable.

A full solution follows. Complete the first step yourself as a short question.

Question   Liquidation

Ascertain the likely result of Crosby & Dawson Co (see above) going into liquidation as at 31 March 20X2.

Answer

Break-up values of assets at 31 March 20X2	$'000
Freehold	3,000
Plant and machinery	1,400
Motor vehicles	120
Patents	800
Current assets	1,050
	6,370

Total liabilities at 31 March 20X2	$'000
Debentures	1,000
Other loans	3,000
Bank overdraft	750
Trade payables	1,960
	6,710

Solution to remainder of the example

If the company was forced into liquidation, the debentures and other loans would be met in full but that after allowing for the expenses of liquidation ($300,000) the bank and trade creditors would receive a total of $2,070,000 or 76c per dollar. The ordinary and preference shareholders would receive nothing.

If the company remains in operation, the cash position will at first deteriorate but will improve from 20X4 onwards. If the figures can be relied on and the trend of results continues after 20X6 the company will become reasonably profitable.

In the immediate future, after taking into account the additional amounts raised from the existing ordinary shareholders, the company will require finance of $400,000 in 20X2 and $500,000 in 20X3.

Vencap might be persuaded to subscribe **cash for ordinary shares**. It is unlikely that the company's clearing bank would be prepared to accept any shares, but as they would only receive 76c per dollar on a liquidation they may be prepared to transfer part of the overdraft into a (say) five year loan whilst maintaining the current overdraft limit. It is unlikely that a suitable arrangement can be reached with the trade payables as many would be prepared to accept 76c per dollar, rather than agree to a moratorium on the debts or take an equity interest in the company.

A possible scheme might be as follows.

1   The **existing ordinary shares** to be **cancelled** and **ordinary shareholders** to be **issued** with **$1,200,000 new $1 ordinary shares** for cash.

2   The **existing preference shares** to be **cancelled** and the holders to be issued with **$320,000 new $1 ordinary shares** at par.

3   The **existing debentures** to be **cancelled** and replaced by **$800,000 15% secured debentures** with a 15 year term and the holders to be issued with $400,000 of new $1 ordinary shares at par.

4   The **loan** 'from other sources' to be **repaid**.

5   The **Vencap Bank to receive $2,000,000 15% secured debentures** with a **15 year term** in part settlement of the existing loan, to be issued **$680,000 new ordinary shares** in settlement of the balance and to **subscribe cash for $800,000** of new ordinary shares.

6   The clearing bank to **transfer the existing overdraft** to a **loan account repayable over five years** and to keep the overdraft limit at $750,000. Both the loan and overdraft to be secured by a floating charge.

Comments

1   **Debenture holders**

    The debentures currently have **more than adequate asset backing**, and their current nominal yield is 10%. If the reconstruction is to be acceptable to them, they must have either **the same asset backing** or **some compensation** in terms of increased nominal value and higher nominal yield. Under the scheme they will receive securities with a total nominal value of $1,200,000 (an increase of $200,000) and an increase in total yield before any ordinary dividends of $20,000. The new debentures issued to Vencap can be secured on the freehold property (see below).

2   **Loans from other sources**

    It has been suggested that the 'loans from other sources' should be **repaid as**, in general, it is easier to arrange a successful reconstruction that involves fewer parties.

3   **Vencap**

    Vencap's existing loan of $2,500,000 will, under the proposed scheme, be changed into $2,000,000 of 15% debentures secured on the property and $680,000 of ordinary shares. This gives total loans of $2,800,000 secured on property with a net disposal value of $3,000,000. This is **low asset cover** which might increase if property values were to rise. The scheme will offer an improvement in security on the first $2,000,000 to compensate for the risk involved in holding ordinary shares. It has also been suggested that Vencap should be asked to subscribe $800,000 for new ordinary shares. The money is required to repay the 'loans from other sources' and to provide additional working capital. The issue of share capital would give the bank a total of 1,480,000 ordinary shares or 43.5% of the equity. From the company's point of view issuing new equity is to be preferred to loan stock as it will improve the gearing position.

4   **The clearing bank**

    In a liquidation now, the clearing bank would **receive approximately $573,000**. In return for the possibility of receiving the full amount owed to them they are being asked under the scheme to **advance a further $750,000**. By way of compensation, they are receiving the **security of a floating charge**.

5   **Preference shares**

    In a liquidation at the present time, the preference shareholders would receive nothing. The issue of 320,000 $1 ordinary shares should be acceptable as it is **equivalent to their current arrears of dividend**. If the preference shares were left unaffected by the scheme, the full arrears of dividend would become payable on the company's return to profitability, giving preference shareholders an undue advantage.

6 Ordinary shareholders

In a liquidation, the ordinary shareholders would also receive nothing. Under the scheme, they will **lose control of the company** but, in exchange for their additional investment, will still hold about 35.3% of the equity in a company which will have sufficient funds to finance the expected future capital requirements.

7 Cash flow forecast, on reconstruction

	$'000
Cash for new shares from equity shareholders	1,200
Cash for new shares from Vencap	800
	2,000
Repayment of loan from other sources	(500)
Cash available	1,500

The overdraft of $750,000 is converted into a long-term loan, leaving the company with a further $750,000 of overdraft facility to use.

8 Adequacy of funds

The statement of financial position below shows the company's position after the implementation of the scheme but before any repayments of short-term debt.

	$'000	$'000
Non-current assets		
Freehold property		2,760
Plant and machinery		1,920
Motor vehicles		200
Deferred development expenditure		790
		5,670
Current assets		
Inventory	1,015	
Receivables	725	
Cash	1,500	
	3,240	
Less current liabilities: Trade payables	(1,960)	
		1,280
		6,950
Less long-term liabilities		
15% debentures		(2,800)
Loan from clearing bank		(750)
		3,400
Ordinary shares of $1		3,400

It would seem likely that the company will have to make a bigger investment in working capital (ignoring cash) for the following reasons.

(a)   Presumably a substantial proportion of the sales will be exports which generally have a longer collection period than domestic sales.

(b)   It is unlikely that the trade creditors will accept the current payment position (average credit takes over two months) in the long term.

9 Will the reconstructed company be financially viable?

Assuming that net current assets excluding cash and any overdraft will, by the end of 20X2, rise from the projected figure of –$220,000 (1,015,000 + 725,000 – 1,960,000) to $500,000 and increase in proportion to sales receipts thereafter, that the equipment required in 20X2 and 20X3 will be leased on five year terms and that the interest charges (including the finance elements in the lease rentals) will be approximately the same as those given in the question, then the expected cash flows on implementation could be as shown below.

	9 months to 31.12.X2	20X3	20X4	20X5	20X6
	$'000	$'000	$'000	$'000	$'000
Receipts from sales	8,000	12,000	15,000	20,000	30,000
Purchase of equipment			1,600	2,700	2,500
Payments to suppliers	6,000	6,700	7,500	10,800	18,000
Other expenses	1,800	4,100	4,200	4,600	6,400
Interest charges	800	900	700	400	100
Lease rentals (excluding finance element) (say)	200	360	360	360	360
Bank loan repayment (say)	150	150	150	150	150
Invt. in working capital	720	250	190	310	630
	9,670	12,460	14,700	19,320	28,140
Net movement	(1,670)	(460)	300	680	1,860
Cash balance b/f	1,500	(170)	(630)	(330)	350
Cash balance c/f	(170)	(630)	(330)	350	2,210

These figures suggest that with an agreed overdraft limit of $750,000 the company will have **sufficient funds** to carry it through the next five years, assuming that the figures are reliable and that no dividends are paid until perhaps 20X4 at the earliest.

This scheme of reconstruction might not be acceptable to all parties, if the **future profits of the company** seem **unattractive**. In particular, Vencap and the clearing bank might be reluctant to agree to the scheme. In such an event, an alternative scheme of reconstruction must be designed, perhaps involving another provider of funds (such as another venture capitalist). Otherwise, the company will be forced into liquidation.

Exam focus point

In a reconstruction question you may be asked to set out the attributes of a successful reconstruction and discuss alternative strategies.

Chapter Roundup

- **Reconstruction schemes** are undertaken when companies have got into difficulties or as part of a strategy to enhance the value of the firm for its owners.

- The impact of a financial reconstruction scheme on the **value** of the firm can be assessed in terms of its impact on the **growth rate** of the company, its **risk**, and its **required rate of return**.

- In an LBO a publicly quoted company is **acquired** by a specialist established **private company.** The private company funds the acquisition by substantial borrowing.

- The **market response** to financial reconstruction has been estimated form **empirical studies** of the **behaviour** of **share prices**.

- A company **goes private** when a small group of individuals buys all the company's shares. Going private may **decrease costs** and make the company **less vulnerable** to hostile takeover bids.

Quick Quiz

1   Describe the procedures that should be followed when designing a financial reconstruction scheme.

2   Give five advantages of a public company going private.

Answers to Quick Quiz

1   (a)   Calculate what each party's position would be in a liquidation
     (b)   Assess possible sources of finance
     (c)   Design the reconstruction
     (d)   Assess each party's position as a result of the reconstruction
     (e)   Check that the company is financially viable

2   (a)   Saving of costs of legal formalities
     (b)   Protection from volatility in share prices
     (c)   Less vulnerability to hostile takeover
     (d)   More concentration on long-term needs of business
     (e)   Closer relationships with shareholders

Now try the question below from the Exam Question Bank

Number	Level	Marks	Time
27	Examination	30	54 mins

Business reorganisation

Topic list	Syllabus reference
1 Business reorganisation	E 2
2 Unbundling	E 2(a), (b)
3 Management buy-outs (MBOs) and buy-ins	E 2(c)
4 Unbundling and firm value	E 2(a), (b)

Introduction

In this chapter we discuss methods of business reorganisations concentrating primarily on methods of unbundling companies. Methods discussed include sell-offs, spin-offs, carve-outs, and management buy-outs.

Study guide

		Intellectual level
E2	**Business re-organisation**	
(a)	Recommend, with reasons, strategies for unbundling parts of a quoted company	3
(b)	Evaluate the likely financial and other benefits of unbundling	3
(c)	Advise on the financial issues relating to a management buy-out and buy-in	3

Exam guide

As with mergers and acquisitions, most questions in this area are likely to be a mixture of calculations (for example assessing the financing mix for a management buy-out) and narrative analysis (discussing the implications of a scheme of reconstruction on various interested parties). You may be asked to consider a reconstruction scheme and advise the board on the various alternatives (liquidation, selling off part or all of the company).

1 Business reorganisation

12/10

FAST FORWARD

Business reorganisations consist of portfolio restructuring and organisational restructuring.

Reorganisations of the operations and the structures of business is a constant feature of business life. Companies are restructuring in the pursuit of long term strategy in order to achieve a higher level of performance or in order to survive when existing structures and activities are problematic. Corporate restructuring is usually the result of extreme changes in corporate governance such as takeovers and bankruptcy, but it can also be initiated as a response to product market pressures and internal corporate controls. Companies which experience negative earnings due to competition, overexpansion, high costs and excessive debt respond in many ways such as cutting research and development expenditure, reducing debt levels, reducing employment levels and introducing changes in the internal organisation.

In Chapter 13 we classified business restructuring as financial, portfolio and organisational. The last two types of restructuring are collectively known as business reorganisations. However, all three types of restructuring are linked and it may be necessary for all types to be undertaken for a restructuring to be successful. In this chapter we concentrate primarily on portfolio restructuring.

1.1 Portfolio restructuring

FAST FORWARD

Portfolio restructuring consists of changes in the mix of assets owned by the firm or the lines of business in which the firm operates in order to increase the performance of the firm.

Key term

Portfolio restructuring is the acquisition or disposal of assets or business units by a company in the form of divestments, demergers, spin-offs or management buy-outs.

Portfolio restructuring involves a number of one-off diverse transactions such as the sale of underperforming assets, spin-offs and acquisitions which have permanent effects on the financial performance of the company. Thus portfolio restructuring can be seen as part of a strategy to increase the performance of the company which involves not only the buying and selling of a business but also the establishment of performance monitoring and evaluation systems.

1.2 Organisational restructuring

FAST FORWARD

Organisational restructuring consists of changes in the organisational structure of the firm, such as divisional changes and hierarchical structures.

Organisational restructuring involves significant changes in the way a company is organised. As part of such a restructuring a company may redraw divisional boundaries, it may flatten the hierarchical structure, it may streamline processes, it may adopt a different system of corporate governance and it may reduce employment.

Organisational restructuring on its own does not seem to have a significant effect on the performance of the company. However when in conjunction with other forms of restructuring it seems to be a more potent means of increasing performance.

2 Unbundling   12/10

FAST FORWARD

Unbundling is a portfolio restructuring strategy which involves the disposal and sale of assets, facilities, production lines, subsidiaries, divisions or product units.

Unbundling can be either voluntary or it can be forced on a company. A company may voluntarily decide to divest part of its business for strategic, financial or organisational reasons. An involuntary unbundling on the other hand may take place for regulatory or financial reasons. The main forms of unbundling are:

(a)   Divestments
(b)   Demergers.
(c)   Sell-offs.
(d)   Spin-offs
(e)   Carve-outs
(f)   Management buy-outs .

2.1 Divestments

FAST FORWARD

Divestment is the partial or complete sale or disposal of physical and organisational assets, the shutdown of facilities and reduction in workforce in order to free funds for investment in other areas of strategic interest.

In a divestment the company ceases the operation of a particular activity in order to concentrate on other activities. The rationale for divestment is normally to reduce costs or to increase return on assets. Divestments differ from the other forms of unbundling because they do not require the formation of a new company.

Key term

A **Divestment** is the disposal of a company's assets.

Divestments are undertaken for a variety of reasons. They may take place as a corrective action in order to reverse unsuccessful previous acquisitions, especially when the acquisition has taken place for diversification purposes. Divestments may also be take place as a response to a cyclical downturn in the activities of a particular unit or line of business. However, divestments may be proactive in the sense that a company may want to exit lines of business which have become obsolete and redeploy resources to activities with a higher return on invested capital.

Where divestments are part of a strategic response for business realignment, the issue of which assets to divest is as important as the decision of which assets to acquire. A company has to decide what constitutes core activities and where the next growth opportunities exist. The growth opportunities may be realized by concentrating on the core business, organic growth and development of the right product lines, or by acquisitions and investment in the right markets.

This refocus of the company priorities may imply that the company may decide to disengage from certain business activities.

2.2 Demergers

FAST FORWARD

> A **demerger** is the splitting up of corporate bodies into two or more separate bodies, to ensure share prices reflect the true value of underlying operations.

Key term

A **demerger** is the opposite of a merger. It is the **splitting up of a corporate body into two or more separate and independent bodies.**

For example, the ABC Group plc might demerge by splitting into two independently operating companies AB plc and C plc. Existing shareholders are given a stake in each of the new separate companies.

Demerging, in its strictest sense, stops short of selling out, but is an attempt to ensure that share prices reflect the true value of the underlying operations.

 Case Study

In March 2010, Liberty International, the UK real estate company, confirmed the demerger of its central London properties from its regional shopping centres. Two new companies – Capital Shopping Centres and Capital & Counties – are expected to be listed on the London Stock Exchange as early as summer 2010.

David Fischel, Liberty's chief executive, commented

'The Capital & Counties business... [is] a very different business to the shopping centre business... The demerger will enable Capital Shopping Centres and Capital & Counties to achieve greater value for shareholders over time than the current Liberty International would as one combined business.'

Source: *Financial Times*, 9 March 2010

2.2.1 Advantages of demergers

The main advantage of a demerger is its greater operational efficiency and the greater opportunity to realise value. A two-division company with one loss making division and one profit making, fast growing division may be better off by splitting the two divisions. The profitable division may acquire a valuation well in excess of its contribution to the merged company.

2.2.2 Disadvantages of demergers

(a)   **Economies of scale** may be **lost**, where the demerged parts of the business had operations in common to which economies of scale applied.

(b)   The **smaller companies** which result from the demerger will have **lower turnover**, profits and status than the group before the demerger.

(c)   There may be **higher overhead** costs as a percentage of turnover, resulting from (b).

(d)   The **ability** to raise **extra finance**, especially debt finance, to support new investments and expansion may be reduced.

(e)   **Vulnerability to takeover** may be **increased**. The impact on a firm's risk maybe significant when a substantial part of the company is spun off. The result maybe a loss in shareholder value if a relatively low beta element is unbundled.

2.3 Sell-offs

FAST FORWARD

A **sell-off** is the sale of part of a company to a third party, generally for cash.

Key term

A **sell-off** is a form of **divestment** involving the sale of part of a company to a third party, usually another company. Generally, cash will be received in exchange.

2.3.1 Reasons for sell-offs

As part of its strategic planning, it has decided to **restructure**, concentrating management effort on particular parts of the business. Control problems may be reduced if peripheral activities are sold off.

It wishes to sell off a part of its business which **makes losses**, and so to improve the company's future reported consolidated profit performance. This may be in the form of a management buy-out (MBO) – see below.

In order to **protect the rest of the business from takeover**, it may choose to sell a part of the business which is particularly attractive to a buyer.

The company may be **short of cash**.

A **subsidiary** with **high risk** in its operating cash flows could be sold, so as to reduce the business risk of the group as a whole. However as in point(e) in section 2.2.2 above, the reverse may actually be the case.

A **subsidiary** could be sold at a **profit**. Some companies have specialised in taking over large groups of companies, and then selling off parts of the newly-acquired groups, so that the proceeds of sales more than pay for the original takeovers.

Case Study

In July 2010, BP announced a £20 billion asset sale to help pay for the cost of the oil spill in the Gulf of Mexico. The plan, which is to take place over an 18 month period, includes the sale of businesses that are 'worth more to other companies than they are to BP'.

Part of the proceeds of the sales will be used to reduce BP's current £15 billion debt to between £6.4 billion and £9.6 billion.

Source: BP seeks sell-offs to plug £20bn hole, www.thisismoney.co.uk

2.3.2 Liquidations

The extreme form of a sell-off is where the entire business is sold off in a **liquidation**. In a voluntary dissolution, the shareholders might decide to close the whole business, sell off all the assets and distribute net funds raised to shareholders.

2.4 Spin-offs

FAST FORWARD

A **spin-off** is the creation of a new company, where the shareholders of the original company own the shares.

Key term

In a **spin-off**, a new company is created whose shares are owned by the shareholders of the original company which is making the distribution of assets.

In a spin-off:

(a) There is **no change** in the **ownership of assets**, as the shareholders own the same proportion of shares in the new company as they did in the old company.

(b) Assets of the part of the business to be separated off are transferred into the new company, which will usually have different management from the old company.

(c) In more complex cases, a spin-off may involve the original company being split into a number of separate companies.

For a number of possible reasons such as those set out below, a spin-off appears generally to meet with favour from stock market investors.

(a) The change may make a **merger** or takeover of some part of the business **easier** in the future, or may protect parts of the business from predators.

(b) There may be **improved efficiency** and more streamlined management within the new structure.

(c) It may be easier to see the value of the **separated parts** of the business now that they are no longer hidden within a conglomerate.

(d) The **requirements** of **regulatory agencies** might be met more easily within the new structure, for example if the agency is able to exercise price control over a particular part of the business which was previously hidden within the conglomerate structure.

(e) After the spin-off, shareholders have the opportunity to **adjust** the **proportions** of their **holdings** between the different companies created.

Case Study

In May 2009, Time Warner announced that it would spin off AOL as a separate independent company. This took effect in December 2009.

Jeff Bewkes, Time Warner Chairman and CEO stated that, with the spin-off, Time Warner had 'returned to [its] roots as one of the leading content companies in the world…[and believed] that AOL will have greater operational and strategic flexibility as a standalone company'.

Source: www.timewarner.com/corp/newsroom

2.5 Carve-outs

FAST FORWARD

A **carve-out** is the creation of a new company, by detaching parts of the company and selling the shares of the new company to the public.

Key term

In a **carve-out**, a new company is created whose shares are owned by the public with the parent company retaining a substantial fraction of the shares.

Parent companies undertake carve-outs in order to raise funds in the capital markets. These funds can be used for the repayment of debt or creditors or it can be retained within the firm to fund expansion. Carved out units tend to be highly valued.

3 Management buy-outs (MBOs) and buy-ins 12/10, 12/11

A **management buy-out** is the purchase of all or part of the business by its managers. Management buy-outs can be the best way of maintaining links with a subsidiary, and can ensure the co-operation of management if a disposal is inevitable.

The main complication with **management buy-outs** is obtaining the consent of all parties involved. Venture capital may be an important source of financial backing.

Key term

> A **management buy-out** is the purchase of all or part of a business from its owners by its managers.

For example, the directors of a subsidiary company in a group might buy the company from the holding company, with the intention of running it as proprietors of a separate business entity.

(a)   **To the managers,** the buy-out would be a method of setting up in business for themselves.

(b)   **To the group**, the buy-out would be a method of **divestment**, selling off the subsidiary as a going concern.

3.1 The parties to a buy-out

There are usually three parties to a management buy-out.

(a)   A **management team** wanting to make a buy-out. This team ought to have the skills and ability to convince financial backers that it is worth supporting.

(b)   **Directors** of a group of companies, who make the divestment decision.

(c)   **Financial backers** of the buy-out team, who will usually want an equity stake in the bought-out business, because of the **venture capital risk** they are taking. Often, several financial backers provide the venture capital for a single buy-out.

The management team making the buy-out would probably have the aims of setting up in business themselves, being owners rather than mere employees; or avoiding redundancy, when the subsidiary is threatened with closure.

3.2 Reasons for a management buy-out

A large organisation's board of directors may agree to a management buy-out of a subsidiary for any of a number of different reasons.

(a)   The **subsidiary** may be **peripheral** to the group's mainstream activities, and no longer fit in with the group's overall strategy.

(b)   The **group may** wish to **sell off a loss-making subsidiary**, and a management team may think that it can restore the subsidiary's fortunes.

(c)   The parent company may need to **raise cash quickly**.

(d)   The subsidiary may be part of a **group** that has just been **taken over** and the new parent company may wish to sell off parts of the group it has just acquired.

(e)   The **best offer price** might come from a **small management group** wanting to arrange a buy-out.

(f)   When a group has taken the decision to sell a subsidiary, it will probably get better co-operation from the management and employees of the subsidiary if the sale is a management buy-out.

(g)   The sale can be arranged more quickly than a **sale** to an **external party**.

(h)   The selling organisation is more likely to be able to maintain beneficial links with a segment sold to management rather than to an **external party**.

A private company's shareholders might agree to sell out to a management team because they need cash, they want to retire, or the business is not profitable enough for them.

To help convince a bank or other institution that it can run the business successfully, the management team should prepare a **business plan** and estimates of sales, costs, profits and cash flows, in reasonable detail.

 Case Study

According to a survey in 2011 by private bank Coutts the number of business owners considering a management buy-out (MBO) has risen by a third in the past three years but only accounts for18 per cent of would-be sellers. In addition only 30 per cent of those who had completed an MBO said that it represented the best form of exit, and 55 per cent said it was the only way they could exit the business or it offered best value.

3.3 The role of the venture capitalist

Knowledge brought forward from earlier studies

Venture capital

- **Venture capital** is risk capital, normally provided in return for an equity stake.

- Examples of **venture capital organisations** in the UK are 3i, Equity Capital for industry and the various venture capital subsidiaries of the clearing banks.

- Venture capital **may be provided to fund** business start-ups, business development, MBOs and the purchase of shares from one of the owners of the business.

- Venture capital can also be provided through **venture capital funds**, which is a pool of finance provided by a variety of investors, which will then be applied to MBOs or expansion projects.

- Venture capitalists will normally require an **equity stake** in the company and may wish to have a **representative on the board** to look after its interests.

- A number of clearly defined **exit routes** will be sought by the venture capitalists in order to ensure the easy realisation of their investment when required.

Venture capitalists are far more inclined to fund MBOs, management buy-ins (MBI) and corporate expansion projects than the more risky and relatively costly early stage investments such as start-ups. The minimum investment considered in the UK will normally be around £100,000, with average investment of £1m - £2m.

Whilst the return required on venture capital for the high-risk, early stage investments may be as high as 80%, where the funding is for a well established business with sound management, it is more commonly around the 25-30% mark. Whilst this may be achieved by the successful investments, of course there will be many more that fail, and the overall returns on venture capital funds averages out at around 10-15%.

For MBOs and MBIs the venture capitalist will not necessarily provide the majority of the finance – a £50m buy-out may be funded by, say, £15m venture capital, £20m debt finance and £15m mezzanine debt, discussed earlier.

Venture capital funds may require:
- A 20–30% shareholding
- Special rights to appoint a number of directors
- The company to seek their prior approval for new issues or acquisitions

3.3.1 Exit strategies

Venture capitalists generally like to have a predetermined **target exit date,** the point at which they can recoup some or all of their investment in an MBO. At the outset, they will wish to establish various **exit routes**, the possibilities including

(a) The sale of shares to the public or to institutional investors following a **flotation** of the company's shares on a recognised stock exchange, or on the equivalent of the UK's Alternative Investment Market (AIM)

(b) The **sale** of the company to another firm

(c) The **repurchase** of the venture capitalist's shares by the company or its owners

(d) The sales of the venture capitalist's shares to an **institution** such as an investment trust

3.4 The appraisal of proposed buy-outs

3.4.1 How likely is a management buy-out to succeed?

Management-owned companies seem to achieve better performance probably because of:

- A **favourable buy-out price** having been achieved
- **Personal motivation and determination**
- **Quicker decision making** and so **more flexibility**
- **Keener decisions** and action on pricing and debt collection
- **Savings in overheads**, eg in contributions to a large head office

However, many management buy-outs, once they occur, begin with some redundancies to cut running costs.

3.4.2 How should an institutional investor evaluate a buy-out?

An institutional investor (such as a venture capitalist) should evaluate a buy-out before deciding whether or not to finance. Aspects of any buy-out that ought to be checked are as follows.

(a) Does the management team have the **full range of management skills** that are needed (for example a technical expert and a finance director)? Does it have the right blend of experience? Does it have the commitment?

(b) **Why** is the **company for sale**? The possible reasons for buy-outs have already been listed. If the reason is that the parent company wants to get rid of a loss-making subsidiary, what evidence is there to suggest that the company can be made profitable after a buy-out?

(c) What are the **projected profits and cash flows** of the business? The prospective returns must justify the risks involved.

(d) What is **being bought**? The buy-out team might be buying the shares of the company, or only selected assets of the company. Are the assets that are being acquired sufficient for the task? Will more assets have to be bought? When will the existing assets need replacing? How much extra finance would be needed for these asset purchases? Can the company be operated profitably?

(e) What is the **price**? Is the price right or is it too high?

(f) What **financial contribution** can be made by members of the management team themselves?

(g) What are the **exit routes** and when might they be taken?

3.5 The financial arrangements in a typical buy-out

Typically, the **buy-out team** will have a **minority** of the equity in the bought-out company, with the **various financial backers** holding a **majority** of the shares between them. A buy-out might have several financial backers, each providing finance in exchange for some equity.

Investors of venture capital usually want the **managers to be financially committed**. Individual managers could borrow personally from a bank, say $20,000 to $50,000.

The suppliers of equity finance might insist on investing part of their capital in the form of **redeemable convertible preference shares**. These often have voting rights should the preference dividend fall in arrears, giving increased influence over the company's affairs. They are issued in a redeemable form to give some hope of taking out part of the investment if it does not develop satisfactorily, and in convertible form for the opposite reason: to allow an increased stake in the equity of a successful company.

3.6 Problems with buy-outs

A common problem with management buy-outs is that the managers have little or no experience in **financial management** or **financial accounting**.

Other problems are:

(a) Tax and legal complications

(b) Difficulties in deciding on a fair price to be paid

(c) Convincing employees of the need to change working practices

(d) Inadequate cash flow to finance the maintenance and replacement of tangible fixed assets

(e) The maintenance of previous employees' pension rights

(f) Accepting the board representation requirement that many sources of funds will insist upon

(g) The loss of key employees if the company moves geographically, or wage rates are decreased too far, or employment conditions are unacceptable in other ways

(h) Maintaining continuity of relationships with suppliers and customers

3.7 Buy-ins

Key term

> **'Buy-in'** is when a team of **outside managers**, as opposed to managers who are already running the business, mount a takeover bid and then run the business themselves.

A management buy-in might occur when a business venture is running into trouble, and a group of outside managers see an opportunity to take over the business and restore its profitability.

Alternatively, research suggests that buy-ins often occur when the major shareholder of a small family company wishes to retire.

Many features are common to management buy-outs and buy-ins, including **financing**.

Buy-ins work best for companies where the existing managers are being replaced by managers of **much better quality**. However, managers who come in from outside may take **time** to get used to the company, and may encounter **opposition** from employees if they seek to introduce significant changes.

4 Unbundling and firm value

FAST FORWARD

> The main effect of **unbundling** on the **value** of the **firm** comes through changes in the **return on assets** and the **asset beta**.

4.1 Effect on growth rate

The impact of unbundling on the value of the firm can be assessed through one of the valuation models that we have considered in previous chapters. For example the growth rate following a restructuring can be calculated from the formula:

Formula to learn

$$g = b\left(ROA + \frac{V_D}{V_E}(ROA - r(1-T)) \right)$$

Where ROA is the return on the net assets of the company

b is the retention rate

V_D is the market value of debt

V_E is the market value of equity

r is the cost of debt

T is the corporate tax rate

When firms divest themselves of existing investments, they affect their expected return on assets, as good projects increase the return on assets, (ROA) and bad projects reduce the return –and any investment decision taken by firms affects their riskiness and therefore the asset beta β_a.

Question

A firm is expected to divest itself of unrelated divisions, which have historically had lower returns on assets. As a result of the divestment the return on equity is expected to increase from 10 percent to 15 percent. Calculate the effect on the earnings growth rate if the debt to equity ratio is 0.30, the tax rate is 0.25, the retention rate is 0.50 and the interest rate on debt is 8 percent.

Answer

Before the restructuring the growth rate is equal to:

$$g = b\left(ROA + \frac{V_D}{V_E}(ROA - r(1-T))\right) = 0.5\big(0.10 + 0.3(0.10 - 0.08(1-0.25))\big) = 0.056$$

After the restructuring the growth rate is equal to:

$$g = b\left(ROA + \frac{V_D}{V_E}(ROA - r(1-T))\right) = 0.5\big(0.15 + 0.3(0.15 - 0.08(1-0.25))\big) = 0.0885$$

The restructuring has increased the growth rate from 5.6 percent to 8.85 percent.

Question

The business risk of an oil company which has diversified into a number of other activities such as leisure and tourism is 1.3. If the oil company divested itself of all other activities and concentrated on its core business, its beta, based on the observed beta of oil companies with similar financial structure is expected to be 1.4 (β_e =1.4). If the tax rate is 0.25 and the debt to equity ratio is 0.30, calculate the business risk following the divestment of business.

Answer

The beta of the company is related to its business beta through the relationship:

$$\beta_e = \beta_a\left(1 + \frac{V_D}{V_E}(1-T)\right)$$

The business risk is calculated from:

$$\beta_a = \frac{\beta_e}{\left(1 + \frac{V_D}{V_E}(1-T)\right)} = \frac{1.4}{\left(1 + 0.3(1-0.25)\right)} = 1.143$$

After the restructuring the business risk of the company is reduced from 1.3 to 1.143 implying a lower cost of equity and consequently a higher value of equity.

Chapter Roundup

- **Business reorganisations** consist of portfolio restructuring and organisational restructuring.

- **Portfolio restructuring** consists of changes in the mix of assets owned by the firm or the lines of business in which the firm operates in order to increase the performance of the firm.

- **Organisational restructuring** consists of changes in the organisational structure of the firm, such as divisional changes and hierarchical structures.

- **Unbundling** is a portfolio restructuring strategy which involves the disposal and sale of assets, facilities, production lines, subsidiaries, divisions or product units.

- **Divestment** is the partial or complete sale or disposal of physical and organisational assets, the shut-down of facilities and reduction in workforce in order to free funds for investment in other areas of strategic interest.

- A **demerger** is the splitting up of corporate bodies into two or more separate bodies, to ensure share prices reflect the true value of underlying operations.

- A **sell-off** is the sale of part of a company to a third party, generally for cash.

- A **spin-off** is the creation of a new company, where the shareholders of the original company own the shares

- A **carve-out** is the creation of a new company, by detaching parts of the company and selling the shares of the new company to the public.

- A **management buy-out** is the purchase of all or part of the business by its managers. Management buy-outs can be the best way of maintaining links with a subsidiary, and can ensure the co-operation of management if a disposal is inevitable

- The main complication with **management buy-outs** is obtaining the consent of all parties involved. Venture capital may be an important source of financial backing.

- The main effect of **unbundling** on the **value** of the **firm** comes through changes in the **return on assets** and the **asset beta**.

Quick Quiz

1 **Fill in the blank**

A .... is a splitting up of a corporate body into two independent bodies

2 **Fill in the blank**

A .... involves the sale of part of a company to a third party.

3 **Fill in the blank**

In a .... , a new company is created whose shares are owned by the shareholders of the old company.

4 Name three factors that an institutional investor will consider when deciding whether to invest in a management buy-out.

5 Give four examples of possible exit strategies for a venture capitalist.

6 What is a management buy-in?

Answers to Quick Quiz

1 Demerger

2 Sell-off

3 Spin-off

4 Any three of:

    (a)   Management skills
    (b)   Reason why company is for sale
    (c)   Projected profits and cash flows of the business
    (d)   What is being bought
    (e)   Price
    (f)   Financial contribution made by the management team
    (g)   Exit routes

5   (a)   Sale of shares to public or institutional investors following a flotation
    (b)   Sale of shares to another company
    (c)   Sale to company itself or its owners
    (d)   Sale to institution management

6 A buy-in is when a team of outside managers mount a takeover bid and run the business.

Now try the question below from the Exam Question Bank

Number	Level	Marks	Time
28	Introductory	12	22 mins

Treasury and advanced risk management techniques

The role of the treasury function in multinationals

Topic list	Syllabus reference
1 The role of financial and money markets	F 1 (a)
2 Banks and other financial institutions in the money markets	F 1 (a)
3 Money market instruments	F 1 (a)
4 The treasury management function	F 1 (a)

Introduction

The purpose of this chapter is to discuss the role of the **treasury function** within a **multinational company**. The treasury function deals primarily with **short-term** decisions but in a way which is consistent with the **long-term** management objective of **maximising shareholder value**.

The chapter starts with a discussion of the role of the **money markets**, and how these provide **short-term finance** to companies. The chapter then discusses the role of banks and **financial institutions** in **financial intermediation** and the various instruments that are traded on this market.

Much of this chapter covers assumed knowledge of material that is now covered in Paper F9 *Financial Management.* However, if you studied Paper F9 before 2013 this material will be new to you and must be studied.

The chapter ends with a discussion of **the treasury management function** in a modern organisation.

Study guide

		Intellectual level
F1	**The role of the treasury function in multinationals**	
(a)	Discuss the role of the treasury management function within:	3
	(i) The short term management of the organisation's financial resources	
	(ii) The longer term maximisation of shareholder value	
	(iii) The management of risk exposure	

The first three sections in this chapter cover material that, from 2013, is part of the Paper F9 *Financial Management* syllabus and becomes assumed knowledge for Paper P4. If you have not covered these topics in Paper F9 then it is important that you read and understand these sections.

1 The role of financial and money markets

1.1 Financial markets

FAST FORWARD

> Financial markets are the markets where economic units with surplus funds, such as individuals, corporations, the government, or overseas investors lend funds to other economic units that want to borrow.

This function is shown diagrammatically below.

Those who have saved and are lending funds, the 'lender savers', are on the left, and those who must borrow funds to finance their spending, the 'borrower spenders', are on the right. The principal lender-savers are **households**, as well as **overseas institutions** and their **governments**, who sometimes also find themselves with excess funds and so lend them out. The most important borrower-spenders are corporations and governments, although individuals also borrow to finance the acquisition of durable goods or houses. The arrows show that funds flow from **lender-savers** to **borrower-spenders** via two routes.

The first route is the direct finance route at the bottom of the diagram, when borrowers borrow funds directly from lenders in financial markets by selling them **securities** (called financial instruments), which are **claims** on the **borrowers' future income** or **assets**.

Securities are **assets** for the **buyer** but **liabilities** for the seller. For example, if British Airways needs to borrow funds to pay for a new aircraft, it might borrow the funds from a saver by **selling** the saver a **bond**, a **debt security** that promises to make payments periodically for a specified period of time.

400 **15: The role of the treasury function in multinationals** │ Part F Treasury and advanced risk management techniques

BPP
LEARNING MEDIA

The channelling of funds from **savers** to **spenders** is a crucial function for the economy because the people who save are frequently not the same people who have profitable investment opportunities available to them, ie the entrepreneurs. Without financial markets, it is hard to transfer funds from a person with surplus funds and no investment opportunities to one who has investment opportunities but no funds. They would be unable to transact and both would be worse off as result. Financial markets are thus essential to promoting **economic efficiency**.

Financial markets not only allow funds to move from people who lack **productive investment opportunities** to people who have such opportunities but they also directly improve the well-being of consumers by allowing them to time their purchases better. They provide funds to young people to buy what they need and can eventually afford without forcing them to wait until they have saved up the entire purchase price. Financial markets that are operating efficiently improve the economic welfare of everyone in the society.

Financial markets can be classified in a variety of ways depending on the criterion selected. The most common groupings are primary and secondary markets, over the counter and exchange -based markets and money and capital markets. A brief description follows.

1.2 Primary and secondary markets

FAST FORWARD

Markets where a security is first issued are known as primary, and markets where a security is subsequently traded are known as secondary.

Key term

A **primary market** is a financial market in which new issues of a security are sold by the issuer to initial buyers. A **secondary market** is a market in which securities that have already been issued can be bought and sold.

1.3 Exchange and over the counter markets

FAST FORWARD

Secondary markets can be organised as exchanges or over the counter (OTC).

Secondary markets for financial securities can be organised as **exchanges**, where buyers and sellers of securities buy and sell securities in one location, the exchange. Examples of exchanges include the **London Stock Exchange** and the **New York Stock Exchange** for the trading of shares, the **Chicago Board of Trade** for the trading of commodities, and the **London International Financial Futures and Options Exchange (LIFFE)** for the trading of derivatives.

Alternatively, secondary markets can operate as **over-the-counter (OTC)** markets, where buyers and sellers transact with each other not through an exchange but through individual negotiation. The prices at which securities are bought over the counter do not differ from the corresponding transactions in an exchange because participants are in constant contact through computers with other market participants and can therefore transact at the most competitive price.

Securities that are issued in an **over the counter market** and can be **resold** are called **negotiable**, and securities that are **not allowed** to be **resold** after they are issued are called **non-negotiable**.

1.4 Money and capital markets

Capital markets are markets in which the securities that are traded have **long maturities**, ie represent **long-term obligations** for the **issuer**. Securities that trade in capital markets include shares and bonds. **Money markets**, on the other hand, are markets in which the securities that are traded have short maturities, less than a year, and the repayment of funds borrowed is required within a short period of time.

2 Banks and other financial institutions in the money markets

Financial intermediaries borrow money from the **lenders-savers** and then in turn make loans to the borrowers-spenders. The most common financial intermediaries are banks, insurance companies, pension funds, mutual funds, and finance companies. The process of **borrowing** and **lending** through **intermediaries** is called **financial intermediation or indirect finance**. As a source of funds for businesses, **indirect finance** is far more common than **direct finance**.

2.1 The importance of financial intermediation

Financial intermediation is important for two main reasons, namely the presence of **transaction costs** and the presence of **credit risk**.

The presence of transaction costs

Transactions costs (time and money spent carrying out financial transactions) are often prohibitively high for individual borrowers and lenders. Financial intermediaries, by handling a large volume of such transactions, develop an expertise that allows them to make additional transactions much more cheaply than any individual could. Financial intermediaries exploit **economies of scale**. By conducting a very **high volume of business,** they reach a point where the unit cost of transactions becomes smaller and smaller.

The presence of credit risk

The second reason for the importance of financial intermediaries is **asymmetric information**. The borrower has much better information about his ability and intention to repay than the lender does. This exposes the lender to **credit risk**. An individual lender will not normally have the ability to ascertain the **credit risk** of another individual. A bank on the other hand employs a number of specialists who are in a better position to evaluate the **credit quality** of an individual and it may have access to information on an individual that would be too costly for an individual lender to acquire.

2.2 Securitisation

FAST FORWARD

Securitisation is the process of converting **illiquid assets** into **marketable asset-backed securities**. The development of **securitisation** has led to **disintermediation** and a reduction in the role of financial intermediaries as borrowers can reach lenders directly.

Securitisation is the process of converting **illiquid assets** into **marketable securities**. These securities are backed by specific assets and are normally called **asset-backed securities** (ABS).

Securitisation started with banks converting their long-term loans such as mortgages into securities and selling them to institutional investors. One of the problems of banks as financial intermediaries, is the fundamental mismatch between the maturities of assets and liabilities. Securitisation of loans and sale to investors with more long-term liabilities reduces the mismatch problem and a bank's overall risk profile.

The oldest and most common type of asset securitization is the **mortgage-backed bond** or **security (MBS)**, although today one can expect virtually anything that has a cash flow to be a candidate for securitisation.

The development of securitisation has led to **disintermediation** and a reduction in the role of financial intermediaries as borrowers can reach lenders directly.

Key term

Disintermediation describes a decline in the traditional deposit and lending relationship between banks and their customers and an increase in direct relationships between the ultimate suppliers and users of financing.

BPP
LEARNING MEDIA

Cash flows before securitisation

Securitisation is also covered further in both Chapter 7a and Chapter 19.

3 Money market instruments

One way in which you can demonstrate competence in the performance objective 'manage cash using active cash management and treasury systems' is to ensure that any financial instruments held to meet liabilities mature on a timely basis. This section introduces various money market instruments and how they can be used to cover liabilities. The various features of each instrument will be useful in practice to determine the best one to use in different situations, not only to cover the risk involved but also to cover the risk for the required period.

FAST FORWARD

Money markets are the markets where **short-term instruments** are traded.

Money markets are the markets where **short-term instruments** are traded. Money markets are over the counter markets and the transactions take place between **institutions** rather than individual investors. The main characteristic of money market instruments apart from their short maturities (up to 12 months) is that they normally have only one cash flow. Money market instruments can be either **negotiable** or **non-negotiable**. They can also be **coupon bearing** or **discount instruments**.

Discount instruments do not pay interest. They are issued and traded at a **discount to the face value**. The discount is equivalent to the interest paid to the investor and is the difference between the purchase price of the instrument and the price at maturity.

Purchase Price = Face value – discount

The table below shows some of the **money market instruments** in the UK.

Coupon Bearing	Discount	Derivatives
Money Market Deposits	Treasury Bill (T-bill)	Forwards and Futures
Certificate of Deposit (CD)	Banker's Acceptance (BA)	Swaps
Repurchase Agreement (Repo)	Commercial Paper (CP)	Options

3.1 Money market deposits

LIBOR (London Interbank Offered Rate) is the rate of interest at which banks borrow from each other in the London interbank market

Money market deposits are **very short-term loans** between banks or other institutions including governments. These deposits can either be **fixed**, where the rate of interest and maturity dates are agreed at the time of the transaction or call deposits where the interest is variable and the deposit can be terminated if notice is given. The table below shows examples of market rates for money market instruments.

	Over-night	7 days notice	One month	Three months	Six months	One year
Interbank Sterling	$5\frac{3}{32} - 5$	$6 - 5\frac{3}{4}$	$6\frac{1}{16} - \frac{15}{16}$	$6\frac{3}{16} - 6\frac{1}{16}$	$6\frac{5}{16} - \frac{3}{16}$	$6\frac{3}{8} - 6\frac{1}{4}$

The table quotes **two rates**. The first figure in each column shows the **interest rate** at which a bank will **lend money**. This is called the **offer price**. The second number is the **rate** at which the bank will pay to **borrow money**. This is called the **bid price**. Note that whereas the convention in London is to quote **Offer/Bid,** in most other markets including the US, what is quoted is **Bid/Offer**.

The rate at which banks borrow from each other in the London market is of particular importance for money market. This is called LIBOR and is the most widely used reference rate for short-term interest rates globally for the settlement of money market derivatives. LIBOR rates are calculated for 10 currencies including the US dollar, pound sterling and the Euro. The following table shows examples of LIBOR rates for three currencies for different maturities.

	EUR	USD	GBP
Overnight	3.413	5.289	5.141
1 week	3.592	5.305	5.150
1 month	3.653	5.350	5.241
3 months	3.672	5.360	5.279
9 months	3.851	5.313	5.420
12 months	3.898	5.250	5.459

The LIBOR rates at **different maturities** define the **short-term yield curve** which is shown below.

LIBOR Yield Curve

Note that whereas the yield curve is given for specific maturities, the yield curve can be constructed by interpolation.

The LIBOR yield curve can also be used to estimate the **forward yield curve** which gives the interest rate between two future periods. The forward yield curve is used to price many money market derivatives.

3.2 Certificates of deposit

Key term

> A **Certificate of Deposit (CD)** is a certificate of receipt for funds deposited at a bank or other financial institution for a specified term and paying interest at a specified rate.

Certificates of deposit can be either **negotiable** or **non-negotiable**. The holder of a **negotiable CD** has two options: to hold it until maturity, receiving the interest and the principal or to sell it before maturity at the market price. A typical range of dollar certificates of deposit in terms of coupon and maturity is shown below, together with the corresponding yield.

Term	Coupon	Annual percentage yield
3 Months	5.950	6.080
3 Months	6.150	6.290
3 Months	6.200	6.350
6 Months	6.200	6.300
6 Months	6.300	6.400
9 Months	6.400	6.450

The coupon is expressed as an annual percentage rate and needs to be adjusted to reflect the fact that its maturity is less than a year. **Sterling CDs** assume there are **365 days** in the year, whilst **US CDs** assume **360 days**.

Formula to learn

> The value of the CD on maturity = face value $\times \left[1+\left(\text{coupon rate}\times\text{days to maturity}\div\text{days in the year}\right)\right]$

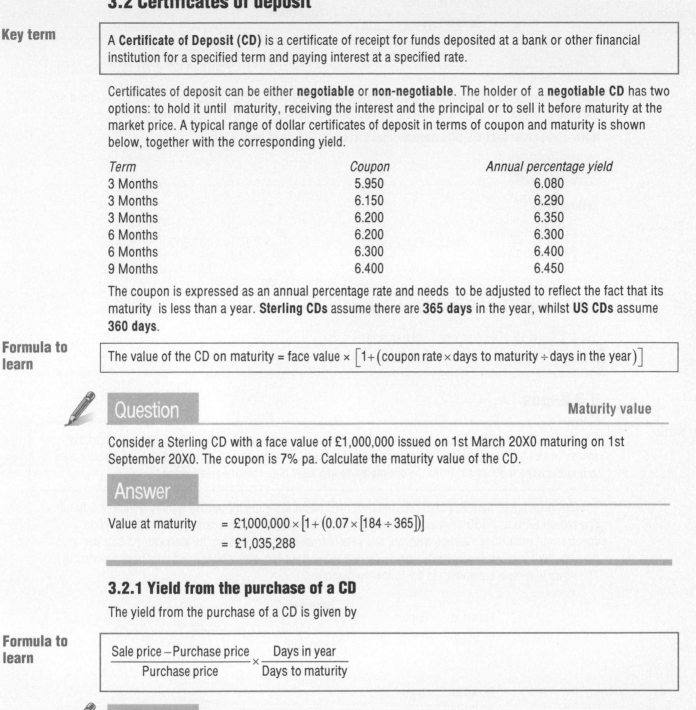

Question

Maturity value

Consider a Sterling CD with a face value of £1,000,000 issued on 1st March 20X0 maturing on 1st September 20X0. The coupon is 7% pa. Calculate the maturity value of the CD.

Answer

$$\text{Value at maturity} = £1,000,000 \times \left[1+\left(0.07 \times \left[184 \div 365\right]\right)\right]$$
$$= £1,035,288$$

3.2.1 Yield from the purchase of a CD

The yield from the purchase of a CD is given by

Formula to learn

> $$\frac{\text{Sale price} - \text{Purchase price}}{\text{Purchase price}} \times \frac{\text{Days in year}}{\text{Days to maturity}}$$

Question

Yield of CD

You have bought a sterling certificate of deposit for £1,012,000 and sold it 28 days later for £1,018,290. What is the yield ?

Answer

$$\frac{1,018,290 - 1,012,000}{1,012,000} \times \frac{365}{28} = 0.0810 \text{ or } 8.10\%$$

3.2.2 Fair price of a CD

The selling price of a CD can be calculated using the following formula.

$$\text{Selling price} = \left[1 + \left[\frac{\text{Days to maturity}}{\text{Days in a year}} \times \text{yield}\right]\right] \times \text{Purchase price}$$

✎ **Question**   **Value of CD after rate increase**

What will be the maturity value of a 90-day US CD yielding 10% if the investor pays $1,000,000 for it at the time of issue? If yields rise to 12% and the security is sold after 5 days, how much will it be worth?

Note: remember that US CDs assume that there are 360 days in a year.

Answer

Selling price

$$\left[1 + \left[\frac{\text{Days to maturity}}{\text{Days in a year}} \times \text{yield}\right]\right] \times \text{Purchase price} = \left[1 + \frac{90}{360} \times 0.10\right] \times 1,000,000$$

$$= \$1,025,000$$

If yield increases to 12% with 85 days remaining, the selling price will be :

$$\left[1 + \left(\frac{85}{360} \times 0.12\right)\right] \times 1,000,000 = \$1,028,333$$

3.3 Repos

A **repurchase agreement** is an agreement between two counterparties under which one counterparty agrees to sell an instrument to the other on an agreed date for an agreed price, and simultaneously agrees to buy back the instrument from the counterparty at a later date for an agreed price.

A repurchase agreement is a loan secured by a marketable instrument, usually a treasury bill or a bond. The typical term is 1-180 days and is an attractive instrument because it can accommodate a wide spectrum of maturities. A repo involves two sets of transactions. First on the start date, the dealer sells the security for cash. On maturity, the dealer will repay the cash with interest and take back the security. The flows in a repo are shown in the following diagram.

✎ **Question**   **Repo cash flows**

A company enters into a repo agreement with a bank and it sells $10,000,000 of government bonds with an obligation to repurchase the security in 60 days. If the repo rate is 8.2% what is the repurchase price of the bond?

Answer

The repurchase price of the bond is the sale price plus the interest on the cash received.

$$Interest = \$10,000,000 \times 0.082 \times \frac{60}{365} = \$134,794.52$$

Repurchase price = \$10,000,000 + \$134,794.52 = \$10,134,794.52

3.3.1 Yield

You should use the following formula when calculating the yield on a repo.

Formula to learn

$$\frac{\text{Number of days in the year}}{\text{Days to maturity}} \times \frac{\text{Selling price} - \text{purchase price}}{\text{Purchase price}}$$

Question

Repo yield

A company enters into a repo agreement with a bank and it sells \$10,000,000 of government bonds with a repurchase price in 60 days of \$10,002,993. What is the yield?

Answer

$$y = \frac{10,002,993 - 10,000,000}{10,000,000} \times \frac{365}{60} = 0.182\%$$

Key term

A **reverse repurchase** agreement (reverse repo) is an agreement for the purchase of an instrument with the simultaneous agreement to resell the instrument at an agreed future date and agreed price.

In a **reverse repo**, the dealer purchases the security initially and then sells it on maturity. Because the two parties in a **repo** agreement act as a buyer and a seller of the security, a **repo** to one party is a **reverse repo** to the other.

3.4 Treasury bills

Treasury bills are debt instruments issued by the government with maturities ranging from one month to one year. The discount rate of a treasury bill can be calculated using the following steps.

Formula to learn

$$\text{Discount rate} = \frac{\text{Number of days in the year}}{\text{Days to maturity}} \times \frac{\text{Face value} - \text{settlement price}}{\text{Face value}}$$

Question

Treasury bill discount

A 91-day Treasury bill with a face value of \$10,000,000 is issued for \$9,870,000. What is the discount rate?

Answer

$$\text{Discount rate} = \frac{365}{91} \times \frac{10,000,000 - 9,870,000}{10,000,000} = 5.2\%$$

3.5 Commercial paper

Commercial paper is **short-term unsecured corporate debt** with maturity up to 270 days. The typical term of this debt is about 30 days. Commercial paper can only be issued by large organisations with good credit ratings, normally to fund short-term expenditure. The debt is issued at a discount that reflects the prevailing interest rates.

Formula to learn

$$\text{Yield on commercial paper} = \frac{\text{Number of days in the year}}{\text{Days to maturity}} \times \frac{\text{Selling price} - \text{purchase price}}{\text{Purchase price}}$$

3.6 Banker's acceptance

Key term

Banker's acceptances are negotiable bills issued by companies and guaranteed by a bank.

Banker's acceptances are issued by firms to finance commercial transactions such as imports or the purchase of goods. The name derives from the fact that the bank has guaranteed the payment to the holder of the banker's acceptance, that is the bank has accepted responsibility for the payment. Banks guaranteed the payment by the company for a fee.

Banker's acceptances are sold on a **discounted basis** like T-bills and commercial paper. Because banker's acceptances are negotiable instruments, they can be bought and sold until they mature. The **rates** on banker's acceptances are **low** because, as they are guaranteed by a bank, the credit risk is low. The yield on a banker's acceptance can be calculated in exactly the same way as the yield on commercial paper given in section 3.5 above.

UK Banker's Acceptance are calculated on a **Actual/365 days** basis while in US they are calculated on an **Actual/360 days** basis.

The typical term is **30 to 180 days** and are issued by firms that do not have a sufficiently high credit rating to issue commercial paper.

4 The treasury management function

FAST FORWARD

Treasury management in a modern enterprise covers a number of areas including **liquidity management**, **funding management**, **currency management** and **corporate finance**.

One way in which you can demonstrate competence in the performance objective 'manage cash using active cash management and treasury systems' is to manage cash on a centralised basis to both maximise returns and minimise charges. This section introduces the treasury management function and how it can be used to pool cash from various sources which can be placed on deposit.

4.1 Treasury management

Large companies rely heavily for both long-term and short-term funds on the financial and currency markets. To manage cash (funds) and currency efficiently, many large companies have set up a separate **treasury department**.

The Association of Corporate Treasurers' **definition of treasury management** is 'the corporate handling of all financial matters, the generation of external and internal funds for business, the management of currencies and cash flows, and the complex strategies, policies and procedures of corporate finance'.

A treasury department, even in a large company, is likely to be quite small, with perhaps a staff of three to six qualified accountants, bankers or corporate treasurers working under a Treasurer, who is responsible to the Finance Director. In some cases, where the company or organisation handles very large amounts of cash or foreign currency dealings, and often has large cash surpluses, the treasury department might be larger.

4.2 The role of the treasurer

The diagrams below are based on the Association of Corporate Treasurers' list of experience it requires from its student members before they are eligible for full membership of the Association. Required experience gives a good indication of the roles of treasury departments.

(a) **Corporate financial objectives**

(b) **Liquidity management**: making sure the company has the liquid funds it needs, and invests any surplus funds, even for very short terms.

(c) **Funding management**

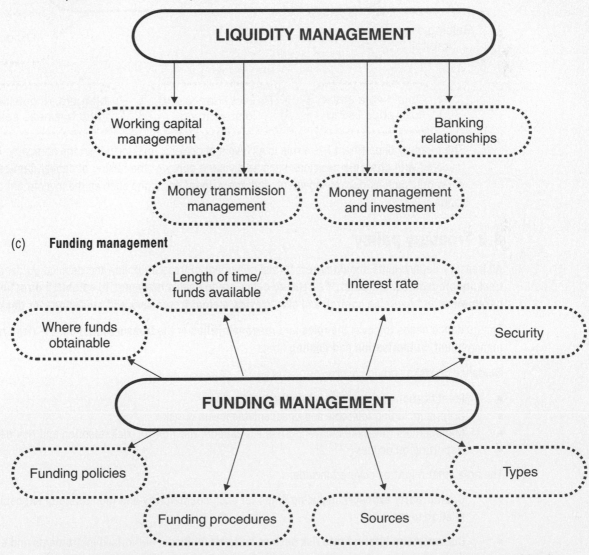

Funding management is concerned with all forms of borrowing, and alternative sources of funds, such as leasing and factoring.

(d) **Currency management**

Currency dealings can save or cost a company considerable amounts of money, and the success or shortcomings of the corporate treasurer can have a significant impact on the income statement of a company which is heavily involved in foreign trade.

(e) **Corporate finance**

The treasury department has a role in all levels of decision-making within the company. It is involved with **strategic** decisions such as dividend policy or the raising of capital, **tactical** decisions such as risk management, and **operational** decisions such as the investment of surplus funds.

4.3 Treasury policy

All treasury departments should have a formal statement of treasury policy and detailed guidance on treasury procedures. The aims of a treasury policy are to enable managers to **establish direction**, **specify parameters** and **exercise control**, and also **provide a clear framework and guidelines for decisions**.

The guidance needs to cover the **roles** and **responsibilities** of the **treasury function**, the **risks** requiring management, **authorisation** and **dealing** limits.

Guidance on **risks** should cover:

- Identification and assessment methodology
- Criteria including tolerable and unacceptable levels of risk
- Management guidelines, covering risk elimination, risk control, risk retention and risk transfer
- Reporting guidelines

The areas that might be covered include:

- **Counterparty exposure** including limits for each counterparty and monitoring of exposures in relation to the limits

- **Currency and interest rate risk** such as hedging methods, authorised instruments and exposure limits

- **Funding risk** including limits and targets for different sources of funding

- **Liquidity management** including permitted banks, netting and inter-group procedures

410   **15: The role of the treasury function in multinationals** | Part F Treasury and advanced risk management techniques

BPP
LEARNING MEDIA

- **Investment management** covering sources of funds, authorised counterparties and instruments, and inter-company funding

- **Bank relationships** specifying criteria for the choice of bank

The guidance must also include guidance on **measurement** of **treasury performance**. Measurement must cover both the **management of risk** and the **financial contribution** the department makes.

4.4 Advantages of a separate treasury department

Advantages of having a treasury function which is **separate from the financial control function** are as follows.

(a)   Centralised liquidity management avoids mixing cash surpluses and overdrafts in different localised bank accounts.

(b)   Bulk cash flows allow **lower bank charges** to be negotiated.

(c)   Larger volumes of cash can be invested, giving **better short-term investment opportunities**.

(d)   Borrowing can be agreed in bulk, probably at **lower interest rates** than for smaller borrowings.

(e)   Currency risk management should be improved, through **matching of cash flows in different subsidiaries**. There should be less need to use expensive hedging instruments such as option contracts.

(f)   A specialist department can employ staff with a **greater level of expertise** than would be possible in a local, more broadly based, finance department.

(g)   The company will be able to benefit from the use of **specialised cash management software**.

(h)   Access to treasury expertise should **improve the quality of strategic planning and decision making**.

4.5 Centralised or decentralised cash management?

Centralising the treasury management function allows businesses to **employ experts**, **deal in bulk cash flows** and hence **take advantage of lower bank** charges and **avoid a mix of surpluses and deficits**. **Decentralised** cash management can be **more responsive to local needs** however.

A large company may have a number of subsidiaries and divisions. In the case of a multinational, these will be located in different countries. It will be necessary to decide whether the treasury function should be centralised.

With **centralised cash management**, the central Treasury department effectively acts as the bank to the group. The central Treasury has the job of ensuring that individual operating units have all the funds they need at the right time.

4.5.1 Advantages of a specialist centralised treasury department

(a)   **Centralised liquidity management** avoids having a mix of cash surpluses and overdrafts in different local bank accounts and facilitates bulk cash flows, so that lower bank charges can be negotiated.

(b)   Larger volumes of cash are available to invest, giving better **short-term investment opportunities** (for example, money market deposits, high interest accounts and Certificates of Deposit).

(c)   Any borrowing can be arranged **in bulk**, at lower interest rates than for smaller borrowings, and perhaps on the eurocurrency or eurobond markets.

(d)   **Foreign currency risk management** is likely to be improved in a group of companies. A central treasury department can match foreign currency income earned by one subsidiary with expenditure in the same currency by another subsidiary. In this way, the risk of losses on adverse exchange

Part F Treasury and advanced risk management techniques | **15: The role of the treasury function in multinationals**   **411**

rate changes can be avoided without the expense of forward exchange contracts or other 'hedging' (risk-reducing) methods.

(e)   A specialist treasury department will employ **experts** with knowledge of dealing in futures, eurocurrency markets, taxation, transfer prices and so on. Localised departments would not have such expertise.

(f)   The centralised pool of **funds required for precautionary purposes** will be smaller than the sum of separate precautionary balances which would need to be held under decentralised treasury arrangements.

(g)   Through having a separate **profit centre**, attention will be focused on the contribution to group profit performance that can be achieved by good cash, funding, investment and foreign currency management.

(h)   Centralisation provides a means of exercising **better control** through use of **standardised procedures** and **risk monitoring**. Standardised practices and performance measures can also create productivity benefits.

4.5.2 Possible advantages of decentralised cash management

(a)   Sources of finance can be **diversified** and can be **matched with local assets**.

(b)   Greater **autonomy** can be given to subsidiaries and divisions because of the closer relationships they will have with the decentralised cash management function.

(c)   The decentralised Treasury function may be able to be **more responsive** to the needs of individual operating units.

However, since cash balances will not be aggregated at group level, there will be **more limited opportunities to invest** such balances on a short-term basis.

4.5.3 Centralised cash management in the multinational firm

If cash management within a **multinational firm** is centralised, each subsidiary holds only the minimum cash balance required for transaction purposes. All excess funds will be remitted to the central Treasury department.

Funds held in the central pool of funds can be returned quickly to the local subsidiary by telegraphic transfer or by means of worldwide bank credit facilities. The firm's bank can instruct its branch office in the country in which the subsidiary is located to advance funds to the subsidiary.

Question	Treasury centralisation

Touten is a US registered multinational company with subsidiaries in 14 countries in Europe, Asia and Africa. The subsidiaries have traditionally been allowed a large amount of autonomy, but Touten is now proposing to centralise most of the group treasury management operations.

Required

Acting as a consultant to Touten prepare a memo suitable for distribution from the group finance director to the senior management of each of the subsidiaries explaining:

(a)   The potential benefits of treasury centralisation; and

(b)   How the company proposes to minimise any potential problems for the subsidiaries that might arise as a result of treasury centralisation

MEMORANDUM

To: Directors of all foreign subsidiaries

From: Group Finance Director

Date: 1 July 20X0

Centralisation of treasury management operations

At its last meeting, the board of directors of Touten made the decision to centralise group treasury management operations. A further memo giving detailed plans will be circulated shortly, but my objective in this memo is to outline the potential benefits of treasury centralisation and how any potential problems arising at subsidiaries can be minimised. Most of you will be familiar with the basic arguments, which we have been discussing informally for some time.

What it means

Centralisation of treasury management means that most decisions on borrowing, investment of cash surpluses, currency management and financial risk management will be taken by an enhanced central treasury team, based at head office, instead of by subsidiaries directly. In addition we propose to set most transfer prices for inter-company goods and services centrally.

The potential benefits

The main benefits are:

(a)   **Cost savings** resulting from reduction of unnecessary banking charges

(b)   **Reduction of the group's total taxation charge**

(c)   **Enhanced control over financial risk**

Reduction in banking charges will result from:

(a)   **Netting off inter-company debts before settlement**. At the moment we are spending too much on foreign exchange commission by settling inter-company debts in a wide range of currencies through the banking system.

(b)   **Knowledge of total group currency exposure from transactions**. Amounts receivable in one subsidiary can hedge payables in another, eliminating unnecessary hedging by subsidiaries.

(c)   **Knowledge of the group's total cash resources and borrowing requirement**. This will reduce the incidence of one company lending cash while a fellow subsidiary borrows at a higher interest rate and will also eliminate unnecessary interest rate hedging. It will also facilitate higher deposit rates and lower borrowing rates.

Reduction in the group's tax charge will be made possible by a comprehensive centrally-set **transfer pricing policy**.

Enhanced control over financial risks will be possible because we will be able to develop a central team of specialists who will have a clear-cut strategy on hedging and risk management. Many of you have requested help in this area.

This team will be able to ensure that decisions are taken in line with **group strategy** and will also be able to provide you with enhanced financial information to assist you with your own decision making.

Potential problems for subsidiaries and their solution

Our group culture is one of **decentralisation** and **enablement of management at individual subsidiary level**. There is no intention to change this culture. Rather, it is hoped that releasing you from specialist treasury decisions will enable you to devote more time to developing your own business units.

The system can only work properly, however, if **information exchange** between head office and subsidiaries is swift and efficient. Enhanced computer systems are to be provided at all centres to assist you with daily reports. It is also important that you keep head office informed of all local conditions that could be beneficial to the treasury function, such as the availability of local subsidised loans, as well as potential local risks such as the threat of exchange control restrictions.

You will find that movements in your cash balances will be affected by **group policy**, as well as reported profitability. Any adjustments made by head office will be eliminated when preparing the performance reports for your own business units and we will ensure that joint venture partners are not penalised by group policy.

Please contact me with any further comments that you may have on our new treasury policy.

4.6 The treasury department as cost centre or profit centre

The treasury department is usually run as a **cost centre** if its main focus is to keep costs within budgeted spending targets. It may be run as a **profit centre** if there is a high level of foreign exchange transactions, or the business wishes to make speculative profits.

A treasury department might be managed either as a **cost centre** or as a **profit centre**. For a group of companies, this decision may need to be made for treasury departments in separate subsidiaries as well as for the central corporate treasury department.

In a cost centre, managers have an incentive only to **keep the costs** of the department within **budgeted spending targets**. The cost centre approach implies that the treasury is there to perform a service of a certain standard to other departments in the enterprise. The treasury is treated much like any other service department.

However, some companies (including BP, for example) are able to make significant profits from their treasury activities. Treating the treasury department as a profit centre recognises the fact that treasury activities such as speculation may earn **revenues** for the company, and may as a result make treasury staff more motivated. It also means that treasury departments have to operate with a greater degree of commercial awareness, in for example the management of working capital.

Question
Treasury profit centre

Suppose that your company is considering plans to establish its treasury function as a profit centre. In what ways are the following issues of potential importance to these plans?

(a) How can we ensure that high quality treasury staff can be recruited?

(b) How might costly errors and overexposure to risk be prevented?

(c) Why will the treasury team need extensive market information to be successful?

(d) Could there be a danger that attitudes to risk in the treasury team will differ from those of the Board? If so, how?

(e) What is the relevance of internal charges?

(f) What problems could there be in evaluating performance of the treasury team?

Answer

If a profit centre approach is being considered, the following issues should be addressed.

(a) **Competence of staff**

Local managers may not have sufficient expertise in the area of treasury management to carry out speculative treasury operations competently. Mistakes in this specialised field may be costly. It may only be appropriate to operate a larger **centralised** treasury as a profit centre, and additional specialist staff demanding high salaries may need to be recruited.

414   **15: The role of the treasury function in multinationals** │ Part F Treasury and advanced risk management techniques

BPP
LEARNING MEDIA

(b)   **Controls**

Adequate controls must be in place to prevent costly errors and overexposure to risks such as foreign exchange risks. It is possible to enter into a very large foreign exchange deal over the telephone.

(c)   **Information**

A treasury team which trades in futures and options or in currencies is competing with other traders employed by major financial institutions who may have better knowledge of the market because of the large number of customers they deal with. In order to compete effectively, the team needs to have detailed and up-to-date market information.

(d)   **Attitudes to risk**

The more aggressive approach to risk-taking which is characteristic of treasury professionals may be difficult to reconcile with the more measured approach to risk which may prevail within the board of directors. The recognition of treasury operations as profit making activities may not fit well with the main business operations of the company.

(e)   **Internal charges**

If the department is to be a true profit centre, then market prices should be charged for its services to other departments. It may be difficult to put realistic prices on some services, such as arrangement of finance or general financial advice.

(f)   **Performance evaluation**

Even with a profit centre approach, it may be difficult to measure the success of a treasury team for the reason that successful treasury activities sometimes involve **avoiding** the incurring of costs, for example when a currency devalues. For example, a treasury team which hedges a future foreign currency receipt over a period when the domestic currency undergoes devaluation may avoid a substantial loss for the company.

Chapter Roundup

- Financial markets are the markets where economic units with surplus funds, such as individuals, corporations, the government, or overseas investors lend funds to other economic units that want to borrow.

- Markets where a security is first issued are known as primary, and markets where a security is subsequently traded are known as secondary.

- Secondary markets can be organised as exchanges or over the counter (OTC).

- **Securitisation** is the process of converting **illiquid assets** into **marketable securities**. The development of securitisation has led to disintermediation and a reduction in the role of financial intermediaries as borrowers can reach lenders directly.

- **Money markets** are the markets where **short-term instruments** are traded.

- Treasury management in a modern enterprise covers a number of areas including **liquidity management**, **funding management**, **currency management** and **corporate finance**.

- Centralising the treasury management function allows businesses to **employ experts**, **deal in bulk cash flows** and hence **take advantage of lower bank charges** and **avoid a mix of surpluses and deficits**. **Decentralised** cash management can be **more responsive to local needs** however.

- The treasury department is usually run as a **cost centre** if its main focus is to keep costs within budgeted spending targets. It may be run as a **profit centre** if there is a high level of foreign exchange transactions, or the business wishes to make speculative profits.

Quick Quiz

1. You have bought a certificate of deposit for £1,028,000 and sold it 45 days later for £1,035,290. What is the yield?

2. A 91-day Treasury bill with a face value of $10,000,000 is issued for $9,830,000. What is the discount rate?

3. Why do you need to calculate the Bond Equivalent Yield for a treasury bill?

4. **Fill in the blanks** in the statement below, using the words in the box. (Words may be used more than once.)

   - Treasury management may be defined as 'the corporate handling of all (1) .... matters, the generation of external and internal (2) .... for business, the management of (3) .... and cash flow, and the complex strategies, policies and procedures of (4) ....

   - A treasury department may be managed either as a (5) .... centre or a (6) .... centre.

   - A (7) .... treasury department has the role of ensuring that individual operating units have all the funds they need at the right time.

   - Futures and options might be employed in (8) .... risk management.

   - Acquisitions and sales of businesses fall within the area of (9) ....

   - Money transmission management is an aspect of (10) .... management.

• Corporate finance	• Centralised	• Profit	• Financial
• Liquidity	• Cost	• Currency/ies	• Funds

5. Give three possible advantages of decentralisation of the treasury function.

Answers to Quick Quiz

1. $y = \dfrac{1{,}035{,}290 - 1{,}028{,}000}{1{,}028{,}000} \times \dfrac{365}{45} = 0.057519$ or 5.75%

2. $d = \dfrac{10{,}000{,}000 - 9{,}830{,}000}{10{,}000{,}000} \times \dfrac{365}{91} = 6.82\%$

3. Because for the US market, the length of a year is different for Treasury bills and bonds.

4. (1) Financial (2) Funds (3) Currencies (4) Corporate finance (5) Cost (6) Profit (7) Centralised (8) Currency (9) Corporate finance (10) Liquidity

5.
   - Diversification of sources of finance and matching with local assets
   - Greater autonomy for subsidiaries and divisions
   - Greater responsiveness to the needs of individual operating units

Now try the question below from the Exam Question Bank

Number	Level	Marks	Time
29	Introductory	11	20 mins

The use of financial derivatives to hedge against foreign exchange risk

16

Topic list	Syllabus reference
1 Translation, transaction and economic risks	F (2) (a)
2 Exchange rates	
3 Internal hedging techniques	F (2) (c)
4 Managing transaction risk – forward contracts	F (2) (b)
5 Money market hedging	F (2) (b)
6 Choosing a hedging method	F (2) (b)
7 Currency futures	F (1) (b), F (2) (b)
8 Currency options	F (1) (b), F (2) (b)
9 Currency swaps	F (2) (b)
10 FOREX swaps	F (2) (b)
11 Devising a foreign currency hedging strategy	F (2) (b)

Introduction

This chapter focuses on how currency derivatives can be used to manage transaction risk. Any company engaged in international trade will be exposed to such risk where movements in exchange rates can have a significant effect on the value of transactions. There are numerous ways in which a company can hedge against transaction risk – both **internal** and **external** methods are available. It is important to know the characteristics of the various techniques and also the **best strategy** to adopt in particular scenarios.

Study guide

		Intellectual level
F1	**The role of the treasury function in multinationals**	
(b)	Discuss the operations of the derivatives market, including:	3
	(i) The relative advantages and disadvantages of exchange traded versus OTC agreements	
	(ii) Key features, such as standard contracts, tick sizes, margin requirements and margin trading	
	(iii) The source of basis risk and how it can be minimised	
F2	**The use of financial derivatives to hedge against forex risk**	
(a)	Assess the impact on an organisation to exposure in translation, transaction and economic risks and how these can be managed.	3
(b)	Evaluate, for a given hedging requirement, which of the following is the most appropriate strategy, given the nature of the underlying position and the risk exposure:	3
	(i) The use of the forward exchange market and the creation of a money market hedge	
	(ii) Synthetic foreign exchange agreements (SAFE's)	
	(iii) Exchange-traded currency futures contracts	
	(iv) Currency swaps	
	(v) FOREX swaps	
	(vi) Currency options	
(c)	Advise on the use of bilateral and multilateral netting and matching as tools for minimising FOREX transactions costs and the management of market barriers to the free movement of capital and other remittances.	3

1 Translation, transaction and economic risks

Translation, transaction and economic risks were covered in Chapter 8 Section 5. It would be a good idea to remind yourself of what each risk is before studying this chapter. The main focus of this chapter is on **transaction risk** – that is, the risk of changes in the exchange rates having an effect on the value of transactions based in a foreign currency (imports or exports).

The effect of exchange rate movements on project values was also covered in Chapter 8. You should review Section 2 of this chapter to remind yourself of how **purchasing power parity**, **interest rate parity** and the **International Fisher effect** can be used to predict exchange rates.

2 Exchange rates

FAST FORWARD

Currency rates can be quoted as **direct quotes** or **indirect quotes**.

The **spot rate** is the rate at which currencies can be exchanged now. The **forward rate** is the rate at which currencies will be exchanged on a set future date.

2.1 Exchange rates

Exchange rates were covered in detail in Paper F9 – *Financial Management*. However it is worthwhile revising the basics here as an understanding of these is essential for the rest of the chapter.

> An **exchange rate** is the rate at which a currency can be traded in exchange for another currency.
>
> The **spot exchange rate** is the rate at which currencies can be bought or sold for **immediate delivery.**
>
> The **forward rate** is an exchange rate set for currencies to be exchanged at a future date.

Every traded currency in fact has many exchange rates. There is an exchange rate with every other traded currency on the foreign exchange markets. Foreign exchange dealers make their profit by buying currency for less than they sell it, and so there are really two exchange rates, a selling rate and a buying rate.

2.2 Direct and indirect currency quotes

> A **direct quote** is the amount of domestic currency which is equal to one foreign currency unit.
>
> An **indirect quote** is the amount of foreign currency which is equal to one domestic currency unit.

In the UK indirect quotes are invariably used but, in most countries, direct quotes are more common.

Currencies may be quoted in either direction. For example, the US dollar and Euro might be quoted as $/€ = 0.7745 or €/$ = 1.2912. In other words €0.7745 = $1 and $1.2912 = €1. One rate is simply the reciprocal of the other.

> If a currency is quoted at £:$1.500, the $ is the **counter currency** (the **reference or term currency**), the £ is the **base currency**.

2.3 Bid and offer prices

> The **bid price** is the rate at which the bank is willing to buy the currency.
>
> The **offer** (or **ask**) **price** is the rate at which the bank is willing to sell the currency.

If an importer has to pay a foreign supplier in a foreign currency, he might ask his bank to sell him the required amount of the currency. For example, suppose that a bank's customer, a UK trading company, has imported goods for which it must now pay $10,000.

(a) In order to pay the bill, the company must obtain (buy) $10,000 from the bank. In other words, the bank will sell $10,000 to the company.

(b) When the bank agrees to sell US$10,000 to the company, it will tell the company what the spot rate of exchange will be for the transaction. If the bank's selling rate (known as the **'offer'**, or **'ask'** price) is, say $1.5500 for the currency, the bank will charge the company:

$$\frac{\$10,000}{\$1.5500 \text{ per } £1} = £6,451.61$$

If a UK exporting company receives $10,000 from a customer, the company will want to sell the dollars to obtain sterling (its home currency). The bank will therefore buy the dollars at a quoted **bid price**. If the bank quotes a **bid** price of, say $1.5595, for the currency the bank will pay the exporter:

$$\frac{\$10,000}{\$1.5595 \text{ per } £1} = £6,412.31$$

Note that the bank buys the dollars for less than it sells them – in other words it makes a net profit on the transactions. In this case the net profit is £39.30. If you are undecided between which price is the bid price and which is the offer price, remember that the bank's customer will always be offered the **worse rate**. An exporter will pay a high price for the foreign currency and an importer will receive a low price.

Just think what happens when you buy currency for a holiday and then sell it back when you come home (ignoring commission).

If you come back to the United Kingdom from a holiday in America with spare dollars, and you are told the spread of £/$ rates is 1.8500 – 1.8700, will you have to pay the bank $1.85 or $1.87 to obtain £1? Answer: you will have to pay the higher price, $1.87.

The rule is that banks buy (currency) low and sell high.

Question

Dollar receipts

Calculate how many dollars an exporter would receive or how many dollars an importer would pay, ignoring the bank's commission, in each of the following situations, if they were to exchange currency at the spot rate.

(a)   A US exporter receives a payment from a Danish customer of 150,000 kroner.

(b)   A US importer buys goods from a Japanese supplier and pays 1 million yen.

Spot rates are as follows.

	Bank sells (offer)		Bank buys (bid)
$/Danish Kr	9.4340	–	9.5380
$/Japanese Yen	203.650	–	205.781

Answer

(a)   The bank is being asked to buy the Danish kroners and will give the exporter:

$$\frac{150{,}000}{9.5380} = \$15{,}726.57 \text{ in exchange}$$

(b)   The bank is being asked to sell the yen to the importer and will charge for the currency:

$$\frac{1{,}000{,}000}{203.650} = \$4{,}910.39$$

2.4 Spread

FAST FORWARD

The difference between the bid price and the offer price is known as the **spread.**

One of the easiest ways to find the closing (end of day) exchange rates is to use the financial press (such as the *Financial Times* or *Wall Street Journal*).

The difference between the bid price and the offer price, covering dealers' costs and profit, is called the **spread**. The spread can be quoted in different ways.

$/£0.6500 +/- 0.0005   or $/£0.6495 – 0.6505

Question

Exchange rate spreads

Pratt Inc, a US based company, is engaged in both import and export activities. During a particular month, Pratt sells goods to Posh plc, a UK company, and receives £5 million. In the same month, Pratt imports goods from a UK supplier, which cost £5 million.

If the exchange rates were $/£0.5075 +/- 0.0003, calculate the dollar values of the sterling receipt and payment.

Answer

(a)   As an exporter, Pratt will pay a high rate to buy dollars (sell pounds) – that is, they will be quoted a rate of 0.5075 + 0.0003 = 0.5078. Pratt will therefore receive

£5 million / 0.5078 = $9,846,396

(b)   As an importer, Pratt will receive a low rate to sell dollars (buy pounds) – that is, a rate of 0.5075 – 0.0003 = 0.5072. Pratt will therefore pay £5 million / 0.5072 = $9,858,044

3 Internal hedging techniques

Internal hedging techniques include **leading and lagging, invoicing in home currency, matching and multilateral netting.**

Internal hedging techniques are cheaper than external techniques and should therefore be considered first. There are various internal techniques available which are discussed below.

3.1 Leading and lagging

Key terms

Leading involves **accelerating payments** to avoid potential additional costs due to currency rate movements.

Lagging is the practice of **delaying payments** if currency rate movements are expected to make the later payment cheaper.

Companies might try to use lead payments (payments in advance) or lagged payments (delayed payments) in order to take advantage of foreign exchange rate movements.

Example

Williams Inc – a company based in the US – imports goods from the UK. The company is due to make a payment of £500,000 to a UK supplier in one month's time. The current exchange rate is as follows:

$1 = £0.6450

(a)   If the dollar is expected to appreciate against sterling by 2% in the next month and by a further 1% in the second month what would be Williams Inc's strategy in terms of leading and lagging and by how much would the company benefit from this strategy?

(b)   If the dollar was to depreciate against sterling by 2% in the next month and by a further 1% in the second month, how would Williams Inc's strategy probably change and what would the resulting benefit be?

Solution

(a)   **Dollar appreciating against sterling**

If the dollar appreciates against sterling, this means that the dollar value of payments will be smaller in two months' time than if payment was made when due. Williams Inc will therefore adopt a 'lagging' approach to its payment – that is it will delay payment by an extra month to reduce the dollar cost.

Payment to UK supplier

	One month's time	Two months' time
Exchange rate ($/£)	£0.6450 x 1.02 = £0.6579	£0.6579 x 1.01 = £0.6645
$ value of payment	£500,000/0.6579 = $759,994	£500,000/0.6645 = $752,445

By delaying the payment by an extra month Williams Inc will save $7,549.

(b)   **Dollar depreciating against sterling**

The opposite strategy should now be adopted. As the dollar depreciates, there is an incentive for Williams Inc to pay as soon as possible. The dollar value of sterling payments will increase as the dollar depreciates therefore to save money the company will want to pay on time.

Payment to UK supplier

	One month's time	Two months' time
Exchange rate ($/£)	£0.6450 x 0.98 = £0.6321	£0.6321 x 0.99 = £0.6258
$ value of payment	£500,000/0.6321 = $791,014	£500,000/0.6258 = $798,977

By paying on time Williams Inc will save $7,963.

Companies should be aware of the potential **finance costs** associated with paying early. This is the interest cost on the money used to make the payment, but early settlement discounts may be available. Before deciding on a strategy of making advanced payments, the company should compare how much they save in terms of currency with the finance costs of making early payment.

By delaying payments there may be a **loss of goodwill** from the supplier which may result in tighter credit terms in the future. Whilst savings may have been made by paying late, the company must compare these savings with potential future costs resulting from, for example, withdrawal of favourable credit terms or early settlement discounts.

3.2 Invoicing in home currency

One way of avoiding transaction risk is for an **exporter** to invoice **overseas customers in its own domestic currency**, or for an **importer** to arrange with its overseas supplier **to be invoiced in its home currency**.

(a)   If a Hong Kong exporter is able to quote and invoice an overseas customer in Hong Kong dollars, then the transaction risk is transferred to that customer.

(b)   If a Hong Kong importer is able to arrange with its overseas supplier to be invoiced in Hong Kong dollars then the transaction risk is transferred to that supplier.

Although either the exporter or the importer avoids transaction risk, the other party to the transaction will bear the full risk. Who ultimately bears the risk may depend on bargaining strength or the exporter's competitive position (it is unlikely to insist on payment in its own currency if it faces strong competition).

An alternative method of achieving the same result is to negotiate contracts expressed in the foreign currency but at a pre-determined fixed rate of exchange.

3.3 Matching receipts and payments

A company can reduce or eliminate its transaction risk exposure by matching receipts and payments. Wherever possible a company that expects to make payments and have receipts in the same foreign currency should plan to **offset its payments against its receipts in that currency**. The process of matching is made simpler by having **foreign currency accounts** with a bank.

Offsetting (matching payments against receipts) will be **cheaper** than arranging a forward contract to buy currency and another forward contract to sell the currency, provided that:

- Receipts occur before payments
- The time difference between receipts and payments in the currency is not too long

Any differences between the amounts receivable and the amounts payable in a given currency may be covered by a forward exchange contract (covered later in this chapter) to buy or sell the amount of the difference.

3.4 Netting

FAST FORWARD
Netting is a process in which credit balances are netted off against debit balances so that only the reduced net amounts remain due to be paid by actual currency flows.

Exam focus point

Netting was examined as a 20 mark optional question in June 2010.

Unlike matching, netting is not technically a method of managing transaction risk. The objective is simply to save transactions costs by netting off inter-company balances before arranging payment. Many **multinational groups** of companies engage in **intra-group trading**. Where related companies located in different countries trade with each other there is likely to be inter-company indebtedness denominated in different currencies.

3.4.1 Bilateral netting

In the case of bilateral netting, only two companies are involved. The lower balance is netted off against the higher balance and the difference is the amount remaining to be paid.

Example

Barlow plc and Orange Inc are respectively UK and US subsidiaries of a Swiss based holding company. On 30th September 20X1 Barlow owed Orange SFr650,000 and Orange owed Barlow SFr450,000. Bilateral netting can reduce the value of the inter-company debts – the two inter-company balances are set against each other, leaving a net debt owed by Barlow to Orange of SFr200,000 (SFr650,000 – SFr450,000).

3.4.2 Multilateral netting

Multilateral netting is a more complex procedure in which the debts of more than two group companies are netted off against each other. There are different ways of arranging multilateral netting. The arrangement might be co-ordinated by the company's own central treasury or alternatively by the company's bankers.

The steps to be followed are:

(1)   Construct a table with companies receiving money down the left side and companies making payments across the top.

(2)   Enter all the amounts each company owes to the others and convert to the agreed settlement currency.

(3)   Add across and down the table to determine total receipts and total payments for each company.

Determine the net receivable or payable for each company.

Example

Maximillian Group is made up of three companies – one in Germany, one in Hong Kong and one in the US. The following inter-company transactions took place during the first quarter of 20X1.

	Paying subsidiary		
Receiving subsidiary	Germany	Hong Kong	US
Germany	-	€10m	€6m
Hong Kong	HK$5m	-	HK$20m
US	$12m	$16m	-

Maximillian has introduced a system of multilateral netting to minimise the number of inter-group payments. The US dollar will be used as the settlement currency. Exchange rates are as follows.

€1 = HK$11.2475   €1 = US$0.6919   US$1 = HK$7.7821

Required

Illustrate the effect of multilateral netting on inter-group receipts and payments.

Solution

Remember the step-by-step guide above – the US dollar is the settlement currency therefore we convert all the receipts and payments to US dollars using the exchange rates given.

Receiving subsidiary	Paying subsidiary			Total receipts (add across)	Total payments (add down)	Net receipt/(payment)
	Germany	Hong Kong	US			
	US$m	US$m	US$m	US$m	US$m	US$m
Germany	-	6.919	4.1514	11.0704	(12.6425)	(1.5721)
Hong Kong	0.6425	-	2.5700	3.2125	(22.9190)	(19.7065)
US	12.0000	16.000	-	28.0000	(6.7214)	21.2786

This policy of multilateral netting will minimise transactions costs for the group and should prevent the need for foreign currency hedging. Only two transactions are now required – Germany pays US$1.5721m to the US and Hong Kong pays US$19.7065m to the US.

A useful check on the accuracy of your currency conversions can be done by adding up the net receipts/payments column. If your calculations are correct (and the signs attached to receipts and payments are consistent) the column should add up to zero. This is because what is a payment for one company is a receipt for another so they cancel out.

Question

Multilateral netting

Robster, Gazza and Howard are all part of the same group – Robster is based in the US, Gazza in the UK and Howard in Singapore. The following transactions took place between the three companies during the previous quarter of the current year.

Receiving subsidiary	Paying subsidiary		
	Robster	Gazza	Howard
Robster	-	US$50m	US$20m
Gazza	£15m	-	£25m
Howard	S$33m	S$45m	-

The settlement currency is £ sterling and the following exchange rates applied at the end of the previous quarter.

£1 = $1.5500   £1 = S$2.800

Required

Illustrate the impact of multilateral netting on the group as a whole and the final transactions that are required to settle the net receipts and payments.

Answer

Receiving subsidiary	Paying subsidiary			Total receipts (add across)	Total payments (add down)	Net receipt/(payment)
	Robster	Gazza	Howard			
	£m	£m	£m	£m	£m	£m
Robster	-	32.26	12.9	45.16	(26.79)	18.37
Gazza	15.00	-	25.0	40.00	(48.33)	(8.33)
Howard	11.79	16.07	-	27.86	(37.90)	(10.04)

The transactions required are reduced to two – Gazza pays Robster £8.33m and Howard pays Robster £10.04m.

3.5 Management of barriers

An overseas government may place **restrictions on remittances**. This means that the amount of profit that can be sent back to the parent company is limited. This may be achieved through **exchange controls** or limits on the amounts that can be remitted. These **barriers** can be avoided / mitigated by the following methods:

(a)   Charge overseas subsidiary companies additional head office overhead charges.

(b)   Subsidiary companies can lend the equivalent of the dividend to the parent company.

(c)   Subsidiary companies can make payments to the parent company in the form of royalties, patents, management fees or other charges.

(d)   Increase the transfer prices paid by the subsidiary to the parent company (see Chapter 18 for further discussion of transfer prices).

(e)   The overseas subsidiary can lend money to another subsidiary requiring funds in the same country. In return the parent company will receive the loan amount in the home country from the other parent company. This method is sometimes known as **parallel loans**.

Foreign governments may put measures in place to stop the above methods being used.

4 Managing transaction risk – forward contracts   6/11

FAST FORWARD

> A **forward contract** is a contract with a bank that covers a **specific amount** of foreign currency for delivery at an **agreed date** at an **exchange rate agreed now**.

Exam focus point

In June 2011 there was a compulsory 30 mark question on foreign currency hedging. This included the recommendation of an appropriate hedging strategy – the use of forward contracts was one of the strategies that had to be considered.

4.1 What is a forward contract?

Key term

A **forward exchange contract** is:

(a)   An immediately firm and binding contract, eg between a bank and its customer which must be exercised regardless of the spot rate at the time of exercise

(b)   For the purchase or sale of a specified quantity of a stated foreign currency

(c)   At a rate of exchange fixed at the time the contract is made

(d)   For performance (delivery of the currency and payment for it) at a future time which is agreed when making the contract (This future time will be either a specified date, or any time between two specified dates.)

Forward contracts hedge against **transaction exposure** by allowing the importer or exporter to arrange for a bank to sell or buy a quantity of foreign currency at an **agreed future date**, at a **rate of exchange determined** when the **forward contract is made**. The trader will know in advance

*   how much local currency he will receive (if he is selling foreign currency to the bank)
*   how much local currency he must pay (if he is buying foreign currency from the bank).

The current spot price is irrelevant to the outcome of a forward contract.

4.2 Forward rates and future exchange rate movements

Interest rate parity predicts that the forward rate is the spot price ruling on the day a forward contract is made plus or minus the interest differential for the period of the contract. **It is wrong to think of a**

forward rate as a forecast of what the spot rate will be on a given date in the future. It will be a coincidence if the forward rate turns out to be the same as the spot rate on that future date.

However the spot rate is likely to move in the direction indicated by the forward rate. Currencies with high interest rates are likely to depreciate in value against currencies with lower interest rates – the attraction of the higher interest persuades investors to hold amounts of a currency that is expected to depreciate.

4.2.1 Forward and spot rates

If the forward rate is higher than the spot rate, the currency is quoted at a discount; if forward rate Is lower than the spot rate, the currency is quoted at a premium.

A forward exchange rate might be higher or lower than the spot rate. If it is higher, the quoted currency will be cheaper forward than spot. For example, if in the case of Swiss francs against sterling (i) the spot rate is 2.1560 – 2.1660 and (ii) the three months forward rate is 2.2070 – 2.2220:

(a)   A bank would sell 2,000 Swiss francs:

    (i)   At the spot rate, now, for   £927.64 $\left(\dfrac{2,000}{2.1560} \right)$

    (ii)   In three months time, under a forward contract, for   £906.21 $\left(\dfrac{2,000}{2.2070} \right)$

(b)   A bank would buy 2,000 Swiss francs

    (i)   At the spot rate, now, for   £923.36 $\left(\dfrac{2,000}{2.1660} \right)$

    (ii)   In three months time, under a forward contract, for   £900.09 $\left(\dfrac{2,000}{2.2220} \right)$

In both cases, the quoted currency (Swiss franc) would be worth less against sterling in a forward contract than at the current spot rate. This is because it is quoted forward 'at a discount', against sterling.

If the forward rate is thus higher than the spot rate, then it is 'at a discount' to the spot rate.

The forward rate can be calculated today without making any estimates of future exchange rates. **Future exchange rates** depend largely on future events and will often turn out to be very different from the forward rate. However, the forward rate is probably an **unbiased predictor of the expected value of the future exchange rate**, based on the information available today. It is also likely that the spot rate will move in the direction indicated by the forward rate.

4.2.2 The rule for adding or subtracting discounts and premiums

Forward rates as adjustments to spot rates	
Forward rate cheaper	Quoted at discount
Forward rate more expensive	Quoted at premium

A **discount** is therefore **added** to the spot rate, and a **premium** is therefore **subtracted** from the spot rate. (The mnemonic **ADDIS** may help you to remember that we ADD Discounts and so subtract premiums.) The longer the duration of a forward contract, the larger will be the quoted premium or discount.

4.3 Expectations theory of forward rates

Expectations theory of forward rates predicts that the **percentage difference between forward and spot rates now equals the expected change in spot rates over the period.**

For example, given expectations of interest rates and inflation rates, the spot rate three months from now is expected to equal the three-months forward rate quoted now. The forward market is said to be an

unbiased predictor of exchange rates as, on average, the forward rate is equal to the future spot rate and overestimates it about as often as it underestimates it.

4.4 Quotation of forward rates

In Section 2.4 we discussed the spread of spot rates, being the difference between the bid and offer prices. A similar situation applies to the quotation of forward rated – banks will quote a spread based on the forward bid and offer prices. For example the €/$ 3-month forward rate might be quoted as:

€1 = $1.3495 - $1.3525   or   €1 = $1.3510 ± 0.0015

As with the spot rate, a company will always be offered the worst rate by the bank. For example if the company is selling € (that is, the bank is buying € and paying $) in 3 months' time, the bank will offer $1.3495. If the company is buying € (that is, the bank is buying $ and paying €) in 3 months' time, the bank will require $1.3525 for every € it sells.

Example

It is now 31st March 20X1. Washington Inc, a US company, has purchased goods from London plc, a UK importer and exporter. Washington is due to pay £5m to London in 3 months' time and wants to hedge the foreign currency payment to reduce transaction risk.

The $/£ spot rates on 31st March 20X1 are $1 = £0.6200 - £0.6230. The 3-month forward rates have been quoted as $1 = £0.6190 - £0.6210.

Calculate the amount in $ that Washington will have to pay if the company hedges the payment using a forward contract.

Solution

Washington will want to buy £ (sell $) in 3 months' time – which means that the bank will be selling £ and buying $. Washington will be offered the 'worst' rate – that is, the bank will pay £0.6190 for each $ received from Washington. The $ cost of the payment to London will be

£5m/0.6190 = $8,077,544

Question

Forward rates

Using the information in the example above, calculate how much in £ London would have to pay Washington if, in 3 months' time, a payment of $5m is due.

Answer

London will be selling £ (buying $) which means that the bank be selling $ The bank will want to sell $ at a high rate therefore will offer London $1 for every £0.6210 the company pays. The total cost of the payment in 3 months' time will be:

$5m x £0.6210 = £3,105,000

4.5 Movement in the spot rate

As discussed above, the forward rate is deemed to be an unbiased predictor of the future spot rate. However the spot rate at the time the forward contract is to be exercised may be more favourable than the forward rate that was agreed when the contract was entered into. Regardless of what the spot rate is at that time, the forward contract **must be exercised** – the holder does not have the option to let it lapse and perform the transaction at the prevailing spot rate.

Example

A US importer knows on 1 April that he must pay a foreign seller 26,500 Swiss francs in one month's time, on 1 May. He can arrange a forward exchange contract with his bank on 1 April, whereby the bank undertakes to sell the importer 26,500 Swiss francs on 1 May, at a fixed rate of say $1 = SF2.6400.

The US importer can be certain that whatever the spot rate is between Swiss francs and US dollars on 1 May, he will have to pay on that date, at this forward rate:

$$\frac{26{,}500}{2.6400} = \$10{,}037.88$$

(a) If the spot rate is **lower than 2.6400**, the importer would have successfully protected himself against a weakening of the dollar, and would have avoided paying more dollars to obtain the Swiss francs.

(b) If the spot rate is **higher than 2.6400**, the dollar's value against the Swiss franc would mean that the importer would pay more under the forward exchange contract than he would have had to pay if he had obtained the francs at the spot rate on 1 May. He cannot avoid this extra cost, because a forward contract is binding.

4.6 Failure to satisfy a forward contract

A customer might be unable to satisfy a forward contract for any one of a number of reasons.

(a) An **importer** might find that:

   (i) His supplier **fails to deliver the goods** as specified, so the importer will not accept the goods delivered and will not agree to pay for them

   (ii) The **supplier sends fewer goods** than expected, perhaps because of supply shortages, and so the importer has less to pay for

   (iii) The supplier is **late with the delivery**, and so the importer does not have to pay for the goods until later than expected

(b) An **exporter** might find the same types of situation, but in reverse, so that he does not receive any payment at all, or he receives more or less than originally expected, or he receives the expected amount, but only after some delay.

4.7 Close-out of forward contracts

If a customer cannot satisfy a forward exchange contract, the bank will make the customer fulfil the contract.

(a) If the customer has arranged for the bank to buy currency but then cannot deliver the currency for the bank to buy, the bank will:

   (i) **Sell currency** to the **customer** at the **spot rate** (when the contract falls due for performance)

   (ii) **Buy** the **currency back**, under the terms of the **forward exchange contract**

(b) If the customer has contracted for the bank to sell him currency, the bank will:

   (i) Sell the customer the specified amount of currency at the forward exchange rate

   (ii) Buy back the unwanted currency at the spot rate

Thus, the bank arranges for the customer to perform his part of the forward exchange contract by either selling or buying the 'missing' currency at the spot rate. These arrangements are known as **closing out** a forward exchange contract.

4.8 Synthetic foreign exchange agreements

In order to reduce the volatility of their exchange rates, some governments have banned foreign currency trading. Examples of affected currencies include the Russian ruble, Indian rupee and Phillipine peso.

In such markets, **synthetic foreign exchange agreements (SAFEs)** – also know as non-deliverable forwards - are used. These instruments resemble forward contracts but no currency is actually delivered. Instead the two counterparties settle the profit or loss (calculated as the difference between the agreed SAFE rate and the prevailing spot rate) on a notional amount of currency (the SAFE's face value). At no time is there any intention on the part of either party to exchange this notional amount.

SAFEs can be used to create a foreign currency loan in a currency that is of no interest to the lender.

Example

A borrower might require US dollars but wants to make the loan repayments in a currency that isn't traded. In this case the borrower will receive dollars and repayments will be calculated in dollars. However actual payment will be in the other preferred currency, calculated using the current exchange rate.

The lender might wish to lend in US dollars and also receive payment in US dollars. Therefore at the same time as lending the dollars to the borrower, the lender may also enter into a SAFE agreement with a counterparty that matches the cash flows from the foreign currency repayments.

What has happened is that the lender has a synthetic dollar loan, the borrower has a synthetic second currency loan and the counterparty has a SAFE agreement with the lender.

It is important to remember that **settlement of SAFEs will always be in dollars** as the counterparty will be unable to settle in the alternative currency (as it is not traded).

Example

A lender enters into a three month SAFE with a counterparty to buy $5m worth of Philippine pesos at a rate of $1 = PHP44.000. The spot rate is $1 = PHP43.850

When the SAFE is due to be settled in three months' time, the spot rate is $1 = PHP44.050. This means that the lender will have to pay 5m x (44.050 − 44.000) = PHP250,000 to the counterparty.

As this will be settled in dollars at the prevailing spot rate, the payment to the counterparty will be PHP250,000/44.050 = $5,675.

5 Money market hedging 6/08

FAST FORWARD

Money market hedging involves borrowing in one currency, converting the money borrowed into another currency and putting the money on deposit until the time at which the transaction is completed, hoping to take advantage of favourable interest rate movements.

Exam focus point

In June 2008, there was an optional question on foreign currency money market hedging. One of the common errors was the incorrect estimation of the appropriate forward rate.

5.1 Using the money market

Because of the close relationship between forward exchange rates and the interest rates in the two currencies, it is possible to 'manufacture' a forward rate by using the spot exchange rate and money market lending or borrowing. This technique is known as a **money market hedge** or **synthetic forward**.

5.2 Hedging payments

Suppose a British company needs to **pay** a US supplier in US dollars in three months' time. It does not have enough cash to pay now, but will have sufficient in three months' time. Instead of negotiating a forward contract, the company could:

- Borrow the appropriate amount in pounds now
- Convert the pounds to dollars immediately
- Put the dollars on deposit in a US dollar bank account
- When the time comes to pay the company:

  (a) Pay the supplier out of the dollar bank account

  (b) Repay the pound loan account

In the exam a tabular approach may be helpful.

	IMPORTER			
	UK £s		**USA $s**	
Now	4	withdraw funds from UK account (1 + borrowing rate)*	3	put money into US account (1 + deposit)*
Three months	5	to compare to a forward	1 2	pay $ invoice from supplier pay off with $ deposit

* remember to take the interest rate quoted and multiply by 3/12 if you have a 3 month loan

What the tabular approach means is that

(1)   The transaction determines whether you are paying or receiving

(2)   This is the loan repayment which determines

(3)   How much money you have to place on deposit in the US$ account (the size of the loan), which determines

(4)   The payment in £

The effect is exactly the same as using a forward contract, and will usually cost almost exactly the same amount (step 5 above gives you the cost of the money market hedge to compare to the cost of a forward contract). If the results from a money market hedge were very different from a forward hedge, speculators could make money without taking a risk. Therefore market forces ensure that the two hedges produce very similar results.

Example: Money market hedge (1)

A UK company owes a Danish supplier Kr3,500,000 in three months' time. The spot exchange rate is £1 = Kr7.5509 – 7.5548. The company can borrow in sterling for 3 months at 8.60% per annum and can deposit kroner for 3 months at 10% per annum.

Required

Calculate the cost in sterling with a money market hedge.

Solution

The interest rates for 3 months are 2.15% to borrow in pounds and 2.5% to deposit in kroner. The company needs to deposit enough kroner now so that the total including interest will be Kr3,500,000 in three months' time. This means depositing:

Kr3,500,000/(1 + 0.025) = Kr3,414,634.

These kroner will cost £452,215 (spot rate 7.5509 – remember the company will always receive the worst rate). The company must borrow this amount and, with three months interest of 2.15%, will have to repay:

£452,215 × (1 + 0.0215) = £461,938.

This can be shown in tabular form as follows.

	IMPORTER			
	UK £s		**Danish Kr**	
Now	4	withdraw funds from UK account Kr3,414,634/7.5509 = £452,215	3	put money into Kr account Kr3,500,000/1.025 = Kr3,414,634
		8.6% x 3/12 = 2.15% (ie 1.0215)		10% x 3/12 = 2.5% (ie 1.025)
Three months	5	to compare to a forward £452,215 x 1.0215 = £461,938	1 2	pay Kr invoice from supplier 3,500,000 pay off with Kr deposit (3,500,000)

* remember to take the interest rate quoted and multiply by 3/12

Cost of hedge = £461,938

Question

A Thai company owes a New Zealand Company NZ$ 3,000,000, payable in 3 months time. The current exchange rate is NZ $1 = Thai Baht 19.0300 – 19.0500.

The Thai company elects to use a money market hedge to manage the exchange risk.

The current annual borrowing and investing rates in the two countries are:

	New Zealand %	Thailand %
Investing	2.5	4.5
Borrowing	3.0	5.2

Required

Calculate the cost to the Thai company of using a money market hedge.

Answer

	IMPORTER	
	Thai Bt	**New Zealand $s**
Now	4 withdraw funds from Thai account $2,981,366 x 19.0500 = Bt56,795,022	3 put money into NZ account $3,000,000/1.00625 = $2,981,366
	5.2% x 3/12 = 1.3% (ie 1.013)	2.5% x 3/12 = 0.625 (ie 1.00625)
Three months	5 to compare to a forward Bt56,795,022 x 1.013 = Bt57,533,357	1 pay $ invoice from supplier 3,000,000 2 pay off with $ deposit (3,000,000)

Cost of hedge = Bt57,533,357

5.3 Hedging foreign currency receipts

A similar technique can be used to cover a foreign currency **receipt** from a customer. To manufacture a forward exchange rate, follow the steps below.

- Borrow an appropriate amount in the foreign currency today
- Convert it immediately to home currency
- Place it on deposit in the home currency
- When the supplier's cash is received:

   (a)   Repay the foreign currency loan
   (b)   Take the cash from the home currency deposit account

This can be shown in tabular form as follows (using an example of a UK exporter receiving $ from a US customer).

	EXPORTER	
	UK £	**US $**
Now	4 pay $ loan into UK bank account (1 + deposit rate)*	3 take out $ loan (1 + borrowing rate)*
Three months	5 to compare to a forward	1 receive $ from export 2 pay off $ loan with export revenue

Part F Treasury and advanced risk management techniques | **16: The use of financial derivatives to hedge against foreign exchange risk** | 433

> Variations on these money market hedges are possible in an examination.

Example: money market hedge (2)

A US company is owed SFr 2,500,000 in three months' time by a Swiss company. The spot exchange rate is $1 = SFr 2.2498 – 2.2510. The company can deposit in dollars for 3 months at 8.00% per annum and can borrow Swiss Francs for 3 months at 7.00% per annum. What is the receipt in dollars with a money market hedge and what effective forward rate would this represent?

Solution

	EXPORTER	
	US $	**Swiss Fr**
Now	**4** pay SFr loan into US account SFr2,457,002/2.2510 = $1,091,516	**3** take out SFr loan SFr2,500,000/1.0175 = SFr2,457,002
	8% x 3/12 = 2% (ie 1.02)	7% x 3/12 = 1.75% (ie 1.0175)
Three months	**5** to compare to a forward $1,091,516 x 1.02 = $1,113,346	**1** receive SFr from export 2,500,000 **2** pay off SFr loan with export revenue (2,500,000)

The exporter would receive $1,113,346.

The effective forward rate that has been manufactured is

SF2,500,000/$1,113,346 = 2.2455 – that is, $1 = SFr2.2455

This effective forward rate shows the Swiss franc at a premium to the US dollar as the Swiss franc interest rate is lower than the US dollar rate.

Question

Money market hedge 2

An Australian company is due to receive ¥15,000,000 from a Japanese company, payable in four months' time. The current exchange rate is Aus$1 = ¥62.6000 – 62.8000.

The Australian company elects to use a money market hedge to manage the exchange risk.

The current annual borrowing and investing rates in the two countries are:

	Australia	*Japan*
	%	%
Investing	4.5	2.7
Borrowing	6.0	3.3

Required

Calculate the amount the Australian company will receive if it uses a money market hedge.

434 | **16: The use of financial derivatives to hedge against foreign exchange risk** | Part F Treasury and advanced risk management techniques

BPP
LEARNING MEDIA

	EXPORTER	
	Australian $	**Japanese ¥**
Now	4 pay ¥ loan into Australian account ¥14,836,795/62.8000 = Aus$236,255	3 take out ¥ loan 15,000,000/1.011 = ¥14,836,795
	4.5% x 4/12 = 1.5% (ie 1.015)	3.3% x 4/12 = 1.1% (ie 1.011)
Four months	5 to compare to a forward Aus$236,255 x 1.015 = Aus$239,799	1 receive ¥ from export 15,000,000 2 pay off ¥ loan with export revenue (15,000,000)

The Australian company will receive Aus$239,799 from the money market hedge.

5.4 Forward exchange contracts versus money market hedge

Is one of these methods of hedging likely to be cheaper than the other? The answer is 'perhaps' but not by much. There will be very little difference between borrowing in foreign currency and repaying the loan with currency receivables and borrowing in the domestic currency and selling forward the currency receivables. This is because the premium or discount on the forward exchange rate reflects the interest differential between the two countries.

5.5 Arbitrage profits

Key term

Arbitrage is the simultaneous purchase and sale of a security in different markets with the aim of making a risk-free profit through the exploitation of any price differences between the two markets.

Arbitrage means exploiting differences

- Between two markets, selling in one market, buying in another

- Between two products, where similarities between those products suggest they should be traded at the **same price**

Arbitrage differences are **short-term**. As others see the differences and exploit them, prices will converge and the opportunities for exploiting differences will disappear as equilibrium is reached.

5.5.1 Arbitrage and exchange rates

Interest rate parity suggests that the spot rate in a year forward will reflect differences in interest rates. If however the difference between the spot rate now and the forward rate being offered now does not reflect differences in the two countries' interest rates, investors can exploit differences. They can:

- Borrow in currency A

- Deposit what they have borrowed in currency B for a period of time

- Take out a forward contract to sell currency B at the end of the period

- At the end of the period, liquidate the investment and convert the currency B proceeds to currency A under the forward contract

- Repay the amount borrowed in currency A and retain the surplus

6 Choosing a hedging method

This is an important section as you may be asked to compare different hedging methods in the exam and recommend the most appropriate course of action.

Exam focus point

In the June 2011 exam there was a compulsory Section A question that required you to recommend an appropriate hedging strategy for a company due to receive foreign currency income in the future.

6.1 Choice of methods

When a company expects to receive or pay a sum of foreign currency in the next few months, it can choose between using the **forward exchange market** and the **money market** to hedge against the foreign exchange risk. The cheaper option available is the one that ought to be chosen. Other methods may also be possible, such as making **lead payments**.

Example

Trumpton, a UK company, has bought goods from a US supplier, and must pay $4,000,000 for them in three months time. The company's finance director wishes to hedge against the foreign exchange risk, and the three methods which the company usually considers are:

- Using forward exchange contracts
- Using money market borrowing or lending
- Making lead payments

The following annual interest rates and exchange rates are currently available.

	US dollar		Sterling	
	Deposit rate	Borrowing rate	Deposit rate	Borrowing rate
	%	%	%	%
1 month	7	10.25	10.75	14.00
3 months	7	10.75	11.00	14.25

	£1 = $
Spot	1.8625 – 1.8635
1 month forward	1.8565 – 1.8577
3 months forward	1.8445 – 1.8460

Which is the cheapest method for Trumpton? Ignore commission costs.

Solution

The three choices must be compared on a similar basis, which means working out the cost of each to Trumpton either **now** or **in three months time**. Here the cost to Trumpton in three months' time will be determined.

Choice 1: the forward exchange market

Trumpton must buy dollars in order to pay the US supplier. The exchange rate in a forward exchange contract to buy $4,000,000 in three months time (bank sells) is £1 = $1.8445

The cost of the $4,000,000 to Trumpton in three months time will be:

$$\frac{\$4,000,000}{1.8445} = £2,168,609.38$$

This is the cost **in three months**.

Choice 2: the money markets

Using the money markets involves lending (depositing) in the foreign currency, as Trumpton will eventually pay the currency.

	IMPORTER	
	UK £s	**USA $s**
Now	4 withdraw funds from UK account $3,931,304/1.8625 = £2,110,767	3 put money into US account $4,000,000/1.0175 = $3,931,204
	14.25 x 3/12 = 3.5625% (ie 1.035625)	7% x 3/12 = 1.75% (ie 1.0175)
Three months	5 to compare to a forward $2,110,767 x 1.035625 = £2,185,963	1 pay $ invoice from supplier $4,000,000 2 pay off with $ deposit ($4,000,000)

The cost of the money market hedge is £2,185,963.

Choice 3: lead payments

Lead payments should be considered when the currency of payment is expected to strengthen over time, and is quoted forward at a premium on the foreign exchange market.

Here, the cost of a lead payment (paying $4,000,000 now) would be:

$4,000,000 ÷ 1.8625 = £2,147,651.01

The cost in three months' time is the cost of lost interest:

£2,147,651 × (1 + 0.11 x 3/12) = £2,206,711

In this example, the present value of the costs are as follows.

	£
Forward exchange contract	2,168,609
Money markets	2,185,867
Lead payment	2,206,711

The cheapest method for Trumpton is the forward exchange contract therefore the company should use this hedging technique to hedge against transaction risk for this transaction.

Question

Hedging techniques

Weft is an importer/exporter of textiles and textile machinery. It is based in the UK but trades extensively with countries throughout Europe, particularly in the eurozone. It has a small subsidiary based in Germany. The company is about to invoice a customer in Germany for 750,000 euros, payable in three months' time. Weft's treasurer is considering two methods of hedging the exchange risk. These are:

Method 1

Borrow €750,000 for three months, convert the loan into sterling and repay the loan out of eventual receipts. The interest payable on the loan will be purchased in the forward exchange market.

Method 2

Enter into a 3-month forward exchange contract with the company's bank to sell €750,000.

The spot rate of exchange is £1 = €1.6006

The 3-month forward rate of exchange is £1 = €1.5935

Annual interest rates for 3 months' borrowing and lending are: euro 3%, sterling 5%.

Required

(a)   Which of the two methods is the most financially advantageous for Weft?

(b)   What are the other factors to consider before deciding whether to hedge the risk using the foreign currency markets?

Answer

(a) **Method 1**

Weft borrows €750,000.

	EXPORTER	
	UK £	**€**
Now	**4** pay € loan into UK bank account €744,417/1.6006 = £465,086	**3** take out € loan €750,000/1.0075 = €744,417
	5% x 3/12 = 1.25% (ie 1.0125)	3% x 3/12 = 0.75% (ie 1.0075)
Three months	**5** to compare to a forward £465,086 x 1.0125 = £470,900	**1** receive € from export €750,000 **2** pay off € loan with export revenue (€750,000)

Using the money market hedge, Weft will receive £470,900.

Method 2

The exchange rate is fixed in advance at €1.5935 by the forward contract. Cash received in three months is converted to produce €750,000/1.5935 = £470,662.

Conclusion

On the basis of the above calculations, Method 1 gives a slightly higher receipt. However, the difference is quite small, and banker's commission has been excluded from the calculation.

(b) **Factors to consider before deciding whether to hedge foreign exchange risk using the foreign currency markets**

Defensive strategy

The company should have a clear strategy concerning how much foreign exchange risk it is prepared to bear. A highly risk-averse or 'defensive' strategy of hedging all transactions can be **expensive** in terms of **commission costs**, but recognises that exchange rates are unpredictable, can be volatile and so can cause severe losses unless the risk is hedged.

Predictive strategy

An alternative **'predictive' strategy** recognises that if all transaction exposures are hedged, the chance of making gains from favourable exchange rate movements is lost. It might be possible to predict the future movement in an exchange rate with some confidence. The company could therefore **attempt** to **forecast foreign exchange movements** and only hedge those transactions where **losses from currency exposures** are **predicted**. For example, if inflation is high in a particular country, its currency will probably depreciate, so that there is little to be gained by hedging **future payments** in that currency. However, **future receipts** in a weak currency would be hedged, to provide protection against the anticipated currency loss.

A predictive strategy can be a risky strategy. If exchange rate movements were certain, **speculators** would almost certainly force an **immediate fall** in the exchange rate. However, some corporate treasurers argue that, if predictions are made sensibly, a predictive strategy for hedging should lead to higher profits within acceptable risk limits than a risk-averse strategy of hedging everything. Fewer hedging transactions will also mean lower commission costs payable to the bank. The risk remains, though, that a single large uncovered transaction could cause severe problems if the currency moves in the opposite direction to that predicted.

Maximum limit

A sensible strategy for a company could be to set a **maximum limit**, in money terms, for a **foreign currency exposure**. Exposures above this amount should be hedged, but below this limit a predictive approach should be taken or, possibly, all amounts could be left unhedged.

438 **16: The use of financial derivatives to hedge against foreign exchange risk** | Part F Treasury and advanced risk management techniques

BPP LEARNING MEDIA

Offsetting

Before using any technique to hedge foreign currency transactions, **receipts and payments** in the same currency at the same date should be **offset**. This technique is known as matching. For example, if the company is expecting to receive €750,000 on 31 March and to pay €600,000 at about the same time, only the net receipt of €150,000 needs to be considered as a currency exposure.

Matching can be applied to receipts and payments which do not take place on exactly the same day by simply hedging the period and amount of the difference between the receipt and payment, or even by using a currency bank account. A company that has many receipts and payments in a single currency such as the euro should consider **matching assets with liabilities** in the same currency.

7 Currency futures   6/11

Key term

> A **currency future** is a standardised contract to buy or sell a fixed amount of currency at a fixed rate at a fixed future date:
> - **Buying** the futures contract means **receiving** the contract currency
> - **Selling** the futures contract means **supplying** the contract currency

7.1 Features of currency futures

Futures are **standardised** contracts that are traded on an organised exchange such as the Chicago Mercantile Exchange or London International Financial Futures and Options Exchange (LIFFE). They fix the exchange rate for a set amount of currency for a specified time period.

When entering into a foreign exchange futures contract, no one is actually buying or selling anything – the participants are **agreeing** to buy or sell currencies on pre-agreed terms at a specified future date if the contract is allowed to reach maturity, which it rarely does. Futures are a **derivative** (their value derives from movements in the spot rate).

Futures are generally **more liquid** and have **less credit risk** than forward contracts as organised exchanges have clearing houses that guarantee that all traders in the futures market will honour their obligations.

Futures contracts are assumed to mature at the end of either March, June, September or December. One of their limitations is that currencies can only be bought or sold on exchanges for US dollars.

7.1.1 Ticks

The price of a currency future moves in '**ticks**'. A tick is the **smallest movement in the exchange rate** and is normally four decimal places.

Tick value = size of futures contract x tick size

For example, if a futures contract is for £62,500 and the tick size is $0.0001, the tick value is $6.25. (Note that the tick size and tick value are **always quoted in US dollars**.)

What this means is that for every $0.0001 movement in the price, the company will make a profit or loss of $6.25. If the exchange rate moves by $0.004 in the company's favour – which is 40 ticks (0.004/0.0001) – the profit made will be 40 x $6.25 = $250 per contract.

Examples of futures contract specifications – including tick size and tick value – are given below.

Currency	Contract size	Price quotation	Tick size	Tick value per contract
British Pound	£62,500	US$/£1	$0.0001	$6.25
Canadian Dollar	C$100,000	US$/C$1	$0.0001	$10.00
Euro	€125,000	US$/€1	$0.0001	$12.50
Japanese Yen	¥12,500,000	US$/¥100	$0.000001	$12.50
Swiss Franc	SFr125,000	US$/SFr1	$0.0001	$12.50
Australian Dollar	A$100,000	US$/A$1	$0.0001	$12.50

Exam focus point

You will usually be given the contract size in the exam.

7.1.2 Basis risk

Key term

Basis risk is the risk that the price of a currency future will vary from the price of the underlying asset (the spot rate).

Basis is the **difference** between the **spot rate** and the **futures price**.

Basis risk is the risk that the price of a futures contract will vary from the spot rate as expiry of the contract approaches. It is assumed that the **difference** between the spot rate and futures price (the 'basis') **falls over time** but there is a risk that basis will not decrease in this predictable way (which will create an imperfect hedge). There is no basis risk when a contract is held to maturity.

In order to **manage** basis risk it is important to choose a currency future with the **closest maturity date** to the actual transaction. This reduces the **unexpired basis** when the transaction is closed out.

Example

A US company trades in Europe and will need to pay €5 million in five months' time. It is now 1 March and futures contracts mature at the relevant month end. The current spot rate is $1.2500/€1. The following futures contracts are available ($ per €1).

September   1.2456
December   1.2382

If September contracts are used, there will be two months of unexpired basis. If December contracts are used there will be five months. If basis is assumed to decline at a constant rate, the unexpired basis on 1 August under each contract would be as follows

	September	December
Spot rate now	1.2500	1.2500
Futures price	1.2456	1.2382
Difference (basis now)	0.0044	0.0118
Months until contract matures	7	10
Unexpired portion of contract on 1 August	2/7	5/10
Unexpired basis	0.0013	0.0059

The September contracts have the lower unexpired basis. Given the shorter time horizon there is less risk of significant differences between the predicted futures price and the actual futures prices on 1 August when the contracts are settled.

In this case however, the September contracts are closed two months before expiry and there is no guarantee that the price of the futures contract will be the same as the predicted price calculated by basis at that date. It is **assumed** that the unexpired basis above is 0.0013 but it could be either more or less.

This creates a problem in that the futures contract, which in theory give a fixed interest cost, may vary and therefore the amount of interest is not fixed or predictable. Typically, this risk is much **smaller** than the risk of remaining unhedged and therefore the impact of this risk is smaller and **preferable** to not hedging at all.

7.2 Hedge efficiency

Hedgers who need to buy or sell the underlying currency or commodity do not use the margin to trade more than they otherwise would. They can use the futures markets quite safely provided they understand how the system operates. The only risk to hedgers is that the futures market does not always provide a perfect hedge. This can result from two causes.

(a)   The first reason is that amounts must be **rounded to a whole number of contracts**, causing inaccuracies.

(b)   The second reason is **basis risk** – as discussed above. The actions of speculators may increase basis risk.

A measure of **hedge efficiency** compares the profit made on the futures market with the loss made on the cash or commodity market, or *vice versa*.

7.2.1 Example: Hedge efficiency

You are given the following details about the results of a hedge by an American company for a payment of SFr 650,000 in n30 days time under two scenarios. In each case compute the hedge efficiency. Assume today's spot rate is SFr1 =$0.5803. Contract size is SFr125,000, and tick size is $12.50.

Number of contracts = 650,000/125,000= 5.2, round to 5.

	Scenario 1		Scenario 2	
Futures hedge (5 contracts)	$/SFr	$	$/SFr	$
Today: Buy 5 at	0.5725		0.5725	
In 30 days: Sell 5 at	0.6030		0.5610	
Gain/(loss) per contract in ticks	305		(115)	
Total gain/(loss) on 5 contracts:				
5 × $12.50 × no. of ticks		19,063		(7,187)
Cash transaction				
In 30 days: SFr 650,000 are				
actually bought at	0.6112	(397,280)	0.5680	(369,200)
Net cost of the Swiss francs		(378,217)		(376,387)

Solution

The futures hedge gives slightly more or less than the target payment of $377,195 (SFr 650,000 × 0.5803) because of hedge inefficiency. To compute the hedge efficiency in each case, compute gain/loss as a percentage. In scenario 1 the gain comes from the futures market. In scenario 2 the gain comes from the cash market.

Hedge efficiency

	$	$
Target payment (650,000 × 0.5803)	377,195	377,195
Actual cash payment	397,280	369,200
Gain/(loss) on spot market	(20,085)	7,995
Futures gain/(loss)	19,063	(7,187)
Hedge efficiency	94.9%	111.2%

The hedge efficiency can be further analysed as follows.

In scenario 1, the futures market gave a gain of 305 ticks on 5 contracts. The spot market price lost 309 ticks on the equivalent of 5.2 contracts.

$$\text{Hedge efficiency} = \frac{305 \times 5}{309 \times 5.2} = 94.9\%.$$

In scenario 2, the spot market gained 123 ticks on 5.2 contracts. The futures price lost 115 ticks on 5 contracts.

$$\text{Hedge efficiency} = \frac{123 \times 5.2}{115 \times 5} = 111.2\%.$$

An alternative measure of the hedge efficiency on the futures market might be its success measured against the **results** of **using a forward contract**.

7.2.2 Margins and marking to market

There are two types of margin – **initial margin** and **variation margin**.

An **initial margin** is similar to a deposit. When a currency future is set up, the trader would be required to deposit some cash (the initial margin) with the futures exchange in a **margin account** – this acts as security against the trader defaulting on their trading obligations. This money will remain in the margin account as long as the currency future remains 'open'.

We mentioned above the process of calculating the profit or loss on a contract when there is movement in the exchange rate. This profit or loss is received into or paid from the margin account on a daily basis rather than in one large amount when the contract matures. This procedure is known as **marking to market**.

The futures exchange monitors the margin account on a daily basis. If the trader is making significant losses, the futures exchange may require additional margin payments known as **variation margins**. This practice creates uncertainty as the trader will not know in advance the extent (if any) of such margin payments.

7.3 Which type of contract?

As mentioned above, one of the limitations of currency futures is that currencies can only be bought or sold on exchanges for US dollars. The basic rules for choosing the type of contract are given below.

7.3.1 Making a payment in a foreign currency (not US$)

If you are going to make a payment in a foreign currency (not US$) on a future date, you will have to **buy** that currency. To hedge, take the following action.

Step 1   **Buy** the appropriate **foreign currency futures** contracts **now** (just as you would with a forward contract).

Step 2   **Sell** the same number of **foreign currency futures** contracts on the date that you buy the actual currency (closing out).

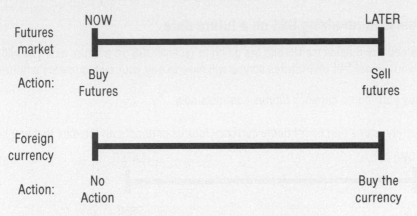

7.3.2 Receiving foreign currency on a future date

If you are going to receive money in a foreign currency on a future date, you will need to sell that currency. To hedge this position take the following steps.

Step 1   **Sell** the appropriate **foreign currency futures** contracts **now**

Step 2   **Buy** the same number of **foreign currency futures** contracts on the date that you sell the actual currency

7.3.3 Non-American wishing to pay in US$ on a future date

If you are from a country outside the US and are going to make a future payment in US$ you will need to buy US$. To hedge, you cannot buy US$ futures so you will have to sell your own currency's futures.

Step 1   Sell your home currency futures contracts now

Step 2   Buy the same number of home currency futures contracts on the date that you buy the US$

7.3.4 Non-American receiving US$ on a future date

If you are from a country outside the US and are going to receive US$ on a future date you will need to sell US$. To hedge you cannot sell US$ futures so you will have to buy your own currency's futures.

Step 1   Buy your home currency futures contracts now

Step 2   Sell the same number of home currency futures contracts on the date that you sell the US$

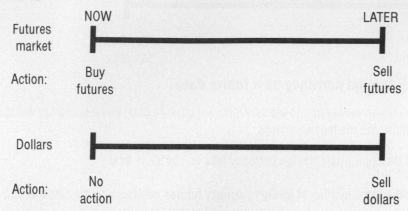

7.4 Dealing with a futures question

A number of possible stages are involved.

Step 1   **The setup process**

This may involve the following steps.

(a)   **Choose which contract**

You must choose an expiry date after the underlying exposure.

(b)   **Choose type of contract**

A €125,000 contract will be used to buy or sell €. If the company **owes €** it will wish to buy this currency so will **buy € futures**.

However a UK company receiving $ will wish to sell $ or buy £. As the contract size is quoted in £ (£62,500 to be precise), the company will **buy £ futures**.

(c)   **Choose number of contracts**

To find the number of contracts required we divide the amount being hedged by the size of the contract.

We may also have to calculate how much of the currency of the future is required. To find this, we use today's price for the futures contract and then divide by the size of the futures contract.

Step 2   **Estimate the closing futures price**

You should be given this in the question.

Step 3   **Hedge outcome**

(a)   **Calculate futures market outcome**

This will be:

Movement in rate x Value of one contract x Number of contracts

(b)   **Calculate net outcome**

444   16: The use of financial derivatives to hedge against foreign exchange risk | Part F Treasury and advanced risk management techniques

BPP
LEARNING MEDIA

Spot market payment or receipt translated at closing rate + Futures market profit/(loss)

The currency used for this calculation will be the opposite to the currency of the receipt/payment being hedged. Ultimately therefore, unless a dollar receipt or payment is being hedged, the value of the futures profit or loss will also have to be converted using the **closing spot rate**.

The gain or loss on the future will accrue during the contract. For exam purposes you will take this gain or loss when the contract is terminated.

Example

A US company buys goods worth €720,000 from a German company payable in 30 days. The US company wants to hedge against the € strengthening against the dollar.

Current spot is €1 = $0.9215 – 0.9221 and the futures rate is 0.9245.

The standard size of a 3 month € futures contract is €125,000.

In 30 days time the spot is 0.9345 – 0.9351. Closing futures price will be 0.9367.

Required

Evaluate the hedge.

Solution

Step 1   Setup

(a) **Which contract?**

We assume that the three month contract is the best available.

(b) **Type of contract**

We need to buy € or sell $.
As the futures contract is in €, we need to buy futures.

(c) **Number of contracts**

$$\frac{720,000}{125,000} = 5.76, \text{ say 6 contracts}$$

Step 2   Closing futures price

We're told it will be 0.9367

Step 3   Hedge outcome

(a) **Outcome in futures market**

Opening futures price	0.9245	Buy at low price
Closing futures price	<u>0.9367</u>	Sell at high price
Movement	0.0122	Profit

Futures profit/loss = 0.0122 x $125,000 x 6 contracts = $9,150

(b)   **Net outcome**

	$
Spot market payment (720,000 x 0.9351)	673,272
Futures market profit	(9,150)
	664,122

In this instance the risk feared was the risk that the payment would go up in $ terms, as you needed more $ to buy each € that you needed to pay the European supplier.

The risk has materialised as in the end you need to pay $0.9351 to buy each € rather than $0.9221.

Buying the € futures has mitigated this loss because at the end you can sell them for more than you paid as € have become more valuable.

7.5 Useful table to remember

You should remember the following table to help you with exam questions on futures.

Transaction on future date		Now		On future date	
Receive	currency	Sell	currency futures	Buy	currency futures
Pay	currency	Buy	currency futures	Sell	currency futures
Receive	$	Buy	currency futures	Sell	currency futures
Pay	$	Sell	currency futures	Buy	currency futures

7.6 Choosing between forward contracts and futures contracts

FAST FORWARD

Although a foreign exchange *futures* contract is conceptually similar to a *forward* foreign exchange contract, there are important differences between the two instruments.

A futures market hedge attempts to achieve the same result as a forward contract, that is to fix the exchange rate in advance for a future foreign currency payment or receipt. As we have seen, hedge inefficiencies mean that a futures contract can only fix the exchange rate subject to a margin of error.

Forward contracts are agreed **'over the counter'** between a bank and its customer. Futures contracts are standardised and traded on futures exchanges. This results in the following advantages and disadvantages.

7.6.1 Advantages of currency futures

(a)   **Transaction** costs should be **lower** than for forward contracts.

(b)   The **exact date** of **receipt** or **payment** of the currency does **not have to be known**, because the futures contract does not have to be closed out until the actual cash receipt or payment is made. In other words, the futures hedge gives the equivalent of an 'option forward' contract, limited only by the expiry date of the contract.

(c)   Because future contracts are traded on exchange regulated markets, **counterparty risk** should be **reduced** and buying and selling contracts should be easy.

7.6.2 Disadvantages of currency futures

(a)   The **contracts cannot be tailored** to the user's exact requirements.

(b)   **Hedge inefficiencies** are **caused** by having to deal in a whole number of contracts and by **basis risk**.

(c) **Only a limited number of currencies** are the subject of futures contracts (although the number of currencies is growing, especially with the rapid development of Asian economies).

(d) The **procedure for converting** between two currencies neither of which is the US dollar is twice as complex for futures as for a forward contract.

(e) Using the market will involve various **costs**, including brokers' fees.

In general, the disadvantages of futures mean that the market is much smaller than the currency forward market.

Question

Currency futures

Allbrit plc, a company based in the UK, imports and exports to the USA. On 1 May it signs three agreements, all of which are to be settled on 31 October:

(a) A sale to a US customer of goods for $205,500

(b) A sale to another US customer for £550,000

(c) A purchase from a US supplier for $875,000

On 1 June the spot rate is £1 = 1.5500 – 1.5520 $ and the October forward rate is at a premium of 4.00 – 3.95 cents per pound. Sterling futures contracts are trading at the following prices:

Sterling futures (IMM) Contract size £62,500

Contract settlement date	Contract price $ per £1
Jun	1.5370
Sep	1.5180
Dec	1.4970

Tick size is $6.25.

Required

(a) Calculate the net amount receivable or payable in pounds if the transactions are covered on the forward market.

(b) Demonstrate how a futures hedge could be set up and calculate the result of the futures hedge if, by 31 October, the spot market price for dollars has moved to 1.5800 – 1.5820 and the sterling futures price has moved to 1.5650.

Answer

(a) Before covering any transactions with forward or futures contracts, match receipts against payments. The sterling receipt does not need to be hedged. The dollar receipt can be matched against the payment giving a net payment of $669,500 on 31 October.

The appropriate spot rate for buying dollars on 1 May (bank sells low) is 1.5500. The forward rate for October is *spot – premium* = 1.5500 – 0.0400 = 1.5100.

Using a forward contract, the sterling cost of the dollar payment will be 669,500/1.5100 = £443,377. The net cash received on October 31 will therefore be £550,000 – 443,377 = £106,623.

(b) **Step 1** Setup

(a) **Which contract?**

December contracts

(b) **Type of contract**

Sell sterling futures in May, we sell the sterling to buy the $ we need

(c) **Number of contracts**

Here we need to convert the dollar payment to £ as contracts are in £.

Using December futures price

$$\frac{669,500}{1.4970} = £447,228$$

No of contracts = $\frac{£447,228}{62,500}$ = 7.16 contracts (round to 7)

Step 2 **Closing futures price**

1.5650 (given in question)

Step 3 Result of futures market

(a) **Futures market outcome**

	$
Opening futures price	1.4970 Sell
Closing futures price	1.5650 Buy
Movement	0.0680 Loss

Futures market loss = 0.0680 x 62,500 x 7 = $29,750

(b) **Net outcome**

	$
Spot market payment	(669,500)
Futures market loss	(29,750)
	(699,250)
Translated at closing spot rate	1.5800
The bank sells low hence we use the rate of 1.5800	£442,563

8 Currency options

6/11

FAST FORWARD

Currency options protect against adverse exchange rate movements while allowing the investor to take advantage of favourable exchange rate movements. They are particularly useful in situations where the cash flow is not certain to occur (eg when tendering for overseas contracts).

8.1 Introduction

A **currency option** is an agreement involving a right, but not an obligation, to buy or sell a certain amount of currency at a stated rate of exchange (the exercise price) at some time in the future.

A forward exchange contract is an agreement to buy or sell a given quantity of foreign exchange, which **must be carried out** because it is a binding contract. However, some exporters might be uncertain about the amount of currency they will earn in several months' time.

An alternative method of obtaining foreign exchange cover, which overcomes much of this problem, is the **currency option**. A currency option **does not have to be exercised**. Instead, when the date for exercising the option arrives, the importer or exporter can either exercise the option or let the option lapse.

The exercise price for the option may be the same as the current spot rate, or it may be more favourable or less favourable to the option holder than the current spot rate.

As with other types of option, buying a currency option involves **paying a premium**, which is the most the buyer of the option can lose. The level of option premiums depends on the following factors:

- The exercise price
- The maturity of the option
- The volatility of exchange and interest rates
- Interest rate differentials, affecting how much banks charge

8.2 Basic terminology

This section covers the basic terminology that you will frequently see in questions relating to currency options. Make sure you understand the meaning of each of the terms as this will help you to interpret questions and make decisions regarding different types of options.

Some of this terminology should be familiar from Chapter 6.

Call option – the right to buy (the contract currency)
Put option – the right to sell (the contract currency)

A **call option** gives the **buyer** of the option the **right to buy** the underlying currency at a **fixed rate of exchange** (and the **seller** of the option would be **required to sell** the underlying currency at that rate).

A **put option** gives the **buyer** of the option the **right to sell** the underlying currency at a **fixed rate of exchange** (and the **seller** of the option would be **required to buy** the underlying currency at that rate).

Exercise price – the price at which the future transaction will take place.

The exercise price is also known as the **strike price**. It is the price with which the prevailing spot rate should be compared in order to determine whether the option should be exercised or not.

In the money – where the option strike price is more favourable than the current spot rate.
At the money – where the option strike price is equal to the current spot rate.
Out of the money – where the option strike price is less favourable than the current spot rate.

For example if a German company holds a call option to purchase £ with a strike price of €1 = £0.9174 and the current spot rate is €1 = £0.9200, the option is '**out of the money**' as the current spot rate is more favourable than the option strike price.

8.3 Types of option – over the counter and exchange-traded

Companies can choose whether to buy:

(a)   A tailor-made currency option from a bank, suited to the company's specific needs. These are **over-the-counter** (OTC) or **negotiated** options, or

(b)   A standard option, in certain currencies only, from an options exchange. Such options are **traded** or **exchange-traded** options.

8.3.1 Over the counter (OTC) options

Over the counter (OTC) options can be purchased directly and are normally **fixed date** (European) options.

Example

It is now 1st March. Robin Inc anticipates that it may receive €6m from the sale of a European investment in June. It wishes to hedge this potential receipt using options. The current spot rate is $1 = €0.7106. June options with a value of €6m and an exercise price of €0.7200 can be purchased for a premium of $150,000.

Required

What will the outcome of the hedge be in each of the following scenarios?

*   The spot exchange rate in June is €0.6500
*   The spot exchange rate in June is €0.7500
*   The sale of the investment does not take place

Solution

(a) The spot rate is better than the option rate therefore the spot rate is used. This will give a value of $9,230769 or $9,080,769 after the premium (which is paid up front).

(b) The option rate is better than the spot rate therefore the option will be exercised. This will give a value of $8,333,333 (or $8,183,333 after the premium).

(c) If the sale of the investment is abandoned then the option is no longer necessary. It will be abandoned (as in (a) above). There is no point in exercising the option as it would cost $8,443,568 to purchase the Euros but Robin Inc would only receive $8,333,333 at the option price (before taking the premium into account). The cost to the company of abandoning the option will be the premium of $150,000.

8.3.2 Exchange traded options

A company wishing to purchase an option to buy or sell sterling might use currency options traded on such US markets as the Philadelphia Stock Exchange (PHLX). The schedule of prices for £/$ options is set out in tables such as the one shown below.

Philadelphia SE £/$ options £31,250 (cents per pound)

Strike price	Calls			Puts		
	Aug	Sep	Oct	Aug	Sep	Oct
1.5750	2.58	3.13	–	–	0.67	–
1.5800	2.14	2.77	3.24	–	0.81	1.32
1.5900	1.23	2.17	2.64	0.05	1.06	1.71
1.6000	0.50	1.61	2.16	0.32	1.50	2.18
1.6100	0.15	1.16	1.71	0.93	2.05	2.69
1.6200	–	0.81	1.33	1.79	2.65	3.30

Note the following points

(a) *What is the contract size?*

The contract size is £31,250

(b) *What is the meaning of the numbers under each month?*

This is the cost in cents per £ (remember that the market is in the US) – for example, September call at a strike price of $1.6100 will cost $0.0116 x £31,250 = $362.50

(c) *What is a put US$ per £ option?*

This is the option to sell £ (eg UK importer having to sell £ to obtain $ to pay a US supplier)

(d) *Why is a August call at $1.5800 more expensive than an August call at $1.5900?*

$1.5800 is a better rate than $1.5900 therefore to secure such a rate will be more expensive.

(e) *Why is a call option exercisable in September more expensive than a call option exercisable in August but with the same strike price?*

This is because there is a longer period until the exercise date and it is therefore more likely that exercising the option will be beneficial. The difference also reflects the market's view of the direction in which the exchange rate is likely to move between the two dates.

8.3.3 Traded v over the counter options

Both types of options have advantages over the other – the choice of option will depend on particular requirements.

Advantages of traded options

(a) Traded options are standard sizes and are thus 'tradable' which means they can be sold on to other parties if not required. OTC options are designed for a specific purpose and are therefore unlikely to be suitable for another party.

(b) Traded options are more flexible in that they cover a period of time (American options, whereas OTC options are fixed date (European options).

Advantages of OTC options

(a) OTC options can be agreed for a longer period than the standard two year maximum offered by traded options. This gives greater flexibility and protection from currency movements in the longer term should the transaction require it.

(b) OTC options are tailored specifically for a particular transaction, ensuring maximum protection from currency movements. As traded options are of a standard size, the full amount of the transaction may not be hedged as fractions of options are not available.

Exam focus point

> Make sure you know these advantages and disadvantages as they may be useful when making a recommendation regarding hedging strategies.

8.4 Choosing the correct type of option

The vast majority of options examples which we consider are concerned with **hedgers** who **purchase** options in order to reduce risk. We are seldom concerned with option writers who sell options.

So, given that we are normally going to *purchase* options, should we **purchase puts or calls**?

(a) A **US company receiving £** in the future and hence wishing to **sell £** in the future can hedge by **purchasing £ put options** (ie options to sell £).

(b) A **US company paying £** in the future and hence wishing to **buy £** in the future can hedge by **purchasing £ call options** (ie options to buy £).

(c) A **UK company receiving $** in the future and hence wishing to **sell $** in the future cannot hedge by purchasing $ put options as they don't exist. They therefore have to **purchase £ call options**.

(d) A **UK company paying $** in the future and hence wishing to **buy $** in the future cannot hedge by purchasing $ call options as they don't exist. They therefore have to **purchase £ put options**.

Exam focus point

The following table will be helpful to remember when answering exam questions on currency options.

Transaction on future date		Now		Option on future date	
Receive	currency	Buy	currency put	Sell	currency
Pay	currency	Buy	currency call	Buy	currency
Receive	$	Buy	currency call	Buy	currency
Pay	$	Buy	currency put	Sell	currency

Note that this table only applies to **traded** options. It would be possible to purchase a dollar put or call option over the counter.

8.5 Choosing the price and the number of contracts to be used

A problem arises when a non-US company wishes to buy or sell US dollars using traded options. The amount of US dollars must first be converted into the home currency. For this purpose the best exchange rate to use is the **exercise price**, which means that the number of contracts may vary according to which exercise price is chosen.

8.6 Closing out when traded options still have time to run

In practice, most traded options are **closed out**, like futures contracts, because the date when the cash is required does not match the option expiry date.

The position with options is equivalent to the position with **futures**; the expiry date of options must be **on** or **after** the date of the key event. Thus if you were told a company was receiving a payment on 10 September, and you were given a choice of using June, September or December options:

- You could most likely choose September as that expires soonest after 10 September (on 30 September)

- You could choose December

- You would not choose June (as June options expire before 10 September, the date on which you will receive the payment)

8.7 Option calculation technique

If an options calculation appears to be complicated, it is best to use a similar method to the method we used for futures to assess the impact of options.

Step 1   Set up the hedge

(a) Choose contract date

(b) Decide whether put or call option is required

(c) Decide which exercise or strike price applies

(d) How many contract are required

(e) Calculate premium (Price in table x 0.01) x Size of contract x Number of contracts

Step 2   Ascertain closing price

You should be given this in the question.

Step 3   Calculate outcome of hedge

You may have to calculate the outcome under more than one closing spot rate.

(a) Outcome in options market. This will include:

    (i)   Exercising the option

    (ii)   Cash flows on exercise

    (iii)   Converting amount uncovered/overcovered at spot rate

(b) Net outcome

Example

A UK company owes a US supplier $2,000,000 payable in July. The spot rate is £1 = $1.5350–1.5370 and the UK company is concerned that the $ might strengthen.

The details for $/£ £31,250 options (cents per £1) are as follows.

Premium cost per contract

	Calls			Puts		
Strike price	June	July	August	June	July	August
1.4750	6.34	6.37	6.54	0.07	0.19	0.50
1.5000	3.86	4.22	4.59	0.08	0.53	1.03
1.5250	1.58	2.50	2.97	0.18	1.25	1.89

Show how traded currency options can be used to hedge the risk at a strike price of 1.525. Calculate the sterling cost of the transaction if the spot rate in July is:

(a)   1.46–1.4620

(b)   1.61–1.6120

Solution

Step 1   Set up the hedge

(a)   Which date contract? July

(b)   Put or call? Put, we need to put (sell) pounds in order to generate the dollars we need

(c)   Which strike price? 1.5250

(d)   How many contracts

$$\frac{2,000,000 \div 1.525}{31,250} \approx 41.97, \text{ say 42 contracts}$$

(e)   Use July Put figure for 1.5250 of 1.25. Remember it has to be multiplied by 0.01.

Premium   = (1.25 × 0.01) × Contract size × Number of contracts

Premium   = 0.0125 × 31,250 × 42

                = $16,406 ÷ 1.5350 (to obtain premium in £)

                = £10,688

We need to pay the option premium in $ now. Therefore the bank sells low at 1.5350.

Step 2   Closing spot and futures price

Case (a) $1.46

Case (b) $1.61

Step 3   Outcome

(a)   **Options market outcome**

Strike price put	1.5250	1.5250
Closing price	1.46	1.61
Exercise?	Yes	No
Outcome of options position (31,250 × 42)	£1,312,500	–

Balance on spot market

	$
Exercise option (31,250 × 42 × 1.5250)	2,001,563
Value of transaction	2,000,000
Balance	1,563

Translated at spot rate $\dfrac{1,563}{1.46}$ = £1,071

(b)   **Net outcome**

	£	£
Spot market outcome translated at closing spot rate $\dfrac{2,000,000}{1.61}$	–	(1,242,236)
Options position	(1,312,500)	–
Difference in hedge at closing rate	1,071	
The difference is a receipt as the amount owed was over-hedged.		
Premium (remember premium has to be added in separately as translated at the opening spot rate)	(10,688)	(10,688)
	(1,322,117)	(1,252,924)

Question   Currency options 1

Edted is a UK company that has purchased goods worth $2,000,000 from an American supplier. Edted is due to make payment in three months' time. Edted's treasury department is looking to hedge the risk using an over-the-counter option, A three month dollar call option has a price of 1.4800.

Required

Ignoring premium costs, calculate the cost to Edted if the exchange rate at the time of payment is:

(a)   £1 = $1.4600
(b)   £1 = $1.5000

Answer

As the option is an over-the-counter option, it is possible to have a dollar call option and to cover the exact amount.

(a)   If the exchange rate is 1.4600, the option will be exercised and the cost will be:

$\dfrac{2,000,000}{1.4800}$ = £1,351,351

(b) If the exchange rate is 1.5000, the option will not be exercised, and the cost will be:

$$\frac{2,000,000}{1.5000} = £1,333,333$$

Question

Vinnick, an American company purchases goods from Santos, a Spanish company, on 15 May on 3 months credit for €600,000.

Vinnick is unsure in which direction exchange rates will move so has decided to buy options to hedge the contract at a rate of $1 = €0.7700.

The details for €10,000 options at 0.7700 are as follows.

Calls				Puts		
July	August	September		July	August	September
2.55	3.57	4.01		1.25	2.31	2.90

The current spot rate is 0.7800.

Required

Calculate the dollar cost of the transaction if the spot rate in August is:

(a) 0.7500
(b) 0.8000

Answer

Step 1 **Set up the hedge**

(a) Which contract date? August

(b) Put or call? Call – we need to buy euros

(c) Which strike price? 0.7700

(d) How many contracts?

$$\frac{600,000}{10,000} = 60$$

(e) Use August call figure of 3.57. Remember it has to be multiplied by 0.01.

Premium = (3.57 x 0.01) x Contract size x Number of contracts

Premium = 0.0357 x 10,000 x 60 = $21,420

Step 2 **Closing spot and futures prices**

Case (a) 0.75

Case (b) 0.80

Step 3   Outcome

(a) **Options market outcome**

Strike price call	0.77	0.77
Closing price	0.75	0.80
Exercise?	Yes	No
Outcome of options position	€600,000	-

(b) **Net outcome**

	$	$
Spot market outcome translated at closing spot rate (600,000/0.80)	-	(750,000)
Options position (600,000/0.77)	(779,221)	-
Premium	(21,420)	(21,420)
	(800,641)	(771,420)

8.8 Graphical illustration of currency options

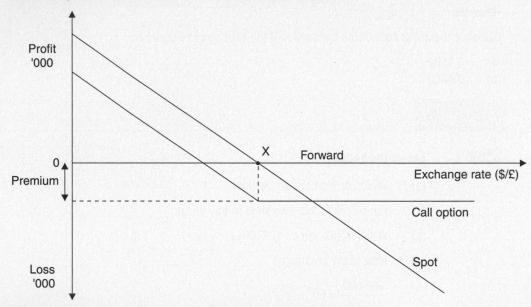

Currency call option, forward and spot markets: profit/loss profile

Suppose that a UK-based company expects to receive an amount of export income in dollars ($) in three months' time. This graph illustrates the profit/loss profile of different strategies.

(a) Selling dollars and buying sterling in the **forward market** eliminates all uncertainty. The outcome is represented by a horizontal line.

(b) Relying on the **spot market** results in a net gain or loss compared with the forward market if the spot exchange rate in three months' time turns out to be below or above $X per pound respectively.

(c) If a **call option** is used, it will not be exercised if the exchange rate is less than $X per pound. A currency call option reduces the potential gain compared with the spot market strategy (b) by the amount of the premium on the option, but has the advantage that potential losses are contained as they will not exceed the value of the premium.

8.9 Currency options v forward and futures contracts

A hedge using a currency future will produce approximately the same result as a currency forward (subject to hedge inefficiencies). When comparing currency options with forward and futures contracts we usually find the following.

(a) If the currency movement is adverse, the option will be exercised. However the hedge will not normally be as good as that of forward or futures contracts – this is due to the premium cost of the option.

(b) If the currency movement is favourable, the option will not be exercised. The hedge will normally be better than that of forward or futures contracts as the option allows the holder to profit from the improved exchange rate.

9 Currency swaps

FAST FORWARD

Currency swaps effectively involve the exchange of debt from one currency to another.

Currency swaps can provide a **hedge** against exchange rate movements for longer periods than the forward market and can be a means of obtaining finance from new countries.

9.1 Swap procedures

Key term

> A **swap** is an arrangement whereby two organisations contractually agree to exchange payments on different terms, for example in different currencies, or one at a fixed rate and the other at a floating rate.

In a **currency swap**, the parties agree to swap equivalent amounts of currency for a period. This effectively involves the exchange of debt from one currency to another. Liability on the main debt (the principal) is not transferred and the parties are liable to **counterparty risk**: if the other party defaults on the agreement to pay interest, the original borrower remains liable to the lender. In practice, most currency swaps are conducted between banks and their customers. An agreement may only be necessary if the swap were for longer than, say, one year.

Example

Consider a US company X with a subsidiary Y in France which owns vineyards. Assume a spot rate of $1 = €0.7062. Suppose the parent company X wishes to raise a loan of €1.6 million for the purpose of buying another French wine company. At the same time, the French subsidiary Y wishes to raise $1 million to pay for new up-to-date capital equipment imported from the US. The US parent company X could borrow the $1 million and the French subsidiary Y could borrow the €1.6 million, each effectively borrowing on the other's behalf. They would then swap currencies.

9.2 Benefits of swaps

(a) **Flexibility**

Swaps are **easy to arrange** and are **flexible** since they can be arranged in any size and are reversible.

(b) **Cost**

Transaction costs are low, only amounting to legal fees, since there is no commission or premium to be paid.

(c) **Market avoidance**

The parties can **obtain the currency they require** without subjecting themselves to the **uncertainties** of the foreign exchange markets.

(d) **Access to finance**

The company can gain **access to debt finance in another country** and currency where it is little known, and consequently has a poorer credit rating, than in its home country. It can therefore take advantage of lower interest rates than it could obtain if it arranged the currency loan itself.

(e) **Financial restructuring**

Currency swaps may be used to **restructure the currency base** of the company's liabilities. This may be important where the company is trading overseas and receiving revenues in foreign currencies, but its borrowings are denominated in the currency of its home country. Currency swaps therefore provide a means of reducing exchange rate exposure.

(f) **Conversion of debt type**

At the same time as exchanging currency, the company may also be able to **convert fixed rate debt** to **floating rate or vice versa**. Thus it may obtain some of the benefits of an interest rate swap in addition to achieving the other purposes of a currency swap.

(g) **Liquidity improvement**

A currency swap could be used to **absorb excess liquidity** in one currency which is not needed immediately, to create funds in another where there is a need.

9.3 Disadvantages of swaps

(a) **Risk of default by the other party to the swap (counterparty risk)**

If one party became **unable to meet its swap payment obligations**, this could mean that the other party risked having to make them itself.

(b) **Position or market risk**

A company whose main business lies outside the field of finance should **not increase financial risk** in order to make **speculative gains**.

(c) **Sovereign risk**

There may be a risk of **political disturbances or exchange controls** in the country whose currency is being used for a swap.

(d) **Arrangement fees**

Swaps have arrangement fees payable to third parties. Although these may appear to be cheap, this is because the intermediary accepts **no liability** for the swap. (The third party does however suffer some spread risk, as they warehouse one side of the swap until it is matched with the other, and then undertake a temporary hedge on the futures market.)

Example

Step 1   Edted, a UK company, wishes to invest in Germany. It borrows £20 million from its bank and pays interest at 5%. To invest in Germany, the £20 million will be converted into euros at a spot rate of £1 = €1.5. The earnings from the German investment will be in euros, but Edted will have to pay interest on the swap. The company arranges to swap the £20 million for €30 million with Gordonbear, a company in the Euro currency zone. Gordonbear is thus the counterparty in this transaction. Interest of 6% is payable on the €30 million. Edted can use the €30 million it receives to invest in Germany.

Step 2   Each year when interest is due:

(a)   Edted receives from its German investment cash remittances of €1.8 million (€30 million × 6%).

(b)   Edted passes this €1.8 million to Gordonbear so that Gordonbear can settle its interest liability.

(c)   Gordonbear passes to Edted £1 million (£20 million × 5%).

(d)   Edted settles its interest liability of £1 million with its lender.

Step 3   At the end of the useful life of the investment the original payments are reversed with Edted paying back the €30 million it originally received and receiving back from Gordonbear the £20 million. Edted uses this £20 million to repay the loan it originally received from its UK lender.

10 FOREX swaps

Key term

> A **FOREX swap** is a spot currency transaction coupled with an agreement that it will be reversed at a pre-specified date by an offsetting forward transaction.

Although the FOREX swap is arranged as a single transaction, it consist of two distinct separate legs. The counterparties agree to exchange two currencies at a particular rate on one date and to reverse payments normally at a different rate on a specified future date. The two legs can therefore be seen as one spot **transaction** and **one forward transaction** going the **opposite direction**.

An FOREX swap is called a *buy/sell* swap when the base currency eg the dollar is bought on the near date and sold on the far date, and is called a *sell/buy* swap when the base currency is sold on the near date and bought on the far date.

A FOREX swap is useful for hedging because it allows companies to shift temporarily into or out of one currency in exchange for a second currency without incurring the exchange rate risk of holding an open position in the currency they temporarily hold. This avoids a change in currency exposure which is the role of the forward contract.

An example of a FOREX swap is where Bank ABC enters into a FOREX swap with Bank 123 to:

- Sell USD1,000,000 worth of Japanese Yen (JPY) today
- Buy USD1,000,000 worth of JPY in one week's time.

This FOREX swap (known as a spot to forward date swap) would look something like this:

	Bank ABC	JPY →	Bank 123
Today	sells JPY and buys USD	← USD	Buys JPY and Sells USD

	Bank ABC	← JPY	Bank 123
One week	buys JPY and sells USD	USD →	sells JPY and buys USD

In the above example the FOREX swap is made up of a spot FOREX transaction and a one-week forward transaction. Other types of FOREX swaps include transactions where both the first and second halves (legs) occur in the future. These are known as forward against forward swaps, and are, in effect, two forward transactions operating in parallel.

11 Devising a foreign currency hedging strategy   6/11

Given the wide range of financial instruments (both internal and external) available to companies that are exposed to foreign currency risk, how can an appropriate strategy be devised that will achieve the objective of reduced exposure whilst at the same time keeping costs at an acceptable level and not damaging the company's relationship with its customers and suppliers?

There is no individual best way of devising a suitable hedging strategy – each situation must be approached on its own merits. Unless you are told otherwise, it should be assumed that the company will be wanting to minimise its risk exposure – it is up to you to come up with the most appropriate way of doing so.

You should be prepared to justify your choice of strategy.

The following example will give you an idea of how to put together a suitable strategy while justifying your choice of doing so.

Example – foreign currency hedging strategy

IOU Inc is a large company based in the USA that trades mainly within the USA and with the UK. It has a significant amount of borrowing in sterling. Debt interest of £725,000 is due to be paid on 31 October and a further £530,000 on 31 December. IOU Inc's policy is to hedge the risks involved in all foreign currency transactions.

Assume it is now 30 September. The company's bank quotes the following rates of exchange, US$ per £:

Spot	1 month forward (mid rate)	3 months forward (mid rate)
1.5584 – 1.5590	1.5601	1.5655

Prices for a £/$ option on a US stock exchange (cents per £, payable on purchase of the option, contract size £31,250) are:

Strike price (£/$)	Calls		Puts	
	October	December	October	December
1.56	2.02	3.00	1.00	2.16
1.57	1.32	n/a	n/a	n/a
1.58	0.84	2.12	2.18	3.14

The treasurer is considering two methods of hedging the risk, forward or option contracts. Market expectations, based on current published economic forecasts, are that sterling will appreciate against the US$ over the next three months. The treasurer thinks the £ might weaken or at least remain stable against the $. He suggests that if options are to be used, one-month options should be bought at a strike price of 1.57 and three-month options at a strike price of 1.58.

Ignore transaction costs.

Required

(a) Recommend, with reasons, the most appropriate method for IOU Inc to hedge its foreign exchange risk on the two interest payments due in one and three months' time. Your answer should include appropriate calculations, using the figures in the question, to support your recommendation and a discussion of the factors to consider when choosing between the two hedging mechanisms.

Assume you are a financial manager with the nationally-owned postal and telecommunications company in Zorro, a country in Asia. In organisations such as this, periodic settlements are made between local and foreign operators. Net receipts or payments are in US$.

(b) Explain the main types of foreign exchange risk exposure that are likely to affect the organisation and advise the company on policies it could consider to reduce exposure to these risks.

Solution

(a) **Spot market position**

The company expects to pay £1,255,000. At today's spot rate this would be converted to $ at $1.5590, giving 1,255,000 × 1.5590 = $1,956,545.

Forward contracts

Forward contracts remove the **risk** from **future short-term currency fluctuations** by fixing an exchange rate in advance. If forward contracts are used, the following dollar costs will be incurred:

One month: £725,000 × 1.5601 = $1,131,073
Three months: £530,000 × 1.5655 = $829,715
Total payment: 1,131,073 + 829,715 = $1,960,788

A forward contract will mean that the interest payment is of a **predictable amount** and the possibility of exchange losses is **eliminated**. However, IOU will not be able to participate in **exchange gains** if the pound weakens.

Options

Options can be used to put a 'ceiling' (or 'cap') on the amount payable while allowing the user to take advantage of **favourable exchange rate movements**.

Option set-up October payment

(i)   Contract date – October

(ii)   Option type – Call option; buy £ with $

(iii) Strike price – Choose $1.57 as recommended by the treasurer

(iv)   Number of contracts

$$\frac{725,000}{31,250} = 23.2 \text{ contracts. Say 23 contracts hedging } 31,250 \times 23$$

$$= £718,750, \text{ leaving } £6,250 \text{ to be hedged on forward market.}$$

(v)   Premium = 23 × 31,250 × $0.0132 = $9,488

Outcome

Option will be exercised if dollar weakens to more than $1.57 in £.

Exercise 23 contracts @ $1.57

	$
Option outcome 1.57 × 23 × £31,250	1,128,438
Option premium	9,488
Unhedged amount covered by forward contract £6,250 × 1.5601	9,751
	1,147,677

Option set-up December payment

(i)   Contract date – December contract

(ii)   Option type – Call option

(iii) Strike price – Choose $1.58

(iv)   Number of contracts

$$\frac{530,000}{31,250} = 16.96 \text{ contracts, say 17 contracts hedging } £31,250 \times 17$$

$$= £531,250, \text{ with difference taken to forward market } (531,250 - 530,000$$

$$= £1,250)$$

(v)   Premium = 17 × 31,250 × $0.0212 = $11,263

Outcome

Option will be exercised if dollar weakens to more than $1.58 in £.

	$
Option outcome 1.58 × 17 × 31,250	839,375
Option premium	11,263
Forward contract receipt £1,250 × 1.5655	(1,957)
Net payment	848,681

Breakeven rate

The disadvantage of options is that they can be expensive to buy because of the premium. The breakeven rate, the rate below which options will give a more favourable outcome than a forward contract, can be calculated as follows, ignoring the issue of whole contracts.

(Breakeven rate × Amount hedged) + Premium = Forward contract payment

For October breakeven rate = $\dfrac{1,131,073 - 9,488}{725,000}$ = $1.5470

For December breakeven rate = $\dfrac{829,715 - 11,263}{530,000}$ = $1.5442

Recommendation

Options should only be used if it is thought to be a good chance that the pound will weaken (but protection is still required against its strengthening). If, as the market believes, the pound is likely to strengthen, forward contracts will offer better value.

(b) **Exchange risks in Zorro**

Transactions exposure

This is the risk that the exchange rate **moves unfavourably** between the **date of agreement** of a contract price and the **date of cash settlement**.

Economic exposure

This is the risk of an **adverse change in the present value** of the organisation's future cash flows as a result of longer-term exchange rate movements.

Netting off

The Zorro postal and telecommunications company will receive **domestic income** in its local currency but will make **settlements** (net receipts or payments) with foreign operators in US dollars. It may appear that most of the **currency risk** is **hedged** because **dollar payments** are balanced against **dollar receipts** before settlement. However, although this is a good way of reducing currency transaction costs, it does not remove currency risk.

Residual risk

Although the foreign transactions are denominated in dollars, the exchange risk involves all the **currencies of the countries** with which the company deals. For example, if money is owed to Germany and the euro has strengthened against the dollar, then the dollar cost of the transaction has increased. Also, although all of these transactions are short term, their combined effect is to expose the company to **continuous exchange risk** on many currencies. The company needs a strategy to manage this form of **economic exposure**.

Management of currency risk

One way to manage currency risk in this situation is to attempt to **match assets and liabilities** in each currency as follows.

(i) The company needs to examine each country with which it deals and, having selected those with which it has a material volume of transactions, **determine in each case** whether there is a **net receipt** or **net payment** with that country and the average amount of this net receipt/payment.

(ii) If for a given country there is normally a net receipt, currency risk can be hedged by **borrowing an amount** in that currency equal to the **expected net receipt** for the period for which hedging is required, and **converting this amount** to the home currency.

(iii) For countries where there is **normally a net payment**, a **deposit account** in this currency should be maintained.

Recommendation

This strategy will go some way towards hedging currency risk in the various countries involved, but will involve **increased currency transaction costs** and possibly **increased interest costs**. It is therefore probably only feasible for major currencies (eg dollar, euro, yen) and for currencies of Asian countries with which there are major transaction volumes.

Chapter Roundup

- Currency rates can be quoted as **direct quotes** or **indirect quotes**.

  The **spot rate** is the rate at which currencies can be exchanged now. The **forward rate** is the rate at which currencies will be exchanged on a set future date.

- The difference between the bid price and the offer price is known as the **spread**.

- Internal hedging techniques include **leading and lagging, invoicing in home currency, matching** and **multilateral netting.**

- Netting is a process in which credit balances are netted off against debit balances so that only the reduced net amounts remain due to be paid by actual currency flows.

- A **forward contract** is a contract with a bank that covers a **specific amount** of foreign currency for delivery at an **agreed date** at an **exchange rate agreed now**.

- If the forward rate is higher that the spot rate, the currency is quoted at a discount; if the forward rate is lower than the spot rate, the currency is quoted at a premium.

- **Money market hedging** involves borrowing in one currency, converting the money borrowed into another currency and putting the money on deposit until the time at which the transaction is completed, hoping to take advantage of favourable interest rate movements.

- Although a foreign exchange *futures* contract is conceptually similar to a *forward* foreign exchange contract, there are important structural and institutional differences between the two instruments.

- **Currency options** protect against adverse exchange rate movements while allowing the investor to take advantage of favourable exchange rate movements. They are particularly useful in situations where the cash flow is not certain to occur (eg when tendering for overseas contracts).

- **Currency swaps** effectively involve the exchange of debt from one currency to another.

- Currency swaps can provide a **hedge** against exchange rate movements for longer periods than the forward market and can be a means of obtaining finance from new countries.

1   A US exporter receives HK$400,000 from a customer. The bank has quoted an offer price of HK$7.7000 and a bid price of HK$7.7425. How many US dollars will the exporter receive from the bank in exchange for HK$400,000?

2   Which factors influence the supply and demand for currencies?

3   Fill in the boxes in the diagram with (A) to (E), to indicate which factors are linked by which theory.

   (A)   Purchasing power parity theory

   (B)   Expectations theory

   (C)   Fisher effect

   (D)   International Fisher effect

   (E)   Interest rate parity

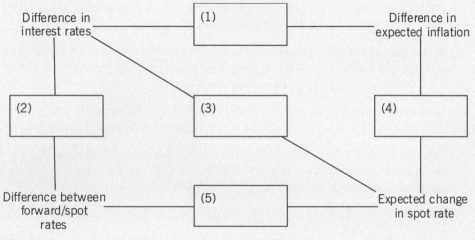

4   Fill in the blanks

   (a)   Forward rate cheaper than spot rate quoted at a ....

   (b)   Forward rate more expensive than spot rate quoted at a ....

5   Complete the following table using Buy or Sell.

Transaction on future date		Now		On future date	
Receive	currency		currency futures		currency futures
Pay	currency		currency futures		currency futures
Receive	$		currency futures		currency futures
Pay	$		currency futures		currency futures

6   Complete the following table using Buy or Sell.

Transaction on future date		Now		Option on future date	
Receive	currency				
Pay	currency				
Receive	$				
Pay	$				

7   What are the key stages in setting up an option hedge?

8   What is the significance of a settlement date in futures?

9   What are the main factors affecting the level of option premiums?

10 Fill in the blank.

.... risk is the risk of one party on a swap defaulting on the arrangement.

11 Swaps, like other derivatives, can be used as methods of speculation.

True ☐

False ☐

12 Trebzon Ltd a UK company plans to use a money market hedge to hedge its payment of €4,000,000 for Spanish goods in one year. The UK interest rate is 6 percent and the Euro interest rate is 4 percent. The spot exchange rate is £1 = €1.46, while the one year forward rate is £1 = €1.46. Determine the amount of £ needed if a money market hedge is used.

13 Thalmes Inc is a multinational company that has a bid on a project funded by the Slovenian government. If the company succeeds in its bid it will have to invest €2,000,000. The decision will be announced in three months from now. The management of Thalmes is afraid that dollar devaluation will increase the cost of investment and would like to hedge against the risk of devaluation. Which of the following three strategies (buy forward, buy futures, buy call option) is in your view the most appropriate?

Answers to Quick Quiz

1 The bank is buying the currency therefore the bid price of HK$7.7425 is relevant (remember than the exporter will always pay the higher price). The exporter will receive:

HK$400,000/7.7425 = $51,662.90

2 (a) Relative rates of inflation   (d) Market sentiment

(b) Relative interest rates   (e) Speculation

(c) Balance of payments position   (f) Government policy

3 (1) C Fisher effect

(2) E Interest rate parity

(3) D International Fisher effect

(4) A Purchasing power parity

(5) B Expectations theory

4 (a) Forward rate cheaper than spot rate quoted at a **discount**

(b) Forward rate more expensive than spot rate quoted at a **premium**

5

Transaction on future date		Now		On future date	
Receive	currency	Sell	currency futures	Buy	currency futures
Pay	currency	Buy	currency futures	Sell	currency futures
Receive	$	Buy	currency futures	Sell	currency futures
Pay	$	Sell	currency futures	Buy	currency futures

6

Transaction on future date		Now		Option on future date	
Receive	currency	Buy	currency put	Sell	currency
Pay	currency	Buy	currency call	Buy	currency
Receive	$	Buy	currency call	Buy	currency
Pay	$	Buy	currency put	Sell	currency

7
- Choose contract date
- Put or call options
- Strike price
- No of contracts
- Premium

8 A settlement date is the date when trading on a futures contract stops and all accounts are settled.

9
- Exercise price
- Maturity of option
- Volatility of exchange/interest rates
- Interest rate differentials

10 **Counterparty** risk is the risk of one party on a swap defaulting on the arrangement.

11 True

12 Deposit amount to hedge in Euro = $\dfrac{4,000,000}{1+0.04} = 3,846,154$

The amount of GBP needed is €3,846,154/1.46 = £2,634,352

13 The most appropriate strategy is to buy a call option which will expire in three months. If the bid is successful Thalmes can use the option to purchase the euros needed. Even if the bid is not accepted it will still exercise the option if the euro spot rate exceeds the exercise price and sell the euros in the open market.

Now try the question below from the Exam Question Bank

Number	Level	Marks	Time
30	Introductory	15	27 mins
31	Introductory	15	27 mins
32	Introductory	15	27 mins
33	Introductory	15	27 mins
34	Examination	30	54 mins

17

The use of financial derivatives to hedge against interest rate risk

Topic list	Syllabus reference
1 Interest rate risk	F (3)
2 Hedging with forward rate agreements (FRAs)	F (3) (a) (i)
3 Interest rate futures	F (3) (a) (ii)
4 Interest rate options	F (3) (a) (iv)
5 Interest rate swaps	F (3) (a) (iii)
6 Hedging strategy alternatives - example	F (3) (a)
7 Issues surrounding the use of derivatives	F (1) (b)
8 The Greeks – measuring the impact of risk factors	F 1 (b)(iv)

Introduction

This chapter continues our discussion and application of derivatives – this time focusing on **interest rate hedging**. In times of volatile interest rates companies borrowing large sums of money may wish to hedge against adverse movements in interest rates that could have a significant effect on the level of interest payments. Similarly companies lending large sums of money may wish to hedge against interest rates falling which will have an adverse effect on interest received.

In this chapter we focus on the different types of interest rate derivatives, their characteristics and how they work. It is important to know how to **apply** these instruments in particular scenarios and also to **recommend** the best instrument for that scenario. Make sure you are familiar with the advantages and disadvantages of the different instruments for **evaluation** purposes.

We also consider various issues surrounding the use of derivatives in general and finish the chapter with The Greeks.

Study guide

		Intellectual level
F1	**The role of the treasury function in multinationals**	
(b)	Discuss the operations of the derivatives market, including:	3
	(i) The relative advantages and disadvantages of exchange traded versus OTC agreements	
	(ii) Key features, such as standard contracts, tick sizes, margin requirements and margin trading	
	(iii) The source of basis risk and how it can be minimised	
	(iv) Risks such as delta, gamma, vega, rho and theta, and how these can be managed	
F3	**The use of financial derivatives to hedge against interest rate risk**	
(a)	Evaluate for a given hedging requirement which of the following is the most appropriate given the nature of the underlying position and the risk exposure:	3
	(i) Forward Rate Agreements	
	(ii) Interest Rate Futures	
	(iii) Interest rate swaps	
	(iv) Options on FRA's (caps and collars), Interest rate futures and interest rate swaps.	

1 Interest rate risk

FAST FORWARD

Factors influencing interest rate risk include

- Fixed rate versus floating rate debt
- The term of the loan

Key term

Interest rate risk is the risk to the profitability or value of a company resulting from changes in interest rates.

1.1 Managing a debt portfolio

Corporate treasurers will be responsible for managing the company's debt portfolio, that is in deciding how a company should obtain its short-term funds so as to:

(a)   Be able to repay debts as they mature

(b)   Minimise any inherent risks, notably invested foreign exchange risk, in the debts the company owes and is owed

There are a number of situations in which a company might be exposed to risk from interest rate movements.

1.2 Risks from interest rate movements

(a)   **Fixed rate versus floating rate debt**

A company can get caught paying **higher interest rates** by having fixed rather than floating rate debt, or floating rather than fixed rate debt, as market interest rates change.

Expectations of interest rate movements will determine whether a company chooses to borrow at a fixed or floating rate. The term structure of interest rates – the rates available on loans of different length - should help businesses determine the market's view on how interest rates are likely to move in the future.

Fixed rate finance may be more expensive: however the business runs the risk of **adverse upward rate movements** if it chooses floating rate finance.

Other factors include:

(i) **Finance term** (the longer the term the more difficult interest rates are to predict)

(ii) The **differences between fixed and floating rates**, plus arrangement costs or new finance

(iii) The **finance risk tolerance** of the directors

(iv) **Existing debt mix** (greater finance diversification may be desirable to hedge all possibilities)

(v) **Current pressures on liquidity** – if the business is stretched in the short-term, it may prefer to take the lower rate available on floating rate debt. In doing so, it is taking the risk that rates may rise and borrowing eventually become more expensive. However the directors are calculating that if this happens, the company will have accumulated sufficient cash to be able to bear the higher rates.

(b) **Currency of debt**

A company can face higher costs if it borrows in a currency for which exchange rates move adversely against the company's domestic currency. The treasurer should seek to **match the currency of the loan** with the **currency of the underlying operations/assets** that generate revenue to pay interest/repay the loans.

(c) **Term of loan**

A company can be exposed by having to **repay a loan earlier** than it can afford to, resulting in a need to re-borrow, perhaps at a higher rate of interest.

(d) **Term loan or overdraft facility**

A company might prefer to **pay for borrowings only when it needs the money** as with an overdraft facility: the bank will charge a commitment fee for such a facility. Alternatively, a term loan might be preferred, but this will cost interest even if it is not needed in full for the whole term.

(e) **Rises in interest rates**

A company may plan to take out borrowing at some time in the future, but face the possibility that **interest rates may rise before the term of borrowing commences**. This problem can be addressed by using financial instruments to fix or cap the rate of interest. This is described later in this chapter.

Exam focus point

> In the exam, watch out for information in the scenario about factors affecting the company's attitude to risk, such as company size or risk appetite of directors. This may determine both the composition of the debt portfolio and the methods used to manage its risks.

1.3 Interest rate risk management

If the organisation faces interest rate risk, it can seek to **hedge the risk**. Alternatively where the magnitude of the risk is **immaterial** in comparison with the company's overall cash flows or appetite for risks, one option is to **do nothing**. The company then accepts the effects of any movement in interest rates which occur.

The company may also decide to do nothing if **risk management costs are excessive**, both in terms of the costs of using derivatives and the staff resources required to manage risk effectively. **Appropriate products** may not be available and of course the company may consider hedging unnecessary as it believes that the **chances of an adverse movement** are **remote**.

Bear in mind the possibility that a company may take the decision to do nothing to reduce interest rate risk – it is a situation you should consider when answering exam questions.

The company's **tax situation** may also be a significant determinant of its decision whether or not to hedge risk. If hedging is likely to **reduce variability of earnings**, this may have tax advantages if the company faces a higher rate of tax for higher earnings levels. The directors may also be unwilling to undertake hedging because of the need to **monitor the arrangements**, and the **requirements to fulfil the disclosure requirements** of IASs 32 and 39 and IFRSs 7 and 9.

Question

Hedging

Explain what is meant by hedging in the context of interest rate risk.

Answer

Hedging is a means of reducing risk. Hedging involves coming to an **agreement with another party** who is prepared to take on the risk that you would **otherwise bear**. The other party may be willing to take on that risk because he would otherwise bear an opposing risk which may be 'matched' with your risk; alternatively, the other party may be a speculator who is willing to bear the risk in return for the prospect of making a profit. In the case of interest rates, a company with a variable rate loan clearly faces the risk that the rate of interest will increase in the future as the result of changing market conditions which cannot now be predicted.

Many financial instruments have been introduced in recent years to help corporate treasurers to hedge the risks of interest rate movements. These instruments include forward rate agreements, financial futures, interest rate swaps and options.

Case Study

In its 2010/11 annual report, **Kingfisher** discussed its management of financial and interest rate risk: 'Borrowings arranged at floating rates of interest expose the Group to cash flow interest rate risk, whereas those arranged at fixed rates of interest expose the Group to fair value interest rate risk. The Group manages its interest rate risk by entering into certain interest rate derivative contracts which modify the interest rate payable on the Group's underlying debt instruments principally the Medium Term Notes and other fixed term debt.'

Tate and Lyle noted in its 2011 annual report that: 'The Group has an exposure to interest rate risk arising principally from changes in US dollar, sterling and euro interest rates. This risk is managed by fixing or capping portions of debt using interest rate derivatives to achieve a target level of fixed/floating rate net debt, which aims to optimise net finance expense and reduce volatility in reported earnings. The Group's policy is that between 30% and 75% of Group net debt (excluding the Group's share of joint venture net debt) is fixed or capped (excluding out of-the-money caps) for more than one year and that no interest rate fixings are undertaken for more than 12 years. At 31 March 2011, the longest term of any fixed rate debt held by the Group was until November 2019. The proportion of net debt at 31 March 2011 that was fixed or capped for more than one year was 85%. A derogation of the maximum percentage of fixed rate debt was approved by the Board until 30 June 2011.'

1.4 Interest rate risk management techniques

Methods of reducing interest rate risk include the following:

- **Netting** – aggregating all positions, assets and liabilities, and hedging the net exposure
- **Smoothing** – maintaining a balance between fixed and floating rate borrowing
- **Matching** – matching assets and liabilities to have a common interest rate
- **Pooling** – (see 1.4.1 below)
- **Forward rate agreements** (FRAs) (Section 2)
- **Interest rate futures** (Section 3)
- **Interest rate options or interest rate guarantees** (Section 4)
- **Interest rate swaps** (Section 5)

1.4.1 Pooling

Pooling means asking the bank to pool the amounts of all its subsidiaries when **considering interest levels and overdraft limits**. It should **reduce the interest payable, stop overdraft limits being breached** and **allow greater control by the treasury department**. It also gives the company the potential to take advantage of **better rates of interest** on **larger cash deposits**.

2 Hedging with forward rate agreements (FRAs)

FAST FORWARD

Forward rate agreements hedge risk by **fixing the interest rate** on future borrowing.

Key term

> A **forward rate agreement** is an agreement, typically between a company and a bank, about the interest rate on future borrowing or bank deposits.

2.1 How do FRAs work?

A **forward rate agreement** (FRA) does not involve the actual transfer of capital from one party to another. A FRA is an agreement to borrow/lend a notional amount for up to 12 months at an agreed rate of interest (the FRA rate). The 'notional' sum is the amount on which the interest payment is calculated. Only the interest on the notional amount between the rate dealt (that is the rate when the FRA is traded) and the rate prevailing at the time of settlement (the reference rate) actually changes hands.

If there is a rise in interest rates between the time that the FRA is traded and the date that the FRA comes into effect, the borrower is protected from paying the higher interest rate. If interest rates fall during that time, the borrower must pay the difference between the **traded rate** and the **actual rate** on the notional sum.

If a borrower wishes to hedge against an increase in interest rates to cover a **three month loan starting in three months' time**, this is known as a **3 x 6 FRA**. A three month loan starting in one month's time would be a 1 x 4 FRA etc.

Important dates

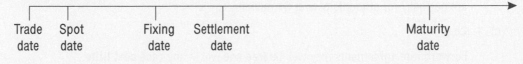

| Trade
date | Spot
date | | Fixing
date | Settlement
date | | Maturity
date |

Trade date	The date on which the contract begins (or when the contract is 'dealt')
Spot date	The date on which the interest rate of the FRA is determined
Fixing date	The date on which the reference rate (which will be compared with the FRA rate on settlement) is determined. The reference rate is the LIBOR on the fixing date. The fixing date is usually 2 business days before the settlement date.
Settlement date	The date on which the notional loan is said to begin. This date is used for the calculation of interest on the notional sum. For example, if you entered into a 3 x 6 FRA, this would be 3 months after the spot date.
Maturity date	The date on which the notional loan expires. For example, in a 3 x 6 FRA, this would be 3 months after the settlement date.

Example

It is 30 June. Lynn will need a $10 million 6 month fixed rate loan from 1 October. Lynn wants to hedge using an FRA. The relevant FRA rate is 6% on 30 June.

What is the result of the FRA and the effective loan rate if the 6 month FRA benchmark rate has moved to

(a)   5%
(b)   9%

Solution

(a)   At 5% because interest rates have fallen, Lynn will pay the bank:

	$
FRA payment $10 million $\times$ (6% − 5%) $\times$ $^6/_{12}$	(50,000)
Payment on underlying loan 5% $\times$ $10 million $\times$ $^6/_{12}$	(250,000)
Net payment on loan	(300,000)

Effective interest rate on loan = 6%

(b)   At 9% because interest rates have risen, the bank will pay Lynn

	$
FRA receipt $10 million $\times$ (9% − 6%) $\times$ $^6/_{12}$	150,000
Payment on underlying loan at market rate 9% $\times$ $10 million $\times$ $^6/_{12}$	(450,000)
Net payment on loan	(300,000)

Effective interest rate on loan = 6%

2.2 Advantages of forward rate agreements

(a)   **Protection provided**

An FRA would protect the borrower from **adverse interest rate movements** above the rate negotiated.

(b)   **Flexibility**

FRAs are **flexible**; they can in theory be arranged for any amounts and any duration, although they are normally for amounts of over $1 million.

(c)   **Cost**

Forward rate agreements may well be **free** and will in any case **cost little**.

2.3 Disadvantages of forward rate agreements

(a)   **Rate available**

The rate the bank will set for the forward rate agreement will reflect **expectations of future interest rate movements**. If interest rates are expected to rise, the bank may set a **higher rate** than the rate currently available.

(b) **Falling interest rate**

The borrower will **not be able to take advantage** if interest rates fall unexpectedly.

(c) **Term of FRA**

The FRA will **terminate on a fixed date**.

(d) **Binding agreement**

FRAs are **binding agreements** so are less easy to sell to other parties.

Question	Forward rate agreements

Rumple Inc will shortly be making a short-term investment and wants to borrow $4m for three months, starting in 3 months' time. However interest rates are currently volatile and it is worried about adverse movements in these rates before it takes out the loan.

LIBOR (the base rate) is currently 3.5% and Rumple has been offered a 3-6 FRA for 3.75%. Rumple can currently borrow at approximately 1% above the base rate.

Required

Advise Rumple of the likely outcome of the FRA if the base rate in 3 months' time is

(a)   4%
(b)   3%

Answer

(a) The actual base rate is above the FRA rate therefore the bank will pay the difference as compensation to Rumple – that is, 0.25%.

Rumple will borrow at the best available rate, which is base rate + 1% - that is 5% (4 + 1).

Net cost to Rumple = 5% - 0.25% = 4.75%

(b) As the actual base rate is below the FRA rate, Rumple will pay compensation of 0.75% to the bank.

Rumple will borrow at the best available rate – that is 4% (3 + 1).

Net cost to Rumple = 4% + 0.75% = 4.75%

This amounts to 0.0475 x 3/12 x $4m = $47,500

3 Interest rate futures   12/08, 12/11

FAST FORWARD

Interest rate futures can be used to hedge against interest rate changes between the current date and the date at which the interest rate on the lending or borrowing is set. Borrowers **sell futures** to hedge against **interest rate rises**. Lenders buy futures to hedge against **interest rate falls**.

3.1 Futures contracts

We covered currency futures in the previous chapter so you should be familiar with how they work. Interest rate futures are similar to currency futures in that they are used to hedge against movements in the underlying (in this case, interest rates).

Interest rate futures are a similar method of hedging to FRAs, except that the terms, amounts and periods are standardised. For example, a company can contract to buy (or sell) $100,000 of a notional 30-year bond bearing an 8% coupon in, say, 6 months' time at an agreed price. The basic principles behind such a decision are:

(a)　The futures price is likely to vary with changes in interest rates. This acts as a hedge against adverse interest rate movements. We will illustrate this in an example shortly.

(b)　The outlay to buy futures is much less than for buying the financial instrument itself.

3.1.1 Borrowing and lending

Borrowers will wish to hedge against an **interest rate rise** by:

- **Selling futures now**
- **Buying futures** on the day that the interest rate is fixed

Lenders will wish to hedge against the possibility of **falling interest rates** by:

- **Borrowing** futures now
- **Lending** futures on the date that the actual lending starts

3.2 Pricing futures contracts

The **pricing** of an interest rate futures contract is determined by prevailing interest rates

- For short-term futures, if three month interest rates are 8%, a three month futures contract will be priced at 92 (100 – 8)

- If interest rates are 11%, the contract price will be 89 (100 – 11)

This decrease in price, or value, of the contract, reflects the reduced attractiveness of a fixed rate deposit in a time of rising interest rates.

The price of long-term futures reflects market prices of the **underlying bonds**. A price of $100 equals par. The interest rate is implied in the price. If a long-term 10% futures contract has a price of $114.00, the implied interest rate on long-term bonds is approximately $^{100}/_{114} \times 10\% = 8.8\%$.

Example

Yew has taken a 3 month $1,000,000 eurodollar loan with interest payable of 8%, the loan being due for rollover on 31 March. At 1 January, the company treasurer considers that interest rates are likely to rise in the near future. The futures price is 91 representing a yield of 9%. Given a standard contract size of $1,000,000 the company **sells** a eurodollar three month contract to hedge against interest on the three month loan required at 31 March (to **sell** a contract is to commit the seller to take a deposit). At 31 March the spot interest rate is 11%.

What is the cost saving to Yew?

Solution

The company will **buy back** the future on 31 March at 89 (100 – 11). The cost saving is the **profit on the futures contract**.

$1,000,000 \times (91 - 89) \times {}^3/_{12} = \$5,000$

The hedge has effectively reduced the net annual interest cost by 2%. Instead of a cost of 11% at 31 March ($27,500) for a three month loan, the net cost is $22,500 ($27,500 – $5,000), a 9% annual cost.

3.3 Use of interest rate futures

The seller of a futures contract does not have to own the underlying instrument. However, the seller may need to deliver it on the contract's delivery date if the buyer requires it. Many, but not all, interest rate contracts are **settled for cash** rather than by delivery of the underlying instrument.

Interest rate futures offer an attractive means of **speculation** for some investors, because there is no requirement that buyers and sellers should actually be lenders and borrowers (respectively) of the nominal amounts of the contracts.

3.4 Basis risk

Basis risk (which was covered in Chapter 16 Section 7) also occurs for interest rate futures.

If a firm takes a position in the futures contract with a view to closing out the contract before its maturity, there is still likely to be basis. The firm can only **estimate what effect** this will **have on the hedge**. 'Basis risk' refers to the problem that the **basis may result in an imperfect hedge**. The basis will be **zero** at the **maturity date of the contract**.

The basis risk can be calculated as the difference between the futures price and the current price (**'cash market' price**) of the underlying security.

3.4.1 Example: Basis and basis risk

To give an example, if three-month LIBOR (the London Inter-Bank Offered Rate) is 7% and the September price of the three-month sterling future is 92.70 now (at the end of March, say) then the basis is:

Libor (100-7)   93.00
Futures   92.70
                        0.30 %
                    or 30 basis points

Exam focus point

In the exam, you might be given other price information and have to calculate the closing futures price from it.

A further cause of basis risk for interest rates is that there are significantly more possible actual interest rates than there are standard contracts. Therefore management may wish to calculate the correlation between the futures price movement and the underlying price movement. This can be used to calculate **hedging ratios** (which were covered in Chapter 16 Section 7) which can be used to determine the overall number of contracts required. **Delta hedging** (covered in Section 8 of this Chapter) can also be used to reduce this risk..

3.5 Setting up a futures hedge

The procedure for setting up an interest rate futures hedge is similar to that for currency futures. The following example illustrates the process.

Example

Panda has taken a 6 month $10,000,000 loan with interest payable of 8%, the loan being due for rollover on 31 March. At 1 January, the company treasurer considers that interest rates are likely to rise in the near future. The futures price is 91 representing a yield of 9%. Given a standard contract size of $1,000,000 the company sells a dollar three month contract to hedge against interest on the three month loan required at 31 March (to sell a contract is to commit the seller to take a deposit). At 31 March the interest rate is 11% and the futures price had fallen to 88.50.

Required

Demonstrate how futures can be used to hedge against interest rate movements.

Solution

The following steps should be taken.

Setup

(a) What contract: 3 month contract

(b) What type: sell (as borrowing and rates expected to rise)

(c) How many contracts: $\dfrac{\text{Exposure}}{\text{Contract size}} \times \dfrac{\text{Loan period}}{\text{Length of contract}} = \dfrac{10m}{1m} \times {}^6/_3 = 20$ contracts

Closing price

Closing futures price = 88.50

Outcome

(a) **Futures outcome**

At opening rate:	0.91 sell
At closing rate:	0.8850 buy
	0.0250 receipt

Futures outcome:

$$\text{Receipt} \times \text{Size of contract} \times \text{Number of contracts} \times \dfrac{\text{Length of contract}}{\text{One year}}$$

$0.0250 \times 1,000,000 \times 20 \times {}^3/_{12} = \$125,000$

(b) **Net outcome**

	$
Payment in spot market $10m $\times$ 11% $\times$ $^6/_{12}$	(550,000)
Receipt in futures market	125,000
Net payments	(425,000)

Effective interest rate $= \dfrac{425,000}{10,000,000} \times {}^{12}/_6 = 8.5\%$

3.6 Advantages of interest rate futures

(a) **Cost**

Costs of interest rate futures are reasonably **low**.

(b) **Amount hedged**

A company can **hedge relatively large exposures of cash** with a **relatively small initial employment of cash**.

3.7 Disadvantages of interest rate futures

(a) **Inflexibility of terms**

Traded interest rate futures are for **fixed periods** and **cover begins in March, June, September or December**. Contracts are for **fixed, large, amounts**, so may not entirely match the amount being hedged

(b) **Basis risk**

The company may be liable to the risk that the **price of the futures contract** may not move in the expected direction.

(c)   **Daily settlement**

The company will have to settle **daily profits or losses** on the contract.

Question   Interest rate futures

Rumple Inc (see question 'Forward rate agreements' in Section 2) is now considering using interest rate futures to hedge the $4m loan. It is now 1st March and the Chicago Board of Trade is quoting the following prices on standardised $1m three month contracts. Note that these prices are quoted in basis points at (100 – annual yield).

March	96.00
June	96.10
September	96.20

Contracts are assumed to expire at the end of the quoted months. LIBOR remains at 3.5% and Rumble can still borrow at a rate of approximately LIBOR + 1%.

Required

Assuming that Rumble takes out a loan at a fixed rate of LIBOR + 1% at the start of the loan, illustrate the outcome of the futures contract if LIBOR is

(a)   4%

(b)   3%

Answer

The solution to this question takes a slightly different approach from the example above. Rather than converting into monetary terms at each stage we leave the answers in % and convert into money at the end. Either approach is acceptable.

Setup

(a)   What contract? **3 months**

(b)   What type? **Sell** (as Rumple is borrowing and rates are expected to rise)

(c)   How many contracts? $\dfrac{\text{Exposure}}{\text{Contract size}} \times \dfrac{\text{Loan period}}{\text{Length of contract}}$ = ($4m/$1m) x (3/3) = **4 contracts**

(d)   Date? **June** (start of the loan)

Closing price

The closing price has to be calculated using basis.

	Now – 1st March	(a) – 1st June	(b) – 1st June
June future	3.90	4.10	3.10
LIBOR	3.50	4.00	3.00
Basis	0.40	0.10	0.10
	This basis represents four months from beginning of December to end of March	One month's basis remains (that is, 0.40/4). We know LIBOR therefore price of June future on 1st March is the balancing figure	

Outcome

	(a)	(b)
Actual loan rate (LIBOR + 1%)	5.00	4.00
Profit/loss on future		
Opening rate (pay)	3.90	3.90
Closing rate (receive)	<u>4.10</u>	<u>3.10</u>
	0.20	0.80
	PROFIT	LOSS
Net rate	4.80	4.80

NOTE THE FIXED OUTCOME

In $ this represents 4.8% x $4m x 3/12 = $48,000

4 Interest rate options

12/11

FAST FORWARD

> Interest rate options allow an organisation to limit its exposure to adverse interest rate movements whilst allowing it to take advantage of favourable interest rate movements.

4.1 What is an interest rate option?

Key term

> An **interest rate option** grants the buyer of the option the right, but not the obligation, to deal at an agreed interest rate (strike rate) at a future maturity date. On the date of expiry of the option, the buyer must decide whether or not to exercise the right.

Clearly the buyer of an option to borrow will not wish to exercise it if the market interest rate is now below that specified in the option agreement. Conversely an option to lend will not be worth exercising if market rates have risen above the rate specified in the option by the time the option has expired.

Tailor-made 'over the counter' interest rate options can be purchased from major banks, with specific values, periods of maturity, denominated currencies and rates of agreed interest. The cost of the option is the 'premium'. Interest rate options offer more flexibility – and are more expensive – than FRAs.

Exchange traded options are also available. These have **standardised amounts** and **standard periods**.

4.2 Exchange traded options

Exchange traded interest rate options are available as options on interest rate futures which give the holder the right to buy (call option) or sell (put option) one futures contract on or before the expiry of the option at a specified price. The best way to understand the pricing of interest rate options is to look at a schedule of prices. The table below is taken from an October issue of the **Financial Times**.

UK long gilt futures options (LIFFE) £100,000 100ths of 1%

Strike price	Calls			Puts		
	Nov	*Dec*	*Jan*	*Nov*	*Dec*	*Jan*
£113.50	0.87	1.27	1.34	0.29	0.69	1.06
£114.00	0.58	0.99	1.10	0.50	0.91	1.32
£114.50	0.36	0.76	0.88	0.77	1.18	1.60

This schedule shows that an investor could pay $^{1.34}/_{100} \times £100,000 = £1,340$ to purchase the right to buy a sterling futures contract in January at a price of £113.50 per £100 stock.

If, say, in December, January futures are priced **below** £113.50 (reflecting an interest rate **rise**), the option will not be exercised. In calculating any gain from the call option, the premium cost must also be taken into account.

If the futures price moves **higher,** as it is likely to if interest rates **fall,** the option will be exercised. The profit for each contract will be current futures prices – 113.50 – 1.34.

4.3 Traded put and call options

> A **call option** is the right to **buy** (in this case to receive interest at the specified rate).
>
> A **put option** is the right to **sell** (that is, the right to pay interest at the specified rate).

To use traded interest rate options for hedging follow exactly the same principles as for traded currency options.

(a)   If a company needs to hedge **borrowing** (where interest will be paid) at a future date it should **purchase put options** to **sell futures**.

(b)   Similarly if a company is lending money (and will therefore be receiving interest) it should **purchase call options** to **buy futures**.

Example

Panda wishes to borrow £4 million fixed rate in June for 9 months and wishes to protect itself against rates rising above 6.75%. It is 11 May and the spot rate is currently 6%. The data is as follows:

INTEREST RATE GUARANTEES

Short sterling options (LIFFE)

£1,000,000 points of 100%

Effective interest rate	Calls			Puts		
%	June	Sept	Dec	June	Sept	Dec
6.75	0.16	0.03	0.03	0.14	0.92	1.62
6.50	0.05	0.01	0.01	0.28	1.15	1.85
6.25	0.01	0.01	0.01	0.49	1.39	2.10

Panda negotiates the loan with the bank on 12 June (when the £4m loan rate is fixed for the full nine months) and closes out the hedge.

What will be the outcome of the hedge and the effective loan rate if prices on 12 June have moved to:

(a)   7.4%
(b)   5.1%

Solution

The following method (similar to currency options) should be used.

Step 1   **Setup**

   (a)   Which contract?   June

   (b)   What type?   Put (as we are borrowing and therefore paying interest)

   (c)   Strike price   93.25   (100 – 6.75)

   (d)   How many? $\dfrac{£4m}{£1m} \times {}^9/_3 = 12$ contracts

   (e)   Premium   At 93.25 (6.75%) June puts = 0.14p

   $\text{Contracts} \times \text{premium} \times \dfrac{\text{Size of contract}}{\left(\dfrac{12 \text{ months}}{\text{Length of contract}}\right)} = 12 \times 0.0014 \times \dfrac{1{,}000{,}000}{\left(^{12}/_9\right)} = £4{,}200$

Step 2   **Closing prices**

   (a)   7.4%

(b)   5.1%

Step 3   **Outcome**

Options market outcome	(a)	(b)
Right to pay interest at	6.75	6.75
Closing rate	7.40	5.10
Exercise?	YES	NO

Net position

	£	£
Spot (£4m x 9/12 x 5.1%)		153,000
Option (£4m x 9/12 x 6.75%)	202,500	
Option premium	4,200	4,200
Net outcome	206,700	157,200
Effective interest rate	(a)	(b)
	(206,700/4,000,000) x (12/9)	(157,200/4,000,000) x (12/9)
	= 6.89%	= 5.24%

Exam focus point

Make sure you read the question carefully to determine whether you have been told which strike price to use. If you have not been told you can choose the exercise price closest to the interest rate – for example if the interest rate is 3% then you would choose an exercise price of 97.00.

Question   Exchange traded options

Rumble Inc (see Section 2 question entitled 'Forward rate agreements') is now considering using options to hedge against interest rate movements on its $4m loan. It is now 1st March and LIBOR remains at 3.5%. Rumble Inc can still borrow at approximately LIBOR + 1%.

Options on three month futures ($1,000,000 contract size, premium cost in %) are as follows.

	Calls			Puts		
	March	*June*	*September*	*March*	*June*	*September*
96000	0.120	0.195	0.270	0.020	0.085	0.180
96250	0.015	0.075	0.155	0.165	0.255	0.335
96500	0	0.085	0.085	0.400	0.480	0.555

Required

Illustrate an option hedge at 3.75%, assuming that the loan is taken out at LIBOR + 1% and LIBOR is

(a)   4%   (b)   3%

Answer

Again this solution takes the approach of leaving everything in % and converting to $ at the end.

Setup

(a)   **Which contract?**   June

(b)   **What type?**   Put (as we are paying interest on borrowings)

(c)   **Strike price**   96.250 (100 – 3.75)

(d)   **How many?** $\dfrac{\text{Exposure}}{\text{Contract size}} \times \dfrac{\text{Loan period}}{\text{Length of contract}}$ = ($4m/$1m) x (3/3) = 4 contracts

(e)   **Premium**   At 96.250 (3.75%) June Puts = 0.255%

$$\text{Contracts} \times \text{premium} \times \dfrac{\text{Size of contract}}{\left(\dfrac{12 \text{ months}}{\text{Length of contract}}\right)} = 4 \times 0.00255 \times [\$4m/(12/3)] = \$10,200$$

Outcome

Options market outcome	(a)	(b)
Right to pay interest at	5.00%	4.00%
Profit/loss on option		
Opening position - put	3.75%	3.75%
Closing position – future (see calculation in Section 3 Question 'Interest rate futures')	<u>4.10%</u>	<u>3.10%</u>
	0.35% (profit)	Do not exercise option
Net outcome	5.00 + 0.255 - 0.35	4.00 + 0.255
	= 4.905%	= 4.255%
In $	0.04905 x $4m x 3/12	0.04255 x $4m x 3/12
	= $49,050	$42,550

4.4 Caps, floors and collars

An **interest rate cap** is an option which sets an interest rate ceiling.

An interest rate **floor** is an option which sets a lower limit to interest rates.

Using a **collar** arrangement, the borrower can buy an interest rate cap and at the same time sell an interest rate floor which reduces the cost for the company.

Various cap and collar agreements are possible.

The cost of a collar is lower than for a cap alone. However the borrowing company forgoes the benefit of movements in interest rates below the floor limit in exchange for this cost reduction.

Example

Suppose the prevailing interest rate for a company's borrowing is 10%. The company treasurer considers that a rise in rates above 12% will cause serious financial difficulties for the company. How can the treasurer make use of a cap and collar arrangement?

Solution

The company can buy an interest rate cap from the bank. The bank will reimburse the company for the effects of a rise in rates above 12%. As part of the arrangements with the bank, the company can agree that it will pay at least 9%, say, as a 'floor' rate. The bank will pay the company for agreeing this. In other words, the company has sold the floor to the bank, which partly offsets the costs of the cap. The bank benefits if rates fall below the floor level.

4.4.1 Traded caps

Say you are a borrower and have bought a put option (a right to sell the future). The exercise price is 93.00, reflecting an interest rate of 7%.

Interest rate rises

- If the interest rate you have to pay **rises to 8%**, the price of the future will fall to 92.00

- You will buy the future at 92.00 and exercise your option to sell it at 93.00

- The profit you make on buying and then selling the future can be set against the 8% interest you have to pay, to give an **effective interest rate of 7%**

Interest rate falls

- If the interest rate **falls to 6%**, you **do not exercise the option**
- Therefore don't worry about buying and selling the future, and just **pay interest at 6%**

4.4.2 Traded floors

In order to set a floor if you are investing/lending, you have to buy a call option – a right to buy a future. Say the exercise price is 95.00, corresponding to an interest rate of 5%.

Interest rate falls

- If the interest rate you receive **falls to 4%**, the price of the future will rise to 96.00

- However you will exercise your option to buy the future at 95.00 and then you will sell it on at 96.00

- The profit you make on the future will be added to the 4% interest you receive to give an **effective interest rate of 5%**

Interest rate rises

- If the interest rate **rises to 6%**, you will not exercise the option
- You will **receive interest at 6%**

4.4.3 Traded collars

With collars, if you're a borrower, you are buying a put and selling a call. Say the exercise price is 96.00, corresponding to an interest rate of 4%.

- Buying a put as above
- Selling a call means that you are selling someone else the right to buy a future from you

Interest rate falls

- If the interest rate **falls to 3%**, the price of the future will rise to 97.00

- You will **pay interest at 3%**

- However the holder of the call option will wish to exercise the option to buy the future at 96.00

- You therefore have to buy the future yourself at 97.00 and sell it to the option holder at 96.00, thus incurring a loss

- The loss you incur will be added to the 3% interest you have to pay to give an effective net interest rate of 4%

- If interest rates **fall further**, you will pay a lower interest rate but incur a larger loss on the option, netting out always at an **interest rate of 4%**

Interest rate rises

- If the interest rate rises above 4%, the option holder will not exercise the option.

- You will pay interest at more than 4%, but be able to offset against this a profit on selling the future, to give an **effective interest rate of 4%.**

Example

Rumple Inc has decided that interest rate options are too expensive and is therefore considering the use of a collar to hedge interest rate payments on its loan. Illustrate the outcome of a collar with a put option at 3.75% and a call option at 3.5% if LIBOR in three months' time is

(a)   4%
(b)   3%

Solution

Setup

(a) Which contract?   June

(b) What type?   Collar (put and call)

(c) How many?   4 (as before)

(d) Premium   0.255% − 0.085% = 0.170%

Outcome

	(a)	(b)
Right to pay interest at	5.00%	4.00%
Profit/loss on option		
Put option at 3.75%	0.35% profit (as before)	
Call option at 3.5%		0.40% loss
		(Holder of call option receives
		3.5% - 3.10% future = 0.40%)
Net outcome	5.00 + 0.170 - 0.35	4.00 + 0.170 + 0.40
	= 4.82%	= 4.57%
In $	0.0482 x $4m x 3/12	0.0457 x $4m x 3/12
	= $48,200	$45,700

4.5 Over the counter options

Over the counter options are tailor-made to the specific requirements of the interested party in terms of size and timing. As these are so specific they will be more expensive than exchange traded options and are much less liquid as they cannot be sold if not required. As with exchange traded options, caps, floors and collars are available.

4.6 Advantages and disadvantages of options

4.6.1 Advantages

(a) **Upside risk** – the company has the choice not to exercise the option and will therefore be able to take advantage of falling interest rates.

(b) **Over the counter options** – these are tailored to the specific needs of the company and are therefore more flexible than exchange traded options for a more exact hedge.

(c) Exchange traded options are useful for **uncertain transactions** – for example you may be unsure if a loan will actually be needed. If it becomes evident that the option is not required it can be sold.

4.6.2 Disadvantages

(a) **Premium** – the premium cost may be **relatively expensive** compared with the costs of other hedging instruments. It will be payable whatever the movement in interest rates and whether or not the option is exercised.

(b) **Collar** – if the company has a collar, this will limit its ability to take advantage of lower interest rates to the lower limit set by the cap.

(c) **Maturity** – the maturity of exchange traded options may be **limited to one year**.

(d) **Traded options** – if the company purchased exchange traded options then the **large fixed amounts** of the available contracts may not match the amount to be hedged. The large amounts of the contracts will also prohibit organisations with smaller amounts to be hedged from using them.

Part F Treasury and advanced risk management techniques | **17: The use of financial derivatives to hedge against interest rate risk**   483

5 Interest rate swaps

> Interest rate swaps allow companies to take advantage of differences in the conditions connected with fixed and floating rate debt.

Key term

> An **interest rate swap** is a transaction that exploits different interest rates in different markets for borrowing, to **reduce interest costs** for either **fixed or floating rate loans**.

There are two main types of interest rate swaps – **coupon swaps** and **basis swaps**.

In a **coupon swap**, one party makes payments at a fixed rate of interest in exchange for receiving payments at a floating rate (which changes for each payment). The other party pays the floating rate and receives the fixed rate.

In a **basis swap**, the parties exchange payments on one floating rate basis (for example at three month LIBOR or at a six month CD rate) for payments on another floating rate basis (for example at six month LIBOR).

Most interest rate swaps are coupon swaps.

5.1 Arranging a swap

An **interest rate swap** is an arrangement whereby two companies, or a company and a bank, swap interest rate commitments with each other. In a sense, each simulates the other's borrowings, with the following effects.

(a)   A company which has **debt at a fixed rate of interest** can make a **swap** so that it ends up paying **interest at a variable rate**.

(b)   A company which has **debt at a variable rate of interest** (floating rate debt) ends up paying a **fixed rate of interest**.

An example is illustrated below.

Interest rate swap

In this example, company A can use a swap to change from paying interest at a floating rate of LIBOR + 1% to one of paying fixed interest of (8½% + 1%) = 9½%.

A swap may be arranged with a bank, or a counterparty may be found through a bank or other financial intermediary. Fees will be payable if a bank is used. However a bank may be able to find a **counterparty more easily**, and may have **access to more counterparties** in **more markets** than if the company seeking the swap tried to find the counterparty itself.

Swaps are generally terminated by agreeing a **settlement interest rate**, generally the current market rate.

Exam focus point

A useful approach to adopt in an exam for a swap organised by a bank is to assume – unless told otherwise – that the variable interest rate payment is at LIBOR.

Example

Goodcredit has been given a high credit rating. It can borrow at a fixed rate of 11%, or at a variable interest rate equal to LIBOR, which also happens to be 11% at the moment. It would like to borrow at a variable rate.

Secondtier is a company with a lower credit rating, which can borrow at a fixed rate of 12½% or at a variable rate of LIBOR plus ½%. It would like to borrow at a fixed rate.

Solution

	Goodcredit	Secondtier	Sum total
Company wants	Variable	Fixed	
Would pay (no swap)	(LIBOR)	(12.5%)	(LIBOR + 12.5%)
Could pay	(11%)	(LIBOR + 0.5%)	(LIBOR + 11.5%)
Potential gain			1%
Split evenly	0.5%	0.5%	
Expected outcome	(LIBOR – 0.5%)	(12%)	(LIBOR + 11.5%)
Swap terms			
Pay interest that could pay	(11%)	(LIBOR + 0.5%)	(LIBOR + 11.5%)
Swap floating	(LIBOR + 0.5%)	LIBOR + 0.5%	
Swap fixed (Working)	12%	(12%)	
Net paid	(LIBOR – 0.5%)	(12%)	(LIBOR + 11.5%)
Would pay	(LIBOR)	(12.5%)	(LIBOR + 12.5%)
Gain	0.5%	0.5%	1%

Working

The floating interest swapped is the amount paid by Secondtier.

Given that the gains are split equally, the fixed interest swap can be calculated as

$$12.5\% - \frac{12.5 - 11.5}{2} = 12\%$$

The starting point, the 12.5%, is what Secondtier would pay without the swap. The [(12.5 – 11.5)/2] is half the gain, half the difference between what Secondtier would pay and could pay.

The results of the swap are that Goodcredit ends up paying variable rate interest, but at a lower cost than it could get from a bank, and Secondtier ends up paying fixed rate interest, also at a lower cost than it could get from investors or a bank.

5.2 Reason for gain

If both parties ended up paying interest at a lower rate than was obtainable from the bank, where did this gain come from? To answer this question, set out a table of the rates at which both companies could borrow from the bank.

	Goodcredit	Secondtier	Difference %
Can borrow at fixed rate	11%	12.5%	1.5
Can borrow at floating rate	LIBOR	LIBOR + 0.5%	0.5
Difference between differences			1.0

Goodcredit has a better credit rating than Secondtier in both types of loan market, but its advantage is comparatively higher in the fixed interest market. The 1% differential between Goodcredit's advantage in the two types of loan may represent a market imperfection or there may be a good reason for it. Whatever the reason, it represents a potential gain which can be made out of a swap arrangement. For a gain to happen:

(a) Each company must borrow in the loan market in which it has **comparative advantage**. Goodcredit has the greatest advantage when it borrows fixed interest. Secondtier has the least disadvantage when it borrows floating rate.

(b) The parties must actually **want** interest of the opposite type to that in which they have comparative advantage. Goodcredit wants floating and Secondtier wants fixed.

Once the target interest rate for each company has been established, there is an infinite number of swap arrangements which will produce the same net result. The example illustrated above is only one of them.

Question · Interest rate swaps

We illustrated above one way in which the swap could work. (Swap fixed 12%, swap floating (LIBOR + 0.5%). Suggest an alternative arrangement for the swap, based on swapping fixed interest at 11%.

	Goodcredit	Secondtier
Could pay	(11%)	(LIBOR + 0.5%)
Swap floating		
Swap fixed		
Net interest cost	(LIBOR − 0.5%)	(12%)

Answer

	Goodcredit	Secondtier
Could pay	(11%)	(LIBOR + 0.5%)
Swap floating (working)	(LIBOR − 0.5%)	LIBOR − 0.5%
Swap fixed	11%	(11%)
Net interest cost	(LIBOR − 0.5%)	(12%)

Working

Given that the gains are split equally, the floating interest swap can be calculated as:

$$LIBOR - \frac{12.5 - 11.5}{2} = LIBOR - 0.5\%$$

The starting point, the LIBOR, is what Goodcredit would pay without the swap.

The $\frac{12.5 - 11.5}{2}$ is half the gain, half the difference between what Goodcredit would pay and could pay.

5.3 Advantages and disadvantages of interest rate swaps

5.3.1 Advantages

(a) **Flexibility and costs**

Swaps are **flexible**, since they can be arranged in any size, and they can be **reversed** if necessary. **Transaction costs are low**, particularly if no intermediary is used, and are potentially much lower than the costs of terminating one loan and taking out another.

(b) **Credit ratings**

Companies **with different credit ratings** can **borrow in the market** that offers each the best deal and then swap this benefit to reduce the mutual borrowing costs. This is an example of the principle of **comparative advantage**.

BPP
LEARNING MEDIA

(c)   **Capital structure**

Swaps allow **capital restructuring** by changing the nature of interest commitments without renegotiating with lenders.

(d)   **Risk management**

Swaps can be used to **manage interest rate risk** by swapping floating for fixed rate debt if rates are expected to rise. Swaps can also be used to swap a variable rate for a fixed rate investment if interest rates are expected to fall.

(e)   **Convenience**

Swaps are relatively **easy to arrange**.

(f)   **Predictability of cash flows**

If a company's future cash flows are uncertain, it can use a swap to ensure it has **predictable fixed rate commitments**.

5.3.2 Disadvantages

(a)   **Additional risk**

The swap is subject to **counterparty risk;** the risk that the other party will default leaving the first company to bear its obligations. This risk can be avoided by using an intermediary.

(b)   **Movements in interest rates**

If a company takes on a floating rate commitment, it may be vulnerable to **adverse movements in interest rates**. If it takes on a fixed rate commitment, it won't be able to **take advantage of favourable movements in rates**.

(c)   **Lack of liquidity**

The **lack of a secondary market in swaps** makes it **very difficult to liquidate a swap contract**.

Exam focus point

An article written by the examiner titled *Determining interest rate forwards and their application to swap valuation* was published in the November 2011 issue of Student Accountant. It follows on from the September 2011 article on bonds.

Exam focus point

Make sure you know the advantages and disadvantages of the different derivatives – it will be useful if you are asked to evaluate them in the context of a particular scenario.

Question   Interest rate swaps 2

Seeler Muller wishes to borrow 300 million euros for five years at a floating rate to finance an investment project in Germany. The cheapest rate at which it can raise such a loan is Euro LIBOR + 0.75%.

The company's bankers have suggested that one of their client companies, Overath Maier, would be interested in a swap arrangement. This company needs a fixed interest loan at €300 million. The cheapest rate at which it can arrange the loan is 10.5% per annum. It could, however, borrow in euros at the floating rate of euro LIBOR + 1.5%.

Seeler Muller can issue a fixed interest 5 year bond at 9% per annum interest. The banker would charge a swap arrangement fee of 0.15% per year to both parties. You are required to devise a swap by which both parties can benefit.

Answer

Company wants	Seeler Muller Floating	Overath Maier Fixed	Sum total
Would pay (no swap)	(LIBOR + 0.75%)	(10.5%)	(LIBOR + 11.25%)
Could pay	(9%)	(LIBOR + 1.5%)	(LIBOR + 10.5%)
Commission	(0.15%)	(0.15%)	(0.3%)
Potential gain (difference between would pay and could pay – commission)			0.45%
split evenly	0.225%	0.225%	
Expected outcome (would pay + potential gain)	(LIBOR + 0.525%)	(10.275%)	(LIBOR + 10.8%)

Swap terms

Could pay	(9%)	(LIBOR + 1.5%)	(LIBOR + 10.5%)
Swap floating	(LIBOR + 1.5%)	LIBOR + 1.5%	
Swap fixed (W)	10.125%	(10.125%)	
Commission	(0.15%)	(0.15%)	(0.3%)
Net paid	(LIBOR + 0.525%)	(10.275%)	(LIBOR + 10.8%)
Would pay	(LIBOR + 0.75%)	(10.5%)	(LIBOR + 11.25%)
Gain	0.225%	0.225%	0.45%

Both companies make a net gain of 0.225%. The swap proceeds as follows.

Step 1   Seeler Muller raises a fixed interest rate 5 year loan for €300m at 9% interest

Step 2   Overath Maier raises a floating rate €300m loan at LIBOR + 1.5%

Step 3   The companies swap loan principals

Step 4   Each year, each company pays its own loan interest and swaps the interest to the counterparty and receives the interest swap from the counterparty. As shown above, the exact payments between the two companies will depend on how the gains are to be split.

Here the floating swap is the floating interest Overath Maier. The fixed interest swap can be calculated as:

$$10.5\% - \frac{11.25 - 10.5}{2} = 10.125\%$$

Step 5   At the end of 5 years the loan principals are swapped back and the companies repay their original loans.

5.4 Interest rate swaptions

Key terms

> **Swaptions** are options on swaps, giving the holder the right but not the obligation to enter into a swap with the seller.
>
> A **payer swaption** gives the holder the right to enter into a swap as the fixed rate payer (and the floating rate receiver).
>
> A **receiver swaption** gives the holder the right to enter the swap as the fixed rate receiver (and the floating rate payer).

A **Bermudan** swaption allows the owner to enter the swap on multiple specified dates.

A **European** swaption allows the owner to enter the swap only on the maturity date.

An **American** swaption allows the owner to enter the swap on any day that falls within a range of two dates.

Swaptions generate a worst case scenario for buyers and sellers. For example an organisation that is going to issue floating rate debt can buy a payer swaption that offers the option to convert to being a fixed rate payer should interest rates increase.

Example

Suppose a party purchases a 1 x 5 payer swaption at a rate of 5%. A year later if the four year swap is 6% the buyer will exercise the swaption and pay 5% fixed rate for LIBOR on a four year swap. If instead the four year swap rate is 4% the buyer will not exercise the swaption.

6 Hedging strategy alternatives – example

It is important to be able to compare and contrast the different hedging instruments in a particular scenario and make recommendations on the best available strategy.

6.1 Hedging instruments

Different hedging instruments often offer alternative ways of managing risk in a specific situation. In this section, we consider the different ways in which a company can hedge interest rate risk.

Example

It is 31 December. Octavo needs to borrow £6 million in three months' time for a period of six months. For the type of loan finance which Octavo would use, the rate of interest is currently 13% per year and the Corporate Treasurer is unwilling to pay a higher rate.

The treasurer is concerned about possible future fluctuations in interest rates, and is considering the following possibilities:

(a)   Forward rate agreements (FRAs)
(b)   Interest rate futures
(c)   Interest rate guarantees or short-term interest rate caps

Required

Explain briefly how each of these three alternatives might be useful to Octavo.

Solution

Forward rate agreements (FRAs)

Entering into an FRA with a bank will allow the treasurer of Octavo to **effectively lock in an interest rate** for the six months of the loan. This agreement is independent of the loan itself, upon which the prevailing rate will be paid. If the FRA were negotiated to be at a rate of 13%, and the actual interest rate paid on the loan were higher than this, the bank will pay the difference between the rate paid and 13% to Octavo. Conversely, if the interest paid by Octavo turned out to be lower than 13%, they would have to pay the difference to the bank. Thus the cost to Octavo will be 13% regardless of movements in actual interest rates.

Interest rate futures

Interest rate futures have the same effect as FRAs, in effectively **locking in an interest rate**, but they are standardised in terms of size, duration (see Chapter 7a Section 5) and terms. They can be **traded on an exchange** (such as LIFFE in London), and they will generally be **closed out before the maturity date**, yielding a profit or loss that is offset against the loss or profit on the money transaction that is being hedged. So, for example, as Octavo is concerned about rises in interest rates, the treasurer can sell future contracts now; if that rate does rise, their value will fall, and they can then be bought at a lower price, yielding a profit which will compensate for the increase in Octavo's loan interest cost. If interest rates fall, the lower interest cost of the loan will be offset by a loss on their futures contracts.

There may not be an **exact match** between the **loan and the future contract** (100% hedge), due to the standardised nature of the contracts, and margin payments may be required while the futures are still held. Basis risk can also cause hedge inefficiency. Basis risk has been covered in Chapter 16 Section 7 and in Section 3 of this Chapter.

Interest rate options

Short-term interest rate options give Octavo the opportunity to **benefit from favourable interest rate movements** as well as protecting them from the effects of adverse movements. They give the holder the **right** but not the **obligation** to deal at an agreed interest rate at a future maturity date. This means that if interest rates rise, the treasurer would exercise the option, and 'lock in' to the predetermined borrowing rate. If, however, interest rates fall, then the option would simply lapse, and Octavo would feel the benefit of lower interest rates.

The main disadvantage of options is that a premium will be payable to the seller of the option, whether or not it is exercised. This will therefore add to the interest cost. The treasurer of Octavo will need to consider whether this cost, which can be quite expensive, is justified by the potential benefits to be gained from favourable interest rate movements.

7 Issues surrounding the use of derivatives

7.1 Rationale for the use of derivatives

FAST FORWARD

Two general arguments have been put forward for the growth in derivatives.

* The first is that derivatives complete the market
* The second argument is that they make markets more efficient.

7.1.1 Market completeness

Derivatives allow investors to achieve payoffs that would be impossible without using them. Although in theory continuous trading can create the payoffs of derivatives, rendering derivatives redundant, in practice this is not possible because investors face **trading costs** that make replicating closely the payoff of even as simple a derivative as a call option **prohibitively expensive**.

In the case of call options the payoff of the call option on shares, for instance, can be replicated by holding treasury bills and shares. When the price of the shares rises, the portfolio is adjusted in favour of shares so that it behaves more or less like the underlying. When the price of shares falls the portfolio is adjusted in favour of treasury bills, creating a minimum value in the portfolio which is the value of the treasury bill position.

Replication also requires the investor to trade every time the price changes. In the absence of continuous trading, the replication is only approximate.

Finally, the correct replicating strategy is often difficult to work out because there is uncertainty as to which is the true statistical process that drives asset prices. For example, if price changes are characterised by trends, then a policy of replication will be successful since a rebalancing of the portfolio in favour of equities following a change in share prices will be followed by further rises in share prices. If on the other hand prices change in a random way, then rebalancing the portfolio in favour of equities, as a result of an increase in share prices, will not be effective if the prices subsequently fall.

7.1.2 Market efficiency

Derivatives make markets more efficient by providing investors with **information** that **cash markets** alone **cannot generate**. For example, swaps can generate **yield curves** even in the absence of corresponding cash markets. The option markets can produce valuable estimates of the implied volatilities in the various markets.

7.2 The role of hedging for the firm

Derivative instruments are used either for **speculation** or for **hedging**. Derivatives are used for speculation when they are used on their own and not in conjunction with the underlying instrument. For example a long position in a futures contract, is a bet that the price of the underlying will move in a certain direction by a certain date. Similarly the writer of a call option bets that the price will not move above a certain range over a period of time. In both cases the derivatives position can result in losses if the price does not move in the anticipated direction. When derivatives are used for **hedging** they are always used in combination with the **underlying**. The principle of **hedging** is that any profits or losses in the **cash position** will be offset by losses or profits in the **derivatives position**. We have seen this in the examples involving derivatives in this chapter and the previous chapter.

The empirical evidence on the use of derivatives by corporations shows that firms primarily use derivatives for **hedging** rather than **speculation**.

One unresolved issue is why companies need to hedge their risks since investors can themselves diversify away all risks by including the shares of the company in a portfolio. Here we review the arguments that have been put forward to explain the use of hedging. The main arguments are:

(a) Hedging reduces the risk imposed on the firm's managers, employees, suppliers and customers

(b) Hedging can control the conflict of interest between bondholders and shareholders, thus reducing the agency costs of debt;

(c) The use of derivatives increases the value of a firm. As we have already discussed in Chapter 7a, Modigliani and Miller showed that firm value and financial policy decisions are unrelated in the absence of market imperfections. Models have been developed that show that hedging can increase the value of a firm if capital market imperfections exist. Thus the following additional justifications have been provided:

   (i) Hedging **lowers the probability** of the firm encountering **financial distress** which in turn lowers the expected costs of financial distress and the cost of capital.

   (ii) Hedging encourages investment by the firm. According to **agency theory** between shareholders and bondholders, the issuance of bonds which have higher priority than equity creates incentives for the firm's equity holders to under-invest. Hedging reduces the incentive to under-invest since hedging reduces uncertainty and the risk of loss. Because firms with more valuable growth opportunities and higher leverage are more likely to be affected by the underinvestment problem, these firms are also more likely to hedge.

7.3 Risks from the use of derivatives

FAST FORWARD

The main risks from the use of derivatives are the role of mispricing (**valuation** or **model risk**), **liquidity risk** and **reporting risk**.

7.3.1 Valuation (model) risk

The most common risk for OTC derivative users is the **risk of mispricing** the derivatives position. Since OTC derivatives do not trade in **liquid markets** where they can always be bought or sold at the market price, valuation models need to be used. These models however are based on assumptions which may not be valid.

For example the Black-Scholes option valuation model assumes that markets have no frictions, that the stock price is lognormally distributed, that interest rates are fixed, that the volatility of return is constant and that trading is possible all the time.

However, it is well known that these assumptions are at variance with reality. Interest rates are not constant and neither is the volatility. Demand and supply may have an impact on prices and there are certainly frictions in the market.

There are many examples of firms losing money due to valuation errors. For example, the National Australian Bank reported currency option losses in excess of $360 million Australian dollars (approximately $280 million in U.S. dollars) that were attributed to rogue traders and risk management failures and involved incorrect valuations and misreporting. It is much harder to value more complicated derivatives.

7.3.2 Liquidity risk

Exchange-traded derivative products are highly liquid and a transaction can take place at the market price. The market value of a derivatives contract is thus realized when it is sold. In the case of OTC derivatives and especially where complex contracts are involved it is not always possible for these contracts to be sold, and their model-calculated value to be realised. The reasons for this are:

(a) Uncertainty about the **valuation model** and the **risks** of the **position**.

(b) In the case of complex contracts, there may be only a small number of counterparties who both want that particular set of risk characteristics and are confident that they understand what they are receiving

7.3.3 Reporting risk

OTC complex derivative positions especially with long maturities can be manipulated so that the true value and the true risks of the positions are not revealed. For example, Enron had a huge portfolio of derivatives, including many contracts with extremely long maturities, whose risks were not revealed before it collapsed.

8 The Greeks—measuring the impact of risk factors 12/10

Changes in the value of an option can be measured in terms of its **Greeks**, that is in terms of its **risk factors**.

We discussed the basic concepts of options in Chapter 6 and have looked at how they are used to hedge currency risk and interest rate risk in Chapters 16 and 17 respectively. In this section we look at how changes in risk factors can affect the value of an option by using '**the Greeks**'.

8.1 Risk factors in options positions

The factors that affect the value of a call or put option are

- The value of the underlying
- The exercise price
- The risk-free interest rate
- The volatility
- The time to expiration

Since these factors are the ones that may adversely affect the value of an option they are also known as **risk factors**.

The Black Scholes model we used in Chapter 6 gives a mathematical expression of the relationship between the **value of an option** and the **factors** that **affect** its **value**. This is reproduced below.

The Black-Scholes model states that the value (P_c) of a call option is given by the following formula.

Exam formula

$$c = P_a N(d_1) - P_e N(d_2)e^{-rt}$$

$$\text{Where} \quad d_1 = \frac{\ln\left(\dfrac{P_a}{P_e}\right) + (r + 0.5s^2)t}{s\sqrt{T}}$$

$$d_2 = d_1 - s\sqrt{T}$$

The model has three main elements.

(a) The share price, P_a

(b) The delta value, $N(d_1)$, which measures how option prices vary with share prices (discussed below)

(c) ($P_e\ N(d_2)e^{-rt}$), which represents the borrowing element that must be combined with the share investment to produce an option equivalent.

Exam focus point

Remember that the volatility is represented by the standard deviation, **not** the variance. The variance is the standard deviation squared.

Within the model

(a) The difference between the share price and the option exercise price ($P_a - P_e$) is the intrinsic value of the option.

(b) e^{-rt} is a discount factor, reflecting the fact that the option will be exercised in the future.

(c)   The model is very dependent upon σ, the factor representing the share price volatility. This is likely to be calculated on the basis of historical movements, and different conditions may apply in the future.

8.2 Measuring the impact of risk factors: the Greeks

FAST FORWARD

The 'Greeks' are an important element in option theory.

- **Delta** – change in call option price/change in value of share
- **Gamma** – change in delta value/change in value of share
- **Theta** – change in option price over time
- **Rho** – change in option price as interest rates change
- **Vega** – change in option price as volatility changes

Various elements of the Black-Scholes model can be analysed separately. Collectively they are known as the Greeks.

Exam focus point

Calculation of deltas in delta hedging is examinable. You will not be required to calculate the other Greeks but you must know what they are and what they are used for.

8.3 Delta   12/10

If we accept the Black-Scholes model, the value of $N(d_1)$ can be used to indicate the amount of the underlying shares (or other instrument) which the writer of an option should hold in order to hedge (eliminate the risk of) the option position.

The appropriate 'hedge ratio' $N(d_1)$ is referred to as the **delta value**: hence the term delta hedge. The delta value is valid if the price changes are **small**.

Key term

Delta = change in call option price ÷ change in the price of the shares $\left(\dfrac{\Delta C}{\Delta S} = \text{delta} \right)$

Delta is used to measure the slope of the option value line at any particular time/price point.

For example, if we know that a change in share price of 3 cents results in a change in the option price of 1 cent, then:

Delta = 1c ÷ 3c = 1/3

For long call options (and/or short put options), delta has a value between 0 and 1.

For long put options (and/or short call options) , delta has a value between 0 and -1.

8.4 Delta hedging

The significance of the delta value is illustrated by the process of delta hedging.

Delta hedging allows us to determine the number of shares that we must buy to create the equivalent portfolio to an option, and hedge it.

We have seen that:

Buying call options = Buying share portfolio + Borrowing at risk free rate

As the opposite of borrowing is investing, therefore:

Buying call options + Investing at risk free rate = Buying share portfolio

As the opposite of buying call options is selling call options therefore:

Investing at risk free rate = Buying share portfolio + Selling call options

Therefore we can eliminate investment risk by buying shares and selling call options, as an adverse movement in the share price will be offset by a favourable movement in the option price. Delta hedging tells us in what proportion shares should be purchased and call options sold.

Delta hedges are only valid for small movements in the share price. The delta value is likely to change during the period of the option, and so the option writer may need to change her holdings to maintain a delta hedge position.

Example: Delta hedge

What is the number of call options that you would have to sell in order to hedge a holding of 200,000 shares, if the delta value ($N(d_1)$) of options is 0.8?

Assume that option contracts are for the purchase or sale of units of 1,000 shares.

Solution

The delta hedge can be calculated by the following formula.

$$\text{Number of contracts} = \frac{\text{Number of Shares}}{\text{Delta of option} \times \text{size of contract}}$$

$$= \frac{200,000}{0.8 \times 1,000}$$

$$= 250$$

If in this example the price of shares increased by $1, the value of the call options would increase by $800 per contract (80c per share). Since however we were selling these contracts the increase in the value of our holding of shares, 200,000 × $1, would be matched by the decrease in our holding of option contracts 250 × $800.

The portfolio would need to be adjusted as the delta value moved. If the delta value moved from 0.8 to 0.9, the number of extra contracts that would be required to maintain the hedge would be:

$250 \times (0.9 - 0.8) = 25$

8.5 Other points about delta values

The table below shows approximate values of delta for different types of options and the position of the exercise price relative to the share price.

	In the money	At the money	Out of the money
Long call/short put	Approaching 1	Approx 0.5	Approaching 0
Long put/short call	Approaching -1	Approx -0.5	Approaching 0

At expiry the value of delta will be as follows.

	In the money	Out of the money
Long call/short put	1	0
Long put/short call	-1	0

The factors influencing delta when the option is either in the money or out of the money can be appreciated by looking at the variables in the $N(d_1)$ formula given earlier. These factors are

- The exercise price of the option relative to the share price (ie its intrinsic value)
- The time to expiration
- The risk-free rate of return
- The volatility of returns on the share

8.6 Uses of delta factors

Delta factors are often used when deciding which options to **sell** or **buy**, with investors considering the delta value of each option and the **trend** – are delta values of options currently held getting stronger or weaker? Not all of the Greeks relate to all the derivatives – delta relates to them all.

8.7 Gamma

Key term

Gamma = Change in delta value ÷ Change in the price of the underlying share

Gamma is important as it measures the extent to which delta changes when the share price changes. We know from above that delta changes as the option moves in or out of the money but we don't know by how much. This is where gamma is useful.

The **higher** the **gamma value**, the more difficult it is for the option writer to **maintain** a **delta hedge** because the delta value increases more for a given change in share price. Gamma is effectively, a measure of **how easy risk management** will be.

Gamma values will be highest for a share which is **close to expiry** and is **'at the money'**. For example, suppose that an option has an exercise price of 340 cents and is due to expire in a few minutes' time.

(a)   If the share price is 338 cents, there is a very low chance of the option being exercised. The delta hedge ratio will be approximately zero. In other words, no hedge is necessary.

(b)   If the share price rises suddenly to 342 cents, it becomes highly probable that the option will be exercised and the delta hedge ratio will approximate to 1, suggesting the need to hedge through holding the underlying shares.

The table below summarises the types of positions of gamma and delta that might arise for different types of options.

Type	Delta value	Gamma Value
Long Call Option	Positive Delta	Positive Gamma
Short Call Option	Negative Delta	Negative Gamma
Long Put Option	Negative Delta	Positive Gamma
Short Put Option	Positive Delta	Negative Gamma
Type	*Delta value*	*Gamma Value*
Long Call Option	Positive Delta	Positive Gamma
Short Call Option	Negative Delta	Negative Gamma

Note that gamma is the same for calls and puts. If you are long a put or call, gamma will be a positive number. If you are short a put or call then gamma will be negative.

8.8 Theta

Key term

Theta is the change in an option's price (specifically its time premium) over time.

Remember that an option's price has two components, its **intrinsic value** and its **time premium**. When it expires, an option has no time premium.

Thus the time premium of an option diminishes over time towards zero and theta measures **how much value is lost over time,** how much therefore the option holder will lose through retaining her options. Theta is usually expressed as an amount lost per day. If a dollar option has a theta of –0.05, it will theoretically lose 5 cents a day, assuming there are no other changes in conditions.

Option
value

Time remaining to expiration   expiry

At **the money options** have the **greatest time premium** and thus the **greatest theta**. Their time decay is not linear; their theta increases as the date of expiration approaches. By contrast, the more in the money or out of the money the option is, the more its theta decays in a straight line.

Generally, options that have a **negative theta** have a **positive gamma** (and vice versa). A **positive gamma** means a **position benefits from movement**. **Negative theta** means that the **position loses money** if the **underlying asset** does **not move**.

8.9 Rho

Key term

> Rho measures the sensitivity of options prices to interest rate changes.

An option's rho is the amount of change in value for a 1% change in the risk-free interest rate. Rho is positive for calls and negative for puts, ie

Prices	Interest rate rises	Interest rate falls
Calls	Increase	Decrease
Puts	Decrease	Increase

If a dollar call option that has one year until expiration has a rho of 0.2, a 1% increase in interest rates will result in a 20 cent increase in the price of the option. However, the impact on the price of an option that has six months left until expiry would only be a 10 cent increase.

Generally, the **interest rate** is the **least significant influence** on change in price, and in addition interest rates tend to change slowly and in small amounts.

Long-term options have larger rhos than short-term options. The more time there is until expiration, the greater the effect of a change in interest rates.

8.10 Vega

Key term

> Vega measures the sensitivity of an option's price to a change in its implied volatility. $\left(\dfrac{\Delta C}{\Delta \sigma} = Vega \right)$

Vega is the **change in value of an option that results from a 1% point change in its volatility**. If a dollar option has a vega of 0.2, its price will increase by 20 cents for a one percentage point increase in its volatility. Vega is the same for both calls and puts

We have seen earlier that the Black-Scholes model is very dependent upon accurately estimating the volatility of the option price. Vega is a measure of the consequences of an incorrect estimation.

Long-term options have **larger vegas** than **short-term options**. The longer the time period until the option expires, the more uncertainty there is about the expiry price. Therefore a given change in volatility will have more impact on an option with longer until expiration than one with less time until expiration.

Volatility means the market's current assessment of volatility. It is influenced by the balance between option **demand** and **supply** (the greater the balance the less the volatility), also matters such as takeover rumours. Once announcements of definite plans have been made volatility will generally decrease.

With company options with the same month of expiry, **vega** is generally greatest **for at the money options**. Vega is small if an option is deeply in the money or out of the money.

BPP
LEARNING MEDIA

Part F Treasury and advanced risk management techniques | **17: The use of financial derivatives to hedge against interest rate risk**   **497**

SUMMARY OF GREEKS		
	Change in	**With**
Delta	Option value	Underlying asset value
Gamma	Delta	Underlying asset value
Theta	Time premium	Time
Rho	Option value	Interest rates

Exam focus point

Both optional and compulsory questions covering the components of the Black-Scholes model are likely to be tested.

8.11 Greeks and risk measurement

The values of the Greek parameters can give an approximate estimate of the value of a position if one or more of the factors that determine the value of an option change. The change in the value of the option can be approximated using the formula

Change in option value = delta × (change in underlying) + ½ × gamma × (change in underlying)^2 + vega × (change in volatility) + theta × (change in time) + rho × (change in interest rate)

$$\Delta C = \text{Delta} \times \Delta S + \tfrac{1}{2}\,\text{Gamma} \times (\Delta S)^2 + \text{Vega} \times \Delta\sigma + \text{Theta} \times \Delta t + \text{Rho} \times \Delta r$$

The gamma term is added to explain the fact that delta itself changes when the price of the underlying changes.

Question

Using the Greeks

Suppose that the Greeks of a call option are as follows:

Delta = 0.5
Gamma = 0.03

What will the value of the call option be if the value of the underlying increase by 5 units?

Answer

The value of the option will change by

$\Delta C = 0.5 \times 5 + \tfrac{1}{2}\,0.03 \times (5)^2 = 2.5 + 0.375 = 2.875$

Note that the changes in the option price could have been calculated directly using the Black-Scholes option pricing model. However, using the Greeks is convenient for two reasons:

- First, this method provides a quick way to calculate the Greeks of a portfolio of options
- The second reason is that the methods allow a simple estimation of the value at risk of an option position to be calculated

Chapter Roundup

- Factors influencing interest rate risk include

    - Fixed rate versus floating rate debt

    - The term of the loan

- Forward rate agreements hedge risk by **fixing the interest rate** on future borrowing.

- **Interest rate futures** can be used to hedge against interest rate changes between the current date and the date at which the interest rate on the lending or borrowing is set. Borrowers sell futures to hedge against **interest rate rises**. Lenders buy futures to hedge against **interest rate falls**.

- Interest rate options allow an organisation to limit its exposure to adverse interest rate movements whilst allowing it to take advantage of favourable interest rate movements.

- Interest rate swaps allow companies to take advantage of differences in the conditions connected with fixed and floating rate debt.

- It is important to be able to compare and contrast the different hedging instruments in a particular scenario and make recommendations on the best available strategy.

- Two general arguments have been put forward for the growth in derivatives.

    - The first is that derivatives complete the market

    - The second argument is that they make markets more efficient

- The main risks from the use of derivatives are the role of mispricing (**valuation** or **model risk**), **liquidity risk** and **reporting risk**.

- Changes in the value of an option can be measured in terms of its **Greeks**, that is in terms of its **risk factors**.

- The 'Greeks' are an important element in option theory.

    - **Delta** – change in call option price/change in value of share

    - **Gamma** – change in delta value/change in value of share

    - **Theta** – change in option price over time

    - **Rho** – change in option price as interest rates change

    - **Vega** – change in option price as volatility changes

Quick Quiz

1   Identify three aspects of a debt in which a company may be exposed to risk from interest rate movements.

2   What are 'FRAs'?

3   Fill in the blanks.

    If a company wishes to hedge borrowing at a future date, it should purchase

    . ... options, if it wishes to hedge lending, it should purchase
    .... options

4   Fill in the blanks.

    With a **collar**, the borrower buys .... and at the same time sells ....

5   What aspect of the valuation of an option does the standard deviation measure?

    A   Asset price   C   Volatility of asset value

    B   Exercise price   D   Time to expiration

6   What happens if one party to a interest rate swap defaults on the arrangements to pay interest?

7   Give three uses of an interest rate swap.

8   Under the terms of a swap arrangement, Louie has paid interest at 10%, Dewie at LIBOR + 1%.

    The parties have swapped floating rate interest at LIBOR + 1%. What amount of fixed rate interest do they need to swap for Louie to end up paying net interest of LIBOR – 0.5%?

Answers to Quick Quiz

1   Any **three** of:

   - Fixed rate *versus* floating rate debt
   - Debt in different currencies
   - Different terms of loan
   - Term loan or overdraft facility

2   Forward interest rate agreements.

3   If a company wishes to hedge borrowing at a future date, it should purchase **put** options, if it wishes to hedge lending, it should purchase **call** options.

4   With a **collar** the borrower buys **an interest rate cap** and at the same time sells **an interest rate floor**.

5   C   Volatility of asset value

6   The original party is liable to the lender.

7   Any three of:

   (a)   Switching from paying one type of interest to another

   (b)   Raising less expensive loans

   (c)   Securing better deposit rates

   (d)   Acting as a cost-effective method of managing interest rate risk

   (e)   Avoiding charges for early termination of loans

   (f)   Accessing a type of finance that could not be accessed directly

8   Fixed interest swapped – Louie interest paid – Floating rate interest swapped = – (LIBOR – 0.5%)
    Fixed interest swapped – 10% – (LIBOR + 1%) = – (LIBOR – 0.5%)
    Fixed interest swapped = 10% + (LIBOR + 1%) – (LIBOR – 0.5%) = 11.5%

Now try the questions below from the Exam Question Bank

Number	Level	Marks	Time
35	Introductory	15	27 mins
36	Introductory	15	27 mins
37	Examination	12	22 mins
38	Introductory	15	27 mins

18

Dividend policy in multinationals and transfer pricing

Topic list	Syllabus reference
1 Forecasting dividend capacity	F (4) (b)
2 Dividend capacity	F (4) (a)
3 Dividend repatriation policies	F (4) (a)
4 Transfer pricing	F (4) (c)
5 Regulation of transfer pricing	F (4) (c)

Introduction

Multinational companies have operations in the form of **subsidiaries**, **affiliates** or **joint ventures** in more than one country and produce and sell products around the world. The revenues of international operations are repatriated to the parent company in the form of dividends, royalties or licences. Overseas operations can therefore have a significant impact on the parent company's ability to pay dividends to its external shareholders or to finance its investment plans.

Multinational companies are either **horizontally integrated** (different affiliates produce the same product in different markets) or **vertically integrated** (upstream affiliates produce intermediate products that are further processed by downstream affiliates prior to final sale) or both. Irrespective of their organisation structure multinational companies are integrated enterprises, their affiliates engage in substantial amounts of intracompany transactions.

This chapter examines the **dividend capacity** of a **multinational company** and how it is affected by dividend repatriation, investment plans and share repurchases. It also discusses factors, such as tax, managerial incentives and timing that may affect dividend repatriation. The chapter then examines the various economic, tax and legal factors which may influence the choice of transfer pricing used in multinational corporations. Motives for the setting of transfer prices are analysed, along with guidelines that multinational companies need to observe in order to prevent them from exploiting the host country.

Study guide

		Intellectual level
F4	**Dividend policy in multinationals and transfer pricing**	
(a)	Determine a corporation's dividend capacity and its policy given:	3
	(i) The corporation's short- and long-term reinvestment strategy	
	(ii) The impact of any other capital reconstruction programmes such as share repurchase agreements and new capital issues on free cash flow to equity	
	(iii) The availability and timing of central remittances	
	(iv) The corporate tax regime within the host jurisdiction	
(b)	Advise, in the context of a specified capital investment programme, on an organisation's current and projected dividend capacity	3
(c)	Develop organisational policy on the transfer pricing of goods and services across international borders and be able to determine the most appropriate transfer pricing strategy in a given situation reflecting local regulations and tax regimes.	3

1 Forecasting dividend capacity

FAST FORWARD

> The dividend capacity of an organisation is measured by its free cash flow to equity.

1.1 How much can be paid as dividends?

Free cash flow to equity (FCFE) was covered earlier in Chapter 7b.

In theory, the entire FCFE can be paid as dividends as this is the amount that is available for this purpose. In practice however only a portion of this figure will be given to the shareholders as dividends as the management team tends to prefer a smooth dividend pattern.

While the dividends can never be less than zero, the free cash flows to equity can be **negative**. This can occur even if earnings are positive, if the firm has **substantial working capital and capital expenditure needs**. Negative free cash flow to equity is not unusual in **small, high growth firms**, at least in the early years, as reinvestment needs will tend to be substantial. However, as growth rates and capital expenditure **slow down**, free cash flow to equity will eventually become **positive**.

We have discussed dividend policy already in Chapter 1 and Chapter 10 (in relation to mergers and acquisitions).

2 Dividend capacity   12/10

FAST FORWARD

> The dividend capacity of a company depends on its after tax profits, investment plans and foreign dividends.

Exam focus point

> There was a six mark section in a compulsory 30 mark question in the December 2007 exam that asked students to calculate a multinational company's maximum dividend capacity.

We have discussed how to estimate the dividend capacity of an organisation above. Here we extend the treatment to the case of a multinational company and highlight the role of special factors such as remittances from subsidiaries, and the timing of payments.

The starting point again is the cash budget identity which may be expressed as follows:

Sources = Uses

$$R_t + FD_t + \Delta S_t + \Delta B_t = OE_t + Int_t + Div_t + Taxes_t + \Delta I_t + \Delta WC_t$$

where subscript (*t*) is used to index these components of cash flow according to date, and

- R = operating revenue from domestic operations
- FD = Dividends from foreign affiliates and subsidiaries
- ΔS = net equity issuance (i.e., new issues net of repurchases)
- ΔB = net debt issuance (i.e., new borrowing net of repayment)
- OE = operating costs
- Int = interest payments on debt, less any interest income
- Div = dividends on common shares
- Taxes = total taxes paid
- Dep = Depreciation
- ΔI = net investment in non-current assets (ie net of asset sales)
- ΔWC = net investment in working capital, inclusive of cash and marketable securities.

The potential dividend that can be paid, ie the dividend capacity of the firm can be estimated by rearranging the terms in the above equation.

$$Div_t = [R_t - OE_t - Int_t - Taxes_t] + FD_t - [\Delta I_t + \Delta WC_t] + \Delta B_t + \Delta S_t$$

Adding and subtracting depreciation the above equation can be restated as the **Free Cash Flow to Equity** (FCFE).

$$FCFE_t = [R_t - OE_t - Dep_t - Int_t - Taxes_t] + Dep_t + FD_t - [\Delta I_t + \Delta WC_t] + \Delta B_t + \Delta S_t$$

$$= \text{Net profit after tax + Depreciation + Foreign Dividends} - \text{Total Net Investment + Net debt Issuance} + \text{Net Share Issuance}$$

The FCFE represents dividends that could be paid to shareholders. This is usually not the same as actual dividends in a given year because normally the management of a company deliberately smoothes dividend payments across time. In the rest of this section we look in greater detail at three of the factors, total net investment, share repurchases and foreign dividends.

<table>
<tr><td>**Exam focus point**</td><td>You should know how the various parts of the FCFE equation affect dividend capacity.</td></tr>
</table>

2.1 Effect of investment plans

Total net investment is the single most important factor in determining dividend payouts to the shareholders. According to pecking order hypothesis funding investments with internal funds is the first choice of management, followed by borrowing or share issues. Consequently, fast growing companies would be associated with low dividend distributions.

2.2 Effect of share repurchases

A company that opts to repurchase its shares transfers funds from the company to the shareholders. The repurchase is financed from the firm's distributable reserves. The effect of a share repurchase is to increase the earnings per share, as the number of issued shares is reduced. The evidence suggests that markets react favourably to announcements of share repurchases. The rationale for the positive reaction is that when there are no investment opportunities then it is preferable for the excess cash to be returned to shareholders rather than to be retained within the company.

Share repurchases as a method of distribution represented a larger amount than dividends in the US. The reason for this is the more favourable tax treatment of share repurchases, which is subject to capital gains tax, whereas dividend payments are subject to income tax which is higher.

2.3 Dividends from overseas operations

Corporations paying dividends to common shareholders could, for example, fund these payments by triggering repatriations. Repatriations help parent companies meet their financing needs as larger dividends to external shareholders are associated with larger dividend repatriations inside the firm, and highly levered parent companies with profitable domestic investment opportunities draw more heavily on the resources of their foreign affiliates. In fact dividend repatriations represent sizeable financial flows for the US companies. For example in 1999 U.S. corporations listed in Compustat paid $198 billion in dividends to common shareholders and foreign affiliates of U.S. multinational firms repatriated $97 billion to the United States as dividends.

The importance of repatriated dividends is not limited to quoted companies, which it may be argued face pressure from the markets to distribute dividends to shareholders. Even private companies rely heavily on their overseas subsidiaries to finance dividend distributions. The evidence suggests that this is happening even when dividend repatriation is not tax efficient.

3 Dividend repatriation policies

FAST FORWARD

The amount of dividends subsidiaries pay to the parent company depend on the parent company's dividend policies, financing needs, taxation and managerial control.

The choice of whether to repatriate earnings from a foreign subsidiary is one of the most important decisions in multinational financial management. As mentioned in the previous section dividend repatriations represent significant financial flows for parent companies and contribute to dividend payments. The factors that affect dividend repatriation policies can be grouped as follows:

(a)   Financing Factors
(b)   Tax Factors
(c)   Managerial Factors
(d)   Timing Factors

3.1 Financing factors

Note that the equation for repatriated dividends can be written in terms of its use as:

$$FD_t = Div_t + \Delta I_t + \Delta WC_t - [R_t - OE_t - Taxes_t - Int_t] - [\Delta S_t + \Delta B_t]$$

The equation shows that the factors that shape **repatriation dividend policy** within the multinational firm are the **payment of dividends to external shareholders**, the le**vel of investment planned by the parent company, after tax profits** and **financing policies**.

Repatriation policies may reflect financing concerns of parents who draw on subsidiary cash flows to finance domestic expenses. Two examples of such domestic expenses are **dividend payments** to **external shareholders** and **capital expenditures in the home countries**.

3.2 Investment financing

Dividend repatriations from foreign affiliates may offer an attractive source of finance for domestic investment expenditures, despite possible associated tax costs especially, when alternative forms of finance are costly. This is true for parent companies with profitable domestic investment opportunities that already maintain large amounts of external debt and do not wish to increase the level of borrowing even further. Another case is when companies need to expand fast into areas and profitability is not sufficient to finance the expansion.

One of the strong implications of the U.S. tax treatment of foreign income is that American multinational corporations should not simultaneously remit dividends from low-tax foreign locations and transfer equity funds into the same foreign locations. Doing so generates a home-country tax liability that could be easily avoided simply by reducing both dividends and equity transfers.

3.3 Dividend policy

Dividend repatriations from foreign affiliates may also offer an attractive source of finance for payments of dividends to common shareholders especially when the parent company may prefer a smooth dividend payment pattern and domestic profitability is in decline. The dividend payments of a subsidiary may also be affected by the dividend policy of the parent company. For example if the parent

 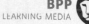

company operates a constant payout ratio policy, then the subsidiary will have to adopt a constant payout ratio policy too.

Empirical evidence shows that dividend payments to parent companies tend to be regular and multinational firms behave as though they select target payouts for their foreign affiliates, gradually adjusting payouts over time in response to changes in earnings.

3.4 Tax regime and dividend payments

Tax considerations are thought to be the primary reason for the dividend policies inside the multinational firm. For example the parent company may reduce its overall tax liability by, for example, receiving larger amounts of dividends from subsidiaries in countries where undistributed earnings are taxed.

For subsidiaries of UK companies, all foreign profits, whether repatriated or not, are liable to UK corporation tax, with a credit for the tax that has already been paid to the host country. Similarly, the US government does not distinguish between income earned abroad and income earned at home and gives credit to MNCs headquartered in the US for the amount of tax paid to foreign governments.

Example

Assume that the corporate tax rate in the home country is 40% and in the overseas country where a subsidiary is located is 30 percent. Assume that both the parent company and the subsidiary have pre-tax profits of $1000.

Taxes to foreign government = $1000 \times 30\% = 300$
MNC's profit after foreign tax = $1,000 - 300 = 700$
US taxes = $1000 \times 40\% = 400$
Foreign tax credit = 300
Net tax to IRS = $400 - 300 = 100$.
Total taxes = $300 + 100 = 400$.

3.5 Managerial control

Another reason that may determine repatriation policies is the inability to fully monitor foreign managers. Regularised dividend payments restrict the financial discretion of foreign managers, thereby reducing associated agency problems. Conflicts of interest are most apt to arise when ownership is divided, as local owners may influence managers to undertake transactions at other than market prices. Control considerations inside the firm may explain the tax-penalized behaviour especially when affiliates are partially owned.

Finally, the desire to control corporate managers around the world carries implications for dividend policies. A multinational firm's central management can use financial flows within the firm to evaluate the financial prospects and needs of far-flung foreign affiliates and to limit the discretion of foreign managers. As this observation suggests, it may be sensible to mandate dividend payments to police and monitor foreign managers, limit their ability to misallocate funds, and to extract returns on investments – much as public shareholders use dividends to monitor and control their firms.

3.6 Timing of dividend payments

So far we have concentrated on the size of repatriated dividends. The timing of payments may also be equally important. For example, a subsidiary may adjust its dividend payments to a parent company in order to benefit from expected movements in exchange rates. A company would like to collect early (lead) payments from currencies vulnerable to depreciation and to collect late (lag) from currencies which are expected to appreciate.

Also given that tax liabilities are triggered by repatriation, these tax liabilities can be deferred by reinvesting earnings abroad rather than remitting dividends to parent companies. The incentive to defer repatriation is much stronger for affiliates in low-tax countries, whose dividends trigger significant parent tax obligations, than they are for affiliates in high-tax countries – particularly since taxpayers receive net credits for repatriations from affiliates in countries with tax rates that exceed the parent country tax rate.

4 Transfer pricing

Transfer prices are set by the multinational corporation not only to recover the cost of services and goods provided but also to achieve objectives such as tax liability minimisation and to offset host country policies.

Multinational corporations supply their affiliates with capital, technology, and managerial skills, for which the parent firm receives a stream of dividend and interest payments, royalties, and license fees. At the same time significant intrafirm transfers of goods and services also occur. For example the subsidiary may provide the parent company with raw materials, whereas the parent company may provide the subsidiary with final goods for distribution to consumers in the host country. For intrafirm trade both the parent company and the subsidiary need to charge prices. These prices for goods, technology, or services between wholly or partly owned affiliates of the multinational are called **transfer prices**.

Key term

> A **transfer price** may be defined as the price at which goods or services are transferred from one process or department to another or from one member of a group to another.

The extent to which costs and profit are covered by the transfer price is a matter of company policy. A transfer price may be based upon any of the following.

- Standard cost
- Marginal cost: at marginal cost or with a gross profit margin added
- Opportunity cost
- Full cost: at full cost, or at a full cost plus price
- Market price
- Market price less a discount
- Negotiated price, which could be based on any of the other bases

A transfer price based on cost might be at **marginal cost** or **full cost**, with no profit or contribution margin but in a profit centre system it is more likely to be a price based on **marginal cost** or **full cost** plus a margin for contribution or profit. This is to allow profit centres to make a profit on work they do for other profit centres, and so earn a reward for their effort and use of resources on the work.

Transfers based on **market price** might be any of the following.

(a) The **actual market price** at which the transferred goods or services could be sold on an external market

(b) The **actual external market price**, minus an amount that reflects the savings in costs (for example selling costs and bad debts) when goods are transferred internally

(c) The **market price** of **similar goods** which are sold on an external market, although the transferred goods are not exactly the same and do not themselves have an external market

(d) A **price** sufficient to give an appropriate share of profit to each party

4.1 The level of transfer prices

The size of the transfer price will affect the costs of one profit centre and the revenues of another. Since profit centre managers are held accountable for their costs, revenues, and profits, they are likely to **dispute** the size of transfer prices with each other, or disagree about whether one profit centre should do work for another or not. Transfer prices affect behaviour and decisions by profit centre managers.

If managers of individual profit centres are tempted to take decisions that are harmful to other divisions and are not congruent with the goals of the organisation as a whole, the problem is likely to emerge in disputes about the transfer price.

Disagreements about output levels tend to focus on the transfer price. There is presumably a profit-maximising level of output and sales for the organisation as a whole. However, unless each profit centre also **maximises** its **own profit** at the corresponding level of output, there will be **inter-divisional disagreements** about output levels and the profit-maximising output will not be achieved.

4.2 The advantages of market value transfer prices

Giving profit centre managers the freedom to negotiate prices with other profit centres as though they were independent companies will tend to result in **market-based transfer prices**.

(a)   In most cases where the transfer price is at market price, internal transfers should be expected, because the buying division is likely to benefit from a **better quality of service**, **greater flexibility**, and **dependability of supply**.

(b)   Both divisions may benefit from **lower costs** of **administration**, **selling** and **transport**.

A market price as the transfer price would therefore result in decisions which would be in the best interests of the company or group as a whole.

4.3 The disadvantages of market value transfer prices

Market value as a transfer price does have certain disadvantages.

(a)   The **market price** may be **temporary**, induced by adverse economic conditions, or dumping, or the market price might depend on the volume of output supplied to the external market by the profit centre.

(b)   A **transfer price** at market value might, under some circumstances, act as a **disincentive** to use up any spare capacity in the divisions. A price based on incremental cost, in contrast, might provide an incentive to use up the spare resources in order to provide a marginal contribution to profit.

(c)   Many products do **not have** an **equivalent market price**, so that the price of a similar product might be chosen. In such circumstances, the option to sell or buy on the open market does not exist.

(d)   There might be an **imperfect external market** for the transferred item, so that if the transferring division tried to sell more externally, it would have to reduce its selling price.

(e)   **Internal transfers** are often **cheaper** than **external sales**, with savings in selling costs, bad debt risks and possibly transport costs. It would therefore seem reasonable for the buying division to expect a discount on the external market price, and to negotiate for such a discount.

4.4 Example: Transfer prices

A multinational company based in Beeland has subsidiary companies in Ceeland and in the UK. The UK subsidiary manufactures machinery parts which are sold to the Ceeland subsidiary for a unit price of B$420 (420 Beeland dollars), where the parts are assembled. The UK subsidiary shows a profit of B$80 per unit; 200,000 units are sold annually.

The Ceeland subsidiary incurs further costs of B$400 per unit and sells the finished goods on for an equivalent of B$1,050.

All of the profits from the foreign subsidiaries are remitted to the parent company as dividends. Double taxation treaties between Beeland, Ceeland and the UK allow companies to set foreign tax liabilities against their domestic tax liability.

The following rates of taxation apply.

	UK	Beeland	Ceeland
Tax on company profits	25%	35%	40%
Withholding tax on dividends	–	12%	10%

Required

Show the tax effect of increasing the transfer price between the UK and Ceeland subsidiaries by 25%.

Solution

The current position is as follows.

	UK company B$'000	Ceeland company B$'000	Total B$'000
Revenues and taxes in the local country			
Sales	84,000	210,000	294,000
Production expenses	(68,000)	(164,000)	(232,000)
Taxable profit	16,000	46,000	62,000
Tax (1)	(4,000)	(18,400)	(22,400)
Dividends to Beeland	12,000	27,600	39,600
Withholding tax (2)	0	2,760	2,760
Revenues and taxes in Beeland			
Dividend	12,000	27,600	39,600
Add back foreign tax paid	4,000	18,400	22,400
Taxable income	16,000	46,000	62,000
	5,600	16,100	21,700
Foreign tax credit	(4,000)	(16,100)	(20,100)
Tax paid in Beeland (3)	1,600	–	1,600
Total tax (1) + (2) + (3)	5,600	21,160	26,760

An increase of 25% in the transfer price would have the following effect.

	UK company B$'000	Ceeland company B$'000	Total B$'000
Revenues and taxes in the local country			
Sales	105,000	210,000	315,000
Production expenses	(68,000)	(185,000)	(253,000)
Taxable profit	37,000	25,000	62,000
Tax (1)	(9,250)	(10,000)	(19,250)
Dividends to Beeland	27,750	15,000	42,750
Withholding tax (2)	0	1,500	1,500
Revenues and taxes in Beeland			
Dividend	27,750	15,000	42,750
Add back foreign tax paid	9,250	10,000	19,250
Taxable income	37,000	25,000	62,000
Beeland tax due	12,950	8,750	21,700
Foreign tax credit	(9,250)	(8,750)	(18,000)
Tax paid in Beeland (3)	3,700	–	3,700
Total tax (1) + (2) + (3)	12,950	11,500	24,450

The total tax payable by the company is therefore reduced by B$2,310,000 to B$24,450,000.

4.5 Motivations for transfer pricing

In deciding on their transfer pricing policies, multinational companies take into account many internal and external factors or motivations for transfer pricing. In terms of internal motivations these include

Performance evaluation

When different affiliates within a multinational are treated as stand-alone profit centres, transfer prices are needed internally by the multinational to determine profitability of the individual divisions. Transfer prices

510 **18: Dividend policy in multinationals and transfer pricing** | Part F Treasury and advanced risk management techniques

BPP
LEARNING MEDIA

which deviate too much from the actual prices will make it difficult to properly monitor the performance of an affiliated unit.

Management incentives

If transfer prices are used for internal measures of performance by individual affiliates deviate from the true economic prices, and managers are evaluated and rewarded on the basis of the distorted profitability, then it may result in corporate managers behaving in an irresponsible way.

Cost allocation

When units within the multinational are run as cost centres, subsidiaries are charged a share of the costs of providing the group service function so that the service provider covers its costs plus a small mark-up. Lower or higher transfer prices may result in a subsidiary bearing less or more of the overheads.

Financing considerations

Transfer pricing may be used in order to boost the profitability of a subsidiary, with the parent company undercharging the subsidiary. Such a boost in the profitability and its credit rating may be needed by the subsidiary in order to succeed in obtaining funds from the host country.

Transfer pricing can also be used to disguise the profitability of the subsidiary in order to justify high prices for its products in the host country and to be able to resist demands for higher wages.

Several external motivations can affect the multinational's choice of transfer prices. Because multinationals operate in two or more jurisdictions, transfer prices must be assigned for intrafirm trade that crosses national borders.

Taxes

Multinational corporations use transfer pricing to channel profits out of high tax rate countries into lower ones. A parent company may sell goods at lower than normal prices to its subsidiaries in lower tax rate countries and buy from them at higher than normal prices. The resultant loss in the parent's high tax country adds significantly to the profits of the subsidiaries . An MNC reports most of its profits in a low-tax country, even though the actual profits are earned in a high tax country.

Tariffs

Border taxes such as tariffs and export taxes, are often levied on crossborder trade. Where the tax is levied on an ad valorem basis, the higher the transfer price, the larger the tax paid per unit. Whether a MNC will follow high transfer price strategy or not may depend on its impact on the tax burden. When border taxes are levied on a per-unit basis (i.e. specific taxes), the transfer price is irrelevant for tax purposes.

Rule of Origin Rule

Another external factor is the need to meet the rule of origin that applies to crossborder flows within a free trade area. Since border taxes are eliminated within the area, rules of origin must be used to determine eligibility for duty-free status. Over-or under-invoicing inputs is one way to avoid customs duties levied on products that do not meet the rule of origin test.

Exchange control and quotas

Transfer pricing can be used to avoid currency controls in the host country. For example a constraint in profit repatriation could be avoided by the parent company charging higher prices for raw materials, or higher fees for services provided to the subsidiary. The parent company will have higher profits and a higher tax liability and the subsidiary will have lower profitability and a lower tax liability.

When the host country restricts the amount of foreign exchange that can be used to import goods, then a lower transfer price allows a greater quantity of goods to be imported.

5 Regulation of transfer pricing

FAST FORWARD

Multinational companies have to adhere to pricing guidelines to prevent exploitation of the host country.

5.1 The problem of transfer price manipulation

As we have discussed in the previous section, transfer pricing is a normal, legitimate, and, in fact, required activity. Firms set prices on intrafirm transactions for a variety of perfectly legal and rational internal reasons, and, even where pricing is not required for internal reasons, governments may require it in order to determine how much tax revenues and customs duties are owed by the multinational corporation. **Transfer price manipulation** on the other hand exists, when multinational companies use transfer prices to evade or avoid payment of taxes and tariffs, or other controls that the government of the host country has put in place.

Governments worry about transfer price manipulation because they are concerned with the loss of revenues through tax avoidance or evasion and they dislike the loss of control. Overall MNC profits after taxes may be raised by either under-or over-invoicing the transfer price; such manipulation for tax purposes, however, comes at the expense of distorting other goals of the firm, in particular, evaluating management performance.

5.2 The arm's length standard

Key term

> The **arm's length standard** states that intra-firm trade of multinationals should be priced as if they took place between unrelated parties acting at arm's length in competitive markets.

The most common solution that tax authorities have adopted to reduce the probability of the transfer price manipulation is to develop particular transfer pricing regulations as part of the corporate income tax code. These regulations are generally based on the concept of the arm's length standard, which says that all MNC intra-firm activities should be priced as if they took place between unrelated parties acting at arm's length in competitive markets. The 1979 OECD Report defines the arm's length standard as

"prices which would have been agreed upon between unrelated parties engaged in the same or similar transactions under the same or similar conditions in the open market" (OECD 1979).

The arm's length standard has two methods.

Method 1: use the price negotiated between two unrelated parties C and D to proxy for the transfer between A and B.

Method 2: use the price at which A sells to unrelated party C to proxy for the transfer price between A and B.

In practice, the method used will depend on the available data. That is the existence of unrelated parties that engage in the same, or nearly the same, transactions under the same or nearly the same, circumstances. Does one of the related parties also engage in the same, or nearly the same, transactions with an unrelated party under the same, or nearly the same circumstances? Where there are differences, are they quantifiable? Do the results seem reasonable in the circumstances?

If the answers to these questions are yes, then the arm's length standard will yield a reasonable result. If the answers are no, then alternative methods must be used.

The main methods of establishing "arm's length" transfer prices of tangible goods include:

- comparable uncontrolled price (CUP)
- resale price (RP)
- cost plus (C+)
- comparable profit method(CPM)
- profit split (PS)

The first three are transactions-based approach, while the latter two are profit-based.

The comparable uncontrolled price (CUP) method

The CUP method looks for a comparable product to the transaction in question, either in terms of the same product being bought or sold by the MNC in a comparable transaction with an unrelated party, or the same or similar product being traded between two unrelated parties under the same or similar circumstances. The product so identified is called a **product comparable**. All the facts and circumstances that could materially affect the price must be considered.

Tax authorities prefer the CUP method over all other pricing methods for at least two reasons. First, it incorporates more information about the specific transaction than does any other method; ie it is transaction and product specific. Second, CUP takes both the interests of the buyer and seller into account since it looks at the price as determined by the intersection of demand and supply.

The resale price method (RPM)

Where a product comparable is not available, and the *CUP* method cannot be used, an alternative method is to focus on one side of the transaction, either the manufacturer or the distributor, and to estimate the transfer price using a functional approach.

Under the resale price method, the tax auditor looks for firms at similar trade levels that perform similar distribution function (ie. a **functional comparable**). The **RPM** method is best used when the distributor adds relatively little value to the product so that the value of its functions is easier to estimate. The assumption behind the **RP** method is that competition among distributors means that similar margins (returns) on sales are earned for similar functions.

The resale price method backs into the transfer price by subtracting a profit margin, derived from margins earned by comparable distributors engaged in comparable functions, from the known retail price to determine the transfer price. As a result, the **RPM** method evaluates the transaction only in terms of **the buyer**. The method ensures that the buyer receives an arm's length return consistent with returns earned by similar firms engaged in similar transactions. Since the resale margin is determined in an arm's length manner, but nothing is done to ensure that the manufacturer's profit margin is consistent with margins earned by other manufacturers, the adjustment is one-sided. Under the RPM method, having determined the buyer's arm's length margin, all excess profit on the transaction is assigned to the seller. Thus the resale price method tends to **overestimate** the transfer price since it gives all unallocated profits on the transaction to the upstream manufacturer. We call this **contract distributor** case, since the manufacturer is contracting out the distribution stage to the lowest bidder.

The cost plus method

The cost plus method starts with the costs of production, measured using recognised accounting principles, and then adds an appropriate mark-up over costs. The appropriate mark-up is estimated from those earned by similar manufacturers.

The assumption is that in a competitive market the percentage mark-ups over cost that could be earned by other arms length manufacturers would be roughly the same. The cost plus method works best when the producer is a simple manufacturer without complicated activities so that its costs and returns can be move easily estimated.

In order to use the cost plus method, the tax authority or the multinational company must know the accounting approach adopted by the unrelated parties. Such as what costs are included in the cost base before the mark-up over costs is calculated? Is it actual cost or standard cost?

Are only manufacturing costs included or is the cost base the sum of manufacturing costs plus some portion of operating costs? The larger the cost base, the smaller should be the profit mark-up, or gross margin, over costs.

The comparable profit (CPM) method

The comparable profits method is based on the premise that companies in similar industries will tend to have similar financial performance and to have similar financial characteristics. This similarity in performance will be indicated by the similarity in financial ratios. For instance if the return on assets (ROA) is the profit level indicator, then knowledge of the rate of ROAs for comparable companies or for the industry coupled with knowledge of the assets of the company would determine the taxable profits of the company.

The comparable profits method (CPM) has the following shortcomings: (1) it is not a transactions-based method, (2) it does not take the contractual obligations of the parties into account, (3) it does not reflect the facts and circumstances of the case, and (4) it could lead to substantial double taxation of income if other governments did not accept the method.

The Profit Split Method (PSM)

When there are no suitable product comparables (the *CUP* method) or functional comparables (the RPM and cost plus methods), the most common alternative method is the profit split (PSM) method, whereby the profits on a transaction earned by two related parties are split between the parties.

The profit split method allocates the consolidated profit from a transaction, or group of transactions, between the related parties. Where there are no comparables that can be used to estimate the transfer price, this method provides an alternative way to calculate or 'back into' the transfer price. The most commonly recommended ratios to split the profits on the transaction between the related parties is return on operating assets (the ratio of operating profits to operating assets).

The profit split method ensures that both related parties earn the same return on assets; the CPM, on the other hand, ensures that one of the two parties earns the average or median of returns earned by comparable uncontrolled parties. CPM is somewhat like the cost plus and resale price methods in that it focuses on only one side of total profits whereas the PS method looks to both sides.

BPP LEARNING MEDIA

Chapter Roundup

- The dividend capacity of an organisation is measured by its free cash flow to equity.

- The dividend capacity of a company depends on its after tax profits, investment plans and foreign dividends.

- The amount of dividends subsidiaries pay to the parent company depend on the parent company's dividend policies, financing needs, taxation and managerial control.

- Transfer prices are set by the multinational corporation not only to recover the cost of services and goods provided but also to achieve objectives such as tax liability minimisation and to offset host country policies.

- Multinational companies have to adhere to pricing guidelines to prevent exploitation of the host country.

Quick Quiz

1   What are the main motivations for transfer pricing?

2   What is meant by transfer price manipulation?

3   What are the main methods of establishing "arm's length" transfer prices?

4   What are the main factors that affect dividend repatriation policies?

Answers to Quick Quiz

The main motivations for transfer pricing are:

1   (a)   Performance evaluation   (e)   Taxes
    (b)   Management incentives   (f)   Tariffs
    (c)   Cost Allocation   (g)   Rule of Origin Rule
    (d)   Financing Considerations   (h)   Exchange Control and Quotas

2   *Transfer price manipulation* is the use of transfer prices to avoid the payment of taxes or tariffs.

3   Comparable uncontrolled price (CUP)   Comparable profit method (CPM)   Cost plus (C+)
    Resale price (RP)   Profit split (PS)

4   (a)   Financing Factors
    (b)   Tax Factors
    (c)   Managerial Factors
    (d)   Timing Factors

Now try the question below from the Exam Question Bank

Number	Level	Marks	Time
39	Introductory	10	18

18: Dividend policy in multinationals and transfer pricing | Part F Treasury and advanced risk management techniques

Emerging issues

Recent developments in world financial markets and international trade

Topic list	Syllabus reference
1 Developments in world financial markets	G (1)
2 Developments in international trade and finance	G (2)
3 Developments in Islamic finance	G (3)

Introduction

In this chapter we discuss developments in global financial markets as well as developments in international trade and finance and how they impact on the operations of a multinational company. We also consider the growth area of Islamic finance.

Study guide

		Intellectual level
G1	**Developments in world financial markets**	
	Discuss the significance to the organisation of latest developments in the world financial markets such as the causes and impact of the recent financial crisis, growth and impact of dark pool trading systems, the removal of barriers to the free movement of capital and the international regulations on money laundering	2
G2	**Developments in international trade and finance**	
	Demonstrate an awareness of new developments in the macroeconomic environment, assessing their impact upon the organisation, and advising on the appropriate response to those developments both internally and externally.	2
G3	**Developments in Islamic financing**	
	Demonstrate an understanding of the role of, and developments in, Islamic financing as a growing source of finance for organisations; explaining the rationale for its use, and identifying its benefits and deficiencies.	2

Introduction

The previous chapters have examined a number of issues regarding the financial decision-making in a corporation, together with the impact of the economic and financial environment on multinational companies. In this chapter we first review the most important developments in financial markets, such as the causes and impact of the recent financial crisis and the growth and impact of dark pool trading systems. We then discuss some recent developments in international trade and finance and how they impact on the operations of multinational companies.

1 Developments in world financial markets 6/12

FAST FORWARD

Developments in international financial markets have facilitated the growth in trade and the funding of overseas expansion strategies and have opened up more opportunities for investors. The main developments are:

- The global financial crisis
- Dark pool trading systems
- The removal of barriers to the free movement of capital
- International regulations on money laundering

1.1 The global credit crisis – the 'credit crunch'

FAST FORWARD

A credit crunch is a crisis caused by banks being too nervous to lend money to customers or to each other. When they do lend, they will charge higher rates of interest to cover their risk.

1.1.1 When it all began

One of the first obvious high-profile casualties of the global credit crisis was New Century Financial – the second largest sub-prime lender in the United States– which filed for Chapter 11 bankruptcy in early 2007. By August 2007, credit turmoil had hit financial markets across the world.

Case Study

In September 2007 in the UK, Northern Rock applied to the Bank of England for emergency funding after struggling to raise cash. This led to Northern Rock savers rushing to empty their accounts as shares in the bank plummeted. In February 2008 the UK Chancellor of the Exchequer, Alistair Darling, announced that Northern Rock was to be nationalised.

In August 2008 US investment bank Lehman Brothers also filed for Chapter 11 bankruptcy after suffering significant losses on sub-prime mortgages. Following substantial losses their trading partners lost confidence in the long-term viability of Lehman Brothers and refused to trade with it knowing that there were substantial 'toxic assets' within the bank. The unknown level of 'toxic assets' also prevented anyone purchasing Lehman Brothers as a going concern.

1.1.2 What caused the crisis?

Years of lax lending on the part of the financial institutions inflated a huge debt bubble as people borrowed cheap money and ploughed it into property.

Lenders were quite free with their funds – particularly in the US where billions of dollars of 'Ninja' mortgages (no income, no job or assets) were sold to people with weak credit ratings (sub-prime borrowers).

The idea was that if these sub-prime borrowers had trouble with repayments, rising house prices would allow them to remortgage their property.

This was a good idea when US Central Bank interest rates were low – but such a situation could not last. In June 2004, following an interest rate low of 1%, rates in the US started to climb and house prices fell in response. Borrowers began to default on mortgage payments and the seeds of a global financial crisis were sown.

1.1.3 How did it turn into a global crisis?

The global crisis stemmed from the way in which **debt was sold onto investors**.

The US banking sector packaged sub-prime home loans into mortgage-backed securities known as **collateralised debt obligations** (CDOs). These were sold onto hedge funds and investment banks who saw them as a good way of generating high returns.

However when borrowers started to default on their loans, the value of these investments plummeted, leading to huge losses by banks on a global scale.

In the UK, many banks had invested large sums of money in sub-prime backed investments and have had to write off billions of pounds in losses.

Case Study

On 22 April 2008, the day after the Bank of England unveiled a £50 billion bailout scheme to aid banks and ease the mortgage market, Royal Bank of Scotland (RBS) admitted that loan losses hit £1.25 billion in just six weeks. In August 2008, RBS reported a pre-tax loss of £691 million (after writing down £5.9 billion on investments hit by the credit crunch) – one of the biggest losses in UK corporate history. At the beginning of 2009, RBS announced that it expected to suffer a loss of up to £28 billion as a result of the credit crunch.

On 3 March 2008, it was reported that HSBC was writing off sub-prime loans at the rate of $51 million per day.

1.1.4 Did IFRS exacerbate the problem?

IAS 39 – *Financial Instruments: Recognition and measurement* requires entities to value financial assets and liabilities at **fair value**. Fair value can be defined as

'*the amount for which an asset could be exchanged, or a liability settled, between knowledgeable, willing parties in an arm's length transaction.*'

However as the global financial crisis deepened, there were calls to **suspend** fair value accounting. Many viewed fair value as **aggravating** the credit crunch problem. As markets collapsed, banks scrambled desperately to establish values for mortgage-related assets, leading to huge write-downs and in some cases runs on the bank. As banks mark assets down, their **lending capacity** is reduced which affects **liquidity**. This in turn creates further uncertainty, leading to further reductions in market price and so it goes on.

Some argued that not all assets are being disposed of immediately, therefore why should they be valued as such? Market prices of sub-prime debt are low due to the fact that no-one is willing to buy, rather than due to the **risk of default**. Fair value prices in the current economic climate are therefore implying a level of default that is **unrealistic**, which is in turn having an adverse effect on market confidence and activity. No banks will be willing to lend or invest if, by doing so, they have to take an **immediate write-down** as a result of being required to mark the asset to an unrealistic market price.

Case Study

Prudential disclosed a £459 million nosedive in the fair value of its US insurance assets for the first quarter of 2008. Under the controversial financial instruments standard IAS 39, the value of the assets were hit by more than £794 million in losses and £335 million in gains, resulting in an overall drop of £459 million.

Accountancy Age, 17 April 2008

However is this criticism of fair value completely reasonable? After all, the credit crunch was in full swing before most of the large write-downs were announced. Is it not the **threat** of write-downs that is the problem rather than the write-downs themselves? In other words, banks are reacting to the **risk** associated with potential write-downs. They do not know how big the problems are with rivals and are unwilling to risk large amounts of capital to find out.

An article in *Accountancy Age* on 17 April 2008 suggested that the **excessive volatility** in the market was caused not by accounting rules but because financial statements do not tell banks whose sub-prime derivatives are better or worse. As mentioned above, banks are unwilling to take the risk of losing large amounts of capital to find out.

1.1.5 How were businesses affected

As banks' confidence was at an all-time low, they stopped lending to each other, causing a liquidity problem. Inter-bank lending funds bank operations – without it banks have insufficient funds to lend to businesses and individuals. By mid-2007 it was obvious there was a severe problem – BNP Paribas had suspended two of its hedge funds blaming 'complete evaporation of liquidity in the asset-backed security market.

2008 was characterised by multi-billion dollar government bail-outs and by the end of the year the US central bank had cut interest rates to 0 – 0.25% in a bid to stem the economic freefall.

With bank lending so low, businesses were unable to obtain funding for investments, resulting in large reductions in output and general business confidence. This lack of confidence had a spiralling effect. As businesses cut back on production and provision of services, workers started to fear for their jobs and thus reduced spending on non-essential items. This led to businesses reducing output further to avoid excessive investment in inventories, workers were made redundant which led to even less consumer spending and so the spiral continued.

1.1.6 Where are we now?

There is little evidence that the global economy is recovering with any rigour. In September 2011 for example the IMF cut its 2011 growth forecast for the UK from 1.7% to just 1.1%, following a meagre 0.2% rise in output in the nine months to June 2011. In April 2012 it was announced that the UK had suffered a second successive quarter of negative growth creating a so-called 'double-dip' recession.

The European Sovereign Debt crisis has spread to such countries as Greece, Portugal, Italy, Ireland and Spain. On 19 September 2011, Standard and Poor's downgraded Italian debt from A+ to A and kept its outlook on 'negative'. The result was the euro losing more than half a cent against the US dollar, thus making US imports more expensive for Eurozone countries.

The US itself has not been without its troubles. In August 2011, Standard and Poor's downgraded US debt for the first time ever, from AAA to AA+, and classified its outlook as 'negative'. This was due to the agency thinking that the US debt reduction plan did not go far enough to tackle its huge debts. The downgrade could lead to an increase in the cost of US government borrowing, which in turn could feed down to companies, consumers and local government in the form of higher interest rates.

We will tackle the European Sovereign Debt crisis in more detail in Section 1.2 below.

1.2 The European Sovereign Debt crisis

Exam focus point

> This section is closely linked to Section B of the syllabus – *Economic Environment* (covered in Chapter 4).

Although the European debt crisis has no one single cause, its roots are in the introduction of the European single currency. This meant that member countries were able to borrow at a cheaper rate than they were previously able to. This was due to the assumption that these countries were following the economic rules of the single currency. This effectively meant that the good credit rating of Germany was improving the credit rating of countries such as Greece, Portugal and Italy.

Some of the European countries used the increased credit offered to increase consumption and build up large balance of payments deficits. The increased borrowing was based on the assumption of certain levels of growth which then did not occur due to the financial crisis of 2007.

The European Sovereign Debt crisis has been increasing in severity since 2010 when Portugal's debt was downgraded and further exacerbated in March 2011 when Greek debt was downgraded to 'junk.' This was followed by Ireland being downgraded in July 2011 and Italy in October 2011. France and Spain have both been downgraded in 2012. In a similar manner to the US downgrade of 2011, this could lead to an increase in the cost of government borrowing, which may lead to rising interest rates.

In May 2010 the European Union (EU) created the European Financial Stability Facility (EFSF) which is guaranteed by the Eurozone countries and provides bailout loans to countries that are in severe financial difficulty. In January 2011 the European Financial Stabilisation Mechanism (EFSM) was created to raise funds by using the EU budget as security. The funds raised can be lent to the IMF or the EFSF.

The EFSF had its credit rating downgraded from AAA to AA+ by Standard and Poor's in January 2012.

1.2.1 Austerity measures

Throughout Europe, and indeed globally, countries have been putting austerity measures in place in an attempt to reduce their spiralling debts. The table below summarises certain European countries' current financial positions and some of the austerity measures in place.

Country	Current position (at April 2012) and austerity measures
Greece	Frozen out of international credit markets because of sovereign debt 'junk' status
	Pensions, tax thresholds and civil service jobs severely affected
	Follow-up bailout of €130 billion by the EU and IMF approved in February 2012, after an initial €110 billion in May 2010
	Second bailout also included €100 billion debt write-off
	Unemployment at 17.7% in 2011
	Greek economy expected to contract 5% in 2012
Irish Republic	EU/IMF bailout of €85 billion in December 2010 (length of time to repay loan extended from 7.5 years to 15 years in 2011)
	Two banks bailed out in 2011 at a cost of €5.8 billion
	Government deficit of 13.1% below the forecast of less than 10% (including bank bailout)
	Government spending slashed by €4 billion – all public servants' pay cut by at least 5% and social welfare reduced
Italy	Debt downgraded from A+ to A in September 2011 (debt stands at 120% of Gross Domestic Product - $2.2 trillion)
	Austerity measures passed in July 2011 features savings worth €70 billion, including increases in healthcare fees, cuts to regional subsidies, family tax benefits and pensions of high-earners
	Original target of balancing budget by 2013 likely to be missed
	Prime Minister Mario Monti has implemented €20 billion in austerity measures since November 2011, but now wants Italy and Europe to promote growth
UK	Savings estimated at about £83 billion to be made over four years, including cutting 490,000 public sector jobs, increase in retirement age from 65 to 66 by 2020
	Budget deficit is currently approximately 10% of Gross Domestic Product, unemployment at highest level since 1994
Spain	Austerity budget for 2011 includes tax rise for the rich and 8% spending cuts
	€27 billion cut from 2012 government spending budget
	Budget deficit of 8.5% in 2011 and economy predicted to shrink by 1.7% in 2012
	Unemployment at 23% in 2012

Such austerity measures go back to times when ailing countries had to prop up their banks and had to find money from somewhere to do so. In 2008, for example, £37 billion of UK taxpayers' money was used to bail out three major banks (Royal Bank of Scotland, Lloyds TSB and HBOS), after which the UK government was forced to borrow a record £44 billion to fund its spending. However such expenditure could not continue without countries running the risk of bankruptcy, hence the severity of the current austerity measures.

1.2.2 Financial contagion

The European Sovereign Debt crisis is a classic example of financial contagion. The initial problems encountered by Greece and Portugal spread throughout Europe as confidence fell in other European economies. Inter-trading amongst European countries meant that, as one country experienced financial difficulties and reduced its imports, those countries providing the imported goods also suffered due to a downturn in trade. For example, the value of Ireland's exports to the UK is approximately 10.6% of Irish Gross Domestic Product (GDP). If the UK cut its spending on exports by 20%, not only would Ireland be losing income amounting to 2% of GDP, it would also be forced to reduce production of the goods and services that are exported to the UK. Economic growth is affected not just in the UK but also in Ireland. This will then have an effect on Ireland's spending on exports and so on.

However it is not just Europe that is suffering. European countries trade worldwide and as their economic growth slows and austerity measures take effect, economies worldwide will be affected. This leads to greater borrowing to fund spending (due to less income from exports and a general slowdown in the economy), leading to increased interest payments on debt and eventually potential downgrade of debt.

1.2.3 Effect on companies

We mentioned above that exporting companies will suffer as economies slow down. However, it is not just their sales that will suffer. As Government debt is downgraded and the cost of debt increases, governments often pass on the cost to companies and consumers in the form of higher interest rates. Therefore companies with debt of their own will find themselves trying to meet increasing interest payments whilst sales revenue is falling.

To try to combat the problem, companies may increase prices to recoup some of their lost sales revenue. Consumers facing austerity measures in the form of pay cuts or freezes, or more expensive essential services, will be unable to afford these higher prices and reduce their spending. Companies will suffer further reductions in sales revenue and the spiral will continue until either confidence grows again or they go out of business.

Currency fluctuations caused by the crisis can also have a significant effect on company performance. The euro has weakened against the dollar due to the crisis, therefore Eurozone companies purchasing goods from the US face increased prices (see Chapter 9 for details on how weakening currencies can affect cash flows).

1.2.4 Where do we go from here?

The full effects of the downgrade of European and US debts have not yet been realised. As the US is the largest economy in the world, its downgrade is bound to have far-reaching global consequences. The European downgrades continue throughout Europe and it is possible that other countries may be downgraded. The euro has already been weakened by the crisis – any further debt downgrades to major Eurozone countries may damage it even further.

The EFSF and EFSM are due to be replaced by the European Stability Mechanisation (ESM) in July 2012. The ESM will be able to guarantee debts and should reduce the risk of default by any one country and therefore also reduce the risk of contagion.

In May 2012, unexpected election results in Greece created political uncertainty as many voters turned to parties that refused to accept the bailout and the austerity conditions that had been imposed. There was also increased speculation that Greece may default on its debts and leave the euro. Many feel that this would cause contagion as outlined above.

1.3 Tranching

FAST FORWARD

A **tranche** is a slice of a security (typically a bond or other credit linked security) which is funded by investors who assume different risk levels within the liability structure of that security.

1.3.1 How tranching works

The structure of securitisation deals, referred to as **tranching**, is standard. In those transactions, claims on cash flows generated by the collateral are split into several classes of notes, at least three and possibly more than five (for example, Class A, Class B). Each class is called a **tranche** and has **absolute priority** in the cash flows over the more junior ones.

All the tranches together make up what is known as the deal's **capital structure** or **liability structure**. They are generally paid sequentially, from the most senior to most junior. The more senior tranches generally have higher ratings than the lower-rated tranches. For example, senior tranches may be rated AAA, AA or A. A more junior tranche may be rated BB. Ratings can fluctuate after the debt is issued – even senior tranches could be rated below investment grade (that is, below BBB).

Typical investors of **senior tranches** are insurance companies, pension funds and other risk-averse investors.

Junior tranches are **more risky** as they are not secured by specific assets. These tranches tend to be bought by hedge funds and other investors looking for higher risk-return profiles.

1.3.2 Example

Suppose you sell $100 million worth of loans. You divide it into 5 tranches with 5 being the most junior and 1 being the most senior. So you sell 20% ($200,000) of the value of the loans as tier 1, 20% as tier 2, etc.

1   During the first year of the loans, $100,000 is expected to be repaid, and $100,000 is repaid. Each tier gets $20,000.

2   During the second year, $100,000 is expected to be repaid, but repayment falls short. Only $90,000 is repaid. Tiers 1, 2, 3, and 4 each get their $20,000; tier 5 takes the loss, and only gets $10,000.

3   During the third year, things get worse - only $50,000 gets repaid. Tiers 1 and 2 each still get $20,000. Tier 3 loses half of its expected payment, collecting $10,000. Tiers 3, 4 and 5 get nothing.

1.3.3 Benefits of tranching

Tranching is a good way of **dividing risk**. Anyone who invests in risky loans is taking a chance, but tranching lets you divide the chances up, so that people who want safety can buy the top (senior) tranches, get less of a profit, but know that they're not going to lose out unless things go seriously wrong. People who are willing to take their chances in the lower (junior) tranches know that they're taking a significant risk, but they can potentially make a lot more money.

1.3.4 Risks of tranching

(a)   Tranches are very **complex**; most investors do not really understand the risks associated with each tranche.

(b)   Tranches **may not be divided properly** and the bundling process may be misleading. Investors are obviously anxious to obtain the most senior tranche – the more junior tranches are more difficult to 'get rid of'. Therefore some bundles of high risk loans may be divided into tranches and, say, 80% of the value of these loans sold as ultra-safe investments. Investors will be unaware of the level of '**rebundling**' that occurred before they managed to obtain their 'senior tranche' low-risk bond.

Exam focus point

Securitisation and tranching were both covered in an exam question in June 2010, including the purpose and methods of credit enhancement and a discussion of the risks in such a scheme.

1.4 Credit default swaps

A credit default swap is a specific type of counterparty agreement which allows the transfer of third party credit risk from one party to the other.

1.4.1 What are credit default swaps?

Credit default swaps act in a similar way to insurance policies. When two parties enter into a credit default swap, the buyer agrees to pay a fixed **spread** to the seller (see below). In return, the seller agrees to purchase a specified financial instrument from the buyer at the instrument's par value in the event of default. You could liken this transaction to a house insurance policy – in the event of a fire, the buyer of the policy will receive whatever the damaged or destroyed goods are worth in monetary terms.

The **spread** of a CDS is the **annual amount** the protection buyer must pay the protection seller over the length of the contract (like an insurance premium), expressed as a **percentage of the notional amount**. The **more likely** the risk of default, **the larger the spread**. For example, if the CDS spread of the reference entity is 50 basis points (or 0.5%) then an investor buying $10 million worth of protection from a bank must pay the bank $50,000 per year. These payments continue until either the CDS contract expires or the reference entity defaults.

Unlike insurance, however, CDS are **unregulated**. This means that contracts can be traded – or swapped – from investor to investor without anyone overseeing the trades to ensure the buyer has the resources to cover the losses if the security defaults.

1.4.2 The CDS market

By the end of 2007, the CDS market was valued at more than $45 trillion – more than twice the size of the combined GDP of the US, Japan and the EU. An original CDS can go through as many as 15 to 20 trades, therefore when a default occurs, the so-called 'insured' party or hedged party does not know who is responsible for making up the default or indeed whether the end party has the funds to do so.

When the economy is booming, CDS can be seen as a means of making 'easy' money for banks. Corporate defaults in a booming economy are few, thus swaps were a low-risk way of collecting premiums and earning extra cash.

1.4.3 Uses of CDS – speculation

The CDS market expanded into **structured finance** from its original confines of municipal bonds and corporate debt and then into the secondary market where **speculative investors** bought and sold the instruments without having any direct relationship with the underlying investment. Their behaviour was almost like **betting** on whether the investments would succeed or fail.

Example

A hedge fund believes that a company (Drury Inc) will shortly default on its debt of $10 million. The hedge fund may therefore buy $10 million worth of CDS protection for say 2 years with Drury Inc as the reference entity, at a spread of 500 basis points (5%) per annum.

If Drury Inc does default after, say, one year, then the hedge fund will have paid $500,000 to the bank but will then receive $10 million (assuming zero recovery rate). The bank will incur a $9.5 million loss unless it has managed to offset the position before the default.

If Drury Inc does not default, then the CDS contract will run for two years and the hedge fund will have paid out $1 million to the bank with no return. The bank makes a profit of $1 million; the hedge fund makes a loss of the same amount.

What would happen if the hedge fund decided to liquidate its position after a certain period of time in an attempt to lock in its gains or losses? Say after one year the market considers Drury Inc to be a greater risk of default, and the spread widens from 500 basis points to 1,500. The hedge fund may decide to sell

$10 million protection to the bank for one year at this higher rate. Over the two years, the hedge fund will pay the bank $1 million (2 x 5% x $10 million) but will receive $1.5 million (1 x 15% x $10 million) – a net profit of $500,000 (as long as Drury Inc does not default in the second year).

1.4.4 Uses of CDS – hedging

Credit default swaps are often used to manage the credit risk (risk of default) which arises from holding debt. For example, the holder of a corporate bond may hedge their exposure by entering into a CDS contract as the buyer of protection. If the bond goes into default, the proceeds from the CDS contract will cancel out the losses on the underlying bond.

Example

A pension fund owns $10 million of a five year bond issued by Drury Inc. In order to manage the risk of losses in the event of a default by Drury Inc, the pension fund buys a CDS from a bank with a notional amount of $10 million. Assume the CDS trades at 300 basis points (3%) which means that the pension fund will pay the bank an annual premium of $300,000.

If Drury Inc does not default on the bond, the pension fund will pay a total premium of 5 x $300,000 = $1.5 million to the bank and will receive the $10 million back at the end of five years. Although it has lost $1.5 million, the pension fund had hedged away the default risk.

If Drury Inc defaults on the bond after say 2 years, the pension fund will stop paying the premiums and the bank will refund the $10 million to compensate for the loss. The pension fund's loss is limited to the premiums it had paid to the bank (2 x $300,000 = $600,000) – if it had not hedged the risk, it would have lost the full $10 million.

1.4.5 The role of CDS in the global economic crisis

Once an obscure financial instrument for banks and bondholders, CDS are now at the heart of the current credit crisis.

American International Group (AIG) – the world's largest insurer – could issue CDSs without putting up any real collateral **as long as it maintained a triple-A credit rating**. There was no real capital cost to selling these swaps; there was no limit. Thanks to **fair value accounting**, AIG could book the profit from say a five-year credit default swap as soon as the contract was sold, based on the **expected** default rate. In many cases, the profits it booked never materialised.

On September 15 2007 the bubble burst when all of the major credit-rating agencies downgraded AIG. At issue were the soaring losses in its credit default swaps. The first big write-off came in the fourth quarter of 2007, when AIG reported an $11 billion charge. It was able to raise capital once, to repair the damage. But the losses kept growing. The moment the downgrade came, AIG was forced to come up with tens of billions of additional collateral, immediately. This was on top of the billions it owed to its trading partners. It didn't have the money. The world's largest insurance company was bankrupt.

As soon as AIG went bankrupt, all those institutions who had hedged debt positions using AIG CDS had to **mark down** the value of their assets, which at once **reduced their ability to lend**. The investment banks had **no ability to borrow** as the collapse of the CDS market meant that no-one was willing to insure their debt. The credit crunch had started in earnest.

Exam focus point

Make sure you read the article entitled 'Toxic assets' which was published in the January 2009 issue of *Student Accountant*.

1.5 Dark pool trading

FAST FORWARD

Dark pools are an 'alternative' trading system that allows participants to trade without displaying quotes publicly.

1.5.1 What is dark pool trading?

Dark pools are off-exchange facilities that allow trading of large blocks of shares. They allow brokers and fund managers to place and match large orders anonymously to avoid influencing the share price. The transactions are only made public after the trades have been completed. Their popularity has increased as electronic trading has resulted in the average size of trades being reduced. Traders placing large orders on the transparent exchanges risk signaling that they are large buyers or sellers. Such signals could cause the markets to move against them and put the order at risk.

1.5.2 What proportion of trading takes place in dark pools?

The proportion of trading that takes place outside the regulated exchanges is difficult to estimate. The Securities and Exchange Commission in the US estimates that dark pools and other alternative platforms accounted for approximately 22% of trade volumes in 2009. In the UK, the London Stock Exchange has lost more than 25% of the market to alternative platforms. In Asia however, stricter regulation and structural differences in the markets mean that dark pools do not pose such a large threat and account for only 1 – 3% of trades in the larger, more liquid markets.

1.5.3 Problems with dark pool trading

The main problem with dark pool trading is that the regulated exchanges do not know about the transactions taking place until the trades have been completed. As a result, the prices at which these trades are executed remains unknown until after the event.

Such a lack of information on significant trades makes the regulated exchanges less efficient. Although the prices in dark pools are based on those in the regulated exchanges, the dark pool trades do not contribute to the changes in prices as their liquidity is not displayed. Dark pools also take trade away from the regulated exchanges, resulting in reduced transparency as fewer trades are publicly exposed. Such a practice could reduce liquidity in the regulated exchanges and hinder efficient price-setting.

Transactions in dark pools can almost be viewed as 'over the counter' as prices are not reported and financial risks are not effectively managed. There is the danger that such risks spread in a manner similar to those attached to credit default swaps and collateralised debt obligations, which triggered the global financial crisis.

Dark pools and their lack of transparency defeat the purpose of fair and regulated markets with large numbers of participants and threaten the healthy and transparent development of these markets. They could lead to a two-tier system whereby the public would not have fair access to information regarding prices and volumes of shares that is available to dark pool participants.

1.5.4 What are regulators doing?

Regulators in both Europe and the US are taking steps to protect market transparency. In 2009, the US Securities and Exchange Commission (SEC) proposed the following measures.

(a) Information about an investor's interest in buying or selling shares should be made publicly available, rather than just the participants in the dark pool (that is, dark pool trades will be treated in the same way as any other trade).

(b) Dark pools should publicly identify that it was their pool that executed the trade.

Such requirements are intended to enhance the transparency of transactions and promote fairer and more efficient markets for US shares.

The European Commission is conducting a review of how dark pools affect share price and market stability before putting forward any regulatory reforms.

1.6 Free movement of capital

1.6.1 Convergence of financial institutions

Traditionally, financial institutions were operating within clearly delineated boundaries. Banks were engaged in **deposit taking** and **loan provision**, **insurance companies** in the **transfer of risks**, **securities firms** and **investment banks** in the provision of **services** related to **capital markets**. The separation of activities was reflected in separate regulatory authorities. In the UK, for example, banks were regulated by the Bank of England, whereas insurance companies were regulated by the Department of Trade and Industry.

Similarly, in the US, the Glass-Steagall Act of 1933 barred banks, brokerages and insurance companies from entering each others' industries, and investment banking and commercial banking were separated.

In the UK, the Financial Services Act 1986 abolished the barriers between the various financial firms, allowing banks to enter the insurance and securities markets and creating a **single regulatory authority**. Similarly, in the US the Financial Services Modernisation Act of 1999 also did away with restrictions on the integration of banking, insurance and stock trading.

The result of abolishing the barriers to entry in the various segments of the financial services industries has led to the creation of **financial conglomerates** with operations in **banking**, **securities** and **insurance**. The effect of this convergence is:

(a) The creation of **economies of scale** as operations that were previously performed by different companies are now performed by one company

(b) The creation of **economies of scope** since one factor of production can be employed in the production of more that one products

(c) The **reduction of volatility of earnings** since some of the earnings are fee-based and not influenced by the economic cycle.

(d) The **saving** of consumers **significant search costs** since they can buy all financial product from one source.

1.6.2 Financial reporting

All EU listed companies must use IFRS for their consolidated financial statements. Common accounting standards increase **transparency** and **comparability** for investors. This should lead to a more **efficient capital market**, much more transparency and greater cross-border investment, thereby promoting growth and employment in Europe. Making IFRS work in the EU will also allow greater access of EU companies to global capital markets since it will include removal of the reconciliation requirement to US GAAP for companies which list in the US.

1.6.3 Effect on the corporate sector

Globalisation and the single European currency have led to the restructuring of the global and European corporate sector, and the emergence of new companies. The raising of capital through **global equity** and **bond markets** has become commonplace and has made easier **cross-border mergers** as well as **foreign direct investment**. These developments can only favour those companies which may have found it difficult in the past to finance themselves, but which will now be able to raise equity more easily.

The ongoing integration process of the national stock exchanges has also been conducive to this development. Primary issues of European equities has been steadily increasing with whole new markets, such as the Neuer Markt in Frankfurt, becoming prominent internationally. In addition, a number of **Europe-wide equity indices** have been established, thereby contributing to extending the trading possibilities and the position-taking opportunities for institutional investors from many European countries. The elimination of exchange rate risks has also allowed many European institutional investors which were previously constrained to investing in the domestic market to invest in any European market, increasing the supply of capital.

Finally, alliances between stock exchanges also foster the integration of stock market infrastructures and trading platforms creating more competition and making the European markets more resilient and fit for the global economy.

1.7 Money laundering legislation

> The growth of globalisation has created more opportunities for money laundering which governments and international bodies are trying to combat with legislation.

One of the side effects of globalisation and the free movement of capital has been the growth in **money laundering**.

Key term

> **Money laundering** constitutes any financial transactions whose purpose is to conceal the identity of the parties to the transaction or to make the tracing of the money difficult.

Money laundering is used by organised crime and terrorist organisations but it is also used in order to avoid the payment of taxes or to distort accounting information. Money laundering involves therefore a number of agents and entities from criminals and terrorists to companies and corrupt officials or states as well as tax havens.

1.7.1 Risks associated with a company's products and services

Some businesses are at a higher risk than others of money laundering. For example, businesses dealing in luxury items of high value can be at risk of the products being resold through the black market or returned to the retailer in exchange for a legitimate cheque from them.

The increasing complexity of financial crime and its increase has prompted national governments and the European Union to legislate and regulate the contact of transactions. The Third Money Laundering Directive of the EU was formally adopted on 26th October 2005 and came into force on 15th December 2007.

At the same time the Financial Services Authority requires that professionals who engage in the provision of financial services should warn the authorities when they discover that illegal transactions have taken place.

1.7.2 The effects of regulation

The following information relates specifically to European companies but similar regulations exist in other countries.

Affected companies must assess the risk of money laundering in their business and take necessary action to alleviate this risk.

Assessing risk – the risk-based approach

The risk-based approach consists of a number of steps.

- Identifying the money laundering risks that are relevant to the business

- Carrying out a detailed risk assessment on such areas as customer behaviour and delivery channels

- Designing and implementing controls to manage and reduce any identified risks

- Monitor the effectiveness of these controls and make improvements where necessary

- Maintain records of actions taken and reasons for these actions

The time and cost of carrying out such assessments will depend on the size and complexity of the business but will require considerable effort to ensure compliance with regulations.

Assessing your customer base

Businesses with certain types of customers are more at risk of money laundering activities and will therefore be required to take more stringent action to protect themselves. Types of customers that pose a risk include the following.

- New customers carrying out large, one-off transactions

- Customers who have been introduced to you by a third party who may not have assessed their risk potential thoroughly

- Customers who aren't local to your business

- Customers whose businesses handle large amounts of cash

Other customers who might pose a risk include those who are unwilling to provide identification and who enter into transactions that do not make commercial sense. Before companies commence business dealings with a customer, they should conduct suitable customer due diligence.

Customer due diligence

This is an official term for taking steps to check that your customers are who they say they are. In practice, the best and easiest way to do this is to ask for official identification such as a passport or driving licence, together with utility bills and bank statements. On a personal level, if you are trying to arrange a loan or open a bank account, it is very likely you will be asked to produce such identification.

If customers are acting on behalf of a third party, it is important to identify who the third party is.

Applying customer due diligence

Businesses should apply customer due diligence whenever they feel it necessary but at least in any of the following circumstances.

(a) When establishing a business relationship. This is likely to be a relationship that will be ongoing therefore it is important to establish identify and credibility at the start. You may have to establish such information as the source and origin of funds that your customer will be using, copies of recent and current financial statements and details of the customer's business or employment.

(b) When carrying out an 'occasional transaction' worth 15,000 euros or more – that is, transactions that are not carried out within an ongoing business relationship. You should also look out for 'linked' transactions which are individual transactions of 15,000 euros or more that have been broken down into smaller , separate transactions to avoid due diligence checks.

(c) When you have doubts about identification information that you obtained previously

(d) When the customer's circumstances change – for example, a change in the ownership of the customer's business or a significant change in the type of business activity of the customer

Ongoing monitoring of your business

It is important that you have an effective system of internal controls to protect your business from being used for money laundering. Staff should be suitably trained in the implementation of these internal controls and be alert to any potential issues. A specific member of staff should be nominated as the person to whom any suspicious activities should be reported.

Full documentation of anti-money laundering policies and procedures should be kept and updated as appropriate. Staff should be kept fully informed of any changes.

Maintaining full and up to date records

Businesses are generally required to keep full and up to date records for financial reporting and auditing purposes but these can also be used to demonstrate compliance with money laundering regulations. Such records will include receipts, invoices and customer correspondence. European money laundering regulations require that such information be kept for each customer for five years beginning on either the date a transaction is completed or the date a business relationship ends.

1.7.3 The costs of compliance

All of the activities listed above do not come cheaply, especially if policies and procedures are being established for the first time. In addition, regulations in the UK state that all accountants in public practice must be supervised and monitored in their compliance and must be registered with a supervisory body.

ACCA is one of the supervisory bodies and is responsible for monitoring its own members. Such supervision comes at a cost however and monitored firms are expected to pay a fee for this service.

 Case Study

Money laundering in the football sector

Italy has experienced an attempt to launder money through the purchase of a famous Italian football club. Investigations to detect the case involved collaboration amongst several Italian public authorities.

Initially, numerous rumours spread concerning a well-known Italian football team and intentions to purchase its shares on the capital market. Almost immediately following the purchase, the shares' value increased rapidly.

Investigations uncovered evidence that the money used to buy the shares was supplied by a criminal association operating in central Italy. Furthermore, some of the money – supposedly offered to the football team as sponsorship – was diverted to another company to purchase real estate. It was found that the criminal association was very interested in purchasing the football team with funds obtained from several criminal offences.

As a result of the investigation, the criminal attempt to purchase the football team failed.

Source: Money Laundering through the Football Sector, *Financial Action Task Force Report*, July 2009

2 Developments in international trade and finance

FAST FORWARD

> The globalisation and integration of financial markets has contributed to expansion of international trade, but it has also created potentially more uncertainty for multinational companies.

The macroeconomic environment has a catalytic effect on business activities. A **stable macroeconomic environment** with **minimal exchange rate** and **interest rate fluctuations** allows business to plan their activities and to predict the key drivers of their value. An economic environment in which there is **uncertainty** about the cost of capital or currency rates, is not conducive to long-term planning. In this section we review some developments that have taken place recently and which have an impact on multinational companies.

2.1 Trade and world deflation

Trade among nations is a common occurrence and normally benefits both the exporter and the importer. In many countries international trade accounts for more than 20 percent of their national incomes. **Foreign trade** can usually be justified on the principle of **comparative advantage**. According to this economic principle, it is economically profitable for a country to specialize in the production of that commodity in which the producer country has the greater comparative advantage and to allow the other country to produce that commodity in which it has the lesser comparative disadvantage. We have already concluded in previous chapters that the risks of foreign trade increase as a company moves from exporting to direct foreign investment and when its activities are directed to less developed countries rather than to developed countries.

The most important application of the principle of **comparative advantage** has been the Chinese economy. China has exploited its comparative advantage stemming from low wages to dominate the production of labour-intensive products which being produced at a fraction of the production cost in developed countries has contributed to the world-wide low inflation regime of the last few years. The reduction of the cost has kept prices down and has increased consumer purchasing power world wide.

2.2 Control of monetary policy

One of the most important developments in the macroeconomic environment has been the way monetary policy has been conducted in the advanced economies. Monetary policy has been assigned the task of controlling inflation and is largely outside the control of the national governments.

The **Bank of England** became independent of the government in 1997 and sets interest rates so as to meet the inflationary target set out by the government. Similarly, the **European Central Bank** sets the interest rates in the euro zone. The **independence of central banks** from government interference has given credibility to their policies and has stabilised the financial markets. This in turn has affected the expectations about inflation of market participants and has lowered inflation. A **low inflation environment** is conducive to **long-term planning** by business and **stimulates investment**.

2.3 Trade zones and international trade

The main obstacles to international trade are capital restrictions and tariffs imposed upon imports as well as restrictions on capital mobility. Tariffs are usually imposed to provide revenue or to protect a home industry. The basic arguments for tariffs are:

(a) To protect infant or key industries
(b) To equalise costs of production between domestic and foreign producers
(c) To protect domestic jobs
(d) To prevent capital being moved to other countries

Other measures that have been used selectively to control imports are **import quotas** which set the maximum absolute amount of a particular commodity that can be imported. **Export subsidies** are also used to encourage exports of certain goods or to prevent discrimination against overseas exporters who sell in a foreign market at a world price lower than the domestic price. **Exchange controls** are also used to control the flow of international trade. Some controls are used to ration a country's scarce foreign exchange. Some countries use different exchange rates for different commodities to encourage or discourage imports.

However, in the last few years there has been an increasing realisation that **tariffs** deny individuals and nations the benefits of **greater productivity** and a higher standard of living and tariffs eliminate or reduce the advantages of specialization and exchange among nations and prevent the best use of scare world resources. The presence of tariffs also hinders the expansion of multinational companies and international trade and inhibits their growth and the benefits of consumers.

As a result of the growing movement towards freer trade which culminated with the creation of the World Trade Organisation many countries have come together to create free trade areas. The European Community was a free trade area, before it became the European Union. The **North American Free Trade Area** is also a free trade area created by the United States, Mexico and Canada in 1994. The members of the trade zone have established preferential tariff treatment for certain products traded between these countries, in the form of reduced or zero rate tariffs. By eliminating **trade barriers**, the **trade zone** facilitates **cross-border movement** of **goods and services**, increases **investment opportunities**, promotes fair competition, and enforces **intellectual property rights** in the three countries.

2.4 Trade financing

A significant development which has boosted international trade is that **trade financing** has become easier to be obtained by companies. Financing sources for international trade transactions include **commercial bank loans** within the host country and loans from **international lending agencies**. Foreign banks can also be used to **discount trade bills** to finance short term financing. Eurodollar financing is another method for providing foreign financing. A **Eurodollar** is a **dollar deposit** held in a bank outside the United States. An active market exists for these deposits. Banks use Eurodollars to make dollar loans to borrowers; the interest rate is usually in excess of the deposit rate. Such loans are usually in very large amounts, are short-term working-capital loans, and are unsecured. U.S. firms frequently arrange for lines of credit and revolving credits from Eurodollar banks. No compensating balances are usually required.

The Eurobond market is widely used for long-term funds for multinational U.S. companies. A Eurobond is a long-term security issued by an internationally recognized borrower in several countries simultaneously. The bonds are denominated in a single currency. Such bonds are usually fixed-income bonds or floating-rate bonds; some bonds are convertible into common stock.

Many countries have organized **development banks** that provide intermediate and long-term loans to private enterprises. Such loans are made to provide **economic development** within a country.

2.5 Developments in the non-market environment

We have discussed so far the impact of developments in financial market and how they may facilitate the funding of investment strategies and the management of risks, These are all the benign effect of globalisation on multinational companies. However, globalisation may also create more uncertainty. This is created in turn by changes in the non-market environments in which multinational companies operate.

The **non-market environments** consist of the **social**, **political**, and **legal arrangements** that determine the firms' interactions outside of, and in conjunction with, markets. These **non-market environments** are shaped by both **global** and **country-specific factors** and the successful implementation of a multi-domestic strategy involves issue-specific action plans that are tailored to the configuration of institutions and interests in individual countries.

2.5.1 Regulation

Many governments have responded to **globalisation** and the loss of control through **tariffs** and other methods of control by introducing regulation. For example the wave of **cross-border mergers** and acquisitions of 1990s, an integral component of globalisation, have created oligopolies in many industries. Major industries (such as automobiles, petroleum exploration, semiconductors, consumer electronics, insurance, banking) now have eight to ten key players that account for 70-80 percent of the global output. Not surprisingly then, there is an increased level of **antitrust scrutiny**, especially in the US and the EU, the scrutiny of the Boeing-McDonnell Douglas merger, British Airways–American Airlines alliance, being notable examples of regulators restraining the emergence of (potential or actual) **cross-border oligopolies**.

Thus antitrust actions become non-tariff barriers or cartel-sponsored private barriers become obstacles to trade and investment flows, key issues are whether, when, and how to establish an international regime (or modify an extant one) on competition policy. Needless to say, this has an immense bearing on multinational corporations' (MNCs) non-market environments.

Globalisation also creates incentives for governments to intervene in favour of domestic MNCs in terms of 'macroeconomic' and 'macro-structural' policies. It was argued in the 1980s that in industries marked by **imperfect competition**, **high positive externalities** and **supernormal profits** (characteristics of the new oligopolies as well), firms are often locked in a zero-sum game, and governments have incentives to intervene in favour of domestic firms. Boundaries between domestic and international are blurred because domestic interventions can tilt the scale in favour of domestic firms in global markets. Arguably, given the fast pace of product obsolescence, a winner-takes-all situation is developing in many industries. Consequently, MNCs have incentives to emerge as winners, if not through market processes then through non-market strategies. Thus, globalisation processes create incentives for MNCs to enlist support from their home governments and create an obligation for governments to support them.

2.5.2 Pressure groups

Although domestic governments may be willing to support MNCs, a major threat has emerged from **globally networked pressure groups**, which influence the public and put pressure on governments to take measures against multinational companies.

Case Study

Greenpeace, the environmental pressure group, has been responsible for numerous protests against environmentally unfriendly corporate practices. For example, in 2010 Greenpeace and its supporters were primarily responsible for Nestle (the global food and confectionery company) agreeing to stop sourcing palm oil from suppliers that destroy the rainforest homes of the last remaining orangutans. Palm oil is used extensively by Nestle in such popular snacks as KitKat. Under Nestle's new policy, it will now stop buying from companies that own or manage 'high risk plantations or farms linked to deforestation'.

2.5.3 Political risks

Because globalisation leads to a high degree of cross -border economic linkages, MNCs become vulnerable to political developments in their home and host countries. Citizen groups in home/host countries can impact MNCs' strategies in yet another country.

Case Study

US citizen groups, notably the Natural Resources Defence Council, in alliance with Mexican groups, forced Mitsubishi to shelve a $100 million investment in a salt plant on the shores of Laguna San Ignacio where gray whales breed: 'And as Mexico had previously received $11.6 billion in long-term investments from abroad, it also discovered that it cannot ignore the other forces, like the environmental movement, that are criss-crossing borders and making politics into a global game'.

The message is clear: if MNCs invest in multiple markets, they need to deal with citizen groups in multiple countries. And this would require MNCs to integrate their supranational and multi-domestic non-market strategies.

3 Developments in Islamic financing

FAST FORWARD

Islamic finance has undergone **rapid growth** in recent years and is considered to be an **alternative** to conventional sources of finance by many organisations.

Islamic finance has undergone **rapid growth** over recent years up to the point today where it is an industry worth more than $1 trillion. Islamic financing is not only the preserve of Islamic banks, but it is also becoming an important revenue stream for some of the worlds biggest lenders and many of the major conventional banks, including HSBC and Standard Chartered, have Islamic banking arms also known as 'Islamic Windows'.

3.1 Rationale for use of Islamic finance

Islamic finance may be used for either cultural/religious or commercial reasons. Commercial reasons include the fact that Islamic finance may be available when other sources of finance are not. Islamic finance may also appeal to companies due to its more prudent investment and risk philosophy

Conventional banks aims to profit by taking in money deposits in return for the payment of interest or (**Riba**) and then lending money out in return for the payment of a higher level of interest. Islamic finance does not permit the charging of interest and invests under arrangements which share the profits and losses of the enterprises.

Taken from the perspective of Sharia'a (Islamic religious law and moral code), the taking of deposits which are subsequently lent out for interest which is paid whether or not the project is profitable is not justifiable. The Islamic bank arranges its business in such a way that the bank's **profitability is closely tied to that of the client**. The bank stands to take profit or make loss in line with the projects it is financing and as such must be more involved in the investment decision making. The bank acts in some ways more like a fund manager than a conventional lending institution. Speculation is not allowed and conventional derivative products are deemed to be un-Islamic.

You have studied some Islamic finance transactions in Paper F9 *Financial Management,* which were also recapped in Chapter 7a of this text.

3.2 Advantages of Islamic finance

Islamic finance operates by the underlying principle that there should be a link between the economic activity that creates value and the financing of that economic activity. The main advantages of Islamic finance are as follows:

(a)   Gharar (uncertainty, risk or speculation) is not allowed, reducing the risk of losses

(b)   Excessive profiteering is also not allowed, only reasonable mark-ups are allowed

(c)   Banks cannot use excessive leverage and are therefore less likely to collapse

3.3 Drawbacks of Islamic finance

The use of Islamic finance does not remove all commercial risk. Indeed there may even be additional risk from the use of Islamic finance. There are the following drawbacks from the use of Islamic finance:

(a)   There is no international consensus on Sharia'a interpretations, particularly with innovative financial products.

(b)   There is no standard Sharia'a model for the Islamic finance market, meaning that documentation is often tailor-made for the transaction, leading to higher transaction costs than for the conventional finance alternative.

(c)   Due to governmental and Sharia'a restrictions, Islamic finance institutions are subject to additional compliance work which can also increase transaction costs.

(d)   Islamic banks cannot minimise their risks in the same way as conventional banks as hedging is prohibited.

Chapter Roundup

- Developments in international financial markets have facilitated the growth in trade and the funding of overseas expansion strategies and have opened up more opportunities for investors. The main developments are:

    - The global financial crisis
    - Deep pool trading systems
    - The removal of barriers to the free movement of capital
    - International regulations on money laundering

- A credit crunch is a crisis caused by banks being too nervous to lend money to customers or to each other. When they do lend, they will charge higher rates of interest to cover their risk.

- A tranche is a slice of a security (typically a bond or other credit linked security) which is funded by investors who assume different risk levels within the liability structure of that security.

- A credit default swap is a specific type of counterparty agreement which allows the transfer of third party credit risk from one party to the other.

- Dark pools are an 'alternative' trading system that allows participants to trade without displaying quotes publicly.

- The growth of globalisation has created more opportunities for **money laundering** which governments and international bodies are trying to combat with legislation.

- The globalisation and integration of financial markets has contributed to expansion of international trade, but it has also created potentially more uncertainty for multinational companies.

- Islamic finance has undergone **rapid growth** in recent years and is considered to be an **alternative** to conventional sources of finance by many organisations.

Quick Quiz

1   Give three effects of the convergence of financial institutions.

2   By what methods do governments try to combat money laundering?

Answers to Quick Quiz

1   Any three of:

   (a)   Create economies of scale
   (b)   Create economies of scope
   (c)   It diversifies revenue sources and reduces risk
   (d)   It reduces search costs for consumers

2   (a)   Legislation that makes it more difficult to happen
     (b)   Asking professionals to report suspect transactions

Now try the question below from the Exam Question Bank

Number	Level	Marks	Time
40	Introductory	10	18 mins

Appendix – Mathematical tables

Present Value Table

Present value of 1 i.e. $(1 + r)^{-n}$

Where r = discount rate
             n = number of periods until payment

Discount rate (r)

Periods (n)	1%	2%	3%	4%	5%	6%	7%	8%	9%	10%	
1	0·990	0·980	0·971	0·962	0·952	0·943	0·935	0·926	0·917	0·909	1
2	0·980	0·961	0·943	0·925	0·907	0·890	0·873	0·857	0·842	0·826	2
3	0·971	0·942	0·915	0·889	0·864	0·840	0·816	0·794	0·772	0·751	3
4	0·961	0·924	0·888	0·855	0·823	0·792	0·763	0·735	0·708	0·683	4
5	0·951	0·906	0·863	0·822	0·784	0·747	0·713	0·681	0·650	0·621	5
6	0·942	0·888	0·837	0·790	0·746	0·705	0·666	0·630	0·596	0·564	6
7	0·933	0·871	0·813	0·760	0·711	0·665	0·623	0·583	0·547	0·513	7
8	0·923	0·853	0·789	0·731	0·677	0·627	0·582	0·540	0·502	0·467	8
9	0·914	0·837	0·766	0·703	0·645	0·592	0·544	0·500	0·460	0·424	9
10	0·905	0·820	0·744	0·676	0·614	0·558	0·508	0·463	0·422	0·386	10
11	0·896	0·804	0·722	0·650	0·585	0·527	0·475	0·429	0·388	0·350	11
12	0·887	0·788	0·701	0·625	0·557	0·497	0·444	0·397	0·356	0·319	12
13	0·879	0·773	0·681	0·601	0·530	0·469	0·415	0·368	0·326	0·290	13
14	0·870	0·758	0·661	0·577	0·505	0·442	0·388	0·340	0·299	0·263	14
15	0·861	0·743	0·642	0·555	0·481	0·417	0·362	0·315	0·275	0·239	15

(n)	11%	12%	13%	14%	15%	16%	17%	18%	19%	20%	
1	0·901	0·893	0·885	0·877	0·870	0·862	0·855	0·847	0·840	0·833	1
2	0·812	0·797	0·783	0·769	0·756	0·743	0·731	0·718	0·706	0·694	2
3	0·731	0·712	0·693	0·675	0·658	0·641	0·624	0·609	0·593	0·579	3
4	0·659	0·636	0·613	0·592	0·572	0·552	0·534	0·516	0·499	0·482	4
5	0·593	0·567	0·543	0·519	0·497	0·476	0·456	0·437	0·419	0·402	5
6	0·535	0·507	0·480	0·456	0·432	0·410	0·390	0·370	0·352	0·335	6
7	0·482	0·452	0·425	0·400	0·376	0·354	0·333	0·314	0·296	0·279	7
8	0·434	0·404	0·376	0·351	0·327	0·305	0·285	0·266	0·249	0·233	8
9	0·391	0·361	0·333	0·308	0·284	0·263	0·243	0·225	0·209	0·194	9
10	0·352	0·322	0·295	0·270	0·247	0·227	0·208	0·191	0·176	0·162	10
11	0·317	0·287	0·261	0·237	0·215	0·195	0·178	0·162	0·148	0·135	11
12	0·286	0·257	0·231	0·208	0·187	0·168	0·152	0·137	0·124	0·112	12
13	0·258	0·229	0·204	0·182	0·163	0·145	0·130	0·116	0·104	0·093	13
14	0·232	0·205	0·181	0·160	0·141	0·125	0·111	0·099	0·088	0·078	14
15	0·209	0·183	0·160	0·140	0·123	0·108	0·095	0·084	0·074	0·065	15

Annuity Table

Present value of an annuity of 1 i.e. $\dfrac{1-(1+r)^{-n}}{r}$

Where   r = discount rate
          n = number of periods

Discount rate (r)

Periods (n)	1%	2%	3%	4%	5%	6%	7%	8%	9%	10%	
1	0·990	0·980	0·971	0·962	0·952	0·943	0·935	0·926	0·917	0·909	1
2	1·970	1·942	1·913	1·886	1·859	1·833	1·808	1·783	1·759	1·736	2
3	2·941	2·884	2·829	2·775	2·723	2·673	2·624	2·577	2·531	2·487	3
4	3·902	3·808	3·717	3·630	3·546	3·465	3·387	3·312	3·240	3·170	4
5	4·853	4·713	4·580	4·452	4·329	4·212	4·100	3·993	3·890	3·791	5
6	5·795	5·601	5·417	5·242	5·076	4·917	4·767	4·623	4·486	4·355	6
7	6·728	6·472	6·230	6·002	5·786	5·582	5·389	5·206	5·033	4·868	7
8	7·652	7·325	7·020	6·733	6·463	6·210	5·971	5·747	5·535	5·335	8
9	8·566	8·162	7·786	7·435	7·108	6·802	6·515	6·247	5·995	5·759	9
10	9·471	8·983	8·530	8·111	7·722	7·360	7·024	6·710	6·418	6·145	10
11	10·37	9·787	9·253	8·760	8·306	7·887	7·499	7·139	6·805	6·495	11
12	11·26	10·58	9·954	9·385	8·863	8·384	7·943	7·536	7·161	6·814	12
13	12·13	11·35	10·63	9·986	9·394	8·853	8·358	7·904	7·487	7·103	13
14	13·00	12·11	11·30	10·56	9·899	9·295	8·745	8·244	7·786	7·367	14
15	13·87	12·85	11·94	11·12	10·38	9·712	9·108	8·559	8·061	7·606	15

(n)	11%	12%	13%	14%	15%	16%	17%	18%	19%	20%	
1	0·901	0·893	0·885	0·877	0·870	0·862	0·855	0·847	0·840	0·833	1
2	1·713	1·690	1·668	1·647	1·626	1·605	1·585	1·566	1·547	1·528	2
3	2·444	2·402	2·361	2·322	2·283	2·246	2·210	2·174	2·140	2·106	3
4	3·102	3·037	2·974	2·914	2·855	2·798	2·743	2·690	2·639	2·589	4
5	3·696	3·605	3·517	3·433	3·352	3·274	3·199	3·127	3·058	2·991	5
6	4·231	4·111	3·998	3·889	3·784	3·685	3·589	3·498	3·410	3·326	6
7	4·712	4·564	4·423	4·288	4·160	4·039	3·922	3·812	3·706	3·605	7
8	5·146	4·968	4·799	4·639	4·487	4·344	4·207	4·078	3·954	3·837	8
9	5·537	5·328	5·132	4·946	4·772	4·607	4·451	4·303	4·163	4·031	9
10	5·889	5·650	5·426	5·216	5·019	4·833	4·659	4·494	4·339	4·192	10
11	6·207	5·938	5·687	5·453	5·234	5·029	4·836	4·656	4·486	4·327	11
12	6·492	6·194	5·918	5·660	5·421	5·197	4·988	4·793	4·611	4·439	12
13	6·750	6·424	6·122	5·842	5·583	5·342	5·118	4·910	4·715	4·533	13
14	6·982	6·628	6·302	6·002	5·724	5·468	5·229	5·008	4·802	4·611	14
15	7·191	6·811	6·462	6·142	5·847	5·575	5·324	5·092	4·876	4·675	15

Standard normal distribution table

	0·00	0·01	0·02	0·03	0·04	0·05	0·06	0·07	0·08	0·09
0·0	0·0000	0·0040	0·0080	0·0120	0·0160	0·0199	0·0239	0·0279	0·0319	0·0359
0·1	0·0398	0·0438	0·0478	0·0517	0·0557	0·0596	0·0636	0·0675	0·0714	0·0753
0·2	0·0793	0·0832	0·0871	0·0910	0·0948	0·0987	0·1026	0·1064	0·1103	0·1141
0·3	0·1179	0·1217	0·1255	0·1293	0·1331	0·1368	0·1406	0·1443	0·1480	0·1517
0·4	0·1554	0·1591	0·1628	0·1664	0·1700	0·1736	0·1772	0·1808	0·1844	0·1879
0·5	0·1915	0·1950	0·1985	0·2019	0·2054	0·2088	0·2123	0·2157	0·2190	0·2224
0·6	0·2257	0·2291	0·2324	0·2357	0·2389	0·2422	0·2454	0·2486	0·2517	0·2549
0·7	0·2580	0·2611	0·2642	0·2673	0·2703	0·2734	0·2764	0·2794	0·2823	0·2852
0·8	0·2881	0·2910	0·2939	0·2967	0·2995	0·3023	0·3051	0·3078	0·3106	0·3133
0·9	0·3159	0·3186	0·3212	0·3238	0·3264	0·3289	0·3315	0·3340	0·3365	0·3389
1·0	0·3413	0·3438	0·3461	0·3485	0·3508	0·3531	0·3554	0·3577	0·3599	0·3621
1·1	0·3643	0·3665	0·3686	0·3708	0·3729	0·3749	0·3770	0·3790	0·3810	0·3830
1·2	0·3849	0·3869	0·3888	0·3907	0·3925	0·3944	0·3962	0·3980	0·3997	0·4015
1·3	0·4032	0·4049	0·4066	0·4082	0·4099	0·4115	0·4131	0·4147	0·4162	0·4177
1·4	0·4192	0·4207	0·4222	0·4236	0·4251	0·4265	0·4279	0·4292	0·4306	0·4319
1·5	0·4332	0·4345	0·4357	0·4370	0·4382	0·4394	0·4406	0·4418	0·4429	0·4441
1·6	0·4452	0·4463	0·4474	0·4484	0·4495	0·4505	0·4515	0·4525	0·4535	0·4545
1·7	0·4554	0·4564	0·4573	0·4582	0·4591	0·4599	0·4608	0·4616	0·4625	0·4633
1·8	0·4641	0·4649	0·4656	0·4664	0·4671	0·4678	0·4686	0·4693	0·4699	0·4706
1·9	0·4713	0·4719	0·4726	0·4732	0·4738	0·4744	0·4750	0·4756	0·4761	0·4767
2·0	0·4772	0·4778	0·4783	0·4788	0·4793	0·4798	0·4803	0·4808	0·4812	0·4817
2·1	0·4821	0·4826	0·4830	0·4834	0·4838	0·4842	0·4846	0·4850	0·4854	0·4857
2·2	0·4861	0·4864	0·4868	0·4871	0·4875	0·4878	0·4881	0·4884	0·4887	0·4890
2·3	0·4893	0·4896	0·4898	0·4901	0·4904	0·4906	0·4909	0·4911	0·4913	0·4916
2·4	0·4918	0·4920	0·4922	0·4925	0·4927	0·4929	0·4931	0·4932	0·4934	0·4936
2·5	0·4938	0·4940	0·4941	0·4943	0·4945	0·4946	0·4948	0·4949	0·4951	0·4952
2·6	0·4953	0·4955	0·4956	0·4957	0·4959	0·4960	0·4961	0·4962	0·4963	0·4964
2·7	0·4965	0·4966	0·4967	0·4968	0·4969	0·4970	0·4971	0·4972	0·4973	0·4974
2·8	0·4974	0·4975	0·4976	0·4977	0·4977	0·4978	0·4979	0·4979	0·4980	0·4981
2·9	0·4981	0·4982	0·4982	0·4983	0·4984	0·4984	0·4985	0·4985	0·4986	0·4986
3·0	0·4987	0·4987	0·4987	0·4988	0·4988	0·4989	0·4989	0·4989	0·4990	0·4990

This table can be used to calculate $N(d_i)$, the cumulative normal distribution functions needed for the Black-Scholes model of option pricing. If $d_i > 0$, add 0·5 to the relevant number above. If $d_i < 0$, subtract the relevant number above from 0·5.

Exam question bank

1 Goals

36 mins

Assume you are Finance Director of a large multinational company, listed on a number of international stock markets. The company is reviewing its corporate plan. At present, the company focuses on maximising shareholder wealth as its major goal. The Managing Director thinks this single goal is inappropriate and asks his co-directors for their views on giving greater emphasis to the following:

(a)   Cash flow generation

(b)   Profitability as measured by profits after tax and return on investment

(c)   Risk-adjusted returns to shareholders

(d)   Performance improvement in a number of areas such as concern for the environment, employees' remuneration and quality of working conditions and customer satisfaction

Required

Provide the Managing Director with a report for presentation at the next board meeting which:

(a)   Evaluates the argument that maximisation of shareholder wealth should be the only true objective of a company, and

(b)   Discusses the advantages and disadvantages of the MD's suggestions about alternative goals

(20 marks)

2 XYZ

27 mins

The table below shows earnings and dividends for XYZ Inc over the past five years.

Year	Net earnings per share $	Net dividend per share $
20W9	1.40	0.84
20X0	1.35	0.88
20X1	1.35	0.90
20X2	1.30	0.95
20X3	1.25	1.00

There are 10,000,000 shares issued and the majority of these shares are owned by private investors. There is no debt in the capital structure.

It is clear from the table that the company has experienced difficult trading conditions over the past few years. In the current year, net earnings are likely to be $10 million, which will be just sufficient to pay a maintained dividend of $1 per share.

Members of the board are considering a number of strategies for the company, some of which will have an impact on the company's future dividend policy.

The company's shareholders require a return of 15% on their investment.

Four options are being considered, as follows.

(1)   Pay out all earnings as dividends.
(2)   Pay a reduced dividend of 50% of earnings and retain the remaining 50% for future investment.
(3)   Pay a reduced dividend of 25% of earnings and retain the remaining 75% for future investment.
(4)   Retain all earnings for an aggressive expansion programme and pay no dividend at all.

The directors cannot agree on any of the four options discussed so far. Some of them prefer option (1) because they believe to do anything else would have an adverse impact on the share price. Others favour either option (2) or option (3) because the company has identified some good investment opportunities and they believe one of these options would be in the best long-term interests of shareholders. An adventurous minority favours option (4) and thinks this will allow the company to take over a small competitor.

Required

(a) Discuss the company's dividend policy between 20W9 and 20X3 and its possible consequences for earnings. **(4 marks)**

(b) Advise the directors of the share price for XYZ Inc which might be expected immediately following the announcement of their decision if they pursued each of the four options, using an appropriate valuation model. You should also show what percentage of total return is provided by dividend and capital gain in each case. You should ignore taxation for this part of the question. Make (and indicate) any realistic assumptions you think necessary to answer this question. **(6 marks)**

(c) Discuss the reliability you can place on the figures you have just produced and on the usefulness of this information to the company's directors. **(5 marks)**

(Total = 15 marks)

3 Remuneration   22 mins

A company is considering improving the methods of remuneration for its senior employees. As a member of the executive board, you are asked to give your opinions on the following suggestions:

(a) A high basic salary with usual 'perks' such as company car, pension scheme etc but no performance-related bonuses

(b) A lower basic salary with usual 'perks' plus a bonus related to their division's profit before tax

(c) A lower basic salary with usual 'perks' plus a share option scheme which allows senior employees to buy a given number of shares in the company at a fixed price at the end of each financial year

Required

Discuss the arguments for and against each of the three options from the point of view of both the company and its employees. Detailed comments on the taxation implications are not required.

(12 marks)

4 Stakeholders   27 mins

(a) Many decisions in financial management are taken in a framework of conflicting stakeholder viewpoints. Identify the stakeholders and some of the financial management issues involved in the situation of a company seeking a stock market listing. **(5 marks)**

(b) XYZ plc is a medium-sized company operating in the chemical industry. It is a profitable business, currently producing at below maximum capacity. It has one large factory located on the outskirts of a small industrial town. It is the region's main employer. The company is evaluating a project which has substantial environmental implications.

Required

Discuss the inclusion of environmental costs and benefits into the investment appraisal procedure and explain how this might be done. **(10 marks)**
(Total = 15 marks)

5 Ethical dimension   36 mins

(a) According to Carroll, what are the four main responsibilities faced by companies when developing an ethical framework, and in what ways can these responsibilities be addressed? **(10 marks)**

(b) Discuss how ethical considerations impact on each of the main functional areas of a firm.

(10 marks)

(Total = 20 marks)

6 Common market

20 mins

(a) State the differences between free trade areas and common markets. **(4 marks)**

(b) Identify the economic benefits countries might gain from forming a common market. **(8 marks)**

(Total = 12 marks)

7 Multinationals

34 mins

By operating in a large number of countries, multinational organisations are exposed to political, cultural and legal risks.

Required

(a) Define each of the three risks mentioned above and the effects they may have on a multinational company's business **(10 marks)**

(b) Explain the steps that a multinational company could take to deal with these risks. **(9 marks)**

(Total = 19 marks)

8 Solden

36 mins

Solden plc is a UK company which is considering setting up a manufacturing operation to make ski-boot warmers in a country called Ober. The currency of Ober is the Gurgle and these are currently G16 to the pound sterling. If the operation were to be set up the plant would be purchased in Ober costing G600,000 now and some equipment would be sent from the UK immediately. This equipment is fully written off in the UK but has a market value of £12,500 or G200,000. All plant and equipment is written off on a straight line basis by Solden plc over 5 years.

The ski-boot warmers will sell for an initial price of G160 but this price will increase in line with inflation in Ober which is expected to continue at its current rate of 10% pa. It is also expected that 4,000 ski-boot warmers will be sold in the first year increasing at a rate of 5% each year. The costs of making ski-boot warmers consist of local variable costs of G80 per unit and selling and administration costs of G40,000 pa, both of which will increase in line with inflation in Ober. The warmers also require some specialist parts sent over from the UK each year. These will be transferred at the beginning of the first year of production at a cost of G40,000 (£2,500) which includes a 25% mark up on cost. The transfer price and cost of these items are expected to increase by 5% pa, and they will be billed to the Ober operation at the beginning of the year and paid for at the end of the year. The working capital for this project will be required at the beginning of each year and will be equal to10% of the expected sales value for the year.

Solden plc estimates that it will lose some of its own exports worth £5,000 now and increasing by 5% pa due to the setting up of the operation in Ober. However, Solden plc will be receiving a licence fee from the Ober operation equal to 10% of sales each year.

Corporation tax in Ober is only 20% and operating costs, licence fees and depreciation at 25% on a straight line basis are all tax allowable expenses. Corporation tax in the UK is at 33%. There is a one year tax delay in both countries.

Solden plc wishes to assess this project from the point of view of both investors in Ober (required return 15%) and investors in the UK (required return 10%). The assessment will take place using Solden's usual 5 year time 'horizon' and valuing the Ober operation at three times its net cash inflow during the fifth year. If the operation were to be sold at this value, tax would be payable at 30% on the proceeds.

It is expected that the Gurgle will depreciate against the pound by 4% pa from year 2, the first depreciation affecting year 2 cash flows. Assume that all prices have just altered, and that all cash flows occur at the end of the year unless specified otherwise.

Required

(a) Calculate (to the nearest 100 Gurgles) whether the operation would be worthwhile for investors based in Ober. **(12 marks)**

(b) If all cash surpluses can be remitted to the UK calculate whether Solden plc should set up the operation. Assume no further UK tax is payable on income taxed on Ober. **(8 marks)**

(Total = 20 marks)

9 Mover   36 mins

(a) You have been asked to provide preliminary advice on whether or not your company's pension fund should make an investment in the shares of Mover Inc, a large construction company which is leading a consortium that is proposing to build a rail tunnel between Gibraltar and Morocco. The tunnel is scheduled to open in 20X4.

Projected cash flows of the tunnel project

	$m
20X0	–450
20X1	–500
20X2	–550
20X3	–650
20X4	–200
20X5	200
20X6	300
20X7	320
20X8	340
20X9	360
20Y0	400
Each year after 20Y0	400

All projections exclude inflation.

The current domestic nominal risk-free rate is 6% whilst the real rate is approximately 4%. The market risk premium for the project has been estimated at 7%.

Required

Undertake an analysis of the proposed tunnel project and advise on whether or not the pension fund should invest in shares of Mover Inc. Relevant calculations must be shown.

State clearly all assumptions that you make. In this question *only* reasoned assumptions regarding a discount rate are encouraged. **(15 marks)**

(b) Explain how inflation affects the rate of return required on an investment project, and the distinction between a real and a nominal (or 'money terms') approach to the evaluation of an investment project under inflation. **(5 marks)**

(Total = 20 marks)

10 PS Ltd   36 mins

(a) A European call option on shares has 3 months to expiry. The exercise price of the option is £2.50, and the current price of the share is £3. The standard deviation of the share is 20% and the risk free rate is 5%.

Required

Calculate the value of the call option per share using the Black-Scholes formula.   **(10 marks)**

(b) Explain

(i)   The five input variables involved in the Black-Scholes pricing model

(ii) How the five input variables can be adapted to value real options as opposed to traded share options   **(10 marks)**

(Total = 20 marks)

11 Nile Inc   27 mins

Nile Inc is considering an investment of capital to be raised from the issue of new ordinary shares and debentures in a mix which will hold its gearing ratio approximately constant. It wishes to estimate its weighted average cost of capital.

The company has an issued share capital of 1 million ordinary shares of $1 each; it has also issued $800,000 of 8% debentures. The market price of ordinary shares is $4.76 per share and debentures are priced at $77 per cent. Dividends and interest are payable annually. An ordinary dividend has just been paid; the next instalment of interest is payable in the near future. Debentures are redeemable at par in 15 years' time.

A summary of the most recent statement of financial position runs as follows:

	$'000		$'000	$'000
Ordinary share capital	1,000	Non-current assets		1,276
Reserves	1,553	Current assets	4,166	
Deferred taxation	164	Less: current		
Debentures	800	liabilities	1,925	
				2,241
	3,517			3,517

Dividends and earnings have been as follows:

	Dividends (excluding tax credit) $'000	Earnings before tax $'000	Earnings after tax $'000
20X4	200	575	350
20X5	230	723	452
20X6	230	682	410
20X7	260	853	536
20X8	300	906	606

Assume that there have been no changes in the system or rates of taxation during the last five years, that the rate of corporation tax is 35% and that the standard rate of income tax is 30%. Assume that 'now' is 20X8.

Required

(a) Calculate Nile plc's weighted average cost of capital.   **(12 marks)**
(b) Discuss briefly any difficulties and uncertainties in your estimation.   **(3 marks)**

(Total = 15 marks)

12 Crystal Inc

27 mins

The following figures have been extracted from the most recent accounts of Crystal plc.

STATEMENT OF FINANCIAL POSITION AS AT 30 JUNE 20X9

	$'000	$'000
Non-current assets		10,115
Investments		821
Current assets	3,658	
Less current liabilities	1,735	
		1,923
		12,859
Ordinary share capital		
Authorised: 4,000,000shares of £1		
Issued: 3,000,000 shares of £1		3,000
Reserves		6,542
Shareholders' funds		9,542
7% Debentures		1,300
Deferred taxation		583
Corporation tax		1,434
		12,859

Summary of profits and dividends

Year ended 30 June:	20X5	20X6	20X7	20X8	20X9
	£'000	£'000	£'000	£'000	£'000
Profit after interest and before tax	1,737	2,090	1,940	1,866	2,179
Less tax	573	690	640	616	719
Profit after interest and tax	1,164	1,400	1,300	1,250	1,460
Less dividends	620	680	740	740	810
Added to reserves	544	720	560	510	650

The current (1 July 20X9) market value of Crystal Inc's ordinary shares is $3.27 per share cum div. An annual dividend of $810,000 is due for payment shortly. The debentures are redeemable at par in ten years time. Their current market value is $77.10 per cent. Annual interest has just been paid on the debentures. There have been no issues or redemptions of ordinary shares or debentures during the past five years.

The current rate of corporation tax is 30%, and the current basic rate of income tax is 25%. Assume that there have been no changes in the system or rates of taxation during the last five years.

Required

(a) Estimate the cost of capital which Crystal Inc should use as a discount rate when appraising new investment opportunities. **(10 marks)**

(b) Discuss any difficulties and uncertainties in your estimates. **(5 marks)**

(Total = 15 marks)

13 Espondera Inc

18 mins

Espondera Inc is a small unquoted company that needs to raise funds in order to invest in a new project. The company wants to issue 10-year bonds and its finance director is trying to work out the cost of debt in order to assess the profitability of the company.

The following information is available for the company

Total assets	$120 million
Net income	$6 million
Type of proposed debt	Subordinated
Long-term debt	$14 million
Income before interest and taxes	$8 million
Interest payments	$1.0 million

The earnings of the company for the last 5 years are as follows

Year	Earnings
20X6	$5m
20X5	$4.2m
20X4	$3.2m
20X3	$3.8m
20X2	$2.2m

The finance director has decided to use the Kaplan Urwitz model for unquoted companies to asses the cost of debt.

The Kaplan-Urwitz model for unquoted companies is given by

Y=4.41+0.001SIZE+6.40PROFITABILITY -2.56DEBT-2.72LEVERAGE + 0.006INTEREST-0.53COV

The classification of companies into credit rating categories is done in the following way

Score (Y)	Rating category
Y > 6.76	AAA
Y > 5.19	AA
Y > 3.28	A
Y > 1.57	BBB
Y > 0	BB

The following table gives the yield to maturity for 10-year corporate bonds by credit category

Rating	Cost of debt (Yield to maturity)
AAA	6.8%
AA	7.3%
A	7.8%
BBB	8.4%
BB	9.4%
B	10.5%

Calculate the cost of debt for Espondera Inc. **(10 marks)**

14 Canada

27 mins

PG plc is considering investing in a new project in Canada which will have a life of four years. The initial investment is C$150,000, including working capital. The net after-tax cash flows which the project will generate are C$60,000 per annum for years 1, 2 and 3 and C$45,000 in year 4. The terminal value of the project is estimated at C$50,000, net of tax.

The current spot rate of C$ against the pound sterling is 1.7000. Economic forecasters expect the pound to strengthen against the Canadian dollar by 5% per annum over the next 4 years.

The company evaluates UK projects of similar risk at 14%.

Required

(a)   Calculate the NPV of the Canadian project using the following two methods:

   (i)   Convert the currency cash flows into sterling and discount the sterling cash flows at a sterling discount rate

   (ii)   Discount the cash flows in C$ using an adjusted discount rate which incorporates the 12-month forecast spot rate and explain briefly the theories and/or assumptions which underlie the use of the adjusted discount rate approach in (ii).   **(10 marks)**

(b)   The company had originally planned to finance the project with internal funds generated in the UK. However, the finance director has suggested that there would be advantages in raising debt finance in Canada.

   Discuss the advantages and disadvantages of matching investment and borrowing overseas as compared with UK-sourced debt or equity.

   Wherever possible, relate your answer to the details in this question for PG plc.   **(5 marks)**

(Total = 15 marks)

15 Organic growth

15 mins

Discuss the advantages to a company of establishing an overseas operating subsidiary by:

either   (a)   Organic growth
or   (b)   Acquisition   **(8 marks)**

16 Canon Burger

36 mins

Canon Burger has been expanding its operation rapidly by acquiring a number of restaurants. Canon has been funding its acquisitions by bank borrowing and it has a high level of gearing. Canon Burger has been specialising in fast food outlets and although the market is supported by a booming young population, the older generation prefer more traditional outlets. Canon is considering the acquisition of Templar Restaurant, a continental type of establishment with a steady clientele and good reputation. The owners of Templar have been rather conservative and have not exploited the brand value of the restaurant to expand, as they approach retirement. The owners of Templar are prepared to accept a cash offer of $200,000. Canon Burger has a cost of capital of 16 percent due to its high gearing. Templar Restaurant on the other hand is free of debt. As a result of the acquisition, Canon Burger expects the debt equity ratio of the combined equity to decrease and the cost of capital to fall to 12 percent. The acquisition of Templar Restaurant is expected to increase Canon's cash flow by $25,000 per year forever.

(a)   What kind of synergies will the acquisition of Templar Restaurants create?   **(6 marks)**

(b)   Should Canon Burger proceed with the acquisition?   **(7 marks)**

(c)   If the acquisition was funded by borrowing so that there is no impact on the level of gearing of the combined entity and the cost of capital was not reduced, should Canon still proceed with the acquisition?   **(7 marks)**

(Total = 20 marks)

17 Takeovers

36 mins

Despite substantial evidence, drawn from different countries and different time periods, that suggests the wealth of shareholders in a bidding company is unlikely to be increased as a result of taking over another company, takeovers remain an important part of the business landscape.

Required

(a) Explain, in economic terms, what a company, which is committed to increasing shareholder wealth, should look for when seeking to acquire another company. **(3 marks)**

(b) Describe four ways in which a takeover may lead to an increase in wealth for the bidding company's shareholders. **(8 marks)**

(c) Discuss four reasons why a takeover may fail to deliver an expected increase in wealth for the bidding company's shareholders. **(9 marks)**

(Total = 20 marks)

18 Univo Inc

27 mins

Summarised financial data for Univo Inc is shown below.

INCOME STATEMENTS

	20W9	20X0	20X1[1]
	$'000	$'000	$'000
Revenue	76,270	89,410	102,300
Taxable income	10,140	12,260	14,190
Taxation	3,346	4,046	4,683
	6,794	8,214	9,507
Dividend	2,335	2,557	2,800
Retained earnings	4,459	5,657	6,707

STATEMENT OF FINANCIAL POSITION

	20X1[1]
	$'000
Non-current assets	54,200
Current assets	39,500
Current liabilities	(26,200)
	67,500
Ordinary shares (50 cents par value)	20,000
Reserves	32,500
10% debentures 20X6 ($100 par value)	15,000
	67,500

[1] 20X1 figures are unaudited estimates.

As a result of recent capital investment, stock market analysts expect post tax earnings and dividends to increase by 25% for two years and then to revert to the company's existing growth rates.

Univo's asset (overall) beta is 0.763, beta of debt is 0.20 and beta of equity is 0.82. The risk free rate is 12% and the market return 17%.

The current market price of Univo's shares is 217 cents cum 20X1 dividend.

Required

(a) Using the dividend growth model estimate what a fundamental analyst might consider to be the intrinsic (or realistic) value of the company's shares. Comment upon the significance of your estimate for the fundamental analyst.

Assume, for this part of the question only, that the cost of equity is not expected to change. The cost of equity may be estimated by using the CAPM. **(10 marks)**

(b) If interest rates were to increase by 2% and expected dividend growth to remain unchanged, estimate what effect this would be likely to have on the intrinsic value of the company's shares.

(5 marks)

(Total = 15 marks)

19 Black Raven Co
54 mins

Black Raven Co is a prosperous private company, whose owners are also the directors. The directors have decided to sell their business, and have begun a search for organisations interested in its purchase. They have asked for your assessment of the price per ordinary share a purchaser might be expected to offer. Relevant information is as follows.

MOST RECENT STATEMENT OF FINANCIAL POSITION

	$'000	$'000	$'000
Non-current assets (net book value)			
Land and buildings			800
Plant and equipment			450
Motor vehicles			55
Patents			2
			1,307
Current assets			
Inventory		250	
Receivables		125	
Cash		8	
		383	
Current liabilities			
Payables	180		
Taxation	50		
		230	
			153
			1,460
Long-term liability			
Loan secured on property			400
			1,060
Share capital (300,000 ordinary shares of $1)			300
Reserves			760
			1,060

The profits after tax and interest but before dividends over the last five years have been as follows.

Year	$
1	90,000
2	80,000
3	105,000
4	90,000
5 (most recent)	100,000

The company's five year plan forecasts an after-tax profit of $100,000 for the next 12 months, with an increase of 4% a year over each of the next four years. The annual dividend has been $45,000 (gross) for the last six years.

As part of their preparations to sell the company, the directors of Black Raven Co have had the non-current assets revalued by an independent expert, with the following results.

	$
Land and buildings	1,075,000
Plant and equipment	480,000
Motor vehicles	45,000

The gross dividend yields and P/E ratios of three quoted companies in the same industry as Black Raven Co over the last three years have been as follows.

	Albatross Inc		Bullfinch Inc		Crow Inc	
	Div. yield %	P/E ratio	Div. yield %	P/E ratio	Div. yield %	P/E ratio
Recent year	12	8.5	11.0	9.0	13.0	10.0
Previous year	12	8.0	10.6	8.5	12.6	9.5
Three years ago	12	8.5	9.3	8.0	12.4	9.0
Average	12	8.33	10.3	8.5	12.7	9.5

Large companies in the industry apply an after-tax cost of capital of about 18% to acquisition proposals when the investment is not backed by tangible assets, as opposed to a rate of only 14% on the net tangible assets.

Your assessment of the net cash flows which would accrue to a purchasing company, allowing for taxation and the capital expenditure required after the acquisition to achieve the company's target five year plan, is as follows.

	$
Year 1	120,000
Year 2	120,000
Year 3	140,000
Year 4	70,000
Year 5	120,000

Required

Use the information provided to suggest alternative valuations which prospective purchasers might make.

(30 marks)

20 Margate   72 mins

Margate Group plc is a large, long-established company whose primary interests are in transport and distribution within the United Kingdom. It is considering a bid to acquire Hastings plc, a company also in the transport and distribution industry. Hastings plc, however, has a strong operations base in Europe as well as in the UK. Both companies are listed on a recognised stock exchange. They both have a wide share ownership including many institutional investors.

Hastings plc has recently fought off a bid from a company based in the United States of America and has made a public statement that it will defend itself against any future bids. The company has recently won a fiercely contested five-year contract to undertake transport and distribution services for a major supermarket group. Margate Group plc also tendered for this contract. Press comment suggests this contract will allow Hastings plc's earnings to grow at 10% a year for at least the next five years. However, some industry experts believe Hastings plc tendered a price that was so low that the contract could result in very little profit, or even losses.

If the acquisition were to succeed, it would create the largest company of its kind in the UK. A concern is that this would attract the interest of the competition authorities. However, as both companies have recently restructured their operations, redundancies are likely to be few and concentrated mainly in central administration.

Financial Statements

Key financial information for the two companies for the latest financial year is given below. All figures are in £ million unless otherwise stated.

INCOME STATEMENTS
FOR THE YEAR TO 31 AUGUST 20X1

	Margate Group plc £m	Hastings plc £m
Revenue	2,763	1,850
Operating costs	1,950	1,380
Operating profit	813	470
Net interest	125	85
Profit before tax	688	385
Tax	185	85
Earnings	503	300
Dividends declared	201	135
Retained profit for the year	302	165
Earnings per shares (pence)	47.90	35.29
EPS for year to 31 August 20X0 (pence)	34.85	29.50

STATEMENTS OF FINANCIAL POSITION AT 31 AUGUST 20X1

	Margate Group plc £m	Hastings plc £m
Non-current assets (net book value)	3,250	2,580
Current assets		
Inventory	125	175
Receivables	550	425
	450	45
Payables: due within 1 year		
Bank overdraft	0	420
Trade payables	755	365
Payables: due after 1 year		
Debentures	1,450	950
Tax	150	40
Net assets	2,020	1,450
Capital and reserves		
Share capital (£1 each)	1,050	850
Share premium	220	150
Retained earnings	750	450
Total shareholders' funds	2,020	1,450

Note. Margate Group plc's debenture is 8%, repayable 20X5. Hastings plc's is 9%, repayable 20X4.

Share price information (prices in pence)

		Margate Group plc	Hastings plc
Share price movements:	High for last financial year	705	590
	Low for last financial year	470	440
Share price today (20 November 20X1)		671	565
P/E ratios today		14	16
Equity betas		1.1	1.2

Other information

- The average P/E for the industry is currently estimated as 13.

- The return on the market is currently estimated as 12%, the risk-free rate as 6%. These rates are expected to remain constant for the next 12 months and are post-tax.

- The average debt ratio for the industry (long-term debt as proportion of total long-term funding) is 30% based on book values.

- Economic forecasts provided by Margate Group plc's financial advisors expect inflation and interest rates to remain at their current levels for the foreseeable future. Inflation is currently 2% a year.

Terms of the proposed bid

Margate Group plc's directors are planning to offer a share exchange to Hastings plc's shareholders.

Required

(a) Calculate and discuss briefly three key ratios for both companies that are relevant to the evaluation of the proposed acquisition. **(7 marks)**

(b) Calculate a range of possible values that Margate Group plc could place on Hastings plc, using both P/E basis and the dividend growth model.

Accompany your calculations by brief comments or explanations. Where necessary, explain any assumptions you have made **(7 marks)**

(c) Assume you are the Financial Manager with Margate Group plc. Write a report to the directors of the group that evaluates the proposed acquisition.

You should use the figures you have calculated in answer to parts (a) and (b) to support your recommendations/advice where relevant. If you have not been able to do the calculations for parts (a) and (b), you should make, and state, appropriate assumptions.

Your report should include the following topics.

(i) Recommendation to the directors of a bid price and offer terms, assuming a share-for-share exchange.

(ii) Advice on a strategy for making the offer to Hastings plc to minimise the likelihood of outright rejection by the Hastings plc board, and a discussion of the other risks involved in making the bid.

(iii) Discussion of the strategic and financial advantages that might arise from the acquisition by Margate Group plc of Hastings plc.

Support your discussion with calculations of the post-acquisition value of the combined group and how the estimated gains are likely to be split between the shareholders of Margate Group plc and Hastings plc. **(26 marks)**

(Total = 40 marks)

21 Canadian Inc   72 mins

Canadian Inc is a regional electricity generating company with several coal, oil and gas powered generating stations. The opportunity to bid for the coal mine supplying one of its local stations has arisen, and you have been asked to assess the project. If Canadian does not bid for the pit, then it is likely to close, in which case coal for the station would have to be obtained from overseas.

Canadian's bid is likely to be successful if priced at $6 million. Regional development fund finance is available at a subsidised interest rate of 4% for the full cost of the purchase, as against Canadian's marginal cost of debt if financed commercially. If Canadian invests a further $6 million in updated machinery, the pit is likely to generate $10 million of coal per annum for the next five years at current domestic coal prices. Operating costs will total $3 million per annum, plus depreciation. Thereafter it will have to close, at a net cost after asset sales of $17 million at current price, which includes redundancy, cleanup and associated costs, at present prices.

You have ascertained the following information about the coal industry.

	Coal industry (average)
Gearing (debt/equity):	
Book values	1 to 0.5
Market values	1:1
Equity beta	0.7
Debt beta	0.2

Capital allowances would be available at 25% on a reducing balance basis for all new machinery. The purchase price of the mine can be depreciated for tax at 25% per annum straight line. All other costs are tax allowable in full.

Other than the regional development fund loan (repayable after 5 years), the project would be financed by retained earnings. The project is likely to add another $3 million of borrowing capacity to Canadian, in addition to the $6 million regional development fund loan. Corporation tax is expected to remain at 30% during the life of the project. The company as a whole expects to be in a tax payable position for all years except the third year of the project.

Assume that all prices rise with the RPI, currently by 3% pa, except coal prices, which in view of reduced demand are set to remain static. You may assume that original investment cash flows arise at the start of the first year, and that all other cash flows arise at the end of the year in which the costs are incurred, except for tax, which lags one year. Treasury bills currently yield 8%, and the return required of the market portfolio is currently 16%.

You have discovered the following information concerning Canadian.

	Canadian Inc
Gearing (debt/equity):	
	1 to 1
	1:2
Equity beta	1.0
Debt beta	0.25
P/E ratio	14
Dividend yield	6%
Share price	220 cents
Number of ordinary shares	8 million

Required

Write a memorandum for the finance director advising on whether the mine should be acquired. you should divide your memorandum into the following sections:

(a)	Overall summary and conclusion	**(6 marks)**
(b)	Detailed numerical workings	**(23 marks)**
(c)	Assumptions behind the report	**(8 marks)**
(d)	Areas for further research	**(3 marks)**

(Total = 40 marks)

22 Peden and Tulen
27 mins

The total values (equity plus debt) of two companies, Peden and Tulen are expected to fluctuate according to the state of the economy.

	Recession	*Economic state* Slow growth	Rapid growth
Probability	0.15	0.65	0.20
Total values			
Peden (£m)	42	55	75
Tulen (£m)	63	80	120

Peden currently has $45 million of debt, and Tulen $10 million of debt.

Required

(a) If the two companies were to merge, and assuming that no operational synergy occurs as a result of the merger, calculate the expected value of debt and equity of the merged company. Explain the reasons for any difference that exists from the expected values of debt and equity if they do not merge. **(11 marks)**

(b) Discuss the importance of financial post-audits following a merger or takeover. **(4 marks)**

(Total = 15 marks)

23 Gasco
45 mins

Gasco, a public limited company with a market value of around £7 billion, is a major supplier of gas to both business and domestic customers. The company also provides maintenance contracts for both gas and central heating customers using the well-known brand name Gas For All. Customers can call emergency lines for assistance for any gas-related incident, such as a suspected leak. Gasco employs its own highly-trained workforce to deal with all such situations quickly and effectively. The company also operates a major new credit card, which has been extensively marketed and which gives users concessions, such as reductions in their gas bills.

Gasco has recently bid £1.1bn for CarCare, a long established mutual organisation (ie it is owned by its members) that is the country's leading motoring organisation. CarCare is financed primarily by an annual subscription to its 4.4 million members. In addition the organisation also obtains income from a range of other activities such as a high profile car insurance brokerage, a travel agency and assistance with all types of travel arrangements. Its main service to members is the provision of a roadside break-down service, which is now an extremely competitive market with many other companies involved. Although many of its competitors use local garages to deal with breakdowns, CarCare uses its own road patrols.

CarCare members have to approve the takeover, which once completed would provide them each with a windfall of around £300 each.

Gasco intend to preserve the CarCare name which is extremely well-known by consumers.

Required

(a) Discuss the possible reasons why Gasco is seeking to buy CarCare. **(9 marks)**

(b) Discuss how the various stakeholders of CarCare might react to the takeover. **(8 marks)**

(c) Discuss the potential problems that may face Gasco in running CarCare now that the takeover has been achieved. **(8 marks)**

(Total = 25 marks)

24 Olivine

36 mins

Olivine is a holiday tour operator that is committed to a policy of expansion. The company has enjoyed record growth in recent years and is now seeking to acquire other companies in order to maintain its growth momentum. It has recently taken an interest in Halite, a charter airline business, as the Board of Directors of Olivine believes that there is a good strategic fit between the two companies. Both companies have the same level of risk. Abbreviated financial statements relating to each company are set out below.

Abbreviated income statement for the year ended 30 November 20X3

	Olivine	Halite
	$m	$m
Sales	182·6	75·2
Operating profit	43·6	21·4
Interest charges	12·3	10·2
Net profit before taxation	31·3	11·2
Company tax	6·3	1·6
Net profit after taxation	25·0	9·6
Dividends	6·0	4·0
Accumulated profits for the year	19·0	5·6

Summarised statements of financial position as at 30 November 20X3

	Olivine	Halite
	$m	$m
Non-current assets	135.4	127.2
Net current assets	65.2	3.2
	200.6	130.4
Payables due after more than one year	120.5	104.8
	80.1	25.6
Capital and reserves		
$0·50 ordinary shares	20.0	8.0
Retained profit	60.1	17.6
	80.1	25.6
Price/earnings ratio before the bid	20	15

The Board of Directors of Olivine is considering making an offer to the shareholders of Halite of five shares in Olivine for every four shares held. It is believed that a rationalisation of administrative functions arising from the merger would reap after tax benefits of $2.4m.

Required

(a) Calculate:

   (i) The total value of the proposed offer

   (ii) The earnings per share of Olivine following the successful acquisition of Halite

   (iii) The share price of Olivine following acquisition, assuming that the benefits of the acquisition are achieved and that the price/earnings ratio declines by 5%. **(10 marks)**

(b) Calculate the effect of the proposed takeover on the wealth of the shareholders of each company.

   (5 marks)

(c) Discuss your results in (a) and (b) above and state what recommendations, if any, you would make to the directors of Olivine. **(5 marks)**

(Total = 20 marks)

25 Takeover regulation

36 mins

(a) Discuss the key aspects of takeover regulation in the UK and continental Europe in the context of European harmonisation.

(b) As hostile takeovers increase discuss some of the defensive measures that could be taken by a target in Europe and compare these briefly with what would be permissible in the US regulatory environment.

(20 marks)

26 Atlas International

27 mins

Atlas International Inc is considering a bid for Olympic Global Inc. The following information is given for both companies:

	Atlas	Olympics
	$	$
Earnings per share	4	0.90
Share price	70	22
Number of shares	1,000,000	500,000

The consensus view is that Olympic will grow at a rate of 5 percent. The management of Atlas believe that without additional investment they can raise the growth rate to 7%.

(a) What is the gain from the acquisition? **(5 marks)**

(b) What is the cost of acquisition if Atlas pays $30 per share in cash for each share of Global? Should the acquisition go ahead? **(5 marks)**

(c) What is the cost of acquisition if Atlas offers one of its own shares for every two shares of Global? Should the acquisition go ahead? **(5 marks)**

(Total = 15 marks)

27 Brive Inc

54 mins

The latest statement of financial position for Brive Inc is summarised below.

	$'000	$'000	$'000
Non-current assets at net book value			5,700
Current assets			
Inventory and work in progress		3,500	
Receivables		1,800	
		5,300	
Less current liabilities			
Unsecured payables	4,000		
Bank overdraft (unsecured)	1,600		
		5,600	
Working capital			(300)
Total assets less current liabilities			5,400
Liabilities falling due after more than one year			
10% secured debentures			3,000
Net assets			2,400
			$'000
Capital and reserves			
Called up share capital			4,000
Income statement			(1,600)
			2,400

Brive Inc's called up capital consists of 4,000,000 $1 ordinary shares issued and fully paid. The non-current assets comprise freehold property with a book value of $3,000,000 and plant and machinery with a book value of $2,700,000. The debentures are secured on the freehold property.

In recent years the company has suffered a series of trading losses which have brought it to the brink of liquidation. The directors estimate that in a forced sale the assets will realise the following amounts.

	$
Freehold premises	2,000,000
Plant and machinery	1,000,000
Inventory	1,700,000
Receivables	1,700,000

The costs of liquidation are estimated at $770,000. However, trading conditions are now improving and the directors estimate that if new investment in plant and machinery costing $2,500,000 were undertaken the company should be able to generate annual profits before interest of $1,750,000. In order to take advantage of this they have put forward the following proposed reconstruction scheme.

(a) Freehold premises should be written down by $1,000,000, plant and machinery by $1,100,000, inventory and work in progress by $800,000 and receivables by $100,000.

(b) The ordinary shares should be written down by $3,000,000 and the debit balance on the income statement written off.

(c) The secured debenture holders would exchange their debentures for $1,500,000 ordinary shares and $1,300,000 14% unsecured loan stock repayable in five years' time.

(d) The bank overdraft should be written off and the bank should receive $1,200,000 of 14% unsecured loan stock repayable in five years' time in compensation.

(e) The unsecured payables should be written down by 25%.

(f) A rights issue of 1 for 1 at par is to be made on the share capital after the above adjustments have been made.

(g) $2,500,000 will be invested in new plant and machinery.

Required

(a) Prepare the statement of financial position of the company after the completion of the reconstruction. **(8 marks)**

(b) Prepare a report, including appropriate calculations, discussing the advantages and disadvantages of the proposed reconstruction from the point of view of:

(i) The ordinary shareholders
(ii) The secured debenture holders
(iii) The bank
(iv) The unsecured payables

Ignore taxation. **(22 marks)**

(Total = 30 marks)

28 Reorganisation   22 mins

(a)   Discuss the potential problems with management buyouts.   **(5 marks)**

(b)   Company X's hotel division is experiencing considerable financial difficulties. The management is prepared to undertake a buyout, and Company X is willing to sell for $15 million. After an analysis of the division's performance, the management concluded that the division required a capital injection of $10 million.

Possible funding sources for the buyout and the additional capital injection are as follows:

From management:

Equity shares of 25c each	$12 million

From venture capitalist:

Equity shares of 25c each	$5.5 million
Debt: 9.5% fixed rate loan	$7.5 million

The fixed rate loan principal is repayable in 10 years' time.

Forecasts of earnings before interest and tax for the next 5 years following the buyout are as follows:

	Year 1	Year 2	Year 3	Year 4	Year 5
	$'000	$'000	$'000	$'000	$'000
EBIT	2,200	3,100	3,900	4,200	4,500

Corporation tax is charged at 30%. Dividends are expected to be no more than 12 % of profits for the first five years.

Management has forecast that the value of equity capital is likely to increase by approximately 15 % per annum for the next 5 years.

Required

On the basis of the above forecasts, determine whether management's estimate that the value of equity will increase by 15% per annum is a viable one.   **(7 marks)**

(Total = 12 marks)

29 Treasury management   20 mins

Many large international organisations have a central treasury department which might be a separate profit centre within the group. The responsibilities of this department will include the management of business risk and market risk for the group as a whole.

Required

(a)   Describe the functions of a central treasury department.

(b)   Describe the information that the treasury department needs, from inside and outside the organisation, to perform its function.

(Total = 11 marks)

30 Expo Inc

27 mins

Expo Inc is an importer/exporter of textiles and textile machinery which trades extensively with countries throughout Europe. It has a small subsidiary based in Switzerland. The company is about to invoice a customer in Switzerland 750,000 Swiss francs, payable in three months' time. Expo Inc's treasurer is considering two methods of hedging the exchange risk. These are:

Method 1: Borrow Fr 750,000 for three months, convert the loan into dollars and repay the loan out of eventual receipts.

Method 2: Enter into a 3-month forward exchange contract with the company's bank to sell Fr 750,000.

The spot rate of exchange is Fr 2.3834 to $1. The 3-month forward rate of exchange is Fr 2.3688 to $1. Annual interest rates for 3 months' borrowing are: Switzerland 3%, US 6%.

Required

(a)   Advise the treasurer on:

(i)   Which of the two methods is the most financially advantageous for Expo Inc, and

(ii)   The factors to consider before deciding whether to hedge the risk using the foreign currency markets

Include relevant calculations in your advice.   **(10 marks)**

(b)   Assume that Expo Inc is trading in and with developing countries rather than Europe and has a subsidiary in a country with no developed capital or currency markets. Expo Inc is now about to invoice a customer in that country in the local currency. Advise Expo Inc's treasurer about ways in which the risk can be managed in these circumstances. No calculations are required for this part of the question.   **(5 marks)**

(Total = 15 marks)

31 Fidden plc

45 mins

(a)   Discuss briefly four techniques a company might use to hedge against the foreign exchange risk involved in foreign trade.   **(8 marks)**

(b)   Fidden plc is a medium sized UK company with export and import trade with the USA. The following transactions are due within the next six months. Transactions are in the currency specified.

Purchases of components, cash payment due in three months: £116,000.
Sale of finished goods, cash receipt due in three months: $197,000.
Purchase of finished goods for resale, cash payment due in six months: $447,000.
Sale of finished goods, cash receipt due in six months: $154,000.

Exchange rates (London market)

	$/£
Spot	1.7106–1.7140
Three months forward	0.82–0.77 cents premium
Six months forward	1.39–1.34 cents premium

Interest rates Three months or six months	*Borrowing*	*Lending*
Sterling	12.5%	9.5%
Dollars	9%	6%

Foreign currency option prices (New York market)
Prices are cents per £, contract size £12,500

Exercise price ($)	Calls			Puts		
	March	June	Sept	March	June	Sept
1.60	–	15.20	–	–	–	2.75
1.70	5.65	7.75	–	–	3.45	6.40
1.80	1.70	3.60	7.90	–	9.32	15.35

Assume that it is now December with three months to the expiry of March contracts and that the option price is not payable until the end of the option period, or when the option is exercised.

Required

(i)   Calculate the net sterling receipts and payments that Fidden might expect for both its three and six month transactions if the company hedges foreign exchange risk on

     1   the forward foreign exchange market
     2   the money market   **(7 marks)**

(ii)   If the actual spot rate in six months time turned out to be exactly the present six months forward rate, calculate whether Fidden would have done better to have hedged through foreign currency options rather than the forward market or the money market.   **(7 marks)**

(iii)   Explain briefly what you consider to be the main advantage of foreign currency options.

(3 marks)

(Total = 25 marks)

32 Exchange rate forecasts   27 mins

(a)   Your managing director has received forecasts of Euro exchange rates in two years' time from three leading banks.

Euro/$ two year forecasts

Lottobank	1.452
Kadbank	1.514
Gross bank	1.782

The current spot mid-rate Euro 1.667/$

A non-executive director of your company has suggested that in order to forecast future exchange rates, the interest rate differential between countries should be used. She states that 'as short term interest rates are currently 6% in the US, and 3.5% in the Euro bloc, the exchange rate in two years' time will be Euro 1.747/$'.

Required

(i)   Prepare a brief report discussing the likely validity of the non-executive director's estimate.
(4 marks)

(ii)   Explain briefly whether or not forecasts of future exchange rates using current interest rate differentials are likely to be accurate.   **(3 marks)**

(b) You have also been asked to give advice to your managing director about a tender by the company's Italian subsidiary for an order in Kuwait. The tender conditions state that payment will be made in Kuwait dinars 18 months from now. The subsidiary is unsure as to what price to tender. The marginal cost of producing the goods at that time is estimated to be Euro 340,000 and a 25% mark-up is normal for the company.

Exchange rates
Euro/Dinar
Spot   0.256 – 0.260

No forward rate exists for 18 months' time.

	Italy %	Kuwait %
Annual inflation rates	3	9
Annual interest rates available to the Italian subsidiary: Borrowing	6	11
Lending	2.5	8

Required

Discuss how the Italian subsidiary might protect itself against foreign exchange rate changes, and recommend what tender price should be used. **(8 marks)**

All relevant calculations must be shown. **(Total = 15 marks)**

33 USA Options   36 mins

(a) Your UK based company has won an export order worth $1.8 million from the USA. Payment is due to be made to you in dollars in six months' time. It is now 15 November. You wish to protect the exchange rate risk with currency options, but do not wish to pay an option premium of more than £10,000.

Your bank has suggested using a particular currency option which has no premium. The option would allow a worst case exchange rate at which the option could be exercised of $1.65/£. If the contract moved in your favour then the bank would share (participate in) the profits, and would take 50% of any gains relative to the current spot exchange rate.

You also have access to currency options on the Philadelphia Stock Exchange.

Current option prices are:

Sterling contacts, £31,250 contract size. Premium is US cents per £.

		Calls			Puts	
Exercise price	Dec	March	June	Dec	March	June
1.55	6.8	7.9	10.1	0.2	0.5	0.9
1.60	2.1	3.8	5.3	1.9	3.1	4.0
1.65	0.6	0.9	1.1	5.1	7.2	9.6
1.70	0.1	0.2	0.4	10.1	12.3	14.1

The current spot rate is $1.6055 – 1.6100/£. Any option premium would be payable immediately.

Required

Evaluate whether a participating option or traded option is likely to offer a better foreign exchange hedge. **(15 marks)**

(b) Your company is trading in and with developing countries and has a subsidiary in a country with no developed capital or currency markets. Your company is now about to invoice a customer in that country in the local currency. Advise your treasurer about ways in which the risk can be managed in these circumstances. **(5 marks)**

(Total = 20 marks)

34 Curropt plc

54 mins

It is now 1 March and the treasury department of Curropt plc, a quoted UK company, faces a problem. At the end of June the treasury department may need to advance to Curropt's US subsidiary the amount of $15,000,000. This depends on whether the subsidiary is successful in winning a franchise. The department's view is that the US dollar will strengthen over the next few months, and it believes that a currency hedge would be sensible. The following data is relevant.

Exchange rates US$/£
1 March spot 1.4461 – 1.4492; 4 months forward 1.4310 – 1.4351.
Futures market contract prices
Sterling £62,500 contracts:
March contract 1.4440; June contract 1.4302.
Currency options: Sterling £31,250 contracts (cents per £)

	Calls	Puts
Exercise price	June	June
$1.400/£	3.40	0.38
$1.425/£	1.20	0.68
$1.450/£	0.40	2.38

Required

(a) Explain whether the treasury department is justified in its belief that the US dollar is likely to strengthen against the pound. **(3 marks)**

(b) Explain the relative merits of forward currency contracts, currency futures contracts and currency options as instruments for hedging in the given situation. **(7 marks)**

(c) Assuming the franchise is won, illustrate the results of using forward, future and option currency hedges if the US$/£ spot exchange rate at the end of June is:

    (i) 1.3500
    (ii) 1.4500
    (iii) 1.5500 **(20 marks)**

Note: Assume that the difference between future and spot price is the same at the end of June as now

(Total = 30 marks)

35 Carrick plc

27 mins

(a) Explain the term risk management in respect of interest rates and discuss how interest risk might be managed. **(7 marks)**

(b) It is currently 1 January 20X7. Carrick plc receives interest of 6% per annum on short-term deposits on the London money markets amounting to £6 million. The company wishes to explore the use of a collar to protect, for a period of seven months, the interest yield it currently earns. The following prices are available, with the premium cost being quoted in annual percentage terms.

LIFFE interest rate options on three month money market futures (Contract size: £500,000).

	Calls		Puts	
Strike price	Jun	Sept	Jun	Sept
92.50	0.71	1.40	0.02	0.06
93.00	0.36	1.08	0.10	0.14
93.50	0.12	0.74	0.20	0.35
94.00	0.01	0.40	0.57	0.80
94.50	–	0.06	0.97	1.12

Required

Evaluate the use of a collar by Carrick plc for the purpose proposed above. Include calculations of the cost involved and indicate appropriate exercise price(s) for the collar. Ignore taxation, commission and margin requirements.

(8 marks)

(Total = 15 marks)

36 Burger-Queen

27 mins

The three-month dollar interest rate futures are quoted as follows on 30 July:

September	92.90
December	92.70
March	92.50

Each futures contract has a notional value of $500,000. Burger Queen will need to borrow $10 million floating at the end of December, for three months and is concerned that interest rates may rise.

(a)   Suggest a hedging strategy that Burger Queen could use to reduce interest rate risk   **(5 marks)**

(b)   What is the effective rate of interest that Burger Queen will have to pay if it hedged its exposure and interest rates have risen to 9 percent in December?   **(5 marks)**

(c)   What is the effective rate of interest after taking into account the derivative transaction if three month spot rates are 6 percent in December?   **(5 marks)**

(Total = 15 marks)

37 Theta Inc

22 mins

(a)   Theta Inc wants to borrow $10 million for five years with interest payable at six-monthly intervals. It can borrow from a bank at a floating rate of LIBOR plus 1% but wants to obtain a fixed rate for the full five-year period. A swap bank has indicated that it will be willing to receive a fixed rate of 8.5% in exchange for payments of six-month LIBOR.

Required

Calculate the fixed interest six-monthly payment with the swap in place.   **(4 marks)**

(b)   Show the interest payments by Theta if

(i)   LIBOR is 10%   **(4 marks)**
(ii)   LIBOR is 7.5%   **(4 marks)**

(Total = 12 marks)

38 Kilber Inc

27 mins

Kilber Inc is a mining company with exclusive rights to the mining of Kilbe. Kilbe is a new metal that used in the construction industry. The demand for Kilbe is highly dependant on the state of the housing and market and the price is highly volatile. Kilber would like to hedge its exposure but there are no traded derivatives for Kilbe. The treasurer of Kilbe has approached a number of banks but have found the OTC market is expensive, as Kilbe is considered to be too risky, and are therefore reluctant to use forward contracts for hedging. One of the bankers they have sought advice from, suggested that they should use futures contracts on copper. She explained that the price of Kilbe is highly correlated with the price of copper and therefore copper futures contracts are good substitutes.

Required

(a) Explain why the company should care about hedging its risks and comment on the risks that Kilber plc may face if it adopts the recommendation and use copper futures contracts as a hedging instrument. **(6 marks)**

(b) Discuss some of the advantages and disadvantages of OTC derivatives. **(3 marks)**

(c) The management of Kilber is currently reviewing its funding strategies. All its borrowing is at variable rate and there are strong indications that interest rates will increase. Advise management on how to reduce the impact of higher rates on its interest payments. **(6 marks)**

(Total = 15 marks)

39 Transfer prices   18 mins

A multinational company based in Beeland has subsidiary companies in Ceeland and in the UK.

The UK subsidiary manufactures machinery parts which are sold to the Ceeland subsidiary for a unit price of B$420 (420 Beeland dollars), where the parts are assembled. The UK subsidiary shows a profit of B$80 per unit; 200,000 units are sold annually.

The Ceeland subsidiary incurs further costs of B$400 per unit and sells the finished goods on for an equivalent of B$1,050.

All of the profits from the foreign subsidiaries are remitted to the parent company as dividends.

Double taxation treaties between Beeland, Ceeland and the UK allow companies to set foreign tax liabilities against their domestic tax liability.

The following rates of taxation apply.

	UK	Beeland	Ceeland
Tax on company profits	25%	35%	40%
Withholding tax on dividends	–	12%	10%

Required

(a) Show the tax effect of increasing the transfer price between the UK and Ceeland subsidiaries by 25%. **(6 marks)**

(b) Outline the various problems which might be encountered by a company which adjusts a transfer price substantially. **(4 marks)**

(Total = 10 marks)

40 Developments   18 mins

International trade has expanded substantially in the last few decades; however this has led to greater uncertainty for multinational companies.

Required

Discuss ways in which increased globalisation may adversely affect multinational organisations.

(10 marks)

Exam answer bank

1 Goals

The conclusion sums up how the possible objectives can be fitted into the overall strategy of the organisation.

(a) and (b)   REPORT

To: Managing Director
From: Finance Director
Date: 17 November 20X5
Subject: Definition of corporate objectives

Introduction

1   This report has been drafted for use as a discussion document at the forthcoming board meeting. It deals with the validity of continuing to operate with the single major goal of **shareholder wealth maximisation**. The remaining sections of the report contain an analysis of the advantages and disadvantages of some of the alternative objectives that have been put forward in recent discussions.

Maximisation of shareholder wealth

2   The concept that the **primary financial objective** of the firm is to **maximise** the **wealth** of shareholders underpins much of modern financial theory. However, there has been some recent debate as to whether this should or can be the only true objective, particularly in the context of the multinational company.

3   The **stakeholder view** of corporate objectives is that **many groups** of people have a stake in what the company does. Each of these groups, which include suppliers, workers, manager, customers and governments as well as shareholders, has its own objectives, and this means that a compromise is required. For example, in the case of the multinational firm with a facility in a politically unstable third world economy, the directors may at times need to place the **interests of local government and economy** ahead of those of its shareholder, in part at least to ensure its own continued stability there.

4   While the relevance of the wealth maximisation goal is under discussion, it might also be useful to consider the way in which this type of objective is defined, since this will impact upon both parallel and subsidiary objectives. A widely adopted approach is to seek to **maximise the present value of the projected cash flows**. In this way, the objective is both made measurable and can be translated into a yardstick for financial decision making. It cannot be defined as a single attainable target but rather as a criterion for the continuing allocation of the company's resources.

Cash flow generation

5   The validity of **cash flow generation** as a major corporate objective depends on the timescale over which performance is measured. If the business maximises the net present value of the cash flows generated in the medium to long term, then this objective is effectively the same as that discussed above. However, if the aim is to **maximise all cash flows**, then decisions are likely to be disproportionately focused on **short-term performance**, and this can work against the long-term health of the business. Defining objectives in terms of long-term cash flow generation makes the shareholder wealth maximisation goal more clearly definable and measurable.

Profitability

6   Many companies use **return on investment (ROI)** targets to **assess performance** and **control the business**. This is useful for the comparison of widely differing divisions within a diverse multinational company, and can provide something approaching a 'level playing field' when setting targets for the different parts of the business. It is important that the **measurement techniques** to be used in respect of both profits and the asset base are **very clearly defined**, and that there is a clear and consistent approach to accounting for inflation. As with the cash flow generation targets discussed above, the selection of the time frame is also important in ensuring that the selected objectives do work for the long-term health of the business.

Risk adjusted returns

7   It is assumed that the use of **risk adjusted returns** relates to the criteria used for investment appraisal, rather than to the performance of the group as a whole. As such, risk adjusted returns cannot be used in defining the top level major corporate goals; however they can be one way in which **corporate goals** are made **congruent** with operating decisions. At the same time, they do provide a **useful input** to the goal setting process in that they focus attention on the company's policy with regard to making risky investments. Once the overall corporate approach to risk has been decided, this can be made effective in operating decisions, for example by **specifying the amount** by which the **cost of capital** is to be **augmented** to allow for risk in various types of investment decisions.

Performance improvement in non-financial areas

8   As discussed in the first section of this report, recent work on corporate objectives suggests that firms should take specific account of those areas which impact only indirectly, if at all, on **financial performance**. The firm has responsibilities towards many groups in addition to the shareholders, including:

    (i)   **Employees:** to provide good working conditions and remuneration, the opportunity for personal development, outplacement help in the event of redundancy and so on

    (ii) **Customers:** to provide a product of good and consistent quality, good service and communication, and open and fair commercial practice

    (iii) **The public:** to ensure responsible disposal of waste products.

9   There are many **other interest groups** that should also be included in the discussion process. Non-financial objectives may often work indirectly to the financial benefit of the firm in the long term, but in the short term they do often appear to compromise the primary financial objectives.

Conclusions

10 It is very difficult to find a comprehensive and appropriate alternative primary financial objective to that of **shareholder wealth maximisation**. However, achievement of this goal can be pursued, at least in part, through the setting of specific **subsidiary targets** in terms of items such as return on investment and risk adjusted returns. The definition of non-financial objectives should also be addressed in the context of the overall review of the corporate plan.

Signed: Finance Director

2 XYZ

(a) **Ratios**

During this period, **earnings per share** have declined by 10.7% while at the same time **dividend per share** has increased by 19.0%. The **payout ratio** has increased from 60% in 20W9 to 80% in 20X3, and thus the proportion of earnings retained has fallen to 20%. If it is assumed that the capital structure has not changed over the period, then it can be seen that both **actual earnings** and the **return on capital employed** have declined over the period.

Retention policy

One possible implication of this policy is that **insufficient earnings** have been **retained** to finance the investment required to at least maintain the rate of return on capital employed. If this means that the company is falling behind its competitors, then this could have a serious **impact** on the **long-term profitability** of the business.

(b) **Rate of return**

For the purposes of calculation it is assumed that any new investment will earn a rate of return equivalent to that **required by the shareholders** (ie 15%), and that this will also be the level of return that is earned on existing investments for the foreseeable future. It is further assumed that investors are indifferent as to whether they receive their returns in the form of dividend or as capital appreciation.

Option 1

The amount of dividend per share is £1 with no growth forecast. The rate of return required by shareholders is 15%. The theoretical share price can be estimated using the dividend valuation model.

$Ke = d_1/p_0$

Where Ke = Cost of equity

$\quad\quad d_1$ = Dividend per share
$\quad\quad p_0$ = Market price per share

$\quad 15\% = 1.00/p_0$

$\quad\quad p_0$ = £6.67, or £7.67 cum div

100% of the total return is provided in the form of dividend.

Option 2

Under the assumptions relating to earnings stated above, the share price will be the same as that calculated for option 1, ie $6.67 per share. However in this case 50% of the expected return is in the form of dividend and 50% as capital appreciation.

A numerical example will clarify the position.

The rate of growth of dividends g may be expressed as:

$g = rb$

Where   r = required rate of return
         b = proportion of profits retained

In this case therefore, with dividends at 50 cents per share:

$g = 0.15 \times 0.5 = 0.075$

$$p_0 = \frac{d_1}{r-g} = \frac{0.5 \times 1.075}{0.15 - 0.075} = \$7.17$$

$7.17 plus 50c dividend at t_0 = $7.67 cum div.

Option 3

This is the same as for option 2, but 25% of the expected return is in the form of dividend and 75% as capital growth.

$g = 0.15 \times 0.75 = 0.1125$

$$p_0 = \frac{0.25 \times 1.1125}{0.15 - 0.1125} = 7.42$$

$7.42 plus 25c dividend at t_0 = $7.67 cum div

Option 4

In this case, for a share price of $6.67, investors would need to believe that retained profits will be invested in projects yielding annual growth of 15% and that the share price will grow at this rate. 100% of the expected return is provided in the form of capital appreciation under this option.

(c)   **Factors influencing share price**

The figures calculated above assume that the **share price** is wholly dependent on the **rate of return required by shareholders** and that the shareholders are indifferent as to the form which the return takes. In practice, this is but one element in the range of factors which influence share prices. Other significant influences include the following.

(i)   The **level of funds available for investment**
(ii)   **Investor confidence**
(iii)   The **tax situation and income requirements of investors**
(iv)   The **availability of alternative investments**

The figures calculated are helpful to the directors only in so far as they direct attention away from the share price: they demonstrate that it is the **level of returns** and the **rate of return required** by investors which drive the share price.

Investment policy

It would be more helpful for the directors to look in detail at the options available to them in terms of **investment** and to assess these against the **cost of capital**, taking account of the differing **degrees of risk** entailed. For the share price to be maximised in the long term, it is the effect of **investment policy** on the net worth of the business which is important, ie the **net present value** of operating cash flows. This may mean that in the short term the share price declines, but the directors may decide that this is a worthwhile sacrifice to make for the long-term profitability of the business. They may also need to consider whether the company needs a further injection of capital in addition to an increase in retentions in order to fund its development.

3 Remuneration

The choice of an appropriate remuneration policy by a company will depend, among other things, on:

(a) **Cost**: the extent to which the package provides value for money.

(b) **Motivation**: the extent to which the package motivates employees both to stay with the company and to work to their full potential.

(c) **Fiscal effects**: government tax incentives may promote different types of pay. In times of wage control and high taxation this can act as an incentive to make the 'perks' a more significant part of the package.

(d) **Goal congruence**: the extent to which the package encourages employees to work in such a way as to achieve the objectives of the firm – perhaps to maximise rather than to satisfice.

High basic salary

In this context, Option (i) is likely to be **relatively expensive** with no payback to the firm in times of low profitability. It is unlikely to encourage staff to maximise their efforts, although the extent to which it acts as a motivator will depend on the individual psychological make-up of the employees concerned. Many staff prefer this type of package however, since they know where they are financially. In the same way the company is also able to budget accurately for its staff costs.

Profit bonus

The firm will be able to gain benefits from operating a **profit-related pay scheme** (Option (ii)), as **costs** will be **lower**, though not proportionately so, during a time of low profits. The effect on motivation will vary with the individual concerned, and will also depend on whether it is an individual or a group performance calculation. There is a further risk that figures and performance may be **manipulated** by managers in such a way as to maximise their bonus to the detriment of the overall longer term company benefit.

Share option scheme

A share option scheme (Option (iii)) carries **fiscal benefits**. It also minimises the cost to the firm since this is effectively borne by the existing shareholders through the dilution of their holdings. Depending on how pricing is determined, it may assist in **achieving goal congruence**. However, since the share price depends on many factors which are external to the firm, it is possible for the scheme to operate in a way which is unrelated to the individual's performance. Thus such a scheme is unlikely to motivate directly through links with performance. Staff will continue to obtain the vast majority of their income from salary and perks and are thus likely to be more concerned with maximising these elements of their income than with working to raise the share price.

4 Stakeholders

> **Top tips.** (a) is an introduction to issues that will often be relevant in questions on mergers as well as questions about change of company status. The answer concentrates on financial benefits, and even just concentrating on these indicates potential conflicts. These may be significant in a merger situation, as co-operation of senior managers and employees will often be essential for the merger to succeed.
>
> The discussion in (b) talks about longer-term technological charges as well as short-term direct costs. Real options may be involved (if action only has to be taken when demand exceeds a certain level). (ii) is important as reputation as a good corporate citizen may be thought to be worth the extra costs incurred in maximising environmental benefits.

(a) **A company seeking a stock market listing**

When an unlisted company converts into a listed company, some of the existing shareholder/managers will sell their shares to outside investors. In addition, new shares will probably be issued. The dilution of ownership might cause loss of control by the existing management.

The stakeholders involved in potential conflicts are as follows.

(i) **Existing shareholder/managers**

They will want to sell some of their shareholding at as high a price as possible. This may motivate them to overstate their company's prospects. Those shareholder/managers who wish to retire from the business may be in conflict with those who wish to stay in control – the latter may oppose the conversion into a listed company.

(ii) **New outside shareholders**

Most of these will hold minority stakes in the company and will receive their rewards as dividends only. This may put them in conflict with the existing shareholder/managers who receive rewards as salaries as well as dividends. On conversion to a listed company there should be clear policies on dividends and directors' remuneration.

(iii) **Employees, including managers who are not shareholders**

Part of the reason for the success of the company will be the efforts made by employees. They may feel that they should benefit when the company seeks a listing. One way of organising this is to create employee share options or other bonus schemes.

(b) **Directly attributable costs**

The way in which **environmental costs and benefits** are included in the appraisal process will depend on the nature of the environmental implications, and the way in which the company intends to approach them. One method is to include in the appraisal only those elements of environmental cost that are **directly attributable** to undertaking the project, and to evaluate any further actions that the company may wish to undertake as a separate issue. In some cases, this may be relatively simple, particularly if legislation exists that defines the environmental standards to be applied.

Technological options

The company will then be faced with a variety of **technological options** that it could use to reduce the contamination to the required levels; for example, if volumes are large enough, it may be appropriate to build a treatment plant to decontaminate the effluent – alternatively it could enter into an agreement with a waste treatment company to tanker away the waste and dispose of it off site. Each of these options will have a **definable cost** which can be evaluated and incorporated into the overall project appraisal. In this situation, there are **no quantifiable benefits** as such, since the environmental issues take the form of a constraint on the project. The costs arise as a direct result of undertaking the project, and as such must be incorporated into the appraisal.

Further expenditure

The problems arise where the company sees the opportunity to go beyond its statutory duties and to act in such a way as to **maximise** the **environmental benefits**. In the example cited above, it may be that the most cost effective method from the point of view of the company is to **tanker the waste** to a remote treatment plant. However, it may view this as unacceptable on the grounds that it wishes to **minimise** the **disturbance** to the area around the site, and thus not to generate high volumes of tanker traffic in the local area. In this situation, the **higher cost option** of **on-site treatment** may become more attractive, although this is not a direct requirement of the project being undertaken. The benefits that arise are difficult to quantify and will not accrue directly to the company undertaking the investment.

In this situation, two approaches are possible.

(i) The company could decide that its own environmental standards form a financial constraint upon the project, and thus that the project should be **evaluated at its full environmental cost**.

(ii) Alternatively, it could decide that the additional costs of on-site treatment over and above the cost of meeting the statutory requirements represent a **separate environmental investment**. If the company sets aside a budget for environmental and social issues, these excess costs could then be taken away from the project and allocated against this environmental budget.

Both approaches are valid and will depend on the objectives and policies of the company with regard to environmental issues.

5 Ethical dimension

(a) The main responsibilities faced by companies when developing an ethical framework are:

(i) Economic
(ii) Legal
(iii) Ethical
(iv) Philanthropic

The ways in which these responsibilities can be addressed are:

Economic

(i) Management should always be acting in the best interests of the company's shareholders, and should therefore always be actively making decisions that will increase shareholders' wealth.

(ii) Projects that have positive NPVs should be pursued as far as funds will allow, as such projects will increase the value of the company and thus shareholders' wealth.

(iii) Whilst management may have a different attitude towards risk than do the shareholders, they should always manage risk according to shareholders' requirements.

(iv) Financing – the optimal financing mix between debt and equity should be chosen as far as possible.

(v) Dividends – there is no legal obligation to pay dividends to ordinary shareholders, but the reasons for withholding dividends must be in the interests of the company as a whole (for example, maintaining funds within the company in order to finance future investment projects).

Legal

(i) Companies must ensure that they are abiding by the rules and regulations that govern how they operate. Company law, health and safety, accounting standards and environmental standards are examples of these boundaries.

(ii) Failure to abide by the rules can cost companies dearly. One only has go look at the fate of WorldCom and Enron bosses, as well as Nick Leeson of Barings Bank, for examples of how failure to operate within the legal framework can cause companies to collapse, taking with them the jobs (and often pension funds) of thousands of employees.

Ethical

(i) Ethical responsibilities arise from a moral requirement for companies to act in an ethical manner.

(ii) Pursuit of ethical behaviour can be governed by such elements as:

- Mission statements
- Ethics managers
- Reporting channels to allow employees to expose unethical behaviour.
- Ethics training and education (including ethics manuals)

Philanthropic

(i) Anything that improves the welfare of employees, the local community or the wider environment.

(ii) Examples include Tesco's "Computers for Schools" campaign (UK); provision of an employees' gym; sponsorship of sporting events; charitable donations.

(b) Main functional areas of a firm include:

(i) Human resources
(ii) Marketing
(iii) Market behaviour
(iv) Product development

Human Resources

(i) Provision of minimum wage. In recent years, much has been made of 'cheap labour' and 'sweat shops'. The introduction of the minimum wage is designed to show that companies have an ethical approach to how they treat their employees and are prepared to pay them an acceptable amount for the work they do.

(ii) Discrimination – whether by age, gender, race or religion. It is no longer acceptable for employers to discriminate against employees for any reason – all employees are deemed to be equal and should not be prevented from progressing within the company for any discriminatory reason.

Marketing

(i) Marketing campaigns should be truthful and should not claim that products or services do something that they in fact cannot. This is why such campaigns have to be very carefully worded to avoid repercussions under Trades Descriptions Acts etc.

(ii) Campaigns should avoid creating artificial wants. This is particularly true with children's toys, as children are very receptive to aggressive advertising.

(iii) Do not target vulnerable groups (linked with above) or create a feeling of inferiority. Again, particularly true with children and teenagers, who are very easily led by what their peer groups have. The elderly are also vulnerable, particularly when it comes to such things as electricity and gas charges – making false promises regarding cheaper heating for example may cause the elderly to change companies when such action is not necessary and may in fact be detrimental.

Market Behaviour

(i) Companies should not exploit their dominant market position by charging vastly inflated prices (this was particularly true when utilities were first privatised in the UK; also transport companies such as railway operators which have monopolies on certain routes).

(ii) Large companies should also avoid exploiting suppliers if these suppliers rely on large company business for survival. Unethical behaviour could include refusing to pay a fair price for the goods and forcing suppliers to provide goods and services at uneconomical prices. In the past this has been a particular problem for suppliers in developing countries providing goods and services to large companies in developed countries.

Product Development

(i) Companies should strive to use ethical means to develop new products – for example, more and more cosmetics companies are not testing on animals, an idea pioneered by such companies as the Body Shop.

(ii) Companies should be sympathetic to the potential beliefs of shareholders – for example, there may be large blocks of shareholders who are strongly opposed to animal testing. Managers could of course argue that if potential investors were aware that the company tested their products on animals then they should not have purchased shares.

(iii) When developing products, be sympathetic to the public mood on certain issues – the use of real fur is now frowned upon in many countries; dolphin friendly tuna is now commonplace.

(iv) Use of Fairtrade products and services – for example, Green and Blacks Fairtrade chocolate; Marks and Spencer using Fairtrade cotton in clothing and selling Fairtrade coffee.

6 Common market

> **Top tips.** This question is a good test of your understanding of the features of a common market. It is probably more straightforward than you would get in the exam; the examiner might be tempted to focus more on implications of recent developments in Europe such as the expansion of the European Union.
>
> If you are tempted to choose a question on this subject, note that the case for the common market is underpinned by economic arguments – comparative advantage, different factor endowments, economies of scale and financial contagion. If you are not confident on the economics, it's best to avoid the question.

(a) **Free trade area**

A free trade area exists when there is **no restriction** on the **movement of goods** and services between countries. This may be extended into a customs union when there is a free trade area between all member countries of the union, and in addition there are common external tariffs applying to imports from non-member countries into any part of the union. In other words, the union promotes free trade among its members but acts as a protectionist bloc against the rest of the world.

Common market

A common market encompasses the idea of a customs union but has a number of **additional features**. In addition to free trade among member countries there is also **complete mobility** of the factors of production. A British citizen has the freedom to work in any other country of the European community, for example. A common market will also aim to achieve stronger links between member countries, for example by harmonising government economic policies and by establishing a closer political confederation.

(b) **Comparative advantage**

The most obvious benefits which countries might gain from forming a common market are associated with **free trade** between them. The benefits of free trade are illustrated by the law of comparative advantage which states that countries should specialise in producing those goods where they have a comparative advantage. Specialisation, together with free trade, will result in an increase in total output and all countries will be able, to a great or lesser extent, to share in the benefits.

Larger range

In particular, different countries have **different factor endowments** and, as the international mobility of these factors tends to be severely limited, **trade increases the range of goods** and services available in a particular country. By becoming part of a common market, imports from other member countries are available more cheaply and easily. Imports of certain raw materials or types of capital equipment not otherwise available in a particular country will improve its productive potential, enabling a faster rate of economic growth to be achieved. Similarly, improvements in the range and quality of consumer goods available will tend to enhance a country's standard of living.

Larger markets

In addition, there is a **larger market for domestic output** and firms may be able to benefit from economies of scale by engaging in export activities. **Economies of scale** improve efficiency in the use of resources and enable output to be produced at lower cost. This also raises the possibility of benefits to consumers if these cost savings are passed on in the form of lower prices. In addition, the extension of the market in which firms operate increases the amount of competition they face and hence should improve efficiency.

Exchange rate agreement

Establishment of a common market is often accompanied by some form of **exchange rate agreement** between members and this in turn is likely to encourage further trade as it reduces uncertainty for both exporters and importers. Stability of exchange rates is also beneficial to a government in formulating its domestic economic policies.

Smaller economies

Membership of a common market may be particularly beneficial to smaller or weaker economies as, in addition to increasing the availability of essential factors of production and the range of goods and services available to domestic consumers, it also enables them to **benefit** from any **economic growth** experienced by their fellow members. Spin-offs may be in the form of larger markets for their exports, lower import prices, improved employment opportunities and so on.

Political links

In addition to fostering economic ties between countries, common markets provide the basis for **stronger political links**. Again, this may be particularly important for smaller countries enabling them to benefit from an enhanced position in the world economy. It may also encourage further international economic co-operation, in turn providing an additional stimulus to growth.

7 Multinationals

(a) **Political Risk**

(i) The risk that political action will affect the position and value of a company.

(ii) This risk can adversely affect multinationals in the following ways:

- Import quotas and tariffs may limit the quantity of goods that a subsidiary can buy from the parent.

- Potential nationalisation of subsidiaries and their assets can lead to financial loss as there may be no compensation from the foreign government for doing so.

- The foreign government may place restrictions on the ability of the parent to purchase domestic companies, particularly in strategic industries.

- Different countries have different legal standards of safety or quality. The subsidiary's country may have stricter standards that the parent is unwilling to adhere to, given that it could lead to inconsistent standards of goods in different countries.

Cultural Risk

(i) The risk that different cultural beliefs and styles will affect the products and services provided and the ways in which the organisation is managed and staffed.

(ii) **Effect on multinationals**:

- The host country's beliefs and cultural approach may affect the means by which the product/service is **advertised or distributed**. Some countries' media is much more rigorously regulated and at times censored therefore it is important to avoid any controversial messages. Poorer countries' residents may have little or no access to television or internet, therefore alternative means of getting the message across may be necessary.

- Customers and consumers may differ depending on the **country** in which multinationals operate. It would be of no benefit in a strictly Muslim country for health clubs to direct marketing campaigns showing men and women exercising in the same complex for example.

- The extent to which cultural differences matter will play a large part in the **exposure to cultural risk**. Although China is a Communist country, its inhabitants respond to many Western marketing campaigns, although there is a much greater emphasis on family. However it would be worthless to advertise pork products in Muslim countries because of religious and cultural beliefs.

Legal Risk

(i) The risk that **legislation** may affect the efficient and effective operations of an organisation.

(ii) Effect on multinationals:

- **Minimum technical standards** may differ in certain countries which may result in a particular product having **different specifications** depending on which country it is manufactured in.

- Some countries do not accept the legality of international trademarks or patents. As such intellectual property is often the core of business, multinationals may find it difficult to accept that local companies can copy their trademarks or have very similar ones. One example is in China where the food chain Pizza Hut operates alongside the Chinese equivalent Pizza Hill, whose company colours and logos are very similar to those of the Western chain.

(b)   Steps to deal with political, cultural and legal risks:

Political Risk

(i)   Negotiate with host government on matters such as transfer of capital and access to local finance.

(ii)   Production strategies – create a balance between contracting out to local sources and producing directly.

(iii) Take out insurance against various threats – for example, war, revolution, currency conversion problems.

Cultural Risk

(i)   Do your homework – identify the best markets to enter based on forecast demand, comparative advantage, risk.

(ii)   Management of human resources – have a balance between local works and ex-pats. Have to look at such matters as:

–   Recruitment and training – ex-pats take away the need to recruit locally and train new people in the ways of the organisation in general and the job in particular.

–   Status of women – certain countries do not allow women to work, or men do not respect women's authority.

–   Locals may have a greater knowledge of the local culture but less appreciation of the wider corporate picture. The reverse is true for ex-pats.

–   Employing locals is generally much cheaper, as ex-pat packages include paying for housing, schools, international health care, air travel and so on.

(iii) Make use of such systems as joint ventures, to take advantage of local knowledge but at the same time using the company's own expertise.

Legal Risk

(i)   Good citizenship – comply with best practice, be responsive to ethical concerns, respect the host country's legal requirements.

(ii)   Keep abreast of changes in the law in the broader sense and human resource policies internally.

(iii) Be aware of the consequences of non-compliance, such as bad publicity and potential court cases and take actions to avoid such exposure.

8 Solden

Top tips. Exam questions would not be purely numerical as this one is, but this question does provide an excellent demonstration of the level of detail you will have to cope with in a foreign investment appraisal. Planning is very important, working out what format you will need and what workings will be required.

You can assume that the rates of return are money rates of return, which means that the sales and costs have to be adjusted for price increases.

Possible pitfalls in this question are getting the timing of the exchange rates movements wrong, forgetting that the working capital figure in the cash flow analysis is the **change** in working capital (not the total amount) and including the full cost of materials in (b) rather than just the contribution (remember the UK company is going to have to pay cost price to obtain new materials).

(a) **Investors in Ober**

Year		0	1	2	3	4	5	6
		G'000	G'000	G'000	G'000	G'000	G'000	G'000
Contribution	1		320.0	369.6	426.9	493.0	569.5	
Materials – UK	2		(40.0)	(43.7)	(47.7)	(52.1)	(56.9)	
Selling costs			(40.0)	(44.0)	(48.4)	(53.2)	(58.6)	
Licence fee (10% sales)			(64.0)	(73.9)	(85.6)	(98.6)	(113.9)	
Tax allowable depreciation (800 × 25%)			(200.0)	(200.0)	(200.0)	(200.0)		
Taxable profit/(loss)			(24.0)	8.0	45.2	89.1	340.1	
Tax at 20%				4.8	(1.6)	(9.0)	(17.8)	(68.0)
Plant		(600.0)						
Equipment		(200.0)						
Tax allowable depreciation			200.0	200.0	200.0	200.0		
Working capital		(64.0)	(9.9)	(11.7)	(13.0)	(15.3)	113.9	
Terminal value (3 × 436.3*)							1,308.9	
Tax on terminal value at 30%								(392.6)
Net cash flow in year		(864.0)	166.1	201.1	230.6	264.8	1,745.1	(460.6)
Discount factor at 15%		1,000	0.870	0.756	0.658	0.572	0.497	0.432
PV		(864.0)	144.5	152.0	151.7	151.4	867.3	(199.0)
NPV		403.9						

*436.3 = Year 5 cash flows to this point.
The project is acceptable to investors in Ober.

Workings

Year		0	1	2	3	4	5	6
Exchange rate		16.00	16.00	16.64	17.31	18.00	18.72	19.47
(1)	Sales – units		4,000	4,200	4,410	4,630	4,862	
	Ober contribution per unit (160 – 80, increasing by 10%)		80.0	88.0	96.8	106.5	117.1	
	Ober contribution (G'000s)		320.0	369.6	426.9	493.0	569.5	
(2)	*Materials (UK) – assuming fixed cost increasing with inflation*							
	Cost in pounds		2,500	2,625	2,756	2,894	3,039	
	Cost in gurgles (G'000s)		40.0	43.7	47.7	52.1	56.9	
(3)	*Working capital*							
	Balance – 10% sales	64.0	73.9	85.6	98.6	113.9		
	Increase/(decrease)	64.0	9.9	11.7	13.0	15.3	(113.9)	

(b) **Investors in UK**

Year		0	1	2	3	4	5	6
		£	£	£	£	£	£	£
From Ober subsidiary	(W1)	(54,000)	10,381	12,085	13,325	14,711	93,221	(23,662)
Adjustments in UK								
Licence fee	(W2)		4,000	4,441	4,946	5,478	6,080	
Contribution on materials			500	525	551	579	608	
Lost exports			(5,000)	(5,250)	(5,513)	(5,788)	(6,078)	
Total adjustments			(500)	(284)	(16)	269	610	
Tax thereon, lagged one year				165	94	5	(89)	(201)
Net		(54,000)	9,881	11,966	13,403	14,985	93,742	(23,863)
DF at 10%		1.000	0.909	0.826	0.751	0.683	0.621	0.564
PV		(54,000)	8,982	9,884	10,066	10,235	58,214	(13,459)

The NPV is positive, at £29,922.

Workings

		0	1	2	3	4	5	6
1	From Ober subsidiary:							
	Cashflow in G'000s	(864.0)	166.1	201.1	230.6	264.8	1,745.1	(460.6)
	Pound equivalent	(54,000)	10,381	12,085	13,325	14,711	93,221	(23,662)
2	Licence fee, in G'000s		64	73.9	85.6	98.6	113.8	
	Licence fee, in pounds		4,000	4,441	4,946	5,478	6,080	

9 Mover

> **Top tips**. Do not assume that because a tunnel is a very high risk project its discount rate must be extremely high. For a diversified investor, the relevant risk in the discount rate is systematic risk. However, construction as an industry does have fairly high systematic risk.
>
> **Examiner's comment**. In (a) candidates needed to use a realistic (not too low) discount rate, justify the discount rate used, and treat estimates beyond year 10 in a sensible fashion. However many discount rates used were too low, and in some cases the inflation rate was used. Some candidates also failed to appreciate the difference between real and nominal rates. Most candidates also failed to discuss wider issues such as the reliability of the cash flows, or the risks, or Mover's activities other than the tunnel project.

(a) **Use of real rate**

The expected cash flows of the tunnel should be discounted at a suitable cost of capital, taking into account the **risk** of the project. Since the cash flow projections exclude inflation, the cost of capital should also be a **real rate.**

Estimate of the real rate

(i) The current domestic **risk free rate** is approximately 6% whilst inflation is approximately 2%, giving an approximate real risk free rate of 4%.

(ii) The market premium is 7%.

(iii) The tunnel project is assumed to have a **high level** of **systematic risk**, say a beta of 1.3.

(iv) The pension fund is well diversified and therefore only subject to **systematic risk.**

This implies a real discount rate of approximately 4% + (7% × 1.3) = approx. 13%

Assuming the tunnel has an indefinite life, post 20Y0 cashflows are discounted in perpetuity:

Year	$m	13% df	PV $m
20X0	(450)	0.885	(398)
20X1	(500)	0.783	(392)
20X2	(550)	0.693	(381)
20X3	(650)	0.613	(398)
20X4	(200)	0.543	(109)
20X5	200	0.480	96
20X6	300	0.425	128
20X7	320	0.376	120
20X8	340	0.333	113
20X9	360	0.295	106
20Y0	400	0.261	104
20Y1 onwards*	400	0.261/0.13	803
			(208)

*These are PVs of perpetuity cash flows.

At this estimated discount rate the NPV is **negative**, and therefore the project should be rejected. For a more comprehensive assessment **sensitivity analysis** should be used.

Other considerations

(i) The use of NPV ignores the value of any **embedded or real options**. Such options might include the option to develop land either side of the tunnel.

(ii) **Economic factors** may be critical to the accuracy of the forecast cashflows.

(iii) **Assumptions** concerning costs and competitive issues (the costs of alternative transport links) should be reviewed. In particular there may be a high probability that costs will be greater than forecast, and also that the project will be delayed, leading to further costs and delays in revenues. In addition the costs of **upkeep** of the tunnel have not been included in the calculations.

(iv) The **contractual role** of the construction company should be reviewed – is the project Government supported?

(v) Whilst the tunnel project is presumably the most important project that Mover will be undertaking over the next few years, the company's continued existence may not depend upon it. The trustees should therefore consider the likely results of the **other contracts** that Mover will be undertaking over the next few years.

On a project of this size, and dependent on the level of the pension fund investment, such factors should be modelled in more detail, perhaps using **sensitivity analysis** or **simulation**.

(b) **Effect of inflation**

Inflation erodes the **purchasing power** of money. It therefore has an **effect** on the **returns** an investor will require, and consequently on the appraisal of capital investment decisions by companies. As the **inflation rate increases so will the minimum return required** by an investor.

Example

A return of 5% on a sum invested of $100 will provide $105 back in one year's time. If inflation is running at 15% then at the end of one year $105 will only buy 105/1.15 = $91.30 worth of goods at today's prices. In order to be able to purchase $105 worth of goods at today's prices the investor will need a nominal return of $1.05 \times 1.15 = 1.2075$, ie 20.75%. Thus with inflation at 15%, a nominal rate of interest of 20.75% is required to give the investor a real return of 5%. This effect can be expressed as:

(1 + money (or nominal) rate) = (1 + real rate) × (1 + inflation rate)

Choice of approaches

Companies therefore have a **choice** of approaches when accounting for inflation in the appraisal of capital projects. They can either **inflate all the elements** of the cash flow at the appropriate rates and then **discount at the nominal (or money) rate of return**. Alternatively they can **exclude inflation** from the cash flows and **discount at the real rate**.

10 PS Ltd

Top tips. Part (a) gives you practice in using the Black-Scholes formula. Go back to Chapter 6 and work again through the example if you got stuck. We have used interpolation to find N (d_1) and N (d_2). However, understanding the principles behind the Black-Scholes formula is more important than being able to plug numbers into the formula. Expect therefore to see discussion parts similar to parts (b)(i) and (ii) featuring in questions on Black-Scholes.

(a) Using the Black-Scholes Formula

$$d_1 = \frac{\ln(P_a \div P_e) + (r + 0.5s^2)t}{s\sqrt{t}}$$

$$d_1 = \frac{\ln(3 / 2.50) + (0.05 + 0.5 \times 0.2^2) \times 0.25}{(0.2 \times \sqrt{0.25})}$$

$d_1 = (0.1823 + 0.0175)/0.1$

$d_1 = 1.998$

$$d_2 = d_1 - s\sqrt{t}$$
$$= 1.998 - 0.2\sqrt{0.25}$$
$$= 1.998 - 0.1$$
$$= 1.898$$

$$N(d_1) = 0.5 + 0.4767 + \frac{82}{100}(0.4772 - 0.4767)$$
$$= 0.9771$$

$$N(d_2) = 0.5 + 0.4706 + \frac{82}{100}(0.4713 - 0.4706)$$
$$= 0.9712$$

$$c = P_s N(d_1) - P_e N(d_2) e^{-rT}$$
$$= (3 \times 0.9771) - (2.50 e^{-0.05 \times 0.25} \times 0.9712)$$
$$= 2.9313 - (2.50 \times 0.9876 \times 0.9712)$$
$$= 53.35p$$

(b) (i) The **Black-Scholes pricing model** was developed to value traded call options on quoted shares and can be adapted to value any options. The input variables are:

(1) **The market price of the underlying share**

If the **share price rises**, the **value** of the **call option** will **increase**.

(2) **The exercise price (or strike price)**

A **call option** gives the holder the **right to buy** the share at a fixed price, known as the **exercise price**. The **higher the price** of the **underlying share** compared with the exercise price (above), the **more valuable** is the **option**.

(3) **The time to expiry**

The longer an option has to run before it expires, the more chance there is that the **value of the underlying share will increase**. Time to expiry therefore **adds value** to an option.

(4) **The volatility of the underlying share (standard deviation of share price variations)**

Options provide **unlimited opportunities for gains** but **losses** are **limited to the purchase price**. This asymmetrical probability distribution of gains/losses means that volatility of the underlying share **adds value** to the option.

(5) **The interest rate**

This is the **risk free rate of interest**, which gives the **time value of money** and is relevant because the option is valued today but is exercisable on a future date.

The difference between 1 and 2 is known as the '**intrinsic value**' of the option, but it has a minimum value of zero. The combination of 3, 4 and 5 gives its '**time value**'. The total value of the option is the sum of intrinsic and time values.

(ii) **Real options**

Real options are **choices** which **arise** in **real capital investments**, for example the opportunity to renew a lease at a fixed price or to renew a license agreement after an introductory period. The party able to make the choice effectively holds an option, the value of which should be considered when appraising the investment.

Example

Suppose a capital project involves paying a franchise fee to a company which has patented a key process. Our agreement gives us the **right** (but not the obligation) to **renew this franchise** after 3 years for a further 5 year period at a fixed cost of $5 million. The value of this option can be estimated by adapting the 5 input variables:

(1) The **current market cost** of a 5-year franchise (say $4m). This would need to take into account potential competitors who may wish to take over our business.

(2) The **$5m cost of the 5 year renewal license** agreed in our contract (i.e. the **exercise price**). This option currently has an intrinsic value of zero.

(3) The **3-year period** until we have to choose.

(4) The **volatility of the franchise price**, which depends on its susceptibility to general market factors and specific factors including our success at using it.

(5) The **risk-free interest rate**, as in the original model.

11 Nile plc

(a) The net dividend has increased 1.5 times from the end of 20X4 to the end of 20X8, a period of 4 years. This represents an approximate annualised growth rate of 10.67% (being $4\sqrt{1.5}$).

Cost of ordinary share capital in after tax terms = $\dfrac{30(1.1067)}{476} + 0.1067 = 0.176$ or 17.6%

Cost of debentures: = $77 (with interest) is the current market price per cent. The cost of debentures (%) is the internal rate of return of the following cash flows:

Year	MV $	Interest $	Tax Saving $	Cash Flow $
0	(77)	8	(2.8)	(71.8)
1-15		8	(2.8)	5.2
15		100		100.0

At a discount rate of 7% the NPV is + $11.8, and at a discount rate of 9% the NPV is – $2.4. The IRR is (by interpolation)

7 + [11.8 / (11.8 + 2.4)] x 2 = 8.7%

It is assumed that the new issue of shares and debentures will be weighted in accordance with the existing gearing ratio as measured by market values.

The weighted average cost of capital is:

	Cost (%)	Market Value		Hash Total
Ordinary share capital	17.6% ×	4,760,000	=	837,760
Debentures	8.7% ×	552,000	=	48,024
		5,312,000		885,784

Weighted average cost of capital = $\dfrac{\$885,784}{5,312,000} \times 100\% = 16.7\%$

(b)   *Difficulties and uncertainties that should be mentioned are:*

(i)   will the growth rate in dividend remain the same as in previous years?

(ii)   should a premium for risk be added to the weighted average cost of capital; e.g. should the test discount rate for projects be, say, 20% or more rather than 16.7% (or 17%)?

12 Crystal Inc

Top tips. (a) demonstrates the complications that may occur in weighted average cost of capital calculations. When you calculate the cost of equity, you will need to do more than just plug the figures into the formula. Don't forget to check whether shares are quoted cum or ex div. Here also you need to use Gordon's growth model to calculate g.

With debentures, the most serious mistake you can make is to treat redeemable debentures as irredeemable. Because the debentures are redeemable, you need to carry out an IRR analysis. Remember this calculation is done from the viewpoint of the **investor**. The investor pays the market price for the debentures at time 0, and then receives the interest and the conversion value in subsequent years. You must bring tax into your calculation, although you could have assumed that tax was paid with a one year time delay.

Lastly don't forget that the weightings in the WACC calculation are based on **market** values, **not book** values.

(b) demonstrates that the calculation of the weighted average cost of capital is not a purely mechanical process. It makes assumptions about the shareholders, the proposed investment and the company's capital structure and future dividend prospects. Given all the assumptions involved, the result of the calculations may need to be taken with a large pinch of salt!

(a)   The post-tax weighted average cost of capital should first be calculated.

(i)   **Ordinary shares**

	$
Market value of shares cum div.	3.27
Less dividend per share (810 ÷ 3,000)	0.27
Market value of shares ex div.	3.00

The formula for calculating the cost of equity when there is dividend growth is:

$$k_e = \frac{D_0(1+g)}{P_0} + g$$

where k_e = cost of equity
D_0 = current dividend
g = rate of growth
P_0 = current ex div market value.

In this case we shall estimate the future rate of growth (g) from the average growth in dividends over the past four years.

$$810 = 620(1+g)^4$$

$$(1+g)^4 = \frac{810}{620} = 1.3065$$

$$(1+g) = 1.069$$

$$g = 0.069 = 6.9\%$$

$$k_e = \frac{0.27 \times 1.069}{3} + 0.069 = 16.5\%$$

(ii) **7% Debentures**

In order to find the post-tax cost of the debentures, which are redeemable in ten years' time, it is necessary to find the discount rate (IRR) which will give the future post-tax cash flows a present value of $77.10.

The relevant cash flows are:

(1) Annual interest payments, net of tax, which are $1,300 × 7% × 70% = $63.70 (for ten years)

(2) A capital repayment of $1,300 (in ten years' time)

It is assumed that tax relief on the debenture interest arises at the same time as the interest payment. In practice the cash flow effect is unlikely to be felt for about a year, but this will have no significant effect on the calculations.

	Present value
Try 8%	$'000
Current market value of debentures (1,300 at £77.10 per cent)	(1,002.3)
Annual interest payments net of tax £63.70 × 6.710 (8% for ten years)	427.4
Capital repayment £1,300 × 0.463 (8% in ten years time)	601.9
NPV	27.0

	$ '000
Try 9%	
Current market value of debentures	(1,002.3)
Annual interest payments net of tax 63.70 × 6.418	408.8
Capital repayment 1,300 × 0.422	548.6
NPV	(44.9)

$$IRR = 8\% + \left[\frac{27.0}{27.0 - -44.9} \times (9-8) \right]\%$$

$$= 8.38\%$$

(iii) **The weighted average cost of capital**

	Market value	Cost	Product
	$'000	%	
Equity	9,000	16.50	1,485
7% Debentures	1,002	8.38	84
	10,002		1,569

$$\frac{1,569}{10,002} \times 100 = 15.7\%$$

The above calculations suggest that a discount rate in the region of 16% might be appropriate for the appraisal of new investment opportunities.

(b) Difficulties and uncertainties in the above estimates arise in a number of areas.

(i) **The cost of equity**. The above calculation assumes that all shareholders have the **same** marginal cost of capital and the same **dividend expectations**, which is unrealistic. In addition, it is assumed that dividend growth has been and will be at a **constant rate** of 6.9%. In fact, actual growth in the years 20X5/6 and 20X8/9 was in excess of 9%, while in the year 20X7/8 there was no dividend growth. 6.9% is merely the average rate of growth for the past four years. The rate of future growth will depend more on the return from future projects undertaken than on the past dividend record.

(ii) **The use of the weighted average cost of capital**. Use of the weighted average cost of capital as a discount rate is only justified where the company in question has achieved what it believes to be the optimal capital structure (the mix of debt and equity) and where it intends to maintain this structure in the long term.

(iii)   **The projects themselves**. The weighted average cost of capital makes no allowance for the business risk of individual projects. In practice some companies, having calculated the WACC, then add a premium for risk. In this case, for example, if one used a risk premium of 5% the final discount rate would be 21%. Ideally the risk premium should vary from project to project, since not all projects are equally risky. In general, the riskier the project the higher the discount rate which should be used.

13 Espondera Inc

In order to calculate the cost of debt we need first to assign a credit rating to the company. The values of the equation variables are as follows

Size = Total Assets = $120 million

$$\text{Profitability} = \frac{\text{Net income}}{\text{Total assets}} = \frac{\$6\,\text{million}}{\$120\,\text{million}} = 0.05$$

Debt = Subordinated = 1

$$\text{Leverage} = \frac{\text{Long term debt}}{\text{Total assets}} = \frac{\$14\,\text{million}}{£120\,\text{million}} = 0.117$$

$$\text{Interest} = \frac{\text{Income before interest and taxes}}{\text{Interest payments}} = \frac{\$8\,\text{million}}{\$1\,\text{million}} = 8$$

$$\text{Cov} = \frac{\text{Standard deviation of earnings}}{\text{Average value of earnings}} = (0.937/3.68) = 0.255$$

Workings

The average value of earnings is: $\dfrac{(5 + 4.2 + 3.2 + 3.8 + 2.2)}{5} = \$3.68\text{m}$

The variance of earnings is:

$$\frac{(5 - 3.68)^2 + (4.2 - 3.68)^2 + (3.2 - 3.68)^2 + (3.8 - 3.68)^2 + (2.2 - 3.68)^2}{5} = 0.878$$

The standard deviation of earnings is the square root of the variance and is: $\sqrt{0.878} = 0.937$

Inserting the values of the variables in The Kaplan – Urwitz model we have:

$$Y = 4.41 + 0.001 \times 120 + 6.40 \times 0.05 - 2.56 \times 1 - 2.72 \times 0.1178 + 0.006 \times 8 - 0.53 \times 0.255 = 1.88$$

The value of the model assigns a credit rating of BBB and on the basis of observed market rates for bonds of this rating the cost of debt is 8.4%.

14 Canada

Top tips. Method (i) involves a year-by-year conversion of the receipts, making sure that you adjust the exchange rate by the correct amount each year. In method (ii) the adjusted discount rate is computed in the same way as a nominal discount rate is computed from a real discount rate and an inflation rate.

Your answer to (b) needs to bring out the costs that will be incurred, and how the risks of loss (and chance of gain) will be limited or enhanced by borrowing abroad.

(a)   **Method (i)**

Years	0	1	2	3	4
Investment C$'000	(150)				50
After tax cash flows C$'000		60	60	60	45
Net cash C$'000	(150)	60	60	60	95
Exchange rate	1.7000	1.7850	1.8743	1.9680	2.0664
Net cash £'000	(88.24)	33.61	32.01	30.49	45.97
14% discount factors	1.000	0.877	0.769	0.675	0.592
PV in £'000	(88.24)	29.48	24.62	20.58	27.21
NPV in £'000	**13.65**				

Method (ii)

Adjusted discount rate: equivalent discount rate in C$, allowing for 5% appreciation of the pound, is given by $1 + r = 1.14 \times 1.05 = 1.197$. Discount rate = 19.7%.

Years	0	1	2	3	4
Net cash C$'000	(150)	60	60	60	95
19.7% discount factors	1.000	0.835	0.698	0.583	0.487
PV C$'000	(150)	50.10	41.88	34.98	46.27
NPV C$'000	23.23				
Exchange rate	1.7000				
NPV £'000	**13.66**				

To provide a 14% rate on return in UK and to cope with a 5% annual strengthening of the pound, a dollar invested in Canada would have to grow by 14% to $1.14 and by a further 5% to $1.14 × 1.05 = $1.197. In other words it would have to show a rate of return of 19.7%. The company's cost of capital, translated into Canadian dollars is therefore 19.7%.

In a system of **free floating exchange rates**, if the C$ depreciates by 5% per year against sterling, the cost of borrowing in C$ is likely to be about 5% more expensive than borrowing in sterling.

(b)   **Finance by borrowing**

The decision to **finance** a **foreign investment** by **borrowing** in the foreign country's currency is influenced by a number of factors.

Loan in the same currency

For any income-generating foreign investment there is a risk that the foreign currency **depreciates**, resulting in a reduced value of income when converted to the home currency. If, however, borrowings are taken out in the **same currency** as that in which the **income** is generated, then the **reduced income** is at least partially offset by reduced **loan interest costs**. It should be noted, however, that this hedging effect also **reduces** the chances of **currency gains**: if the foreign currency appreciates, then the increased value of income is offset by an increased loan interest cost when converted to the home currency.

Unexpected losses

In the example, the Canadian dollar steadily devalues against the pound. Borrowing in Canadian dollars would therefore enable currency risk to be managed better than if borrowing is arranged in sterling. However, in a system of free floating exchange rates, if the C$ depreciates by 5% per year against sterling, the cost of borrowing in C$ is likely to be about 5% **more expensive than borrowing** in sterling. This **increased interest cost** will take away the advantage of the devaluation of the C$ loan. If currencies always moved in predictable ways, there would be little advantage in financing the Canadian investment with a Canadian loan. However, currency **devaluations** can sometimes be **unexpected** and much larger than predicted. It is to prevent these **unexpected losses** that hedging using a foreign loan is recommended.

Cost of foreign loans

The **cost of foreign loans** may be higher than the theoretical equivalent cost of a domestic loan because the company does not have such a **good credit standing** in the foreign country. Better rates may be obtained from the **euromarkets** or by arranging a **currency loan swap**. Care should be taken to match the duration of the loan with the **expected duration** of the project (4 years in this question), unless further foreign investments are anticipated. A further consideration is the availability of **tax savings** on the loan interest. The effect on the company's **overall tax charge needs** to be included in the decision process.

Impact of political risk

For countries with high political risk, which may impose exchange controls, or even expropriate assets, **borrowing** in the **local currency** is recommended to **offset** investment losses which might result from political action.

15 Organic growth

(a) **Advantages of organic growth**

    (i)   The company will be developing a new vehicle that has the group's existing culture rather than acquiring a **subsidiary** with a **different culture**.

    (ii)   Growing organically may be cheaper in the long-run as it is more likely to **be financed** by **retained earnings** rather than new sources with issue costs, and it will not involve paying a premium for a desirable subsidiary.

    (iii)   Planned development of a subsidiary should mean that there is **no duplication of resources** with existing operations.

    (iv)   Organic growth offers **more opportunities** for **current employees**.

    (v)   Organic growth is more likely to be in areas where a company **currently has expertise**, limiting the risk of failure.

(b) **Advantages of acquisition**

    (i)   Acquisition can offer **speedier entry** into an overseas market than organic growth.

    (ii)   Merging with **established firms abroad** can be a means of **purchasing market information**, **market share**, **distribution channels** and **reputation**.

    (iii)   **Other synergies** include **acquisition of management skills** and **knowledge**, **intangibles** such as brands and trademarks, or **additional cash** and **debt capacity**.

    (iv)   Acquiring a subsidiary may be a means of **removing trade barriers**.

    (v)   Acquisition can be a means of **removing a competitor**.

    (vi)   **Start-up costs** will not be incurred.

Ultimately the risk of acquiring an established operation may well be less than starting up a subsidiary in an area where the company has **not previously operated**.

16 Canon Burger

(a) There are a number of synergies that the acquisition of Templar can create.

Financial synergies arising from the diversification into other areas reducing the volatility of earnings. The acquisition will also increase the debt capacity of Canon as Templar has no debt.

Revenue synergies are also expected to arise as Templar will be able to use the marketing and advertising services of Canon

The management of Canon may also improve the performance of Templar and may exploit its brand value and clientele.

(b)   Present value of additional cash flow in perpetuity = $\dfrac{\$25,000}{0.12}$ = $208,333

The net present value of the acquisition is given by value from the acquisition minus the cost of the acquisition

NPV = $208,333 − $200,000 = $8,333

The acquisition should proceed

(c)   Unchanged level of gearing of the combined entity means that the cost of capital remains the same at 16%

$$\text{NPV} = \dfrac{\$25,000}{0.16} - \$200,000 \;\; = \$156,950 - \$200,000$$
$$= -\,\$43,750$$

The acquisition should not proceed if there is no reduction in the cost of capital.

17 Takeovers

> **Top tips.** This question discusses the issues surrounding mergers and takeovers. (b) illustrates why companies are acquired. (c) what can go wrong. Together they constitute a checklist of the sorts of issues to look out for in a takeover question.

(a)   **Shareholder wealth** in a company can be expressed as the **present value of the future cash flows** of the business. Therefore if a takeover of another company is to increase shareholder wealth then the present value of the combined entity must exceed the sum of the present values of the two individual businesses.

PV combined business > PV bidding company + PV target company

(b)   In order for a takeover to lead to an increase in wealth for the bidding company's shareholders there must be gains that would not have arisen if the two companies had not combined.

Economies of scale

When two businesses combine this creates a **larger business** which can **lead to economies of scale**. For example there could be direct cost savings by eliminating duplication of costs, or market power could be exerted by the larger entity in order for example to gain lower purchase prices for buying larger quantities.

Complementary resources

One company may decide to buy another company as a method of directly acquiring resources the other company may have. For example a manufacturing company may acquire a company with a strong research and development division which will eventually improve the bidding company's products.

Competition

The motivation for a bidding company to acquire a competitor may be in order to eliminate that market competition and improve market share. This in turn might mean that the combined entity is in more of a position to influence prices and increase profits. However as this will not always benefit the final consumer such an acquisition may not be allowed by government.

Undervalued shares

In some circumstances, due to market imperfections, the shares in the target company may be undervalued and therefore the bidding company is effectively buying a bargain.

BPP
LEARNING MEDIA

Underutilisation of resources

The target company may have been chosen due to a perception by the bidding company management that the resources of the target are being underutilised and by introducing a new management team additional profits can be earned.

(c) In other cases although the bidding company management might have expectations of an increase in wealth for its shareholders this may not always transpire.

Paying too high a price

In a takeover bid, particularly a contested one, it is entirely possible that the bidding company may pay a **higher price for the target company shares** than they are worth. This is often the case as it is common for a **premium** to be offered to the target company shareholders in order to persuade them to sell their shares. If the premium is greater than the benefits from the takeover then this will be a direct transfer of wealth from the bidding company shareholders to the target company shareholders.

Integration of the businesses

After a takeover it is often **hard to integrate the two businesses** to such an extent that any anticipated benefits can be realised. This may be due to **differences in culture, management style or operational or organisational matters**. The problem is particularly highlighted where the bidding company tries to impose its own systems, culture and management on the target company.

Unforeseen problems

Despite thorough investigation and due diligence procedures being carried out during a takeover bid it is entirely possible after the combination to **discover problems** in the target company which were not evident before the bid and which will eliminate any anticipated increases in wealth.

Management problems

In some cases the management of the bidding company **lose motivation** after a takeover and assume that the benefits foreseen will just happen without additional effort on their behalf. This is rarely the case and continued management effort and motivation will be required in order to achieve the desired results.

18 Univo Inc

Top tips. Hopefully you remembered that the fundamental theory of share values is based on linking share values with **future** dividend patterns, whatever these patterns are assumed to be. (Chartism assumes that past dividend patterns will be repeated in the future).

This question gives you the beta of equity, so you can just insert it into the formula. In the exam you are more likely to have to calculate it using the principles of gearing and ungearing betas (which we covered in the appendix to Chapter 4). The main complication in (a) is knowing how to cope with the different dividend growth rates. The calculation of the intrinsic value of share has two elements:

(a) The present value of dividends in 20X2 and 20X3
(b) The market value of the shares in 20X3, using the formula but remembering to discount its result.

In (b) you have to carry out the same calculation making the assumption that as the return on fixed interest securities has increased, the return required from shares must also have increased. Don't get confused into making adjustments to the actual dividends received (the question tells you that they are unaffected by the change in interest rates); it is the discount factor that needs to change.

(a) The **dividend growth model** may be formulated as follows.

$$P_0 = \frac{D_0(1+g)}{(r-g)}$$

where: P_0 = market price of the share (ex div)
D_0 = current net dividend
r = cost of equity capital
g = expected annual rate of dividend growth

In this example, the first step is to calculate the cost of equity capital. This may be done using the CAPM, assuming that debt and equity betas are weighted using market values. The CAPM takes the form:

$$E(r_j) = r_f + [E(r_m) - r_f]\beta_i$$

where: $E(r_j)$ = cost of capital
β_j = beta factor relating to the type of capital in question
$E(r_m)$ = expected market rate of return
F_r = risk free rate of return
$E(r_j)$ = $12\% + (17\% - 12\%) \times 0.82 = 16.1\%$

Dividend growth between 20W9 and 20X1 has been 9.5% per year. It is estimated that growth in 20X2 and 20X3 will be 25%, thereafter reverting to 9.5%. Dividends for the next three years can be estimated as follows.

	Total dividend $	Dividend per share cents
20X1	2,800,000	7.00
20X2	3,500,000	8.75
20X3	4,375,000	10.94
20X4	4,790,625	11.98

Then we can estimate the intrinsic share value as follows.

	ρ	Discount factor @ 16%	PV Cents
20X1 Dividend	7.00	–	–
20X2 Dividend	8.75	0.862	7.54
20X3 Dividend	10.94	0.743	8.13
20X3 Value of shares in			
20X3 per dividend model	181.50*	0.743	134.85
			150.52

$$* \quad \frac{d_{20X3}(1+g)}{K_e - g} = \frac{10.94(1+0.095)}{0.161 - 0.095} = 181.50 \text{ cents}$$

Estimated intrinsic value = 150.52c

The actual market price of the shares (ex div) is 210 cents per share. A fundamental analyst would therefore regard the shares as being overpriced and would recommend their sale.

(b) If the interest rate increased by 2%, the return required on equity is likely to increase by a similar amount to approximately 18%. The PV of dividends to be used in calculations will therefore fall.

	Total dividend $	Dividend per share Cents	Discount factor @ 18%	PV Cents
20X1	2,800,000	7.00		
20X2	3,500,000	8.75	0.847	7.41
20X3	4,375,000	10.94	0.718	7.85
20X4	4,790,625	11.98		
				15.26

The PV of the expected dividend from 20X4 onwards will fall to 8.6c (11.98c × 0.718).

$$P_0 = \frac{D_1}{(k_e - g)}$$

where: P_0 = market price of the share (ex div)

D_1 = net dividend in the following year (8.6c)

k_e = cost of equity capital (18%)

g = expected annual rate of dividend growth (9.5%)

$$P_0 = \frac{8.6}{(0.18 - 0.095)} = 101.18c$$

To this must be added the PV of the dividend for 20X2 and 20X3:

Estimated intrinsic value = 101.18 + 15.26 = 116.44c

19 Black Raven Co

Top tips. This question provides comprehensive practice of valuation techniques. In the exam you would most likely be expected to use three or four of these techniques to carry out calculations that would form the basis of discussions. Even in this question, you do need to make clear the basis of your calculations and the assumptions you are making (in (a) the assumptions are that the purchaser will accept the valuation, that the last five years are an appropriate indicator and so on).

Other important issues which this question raises include:

- Valuation (if any) of intangible assets
- Lack of likelihood that asset valuation basis would be used
- Adjustment to P/E ratios used in calculations because company is unquoted

Don't take all of the figures used in this answer as the only possibilities. You could for example have made adjustments to estimated earnings in (c) to allow for uncertainty, or used a different figure to 17%.

(a) **Earnings basis valuations**

If the purchaser believes that earnings over the last five years are an appropriate measure for valuation, we could take average earnings in these years, which were:

$$\frac{\$465,000}{5} = \$93,000$$

An appropriate P/E ratio for an earnings basis valuation might be the average of the three publicly quoted companies for the recent year. (A trend towards an increase in the P/E ratio over three years is assumed, and even though average earnings have been taken, the most recent year's P/E ratios are considered to be the only figures which are appropriate.)

	P/E ratio	
Albatross Inc	8.5	
Bullfinch Inc	9.0	
Crow Inc	10.0	
Average	9.167	(i)
Reduce by about 40% to allow for unquoted status	5.5	(ii)

Share valuations on a past earnings basis are as follows.

	P/E ratio	Earnings $'000	Valuation $'000	Number of shares	Value per share
(i)	9.167	93	852.5	300,000	$2.84
(ii)	5.5	93	511.5	300,000	$1.71

Because of the unquoted status of Black Raven Co, purchasers would probably apply a lower P/E ratio, and an offer of about $1.71 per share would be more likely than one of $2.84.

Future earnings might be used. Forecast earnings based on the company's five year plan will be used.

Expected earnings:		$
	Year 1	100,000
	Year 2	104,000
	Year 3	108,160
	Year 4	112,486
	Year 5	116,986
	Average	108,326.4 (say $108,000)

A share valuation on an expected earnings basis would be as follows.

P/E ratio	Average future earnings	Valuation	Value per share
5.5	$108,000	$594,000	$1.98

It is not clear whether the purchasing company would accept Black Raven's own estimates of earnings.

(b) **A dividend yield basis of valuation with no growth**

There seems to have been a general pattern of increase in dividend yields to shareholders in quoted companies, and it is reasonable to suppose that investors in Black Raven would require at least the same yield.

An average yield for the recent year for the three quoted companies will be used. This is 12%. The only reliable dividend figure for Black Raven Ltd is $45,000 a year gross, in spite of the expected increase in future earnings. A yield basis valuation would therefore be:

$$\frac{\$45,000}{12\%} = \$375,000 \text{ or } \$1.25 \text{ per share}.$$

A purchasing company would, however, be more concerned with earnings than with dividends if it intended to buy the entire company, and an offer price of $1.25 should be considered too low. On the other hand, since Black Raven is an unquoted company, a higher yield than 12% might be expected.

(c) **A dividend yield basis of valuation, with growth**

Since earnings are expected to increase by 4% a year, it could be argued that a similar growth rate in dividends would be expected. We shall assume that the required yield is 17%, rather more than the 12% for quoted companies because Black Raven Co is unquoted. However, in the absence of information about the expected growth of dividends in the quoted companies, the choice of 12%, 17% or whatever, is not much better than a guess.

$$P_0 = \frac{D_0(1+g)}{(r-g)} = \frac{45,000(1.04)}{(0.17-0.04)} = \$360,000 \text{ or } \$1.20 \text{ per share}$$

(d) **The discounted value of future cash flows**

The present value of cash inflows from an investment by a purchaser of Black Raven Ltd's shares would be discounted at either 18% or 14%, depending on the view taken of Black Raven Co's assets. Although the loan of $400,000 is secured on some of the company's property, there are enough assets against which there is no charge to assume that a purchaser would consider the investment to be backed by tangible assets.

The present value of the benefits from the investment would be as follows.

Year	Cash flow $'000	Discount factor 14%	PV of cash flow $'000
1	120	0.877	105.24
2	120	0.769	92.28
3	140	0.675	94.50
4	70	0.592	41.44
5	120	0.519	62.28
			395.74

A valuation per share of $1.32 might therefore be made. This basis of valuation is one which a purchasing company ought to consider. It might be argued that cash flows beyond year 5 should be considered and a higher valuation could be appropriate, but a figure of less than $2 per share would be offered on a DCF valuation basis.

(e) **Summary**

Any of the preceding valuations might be made, but since share valuation is largely a subjective matter, many other prices might be offered. In view of the high asset values of the company an asset stripping purchaser might come forward.

20 Margate

> **Top tips.** In this case study there are *many* alternative answers for all parts of the question, but the main requirement throughout the question is to demonstrate your knowledge of the principles involved by writing explanatory notes and comments.
>
> In part (a), try to choose three ratios with different purposes (e.g. profitability, liquidity, gearing) – but the P/E ratios are already given – so presumably no marks for calculating them, even though it is a relevant ratio!
>
> In part (b), there is a huge range of justifiable values for the company, even without estimating possible merger gains, on which no information is given. Again, the key is to justify the assumptions you make, Giving a range of possible answers means the expectations of different commentators are taken into account, and an indication of the risk involved is given.
>
> For the report in part (c), the most sensible figure to choose for a bid price would be something with a premium over current market value. The 'offer terms' means suggesting how many shares of Margate would be exchanged for a given number of Hastings' shares (eg 7 for 8). The bulk of the discussion marks can be earned by considering principles of takeover defences and reasons for merger synergy and needs to range quite widely. Your calculation for the value of the combined company should show how much would be owned by the original shareholders of Margate and how much by former Hastings shareholders.

(a) **Three key ratios**

Profitability: Return on shareholders' funds

	Margate Group plc £m	Hastings plc £m
Earnings £m	503	300
Shareholders' funds £m	2,020	1,450
Return on shareholders' funds	25%	21%

This ratio shows the **rate of return of equity earnings** compared with the book value of shareholders' funds. Margate Group plc has a **higher return** at present, a fact that is consistent with its lower P/E ratio, but inconsistent with its lower equity beta. The measure is **limited** by the fact that **book values** are used.

Gearing: Debt ratio

	Margate Group plc £m	Hastings plc £m
Long term debt	1,450	950
Shareholders' funds	2,020	1,450
Total long term funds	3,470	2,400
Debt ratio	42%	40%

Both companies have **higher debt ratios** than the industry average (30%), indicating that use of **debt finance** for the merger would probably be **inadvisable**. The figure for Hastings could be understated if its substantial overdraft is effectively used as long-term debt. Including the overdraft of £420 million, the debt ratio becomes 1,370/2,820 = 49%.

Liquidity: Current ratio

	Margate Group plc £m	Hastings plc £m
Current assets £m	1,125	645
Current liabilities £m	755	785
Current ratio	1.490	0.822

At less than 1, the current ratio of Hastings looks low. This is despite the fact that it carries **higher inventory levels** than Margate. The high overdraft probably needs restructuring into long term funds, otherwise a period of rapid growth may cause severe liquidity difficulties.

(b) **Range of possible values for Hastings plc**

P/E ratios

Hastings' **current P/E ratio** is 16, giving its equity shares a current market value of 16 × equity earnings £300 million = £4,800 million. It is highly unlikely that any offer below this figure would be attractive to shareholders, who would have no incentive to sell. Measured by the industry average P/E of 13, Hastings would be worth 13 × £300 million = £3,900 million. The higher value that Hastings enjoys at present is because of its **above-average growth expectations** and, probably, expectations of gains from a merger with another company.

The dividend valuation model

> **Top tips.** Many different calculation assumptions may be offered here. Two or three valuations would be sufficient.

The current dividend is £135 million. The cost of equity for Hastings can be estimated from the **Capital Asset Pricing Model**, k_e = 6% + (12% − 6%) 1.2 = 13.2%.

Possible valuation method

Using this cost of equity in the dividend valuation model, we obtain the following possible valuation figures:

(i) If, as some experts believe, the **supermarket contract results in zero growth**, the company's equity value would be 135/0.132 = £1,023 million, well below current market value.

(ii) On the optimistic side, if there was **dividend growth of 10% per year to perpetuity**, the equity value would be 135 × 1.1 / (0.132 − 0.10) = £4,640 million. This is more in line with current market value.

(iii) Dividend growth of 10% per annum for 5 years followed by a period of lower growth would result in a **valuation figure between these two values**.

Adjusted present value method

Hastings is relatively highly geared, which has the effect of increasing its equity beta. Since the acquisition would be financed by equity shares, the Adjusted Present Value method would use a discount rate based on the **cost of ungeared equity** to value Hastings, and there would be no gearing side effect. The cost of ungeared equity for Hastings would be lower than 13.7%, let us say 1.0, giving a cost of equity of 12%. The computations above would then lead to higher figures:

(i) **No dividend growth**: $135/0.12 = £1,125$ million

(ii) **Growth of 10% p.a. to perpetuity**: $135 \times 1.1 / (0.12 - 0.10) = £7,425$ million

(iii) **Growth of 10% for 5 years**, followed by slower growth: a figure between these two values

Summary

Based on existing information, the value of Hastings' equity can be calculated as somewhere between £1,023 and £7,425 million, with its **current market value** at £4,800 million.

(c)

To:	Board of Directors, Margate Group plc
From:	Financial Manager
Date:	13 December 20X1
Subject:	Report on the proposed acquisition of Hastings plc

Introduction

This report provides a financial evaluation of the proposed acquisition, recommends offer terms and discusses strategic issues.

(i) **Recommended bid price and offer terms**

Our calculations show that the intrinsic value of Hastings as a stand-alone company is somewhere in the **range £1,000 million to £7,400 million**. On the basis of the efficient market hypothesis, the **current market value** of £4,800 million is probably as good a guide to the company's value as any, but it should be remembered that the market will undoubtedly have factored some expected merger gains (see below) into the share price as a result of the recent bid by the US company.

Premium

However, if we are to make a bid, we will not be successful unless we offer a **premium over current market value**, giving the Hastings shareholders an incentive to sell. An offer price of approximately £5,000 million is suggested.

Synergy

It should be noted that if the possibility of merger gains is already factored into Hastings' share price, this offer price can only be justified if we have clear **plans** for **creating synergy** from the combination. Before going ahead, I suggest that we thoroughly investigate the possibilities, as indicated below.

Consideration

A share-for-share exchange should be offered as the terms for this merger, because:

(1) We have **insufficient cash**.

(2) As the **debt ratios** of both companies are above the industry average, I do **not recommend** any further **increase in borrowings** to finance this deal.

(3) Our company's shares have an **above average P/E ratio that**, though not as high as Hastings', indicates that they are a relatively good 'currency' at the moment.

I recommend that we offer **7 of our own shares for every 8 in Hastings**. At our current share price this would value Hastings shares at $7 \times 671p / 8 = 587.125$ pence, giving a total market value for Hastings equity of £4,991 million, a premium of 3.9% over the current market value.

Workings

Our share price is currently 671 pence.

Hastings' total number of shares in issue are 850million. At a total value of £5,000 million, Hastings' share price would be 588 pence.

The terms of the offer should be 588 of our shares for 671 of Hastings, which are approximately 7 of ours for 8 of theirs.

Revised bid

When we make our initial bid, the market will assess it. The effect on the share price will depend on whether the market anticipated the sort of bid that we shall be making, but it is possible that we may have to make a revised offer.

(ii)   **Strategy for making the offer**

To minimise the **risk of outright rejection** by the Hastings plc board, our strategy needs to take the following factors into account.

(1)   We must follow the **City Code** on Takeovers and Mergers, Stock Exchange regulations and the law, especially that on **insider dealing**. We are allowed to approach the board of directors of Hastings for informal talks, but must maintain **absolute secrecy** until we make a formal offer.

(2)   We will need to ensure that Hastings' directors are given **key roles** on the board of the combined company. This bid is most likely to succeed if management arrangements are those of a genuine merger rather than a takeover by ourselves.

(3)   We need to **emphasise the similarities** between the management styles of our companies, and the advantages of joining forces to compete effectively in Europe against world competition.

Risks in making the bid

(1)   The American company may decide to make a **counter offer**, resulting in an auction for Hastings' business, bidding up the price to an unrealistic level.

(2)   Hastings may appeal for an **investigation** by the Competition Commission, on the grounds that our bid is against the public interest.

(3)   Hastings' board may decide to **counter our offer** by making an offer to acquire us.

(4)   Hastings staff may decide to **mobilise public opinion** against us. Some key members may leave (see below).

(5)   Hastings' directors may have strengthened their **contract termination terms**: this needs to be investigated.

Risks of post-merger failure

(1)   There may be a **conflict of cultures** between the management of the two companies. Disagreements at board level may lead to widespread loss of morale. Key staff of Hastings may leave and set up on their own or join another competing company. For example the American company may decide to poach staff rather than making an increased offer for Hastings' business.

(2)   Our objective of achieving synergy may not be realised because of **poor planning**, lack of resolve to tackle the key issues, or shortage of funds for necessary capital investment.

(3)   **Incompatibility of information systems** between the companies is a common merger problem.

(iii) **Strategic and financial issues**

The rationale for the bid depends on the advantages that a combination of our companies would have over the existing 'stand-alone' businesses. Such combinations can create synergetic merger gains (the whole is worth more than the sum of the parts) by a number of mechanisms.

Increased market power

Elimination of Hastings as a major competitor might allow us to charge **more realistic prices** to customers on some of our less profitable operations. We are also likely to be able to negotiate **more favourable deals** with suppliers in terms of costs and payment terms. However, in this respect we must be careful to avoid the accusation that we have become a monopoly. Our combination will have more than a 25% share of the UK market and the Competition Commission may decide to mount an investigation.

Access to new market

The merger would enable us to **grow more rapidly** in Europe, where Hastings already has a strong base.

Combining complementary resources

Hastings' **superior knowledge of markets in Europe** fits well with our dominant position in the UK.

Achieving critical mass to enable effective competition

As trade barriers fall, our competition is worldwide rather than just the UK. Our defence to the potential monopoly accusation is that our **market share** in the **European Union** is still relatively small and we need this merger in order to be able to compete effectively in international markets.

Elimination of duplicated resources

Our research shows that recent restructuring of both our companies does **not** leave **much scope** for **staff reductions** except at the head offices, but there will be possibilities for rationalising our warehouse and depot locations, for example.

Elimination of management inefficiencies

For example, Hastings' **financial management** could be **improved** with savings in financing costs.

Post-acquisition value of combined group

Our company has 1,050 million shares in issue and Hastings has 850 million.

At offer terms of 7 for 8, we will issue 7/8 × 850m new shares in Margate = 743.8m.

Total Margate shares in issue would then be 1,050 +743.8 = 1,793.8m shares.

To maintain our existing share price, the value of the combined company would need to be 1,793.8 × 671p = £12,036m, shared as follows:

	No of shares	Share price (p)	Value £m
Original Margate shareholders	1,050.0	671	7,045
New shareholders from Hastings	743.8	671	4,991
	1,793.8		12,036

The existing market capitalisation of the two companies is as follows:

		£m
Margate	as above	7,045
Hastings	£300m × P/E16	4,800
		11,845

Size of synergistic gains

To maintain our existing share price, we would need to generate synergetic gains of £191 million (above those gains which have already been factored into the current share prices), which would accrue to the new shareholders from Hastings (£4,991m – £4,800m).

(1) On the down side, if we assume that a more realistic value for Hastings as a stand-alone company is in the region of £4,000 million, the synergy needed is closer to £1,000 million. Clearly we need to start work immediately on evaluating whether this is a **realistic proposition** and, if so, developing plans for implementing our ideas as swiftly as possible.

(2) On the optimistic side, if the market value of Hastings is realistic and our offer is accepted and we can generate an **additional synergy** of **£500 million**, say, the value of the company would be £12,345 million, split as follows:

	No of shares	Value £m	Original value £m	Gain £m	% gain
Original					
Margate shareholders	1,050.0	7,226	7,045	181	2.6%
New shareholders from Hastings	743.8	5,119	4,800	319	6.6%
	1,793.8	12,345		500	

The gains made by Hastings shareholders would be higher in percentage terms.

Financial advantages

Given that the preferred bid strategy is a share-for-share exchange, if the bid goes through the combined group's debt: equity ratio will be lower than either of the current companies. We can either accept that this reduction in financial risk would be beneficial (as the gearing of both companies currently is high for the industry), or we can take the opportunity to issue further debt. Perceived business risk is unlikely to fall because the merger does not involve diversification, and because of the uncertainties surrounding the supermarket project.

Conclusion

Whilst a merger would have some significant benefits, we would need to convince our shareholders that Hastings is not overvalued, before they approve the issue of the consideration shares. Other issues, in particular the reaction of Hastings and the Competition Commission, also need to be considered carefully.

21 Canadian Inc

MEMORANDUM

To: The Finance Director
From: Accountant
Date: 12 December 20X5
Subject: Proposed investment in local coal mine

(a) **Overall summary and conclusion**

I have performed an analysis of the available figures using the adjusted present value technique (APV). This method is appropriate because the project:

(i)   Represents an activity **fundamentally different** from that of the company
(ii)   Has a **different risk profile**, as evidenced by the differing betas, from Canadian
(iii)   Is to be financed using a **gearing ratio different** from the company
(iv)   Is a **significant investment** for the company (ie is not a marginal investment)

An alternative to this method might be the **adjusted discount rate method**, in which an estimate is made of the appropriate discount rate to use and the project cash flows discounted at this rate. However, insufficient data is available to perform this sort of analysis.

APV demonstrates that while the project appears to be marginally attractive under the stated assumptions (a positive NPV of $86,000), the total project allowing for the financing effects has a positive net present value of $2,010,000. These positive financing effects result from the interest savings on the Regional Development Board loan, plus the tax effects of the additional debt capacity of the firm.

However, I should stress that these figures assume a great deal about the future, both as regards the values of the factors that have been taken into account, and the factors that have been ignored. I would refer you to the later sections of this memo, but broadly:

(i)   There would be **substantial implications** for power station X if this pit were to close. These costs should also be considered in coming to our conclusion.

(ii)   Even if the power station is judged viable in the absence of the pit, **buying coal from overseas** will expose us to **currency fluctuations** which would need to be managed.

(iii)   **No sensitivity analysis** has been carried out. It would appear likely that the project is highly sensitive to the price of coal, and to the level of redundancy and environmental cleanup costs. This implies a high degree of political risk, which will be outstanding for five years

(b) **Workings**

The adjusted present value represents the NPV of the project based on an all equity financed situation, adjusted for any finance costs/benefits.

The appropriate discount rate is found from the formula:

$$\beta_a = \beta_e \frac{E}{E + D(1-t)} + \beta_d \frac{D(1-t)}{E + D(1-t)}$$

This should be based on the betas for the coal mining industry, which obviously has a different risk profile from that of the power generation industry.

$$\beta_a = 0.7 \times \frac{1}{1 + 1(1 - 0.3)} + 0.2 \times \frac{(1 - 0.3)}{1 + 1(1 - 0.3)} = 0.494$$

Therefore the appropriate discount rate is:

$$\begin{aligned} K_e &= 8\% + (16\% - 8\%) \times 0.494 \\ &= 12\% \end{aligned}$$

The cashflows generated by the project are therefore discounted at 12% to find the base NPV.

Cashflow forecast, $'000s

Year	0	1	2	3	4	5	6
Inflows							
Value of coal production		10,000	10,000	10,000	10,000	10,000	
Outflows							
Operating costs (3,000 × 3% inflation factor)		(3,090)	(3,183)	(3,278)	(3,377)	(3,478)	
Initial investment	(12,000)						
Final payment (17,000 × 1.03⁵)						(19,708)	
Tax			(1,173)		(1,313)	(1,347)	4,525
Tax from year 3					(1,258)		
Net cashflow	(12,000)	6,910	5,644	6,722	4,052	(14,533)	4,525
PV factor (12%)	1.000	0.893	0.797	0.712	0.636	0.567	0.507
Present value	(12,000)	6,171	4,498	4,786	2,577	(8,240)	2,294
NPV	86						

Working

Year	1	2	3	4	5
Tax calculations					
Operating cashflows					
Inflows	10,000	10,000	10,000	10,000	10,000
Outflows	(3,090)	(3,183)	(3,278)	(3,377)	(3,478)
Capital allowances					
On equipment	(1,500)	(1,125)	(844)	(633)	(1,898)
On mine	(1,500)	(1,500)	(1,500)	(1,500)	
Termination costs					(19,708)
Net taxable flow	3,910	4,192	4,378	4,490	(15,084)
Tax on taxable flow	1,173	1,258	1,313	1,347	(4,525)

Financing effects are as follows.

Borrowing effect

The company can borrow a total of $6 million (the regional development loan) plus the $3 million increase in the borrowing capacity as a result of this project. This means that debt benefits flow on a total of $9 million of additional debt. This is worth:

Debt benefit = Total debt × Canadian's borrowing rate × tax rate

Canadian's borrowing rate can be found using CAPM as:

$K_d = 8\% + (16\% - 8\%) \times 0.25 = 10\%$

Therefore the increase in debt capacity is worth:

$9 million × 10% × 30% = $270,000 pa

This tax benefit will be received between the years 2 and 6, and should be discounted at the cost of debt (10%).

$$\$270,000 \times 3.791 \times \frac{1}{1.10} = \$931,000$$

Regional development loan

The value of the subsidy can be related directly to the cost of debt that Canadian Inc would otherwise have paid (10%).

Therefore the saving in interest charges is:

$6 million × (10% − 4%) = $360,000 pa

Again, this is discounted at the cost of debt. However, there are two things to notice:

(i)   The benefit of the interest rate reduction is received in years 1-5.

(ii)   There is an associated reduction in the tax benefit, detrimental in years 2-6, of the interest cost × tax charge.

Present value of interest saved in years 1-5:

$360,000 × 3.791 = $1,365,000

Present value of tax benefit foregone in years 2-6:

$$6m \times 6\% \times 30\% \times 3.791 \times \frac{1}{1.10} = \$372,000$$

The expected APV of the project, including financing effects, will therefore be:

	$'000
NPV of project	86
NPV of tax shelter on interest	931
NPV of interest saved	1,365
NPV of tax benefit forgone on interest saved	(372)
	2,010

(c)   **Assumptions behind this report**

As regards the data used in the report, it assumes the following.

(i)   The various output and costing **figures** are reasonably **accurate**.

(ii)   The **cleanup** and **redundancy costs** are **correctly estimated** – this assumes a stable political environment over the next five years.

(iii)   The **price of coal** will **stay at the current level** for the foreseeable future.

(iv)   The **RPI** can be **accurately used** as a measure of the cost inflation factors that will affect the pit.

(v)   The Regional Development Board **loan is obtained**.

(vi)   **Retained earnings** are **available** to finance the equity component of the project. If additional equity finance were required then issue costs could make this project unviable.

(vii)   That the **debt capacity** added to the firm is **accurate**. It is not known how this figure is arrived at, but the project might well affect the total perceived risk of the firm for both equity and debt, and therefore change borrowing capacities for the rest of the firm.

(viii) The **tax regime** is at least as **favourable** as regards capital allowances as at present over the next five years

As regards the APV model, it assumes the following.

(i)   The value of the **tax shield** is the **full corporate tax rate**. This is questionable when shareholders obtain the benefit of a dividend imputation system and annual capital gains tax allowances.

(ii)   The **project** will **contribute** a **full $9 million** to the borrowing capacity of the group for the whole of its useful life. In reality it is likely that the asset base, and hence the borrowing capacity, will diminish over time.

(iii) The **CAPM** can be used to arrive at an **ungeared cost of capital**, which can then be used to discount the cash flows over five years. The CAPM is an annual model, so the assumption must be questioned.

(d) **Areas for further research**

(i) This memo is incomplete without a **detailed sensitivity analysis** being carried out. Such an analysis would seek to determine which of the above assumptions was likely to change, and by how much.

(ii) It is also not possible to assess whether this project is advisable in isolation from other **capital opportunities** and needs of the firm. It is unclear whether capital is in short supply.

(iii) The scenario presumes that there is **no alternative bidder for** the mine. However, it is possible that supplies to Station X might be secured by offering a fixed price contract to an alternative bidder for the supply of coal. In this case we ourselves can avoid the risks inherent in this industry, about which we know so little, and concentrate on our strengths.

22 Peden and Tulen

Top tips. (a) illustrates how shareholders gain from creditors in a bankruptcy scenario because of their limited liability. The key is that when Peden is a stand-alone company, the minimum value of its equity is zero, causing a drop in the value of debt, but when combined with a low-geared company the debt recovers its value at the expense of equity.

Examiner's comment. Many candidates aggregated equity and debt without considering their individual values, and produced implausible solutions. Candidates also ignored the narrative in the question that stated that operational synergy did not occur.

(a) **Value of Peden's shares**

To find the **value of Peden's equity shares**, subtract debt of $45m from the total value:

Peden	Recession	Slow growth	Rapid growth
	$m	$m	$m
Equity	(3)	10	30
Debt	45	45	45
Total	42	55	75

This gives a **negative value to equity** in the recession scenario, which cannot happen because the shares have limited liability. Assume the shares are zero value and the debt has declined to $42m because of bankruptcy risk. The expected value of equity of debt can then be computed:

Peden	Recession	Slow growth	Rapid growth	Expected value
Equity	0	10	30	12.50
Debt	42	45	45	44.55
Total	42	55	75	57.05

Value of Tulen's shares

To find the value of Tulen's equity shares, subtract debt of $10m from the total value:

Tulen	Recession	Slow growth	Rapid growth	Expected value
Equity	53	70	110	75.45
Debt	10	10	10	10.00
Total	63	80	120	85.45

Effect of merger

When the companies merge, **add** the **economic values** of **equity** and **debt** together. This means using the negative $3 million value for Peden's equity in the recession scenario. Its debt will be restored to $45 million because the bankruptcy risk will have disappeared by combination with a low geared company. This is known as the **coinsurance** effect.

Combined	Recession	Slow growth	Rapid growth	Expected value
Equity	50	80	140	87.50
Debt	55	55	55	55.00
Total	105	135	195	142.50

Summary

Expected equity values

	$m
Peden	12.50
Tulen	75.45
Total	87.95
Combined company	87.50
Loss in equity value after combination	0.45

Expected debt values

	$m
Peden	44.55
Tulen	10.00
Total	54.55
Combined company	55.00
Gain in debt value after combination	0.45

After the combination, in the absence of synergy, the total economic value of the businesses remains at $142.5 million, but the total expected value of debt has increased by $0.45m at the expense of equity. This is because, under the recession scenario, there is **no longer** a **bankruptcy risk** for the debt holders of Peden. The previous advantage conferred on Peden equity by limited liability has now disappeared.

Furthermore, the cash flows of the combined company may **reduce in volatility** because of the portfolio effect and this may further reduce the cost of debt, increasing its value.

(b) **Significance of financial post-audits**

(i) **Incentive for strategic planning**

The knowledge that a post-audit will take place will **discourage growth** by acquisition **without** proper strategic **analysis** and **planning**.

(ii) **Problem identification**

They **identify problems** which have occurred since the merger or acquisition, identify whether these were unexpected or whether contingency plans had been made, and ensure that management confront the problems.

(iii) **Forecasting methods assessment**

By **analysing results** against **forecasts** made before the merger or takeover, they provide valuable feedback on the **reliability** of the **forecasting** and **planning** methods used.

(iv) **Future plans**

They identify **factors** which may have been **overlooked** and which need to be incorporated into future merger and takeover proposals.

23 Gasco

> **Top tips.** This case study is a welcome change to most 'general questions' on mergers and takeovers as it provides a lot of detail for use as illustrations of synergy, stakeholder expectations and post-merger problems. You should state the general principles involved and illustrate them with examples drawn from the question.

(a)　There is frequently a mix of good and bad reasons behind a takeover bid. Amongst the good reasons, the most significant is the possibility of creating **synergy,** which means that the value of cash flows from the combined business is higher than the value of cash flows from the two individual businesses. Although CarCare and Gasco are in different market sectors, there are a number of areas which may generate synergy.

(i)　**Elimination of duplicated resources**. The most obvious areas are the marketing systems, the call centre systems and local offices and training facilities for mobile repair/emergency staff. Head office overheads may also be reduced.

(ii)　**Cross-selling**. Opportunities exist to cross-sell products to customers on the other company's database.

(iii)　**Building a critical mass** for non-core business. This might apply to the financial services areas of both businesses. The credit card and insurance businesses may gain from a combined brand name.

(iv)　**Reduction in the risk of the company's cash flow profile**. CarCare receives membership subscriptions in advance, whereas Gasco's customers will pay mainly in arrears. The combined cash flows will be perceived as less risky by shareholders and lenders.

(v)　The takeover of CarCare will **abolish its mutual status** and will allow equity funds for expansion to be raised more easily, by share issues made by the parent company, reducing the cost of capital.

Amongst the many possible bad reasons for takeover are:

(i)　The directors of Gasco **seeking the prestige** of a larger company
(ii)　Diversification with **no real strategic objective**
(iii)　Gasco using up surplus cash, **again with no strategic objective**

(b)　**Stakeholders**

The major stakeholders of CarCare are its members, who are both owners and customers, its directors and employees, and its creditors. Competitors will also be highly interested in the takeover.

Members

The members will have **mixed reactions.** The replacement of mutual status with marketable equity shares or cash will give them an immediate **'windfall' gain,** which many will welcome. However, the cost of this is **lost influence** on the future direction of CarCare. As customers, many may fear a reduction in the quality of service, particularly in the light of increased competition in the market and the fact that Gasco has to demonstrate that it is making a **return on its investment**. Others may disagree, on the basis that Gasco will be able to raise money for expansion, modernisation and improvements more easily than CarCare could as a mutual organisation.

CarCare's directors have a duty to ensure that they act in the **best interest** of **members.** However they will also be concerned about their own positions after the takeover and will wish to seek suitable positions in the new company's management structure. Some may fear loss of their jobs.

Employees

Employees will have **mixed reactions** depending on whether they are likely to be presented with additional opportunities or loss of status or redundancy. There is likely to be some **rationalisation** of the workforce except for those with highly specific skills, and for those who remain there may also be the threat of relocation. Employees will be seeking answers to these questions before the takeover happens, but are unlikely to receive comprehensive answers.

Payables

Payables, including bankers, will probably be **happy** with the **merger** provided that Gasco has no financial problems.

Competitors

Some competitors will fear that they will **lose market share** if the takeover enables new finance for expansion, improvement and marketing of CarCare. Others will be more optimistic, believing that CarCare will become less sensitive to the needs of customers.

(c)   Gasco may face a number of problems after the takeover has been achieved.

(i)   Former members of Gasco who did not agree with the takeover, and who may have been actively resisting it, may decide to **change their service provider** to another organisation. The parent company will have to be pro-active in giving confidence to all its CarCare customers.

(ii)   The two organisations probably had **different management styles**, Gasco being a stock exchange quoted company with a clear need for financial results and CarCare being more orientated to serving its customers and acting as a pressure group to represent their needs. Conflicts may arise between directors, managers and employees of CarCare after the takeover as a result of an enforced change in management style from Gasco.

(iii)   Actual and feared redundancies, relocations, changes in work practice, training methods and other problems may **demotivate CarCare employees,** causing resistance and a drop in productivity. In this respect, delays in information provision and decision making can make the situation worse.

(iv)   **Competitors may take advantage** of reorganisation problems at CarCare in order to gain market share.

24 Olivine

> **Top tips.** Our answer to part (a)(ii) assumes that the administrative savings have been achieved. Otherwise the answer to (a)(ii) is £(25 + 9.6)m/60m = 57.7 pence per share, and subsequent answers also change.
>
> **Examiner's comments.** The calculations in the first two parts of the question were generally well answered but the final part which required discussion of the calculations was not particularly well done. The terms of the proposed takeover favoured the target company's shareholders and candidates should have identified the need to achieve a more equitable outcome between the two shareholder groups by changing the offer price.

(a)   (i)   **The total value of the share offer**

Earnings per share = $25m/40m = $0.625
P/E ratio = 20
Share price = 20 × $0.625 = $12.50 per share
Share offer = 5 shares × (16m shares/4) = 20m shares issued
Value of share offer = $12.50 × 20 million = $250 million

(ii)   **Olivine earnings per share**

Earnings = $25m + $9.6m + $2.4m = $37.0m
Number of shares = 40m + 20m = 60 million
Earnings per share = $37.0m/60m = 61.7 cents per share

(iii) **Share price of Olivine**

Earnings per share (part ii) = 61.7 cents per share
Price earnings ratio = 20 × (100 − 5)% = 19
Share price = 19 × $0.617 = $11.72 per share

(b) **Effect on wealth of shareholders**

Olivine shareholders

Original holding = 40m shares @ $12.50 per share = $500m
New share price = $11.72
New share value = 40m shares @ $11.72 = $468.8m
Loss in shareholder wealth = $500m − $468.8m = $31.2m or 6.24%

Halite shareholders

Original earnings per share = $9.6m/16m shares = $0.60
Price/earnings ratio = 15
Share price = 15 × $0.60 = $9.00 per share
Original holding = 16m shares @ $9.00 = $144m
New holding = 20m shares @ $11.72 = $234.4m
Gain in shareholder wealth = $234.4m − $144m = $90.4m or 62.78%

(c) The market capitalisation of the separate businesses is (40m × $12.50) + (16m × $9.00) = $644m. When combined the market capitalisation will be 60m × $11.72 = $703.2m so there are benefits to be gained in overall terms.

Effect on share price

The **total share value** of Halite prior to the acquisition is $144 million. However the intended share issue by Olivine of 20 million shares has a value at Olivine's current share price of $250 million. The issue of so many shares to achieve this premium means that there is a small reduction in the size of the earnings per share of Olivine even when the earnings of Halite and the benefits of the acquisition are taken into account. This reduction in earnings per share together with a 5% reduction in the price/earnings ratio of Olivine after the acquisition would lead to a reduction in Olivine's share price from $12.50 per share before the acquisition to $11.72 per share after the acquisition. The estimate of the revised P/E ratio is possibly too high and needs further scrutiny.

This reduction in share value for Olivine shareholders would **result in a loss in shareholder value** from the acquisition of $31.2 million (6.24%). In contrast the generous premium being considered for the shares of Halite would lead to an increase in the value of the shares held by former Halite plc shareholders of $90.4 million (62.78%).

Beneficiaries of offer

If the proposed offer is made all of the benefit of the acquisition will accrue to the Halite plc shareholders and the Olivine shareholders will suffer a loss in share value. However, the dividend per share for Halite shareholders is likely to be lower in the future than it is at present.

The directors of Olivine might wish to consider a less generous offer than the current premium of $106 million ($250m − $144m) on the purchase of Halite. For example a share for share exchange would value the offer at $200 million (16 million shares @ $12.50 per share) thereby still providing a substantial premium to the Halite shareholders but with no loss to the Olivine shareholders.

25 Takeover regulation

(a) Takeover regulation in the UK, centred around the City Code, is based upon what is often referred to as a **'market-based model'** designed to protect a wide and **dispersed shareholder base**. This system which also prevails in the Commonwealth countries and the US is based on **case law** and the legal rules resulting from it. These seek to a great extent the protection of shareholder rights.

The second system, prevalent in continental Europe, is referred to as the **'block-holder'** or **stakeholder system** and relies on codified or civil law seeking to protect a broader group of stakeholders such as creditors, employees and the wider national interest.

The two systems differ not only in terms of their **regulatory framework** (**civil** versus **common law**) but also in terms of the underlying structure of ownership and control that they seek to address.

In the UK and the US the system is characterised by **wider share ownership** than in continental Europe where companies tend to be owned by **majority** or **near-majority stakes** held by a small number of investors.

In the Anglo-American model, the emphasis is on the **agency problem** and the protection of the **widely distributed shareholder base**.

The civil law countries rely via **legislation** on the monitoring by large shareholders, **creditors** and **employees**.

The **Takeovers Directive** lays down for the first time minimum EU rules concerning the regulation of takeovers of companies whose shares are traded on regulated markets. It is one of the measures adopted under the EU Financial Services Action Plan and aims to strengthen the single market in financial services.

The **Takeovers Directive** requires that certain of the activities of the **Takeover Panel** are placed within a legal framework bringing an end to the non-statutory approach to regulation in the UK. In terms of approach, the new regulatory model leads to the **convergence** of the **European system** to the **UK-US** one by adopting many of the elements of the **City Code**.

The City Code is divided into general principles and detailed rules which must be observed by persons involved in a merger or takeover transaction. The ten principles of the City Code are the following:

1 All the shareholders of the target company must be treated similarly

2 All information disclosed to one or more shareholders of the target company must be disclosed to all

3 An offer should only be made if it can be implemented in full

4 Sufficient information, advice and time to be given for a properly informed decision

5 All documentation should be of the highest standards of accuracy

6 All parties must do everything to ensure that a false market is not created in the shares of the target company

7 Shareholder approval

8 'Rights of control must be exercised in good faith and the oppression of a minority is wholly unacceptable'

9 The directors of both target and bidder must act in the interest of their respective companies

10 'Where control of a company is acquired ... a general offer to all other shareholders is normally required'

BPP
LEARNING MEDIA

(b) Some mergers, referred to as friendly, take place when the management of the respective firms negotiate an agreement that is beneficial to both sides.

However, not all takeovers are negotiated in this way and those that are perceived as hostile are likely to be resisted by the directors.

The defensive measures that can be taken to resist a hostile bid have developed over the years, mainly in the US during the wave of takeover bids of the 1980s.

The more aggressive tactics are designed to make the target less attractive to the bidder, often risk shareholders interests in favour of those of management.

Examples of such aggressive tactics include the following:

Golden parachute

This is where large compensation payments are agreed with top management in the case of a takeover.

Poison pill

Poison pills have many variants but the basic objective behind them is to give rights to existing shareholders to buy shares at a very low price or special preferential terms.

Crown jewels

This tactics is where the directors decide to sell the firm's most valuable assets making the firm less attractive as a result.

Restricted voting rights

Multiple voting rights can often be used as a means of allocation to certain shareholders disproportionate voting rights, enabling them to frustrate a bid.

In the US these takeover defences are allowed to a greater extent as they are subject to a very sophisticated and ever-developing set of rulings based on case law established during a period of over 25 years of court judgements.

In the UK, one of the principles of the Takeover Code is the requirement that the directors of the target company are not permitted to take any steps to frustrate a bid without the prior approval of the shareholders. This principle seeks to minimise the danger of the directors adopting measures that would risk the shareholders' interests in favour of their own.

In Europe an attempt was made by the Takeover Directive to introduce the break-through rule whereby a bidder with a specified proportion of shares would be able to break-through the company's multiple voting rights and exercise control as if one share one vote existed. However, this was considered unpopular and was introduced as an optional measure in continental Europe.

26 Atlas International

(a) We need to find the value of Global under the assumption that it will grow at 7%. We do not know the cost of equity for Global so we find it implicitly for the share price.

$$P = \frac{EPS}{k - g}$$

Or $22 = \dfrac{\$0.90}{k - 0.05}$ or $k = \dfrac{\$0.90}{\$22} + 0.05 = 0.0909$

The value of the target company is:

$$\frac{\$0.90}{0.0909 - 0.07} = \$43.04 \text{ per share}$$

The value of Global's equity will therefore be:

$43.04 \times 500,000 = \$21,521,739$

The value will increase by:

$21,521,739 - 11,000,000 = 10,521,739$

(b) The acquisition premium is:

$30 - $22 = $8 per share

or $4,000,000

The NPV of acquisition is:

NPV = Additional Revenues – Costs of Acquisition
   = 10,521,739 – 4,000,000
   = 6,521,739

The acquisition should proceed

(c) Atlas needs to issue another 250,000 shares. The value of the combined company will be $70,000,000 + 21,521,739 = 91,521,739$

The value of each share will be:

$$\frac{91,521,739}{1,250,000} = \$73.22$$

Cost of acquisition = $250,000 \times 73.22 - 11,000,000 = 7,304,348$

NPV of acquisition = $10,521,739 - 7,304,348 = 3,217,391$

The acquisition should proceed

27 Brive Inc

(a) and (b)

REPORT

To: Board of Directors
From: M Accountant
Date: 17 September 20X1
Subject: Proposed capital reconstruction

Introduction

The purpose of this report is to evaluate the implications of the proposed capital reconstruction of Brive Inc for the various affected parties, including the shareholders, debenture holders, unsecured payables and the bank. Calculations showing the effect of the reconstruction on the statement of financial position are included as an appendix to this report.

Ordinary shareholders

In the event of Brive going into liquidation, the ordinary shareholders would be most unlikely to receive anything for their shares, since the net proceeds of the liquidation would be as follows.

	$
Property	2,000,000
Plant	1,000,000
Inventory	1,700,000
Receivables	1,700,000
Liquidation costs	(770,000)
	5,630,000

The total amount due to the payables, bank and debenture holders is $8,600,000, leaving nothing available for the shareholders.

If the reconstruction is undertaken, the existing shareholders will have to provide an additional $1m of capital in subscribing to the rights issue. However, if the projections are correct the effect of this should be to bring Brive back into profit, with earnings after interest amounting to $1.4m ($1.75m – $0.35m) per annum. This amounts to earnings per share of 28c which should permit Brive to start paying a dividend and providing some return to the shareholders again. The fact that the company is returning to profit should also make it possible to sell the shares if required which is presumably difficult at the present time. However there would be a substantial shift in the balance of control with the existing shareholders being left with only 40% of the equity, the balance being in the hands of the present debenture holders.

Secured debenture holders

Under the existing arrangements, the amount owing to the debenture holders is $3m. Although the debentures are secured on the property which has a book value of $3m, in the event of a forced sale this would only be likely to realise $2m giving a shortfall of $1m. The debenture holders would rank alongside the bank and the other payables for repayment of this balance. As has been calculated above, the amount that would be realised on liquidation and available to the unsecured payables would be $3.63m (net of property proceeds). The total amount owed is:

	$m
Debenture holders	1.0
Bank (overdraft)	1.6
Payables	4.0
	6.6

The debenture holders would therefore only receive 55 cents in the pound on the balance owing, giving a total payout of 85 cents in the pound (($2m + $0.55m)/$3.0m).

Under the proposed scheme, the debenture holders would receive $2.8m of new capital in return for the old debentures ie 93.33 cents in the dollar in the form of capital rather than cash. Of this, $1.3m would be in the form of 14% unsecured loan stock, and the remainder in the form of equity. They would also have to subscribe an additional $1.5m to take up the rights issue. Their total investment in the reconstruction would therefore be:

	$m
Cash foregone from liquidation	2.55
Additional cash investment	1.50
	4.05

Returns would be:

	$
Interest ($1.3m × 14%)	182,000
Return on equity ($3m × 0.28)	840,000
	1,022,000

This represents a return of 25.23% which is likely to be above that which could be earned elsewhere thus making the scheme attractive to the debenture holders. However, in addition they would have to forgo their security on the property and rank partly with the unsecured payables and partly with the equity. They should therefore be confident of the ability of the management to deliver the projected returns before consenting to the scheme.

The bank

Since the overdraft is unsecured, the bank would rank for repayment alongside the unsecured payables. As calculated above, the amount to be repaid would be 55 cents in the dollar, and the bank would thus recover $880,000 in the event of a liquidation. In the reconstruction, the bank would have to write off $400,000 ($1,600,000 debt – $1,200,000 loan stock), but would receive interest of 14% per annum leading to repayment of the balance in five years' time.

The investment that the bank would be making would therefore be the cash forgone from the liquidation of $880,000. The annual returns would be $168,000 (14% × $1.2m) which represents a return on the incremental investment of 19.1%. Provided that the bank is confident of the financial projections of the management, it stands to receive $1.2m in five years' time. The effective return of 19.1% in the meantime should be in **excess of current overdraft rates**, and the level of security is improved since there would no longer be secured debenture holders ranking ahead of the bank for repayment. The scheme is therefore likely to be attractive to the bank.

Unsecured payables

If Brive goes into liquidation the unsecured payables will receive 55 cents in the dollar ie $2.2m. Under the proposed scheme they would stand to receive 75 cents (25% written down) in the pound with apparently no significant delay in payment. If Brive continues to operate they will be able to continue to trade with the company and generate further profits from the business. The proposed scheme therefore seems **attractive** from their point of view.

Conclusions

The proposed scheme appears to hold benefits for all the parties involved. It is also in the interests of Brive's customers and workforce for the company to continue to trade. However these benefits will only be realised if the directors are correct in their forecast of trading conditions and if the new investment can achieve the projected returns. All parties should satisfy themselves as to these points before considering proceeding further with the reconstruction.

	Before $'000	a	b	c	d	e–g	After $'000
Non-current assets	5,700	(2,100)				2,500	6,100
Current assets							
Inventory	3,500	(800)					2,700
Receivables	1,800	(100)					1,700
	5,300						4,400
Payables	(4,000)					1,000	(3,000)
Overdraft	(1,600)				1,600		0
Working capital	(300)						1,400
Total assets less current liabilities	5,400						7,500
10% Debentures	(3,000)			3,000			0
14% Stock				(1,300)	(1,200)		(2,500)
Net assets	2,400						5,000
Capital and reserves							
Share capital	4,000	(3,000)	1,500			2,500	5,000
Income statement	(1,600)		1,600				0
	2,400						5,000

28 Reorganisation

(a)   Potential problems with management buy outs:

(i)   Deciding on a fair price – management will obviously want to pay the lowest price possible, whilst the vendor will want to secure the highest possible price.

(ii)   Any geographical relocation may result in the loss of key workers.

(iii)   Maintaining a good relationship with suppliers and customers, particularly if key contacts that suppliers and customers were used to dealing with decide to leave as a result of the buy out.

(iv)   Availability of sufficient cash flow to maintain and replace fixed assets. This is one of the main problems with buy outs – cash is often very tight at the beginning of the venture.

(v)   Changes in work practices may not suit all employees.

(vi)   Maintaining financial arrangements with previous employees may be difficult – for example, pension rights.

(vii)   Many suppliers of funds will insist on representation at board level in order to maintain some control over how the funds are being used.

(b) In order to estimate the change in the value of equity, we can use forecast retained earnings figures, assuming dividends to be at the maximum 12 % level:

(All figures are in $000)

	0	1	2	3	4	5
EBIT	–	2,200	3,100	3,900	4,200	4,500
9.5% interest	–	713	713	713	713	713
Earnings before tax	–	1,487	2,387	3,187	3,487	3,787
Tax	–	446	716	956	1,046	1,136
Earnings after tax	–	1,041	1,671	2,231	2,441	2,651
Dividend (12%)	–	125	201	268	293	318
Retained earnings	–	916	1,470	1,963	2,148	2,333
Equity	17,500	18,416	19,886	21,849	23,997	26,330

$$\text{Compound growth interest rate} = \left[\sqrt[5]{\frac{26,330}{17,500}} \right] - 1 = 8.5\%$$

The 8.5% growth rate is considerably less than the 15% rise predicted by management, therefore it can be concluded that the management's estimate does not appear to be viable.

29 Treasury management

Top tips. A few easy marks may be available for discussing the role of the treasury function. (b) looks at the role from another angle.

(a) **Management of cash**

A central treasury department will normally have the responsibility for the **management of the group's cash flows** and borrowings. Subsidiaries with surplus cash will be required to submit the cash to the treasury department, and subsidiaries needing cash will borrow it from the treasury department, not from an external bank.

Borrowing

A central treasury will also be given the **responsibility for borrowing** on behalf of the group. If a subsidiary needs capital to invest, the treasury department will borrow the money required, and lend it on to the subsidiary. The subsidiary will be responsible for **paying interest** and **repaying the capital** to the treasury department, which will in turn be responsible for the interest and capital payments to the original lenders.

Risk management

Another function of the treasury department will be to **manage the financial risk** of the group, such as currency risk and interest rate risk. Within broad guidelines, the treasurer might have authority to decide on the balance between fixed rate and floating rate borrowing, and to use swaps to adjust the balance. The department would also be responsible for arranging forward exchange contracts and other hedging transactions.

Taxation

The central treasury department could also be responsible for the **tax affairs** of the group, and an objective would be to minimise the overall tax bill. To accomplish this effectively, the treasury must have **authority to manage transfer prices** between subsidiaries in the group, as a means of transferring profits from high-tax countries to lower-tax countries.

(b) The treasury function needs information from within and from outside the organisation to carry out its tasks.

(i) From each subsidiary within the group, it will need **figures for future cash receipts and payments**, making a distinction between definite amounts and estimates of future amounts. This information about cash flows will be used to **forecast the cash flows of the group**, and identify any future borrowing needs, particularly short-term and medium-term requirements. Figures should be provided regularly, possibly on a daily basis.

(ii) Information will also be required about **capital expenditure requirements**, so that long-term capital can be made available to fund it.

(iii) Subsidiary finance managers should be encouraged to **submit information** to the **treasury department** about local market and business conditions, such as prospects for a change in the value of the local currency, or a change in interest rates.

(iv) From outside the group, the treasury will need a **range of information** about current market prices, such as exchange rates and interest rates, and about which banks are offering those prices. Large treasury departments will have a link to one or more information systems such as Reuters and Bloomberg.

(v) The treasury department should be alert to any **favourable market opportunities** for raising new debt capital. The treasurer should maintain regular contact with several banks, and expect to be kept informed of opportunities as they arise.

(vi) Where the treasury is responsible for the group's tax affairs, information will also be needed about **tax regulations** in each country where the group operates, and changes in those regulations.

30 Expo plc

> **Top tips.** The numerical part of this question is a good example of how you might be tested on forward and money market alternatives to hedging. However the rest of the question demonstrates that you need to be able to discuss why and how risk can be dealt with. Remember that hedging everything will be expensive, but only hedging certain transactions may be more expensive still. (b) shows the importance of matching; remember that the company may be able to use a hard currency if the local currency cannot be used. There are however other possibilities and your answer should briefly mention these.

(a) To: The Treasurer
From: Assistant
Date: 12 November 20X7

(i) Comparison of two methods of hedging exchange risk

Method 1

Expo borrows SFr750,000.

Three months interest is SFr750,000 $\times$ 3% $\times$ 3/12 = SFr5,625.

The customer pays SFr750,000, which repays the loan principal but not the interest. The interest must be paid by converting dollars. Since the interest is known in advance, this can be covered on the forward market at a cost of 5625/2.3688 = $2,375.

Meanwhile, the SFr750,000 is converted to dollars at the original spot rate 2.3834 to give $314,677. Assume that this is used to repay the company's short-term borrowings. Interest saved will be $314,677 $\times$ 6% $\times$ 3/12 = $4,720.

So, at the end of three months, the net dollar cash from the transaction is:

$314,677 + $4,720 – $2,375 = $317,022.

Method 2

The exchange rate is agreed in advance. Cash received in three months is converted to produce 750,000/2.3688 = $316,616.

Conclusion

On the basis of the above calculations, Method 1 gives a slightly better receipt. Banker's commission has been omitted from the figures.

(ii) **Factors to consider before deciding whether to hedge foreign exchange risk using the foreign currency markets**

Risk-averse strategy

The company should have a clear strategy concerning how much foreign exchange risk it is prepared to bear. A highly risk-averse or 'defensive' strategy of hedging all transactions is expensive in terms of commission costs but recognises that floating exchange rates are very unpredictable and can cause losses high enough to bankrupt the company.

Predictive strategy

An alternative 'predictive' strategy recognises that if all transactions are hedged, then the chance of currency gains is lost. The company could therefore attempt to forecast foreign exchange movements and only hedge those transactions where currency losses are predicted. The fact is that some currencies are relatively predictable (for example, if inflation is high the currency will devalue and there is little to be gained by hedging payments in that currency).

This is, of course, a much more risky strategy but in the long run, if predictions are made sensibly, the strategy should lead to a higher expected value than that of hedging everything and will incur lower commission costs as well. The risk remains, though, that a single large uncovered transaction could cause severe problems if the currency moves in the opposite direction to that predicted.

Best strategy

A sensible strategy for our company could be to set a cash size for a foreign currency exposure above which all amounts must be hedged, but below this limit a predictive approach is taken or even, possibly, all amounts are left unhedged.

Matching

Before using any technique to hedge foreign currency transactions, receipts and payments in the same currency at the same date should be offset. This technique is known as 'matching'. For example, if the company is expecting to receive SFr750,000 on 31 March and to pay SFr600,000 on the same day, only the net amount of SFr150,000 needs to be considered.

Matching can be extended to receipts and payments which do not take place on exactly the same day by simply hedging the period and amount of the difference between the receipt and payment. A company like ours which has many receipts and payments in European currencies should consider matching assets with liabilities in the same currency. For example if we have total Swiss debtors of SFr2million, we should borrow SFr2million on overdraft to match the debtor.

(b)   **Matching**

If the foreign subsidiary is selling predominantly **matching** in its own country, the principle of matching assets and liabilities says that the subsidiary should be **financed as far as possible** in the **currency of that country**. Ideally the subsidiary will be highly geared with loans and overdrafts in the developing country's currency. If local finance has not been used and the sales invoice which is about to be sent is large, then an overdraft in the same currency should be taken out and the receipt converted to sterling immediately.

Positively correlated currency

If it is impossible to borrow in the local currency, Expo plc should attempt to find a **hard currency** which is **highly positively correlated** with the local currency. For example, some countries have a policy of pegging their currency to the US dollar. The receipt can then be hedged by selling the US dollar forward.

This technique is, however, open to the risk that the local currency suddenly devalues against the dollar, as happened in 1997 with a number of Asian currencies. The likelihood of this happening is high if there is high inflation in the country and it has low reserves.

If Expo Inc is fairly certain that the local currency is going to devalue and that it cannot borrow in that currency, the remaining alternatives are:

(i)   To **increase the sales price** by the amount of the expected devaluation and bear the risk

(ii)   To **invoice in a hard currency**, for example US dollars, which can then be sold forward

(iii)   To **arrange a 'counter-trade' agreement** (ie barter) in which the sale of Expo's textiles is paid for by the purchase of local raw materials or other products

31 Fidden plc

(a)   Techniques for protecting against the risk of adverse foreign exchange movements include the following.

(i)   A company could trade only in its own currency, thus transferring all risks to suppliers and customers.

(ii)   A company could ensure that its assets and liabilities in any one currency are as nearly equal as possible, so that losses on assets (or liabilities) are matched by gains on liabilities (or assets).

(iii)   A company could enter into forward contracts, under which an agreed amount of a currency will be bought or sold at an agreed rate at some fixed future date or, under a forward option contract, at some date in a fixed future period.

(iv)   A company could buy foreign currency options, under which the buyer acquires the right to buy (call options) or sell (put options) a certain amount of a currency at a fixed rate at some future date. If rates move in such a way that the option rate is unfavourable, the option is simply allowed to lapse.

(v)   A company could buy foreign currency futures on a financial futures exchange. Futures are effectively forward contracts, in standard sizes and with fixed maturity dates. Their prices move in response to exchange rate movements, and they are usually sold before maturity, the profit or loss on sale corresponding approximately to the exchange loss or profit on the currency transaction they were intended to hedge.

(vi)   A company could enter into a money market hedge. One currency is borrowed and converted into another, which is then invested until the funds are required or funds are received to repay the original loan. The early conversion protects against adverse exchange rate movements, but at a cost equal to the difference between the cost of borrowing in one currency and the return available on investment in the other currency.

(b) (i) 1 Forward exchange market

The rates are:

	$/£
Spot	1.7106 – 1.7140
3 months forward	1.7024 – 1.7063
6 months forward	1.6967 – 1.7006

The net payment three months hence is $£116,000 - \dfrac{\$197,000}{1.7063} = £546$.

The net payment six months hence is $\dfrac{\$(447,000 - 154,000)}{1.6967} = £172,688$.

Note that the dollar receipts can be used in part settlement of the dollar payments, so only the net payment is hedged.

2 Money market

$197,000 will be received three months hence, so:

$$\frac{\$197,000}{(1 + 0.09 \times \frac{3}{12})} = \$192,665$$

may be borrowed now and converted into sterling, the dollar loan to be repaid from the receipts.

The net sterling payment three months hence is:

$$£116,000 - \frac{\$197,000}{1 + (0.09 \times \frac{3}{12})} \times \frac{1}{1.7140} \times (1 + (0.095 \times \frac{3}{12})) = £924$$

The equation for the $197,000 receipt in three months is to calculate the amount of dollars to borrow now (divide by the dollar borrowing rate) and then to find out how much that will give now in sterling (divide by the exchange rate). The final amount of sterling after three months is given by multiplying by the sterling lending rate.

$293,000 (net) must be paid six months hence. We can borrow sterling now and convert it into dollars, such that the fund in six months will equal $293,000. The sterling payment in six months time will be the principal and the interest thereon. A similar logic applies as for the equation above except that the situation is one of making a final payment rather than a receipt.

The sterling payment six months hence is therefore

$$\frac{293,000}{1 + 0.06 \times \frac{6}{12}} \times \frac{1}{1.7106} \times (1 + 0.125 \times \frac{6}{12}) = £176,690$$

(ii) Available put options (put, because sterling is to be sold) are at $1.70 (cost 3.45 cents per £) and at $1.80 (cost 9.32 cents per £).

Using options at $1.70 gives the following results.

$$\frac{\$293,000}{1.70\$/£} = £172,353$$

Contracts required $= \dfrac{£172,353}{£12,500} = 14$ (to the next whole number)

Cost of options $= 14 \times 12,500 \times 3.45$ cents $= \$6,038$

(translated at today's spot rate $= £3,530$)

14 contracts will provide, for $£12,500 \times 14 = £175,000$, $\$(175,000 \times 1.70) = \$297,500$.

The overall cost is £175,000 + $\dfrac{\$293{,}000 + \$6{,}038 - \$297{,}500}{1.6967} = £175{,}906$

As this figure exceeds the cost of hedging through the forward exchange market (£172,688), use of $1.70 options would have been disadvantageous.

Using options at $1.80:

$\dfrac{\$293{,}000}{1.80\$/£} = £162{,}778$

Contracts required = $\dfrac{£162{,}778}{£12{,}500} = 14$ (to next whole number)

Cost of options = $14 \times 12{,}500 \times 9.32$ cents = $16,310 (÷ 1.7106 = £9,535)

14 contracts will provide, for £12,500 × 14 = £175,000, 175,000 × 1.80 = $315,000.

The overall cost Is £175,000 + $\dfrac{\$293{,}000 + \$16{,}310 - \$315{,}000}{1.7006} = £171{,}654$

This figure is less than the cost of hedging through the forward exchange market, so use of $1.80 options would have been preferable.

(iii)   Foreign currency options have the advantage that while offering protection against adverse currency movements, they need not be exercised if movements are favourable. Thus the maximum cost is the option price, while there is no comparable limit on the potential gains.

32 Exchange rate forecasts

> **Top tips**. In (a) (i) and (b) there are two alternative versions of the International Fisher Effect and Purchasing Power Parity formulae. Either one will give the correct result. In (a)(ii) you must distinguish between the terms 'unbiased' and 'accurate', and state some of the assumptions behind the IFE formula. In (b) the best type of hedge where it is uncertain whether cash is needed is a currency option.
>
> In (a) marks were split 50% IFE calculations, 50% comment. 5 out of 8 marks were available in (b) for calculations of the tender price and conclusion, with 3 marks being available for the alternative hedges.

(a)   (i)   To: Managing Director

From: Financial analyst

Predictions of Euro/$ exchange rate

If exchange rates are freely floating and interest rates are also freely determined by market forces, then, according to the International Fisher Effect, interest rate differentials between two countries can be applied to the current exchange rate to give an unbiased predictor of the future exchange rate.

Predicted future exchange rate = spot rate × $(1 + i_f)/(1 + i_{US})$

This gives year 1 exchange rate as 1.667 × 1.035/1.06 = 1.6277, and year 2 as 1.6277 × 1.035/1.06 = 1.589 Euro/$.

The non-executive director is wrong, having applied the formula wrongly as 1.667 × (1 + $0.02358)^2$ = 1.747 Euro/$.

> **Top tips**. An alternative version of the formula gives the predicted figure as follows:
>
> Using the formula $(i_f - i_{uk})/(1 + i_{US})$, the predicted future exchange rate would change by:
>
> (0.035 − 0.06)/1.06 = -2.358%. This implies that the Euro is predicted to strengthen against the dollar by 2.36%.

> If this happens for two years, the predicted exchange rate will be $1.667 \times (1 - 0.02358)^2 = 1.667 \times 0.97642^2 = 1.589$ Euro/\$.

(ii) **Errors in prediction**

The fact that a predicted exchange rate is **unbiased** does not make it accurate. Unbiased simply means that the rate is as likely to be above the prediction as below it. The margin of error on the prediction over two years will be very large, even if other factors remain the same, which is unlikely. Over the next two years interest rates are almost certain to change with changing economic conditions.

Assumptions

The **assumptions** behind the IFE model are also **unlikely to hold**. The model assumes that the currencies are freely traded on the market with, for example, no government intervention, and that the current exchange rate represents an equilibrium position. The forecast exchange rate is therefore very unlikely to be accurate.

(b) **Currency options**

The best form of protection against foreign exchange risk, in a situation where it is uncertain whether there will be a need for the currency to be exchanged, is a **currency option**. A forward contract cannot be avoided if the contract is lost and could create a currency loss, whereas a currency option can be allowed to lapse if it is not advantageous. The disadvantage of a currency option is the 'up-front' premium, which is non-refundable and can be expensive.

Period of option

The option is needed **from the date** the **tender is made** to **the date the results are announced**. Beyond that point, if the contract is won, currency protection could be achieved by a money market hedge (borrowing Dinars on the strength of the future sales proceeds), or by another option, but forward contracts do not appear to be available.

Since the date of award of the contract is unknown, an alternative hedge would be to take out an **option** for the **whole 18 month period**. The company would purchase an option to sell (put) Dinars for Euros in 18 months' time.

Prediction of exchange rate

If no hedge is used, a prediction of the exchange rate in 18 months is needed to estimate the tender price.

The spot rate is 0.256 – 0.260 Euros per Dinar. The rate for selling Dinars is 0.256 (when you sell Dinars you will get the lower number of Dinars).

The formula is: $\dfrac{\left(i_E - i_D\right)}{\left(1 + i_D\right)}$

The Euro is predicted to strengthen against the Dinar: $\dfrac{(3\% - 9\%)}{1.09} = -5.505\%$ per year.

In 18 months (1.5 years) the exchange rate is predicted to be:

$0.256 \times (1 - 0.0505)^{1.5} = 0.235$ Euros per Dinar.

Purchasing power parity has been used instead of the International Fisher effect as it is regarded as more reliable.

The Euro cost in 18 months' time is predicted to be €340,000. A 25% margin gives a price of €425,000.

If no hedge is used, the recommended tender price is: $\dfrac{425,000}{0.235} = 1,808,511$ Dinars.

If an option hedge using today's exchange rate is used, the price should be 425,000/0.256 = 1,660,156 Dinars *plus* the cost of the option.

33 USA Options

(a) **Current spot rate**

At the current exchange rate of £1 = $1.6100, the receipt of $1,800,000 will produce £1,118,012.

Participating option

Using the **participating option**, there is no premium. An examination of possible receipts under 4 possible exchange rates in 6 months time shows the following.

	$1.55	$1.60	$1.65	$1.70
	£	£	£	£
Spot market				
At opening spot rate $1.8 million/$1.61	1,118,012	1,118,012	1,118,012	1,118,012
At closing spot rate $1.8 million/closing rate	1,161,290	1,125,000	1,090,909	1,058,824
Gain/(loss)	43,278	6,988	(27,103)	(59,188)
Options market				
Buy at	1.65	1.65	1.65	1.65
Sell at	1.55	1.60	1.65	1.70
Exercise?	No	No	Yes/No	Yes

Outcome of option position

			As for $1.65 on spot market	As for $1.65 on spot market
Net outcome	£	£	£	£
Gain/(loss)	43,278	6,988	(27,103)	(27,103)
Half gain to bank	(21,639)	(3,494)		
Net gain/(loss)	21,639	3,494		

Traded option

Set up option

(i) Contract date June

(ii) Option type call

(iii) Strike price $1.65 and $1.70 have premium costs less than £10,000. Choose $1.65 for comparison

(iv) Number of contracts

$$\frac{1,800,000 \div 1.65}{31,250} \approx 34.9 \text{ contracts, say } 35$$

(v) Tick size = 31,250 × 0.0001
= $3.125

(vi) Premium $= \dfrac{1.1}{100} \times 31{,}250 \times 35$

$\qquad\qquad\qquad = \$12{,}031 @ 1.605$

$\qquad\qquad\qquad = £7{,}494$

Closing prices

As for participating option.

Outcome

		$1.55	$1.60	$1.65	$1.70
(i)	Options market				
	Strike price call	$1.65	$1.65	$1.65	$1.65
	Closing price	$1.55	$1.60	$1.65	$1.65
	Exercise ?	No	No	Yes/no	Yes
	Tick movement			500	
	Options outcome			$500 \times 35 \times 3.125 = \$54{,}688$	

		£	£	£	£
(ii)	Net outcome				
	Spot market gain/(loss) as for participating option	43,278	6,988	(27,103)	(59,188)
	Options market gain ÷ spot rate				32,169
	Options premium	(7,494)	(7,494)	(7,494)	(7,494)
		35,784	(506)	(34,597)	(34,513)

Comparison of the two pay-off schedules shows that using the participating option is probably preferable, as the resulting cash receipt is less sensitive to exchange rate fluctuations and, in particular, shows a lower maximum loss.

Creation of straddle option

As a more advanced use of traded options, the company could consider creating a straddle option. In order to hedge the purchase of pounds with dollars, the company should buy call options and sell put options at the same exercise price.

For example, the cost of purchasing $1.60 call options (5.3 cents) can be offset by selling $1.60 put options (4.0 cents). The net premium cost per £ is 1.3 cents.

Receipt $= 1{,}800{,}000/1.60$

$\qquad\quad = £1{,}125{,}000$

Premium $= \$1.3/100 \times 1{,}125{,}000$

$\qquad\quad = \$14{,}625$, which at today's spot rate of $1.6055 would be £9,109, which is within the £10,000 limit.

Effect of straddle

The combination of two options on the same exercise price *fixes* the exchange rate to £1 = $1.60. When the net premium cost is added, the effective exchange rate for buying pounds with dollars is £1 = $1.613. This is an alternative to using forward or futures contracts.

Collars

Use of collars with calls and puts on different exercise prices gives a **pay off schedule** with a **risk profile intermediate** between a fixed return and the call option pay off shown above.

(b)   **Matching assets and liabilities**

If the foreign subsidiary is selling predominantly in its own country, the principle of **matching assets and liabilities** says that the subsidiary should be financed as far as possible in the currency of that country. Ideally the subsidiary will be highly geared with loans and overdrafts in the developing country's currency. If local finance has not been used and the sales invoice which is about to be sent is large, then an overdraft in the same currency should be taken out and the receipt converted to sterling immediately.

Use of hard currency

If it is impossible to borrow in the local currency, the company should attempt to find a hard currency which is highly positively correlated with the local currency. For example, some countries have a policy of pegging their currency to the US dollar. The receipt can then be hedged by selling the US dollar forward.

This technique is, however, open to the risk that the local currency suddenly devalues against the dollar, as happened in 1997 with a number of Asian currencies. The likelihood of this happening is high if there is high inflation in the country and it has low reserves.

Other options

If the company is fairly certain that the local currency is going to devalue and that it cannot borrow in that currency, the **remaining alternatives** are:

(i)   **Increase the sales price** by the amount of the expected devaluation and bear the risk

(ii)   **Invoice in a hard currency**, for example US dollars, which can then be sold forward

(iii)   **Arrange a 'countertrade' agreement** (ie barter) in which the sale of the company's textiles is paid for by the purchase of local raw materials or other products

34 Curropt plc

(a)   The department's view that the US dollar will strengthen is in **agreement** with the **indications** of the forward market and the futures market. Forward and futures rates show a **stronger dollar** than the spot rate. The forward rate is often taken as an **unbiased** predictor of what the spot rate will be in future. However, future events could cause large currency movements in **either direction**.

(b)   The **company needs to buy dollars in June.**

Forward contract

A forward currency contract will fix the exchange rate for the date required near the end of June. If the exact date is not known, a range of dates can be specified, using an **option forward contract**. This will remove currency risk **provided that the franchise is won**. If the **franchise is not won** and the group has no use for US dollars, it will still have to buy the dollars at the forward rate. It will than have to sell them back for pounds at the spot rate which might result in an exchange loss.

Futures contract

A currency hedge using futures contracts will attempt to create a **compensating gain** on the futures market which will **offset** the **increase** in the **sterling cost** if the dollar strengthens. The hedge works by **selling sterling futures** contracts now and closing out by **buying sterling futures** in **June** at a lower dollar price if the dollar has strengthened. Like a forward contract, the exchange rate in June is effectively fixed because, if the dollar weakens, the futures hedge will produce a loss which counter-balances the cheaper sterling cost. However, because of inefficiencies in future market hedges, the exchange rate is not fixed to the same level of accuracy as a forward hedge.

A futures market hedge has the same weakness as a forward currency contract in the franchise situation. If the franchise is not won, an **exchange loss** may result.

Currency option

A currency option is an ideal hedge in the franchise situation. It gives the company the **right but not the obligation** to sell pounds for dollars in June. It is only exercised if it is to the company's advantage, that is if the dollar has strengthened. If the **dollar strengthens** and the franchise is won, the exchange rate has been **protected**. If the dollar strengthens and the **franchise is not won**, a **windfall gain** will result by **selling pounds** at the exercise price and buying them more cheaply at spot with a stronger dollar.

(c) **Results of using currency hedges if the franchise is won**

Forward market

Using the forward market, the rate for **buying dollars** at the end of June is 1.4310 US$/£. The cost in sterling is 15 million/1.4310 = £10,482,180.

Futures

Date of contract

June future

Type of contract

Sell sterling futures

Number of contracts

$$\frac{15,000,000}{1.4302 \times 62,500} = 167.8 \approx 168 \text{ contracts}$$

Tick size

0.0001 × 62,500 = $6.25

Closing futures price

Three possible spot price scenarios

1.3500
1.4500
1.5500

As told futures price is in the same relationship to spot price, futures price at end of June

(i)   1.3500 + (1.4302 – 1.4461) = 1.3341
(ii)   1.4500 + (1.4302 – 1.4461) = 1.4341
(iii)   1.5500 + (1.4302 – 1.4461) = 1.5341

Hedge outcome

	1.3500	1.4500	1.5500
	$	$	$
Opening futures price	1.4302	1.4302	1.4302
Closing futures price	1.3341	1.4341	1.5341
Movement in ticks	961	(39)	(1,039)
Futures profits /(losses)	1,009,050	(40,950)	(1,090,950)
168 × tick movement × 6.25	1,009,050	(40,950)	(1,090,950)

Net outcome

	$	$	$
Spot market payment	(15,000,000)	(15,000,000)	(15,000,000)
Futures market (profits)/losses	1,009,050	(40,950)	(1,090,950)
	(13,990,950)	(15,040,950)	(16,090,950)
Translated at closing rate	£10,363,667	£10,373,069	£10,381,258

Options

Date of contract

June

Option type

Buy put

Exercise price

Exercise price	Premium	Net
1.4000	0.0038	1.3962
1.4250	0.0068	1.4182
1.4500	0.0238	1.4262

Choose 1.4500

Number of contracts

$$\frac{15,000,000 \quad 1.4500}{31,250} = 331.03 \approx 331 \text{ contracts}$$

Tick size

$31,250 \times 0.0001 = \$3.125$

Premium

$0.0238 \times 31,250 \times 331 = \$246,181$ at 1.4461
$\qquad\qquad\qquad\qquad\quad = £170,238$

Outcome

	1.3500 $	1.4500 $	1.5500 $
Option market			
Strike price	1.4500	1.4500	1.4500
Closing price	1.3500	1.4500	1.5500
Exercise?	Yes	No	No
Tick movement	1,000	–	–
Outcome of	1,000		
options position	× 331		
	× 3.125		
	= 1,034,375		

Net outcome

	1.3500 $	1.4500 $	1.5500 $
Spot market payment	(15,000,000)	(15,000,000)	(15,000,000)
Options	1,034,375		
	(13,965,625)	(15,000,000)	(15,000,000)
	£	£	£
Translated at closing spot rate	(10,344,907)	(10,344,828)	(9,677,419)
Premium	(170,238)	(170,238)	(170,238)
	10,515,145	10,515,066	9,847,657

Summary

The company will either choose to purchase a **future** or an **option**. Although futures are more advantageous at lower exchange rates, the net benefits of using an option if the rate is $1.5500 are much greater than the difference between futures and options at 1.3500 and 1.4500.

35 Carrick plc

> **Top tips.** The first part of this question should be fairly straightforward. It is easy however to write more than is strictly necessary on these areas, and leave yourself insufficient time for the rest of the question. The key things to bring out is how each instrument limits interest rate risk by limiting or eliminating the effects of interest rate changes on the company.
>
> In (b) remember that Carrick is **receiving** interest so it must buy a call option to limit its exposure to falls in interest rates. As a collar is being constructed, Carrick must sell a put option to counterbalance buying the call option.
>
> The answer works through the key stages:
>
> - Choice of options
> - No of contracts
> - Premium payable
> - Effects of collar
> - Results of collar
>
> You need to show in the answer:
>
> - Technical expertise (choosing 9400 for the initial option, evaluating the other possible prices but ignoring 9450 as it's not relevant)
>
> - Numerical abilities (getting the premium, number of contracts and gain calculation right)
>
> - Depth of discussion (the question asks you to evaluate and that implies detailed analysis, explaining what will happen at the various rates, and also explaining that the choice is not clear-cut – 9250 has the largest potential benefits but also the largest definite costs)

(a) **Interest rate exposure**

Interest rate exposure arises when a company's borrowing is such that a change in interest rates might expose it to interest charges that are unacceptably high. For example, if a company has a large tranche of debt at a fixed rate of interest that is due for repayment in the near future, and the loan is to be replaced or renegotiated, the company would be vulnerable to a sudden increase in market interest rates.

Risk management

Risk management in this context involves using **hedging techniques** to reduce or 'cover' an exposure. However, hedging has a cost, which will either take the form of a **fee** to a financial institution or a **reduction in profit**, and this must be weighed against the reduction in financial risks that the hedge achieves. The extent to which the exposure is covered is known as the '**hedge efficiency**'. A perfect hedge has an efficiency of 100%.

Methods of managing interest rate risk include the following.

Forward interest rate agreements (FRAs)

A FRA is an agreement, usually between a company and a bank, about the **interest rate** on a future loan or deposit. The agreement will **fix the rate of interest** for borrowing for a certain time in the future. If the actual rate of interest at that time is above that agreed, the bank pays the company the difference, and vice versa. Thus the company benefits from effectively fixing the rate of interest on a loan for a given period, but it may miss the opportunity to benefit from any favourable movements in rates during that time. A FRA is simply an agreement about rates – it does not involve the movement of the principal sum – the actual borrowing must be arranged separately.

Futures

A financial future is an agreement on the **future price** of a **financial variable**. Interest rate futures are similar in all respects to FRAs, except that the terms, sums involved, and periods are **standardised**. They are traded on the London International Futures and Options Exchange (LIFFE).

Their standardised nature makes them less attractive to corporate borrowers because it is not always possible to match them exactly to specific rate exposures. Each contract will require the payment of a small initial deposit.

Interest rate options

An interest rate guarantee (or option) provides the **right to borrow** a **specified amount** at a guaranteed rate of interest. The option guarantees that the **interest rate will not rise** above a specified level during a specified period. On the date of expiry of the option the buyer must decide whether or not to exercise his right to borrow. He will only exercise the option if actual **interest rates** have **risen above the option rate**. The advantage of options is that the buyer cannot lose on the interest rate and can take advantage of any favourable rate movements. However, a **premium** must be paid regardless of whether or not the option is exercised. Options can be negotiated directly with the bank or traded in a standardised form on the LIFFE.

Caps and collars

These can be used to set a **floor** and a **ceiling** to the range of interest rates that might be incurred. A **premium** must be paid for this service. These agreements do not provide a perfect hedge, but they do limit the range of possibilities and thus reduce the level of exposure.

(b) Collars make use of **interest rate options** to limit exposure to the risk of movement in rates. The company would arrange both a ceiling (an upper limit) and a floor (a lower limit) on its interest yield. The use of the ceiling means that the cost is lower than for a floor alone.

Choice of options

Since Carrick requires protection for the next seven months, it can use **September options** in order to cover the full period. It is assumed that the floor will be fixed at the current yield of 6%. This implies that it will buy call options at 9400. At the same time, Carrick will limit its ability to benefit from rises in rates by selling a put option at a higher rate, for example 7% (or 9300).

The level of **premiums payable** will **depend** on the different **sizes of collar**. The number of three-month contracts required for seven months' cover will be:

$$\frac{£6m}{£0.5m} \times \frac{7}{3} = 28 \text{ contracts (£14m)}$$

The premiums payable at different sizes of collar (in annual percentage terms) will be:

Call	Premium	Put	Premium	Net premium	£ cost*
9400	0.40	9350	0.35	0.05	1,750
9400	0.40	9300	0.14	0.26	9,100
9400	0.40	9250	0.06	0.34	11,900

(* eg £14m × 0.05% × ¼ = £1,750)

If Carrick does take out the options as described above, the effect will be as follows.

(i) If interest rates fall below 6%, Carrick will **exercise the call option** and effectively fix its interest rate at 6%. The loss on the interest rate will be borne by the seller of the call option.

(ii) If interest rates remain between the 6% floor and the 7% ceiling, Carrick will **do nothing** but will benefit from the effect of any increase in rates above 6% within this band.

(iii) If interest rates rise above 7% the buyer of the put option will **exercise** their **option**, provided that the futures price falls below 9300. Carrick will effectively achieve an interest rate of 7%, but the benefit of any premium on rates above 7% will accrue to the buyer of the put option.

In practice, costs will be higher due to the transaction costs that will be incurred.

The potential gross interest rate gain, and the net gain taking premiums into account if rates do rise to the various exercise prices, are as follows. The interest rate gain is calculated on £6m for seven months.

	Interest rate % rise	Interest gain £	Premium £ cost (above)	Net gain £
9350	0.50	17,500	1,750	15,750
9300	1.00	35,000	9,100	25,900
9250	1.50	52,500	11,900	40,600

This suggests that Carrick could make the greatest potential gain by **selling put options** at 9250. However, this gain will only be realised if actual rates rise to 7.5%. If they stay at around 6% then Carrick will still incur costs without realising benefits. The actual put price chosen will depend on the view of the directors on the likely movements in rates over the period in question, but if it seems likely that rates will increase by up to 1%, then a put price of 9300 would be the most appropriate.

36 Burger-Queen

(a) Burger-Queen could sell the December futures contract for 92.70. Since each contract has a notional value of $500,000 it should sell

$$\frac{\$10,000,000}{\$500,000} = 20 \text{ contracts}$$

(b) Since interest rates have risen to 9% the price of the futures contract will fall to 91 (=100-9).

The gain on the futures contract is as follows:

92.70 – 91 = 170 ticks

Each tick is worth $12.50 and the profit on the futures contract is

$170 \times £12.5 \times 20 = £42,500$

Although there is gain in the futures position, the company has to pay a higher rate for the loan. The extra amount of interest paid on the loan is: 9 – 7.3 = 1.70 percent or

$10 million $\times 0.017 \times {}^{3}/_{12}$ = $42,500

This extra cost is offset by the profit on the futures position so the effective rate is 7.3% even though interest rates have risen

(c) The effective rate is still 7.3%

This time there will be loss on the futures contract since the price of the futures contract has risen. The price of the futures contract is now 94 (= 100 - 6). The loss is 94 - 92.70 = 130 ticks or

$130 \times \$12.50 \times 20 =$ $32,500

The lower interest rate on the loan means that there is a saving on interest payments equal to

$10 million $\times (0.073 - 0.06) \times {}^{3}/_{12}$ = $32,500

The gain on the interest is again offset by the loss on the futures position, so that the cost of borrowing remains the same at 7.3%.

37 Theta Inc

(a) Theta borrows $10 million with interest at six-month LIBOR plus 1%. In the swap, it receives six-month LIBOR and pays fixed interest at 8.5%. The net effect is to acquire a fixed rate obligation at 9.5% for the full term of the swap.

	%
Borrow at LIBOR plus 1%	– (LIBOR + 1%)
Swap: receive (floating rate)	+LIBOR
pay (fixed rate)	–8.5%
Net payment (fixed rate)	–9.5%

Theta will therefore fix its payments at $475,000 (10 million × 9.5% × 6/12) every six months for the five-year term of the swap.

At each six-monthly fixing date for the swap, the payment due from Theta to the swaps bank or from the bank to Theta will depend on the market rate for six-month LIBOR at that date.

(b)   (i)   **LIBOR 10%**

Suppose that on the first fixing date for the swap, at the end of month six in the first year, six-month LIBOR is 10%. The payments due by each party to the swap will be as follows:

	$
Theta pays fixed rate of 8.5%	
($10 million × 8.5% × 6/12)	425,000
Swaps bank pays LIBOR rate of 10%	
($10million × 10% × 6/12)	500,000
Net payment from bank to Theta	75,000

This payment will be made six months later at the end of the notional interest rate period. Theta will pay interest on its loan at LIBOR + 1% which for this six-month period is 11% (10% + 1%). Taken with the payment received under the swap agreement, the net cost to Theta is equivalent to interest payable at 9.5%.

	$
Loan payment at 11%	
($10 million x 11% x 6/12)	550,000
Payment received from the swap bank	(75,000)
Net payment (equivalent to 9.5% interest)	475,000

(b)   (ii)   **LIBOR 7.5%**

Suppose that at the next six-monthly fixing date, six-month LIBOR is 7.5%. The swap payments will be as follows:

	$
Theta to swap bank (fixed at 8.5%)	425,000
Swap bank to Theta (at 7.5%)	375,000
Net payment by Theta to swaps bank	50,000

Under its loan arrangement, Theta will pay 8.5% (LIBOR + 1%) for the six-month period. Adding the net swap payment gives a total cost for the six-month period of £475,000, equivalent to an interest rate of 9.5% for the period.

	$
Loan payment at 8.5%	
($10 million × 8.5% × 6/12)	425,000
Swap payment	50,000
Total payment (equivalent to 9.5% interest)	475,000

38 Kilber Inc

(a)   The management of risk is one of the most important aspects of the treasury function. Excessive volatility in the cash flows of the company, caused by changing business conditions, changes in exchange rates or interest rates will affect adversely the value of the firm. Hedging is in general considered to enhance the value of the company.

The most serious risk that Kilber faces is the falling kilbe prices. Since kilbe prices are highly correlated with copper prices, it is reasonable to use copper futures contract to lock into certain future value. Suppose that Kilber has sold a sufficient number of copper futures contracts maturing in three months. Suppose further that during this period, the price of both kilbe and copper have fallen. On expiration of the contract, the company will have a loss due to the fall in the price of the kilbe but a gain on the copper futures contract.

Whether the gain in the futures contract will offset the loss due to the fall in the price of the kilbe it will depend on whether the price of copper has fallen by the same percentage as the price of kilbe.

If it has fallen by the same percentage then the price of copper will be behaving exactly like the price of kilbe, the copper futures contract will be the exact equivalent of a kilbe futures contract.

However when the price of kilbe and copper is not perfectly correlated, then the copper futures contract is an imperfect hedge.

The remaining risk is called basis risk and arises from the imperfect correlation between the hedging instrument and the hedged asset.

(b) The main benefit of OTC derivatives is that they can be tailored to the needs of the two parties; their major drawback is that they pose a higher risk of default than do exchange-traded derivatives. Some very specialized agreements may also be illiquid.

(c) Kilber could use a variety of instruments to hedge interest rate risk depending on its time horizon. For short-term protection the company could use forward rate agreements, short-term interest rate futures and interest rate options. For long-term protection, it could use interest rate swaps to convert the variable interest rate debt to fixed rate.

Note that forward rate agreements, futures and swaps lock into a particular borrowing rate and the company does not benefit from a fall in interest rate. Interest rate options on the other hand set a ceiling on the interest rate to be paid but allow the company to benefit from a fall in interest rates.

39 Transfer prices

Top tips. You can go wrong quite easily in part (a) if you don't think carefully about the layout of your computation. For each of the options you need to split the calculation between what happens in the countries where the subsidiaries are located, and what happens in the country where the holding company is located. Remember also to assess the effect of the withholding tax separately from the other local taxes.

(b) demonstrates how strategic issues can be brought into the discussion part of an answer. It is not sufficient just to discuss government action. Local issues are important, also trying to ensure goal congruence throughout the group.

(a) The current position is as follows.

	UK company B$'000	Ceeland company B$'000	Total B$'000
Revenue and taxes in the local country			
Sales	84,000	210,000	294,000
Production expenses	(68,000)	(164,000)	(232,000)
Taxable profit	16,000	46,000	62,000
Tax (1)	(4,000)	(18,400)	(22,400)
Dividends to Beeland	12,000	27,600	39,600
Withholding tax (2)	0	2,760	2,760
Revenue and taxes in Beeland			
Dividend	12,000	27,600	39,600
Add back foreign tax paid	4,000	18,400	22,400
Taxable income	16,000	46,000	62,000
Beeland tax due	5,600	16,100	21,700
Foreign tax credit	(4,000)	(16,100)	(20,100)
Tax paid in Beeland (3)	1,600	–	1,600
Total tax (1) + (2) + (3)	5,600	21,160	26,760

An increase of 25% in the transfer price would have the following effect.

	UK company B$'000	Ceeland company B$'000	Total B$'000
Revenues and taxes in the local country			
Sales	105,000	210,000	315,000
Production expenses	(68,000)	(185,000)	(253,000)
Taxable profit	37,000	25,000	62,000
Tax (1)	(9,250)	(10,000)	(19,250)
Dividends to Beeland	27,750	15,000	42,750
Withholding tax (2)	0	1,500	1,500
Revenues and taxes in Beeland			
Dividend	27,750	15,000	42,750
Add back foreign tax paid	9,250	10,000	19,250
Taxable income	37,000	25,000	62,000
Beeland tax due	12,950	8,750	21,700
Foreign tax credit	(9,250)	(8,750)	(18,000)
Tax paid in Beeland (3)	3,700	–	3,700
Total tax (1) + (2) + (3)	12,950	11,500	24,450

The total tax payable by the company is therefore reduced by B$2,310,000 to B$24,450,000.

(b) **Government action**

In practice, governments usually seek to prevent multinationals reducing their tax liability through the manipulation of transfer prices. For tax purposes governments will normally demand that an **'arms length' price** is used in the computation of the taxable profit and not an artificial transfer price. If no such 'arms length' price is available then there may be some scope for tax minimisation through the choice of transfer price.

Other factors

If it is possible to manipulate the transfer price in this way, there are further factors that the company must take into consideration before making a final decision.

(i) The level of transfer prices will affect the **movement of funds** within the group. If inter company sales involve the use of different currencies the level of the transfer price will also affect the group's **foreign exchange exposure**. These factors must be taken into account as well as the tax situation.

(ii) The level of profit reported by the subsidiary could affect its **local credit rating** and this could be important if the company wishes to raise funds locally. It could also affect the ease with which credit can be obtained from suppliers.

(iii) The reported profit is likely to have an **effect** on the **motivation** of managers and staff in the subsidiary. If reported profits are high then they may become complacent and cost control may become weak. If on the other hand profits are continually low they may become demotivated.

(iv) Transfer prices that **do not reflect market levels** may lead to subsidiaries making 'make or buy' decisions that do not optimise the performance of the group as a whole.

40 Developments

Adverse effects of increased globalisation on multinational companies:

Government regulation

(a)   Increased regulation due to greater number of industries being characterised by oligopoly.

(b)   Anti-trust scrutiny – for example, British Airways and American Airlines alliance to prevent cross-border oligopolies.

(c)   Such regulation creates obstacles to trade, as companies must comply with regulations that may prevent efficient and effective operations.

Pressure groups

Pressure is being put on governments to take measures against multinational companies – in the UK for example there is increasing resistance to supermarket chains setting up in opposition to small shops in city suburbs. The pressure groups are becoming more and more successful at curbing multinationals' activities.

Political risks

(a)   Multinational companies are becoming more vulnerable to political developments in home and host countries. Global conflicts have led to trade embargoes, restrictions on operating in certain countries and sanctions.

(b)   Tariffs and capital restrictions; import quotas; export subsidies; exchange controls are all barriers that can affect multinational activity, as host countries try to protect domestic industries.

Index

BPP
LEARNING MEDIA

Notes

Notes

Review Form – Paper P4 Advanced Financial Management (8/12)

Please help us to ensure that the ACCA learning materials we produce remain as accurate and user-friendly as possible. We cannot promise to answer every submission we receive, but we do promise that it will be read and taken into account when we update this Study Text.

Name: _____   Address: _____

_____

_____

How have you used this Study Text?
(Tick one box only)

☐ Home study (book only)

☐ On a course: college _____

☐ With 'correspondence' package

☐ Other _____

Why did you decide to purchase this Study Text? *(Tick one box only)*

☐ Have used BPP Texts in the past

☐ Recommendation by friend/colleague

☐ Recommendation by a lecturer at college

☐ Saw information on BPP website

☐ Saw advertising

☐ Other _____

During the past six months do you recall seeing/receiving any of the following?
(Tick as many boxes as are relevant)

☐ Our advertisement in *ACCA Student Accountant*

☐ Our advertisement in *Pass*

☐ Our advertisement in *PQ*

☐ Our brochure with a letter through the post

☐ Our website www.bpp.com

Which (if any) aspects of our advertising do you find useful?
(Tick as many boxes as are relevant)

☐ Prices and publication dates of new editions

☐ Information on Text content

☐ Facility to order books off-the-page

☐ None of the above

Which BPP products have you used?

Text	☑	Success CD	☐
Kit	☐	i-Pass	☐
Passcard	☐	Interactive Passcard	☐

Your ratings, comments and suggestions would be appreciated on the following areas.

	Very useful	Useful	Not useful
Introductory section	☐	☐	☐
Chapter introductions	☐	☐	☐
Key terms	☐	☐	☐
Quality of explanations	☐	☐	☐
Case studies and other examples	☐	☐	☐
Exam focus points	☐	☐	☐
Questions and answers in each chapter	☐	☐	☐
Fast forwards and chapter roundups	☐	☐	☐
Quick quizzes	☐	☐	☐
Question Bank	☐	☐	☐
Answer Bank	☐	☐	☐
Index	☐	☐	☐

Overall opinion of this Study Text	Excellent ☐	Good ☐	Adeqate ☐	Poor ☐

Do you intend to continue using BPP products?   Yes ☐   No ☐

On the reverse of this page is space for you to write your comments about our Study Text We welcome your feedback.

The BPP Learning Media author of this edition can be e-mailed at: andrewfinch@bpp.com

Please return this form to: Nick Weller, ACCA Publishing Manager, BPP Learning Media Ltd, FREEPOST, London, W12 8BR

TELL US WHAT YOU THINK

Please note any further comments and suggestions/errors below. For example, was the text accurate, readable, concise, user-friendly and comprehensive?